FIFTH EDITION

CITIES AND URBAN LIFE

JOHN J. MACIONIS
KENYON COLLEGE

VINCENT N. PARRILLO
WILLIAM PATERSON UNIVERSITY

Boston   Columbus   Indianapolis   New York   San Francisco   Upper Saddle River
Amsterdam   Cape Town   Dubai   London   Madrid   Milan   Munich   Paris   Montreal   Toronto
Delhi   Mexico City   Sao Paulo   Sydney   Hong Kong   Seoul   Singapore   Taipei   Tokyo

Editorial Director: Leah Jewell
Editor-in-Chief: Dickson Musslewhite
AVP, Publisher: Nancy Roberts
Editorial Project Manager: Vanessa Gennarelli
Editorial Assistant: Nart Varoqua
Director of Marketing: Brandy Dawson
Senior Marketing Manager: Kelly May
Marketing Assistant: Elaine Almquist
Project Manager: Cheryl Keenan
Senior Operations Supervisor: Sherry Lewis
Operations Specialist: Christina Amato/Amanda A. Smith
Cover Design: Jodi Notowitz
Manager, Visual Research: Beth Brenzel

Photo Researcher: Kathy Ringrose
Manager, Rights and Permissions: Zina Arabia
Image Permission Coordinator: Debbie Hewitson
Manager, Cover Visual Research and Permissions:
   Karen Sanatar
Supplements Editor: Mayda Bosco
Full-Service Project Management: Doug Bell,
   PreMedia Global, Inc.
Composition: PreMedia Global, Inc.
Printer, Binder, and Cover Printer: R. R. Donnelley
   & Sons
Text Font: Baskerville

Credits and acknowledgments borrowed from other sources and reproduced, with permission, in this textbook appear on the appropriate page within text or on pages 445–446.

If you purchased this book within the United States or Canada you should be aware that it has been wrongfully imported without the approval of the Publisher or the Author.

10 9 8 7 6 5 4 3 2 1

ISBN 13: 978-0-205-74104-5
ISBN 10:   0-205-74104-5

CONTENTS

Chapter 9   Comparative Urbanism: The City and Culture   235

PART   IV   GLOBAL URBAN DEVELOPMENTS

SPECIAL FEATURES

URBAN LIVING

CITYSCAPE

URBAN TRENDS

PREFACE

The world stands on the brink of an historic landmark: In a few years, a majority of the planet's people will live in cities. Urban living is rapidly becoming the *norm* for members of our species. Surely, no more compelling reason exists for us to undertake the study of cities and urban life.

THE BASIC APPROACH

The approach of this text is multidisciplinary but fundamentally sociological. Readers will find here the enduring contributions of the classical European social thinkers, including Max Weber, Karl Marx, Ferdinand Tönnies, Georg Simmel, and Emile Durkheim, as well as those of early pioneers in North America, including Robert Park and Louis Wirth. Of course, many men and women have stood on the shoulders of these giants and extended our understanding. Thus, this text also considers the ideas of a host of contemporary urbanists, including Manuel Castells, Michael Dear, Herbert Gans, Jane Jacobs, Henri Lefebvre, Lyn Lofland, John Logan, Kevin Lynch, Harvey Molotch, Allen Scott, Edward Soja, and Michael Sorkin.

Yet, as this string of well-known names suggests, urban studies rests on research and theory developed within many disciplines. *Cities and Urban Life,* therefore, is truly a multidisciplinary text that draws together the work of historians (Chapter 2: "The Origins and Development of the World's Cities," and Chapter 3: "The Development of North American Cities"), sociologists (Chapter 4: "Today's Cities and Suburbs," Chapter 5: "Urban Sociology: Classic and Modern Statements," Chapter 10: "Stratification and Social Class: Urban and Suburban Lifestyles," Chapter 11: "Race, Ethnicity, and Gender: Urban Diversity," and Chapter 12: "Housing, Education, Crime: Confronting Urban Problems"), geographers and urban ecologists (Chapter 6: "Spatial Perspectives: Making Sense of Space"), political economists working within various disciplines (Chapter 7: "Critical Urban Sociology: The City and Capitalism"), social psychologists (Chapter 8: "Social Psychology: The Urban Experience"), anthropologists (Chapter 9: "Comparative Urbanism: The City and Culture," and Chapter 13: "Cities in the Developing World"), and architects as well as city planners (Chapter 14: "Planning the Urban Environment").

THE ORGANIZATION OF THIS TEXT

Part I of the text, "Understanding the City: Its Origin and Development," introduces the main concepts and themes that resonate throughout the book; surveys the historical development of cities, noting how urban life has often differed in striking ways from the contemporary patterns we take for granted (Chapters 2 and 3); and examines the current trends of sprawl, edge cities, and gated communities now shaping cities and suburbs (Chapter 4). Part II, "Disciplinary Perspectives," highlights the various disciplinary orientations that, together, have so advanced our understanding of cities (Chapters 5–9). Part III, "The Structure of the City," focuses on the social organization of today's cities in North America, highlighting how urban living reflects the importance of stratification and social class (Chapter 10) and of race, ethnicity, and gender (Chapter 11), as well as forcing us to confront vexing problems such as housing, education, and crime (Chapter 12). Part IV, "Global Urban Developments," first offers a look at urbanization in four major world regions: Latin America, Africa, the Middle East, and Asia (Chapter 13). It is in these areas of the world that urbanization is now most rapid, with cities reaching unprecedented size. Finally, Chapter 14 examines the architectural, social, and political dimensions of urban planning, and discusses approaches to help cities achieve their potential for improving everyone's lives.

FOUR KEY THEMES

This attempt to tell the urban story will lead us to consider a wide range of issues and to confront countless questions. Four main themes guide this exploration, however, and it is useful to make these explicit. Whatever else a student entering the field of urban studies might learn, he or she must pay attention to these themes:

1. *Cities and urban life vary according to time and place.* Since the idea of the city first came to our ancestors some 10,000 years ago, the urban scene has been re-created time and again, all around the world, in countless ways. The authors—informed by their own travels to some 60 of the world's nations—have labored to portray this remarkable diversity throughout this text.
2. *Cities reflect and intensify society and culture.* Although cities vary in striking ways, everywhere, they stand as physical symbols of human civilization. For example, nowhere do we perceive the inward-looking world of the Middle Ages better than in the walled cities of that era. Similarly, modern U.S. cities are powerful statements about the contemporary forces of industrial capitalism.
3. *Cities reveal the best and the worst about the human condition.* Another way to "read" cities

is as testimony to the achievements and failings of a way of life. Thus, while New York boasts some spectacular architecture, exciting public parks, vital art galleries, and vibrant concert halls, it also forces us to confront chronic prejudice and wrenching poverty.
4. *Cities offer the promise—but not always the reality—of a better life.* Since at least the time of the ancient Greeks, people have recognized that the city holds the promise of living "the good life." Yet all urban places fall short of this ideal in some ways, and in many of today's cities, people are struggling valiantly simply to survive. The great promise of urban living, coupled with the daunting problems of actual cities, provokes us to ask how we can intentionally and thoughtfully make urban places better. Although we are realistic about the problems, we remain optimistic about the possibilities.

SPECIAL FEATURES OF THE TEXT

Two special features warrant the attention of readers.

Boxes Each chapter contains several boxed inserts. These boxes are of three kinds. *Urban Trends* boxes depict a pattern, either past or present, shaping people's way of life. *Urban Living* boxes provide a picture of the city "at street level"—that is, a close-up look at how people really live. Finally, *Cityscape* boxes present a literary account or scholarly analysis of some significant dimension of urban life.

Case Studies The text includes eight case studies that offer a broad sociohistorical look at major cities in various regions of the world as they illustrate a chapter's key points. The cities profiled in these case studies are London (Chapter 2), New York (Chapter 3), Portland, Oregon (Chapter 4), Ming Peking (Chapter 9), Hellenic Athens (Chapter 9), Communist Beijing (Chapter 9), Chicago (Chapter 11), and Toronto (Chapter 14).

WHAT'S NEW IN THE FIFTH EDITION

This new edition reflects a number of changes. First, and most important, is the continuance of our policy to provide a thorough updating of all data and information and to include the most recent and relevant studies not only in sociology but in many other related fields as well.

Second, Chapter 1 has been extensively revised to offer a more thorough introduction to all the major concepts in the field of urban sociology. This chapter now provides the reader with a strong framework for approaching the subject.

Third, throughout the book, a concerted effort has been made to include the Canadian urban experience in every chapter to encourage students to think beyond national boundaries.

Fourth, a few chapters have been rearranged in sequence for greater cohesiveness. Thus, the chapter on urban political economy now immediately follows Chapter 6 on urban ecology and social area analysis to allow for clearer contrasts between the two perspectives. The chapters on social psychology and culture then follow consecutively, to enhance an understanding of their interconnectivity.

Fifth, Chapter 4 on today's cities and suburbs contains an expanded discussion on the environmental consequences of sprawl and on smart growth alternatives, with the addition of a chart explaining the main differences between the two.

Sixth, several other chapters now contain expanded discussions on important topics: eminent domain (Chapter 4); political fragmentation (Chapter 4); the Los Angeles School (Chapter 6); and world-systems analysis (Chapter 7).

Seventh, Chapter 6 on spatial perspectives includes information regarding the use of social area analysis for thematic mapping. The use of GIS mapping for understanding the interplay of geography and the built environment is also discussed.

Eighth, Chapter 8 contains new sections on social movements and city life and on the social psychology of suburban life.

Ninth, Chapter 13 has been extensively revised, with greater emphasis on modern cities in the developing world, their role in world-systems analysis, and their environmental impact.

Tenth, Chapter 14 contains information on newer urban utopian visions, such as TRY-2004 and Crystal Island.

Eleventh, new special features boxes have been added: on sprawl ("As American as Apple Pie" in Chapter 4), on the texture of cities ("The Personality of Cities" in Chapter 8), on Bobos ("The Bourgeois and Bohemians Merge" in Chapter 10), on women in public space ("Targets of Public Harassment" in Chapter 11), on inner-city coping skills ("Inner City Toughness" in Chapter 12), and on the new urbanism ("Defining New Urbanism" in Chapter 12).

Twelfth, each chapter concludes with Internet activities, many of them interactive, and all especially chosen to further an understanding and appreciation for that chapter's content.

Thirteenth, an end-of-book glossary has been added to facilitate understanding of key terms and concepts.

In addition, a new photo program and supplemental materials further enhance the fifth edition, both for readers and for instructors.

ACKNOWLEDGMENTS

The authors wish to thank the editorial team at Prentice Hall for their efforts in making this text a reality. Particular thanks go to Nancy Roberts, publisher–sociology, for originally signing the project and helping to get the work under way, and to Vanessa Gennarrelli, our project manager at Prentice Hall, for her truly excellent work in guiding this new edition from conceptualization through its publication. We are also grateful to Wesley Morrison for copyediting, to Lee Lawton for preparing the index, and to Kathy Ringrose for photo research.

The authors also wish to acknowledge the role played by James L. Spates, of Hobart and William Smith Colleges, in a 1980s version of this book, entitled *The Sociology of Cities,* coauthored by Spates and Macionis. Although Vince Parrillo and John Macionis have significantly revised that effort at many levels, some elements of Jim's ideas still remain.

For their efforts reviewing part or all of the manuscript and generously sharing their ideas with us, we gratefully acknowledge the reviewers for this edition: Robert L. Boyd, Mississippi State University; Ivan Chompalov, Edinboro University; Patrick Donnelly, University of Dayton; Matthew Green, University of Arizona; Richard S. Muller, Monmouth University; Lee L. Williams, Edinboro University. For the fourth edition: Daniel J. Monti, Jr., Boston University; Stephanie Moller, University of North Carolina at Charlotte; and Robert J. S. Ross, Clark University. For the third edition: Mark Abrahamson, University of Connecticut; Robert L. Boyd, Mississippi State University; and Jerome Krase, Brooklyn College. For the second edition: Leo Pinard, California Polytechnic State University–San Luis Obispo; David Prok, Baldwin Wallace College; and James D. Tasa, Eric Community College–North. For the first edition: Ronald S. Edari, University of Wisconsin; and Daniel J. Monti, Boston University.

John J. Macionis
Kenyon College
Gambier, Ohio 43022
E-mail: macionis@kenyon.edu
http://www.TheSociologyPage.com

Vincent N. Parrillo
William Paterson University
Wayne, New Jersey 07470
E-mail: parrillov@wpunj.edu
http://www.wpunj.edu/cohss/sociology/faculty/parrillo.htm

Vancouver

Seattle

Portland

Denver

San Francisco
Los Angeles

Phoenix

Toronto

Detroit

Chicago

Pittsburgh

St. Louis

Atlanta

Houston

(Teotihuacan)

Montreal

Boston
Newport
New York

Philadelphia

Charleston

Miami

New Orleans

Mexico City
(Tenochtitlan)

Caracas

Lima

La Paz

Brasilia

Rio de
Janeiro

Buenos Aires

Amsterdam

Stockholm

Moscow

London

Warsaw

Berlin

Paris

Istanbul
(Constantinople)

Rome

Venice

Baghdad

Athens

Tehran

Beirut

Isfahan

Algiers

Jerusalem

Jericho

Beijing

Tokyo

Marrakech

Alexandria

Shanghai

Cairo

b

Delhi

Mecca

Calcutta

Hanoi

SAHARA DESERT

Kano

Bombay

Hong Kong

Manila

Lagos

Madras

Bangkok

Addis Ababa

Ibadan

Nairobi

Ho Chi Minh City

Singapore

Jakarta

Johannesburg

Cape Town

Sydney

Melbourne

Canberra

CHAPTER 1

EXPLORING THE CITY

"This music crept by me upon the waters"
And along the Strand, up Queen Victoria Street.
O City, city, I can sometimes hear
Beside a public bar in Lower Thames Street,
The pleasant whining of a mandolin
And a clatter and a chatter from within
Where fishmen lounge at noon: where the walls
Of Magnus Martyr hold
Inexplicable splendour of Ionian white and gold.

T. S. Eliot, "The Waste Land"

Let us go then, you and I,
When the evening is spread out against the sky
Like a patient etherised upon a table;
Let us go, through certain half-deserted streets,
The muttering retreats
Of restless nights in one-night cheap hotels
And sawdust restaurants with oyster-shells:
Streets that follow like a tedious argument

Of insidious intent
To lead you to an overwhelming question . . .
Oh, do not ask, "What is it?"
Let us go and make our visit.

T. S. Eliot, "The Love Song of J. Alfred Prufrock"

WHY STUDY THE CITY?

Cities! Most of us share poet T. S. Eliot's fascination with urban places—settings of intense excitement, great mystery, and striking human diversity. With the poet, most of us probably agree that cities (London was the object of Eliot's interest) are places we would love to visit—but, of course, many of us wouldn't want to live there! On the one hand, little compares with the excitement of visiting a major city such as New York, Toronto, Chicago, or San Francisco.

When we go into the city, we often find block after block of shops selling all kinds of things we never find at home, and we pass by every imaginable sort of person— the old and the young, the rich and the poor, the up and coming as well as the down and out. People say that virtually anything can and does happen in big cities—and it doesn't take long to realize that they're right!

Across North America, about four out of five of us live in urban places, and even more of us build our lives around cities. We are born in cities (or near them), grow up in or near one (probably in a suburb), go to a college in or near a city (maybe one some distance away from our hometowns), and eventually settle down in or near a city that becomes "home." Across the continent, much of our favorite entertainment— including clubs, musical events, sports contests, and theatre—is city based. We might as well admit it: We are a nation of city slickers, and the urban way of life has become the norm in both Canada and the United States. To study the city, therefore, is to study ourselves.

Yet the city is more than what our personal experiences reveal. It is a dynamic entity unto itself, the most powerful drawing card in human history. In 1900, cities were home to just 9 percent of the world's population. In 1950, cities were home to 30 percent, and then to 47 percent in 2000. If present trends continue, by 2030 cities will be home to 60 percent of humanity (United Nations Population Division 2008).

The city is thus the setting for all aspects of the human drama: the highest learning colliding with the grossest ignorance, unimaginable wealth juxtaposed with the most abject poverty. Historically, most people drawn to the city have been able to realize their hopes of a higher standard of living—but will this continue to be true in the new megacities, such as Mexico City, Rio de Janeiro, Cairo, New Delhi, and Tokyo? (See the world map preceding this chapter to locate these and other prominent cities.) Such places are adding millions of new residents so rapidly that they cannot provide basic services (water, housing, and electricity) to many of their people. If such growth is not checked soon, poverty and suffering for billions, not to mention ecological disasters unparalleled in history, may be inescapable. To study the city, therefore, is also to study a uniquely powerful form of human settlement: a physical and social environment with the potential for both satisfying and frustrating the entire spectrum of human needs.

An important theme of this book is that cities do not exist entirely by themselves. They are inextricably bound up with the larger societies of which they are a part. For centuries, the city has been the heart, the lifeblood, of various civilizations—the center of economic, political, and artistic events. In cities, we find both the triumphs and the tragedies of the human story. For example, we associate Hellenic Athens, Renaissance Florence, and Elizabethan London with great achievements of the human spirit, while we link classical Rome and Nazi Berlin with savage human degradation. In each case, a cultural setting helped shape the city's character: During the fourth century

B.C.E.,[1] the Greeks raised Athens to a pinnacle of human accomplishment, while the rise of Nazism in Germany after World War I led to Berlin's infamous decadence.

The connection between the city and a broader culture is no less evident today. In its cities exists much of what is great about the United States: intellectual excellence, political freedom, and artistic vitality. Of course, these same cities also exhibit this country's greatest failings, including grinding poverty and sometimes-savage crimes. To study the city, then, is also to examine the society in which it exists. The impact of economics can be as significant as that of culture, particularly in today's global economy, so we must also examine closely the forces of globalization in shaping a city's structure and well-being.

Understanding the city, therefore, is crucial in comprehending modern existence. But how we choose to study the city is also important. The city is a complex reality that yields few easy answers. Our approach here is to study the city much as we would a poem. In encountering a new poem, most people wonder, "What does it mean?" For example, someone might ask what T. S. Eliot means by "the walls of Magnus Martyr" in the lines that opened this chapter—a reference to a particularly beautiful London church, Saint Magnus Martyr, built by Sir Christopher Wren in the seventeenth century. Or we might examine the phrase "inexplicable splendour of Ionian white and gold"—a reference to the startling white and gold interior of Magnus Martyr, which reminded Eliot of the glories of the Ionian period of classical Greece.

Central as these "what" questions are, U.S. poet John Ciardi (1990, chap. 1) believed, that we also need to consider the mood the poem creates in us, its readers, as well as the deeper subtleties conveyed in how the poem's words play together. Our concern, wrote Ciardi, should not be "to arrive at a definition and close the book, but to arrive at an experience." In other words, Ciardi maintains, only by asking *how* a poem transmits its meaning—by experiencing how all its complex elements fit together—will we fully comprehend the poem. The same is true of cities.

If we look only at the facts of urban life, we will surely miss its dynamic soul. The city will appear dull and lifeless—a collection of concrete buildings, bureaucracies, and unemployment rates. But if we also ask the "how" questions, which link these factual elements to human lives, the city springs to life as a set of vital, dynamic forces.

In studying the city, then, we must not ask merely "What is it?" We must, as Eliot suggests in his poem, "go and make our visit." We must probe beyond the descriptions and the statistics to the broader and deeper reality of urban life. This book will help you do just that.

DECIDING WHAT IS "URBAN"

Urban seems like a simple enough concept to grasp, but it actually has many interpretations. Derived from the Latin word *urbanus*—meaning characteristic of, or pertaining to, the city—*urban* essentially holds that same connotation to most people.

Complicating that understanding, however, are the varying criteria for defining an urban area that exist among the 195 countries with urban populations. These criteria include *administrative function* (a national or regional capital), *economic characteristics* (more than half the residents in non-agricultural occupations), *functional nature* (existence of paved streets, water supply, sewerage, and electrical systems), and *population size* or *population density* (the number of people living within a square mile or kilometer). Administrative function is used solely in 89 countries and in combination with other criteria in an additional 20. Economics is one of several criteria in 27 countries, as is function in 19 countries. Function is also used solely in only five

---

[1] The designation B.C.E. ("before the common era") is used in place of B.C. ("before Christ") in recognition of the religious pluralism of North American society. Similarly, we use C.E. ("common era") in place of A.D. (*Anno Domini,* "in the year of our lord").

countries. Population size or density is the sole criterion in 46 countries and is used in combination in an additional 42. No definition exists in 24 countries—while in Guadeloupe, Hong Kong, Kuwait, Monaco, Nauru, and Singapore, the entire population is designated as urban.

Canada and the United States both use population density to identify an urban area, and these areas are delineated without regard to local boundaries. In Canada, an urban area must contain more than 400 people per square kilometer, with a total population exceeding 1,000 people. The United States defines an urban area as contiguous census blocks with a population density of 1,000 persons per square mile, which is equivalent to the Canadian standard. **Urban cluster** is the U.S. Census Bureau term for a combination of these contiguous urban areas that extend across city, county, or state boundaries. (All areas that the Census Bureau does not classify as urban—generally places of less than 2,500 persons—it defines as rural.)

Such differences worldwide make cross-national comparisons difficult. For example, the lower-range limit for population of an urban area ranges from 200 in Iceland to 10,000 in Greece. A universal standard—say, a midpoint from these two extremes of 5,000 inhabitants—would be inappropriate in populous countries such as China or India, where rural settlements—with no urban attributes at all—could easily contain such large numbers. Using each country's own criteria, the United Nations Population Division (2008) reported that 47 percent of the world's population was urban. Significant variations existed: Africa, 36 percent urban; Asia, 37 percent urban; Europe, 71 percent urban; Latin America and the Caribbean, 75 percent urban; North America, 79 percent urban. The lowest urban population (10 percent) was in Burundi, while the highest (100 percent) were in the six countries previously identified.

Worldwide projections show the percentage of urban population increasing everywhere (see Table 1–1). Reporting the percentage of urban people living in the world's seven major geographical areas between the years 1950 and 2000, the table shows that urbanization is an unmistakable trend everywhere. In fact, the world's cities are growing by 1 million people each week. This dramatic pattern means that by 2050, more than two-thirds of the planet's people will be urban dwellers.

Distinct regional patterns, however, can be seen in urban growth. If we examine Table 1–1 for the percentages of growth between 1950 and 2000, we see that all regions gained urban population. Yet in the more industrialized

TABLE 1–1   Percentage of Urban Population in Major Areas of the World

Area	1950	2000	2050
Africa	14.5	35.9	61.8
Asia	16.8	37.1	66.2
Europe	51.2	71.4	83.8
Latin America and Caribbean	41.4	75.3	88.7
North America	63.9	79.1	90.2
Oceania	62.0	70.4	76.4
World	29.1	46.6	69.6
More developed regions	52.5	73.1	86.0
Less developed regions	18.0	40.2	67.0

Source: From *World Urbanization Prospects,* 2007 Revision. Copyright © 2007 by the United Nations, Population Division. Reprinted with permission.

areas of the world—North America and Europe—urban growth has slowed considerably in recent years. The area of greatest urban growth is now in the developing world—Latin America, Africa, the Middle East, and Asia (see Figure 1–1, page 6). In fact, when we consult the figures on urban growth rates by country, we find that the 10 countries with the highest urban growth rates are all in these four regions; those with the lowest rates, with one exception (Uruguay in South America), are all in Europe, North America, and Japan. Moreover, when we scan a list of all the world's nations ranked in order of their urban growth rates, we must look down through 150 countries before we encounter an industrial nation—Canada (UN 2008).

THE URBAN TRANSFORMATION

If any one thing should astound us, it is how popular cities have become the world over. As a human invention, cities are scarcely 10,000 years old, but as the centuries have passed, they have become both much larger and far more numerous. For example, in 1800 only one city, Beijing, had 1 million residents; now the world contains 130 cities where a million or more people reside. The increase in world population alone cannot explain this phenomenon. Once people become aware of the advantages of cities—protection, increased material standard of living, a more stimulating mental and social life—they don't want to live anywhere else. Because this urban growth and development can occur in different ways and on several levels, however, we need to know some basic concepts about these processes and their consequences if we are to understand fully what is happening.

Urbanization as a Process

The changes resulting from people moving into cities and other densely populated areas is what we mean by **urbanization.** This process of increased population concentration can be deliberate and planned, such as Brazil's capital, Brasilia, which was inaugurated in 1960. It can also be spontaneous and unplanned, as in the rapid urban growth occurring in many developing countries. However it occurs, urbanization transforms land use from rural to urban economic activities—and often the land itself, from a porous surface to a non-porous one of asphalt and concrete. In addition, this progression in greater population density also transforms many patterns of social life, altering both the social structure and the social organization of that area. As we will discuss shortly, these changes include a more complex division of labor and social stratification, the growth of subcultures, and more formal social controls.

As an example of urbanization, consider the massive changes that San Francisco experienced. Today, it is a thoroughly modern U.S. city, famed for its hills, cable cars, fog, and natural beauty. It also has a particularly easy-going lifestyle, about which Geoffrey Moorhouse once wrote:

> No one who visits San Francisco for the first time can fail to be aware of the pleasantly relaxed atmosphere. You are not perpetually admonished by well-wishers about the dangers of getting mugged, as visitors usually are in New York. It seems true that shop assistants here are more amiable than elsewhere, less bent on treating their customers as components of the cash register; when they say "Have a nice day," they sound as though they mean it and not as if it were a ritual phrase learned to help trade. Watch people move about the streets if you want to appreciate what San Francisco has done to them. Except at rush hour, they tend to stroll. There is nothing comparable here to downtown New York or the heart of London, where the word "perambulation" may now be considered redundant except at weekends, having long since been banished by the general push and shove. (1979:24)

Such was not always the case, however. The changes to San Francisco since its early existence have been profound, as historic documents attest. One such document is Richard Henry Dana's *Two Years Before the Mast* (2001, originally published in 1862), one of the greatest of nineteenth-century seagoing journals, a

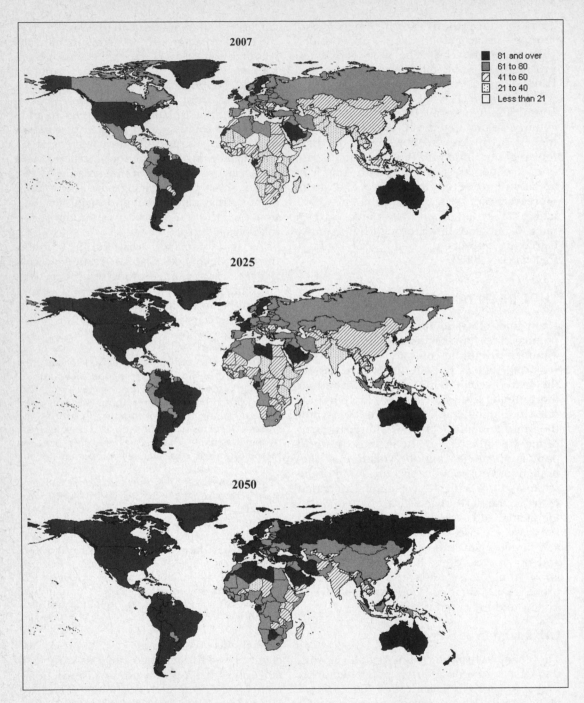

FIGURE 1–1 Percentage of Population in Urban Areas, 2007, 2025, and 2050

Source: From *World Urbanization Prospects,* 2007 Revision. Copyright © 2007 by the United Nations, Population Division. Reprinted with permission.

part of which you can read in the *Cityscape* box on page 8.[2]

What happened to San Francisco between Dana's two visits was gold, discovered in 1849. Almost overnight, the sleepy little village of Yerba Buena, the nearest port for outfitting the Sierra Nevada mines, was transformed into a feverish city. Not for another 70 years would Moorhouse's sophisticated, "laid-back" San Francisco begin to appear.

Levels of Urbanization

As the process of urbanization expands into ever-increasing concentrations and areas of land, other terms and concepts are necessary to understand the complexity and scale of human organization and interaction. Although we will explore these topics more fully in subsequent chapters, here is a brief introduction to them:

Metropolitan Area. A large population center and its adjacent communities, with which it has a high degree of economic and social integration, constitute a *metropolitan area*. Also known as an *urban agglomeration*, such a region typically has a large city (100,000 residents or more) as the hub that extends its sphere of influence into the surrounding communities. These communities may not be urban in character themselves, but they link closely with that city through transportation (roads and public transit), employment (commuters), media (city newspapers, and radio and TV stations), and leisure activities (clubbing, dining, entertainment, and professional sports).

Megalopolis. When two or more metropolitan areas expand so that they intermingle with one another to form a continuous (or almost continuous) urban complex, we have a *megalopolis*, which is sometimes referred to as a *conurbation*. This merged conglomeration typically contains a population in the tens of millions, such as that along the Eastern Seaboard, although the cities therein retain their individual names (Boston, New York, Philadelphia, Baltimore, and Washington, D.C.).

Megacity. A metropolitan area can constitute its own megalopolis if the population within its municipal boundary numbers at least 10 million people. In the past 35 years, the number of megacities has rocketed from three in 1975 to 19 in 2007, with an expected increase to 27 by 2025 (see Table 1–2, page 9). Today, 1 in 11 people worldwide live in a megacity (UN Population Division 2008:10).

Global City. Also called a *world city*, a *global city* occupies an influential position in the global economic system, attracting global investments and exercising considerable economic power worldwide. London, New York, and Tokyo are at the top of the hierarchy of cities because of their role in the world system of finance and trade (Sassen 2001). **World-systems analysis,** an approach we will examine more closely in Chapter 7 on critical urban sociology, suggests that the economic well-being of most cities is heavily dependent on their placement within this world hierarchy.

Urbanism as a Way of Life

As implied earlier, the companion concept to urbanization (population growth and concentration) is **urbanism,** the culture or way of life of city dwellers. Here we are not only speaking about changes in values, attitudes, norms, and customs but also about lifestyle patterns and behavioral adaptations influenced by one's residential and/or work environment. Numerous elements affect this interactive relationship between human behavior and environment, and one of the main ones is social structure.

By **social structure,** we mean the recurrent patterns of city life that are shaped significantly by the unequal distribution of important urban resources, including wealth, power, and prestige. One aspect of social structure concerns the wide variety of lifestyles within

[2]Various kinds of boxes are included in each chapter to illustrate key points and themes. When you encounter a reference to a particular box, take a minute or two to read it before going on with the chapter.

CITYSCAPE

San Francisco's Massive Changes

Shipping from New York, Richard Henry Dana first visited San Francisco, then called Yerba Buena ("good herbs"), in 1835. Here is what he saw:

[Near the] mouth of the bay . . . is a high point on which the [Presidio Mexican military outpost] is built. Behind this point is the little harbor, or bight, called Yerba Buena, in which trading vessels anchor, and, near it, the Mission of Delores. There was no other habitation on this side of the Bay, except a shanty of rough boards put up by a man named Richardson, who was doing a little trading between the vessels and the Indians. . . . We came to anchor near the mouth of the bay, under a high and beautifully sloping hill, upon which herds of hundreds and hundreds of red deer, and the stag, with his high branching of antlers, were bounding about, looking at us for a moment, and then starting off, affrighted at the noises we made at seeing the variety of their beautiful attitudes and motion.

That was not the San Francisco of Geoffrey Moorhouse; nor does it much resemble this description of Dana's, written in 1859 after a second visit:

We bore round the point toward the old anchoring ground of hide ships, and there, covering the sand hills and the valleys, stretching from the water's edge to the base of the great hills, and from the old Presidio to the Mission, flickering all over with lamps of its streets and houses, lay a city of one hundred thousand inhabitants. . . . The dock into which we drew, and the streets about it, were densely crowded with express wagons and hand-carts to take luggage, coaches and cabs for passengers, and with men. . . . Through this crowd I made my way, along the well-built and well-lighted streets, as alive as by day, where boys in high keyed voices were already crying the latest New York papers; and between one and two o'clock in the morning found myself comfortably abed in a commodious room, in the Oriental Hotel, which stood, as well as I could learn, on the filled-up cove, and not far from the spot where we used to beach our boats from the Alert.

When I awoke in the morning, and looked from my windows over the city of San Francisco, with its townhouses, towers, and steeples; its courthouses, theaters, and hospitals; its daily journals; its well-filled learned professions; its fortresses and light houses; its wharves and harbor, with their thousand-ton clipper ships, more in number than London or Liverpool sheltered that day . . . when I looked across the bay to the eastward, and beheld a beautiful town on the fertile wooded Shores of the Contra Costa [the area of today's Oakland and Berkeley] and steamers, large and small, the ferryboats of the Contra Costa, and capacious freighters and passenger-carriers to all parts of the great bay and its horizon—when I saw all these things, and reflected on what I once was and saw here, and what now surrounded me, I could scarcely keep my hold on reality at all, or the genuineness of anything, and seemed to myself like one who had moved in "worlds not realized."

Source: Richard Henry Dana, *Two Years Before the Mast* (New York: Heritage, 2001), pp. 196, 203, 320–22.

our cities. Often, these lifestyles coincide with different geographical districts of the city. In downtown areas, for example, we are likely to see well-dressed businesspeople—many of whom live in apartments. Older residential neighborhoods may provide the sights, sounds, and even smells of exotic cultural diversity. Still other neighborhoods contain the city's poor, who struggle every day to survive. In many suburban areas, single-family homes—replete with children and the ever-present automobile—dominate.

TABLE 1–2   Population of the World's Megacities in Millions

2007			2025		
Rank	Urban Agglomeration	Population	Rank	Urban Agglomeration	Population
1	Tokyo, Japan	35.7	1	Tokyo, Japan	36.4
2	New York–Newark, USA	19.0	2	Mumbai (Bombay), India	26.4
3	Mexico City, Mexico	19.0	3	Delhi, India	22.5
4	Mumbai (Bombay), India	19.0	4	Dhaka, Bangladesh	22.0
5	São Paulo, Brazil	18.8	5	São Paulo, Brazil	21.4
6	Delhi, India	15.9	6	Mexico City, Mexico	21.0
7	Shanghai, China	15.0	7	New York–Newark, USA	20.6
8	Kolkata (Calcutta), India	14.8	8	Kolkata (Calcutta), India	20.6
9	Dhaka, Bangladesh	13.5	9	Shanghai, China	19.4
10	Buenos Aires, Argentina	12.8	10	Karachi, Pakistan	19.1
11	Los Angeles–Long Beach–Santa Ana, USA	12.5	11	Kinshasa, DR Congo	16.8
12	Karachi, Pakistan	12.1	12	Lagos, Nigeria	15.8
13	Al-Qahirah (Cairo), Egypt	11.9	13	Al-Qahirah (Cairo), Egypt	15.6
14	Rio de Janeiro, Brazil	11.7	14	Manila, Philippines	14.8
15	Osaka–Kobe, Japan	11.3	15	Beijing, China	14.5
16	Beijing, China	11.1	16	Buenos Aires, Argentina	13.8
17	Manila, Philippines	11.1	17	Los Angeles–Long Beach–Santa Ana, USA	13.7
18	Moskva (Moscow), Russia	10.5	18	Rio de Janeiro, Brazil	13.4
19	Istanbul, Turkey	10.1	19	Jakarta, Indonesia	12.4
			20	Istanbul, Turkey	12.1
			21	Guangzhou, Guangdong, China	11.8
			22	Osaka–Kobe, Japan	11.4
			23	Moskva (Moscow), Russia	10.5
			24	Lahore, Pakistan	10.5
			25	Shenzhen, China	10.2
			26	Chennai (Madras), India	10.1
			27	Paris, France	10.0

Source: From *World Urbanization Prospects,* 2007 Revision. Copyright © 2007 by the United Nations, Population Division. Reprinted with permission.

Lifestyles are, of course, much more than matters of individual choice. They reflect dimensions of social difference, often taking the form of social inequality. Like virtually all other societies, the United States and Canada contain marked **social stratification,** the hierarchical ranking of people in terms of valued resources. Wealth is certainly one important dimension of social stratification, and North American cities often provide striking contrasts between well-heeled urbanites who have lives of material comfort and others who must persevere just to survive.

Such differences are typically related to other dimensions of social difference: race, ethnicity, and gender. Once ignored in the urban public sphere, women are now more likely to hold public office, at least in cities with populations of 25,000 or more (MacManus and Bullock 1995:162). From both historical and contemporary viewpoints, however, women's lives and city experiences have reflected the realities of gender, interwoven with those of social class, race, and ethnicity. In a still-continuing historic pattern, North American cities attract immigrants of different races and ethnicities; on arrival, many find themselves at or near the bottom of the urban hierarchy. With time, many improve their situation, but others continue to suffer from a wide range of problems associated with poverty and/or prejudice.

Social power—the ability to achieve one's goals and to shape events—is yet another important dimension of inequality. For those with considerable wealth, urban living is often the experience of shaping their own lives (and, indeed, the lives of others). By contrast, for poorer urbanites, many of whom are members of racial and ethnic minorities, life in the city is a grim matter of trying to cope with forces that seem overwhelming.

Of course, none of these structural patterns exists exclusively in cities. Social stratification is as important in small towns in North Carolina as it is in Raleigh, the state capital; people perceive racial distinctions as keenly in rural Ohio as they do in Columbus; and "power politics" is the name of the game in rural Wyoming, just as it is in Cheyenne. Nevertheless, because these structural patterns shape our cities so strongly, we can hardly ignore them.

On another level, however, cities intensify the effects of class, race, ethnicity, gender, and power, because they concentrate everything human in a small space. If we care to look, we can find examples of wealth and poverty, of power and powerlessness, of such extremity as to be nearly incomprehensible. A walk through the poor neighborhoods of almost any major North American city will reveal numerous examples of numbing poverty. Indeed, poverty for millions continues as only one of the significant problems that beset the urban environment.

THE COMPLEXITY OF THE CITY: VARIOUS PERSPECTIVES

The city may well be the most complex of all human creations. As a result, it cannot be understood using any single point of view. While this book is fundamentally sociological in its orientation, it draws together insights, theories, and statistics from a wide variety of related disciplines, including history, archaeology, psychology, geography, economics, and political science. As we now explain, all these perspectives are vital for grasping the living entity that is the contemporary city.

The City in History

Today, cities are so much a part of our lives that they seem both natural and inevitable. You may be surprised to learn, then, that in the larger picture of human history, cities are a very new idea. Although the human species has existed on the earth for at least 100,000 years, cities began to appear a scant 10,000 years ago. Moreover, it wasn't until the last 3,000 years that cities became relatively numerous and inhabited by significant numbers of people. And only today are we reaching the point at which most of the world's people will be urbanites.

Thus, we can see the importance of studying the city historically. Without the benefit of hindsight, we might easily fool ourselves into thinking that cities, although perhaps smaller in the past, were always more or less like those we know today.

Luckily, our understanding of past cities doesn't rely only on historical documents, such as Dana's account of early San Francisco. In recent years, urban archaeologists have made major strides in the study of urban settings about which little or no written material is available.

Abandoned cities, or cities rebuilt on earlier foundations, still contain traces of their earlier existence, providing clues for archaeologists trained in the careful excavation and analysis of artifacts. From such clues, archaeologists can piece together a picture of how a city's people lived: how they built their houses and organized their families, what they thought important enough to portray in paintings, what level of technology they employed, what they commonly drank or ate. By unearthing many such clues, archaeologists allow long-dead cities to spring back to life in our minds.

One of the most important finds during recent years was the 2001 carbon dating of Caral, an ancient, sacred city of about 160 acres located approximately 62 miles north of the Peruvian capital of Lima. Imagine the excitement of discovering it was founded before 2600 B.C.E.—pushing back the date for the first known urban settlement in the Western Hemisphere by at least 1,000 years! This settlement predates the Incan civilization by 4,000 years, but even more astonishing is the impressive construction of its six pyramids, which are a century older than the pyramids of Gizeh in ancient Egypt. It appears that other nearby sites may be even older, but that Caral was the regional center for the approximately 10,000 people living in that area.

Lost for centuries, archaeologists regard the Caral as the most important pre-Columbian ruins discovered since the 1911 discovery of Machu Picchu, also in Peru but hundreds of miles to the south. The Caral site is so old that it predates the ceramic period, which explains why archaeologists did not find any pottery shards. Caral's importance resides in its domestication of plants, especially cotton but also beans, squashes, and guava. This civilization knew how to use textiles and built many residential structures around the pyramids. Among the numerous artifacts discovered were 32 flutes made from pelican and animal bones, engraved with the figures of birds and monkeys, thus revealing that although the inhabitants lived by the Pacific coast, they were nevertheless aware of the animals of the Amazon (Isbel and Silverman 2006).

Archaeology also plays a role in contemporary cities. Most cities exist on the rubble of their own past. Take London, for example. Over the course of its 2,000-year history, this city has risen some 30 feet, building on its own refuse. In 1997, ten excavation sites in and around London Bridge unearthing Roman London—established in the first century C.E.—brought new discoveries. Archaeologists found two different types of Roman

Built by the Incas in the mid-fifteenth century, Machu Picchu remained hidden until 1911. Now a tourist attraction receiving 400,000 visitors annually, it is one of the world's most impressive archaeological sites. It is a masterpiece of urban planning, civil engineering, architecture, and stonemasonry, its many buildings still intact except for their thatch-and-reed roofs.

buildings, one type made with timber frames and clay walls and floors, and later, more substantial masonry buildings, some with mortar floors and plaster walls, both of which served as the homes of artisans, with shops or workshops in front and living quarters behind. Also uncovered were many artifacts of everyday life, including oil lamps for lighting homes and vessels for cooking and drinking (Jubilee Line Extension 1997).

Closer to home, archaeologists completed an excavation on New York's Wall Street in 1979–1980, uncovering artifacts from the original Dutch settlement of 1625. In 1991, excavation for a new federal building between Broadway and Duane Street in Lower Manhattan unearthed an eighteenth-century African American burial ground.

Two chapters of this text survey cities in human history. Chapter 2 reviews major urban developments from the beginnings of cities some 10 millennia ago right up to the urban events of this century. We will see that the urban story is one of continuous and striking change. Chapter 3 highlights how cities have developed in the United States and Canada. Here, too, we will find astonishing changes— changes hinted at in Dana's account of San Francisco. We will see the alterations of North American urban life as cities grew from the small, isolated colonial centers of the seventeenth century to sprawling environments with populations often reaching into multimillions. Then, in Chapter 4, we will examine recent urban trends that are shaping urban and suburban lifestyles in this century: sprawl, edge cities, gated communities, and common-interest developments (CIDs).

The Emergence of Urban Sociology

One key goal of this text is to understand how sociologists study the city. Although historians have been looking at cities for centuries, sociologists are more recent investigators. As Chapter 5 explains, early sociologists in the late nineteenth century lived during a period of dramatic urban upheaval, and naturally, they turned their attention to cities. They tried to understand just how the Industrial Revolution transformed the small villages of both Europe and North America into huge, chaotic metropolises.

Many early sociologists shared a pessimistic vision of the city. Their works portray the city as a dangerous place where the traditional values of social life—a sense of community and caring for other people—were systematically torn apart. Recent sociological research, however, shows that many of these concerns about the destructiveness of urban living were based on faulty evidence. In the light of contemporary research, the city emerges as a more neutral phenomenon. Neither good nor bad in and of themselves, cities have been pushed in one direction or the other by the cultural forces at work in a particular time and place. Thus, the horrors of nineteenth-century London appear to be primarily a product of the massive industrialization that took place within a capitalist society, not a result of something inherently urban.

Geography and Spatial Perspectives

Why did people cluster together to form cities in the first place? Aristotle, an ancient Greek philosopher, provided a timeless answer: People come together in cities for security; they remain there to live the good life. For the ancient Greeks, cities satisfied a need for security, because in an age of few laws and fewer treaties, groups frequently preyed on one another. For protection, people came together in a single location, often a natural fortification, such as the Acropolis in Aristotle's Athens. Where natural defenses were not available, people built walls. But a site could become a city only with other geographical assets: water, access to transportation routes, and the ability to produce or import enough goods to meet the population's needs.

Once cities began, however, people made a remarkable discovery. Mixing together in large numbers not only afforded protection; it generated more profitable trade and stimulated intellectual life as well. People began to hail the city as offering the potential for what Aristotle termed "the good life."

The importance of a city's physical location, and of how people come to arrange themselves within the urban area, has led urbanists to develop two related areas of study: (1) **urban geography,** which focuses on the significance of the city's location and natural resources; and (2) **urban ecology,** which analyzes how people spread out within an urban area. Let us illustrate each of these areas of study.

A city's geographical location has a great deal to do with how life in that city is lived. Take the two largest U.S. cities, New York and Los Angeles. Centered on Manhattan Island and surrounded by rivers, New York City has a land base of bedrock that is physically able to support tall buildings. By contrast, Los Angeles stretches out across a semi-arid basin that, geologically speaking, makes the building of skyscrapers a shaky business indeed. These different settings translate into very different daily routines, as Joseph Giovannini, a part-time resident of both cities, noted:

New York and Los Angeles have fundamentally different spatial premises. Space in New York collects people; in Los Angeles it separates them. New Yorkers occupy a community; Angelenos occupy their own privacy. New York is an environment of people; Los Angeles is an environment of vehicular movement. New York is a vertical city, and Los Angeles, despite its hills and mountains, is horizontally organized. . . .

The urban patterns that shape attitudes in the two cities are as simple as the daily commute. In Los Angeles, I coasted downhill in my '59 Studebaker Lark, accompanied by FM music. If I timed the freeways correctly to avoid bottlenecks, the drive to work from my office in Venice was a rumination. . . .

In New York, the half-hour commute is a very different half hour. It starts in the elevator, where I might encounter another tenant: We chat. Then, a brief conversation with the doorman; perhaps a passing greeting to a neighbor on the street, and then another chat at the corner newsstand. [After my subway ride, when] I arrive at Times Square, I sometimes head for my morning coffee and pastry at the Lucky Star Delicatessen, where I talk to Mervat, an Egyptian

waitress; then, on the elevator in The Times building, I meet more people before sitting down at my desk. (1983:147)

Geography is only one cause of the differing social dynamics that distinguish cities. Various categories of people stake out particular areas within the city, and particular activities come to dominate certain districts—and both of these change over time. Such shifts interest urban ecologists, who seek to understand how people choose to locate and rearrange themselves in urban space. One well-documented ecological process is **invasion-succession,** by which whole sections of a city change. A new "high-tech" area in an adjacent suburb may rather suddenly upstage an old industrial district. Almost overnight, the older district starts to look tawdry; second-hand stores, "gentlemen's clubs," and pornographic bookstores replace the older, more respectable businesses. Before long, income levels in the area drop, and the few remaining original businesses close their doors. Where once executives and working people trod the city sidewalks, now one finds only prostitutes, drug dealers, and petty criminals. With this succession, the process of change is complete. Invasion-succession may also occur in residential areas as new categories of people enter an established neighborhood.

For many contemporary social scientists, the ecological model has fallen into disfavor. The critical urban sociology field mentioned earlier is the more emphasized approach. Of particular note is the influence of postmodernism on urban studies. **Postmodernism** is primarily a reaction against the assumed certainty that rational, objective efforts can explain reality. Instead, it insists there are multiple interpretations based on concrete experiences, not abstract principles, so urban planning should entail notions of community, diversity, small-scale approaches, restoration of the older urban fabric, and creation of new spaces that use modern technologies and materials but express traditional visions (Harvey 1992).

Both the older and the newer studies of physical arrangements, spatial perspectives, and the social dynamics for city life provide the subject matter of Chapter 6.

Critical Urban Sociology: The City and Capitalism

Just as important as a city's geographical setting and its cultural framework is its ability to generate trade—to be economically prosperous. In the fourth century B.C.E., Aristotle, as previously mentioned, said that initially, people came to cities for security. True enough, particularly at the time he was writing. But throughout history, people have flocked to the city for many reasons, chief among them the belief that in the city, they would significantly improve their material standard of living. For example, the hope for a better life spurred millions upon millions of immigrants from rural and poor backgrounds to come to the cities of Canada and the United States during the late nineteenth and early twentieth centuries. These people, including many of our grandparents and great-grandparents, settled in cities across both nations in an attempt to make their fortunes.

Comparisons of medieval and contemporary cities reveal the growing importance of the economic function of cities over the centuries. In the Middle Ages, although cities were already important centers of trade, other areas of life also were thriving. All one has to do is look at the physical layout of cities built during the Middle Ages—with their central cathedral as the tallest building—to see the importance of religion in the lives of the people. With the coming of the Industrial Revolution, however, all that began to change. Cities became ever more important as centers of wealth. Skyscrapers, large factories, and office buildings sprang up to meet the economic demands of millions. The churches that previously dominated the skyline were dwarfed by the new "central business district."

Looking at the decline of manufacturing in cities, the migration to the suburbs and the Sunbelt, the mushrooming cities in poor nations, and a growing world economy, a new

The Church of Our Lady before Tyn, with its magnificent Gothic steeples, dominates the cityscape of Prague, Czech Republic. The Old Town retains many medieval qualities: visual domination by the cathedral, no central business district, narrow streets, and buildings with commercial enterprises at street level and residences on the floors above.

Unlike the medieval Old Town section of Prague with its central cathedral and lower surrounding buildings, North American cities typically include a central business district with residences but also expressways, wider streets for cars, and a skyline dominated by tall commercial buildings, as illustrated in this view of Atlanta, Georgia.

breed of urban researchers concluded that natural processes could not explain these changes and their economic impact on cities. Instead, they argue, decision making within political and economic institutions, often thousands of miles away, affects a city economically, politically, socially, and even physically. Some, but not all, advocates of this **urban political economy,** or critical urban sociology perspective, are neo-Marxists. Regardless of their ideological orientation, they focus on investment decisions and economic trends that determine a city's fortunes.

Recent analytical thinking in this area includes postmodern theory, an emphasis on fragmented and nontraditional elements. World-systems analysis—examining a city as one interdependent part of the global whole—is another prominent aspect of contemporary thinking.

We will look at all of these structural imperatives and their ramifications on urban poverty in Chapter 7.

Social Psychology: The Urban Experience

With about four-fifths of North Americans living in cities, any student of cities needs to explore the urban experience. How and why do cities stimulate us so much? Do cities change people in one way or another?

We know that the city trips our emotions, for some in positive ways and for others in negative ways. Although these reactions are certainly personal, they are also *social* in two senses. First, it is the social environment of the city itself that generates them. Second, they are social in that they are common; they resonate in one of those ways with virtually all of us.

These social dimensions of the urban experience also figure in our analysis. *Urbanism*—a concept referring to those social–psychological aspects of life, personality patterns, and behavioral adaptations influenced by the city—is the focal point of Chapter 8.

Comparative Urbanism: The City and Culture

As we have already suggested, the city does not exist in a vacuum. It is "powered" by its people, who represent a particular way of life, or culture. By the term **culture,** we mean the basic beliefs, values, and technology that characterize a city in a particular historical era. Any society's culture is reproduced and intensified in the city.

Technology provides a good example. If we were to visit the London of a century and a half ago, we likely would be shocked to see how different it was from the cities of today. Yes, we would find a bustling business district and lots of people—but there the similarity would end. Rather than a sprawling metropolitan area with extensive suburbs and shopping centers, crisscrossed by superhighways and adorned with skyscrapers, we would find a relatively compact city, with all its hustle going on in narrow, winding streets of astonishing filth. Charles Dickens, who lived there, described this very scene in his novel *Bleak House*:

> LONDON. . . . Implaccable November weather. As much mud in the streets as if the waters had but newly retreated from the face of the earth. . . . Smoke lowering down from chimney pots, making a soft black drizzle, with flakes of soot in it as big as full-grown snow-flakes—gone into mourning, one might imagine, for the death of the sun. Dogs, undistinguishable in mire. Horses, scarcely better; splashed to their very blinkers. Foot passengers, jostling one another's umbrellas, in a general infection of ill-temper, and losing their foothold at street-corners, where tens of thousands of other foot passengers have been slipping and sliding since the day broke (if this day ever broke), adding new deposits to the crust upon crust of mud . . . and accumulating at compound interest. (1853:1)

Inevitable as they may seem, clean and paved streets, clean air, the skyscraper, the superhighway, and the large, sprawling suburb are very recent urban phenomena—all products of a certain level of technological development. The skyscraper only became feasible in the latter part of the nineteenth century, when steel-frame buildings and electrically powered elevators were developed. Similarly, sprawling suburbs are unthinkable without superhighways or mass public transportation linking cities and suburbs; these, in turn, are dependent on technological innovations, such as steel, railroads, electricity, and the private automobile. Finally, paved streets became common in cities only in the twentieth century, and it wasn't until the 1950s and 1960s that clean air legislation was passed in the United States to curtail exhaust excesses like those Dickens described. A given level of technology, then, has much to do with the urban experience.

At the same time, cultural beliefs play a major role in shaping city life, including certain uses of technology. Take the mobile phone, for instance. Although larger, clumsier predecessors existed in earlier decades, the 1990s were when cellular phones came into widespread use. Once a mostly private means of communication via landlines in the home, office, or enclosed phone booth, the mobile phone today has redefined our sense of private and public space.

On the one hand, mobile phones are decidedly private; only a limited circle of people know the user's mobile phone number, the number is typically not listed in a directory, and the user may have fewer disruptions or eavesdropping than at home, essentially by using an "improvised open-air wireless phone booth" (Lasen 2003:1). At the same time, however, the mobile phone intrudes into the public sphere, its ringing heard by all in the vicinity, who are forced to hear only one side of a conversation—particularly if the speaker does not talk quietly.

Almost everywhere, these third parties to such calls consider them a nuisance when they occur in a theater, museum, classroom, church, waiting room, and restaurant or at social events and work. Of less annoyance, but still viewed as a nuisance, are mobile calls on a bus or train and in bars, cafés, stores, or other people's houses (Höflich 2006:63). Reaction to mobile calls in these situations is nearly

The congested, bustling activity captured in this woodcut of London in the 1870s helps us visualize the sights and sounds, the grandeur and squalor, that attracted millions of people to live, work, play, or visit the city and participate in all that it offered.

universal, but cultural differences—along with such variables as education and social class—affect phone usage behavior and acceptance of that behavior.

In a comparative study of Europeans, Joachim Höflich (2006) reported that Italians are far more likely than Finns, Germans, or Spaniards to use a mobile phone to maintain communication with family members but feel more uncomfortable making a call with strangers around them. At the same time, Southern Europeans (e.g., Greek, Italian, Portuguese, and Spanish) tend to speak more loudly in public than Northern Europeans (e.g., Finns, Germans, and Scandinavians). Finns in particular feel a strong need for a private sphere respected by others, while use of mobile phones in public by Italians and Spaniards is extremely common.

The above is but one example of the role that cultural beliefs play in the urban setting. So central is this issue to the study of cities that we devote all of Chapter 9 to it.

THE ANATOMY OF MODERN NORTH AMERICAN CITIES

Chapters 2 through 9 provide the basic framework for a detailed analysis of the cities of the contemporary world. Then, our attention returns to North America for a detailed analysis of the cities that most of us know best. Even though urban population growth has slowed in Canada and the United States, this by no means suggests that the situation of our cities today is stagnant and unchanging. In fact, the situation is far from it. Recent decades have been a period of enormous change for North American cities.

In the United States, the much-publicized movement to Sunbelt (southern and western) cities is one such change. As Table 1–3 indicates, with a few exceptions, Sunbelt cities have gained markedly in population during the last decade, while midwestern and northeastern cities have generally declined. Growing significantly were the cities of Austin, Phoenix, San Jose, Charlotte, and San Antonio—all in the South and West. Declining substantially

were Detroit, Milwaukee, Washington, D.C., Baltimore, and Philadelphia—all in the Midwest or Northeast. Moving against the trend were New York City, which increased in population, and New Orleans and Birmingham, which lost people.

A second recent development is a nationwide trend toward living in smaller cities or in areas farther away from the central cities. For instance, the census shows that the areas surrounding suburbs are growing most rapidly. Thus, just as people moved from central cities to suburbs a generation ago, now they are moving still farther from the urban core.

What accounts for these marked changes? Demographers suggest that although many older Americans prefer to remain in the community where they spent most of their adult lives ("aging in place"), retirement magnet areas attract many affluent seniors. A retirement home in Dade County, Florida (Miami's home county); Austin, Texas; or Sun City, Arizona (near Phoenix) has become an attraction that millions have no desire to resist. Second, the last several decades have seen an increasing exodus of business and industry from center cities, occasioned by a desire to escape high taxation, congestion, outmoded plants, high union wages, and excessive heating costs (the latter two factors primarily in the North). In many cases, firms have moved to the South or West. In other instances, they have moved to areas on the periphery of the center city. In either case, they have pulled their employees with them. Employees choose to live in smaller cities, towns, and rural areas partly from their desire to be near relocated businesses or industries and partly from the long-standing desire to be free of congestion and have "living space" in affordable housing. Earlier suburbs, built primarily in the 1950s and 1960s, were the first manifestation of this cultural value. The decentralization indicated by recent census data confirms that this trend is continuing.

Whatever the final explanations for these demographic changes, their effects are profound. Those cities with declining population lose federal funding and political representation. As a result, such cities must cut budgets,

TABLE 1–3   Population of the 30 Largest U.S. Cities, 2000 and 2006

2006 Ranking	City	2000 Population	2006 Population	2000 Ranking	Percentage Change
1	New York	8,008,000	8,214,000	1	+2.6
2	Los Angeles	3,695,000	3,849,000	2	+4.2
3	Chicago	2,896,000	2,833,000	3	−2.2
4	Houston	1,954,000	2,144,000	4	+8.8
5	Phoenix	1,321,000	1,513,000	6	+33.6
6	Philadelphia	1,518,000	1,448,000	5	−4.6
7	San Antonio	1,145,000	1,297,000	9	+11.8
8	San Diego	1,223,000	1,257,000	7	+2.7
9	Dallas	1,189,000	1,233,000	8	+3.7
10	San Jose	895,000	930,000	11	+3.9
11	Detroit	951,000	871,000	10	−8.4
12	Jacksonville	736,000	7955,000	14	+8.0
13	Indianapolis	782,000	786,000	12	+0.5
14	San Francisco	777,000	744,000	13	−4.2
15	Columbus	711,000	733,000	15	+3.0
16	Austin	657,000	710,000	16	+7.6
17	Memphis	650,000	671,000	18	+8.1
18	Fort Worth	535,000	653,000	29	+20.7
19	Baltimore	651,000	631,000	17	−3.0
20	Charlotte	541,000	630,000	26	+11.2
21	El Paso	564,000	609,000	22	+8.1
22	Boston	589,000	591,000	20	+0.3
23	Seattle	563,000	582,000	23	+3.4
24	Washington, D.C.	572,000	582,000	21	+1.7
25	Milwaukee	597,000	573,000	19	−4.0
26	Denver	555,000	567,000	24	+2.4
27	Louisville	552,000	554,000	—	+0.6
28	Las Vegas	478,000	553,000	—	+15.1
29	Nashville–Davidson	546,000	552,000	25	+1.2
30	Oklahoma City	506,000	538,000	29	+6.2

Source: U.S. Bureau of the Census.

services, and aid to the poor and elderly, further decreasing their attractiveness as places to live. Because of lost revenues, inner suburbs also begin to deteriorate as people move away. On the other hand, the small cities and towns that gain population are likely to "get rich quick." This growth is a mixed blessing, however—many long-time residents of outlying areas, accustomed to traditional rural lifestyles, now find themselves assailed by an invasion of "city slickers."

What is life like in these cities of ours? Who lives in them? Why do they live there? What are the problems these cities face? Such questions will be answered in three chapters (Chapters 10–12) that look at North American urban social structure.

THE CITY IN GLOBAL PERSPECTIVE

As mentioned earlier, the greatest urban growth is occurring in developing countries. Why should this concern us? Aren't growing cities generally a good thing? After all, cities produce jobs, generate better health care, and stimulate improvements in technology and the arts. The answer to this question is double-edged, however: Sometimes cities do these things, but not always; and often, they do them for only some of the city's people.

In fact, throughout most of the developing world, the urban situation is desperate—and, in some places, the situation is even getting worse. Recent decades have witnessed hundreds of millions of people, enticed by the promise of a better life, moving into the cities of Latin America, Africa, the Middle East, and Asia. Most of these cities cannot keep up with the incoming tide. The results are poverty, malnutrition, and disease for many people. The *Urban Living* box below provides tragic examples of even worse outcomes. Fortunately, these kinds of disasters do not happen often, but the conditions reported still exist in many shantytowns throughout the world.

The grave situation in these countries is common throughout the world's poor nations. Chapter 13 examines the cities of Latin America, Africa, the Middle East, and Asia and offers analysis highlighting their urban problems and successes.

THE QUALITY OF CITY LIFE

The city is a living, dynamic entity. Its capacity to concentrate human efforts means that urban places contain the greatest potential for improving the quality of human life.

For millennia, people have come to the city with hopes and dreams of living "the good life." When all is said and done, however, has the city lived up to its billing? True, many cities boast material living standards that are higher than they ever have been in history, but this is not the case for everyone. Furthermore, in many cities of the developing world, material living standards are appallingly low—destitution in many cities is not the exception but the rule. Then, too, focusing on material standards alone may be a mistake. What about security, which was Aristotle's first concern? Despite a steadily declining urban crime rate during

---

URBAN LIVING

The Shantytowns of the Developing World

Communities of squatters, so poor that they cannot pay any amount of rent, exist on the outskirts of major cities throughout Africa, Asia, the Caribbean, and Latin America. Millions of people throughout the developing world live in comparably unhealthy and dangerously situated shantytowns, most of them without indoor plumbing or electricity. Built from cast-off scraps of lumber and tin by people who often have not even heard of building codes, they sprawl either across river flood plains and low-lying coastal strips, where tidal flooding is common, or else on hillsides, where deadly mudslides take their toll. The mudslides are a chronic problem. Clearing grass and shrubs from the hillsides to make way for the shantytowns causes erosion, leaving these communities vulnerable during heavy rains.

Almost every year during the hurricane and monsoon seasons come tragic stories of hundreds of deaths from these mudslides. In July 2005, for example, a monsoon deluged Mumbai (Bombay), India, with 37 inches of rain in a 24-hour period. In Saki Naka, a shantytown in the city's northern area, a water-soaked hill collapsed and buried more than 150 people.

As this scene of New Year's revelers in Times Square shows, a city is a dynamic, living entity, but not just on such special occasions. A city's night life—with its excitement, bright neon lights, large digital screens, variety of activities, crowds of people, and sense of adventure—lures people of all ages and backgrounds to come and be part of one of its many simultaneous happenings.

In the same year, torrential rains from Hurricane Stan triggered a mudslide that killed hundreds in the Guatemalan village of Panabaj. In 2004, flooding and mudslides caused by Hurricane Jeanne killed an estimated 3,000 people in Haiti. In 2007, large chunks of earth slid off the soaked hillsides into a shantytown in the Bangladeshi port city of Chittagong, killing nearly 100, while a similar number who had lived in crudely built shacks outside Rio de Janeiro, Brazil, also perished.

In each of these areas, and in many others, relief agencies attempted to provide food, provisions, and emergency shelter. Governments, working in tandem with these agencies, built new housing and pledged not to allow residents to again live in dwellings on such unstable ground. This relief effort has not been enough, however, for the displaced, ever-growing population people who abandon the countryside in search of better jobs and are unable to find affordable housing. Instead, they continue to occupy these shantytowns throughout the developing world. Until the economic problems in these countries are solved, better housing will not be the answer, because people still won't be able to pay even a minimal amount for housing. So the shantytowns exist again, with the squatters living in houses stacked so close to one another that the edges often overlap, hoping they will be spared when the next heavy rains come.

recent years, some areas in many cities are so dangerous that people cannot go out alone, especially at night, without fear of being mugged, raped, or murdered. What about strong, community-oriented neighborhoods? Once a primary element of cities, these, too, have weakened in recent decades—and, in some areas, have disappeared altogether.

We need to understand the whole range of conditions that contribute to a more stimulating, fulfilling urban life. In bits and pieces throughout this book, evidence regarding the positive and negative elements of the city will emerge. We will comment on some of this evidence as we proceed, and in the final chapter, we will pull together these ideas as we examine urban planning and offer some thoughtful speculation about the future of cities.

Because of the ever-increasing importance of the city to the future of human civilization, sizing up the potential of urban places for meeting human needs is clearly essential. Is the city a place of alienation, danger, dehu-

manization, and exploitation, as some people fear? Or can the city become the ideal suggested by historian Lewis Mumford in the following passage:

> The mission of the city is to further [the human being's] conscious participation in the cosmic and historic process. Through its own complex and enduring structure, the city vastly augments [human beings'] ability to interpret these processes and take an active, formative part in them, so that every phase of the drama it stages shall have, to the highest degree possible, the illumination of consciousness, the stamp of purpose, the color of love. That magnification of all the dimensions of life, through emotional communion, rational communication, technological mastery, and above all, dramatic representation, has been the supreme office of the city in history. And it remains the chief reason for the city's continued existence. (1989:576; orig. 1961)

To find the answers to those questions, we must "go and make our visit."

KEY TERMS

culture (16)
global city (7)
invasion-succession (13)
megacity (7)
megalopolis (7)
metropolitan area (7)
postmodernism (13)
social power (10)
social stratification (9)

social structure (7)
urban cluster (4)
urban ecology (13)
urban geography (13)
urban political economy (15)
urbanism (7)
urbanization (5)
world-systems analysis (7)

INTERNET ACTIVITY

To explore New York City's Times Square area, go to *http://maps.google.com*, and in the box at the top, type in "1500 Broadway New York NY." In the balloon in the middle of the map that appears, click "Street view." When the street scene appears, click "Full-screen." Next, in the upper-left corner, click the left or right rotation arrows. How many different kinds of elements can you find as you completely rotate your view?

CHAPTER 2

THE ORIGINS AND DEVELOPMENT OF THE WORLD'S CITIES

Can you imagine the United States without great cities such as New York, Chicago, or San Francisco? It would be like thinking about Egypt without Cairo, Japan without Tokyo, France without Paris, or England without London. Why are entire countries so closely bound up with cities? The answer, as this chapter explains, is that much of the story of human history is centered in cities. In fact, the words city and civilization are both derived from a single Latin root—civitas. Indeed, to be civilized is to live in or near a city.

This was not always the case, however. Most knowledgeable people today recognize the importance of cities, because in our era, the city not only is the dominant form of human association but also is becoming more so every day. In the larger picture of human history, however, the city is a "wide-eyed infant"—a very recent arrival on the human scene.

URBAN ORIGINS

When and where did the first cities develop? What were they like? How did they change over time? Here we will offer brief answers to these crucial questions. Before we can do so, however, we must look far back in time to see just how recently human beings began making history on this earth.

To get a better perspective on where we are in relation to human history, let's use astronomer Carl Sagan's concept of a **cosmic calendar.** Sagan (1977) suggested that we imagine the entire history of our planet compressed into a single calendar year. What does such a vision suggest? To begin with, for almost the entire history of the universe (beginning with the "Big Bang"—corresponding to January 1st), the human species did not exist. In fact, our species, *Homo sapiens,* appeared on earth roughly 200,000 years ago (December 31st in Sagan's year). Another 190,000 years passed before permanent settlements—even in the form of small villages—existed. The emergence of the first cities, then, and with them the way of life that we commonly call "civilization," occurred only about 10,000 years ago (8000 B.C.E.)—in the last minute of Sagan's year! It would be several thousand years more, around 3000 B.C.E., before cities became common. Even then, however, they contained only a small proportion of the world's population.

Only in the last several centuries (the last second in Sagan's year) has the world acquired a sizable urban population. As recently as 1940, the proportion of the world's population living in cities was only 19 percent. In 2000, this figure had grown to 47 percent. In other words, the existence of the city—and of the urban way of life that we so readily take for granted—is a very recent and momentous change in the history of the world.

Archaeology: Digging the Early City

Learning about the first cities has been a gradual process filled with difficulties. Urban scholars have relied heavily on the work of archaeologists to gain an understanding of early settlements. Through excavation and techniques for determining the age of artifacts, we have learned much about the social life of people who left little formal record of their existence. Often, however, simply finding the sites of early cities—frequently buried beneath the surface, hidden by dense plant growth, or even covered by a current metropolis—is a matter of hard work as well as a bit of luck. Once an ancient city is found, excavation must proceed carefully to avoid damaging the remains. Finally, even when a city has been excavated successfully, archaeologists do not always offer the same interpretations of findings at a given site.

Moreover, our understanding of early urban settlements is subject to continuous revision. Ongoing investigations at old sites and the discovery of new locations, such as the recent excavation of Caral in Peru, provide a steady stream of new data. In addition, techniques of analysis continually improve, often leading to a reformulation of beliefs that urbanists held with certainty only a few years before.

We still have much to learn. Nevertheless, there is much that we do know about early cities, and this chapter summarizes a great deal of that knowledge. First, we examine cities as they took form in the ancient world, and then we consider how, as the centuries passed, cities reflected the changing character of human civilization.

The First Permanent Settlements

Human beings like us first appeared on the earth about 200,000 years ago. For the next 190,000 years, our ancestors lived as hunters and gatherers—hunting game and gathering vegetation over large areas. Most followed the animals and moved with the seasons, without permanent settlements, in small groups ranging in size from 25 to 50 individuals. Frequently, these family bands would camp in a place for a few weeks because the hunting was good or the vegetation was plentiful. When the game left the area or the vegetation went out of season, the people moved on.

Around 10,000 years ago, near the end of the last Ice Age, a change occurred. It happened slowly and without any evident drama. Nonetheless, it was one of the most momentous changes in human history: People began to settle down in one place and to evolve more complex social structures. Civilization as we know it was beginning, but why did it happen?

As time passed, the number of hunter-gatherer tribes grew. Gradually, they began to deplete the natural resources that had formed the mainstay of their existence for millennia. Game became scarce, and vegetation was depleted. How could these nomads solve the food shortage problem? They could wander over larger areas, but that was difficult and threatened to place them in direct competition with other groups. They could carry extra food from areas of abundance, but this would be burdensome without the use of animals—which had not yet been domesticated. A better possibility was to settle in the most fertile areas and raise their own food. This option was the one that won out. Many experts view the domestication of plants, sometimes called the *agricultural revolution,* as the single most important event in human history (Mumford 1989:55; orig. 1961). For the first time, people could stay in one place and—once a food surplus could be produced—could allow some members of the group to pursue interests other than seeking food, such as crafts and science.

Over a period of some 5,000 years, villages began and multiplied. Humans created permanent settlements where they raised crops and learned to domesticate animals for use in the fields or as a food supply. Permanent settlements also transformed patterns of social structure. Most important, these settlements were all characterized by a more complex **division of labor.** For the first time, people began doing many different, specialized tasks to "earn a living." This was a radical shift from the social structure that prevailed in hunter-gatherer tribes. In nomadic groups, everyone knew a bit about everything; no one was a full-time doctor, lawyer, priest, or trader. Only permanent settlements afforded people the opportunity to specialize, not just in food production but also in religion, military affairs, trade, and a host of other occupations.

Specialization benefited everyone: The farmer gained the protection of the military and the benefit of the priest's greater insight into religious matters, while the priest and the soldier received the fruits of the farmer's labors. In short, these early settlements provided the possibility of living a life based more on choice than on tradition. No longer did each man face the limited choice of becoming a farmer or hunter, and each woman a housekeeper and mother. Now a widening variety of options emerged that allowed personal choice instead of merely following in a parent's footsteps. Such opportunities were probably as strong an inducement thousands of years ago as they are today.

Linked to the more complex division of labor was a second major element in the social structure of these early settlements: a **hierarchical power structure.** Hunting and gathering societies tend to be egalitarian—that is, while people perform a few different tasks in daily life, all work is deemed to be equally important for the welfare of the group. For example, hunting (typically done by men) is no more important than gathering food or caring for children (usually done by women). Furthermore, with the limited productive technology possessed by hunter-gatherers, few resources are available beyond those needed for daily life; no one is able to amass much more wealth than anyone else.

Given a more complex division of labor and the development of an hierarchical power structure, a third element was necessary for cities to emerge: the development of a **productive surplus.** Earlier, we noted that many archaeologists believe that the rise of agriculture was the main reason people traded hunting and gathering for permanent settlements. A similar process was at work in the gradual transition from village to town to city. Specifically, a growing population could not be supported without an increasing surplus of food. This notion of "agricultural primacy"—of food surplus supporting permanent settlements—has been reinforced by the discovery of the remains of domesticated plants and animals at early urban sites around the world.

To sum up, around 8000 B.C.E., hunting and gathering societies began to increase in size. As a response to population increase, people began to settle down and take up agriculture as a way of life. These permanent settlements were characterized by increasingly complex social structures organized around a division of labor and a hierarchical power structure. Such settlements depended on a productive surplus. As these elements coalesced, they reinforced each other: The division of labor led to more efficient use of human and natural resources, which in turn led to a greater division of labor and a more intricate power structure, and so on. As this happened, villages turned into towns, and then towns became the first cities.

The City Emerges

What do we know of these earliest cities? We begin with what is thought to be the first city: Jericho. The modern city of Jericho and its ancient ruins lie just to the north of the Dead Sea, in present-day Israel (see Figure 2–1 on pages 28–29).

Jericho.   With careful excavation, archaeologists found evidence to identify Jericho as the oldest city yet to be discovered anywhere in the world. We now know that Jericho was constructed as a walled city over 10,000 years ago. Put differently, it was already an ancient city when the pyramids were built.

Research at Jericho, however, sparked a debate: At what point can we speak of a permanent settlement as being a "city"? Some archaeologists argue that given total population statistics in that period, a population of about 600 people and substantial buildings allow Jericho to be considered a city by about 8000 B.C.E. Others disagree, citing Jericho's small size by today's standards. Size, however, is not the only important factor. Population density and the complexity of social life—involving a broad range of activities and a hierarchy of power relations—add to Jericho's claim to city status.

What made Jericho different from other settlements of its time was the presence of houses made of sun-dried brick, a surrounding wall, a tower, and a large trench, all suggesting an advanced division of labor and an hierarchical social order that could oversee large-scale public works. The wall further indicates a recognition of the need for defense and for protection from the elements. Even after 10,000 years of erosion, its ruins are some 12 feet high and 6 feet thick at the base. The trench, cut into solid rock, is about 27 feet across and 9 feet deep. Although archaeologists are not sure what it was used for (to hold water?), certainly a complex, cooperative effort was necessary to create it.

A short account of the later history of Jericho holds an interesting lesson in the history of urban settlements. It would seem that the original settlers of Jericho did not remain after about 7000 B.C.E., when a second group took up residence. This second group was more technologically advanced than the original settlers, constructing rectangular houses of bricks and mortar with plaster walls and floors. Around this time, trade with outsiders appears to have developed, adding to Jericho's cosmopolitan character. Then, about 1,000 years later—close to 6000 B.C.E.—the site was inexplicably abandoned, and it remained so for a millennium.

Resettlement began about 5000 B.C.E., providing yet another twist to Jericho's story. The later settlers were markedly less advanced in their technology, digging only primitive shelters, and no public works are traceable to this period. Then, with the coming of the Bronze Age at about 3000 B.C.E., a far more advanced culture prevailed. Artwork is evident, possibly linked to the civilization in Mesopotamia to the east or in Egypt to the southwest. By the time settlement of ancient Jericho came to an end at about 1500 B.C.E., many other groups had lived within the city.

The story of Jericho teaches us that the history of cities must not be oversimplified. Cities do not always grow in population and gain technical capacity. Discontinuity and unexpected events change developmental patterns again and again, as we shall see in the remainder of this chapter.

Catal Hüyük. Evidence produced by excavation at Jericho places the beginning of city life between 8000 and 7000 B.C.E. By 6000 B.C.E., other sites, such as Catal Hüyük (pronounced Sha-tal Hoo-yook) in present-day Turkey, had become well developed. Originally settled on a 32-acre site (three times larger than Jericho), Catal Hüyük eventually supported a population of some 6,000. This strange, streetless city was composed of mud-brick dwellings clustered together like the cells of a beehive, with windowless walls facing outward. Small windows built high in the inner walls provided light, and the only entrances were on the roofs, reachable by ladders. This construction design was so secure that no trace has been found of any plunder or massacre during the city's nearly 1,000 years of existence. The *Cityscape* box on page 30 offers a portrait of life in this early city.

The partial excavation of the Neolithic city of Catal Hüyük has already provided archaeologists with many clues about the social life of its inhabitants. Discovered in the late 1950s, the site became internationally famous for the large size and dense occupation of the settlement as well as for the spectacular wall paintings and other art uncovered inside the houses.

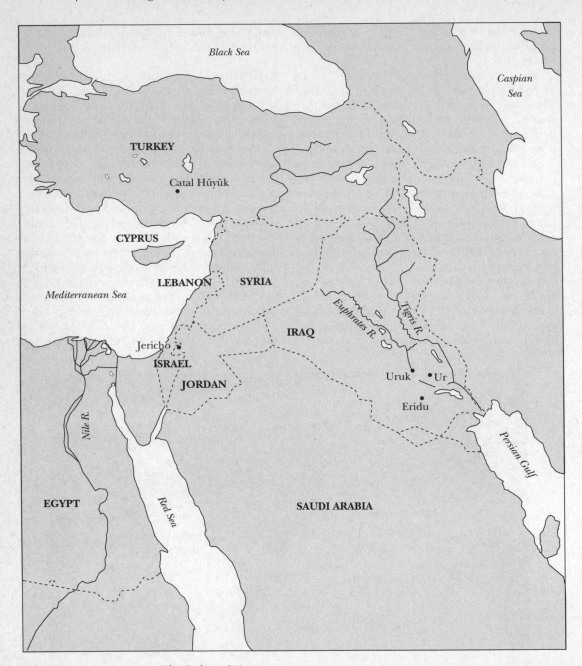

FIGURE 2–1   Asia Minor: The Earliest Cities

FIGURE 2–1   Asia Minor: The Earliest Cities *(continued)*

CITYSCAPE

Daily Life in Catal Hüyük, 6000 B.C.E.

When the first light of dawn struck . . . on a spring morning in the year 6000 B.C.E., it brushed lightly across the flat roofs of tightly built mud-brick houses. . . . The houses turned blank, doorless walls to the world. The household entrance was by way of the roof through either a wooden doorway or a thatch opening onto a ladder. Doors at ground level could have let in anything from floodwaters to wild animals: the roof holes and ladders provided security. . . .

Inside one of the houses the father stirred. . . . From his leather pouch he grasped a lump of yellowish, crystalline sulfur collected on his last trip to the hills, and a flint tool that he had fashioned to his needs. . . . With this prehistoric Boy Scout knife the man could make wood shavings, strike a spark, feed the spark with sulfur and produce a fire within minutes. . . . The man made a fire on the hearth while his wife went through a small doorless opening in the mud-brick wall to the family food-storage niche. In it was a bin about a yard high, made of clay and very clean. She drew some grain from a small hole at the bin's bottom: it was always filled from the top and emptied from the bottom so

that the oldest grain, or that most exposed to damp, would be used first. The wife moved slowly. She was heavy with another child, and she was getting old: almost 28.

On that mythical morning the family ate a gruel of grain and milk, supplemented by bits of meat left over from a previous meal. The mother nursed the baby while she fed the next-oldest with a spoon made from a cow's rib bone. . . .

Then there was work to do. . . .

The man and the woman might have tended fields or flocks, but not many townsfolk could have been farmers—no compact community of 6,000 people could have grown enough food to support itself while doing all the other things that Catal Hüyük residents did. The city must have traded goods and services for supplies from the surrounding region. The woman of the house might conceivably have made baskets for such trade. Or the man might have spent his days as a craftsman, for although no specialized tools were found in his home, there is ample evidence in the city of skillfully woven textiles, good pottery and beautiful art work.

Source: Dora Jane Hamblin, *The First Cities* (New York: Time–Life, 1973), pp. 43–46, excerpts.

THE FIRST URBAN REVOLUTION: CITY-STATES AND URBAN EMPIRES

Although scattered cities such as Jericho and Catal Hüyük thrived in the period between 7000 and 4000 B.C.E., it was not until about 3500 B.C.E. that urban development accelerated to a point where large numbers of cities flourished.

The earliest cities, like Jericho, clearly demonstrated their ability to generate security

and wealth for fairly large numbers of people. Thus, more and more people came to the city to share in these benefits. The *idea* of the city was taking hold. No longer were many people content to live the relatively backward life of the tribe, the village, or the town. They wanted the benefits of the city: more choice, unprecedented material wealth, and ongoing excitement.

So cities grew in number and in population, but growth also brought problems. A rising population demanded more and more goods and services, and the needs of the city's inhabitants had to be managed in some way. Some cities responded to this challenge by making their social structure even more complex: They created the state.

The central feature of the state is its ability to wield power over many people—essentially, to dictate everyone's rights and responsibilities: who has to live where, who has to serve in the military, and so on. With such power, the city's leaders can do pretty much what they like in order to solve (or create) the city's problems—they can reorganize production, determine who will be educated, and perhaps most important, make alliances and wage war to capture land, population, and resources.

With the emergence of the state as a form of social organization came the first **city-states**— cities that controlled the surrounding regions, including a number of other towns, villages, and rural lands. As time passed, some of these city-states conquered or made alliances with others to form the world's first urban empires— much larger regions, usually dominated by a single central city. These early urban empires emerged around the world—in Mesopotamia, Egypt, the Indus River Valley, China, Central America, and South America—and they "pushed" the city as a form of human settlement to ever-greater complexity and population size.

This, then, was the period of the *first urban revolution* (Childe 1950). From approximately 4000 B.C.E. to 500 C.E., urban sites multiplied and their populations grew to sizes previously unknown in human history (Rome at its apex, for example, surpassed a million people). In retrospect, the first urban revolution appears to have been something of a mixed blessing. The city's greatest positive attributes were its ability to improve people's standard of living, provide choice in the conduct of life, and stimulate the human imagination. On the other hand, these first cities also had rigid divisions of social class that extended the city's benefits to only a small minority of the urban population. With the emergence of city-states and urban empires, human warfare and bloodshed rose to unparalleled levels as well.

With all this in mind, then, we now turn to brief descriptions of some of the first urban empires.

The Near East: Mesopotamia and Egypt

The first urban empire was in the Fertile Crescent region of the Tigris and Euphrates rivers in the southern portion of present-day Iraq. This region, known in ancient times as Mesopotamia or Sumer, began evolving significant cities as early as 4000 B.C.E. Cities such as Uruk, Eridu, and Ur (see Figure 2–1) represent a significant extension of world urbanization not only because they were larger than their earlier counterparts but also because of their more complex social structures. Wheat and barley were important domesticated crops, and city dwellers enjoyed the advantages of major technological advances, such as oxen-pulled plows and the wheel (Schomp 2005).

Rise of Mesopotamian Cities.   The cities of the region reached their greatest development at about 2800 B.C.E. Uruk, it is estimated, covered an area of approximately 1,100 acres and supported a population as high as 50,000 (Liverani 2006). All the Mesopotamian (Sumerian) cities were theocracies, ruled by a priest-king. A ruling elite that controlled and protected the area around the city, including its agricultural land, exacted a portion of the agricultural surplus as tribute and stored it in the major temple (Schomp 2005:17).

Uruk and other Mesopotamian cities had highly complex social structures, including a power hierarchy and a pronounced division of labor. Excavations have established the existence of monumental public buildings, including ziggurats (religious shrines); extensive trade arrangements; a system of writing (cuneiform); mathematics; and a code of law. Sumerian texts noting the concerns of everyday life still survive. In these accounts, sheep, goats, and cattle are tabulated, taxed, and exchanged; children are shepherded to school— as today, often against their will—by concerned parents; a council of elders meets to consider grievances against the inhabitants of an adjoining city-state; and a politician attempts to win the favor of the populace with tax reductions (Wenke 2005). Clearly, these cities had advanced to a point at which parallels may easily be drawn with cities of our own experience.

Early Mesopotamian urban life, however, was centered on the temple and on religious beliefs. The populace recognized thousands of gods, and the temples, like the palaces, were large and opulently decorated. People of less favorable social position lived in irregularly organized houses along the narrow, unpaved, winding streets. The complex social structure also resulted in a strong military elite and made possible an increasing capacity to wage war. Frequently under attack, Mesopotamian cities were walled defensively.

After about 3500 B.C.E., the cities began to be organized as politically distinct city-states, each exerting its influence over a broad region. Although these city-states were independent of one another and often at war, they did represent a common civilization. They shared a common cultural heritage and, as far as the outside world was concerned, saw themselves as possessors of a unique, even superior culture (Wenke 2005). By 700 B.C.E., the Assyrian Empire dominated the region, and the Persian Empire followed around 500 B.C.E.

The importance of this continual trading of urban dominance was that it spurred the development of cities and their influence throughout the Near East. In an effort to maintain control of their empires, each set of rulers tried to develop their cities as much as their culture and technology would permit. The cities of the region were continually renewed with inventions, innovations, and new ideas supplied by trade and people of different backgrounds.

Although it would be too much to say that these cities contained all of the civilization that existed in their era, they were key centers. They were "containers" in a double sense: They literally encircled their population and their valued goods with walls, and more figuratively, they served as the place where all the themes of Mesopotamian culture could be found.

Egyptian Cities. The Great Pyramids of Gizeh are modern reminders of another empire that flourished shortly after the rise of cities in Mesopotamia. The archaeological record of Egyptian cities is less detailed than that of their Mesopotamian counterparts, but it appears that by 3100 B.C.E., Menes, the first pharaoh of a united Egypt, was in control of the cities of Memphis and Hierakonopolis to its south along the Nile River.

Several reasons explain why the record of the earliest Egyptian cities is less clear. First, their buildings were made of unbaked brick and other materials that have not stood the test of time. Second, the early Egyptians apparently built and abandoned their cities with some frequency. As a result, even though the cities were crucial centers of Egyptian civilization, none maintained its dominance long enough to reach a very large size (Kemp 1992; Sjoberg 1965).

Although the cities that emerged in Egypt went through what we now think is the normal process of early development—from village to town and, finally, to city—they were rather distinct from those in Mesopotamia. Egyptian civilization was focused on the ruling pharaoh, and each had his own city—a religious and political center built to reflect his power, which by 2500 B.C.E. was virtually absolute. More than a secular leader or priest, the pharaoh was believed to be a god, and his singular dominance of the Nile region created a relatively peaceful history.

Thus, we find little evidence in early Egypt of city walls. Each capital city became a pharaoh's administrative center, and much of the activity of urban artisans was directed toward construction of a palace for his pleasure in this life and an opulent tomb for his needs in the life to come. Although not as large as those of Mesopotamia, these Egyptian cities were characterized by distinctive urban traits, including a clear power structure and division of labor, social inequality, and an administrative organization (utilizing hieroglyphic writing, papyrus paper, and ink) to oversee public needs and maintain the pharaoh's control.

If the early Egyptian cities were peaceful, however, those that followed were not. Egypt's later history, like that of Mesopotamia, is riddled with conflict both within the empire and with other empires. During the period known as the Old Kingdom (2700–2180 B.C.E.), the pharaohs made forays into neighboring territories to procure goods. Successful in many of these adventures, they used their plundered wealth and captured slaves to build cities and palaces. It was two pharaohs of this period (Cheops and his son, Cephren) who built the Great Pyramids of Gizeh—still the most colossal monuments ever constructed—between 2600 and 2500 B.C.E. Cephren was also responsible for the Sphinx at Gizeh.

Then, around 2180 B.C.E., the Old Kingdom collapsed, famine spread, and rioting in the cities was rampant. For the next 600 years, Egypt went through several alternating periods of disarray and reunification. Urban greatness once again reappeared in the New Kingdom period (1500–1100 B.C.E.). This was the time of the minor pharaoh Tutankhamun—the only pharaoh whose gravesite in the Valley of the Kings was undisturbed by pillaging robbers—and of Ramses II, the pharaoh who conquered much of the Near East for Egypt and who may have been Moses' adversary in his attempts to free the Jews from Egyptian servitude. Ramses rebuilt many of Egypt's cities; created a new capital, Pi-Ramesse, on the Mediterranean; and constructed self-glorifying yet magnificent temples at Karnak, Luxor, and Abu Simbel. The Asian territories were lost around 1100 B.C.E., and the next 300 years saw the final decline of pharaoh-ruled Egypt. From 800 to 671 B.C.E., the African rulers of Kush—a former Egyptian outpost to the south—controlled Egypt.

Near Eastern empires inflicted the final indignities. The Assyrians conquered Egypt in 671 B.C.E. and, though expelled less than 20 years later, were followed by the Persians in 525 B.C.E. The Persians more or less dominated the region until 332 B.C.E., the year that Alexander the Great arrived, was accepted as pharaoh, and built his city, Alexandria, at the head of the Nile. From then on, Egypt was at the mercy of foreign overlords.

The development of cities in the Nile region raises an interesting question as to the possible diffusion of urban influence from Mesopotamia. History records frequent contact between the two regions. Were the Egyptian cities created independently, or was the idea of the city imported? Debate continues, but the currently dominant belief is that traders or nomads from early cities in Mesopotamia carried at least some urban influences toward both Egypt in the west and the Indus Valley in the east (Rice 2003). In all three regions, however, city life emerged in its own special fashion and included clearly distinct and unique aspects that revealed the stamp of the local civilization (Sjoberg 1965:49).

The Indus Region

To the east of Mesopotamia, along the Indus River of present-day India and Pakistan, was a third ecologically favorable area where early cities emerged. Trade routes linked the Indus cities with Mesopotamian cities through other outposts, such as Tepe Yahya, midway between the two areas (see Figure 2–1). It is also likely that trading in such products as jade linked this area with Central Asia to the east (Magee 2005).

Excavations have yielded the remains of two highly developed cities that were centers of a regional civilization beginning about 2500 B.C.E. Both were prominent in urban history until about 1500 B.C.E. Moenjo-Daro was situated on the Indus River about 175 miles from the Arabian Sea; Harappa was about 350 miles further north, on one of the Indus River's tributaries. Each had a population as high as 40,000 and represented an urban civilization distinct in many ways from those we have considered thus far. Unlike either Mesopotamia or Egypt, for example, Moenjo-Daro does not show evidence of a single, all-powerful leader or a preoccupation with temples and god-monuments, but it does show evidence of extensive "good living."

Moenjo-Daro would have seemed familiar to a modern visitor, with the same gridiron pattern common to most Western cities today. Its remarkable structures of mud-baked bricks and burnt-wood framing were up to two stories high and included an elaborate, well-built bath

The excavated site of ancient Moenjo-Daro in the Indus River Valley reveals a surprisingly modern grid pattern of housing (left) and a sanitation system of brick-lined, open sewers (trench, bottom and right). What the photo does not reveal is the uniformity of its north–south boulevard, which is 30 feet wide, and the east–west cross streets about every 200 yards.

area with a layer of natural tar to keep it from leaking. Remarkably, it even had a building with an underground furnace, like the Roman hypocausts, for heated bathing. Other city features were a central marketplace, a large common well, and a citadel or administrative center that may have included a granary for storage of food surplus.

Perhaps the most remarkable discovery about this city was its well-constructed sanitation system. Along the streets were brick-lined, open sewers that carried away house drainage. Archaeologists discovered several bathrooms with sit-down toilets, indicating the presence in 2500 B.C.E. of an urban luxury not commonly found in European cities until the nineteenth century.

Within the city, numerous craft specialists were in operation, including potters, weavers, brick makers, and copper and bronze metalworkers (Kenoyer 1998). In fact, the presence of extensive residential areas displaying

a uniformity of mud-brick houses, streets, and drainage systems suggests the extensive existence of a comparatively high standard of living. This would make Moenjo-Daro one of the first cities to provide such a widespread state of well being—essentially, a kind of middle-class lifestyle—among its citizenry.

Until the mid-twentieth century, it was commonly thought that Mesopotamia, Egypt, and the Indus River Valley contained the cities from which all later ones took their pattern. Archaeological research since then, however, showed otherwise. Apparently, cities emerged in many places around the world independently of one another. Two other regions where this occurred were China and the Americas.

A Glance Eastward: China

Cities in China date back at least 4,300 years. A 2006 archaeological discovery suggests that the earliest was Liangzhu, in Yuhang County,

Zhejiang. This city had an area of 31 million square feet, a 131-foot canal of hardened earth, and a defensive wall that was 13 to 20 feet thick. In the stratified society, as evidenced by jade and silk found at elite burial sites and simply pottery shards for the nonelite, it appears that religion held considerable importance, given the elaborate religious structures and carefully positioned altars and piles of stones (Stark 2006).

We know much more about the second and third capital cities of the Shang Dynasty than the first, thought to be Bo. The second capital, Cheng-chou, was at its height about 1600 B.C.E. A rectangular wall 4.5 miles in length and more than 30 feet high enclosed an area of about 1.5 square miles, which contained the city's administrative and ceremonial centers. In this fortified area, the political and religious elite lived apart from the common people. Outside the enclosure lived artisans—bronze workers and craftspeople.

An-yang was the third Shang capital. Archaeological excavation has uncovered remnants of its larger pattern, by which the central city was linked to the surrounding area. As in Cheng-chou, the residences of artisans and craft workers were just outside a walled area. In the region immediately beyond, numerous villages formed a network of trade, supplying agricultural and other specialized products to the city (Thorp 2005).

What existed in China, then, was a type of urban settlement somewhat more diffused than that in the areas already considered. Rather than concentrating all their political, religious, and craft activities in a single, center-city area, the Chinese set priests and rulers apart from the remainder of the urban population. At some distance from their protected, walled enclosure, residents of satellite villages participated in the life of the urban area as a whole.

A Glance Westward: The Americas

The last major region in which early cities developed was nearer to home—in Mesoamerica, specifically the area of present-day central Mexico, the Yucatan Peninsula, and Guatemala; and in South America, particularly the western part of that continent. The history of these areas reveals, once again, several familiar patterns: A more productive agricultural technology and the formation of a complex social structure accompanied the rise of cities. The case of Mesoamerica, however, also represents several significant areas of contrast to urban development elsewhere.

People inhabited the area at least as early as 20,000 B.C.E. Cultivation of plants had been achieved by 7000 B.C.E., but in contrast to other parts of the world where cities arose, this area was not well suited to the production of large surpluses, partly because of its rocky, mountainous terrain and partly because the inhabitants lacked domesticated animals and a solid source of agricultural protein. The traditional digging stick rather than the plow remained the primary tool of cultivation for millennia, and Mesoamerica never embraced farming in the sense that other regions did. Rather, its groups developed a mixed economy in which hunting and other undomesticated resources continued to play a very important part. Nevertheless, one cultivated crop, maize (corn), contributed to a sturdy and nutritious diet.

By 1500 B.C.E., early villages of mud-walled houses had been established. Because hunting continued to play a major role in the economy, these village sites moved with some frequency. In some villages, Olmec and Mayan tribes built elaborate ceremonial centers that served large populations, employing many craftspeople in their design and construction. Serving as a place of permanent residence for only a small number of priests at the outset, these ceremonial centers slowly grew in size and complexity. Before the time of the birth of Christ, they had become full-fledged cities.

The same process occurred on the western coast of South America in present-day Peru and Bolivia. Perhaps the most famous urban empire of this region was that of the Incas, with its capital in the city of Cuzco. Less well known, but as important, was the urban empire of Chimor on the north coast of Peru. Its capital, Chan Chan, began as a city around the same time that the Incan urban centers evolved—about 800 C.E. At its height (approximately 1450 C.E.), Chan Chan ruled over a large hinterland as a major challenger to the Incas.

Note that Chan Chan was a **regal/ritual city**—an important urban center with a population of no more than 30,000. As the term suggests, a regal/ritual city is used primarily by the ruling class: Chan Chan's rulers lived there year-round in magnificent palaces and used most of the city's buildings for their own pleasure and for the rituals of Chimor culture. Only small numbers of artisans, servants, and peasants were allowed to share in that part of the urban environment. All the rest of the empire's people were forced to live in the surrounding towns or rural areas and do the bidding of the ruling class, including producing food, paying taxes, and laboring on city projects.

In 1470, Chan Chan's challenge provoked the Incas to conquer the Chimor Empire and subjugate its inhabitants, but even this dominance was not to last. By the end of the century, Columbus would land in the New World. Not long after that, the Spanish and, later, the Portuguese would arrive in Mesoamerica and South America in force. Under the European onslaught, these proud urban empires would fall like dominoes, and a new type of city would arise—a process described in Chapter 13.

Despite conditions that were unique to the hemisphere, cities arose indigenously in the Americas as they had in other regions of the world. These cities, from a historical standpoint, were highly sophisticated and equal in complexity to those found elsewhere. For example, a thousand years before the Aztecs, Teotihuacan was the religious capital of Mexico. An urban center of massive structures that was at its peak around 600 C.E., it supported a population of perhaps 200,000 in a city physically larger than imperial Rome itself (Austin and Lujan 2001:109). Its eight square miles were laid out in a specific grid plan, its north–south avenues containing palaces and pyramid temples with impressive sculptures. The city's housing complexes were large and contained a number of rooms, all opening onto patios. Some were built, like the pyramid temples, of a red volcanic rock that was mined locally. Towering over the city

was the Pyramid of the Sun, rising at a sharp angle from its 720- by 760-foot base to a height of 216 feet. Probably constructed in the first century C.E., it would have taken, according to expert estimates, thousands of laborers 50 years to build (Braswell 2004).

Summary: Traits of Early Cities

Human beings first devised cities about 10,000 years ago. As shown graphically in Figure 2–2, they had become quite common in the Near East by 4000 B.C.E., in the Indus River Valley by 2500 B.C.E., and in China by 2000 B.C.E. Their appearance in the Americas came somewhat later, around 500 B.C.E

All early cities were characterized by some combination of favorable ecological conditions, some sort of trade or food surplus, and a complex social structure (a fairly sophisticated division of labor and a power hierarchy). Beyond these important characteristics, some other similarities, and a few differences, may be mentioned.

First, early cities do not show any smooth progression of growth. On the one hand, the transition from the first permanent settlements to full-fledged cities took a long time—from about 8000 B.C.E. to 3000 B.C.E. On the other hand, city histories the world over are marked by discontinuity and change, by rise and fall. Sometimes, as in Teotihuacan, one group occupied a city for its entire duration; sometimes, as in Jericho, many groups came and went.

Second, as population centers, early cities were small. Most were mere towns by today's standards. A population of about 10,000 was usual, and even the largest settlements never went much beyond the quarter-million mark.

Third, regarding the power structure, many early cities had a theocratic character— a fused religious and political elite in which kings were also priests and, not infrequently, "gods." This fusion allowed a type of double control over the city's population and its problems. Royalty could, in the name of heaven, impose taxes and even servitude. Of course, the character of this elite structure varied. It was sharply evident in Egypt, China,

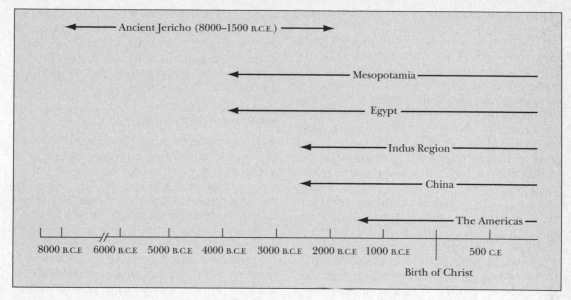

FIGURE 2–2   The Chronology of the First Cities

and Teotihuacan but was more subdued in the Indus city of Moenjo-Daro. Everywhere, however, the first cities were characterized by inequalities in power and benefits: Usually, the few prospered, and the many got by as best they could.

Finally, what of the quality of life in early cities? In comparison with modern Western cities, it was probably not very high—life was usually hard, relatively short, and subject to considerable uncertainty. Yet there is substantial variation here as well. Moenjo-Daro appears to have afforded a higher standard of living to more residents than was the case in other cities that were more sharply divided by class.

Other factors, such as war and slavery, also must have had a powerful effect on the quality of life experienced by many early city dwellers. The city, particularly after it reached the state and empire stage, was more often than not an instrument of death and destruction as one urban center tried to conquer another. To some extent, this increase in bloodshed cannot be blamed on the city as such. Rather, the use of systematic warfare

seems more coincident with primitive agriculture and the coming of the first permanent settlements around 8000 B.C.E. Apparently, agricultural techniques produced a productive surplus for the first time, and this surplus, in turn, attracted people to settlements and induced some of them to conquer other groups in an effort to procure even more surplus. When urban areas became common around 4000 B.C.E., however, the human appetite for conquest rose to a level unknown before in history.

In short, the development of the city was a most decisive event in human history. The early city magnified human activity in all its dimensions. People knew more, did more, and found more possibilities open to them. Such has always been the city's promise: to provide a better life. Early Western cities, discussed next, also held out the promise of "the good life." Although certainly some progress was made along that road, these cities, like their earlier counterparts, also had a tragic capacity for harboring the human indignities of coercive inequality, militaristic expansion, and war.

Crete and Greece

Western cities—those of Europe and North America—are relative latecomers in the urban story. Cities had been in existence for many thousands of years before urbanization took hold in the northern Mediterranean region on the island of Crete.

About 1800 B.C.E., settlements were established in Crete, possibly by traders or migrants from the urban settlements of Mesopotamia. Little is known of these early cities, yet by all accounts, they were thriving overseas trade centers. Stone-paved roads, made from blocks cut by bronze saws, connected the cities. Lining the paved city streets that had drainage capabilities were two- to three-story buildings with flat-tiled roofs held up by ceiling timbers. Their court buildings contained inverted columns, wider at the top than the bottom (Chadwick 1999). For some reason, these cities come to an end about 1400 B.C.E. The cities of Crete were destroyed, like Teotihuacan would be in another two centuries, either by a catastrophic earthquake or volcanic eruption or by invaders. Not until seven centuries later would urban development appear again in Europe, this time in Greece.

The early Greek *polis*, or city-state, did not follow the pattern of the cities of Mesopotamia and Egypt, which magnified the power of the elite at the expense of their other citizens. The fiercely independent Greek city-states— among them Athens, Corinth, and Sparta— experienced war as well as peaceful rivalry, as symbolized by the Olympic games. Compared with earlier cities of the Near East with powerful rulers, Greek cities were more egalitarian, though few matched Athens in having most of its free citizenry (the Greeks had slaves) directly participating in legislative decisions.

Classes whose commercial influence reached outward from Sicily to northern Africa ruled these cities. The Greeks founded such cities as Messina in Sicily and Marseilles in France. Unfortunately, however, in the end the Greek city-states turned on each other in the destructive Peloponnesian War (431–404 B.C.E.), leaving behind a remarkable legacy that highlighted the positive possibilities of urban civilization, including outstanding painting, sculpture, and architecture as well as a political system and body of philosophy that influence the world to this day (Waterfield 2005).

Rome

As Greek culture slipped into decline, another great civilization was gathering strength to the west. It was centered, perhaps more than any cultural system before or since, on a single city; indeed, the city's name is synonymous with the culture itself. In his oft-cited oration *To Rome*, written in the mid-second century B.C.E., Aelius Aristides claimed "Rome! Everything is found here. All the skills which exist or have existed, anything that can be made or grown. If something can't be found here, then it simply doesn't exist!"

Aristedes was right. By the final centuries of the pre-Christian era, Rome was the dominant power of the Western world. By the time of Christ, the city on which the Roman Empire was based was gargantuan by all previous urban standards, possibly containing a population of more than 1 million.

Rome displayed the same characteristics we have encountered in the earliest cities: a favorable ecological setting, the ability to produce an economic surplus, and a complex social structure. Also, like the Greek cities, Rome was characterized by developed arts and sciences and by public monuments and buildings. Yet Rome was an urban civilization almost exclusively based on the expression of militaristic power. For the several centuries during which the city thrived, Rome explored and revealed for all history the consequences of concentrating a city's resources almost entirely on the accumulation of power and wealth.

If the Greek conception of the good life was a city founded on the principles of moderation, balance, and human participation, the Roman conception was based on the celebration of sheer excess and unremitting domination. At its height, the empire extended from Rome across the Mediterranean to

At its height, Imperial Rome was the center of a vast, militaristic empire. The city, a mixture of magnificent buildings and squalid slums, contained carefully planned, broad thoroughfares and an impressive water supply and drainage system. Here, the Roman Forum—the heart of the city's ceremonial life—was crowded with temples, arches, statues, and public buildings.

northern Africa, to present-day Germany, to Hadrian's Wall on the border between England and Scotland, and to Mesopotamia, where the Tigris and Euphrates rivers flowed. It included almost half the world's population, and Rome ruled this territory mostly in its entirety for an amazing 450 years (Heather 2007:13-14).

What can we say of the city that served as the center of this vast empire? In physical design, Rome was similar to the cities discussed earlier. At its center were a market, a forum, and a complex of monumental buildings. Radiating outward in orderly fashion across the breadth of the city—some 7 square miles overall—were major, broad thoroughfares constructed according to a careful plan. Indeed, roads were one of Rome's greatest achievements. In all, the Roman work force constructed more than 50,000 miles of roads. Extremely well built, these roads served as links between Rome and the empire's vast hinterland, from which the city drew tribute.

Many of the major cities of Europe today—including London, York, Vienna, Bordeaux, Paris, and Cologne—were once provincial outposts of Rome.

Perhaps most striking was the city's aqueduct system, considered to be among the greatest engineering feats of the ancient world. Between 312 B.C.E. and 222 C.E., the Romans built 11 separate aqueducts, which together could deliver up to 264 gallons per person to its 1 million residents—more than the capability of most cities today. Benefiting from such a generous water supply, Rome had large public baths, fountains, hydrants along main streets, and a system of water drainage begun as early as the sixth century B.C.E. In addition, the Romans constructed aqueducts for about 200 provincial cities they founded throughout Europe (Carcopino 2003). These spillways—some of which are still in use today—brought freshwater from as far away as 59 miles, just as today's aqueduct systems bring water from as far away as 120 miles to

New York City or from many hundreds of miles away in California.

The motive for Rome's impressive engineering was ultimately to serve the interests of the ruling military and political elite. While the elite enjoyed incredible riches, Rome's poorer residents, living in largely unplanned and squalid tenements, benefited little from the wealth that was brought continuously to the city. Like their modern counterparts, these tenement districts were typically overcrowded, stifling, foul smelling, disease ridden, and filled with brutal actions that desensitized its people and cheapened the value of life. This underside of Roman life had a further dimension—one that could hardly find a sharper contrast with the Greek ideal of human dignity. The enduring, if horrible, example of Rome's descent into sadistic escapism was the Circus, as described in the *Cityscape* box on page 41.

Taken as a whole, Rome was a parade of contrasts: engineering excellence and technical achievement juxtaposed with human debasement and militaristic cruelty. Eventually, its empire extended so far that it could no longer control its home base, and rotting from within, Rome sank into decline. It fell in 476 C.E. under the onslaught of northern invasion, and by the sixth century, it had become a mere town of 20,000.

Decline: The Middle Ages

As Rome collapsed, so did the empire that had sustained urban life throughout much of Europe. With this eclipse came a period of about 600 years during which European cities either fell into a pattern of minimal survival or ceased to exist entirely. The commercial trade that had been the source of life to the empire and its cities was drastically curtailed. The danger of pillaging by barbarians increased. Oncegreat cities, which had boasted populations in excess of 100,000, became virtually isolated hamlets. There evolved an almost singular concern for security. Surviving cities were fortified—surrounded by great walls, a revival of an older urban feature that had been rendered unnecessary by the establishment of Roman control over nearly the entire continent.

The pattern of settlement typical of the fifth through the eleventh centuries was a mosaic of local manors, villages, and small towns that in many ways were reminiscent of the earliest urban settlements we considered at the beginning of this chapter. The dominance over a large hinterland so characteristic of Greek and Roman cities all but vanished. This is, of course, the essence of the image conveyed by the phrase "Dark Ages."

During this period, a feudal system arose in which a local lord provided security in exchange for service on his lands. In most cases, however, manors were situated in the countryside, weakening urban influence even further. A few highly fortified small cities and manor towns survived, but a delicate balance was struck in these settlements. Given the state of medieval technology, protection could be provided for only a limited population. A small population made a low level of production inevitable, however, and this, in turn, caused the city to stagnate.

Revival: Medieval and Renaissance Cities

The low point of urban life in Europe was reached in the ninth century (Holmes 2002). Then, around the eleventh century, a general "awakening" began. The reasons for this change, which occurred gradually over several centuries, are numerous and complex, but a general development of urban trade and crafts was a key factor.

The Crusades—armed marches by Christian European groups against the Islamic possessors of "The Holy Land," where more often than not the Europeans found ultimate defeat—took place between 1096 and 1291. Even so, the Crusades contributed to a rebirth of trade routes linking Europe and the Near East, as did the growth of local trade, both of which began stimulating the long-dormant urban division of labor.

The emergence of a complex and competitive commercial class at the center of this trade, dominated from the eleventh century onward by craft guilds, contributed to a newly vibrant city life. Merchants alone did not

CITYSCAPE

Classical Rome: The Dance of Death

The existence of a parasitic economy and a predatory political system produced a typically Roman urban institution that embraced both aspects of its life and gave them a dramatic setting: the old practice of the religious blood sacrifice was given a new secular form in the arena.

Roman life, for all its claims of peace, centered more and more on the imposing rituals of extermination. In the pursuit of sensations sufficiently sharp to cover momentarily the emptiness and meaninglessness of their parasitic existence, the Romans took to staging chariot races, spectacular naval battles set in an artificial lake, theatrical pantomimes in which the strip tease and lewder sexual acts were performed in public. But sensations need constant whipping as people become inured to them: so the whole effort reached a pinnacle in the gladiatorial spectacles, where the agents of this regime applied a diabolic inventiveness to human torture and human extermination. . . . To make attendance at these spectacles even easier, as early as the reign of Claudius, 159 days were marked as public holidays, and as many as 93, a quarter of the whole year, were devoted to games at the public expense. Vast fortunes were spent on staging even a single one of these events. . . .

No body of citizens, not even the Athenians at the height of their empire, ever had such an abundance of idle time to fill with idiotic occupations. . . . after the hour of noon, in addition, the Roman workers, who had doubtless risen at daybreak, suffered no further demand on their time. The transformation of the active, useful life of the early Republican city into the passive and parasitic life that finally dominated it took centuries. But in the end, attendance at public spectacles, terrestrial and nautical, human and animal, became the principal occupation of their existence; and all other activities fed directly or indirectly into it. . . .

The gladiatorial games were first introduced into Rome in 264 B.C. by the consul Decimus Junius Brutus on the occasion of his father's funeral; but the Romans gave them a more utilitarian turn by employing the deadly contests as a popular means for the public punishment of criminals, at first presumably as much for an admonitory deterrent as an enjoyment. Too soon, unfortunately, the ordeal of the prisoner became the welcome amusement of the spectator; and even the emptying of the jails did not provide a sufficient number of victims to meet the popular demand. As with the religious sacrifices of the Aztecs, military expeditions were directed toward supplying a sufficient number of victims, human and animal. Here in the arena both degraded professionals, thoroughly trained for their occupation, and wholly innocent men and women were tortured with every imaginable body-maiming and fear-producing device for public delight.

Source: Excerpts from "The Crystallization of the City," in *The City in History: Its Origin, Its Transformation, and Its Prospects,* copyright © 1961 and renewed 1989 by Lewis Mumford, reprinted by permission of Houghton Mifflin Harcourt Publishing Company and Random House Ltd. This material may not be reproduced in any form or by any means without the prior written permission of the publisher.

dominate these cities, however. Many groups—including the church, the landed gentry, and the feudal royalty—vied for position. Small and self-contained, medieval cities allowed no single focus to dominate urban life in the way the military and political elements had dominated Rome (Nicholas 2003).

As for their populations, medieval cities were small—both in relation to Roman cities (many of which supported more than 100,000 people) and in comparison with the industrial cities that would follow. Although a few cities, such as Paris and Venice, were much larger in area, the physical dimensions of most medieval cities also were modest. Cities typically occupied a few hundred acres, or the size of a small town of about 5,000 people today. Walls surrounding the cities often were supplemented by a moat, as shown in Figure 2–3. Major roads connected the city gates to the center of the city—generally the cathedral, the marketplace, or major buildings, such as the guilds or town halls.

If any one center was of greatest importance, it was the cathedral, which often towered over the rest of the city. Indeed, the importance of the church to the social life of medieval Europe is difficult to exaggerate. All members of mainstream medieval society—both urban and rural—were Roman Catholics. The Catholic Church was an unchallenged dominant force, and exclusion from it—whether through excommunication or as a member of a religious minority (particularly Jews)—relegated one to the status of a social outcast on the fringe of society.

The medieval city did not produce the sense of awe and massive scale that mark the modern Western city. Other than the cathedral and, perhaps, a palace, there were no tall buildings, and streets were narrow and winding rather than wide and straight, as they are today. Paving of streets, done on a large scale in Rome during its empire, did not become common in medieval European cities until the twelfth and thirteenth centuries. Houses, typically built together in rowhouse fashion, often had open space for cultivation in the rear. Despite the lack of such conveniences as indoor plumbing, the small population and relatively low density of these cities allowed life to proceed under conditions far more healthful than those of many cities in the developing world today.

FIGURE 2–3   The medieval city, circa 1350, developed on a new site in response to the needs and patterns of the new trading system and for defense. The site was chosen at the intersection of rivers and roads, a natural route center that offered plentiful water, natural defenses, and an ample food supply from the surrounding agrarian area of the valley. The city was a trading and commercial center; craft industries produced goods for trade and for exchange with farmers of the surrounding area who supplied food as well as many of the items involved in long-distance trade. Movement within the city was mainly pedestrian, so narrow streets with many angles were not constricting. Some wider, more open streets allowed passage of horse traffic involved in long-distance trade.

1. Cathedral
2. Market plaza
3. Guildhalls, craft and trade centers
4. Fortress of local lord
5. Defensive walls with turrets at intervals
6. Moat outside defensive wall

Source: Janet Roebuck, *The Shaping of Urban Society*, pp. 48–49. Copyright © 1974 by Janet Roebuck.

The city of Carcassonne in France remains an outstanding example of a medieval walled city. Compare this picture to Figure 2–3. The local lord's fortress is on the right, and the cathedral is slightly to the left and above it. Such cities were characteristic of Europe for nearly 1,000 years after the fall of Rome (479 C.E.).

These European cities gradually grew in population size and density. First, the rear yards were built over, and then, when there was no more space for construction, they built upward, with floor added to floor (Pounds 2005). The period from the twelfth century until about the sixteenth century was an age of general urban rebirth, or renaissance. First evident in Italian city-states, such as Venice, Florence, Palermo, and Milan, this rebirth is easily linked to the humanistic conception of city life that flourished some 1,500 years earlier in Athens. During the Renaissance, the city gradually recaptured an interest in art, literature, and architecture.

Although once again the city generated the ideal of full human development, the real contradiction of the era was that it was an ideal the great bulk of its citizens had little chance to realize. Wealth, for example, was highly concentrated. For example, in 1545, more than half the wealth in the French city of Lyon belonged to a mere 10 percent of the population (Hohenberg and Lees 1996:147).

THE SECOND URBAN REVOLUTION: THE RISE OF MODERN CITIES

Within the walls of the Renaissance city, the seeds of another type of city altogether were being sown. The old feudal power structure was breaking down, giving people more freedom to live their lives where they chose. Trade was becoming more important, increasing the available wealth, and cities were gaining rapidly in prominence.

Throughout Europe, commerce slowly began to replace agriculture as the dominant mode of making a living. A new middle class began to rise to power. This class—the **bourgeoisie** (the French word means, literally, "of the town")—was composed of shopkeepers, traders, bureaucrats, government officials, and people engaged in commercial ventures of all sorts. As wealth increased in the cities, they began to attract ever more people who hoped to share in the obvious material benefits of this process.

By the mid-seventeenth century, feudalism was all but dead, and with it went the last remnants of the rural-centered life of the Middle Ages. In its place stood capitalism, a mode of life fundamentally grounded in the possibilities for trade offered by the city. By the eighteenth century, the Industrial Revolution had begun a process that fueled even more strongly the dominance of the city-based market economy. The change was striking: City populations everywhere exploded (see Table 2–1). If the first urban revolution took place when cities first appeared some 10,000 years before, the second urban revolution occurred from about 1650 on, as Europe became a continent of cities.

The preindustrial era had been characterized by low-efficiency technology and primitive

health care and by high birth and death rates. In other words, people typically had many children, but only some lived to become adults. Even for those who did, life expectancy was much lower than today (usually less than 40 years). As a result, natural population growth (the difference between the birth and death rates) was slow and frequently checked by massive numbers of deaths occasioned by outbreaks of plague. From the 1340s to the early 1350s, for example, the Black Plague raced across Europe, killing one-third of the population overall and up to 60 percent in the continent's cities (Kelly 2005).

Fortunately, plague did not wreak its vengeance forever. In time, a larger portion of the urban population enjoyed more wealth, more efficient means of production, and better health and sanitation conditions. Death rates fell dramatically, while birth rates remained high: What population experts call a *demographic transition* was underway. A major population explosion began throughout Europe, primarily centered in the cities. Although migration caused much urban growth—that is, from people coming to the city from the countryside—natural population growth was also extremely high. Together, both forces began to produce cities with population sizes undreamed of in antiquity. Recall that Rome, at its peak, contained around a million people. London in 2009 contained more than seven times that number.

In European and North American countries, this urban demographic transition continued well into the twentieth century. Then, the third and last phase of demographic transition took place. A rising standard of living—making more children for "productive purposes" unnecessary—and effective means of contraception led to a lowered birth rate. In most industrial nations, population growth not only has slowed but actually has begun to decline, as in many European countries and Japan. Although the birth rate also has dropped in much of the developing world, it still remains high, leading to burgeoning growth and problems of overpopulation (see Figure 2–4).

To conclude this chapter, we turn to a case study focusing on London, a city that many

TABLE 2–1 Population of Selected European Cities, 1700–2009, in Thousands

City	1700	1800	1900	2009
Amsterdam	172	201	510	753
Berlin	—	172	2,424	3,418
Hamburg	70	130	895	1,774
Lisbon	188	237	363	483
London	550	861	6,480	7,683
Madrid	110	169	539	4,590
Naples	207	430	563	959
Paris	530	547	3,330	2,184
Rome	149	153	487	2,492
Vienna	105	231	1,662	1,690

Source: Adapted from T. Chandler and G. Fox, *3000 Years of Urban History* (New York: Academic Press, 1974); *The World Gazetteer,* accessed online at http://www.gazetteer.de on February 16, 2009.

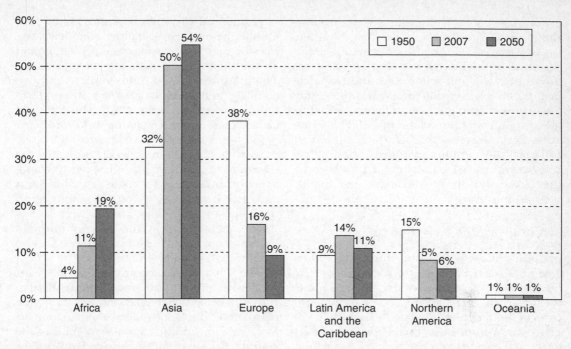

FIGURE 2–4   Distribution of the World Urban Population by Major Area, 1950, 2007, 2050
Source: United Nations Population Division.

consider, perhaps with Paris and Rome, to be the greatest of European urban centers. As we examine this city of kings, queens, Shake-speare, Dickens, and Churchill, we shall see reflected all the stages of urban development we have just discussed.

CASE STUDY

London—The History of a World City

When a man is tired of London, he is tired of life; for there is in London all that life can afford.

Dr. Samuel Johnson (1709–1784)

There are certain great cities, suggests Saskia Sassen (2006:50), that conduct a dispropor-tionate part of the world's most important business. These are the "world cities," such as London.

For approximately 1,000 years, London has been a focus of European urban life. It is one of the four or five most important economic centers of the world. Its metropolitan area has a population exceeding 8.5 million people, and it is one of the world's leading destinations for tourists (nearly 12 million annually). Even though tourism provides employment for up to 13 percent of London's work force and brings in over $11 billion annually, the time-honored image of a relatively sedate city is changing rapidly. Some Londoners feel the quality of life is being destroyed as a fleeing middle class and growing racial/ethnic diversity change the city's texture. They see "too many" foreign-born who come to stay without regard for traditions and customs and who fill up hospital casualty wards, police stations, and magistrate's courts (Government Office for London 2008).

More seriously, the city has lost over 1 million jobs in recent decades, including more than 100,000 between 2001 and 2003 when the dot.com bubble burst and more than that in the 2007–2008 finance market crisis (Condie 2008). Even so, an occupational bipolarization continues, with higher unemployment among the less skilled and less educated but increased demand and good pay for business professionals. Most of London's middle class, however, has moved to the suburbs, leaving the city bereft of its traditional tax base and increasingly polarized into a home for the very rich and the poor. Tension between whites and minorities still exists, although not with the violent confrontations of the mid-1980s.

So London remains, as Dr. Johnson put it, a mix of "all that life can afford." Why? What forces are at work in making a city a world city? To answer this question, we need to look at London's history.

Beginnings: 55 B.C.E.–1066 C.E.

London's story begins with Rome and Julius Caesar. After his conquest of Gaul in the first century B.C.E., Caesar was told of a large island to the north that had important natural resources. His expedition to the island in 55 B.C.E. met with little success: He encountered fierce resistance from the local Celtic tribes, so he retreated to Rome to enjoy his other victories. But he brought back with him knowledge of the island.

A hundred years later, in 43 C.E., the fifth Caesar, the emperor Claudius, conquered the island. Claudius set up his main encampment at the first point upstream on the River Thames (pronounced "tems") where a bridge could be built, thereby allowing access across the river by troops to the south. The place was called "Londinium" (meaning "wild" or "bold" place), after the Celtic name for the area. A deep-water port, London's site facilitated the shipment of goods into the heart of England. The Romans built major roads in all directions and enclosed the city within a wall for protection. By 60 C.E., London was thriving: In *The Annals* (110-120 C.E.), the Roman historian Tacitus wrote that the city was "famed for commerce and crowded with traders."

The Romans remained for nearly 400 years. By the beginning of the fifth century, Roman rule was being challenged continually by the remnants of the Celtic tribes (who had long before been forced into the outer regions of the country: Cornwall, Wales, and Scotland) and by invading tribes from northern Europe. Eventually, the cost of maintaining the British Isles, combined with the necessity of protecting the

Ancient Rome's domination of Europe had a profound influence on the continent's urban development, both physically and culturally. In many European cities today, we can find the remains of vast building projects, roads, bridges, enormous baths and aqueducts, temples, and theaters. Situated near the Tower of London, for example, is this portion of a Roman wall built in 200 B.C.E parts of the empire closer to Rome itself, became too great, and the islands were abandoned in 410 C.E. Virtually all remnants of the Roman occupation, including the Roman remains in London, were destroyed with great relish by the reemergent tribes. Nevertheless, the Romans left two legacies that would be crucial to London's later history: the established city and a superior road system that linked it with the hinterland.

From the time of the Roman retreat until the Norman Conquest in 1066, Britain came under a variety of political overlords. Different tribes—the original Celts, Danes, Angles, Saxons, and Vikings—vied for control of the island, gaining and losing it numerous times. To take but one example, in 1013 the Danes conquered the city, driving out the Saxon king, Ethelred. Ethelred formed an alliance with King Olaf of Norway, and together, they quickly attacked the city again. Knowing that London Bridge was the key to London's southern supply route, they attached ropes to its huge pilings and sailed downstream, pulling the bridge in their wake (hence the origin of the eleventh-century song "London Bridge Is Falling Down"). Following the Saxon–Norwegian takeover, the Danes returned in 1016, and again, they took the city. This seesaw pattern was typical.

Despite changing political fortunes, London thrived. Eager to maintain their success, its merchants usually threw in with whoever was in power, thus maintaining and strengthening London's importance as the economic center of England.

The Medieval City: 1066–1550

The year 1066 brought political stability. The Norman invader, William the Conqueror, defeated the Saxon king, Harold, at the Battle of Hastings and then marched on London. Finding the city well fortified and recognizing the vital importance of the trade connections it maintained elsewhere, William attacked the community of Southwark (pronounced "sutherk") at the opposite end of London Bridge. Leaving a standing army, he took the remainder of his forces to the smaller, less protected cities in the west and north. These he systematically destroyed (ravaged might be a better word), always sending back news of his conquests. The message to Londoners was all too clear: Surrender or face utter devastation. Londoners opened the gates of the city and welcomed William as their king. Without a shot fired, William had gained his prize. And by not sacking the city, William not only gained access to virtually all its wealth but also ensured that the city would be able to produce more wealth in the future. Slaughtered merchants, after all, trade with no one.

Twenty-five years before William's conquest, the Saxon king, Edward the Confessor, a devout Christian, had decided to build a great abbey west of the original City of London, around a sharp bend in the Thames. (Technically, and still true today, the "City of London" is the original one-square-mile area encompassed by the Roman walls.) It was in this abbey, called Westminster (literally, "the church in the west"), where William chose to have himself crowned king of all England. William then took up residence in the nearby palace that had been constructed by Edward.

The site of William's coronation and residence was critical to the history of London for three reasons. First, an important political residence was established in the immediate vicinity of the financial capital, giving London the power of a "double magnet"—both a financial center and a political center. Second, the establishment of the City of Westminster to the west of the City of London meant that the land between would be filled with incoming people, thus "dragging" greater London in a westward sprawl out of the original walled, Roman city. Third, the establishment of the royal residence in London inextricably tied London's local history to the nation's history. Henceforth, the history of London would be, to a large degree, part of the history of England.

For five and a half centuries, medieval London grew steadily. Nevertheless, it was an out-of-the-way place—an important, but not major, European city. This changed radically, however, with the onset of world exploration. By 1550, London had become a world city.

The World City Emerges: 1550–1800

There are three reasons for the transformation of London. First, with the discovery of the Americas, London suddenly became a stop "on the way" for most northern European expeditions heading west to the Americas. It thus became a place where goods could be unloaded conveniently and transferred to the ships of other nations or processed in some manner for reshipment.

Second, because of its geographical isolation from the rest of Europe and paucity of natural resources, England became a seafaring nation, with the world's most efficient sailing fleet.

Third, there was wool. Isolated from war-ravaged Europe for centuries, England was able to produce more of this precious material than any other country. With wool in ever-increasing demand, London quickly became the port where the largest proportion by far of the world's wool was traded. In fact, London merchants established a virtual monopoly.

As a result of all these factors, London exploded in population, wealth, power, and influence. By the mid-1500s, the English Renaissance—comparable to those of Florence and Venice—had begun. Not only did commerce thrive, so did art, literature, music, and drama. It was the era of Henry VIII, Sir Thomas More, Elizabeth I, Roger Bacon, Sir Walter Raleigh, and of course, Shakespeare.

Shakespeare, in fact, is a marvelous example of a city's nourishing effect on human creativity. In the late 1500s, Shakespeare arrived in London—the only place where serious dramatists could have their work produced. There, he found patrons and competitors who pushed him to his peak. All his greatest works were written in London. As Oscar Wilde, the great nineteenth-century poet and playwright, put it, "Town life nourishes and perfects all the more civilized elements in man. . . . Shakespeare wrote nothing but doggerel lampoon before he came to London and never penned a line after he left" (Keyes 1999:126).

It is important to see the link between a thriving city and the advance of cultural ideas.

First, a dynamic city draws to it people from different backgrounds. As the population grows, the possibilities for permutations and combinations of ideas and lifestyles become legion. Second, a thriving city is usually a wealthy city, and an intimate historical link has long existed between wealth and the development of cultural ideas. Simply put, wealth supports leisure. Creative artists with wealthy patrons or buyers for their work can literally afford to develop their art in ways that would be impossible if leisure time were not available. In addition, affluent people enjoy theater, architecture, and music, thereby enhancing the creative arts in another way.

People came to Renaissance London in droves. In 1500, the city was home to 75,000 people. By 1600, that number had nearly tripled to 220,000, and by 1650, it had doubled again to more than 450,000. London, however, had no plan for accommodating these huge numbers of people. Housing became scarce and overcrowded, the streets virtually impassable. The water became polluted, and not surprisingly, so did the streets themselves. As one historian notes:

> A whole network of officials, from the mayor down to the four [officials] attached to each ward, were continuously battling with the problems of street cleaning. People like William Ward, who caused great nuisance and discomfort to his neighbors by throwing out horrible filth onto the highway, the stench of which was so odious that none of his neighbors could remain in their shops, were prosecuted as public menaces. Many people defied regulations and simply emptied their slops into the street, or, like one ingenious fellow, piped them into the cellar of a neighbor. (Gray 1997:133–34)

Then, in a single year, the city was hit twice by catastrophe. The first was directly connected with the unsanitary conditions we have just described. The Black Plague had visited London before, but never with the virulence of the epidemic of 1665–1666. The population of the city was nearly halved; more than 100,000 people died in the space of eight months.

A major contributor to ending the bubonic plague by killing the rats who transmitted it was the Great Fire that began the evening of September 2, 1666. By the end of the fire four days later, some four-fifths of the City of London had been destroyed—approximately 13,200 houses, 87 churches, and 50 Livery Halls over an area of 436 acres. But, like the mythical phoenix, London rose from its own flames. Less than 40 years later, in 1700, the London area had a population of over half a million people, and the city had been entirely, even spectacularly, rebuilt. It was more powerful than ever. By 1750, the population had grown to more than 675,000, and by 1800, it was nearly 900,000, almost twice the size of Paris.

Industrialization and Colonization: 1800–1900

The onset of the Industrial Revolution in the late 1700s spurred the growth of London as never before. London was already the center of British trade: What the city did not produce, it shipped; what it did not ship was simply not available for human consumption. To fuel its voracious industrial machine, England needed cheap raw materials in huge portions. Unable to supply all these materials itself, England, like many European nations of the period, colonized much of the globe as quickly as possible. Thus grew the British Empire, on which the sun never set and which, from its center in London, controlled the destinies of a quarter of the earth's population.

To accommodate the burgeoning empire and its industry, the city grew immensely. The docks expanded and provided huge numbers of jobs in the East End; the government civil service expanded to oversee the empire; growing industry provided still more jobs. London became like a huge, expanding mouth, swallowing up people by the millions. By 1861, the population of London had risen to nearly 3 million. By 1901, the figure was almost 6.5 million, thus increasing by more than 3 million in just 40 years.

The city also developed a level of poverty among millions of its residents that was unlike anything experienced before. Many— including Charles Dickens, Karl Marx, and

The Industrial Revolution brought migrants by the millions to cities such as London. Misery and despair, a life of squalor in unbelievable slum conditions, were the lot of many, as poignantly shown in this picture of London's Harrow Alley, drawn by French artist Gustav Doré in the 1870s.

Friedrich Engels—described the suffering of the poor in nineteenth-century London, but few captured it as well as the French illustrator Gustave Doré, whose drawing accompanies this discussion.

The Modern Era: 1900 to the Present

After 1900, life improved. World War I united the country against a common enemy, and ironically, the Great Depression of the 1930s helped equalize the suffering by cutting the economic bottom out from under the country's middle and upper-middle classes. Then, in 1940, Adolf Hitler's *Luftwaffe*, through continuous bombings, destroyed much of the city once again.

After World War II, the city regenerated it-self once more. Rebuilt offices in the devas-tated city boomed, and tourists came by the millions. Yet much also was lost. London lost population, partly because of the policy of shift-ing people out of the slums and into new towns and partly because of the decline in heavy in-dustries. The docklands—an 8.5-square-mile area in the East End that housed the world's largest complex of enclosed docks and ware-houses—went into rapid decline as the advent of container ships and other technological changes rendered the docks obsolete (see *Cityscape* box on page 52). As England's colonies became independent states, the em-pire disappeared as well—and with it the im-mense wealth that enabled growth.

Long-term unemployment was virtually un-known in London until the 1960s and 1970s, when massive Commonwealth immigration brought racial and ethnic minorities (primar-ily Indians, Pakistanis, and Bangladeshis) into the city's inner districts. Roy Porter (1994) noted that Londoners viewed these areas as decaying and dangerous, filled with an emerging outcast group that was poorly inte-grated into the ties of workplace and neigh-borhood as unemployment remained two to three times above the city average. With an in-crease in crime and violence and a decrease in social services, many thought London's fu-ture lay somewhere between dismal and dire. Commerce no longer served as a unifying force, and poor areas were becoming urban ghettos. Race riots in the city's Brixton district in 1981 and 1985 demonstrated that its social fabric was unraveling as well. Londoners began to fear that the city had lost its ability to integrate diverse elements of society and sur-vive social upheaval without shattering into fragments. As Porter further observed:

London's problems mirror those of many U.S. and other world cities, and its plight worries many Londoners: Homelessness, single-parent families, the isolation of the old, classroom violence, joblessness, rising crime, poverty, drug-dealing, neo-Nazi racial attacks—all these

London effectively blends its past and present, its modern buildings serving as a backdrop to the eleventh-century Tower of London and complex along the River Thames. The city continues successfully modernizing to remain competitive, but its rich traditions and charm of bygone years remain an important part of London and are major attractions for millions of visitors annually.

now-familiar troubles foretell alienation, anti-social behaviour and despair. Poverty and de-privation deepen, and fears rise of the emergence of a new, permanent underclass, re-sented by the rest, reinforcing polarization. . . . As the able and the aspirant leave, quitting Greater London for cleaner, greener pastures elsewhere, the capital is being saddled with a disproportionate population of problem people—resource consumers rather than pro-ducers: the old, sick and disabled, broken and lone-parent families, the chronic unemployed, children in care, alcoholics, addicts, new immi-grants (some illegal) and derelicts. (Porter 1994:30)

In analyzing occupational and housing im-provements in London during the 1970s and 1980s, Peter Congdon (1995) offered a more optimistic view. While acknowledging the city's problems, he also found revitalization underway:

The continuing growth of financial, business and information services in the central city, and their deregulation in the 1980s, increased demand for . . . higher-income professional and managerial workers as a proportion of the London work force. Despite the recent rise in regional unemployment [the city experi-enced] an improvement in average prosperity exceeding the national average. (Congdon 1995:523)

As the first city to develop an infrastructure able to sustain millions of people living and working in a relatively confined area, London can rightly be called the "mother of the mod-ern megacity." That infrastructure—including water, gas and electricity supplies, sewage and waste disposal systems, an underground and suburban railway network—has since been copied by other large cities worldwide. How-ever, although it was once a forerunner in cre-ating a livable, modern metropolis, voters in London, beset by a recession, high inflation, and burdensome costs during the 1980s, elected a conservative government that elimi-nated the Greater London Council, which was responsible for maintaining the infra-structure of the London metropolitan area (Girardet 1994:12). Now, the mayor of London works with a wide range of environmental groups to draw up strategies and implement them, while the 25-member London Assem-bly scrutinizes the mayor's approach and issues reports that comment on those strategies.

Today, mixed trends still are evident. After an upturn in office rentals in 2004-6, the subsequent credit crisis led to serious de-clines in commercial property vaules and rentals (*Economist* 2008:49). Despite the cur-rent setbacks, Canary Wharf remains one of the busiest and most important areas of com-merce. This thriving community is in the docklands area, at the famous "U" bend in the River Thames, with its blend of restored warehouses and historic buildings as well as contemporary housing complexes and office developments, many with award-winning glass-and-steel designs. In two decades, this area has undergone a massive, landscape-changing development, with towering sky-scrapers, including Britain's tallest building, the 50-story Canary Wharf Tower, and the uniquely designed, 41-story Swiss Re build-ing, known to Londoners as "the Gherkin." Nearby is the popular promenade on the south bank of the Thames, with its new at-traction, the London Eye, the world's largest observation wheel, standing at about 443 feet and attracting approximately 10,000 visi-tors daily.

Meanwhile, the influx of immigrants has placed a serious strain on public services and resulted in more children with a poor com-mand of English in the schools. As Londoners flee the crime, congestion, and higher cost of living, the city has become more foreign and diverse than the rest of Britain. London has also become more economically polarized, with its high cost of living making it difficult for those struggling to find economic secu-rity and a home of their own. Thus, even as London improves, not everyone is necessarily better off.

Perhaps Dr. Johnson was right after all. With several trends occurring simultaneously, there is no one portrait of this city. London in the modern era is still as it was in Johnson's day: a world city that inevitably contains "all that life can afford."

CITYSCAPE

The East End and West End of London

These two ends of central London appear to have little in common. The West End and its neighbours, Whitehall and Westminster, are linked together by centuries of state power and by the wealth of its royal, aristocratic, and (more recently) bourgeois residents. They contain most of the principal contemporary tourist sites, as well as monuments and buildings redolent of empire and pre-colonial, medieval elites. The East End, on the other hand, has long been a poor suburb of the City of London. During the nineteenth century it rapidly expanded into a vast working-class area containing substantial pockets of intense poverty. Its residents were excluded from the centers of political and social power until the early twentieth century. Here the struggle for survival operated over a terrain sharply divided by occupational, ethnic, racial, and gender distinctions.

While Soho shares many of the characteristics associated with the East End, it is nevertheless a small enclave contained within a generally prosperous area of central London. Soho became a central London locality where middle- and upper-class visitors could easily find "low life" entertainment. In the East End the scale of its social and economic problems, and its overwhelmingly working-class population, has deterred all but the most determined visitors from the West End and other more prosperous areas of London.

The terms "West End" and "East End," therefore, conjure up two sharply different images of London—images shaped by the realities of social and economic inequality. Yet the gap between these two ends of central London has recently narrowed as the dockland neighbourhoods have been redeveloped.

Source: John Eade, *Placing London: From Imperial Capital to Global City* (London: Berghahn Books, 2000), p. 123.

SUMMARY

Cities have been with us for 10,000 years. They began after the last Ice Age in favorable ecological settings in many areas of the world. Slowly and tentatively, they established themselves, fueled by a surplus of goods and materials, whether developed by agriculture, trade, or military dominance. As they grew, they evolved a complex social structure—most particularly, a specialized division of labor and an hierarchical power structure. All these elements allowed cities, over time, to increase their dominance in human affairs. Thus began the first urban revolution.

The earliest cities, such as Jericho and Catal Hüyük, were scattered, independent units, often linked by trade but not much more. Sometime after 4000 B.C.E., however, the first urban empires began to appear. First in Mesopotamia and then in Egypt, China, the Indus River Valley, and the Americas, systems of cities emerged. These became not only centers of culture but also centers of regional domination. This link between city and empire was a central factor in the development of civilization for nearly 5,000 years. Urban empires pulled into their sphere diverse peoples, ideas, and great wealth and power. This was as true of Teotihuacan in North America as it was of Egypt in the Middle East.

Early Western civilization also centered around its cities—first those of Greece and then those of the Roman Empire. When the latter finally crumbled in the late fifth century C.E., most of the other cities of Europe—outposts in the Roman chain—lost their reason for being. The next 500 years—roughly from 500 to 1000 C.E.—were a decidedly anti-urban period. Many cities disappeared entirely, and the few that managed to survive limped along as shadows of what they had been.

In the first few centuries of the second millennium C.E., a halting urban revival began. Slowly, trade began to revive, and the old feudal system began to break down as a new merchant class gained power. This revival reached its peak between 1400 and 1600 with the evolution of the Renaissance cities—most effectively symbolized by the Italian city-states of Florence, Venice, and Milan.

Then, around 1600, a turning point was reached. The old feudal social order was weakened beyond repair, and the merchant class, generating greater wealth through increasingly successful business ventures, began to control urban life throughout Europe. Seeing new possibilities for a better life in material terms, people streamed into cities all over the continent. This influx, coupled with technological improvement and advances in health and sanitation services, created a demographic transition. Europe in general, but cities in particular, exploded in population as death rates plummeted, birth rates stayed high, and migrants arrived by the millions. From 1650 on, cities—many huge in population and dominance—began sprouting all over Europe and in North America. This was the second urban revolution, spurred on primarily by the twin engines of capitalism and industrialization.

Today, cities exist in the farthest reaches of the globe. In many cases, the growth of cities created immense problems and widespread suffering amid successes. Now, in areas of the world where the urban demographic transition first occurred (notably Europe and North America), urban growth has slowed dramatically. Unhappily, in other areas—as Chapter 13 explains—urban growth has not.

Our case study of London illustrates, in the life of a single city, nearly all of these processes. London began as an outpost of the Roman Empire, achieved initial success, and then, with the Roman retreat in 410, fell into its own dark age—unheard of for centuries and the object of multiple invasions. It began to recover after the victory of William the Conqueror in 1066. For five centuries, it built its prominence as the center of British life and, around 1600, blossomed into one of the greatest Renaissance cities in history. Its success was linked primarily to international trade. Through the next two centuries, London grew and gained even greater control of world markets. Then, with the Industrial Revolution and intensive British colonization during the nineteenth and early twentieth centuries, the city exploded in population, undergoing a major demographic transition. Despite its incredible wealth-generating capacity, London has had massive problems that it has carried into this century. It now faces, as do many Western industrial cities, a future of changing demographics and a transformation of its economic activities.

CONCLUSION

The emergence of cities as a dominant force in human affairs is one of the crucial events of history. In many instances, cities have been the driving wheel behind the development of civilization. They have combined ideas in new ways, produced great wealth, wielded incredible power (often injudiciously and inhumanely), and become home to an increasing proportion of the world's population.

Yet throughout history, cities have not always had the same character. As we suggested at the opening of this chapter, the city is largely synonymous with civilization itself. Each chapter in the story of human civilization has thus brought distinctive cities: cities of the early empires, the medieval city, the Renaissance city, and most recently, the industrial–capitalist city.

Thus, there is both constancy and flux to the history of cities. Together, these processes create urban living. Both shall be clearly evident again as we consider the development of North American cities in the next chapter.

KEY TERMS

bourgeoisie (44)
city-states (31)
cosmic calendar (24)
division of labor (25)

hierarchical power structure (25)
productive surplus (26)
regal/ritual city (36)

INTERNET ACTIVITIES

1. You can learn much about ancient cities and structures if you go to *http://www.goldenageproject.org.uk/294jericho.html*. The first page will show you photos of the ruins of Jericho. At the bottom of the page are red arrows to click that will take you to illustrations of many other locales worldwide.

2. You can explore the archaeological ruins at Moenjo-Daro if you go to *http://www.world-heritage-tour.org/asia/south-asia/pakistan/moenjodaro/map.html*. Once there, if you click on any small photo, then click and drag inside that enlarged image, you can get a 360° view of each part of the site.

CHAPTER 3

THE DEVELOPMENT OF NORTH AMERICAN CITIES

Come hither, and I will show you an admirable Spectacle! 'Tis a
Heavenly CITY. . . . A CITY to be inhabited by an Innumer-
able Company of Angels, and by the Spirits of Just Men. . . .
Put on thy beautiful garments, O America, the Holy City!
    Cotton Mather, Seventeenth-century preacher

American urban history began with the small town—five
villages hacked out of the wilderness . . . each an "upstart"

town with no past, an uncertain future, and a host of confounding and novel problems.

Alexander B. Callow, Jr. (1982:37)

To the visitor from London, the cities of North America may seem to lack the rich texture that accumulates over centuries of history. In no city of North America, for example, does a single building rival in age the Tower of London—the foundations of which were erected in the eleventh century during the reign of William the Conqueror. Even the current Houses of Parliament and Buckingham Palace—relative newcomers on the London scene, dating from the mid-nineteenth century—are older than all but a few urban structures in the United States and Canada. Indeed, throughout Europe and much of the non-Western world, one can find abundant examples of exquisite, old architecture that suggests a vibrant, urban past that long predates the founding of Canada and the United States.

If the cities of North America are rather recent developments in the course of world urban history, however, they have a fascinating history of their own, spanning five centuries. The first European settlements in North America were founded in the early seventeenth century, at the time when industrialization was transforming the medieval cities in Europe. Perhaps not surprisingly, the New World cities were founded specifically as trade- and wealth-generating centers to fuel the growth of cities across the Atlantic in Europe. The forces of postmedieval culture—commercial trade and, shortly thereafter, industrial production—were the primary shapers of urban settlement. These cities, like the new nations themselves, began with the greatest of hopes. Cotton Mather was so enamored of the idea of the city that he saw its growth as fulfilling the biblical promise of a heavenly setting here on earth. Has that promise been realized? To find out, this chapter examines the development of urban North America in terms of four phases: the colonial, growth and expansion, metropolitan, and modern eras.

THE COLONIAL ERA: 1600–1800

The potential of a good river or seaport and a strategic location for trade were principal reasons for the founding of the early cities of Boston, Charles Town (Charleston), New Amsterdam (New York), Newport, Philadelphia, and Quebec City. With the exception of Newport (eclipsed in prominence by Providence during the nineteenth century), all of these settlements became important North American cities.

Characteristics of Colonial Cities

Colonial cities were exceptionally small, both in physical size and in population. New Amsterdam, for example, occupied only the southernmost tip of Manhattan Island, a far cry from the huge, five-borough City of New York that was incorporated in 1898. Until the eighteenth century, neither New Amsterdam nor any other North American urban settlement had a population approaching even 10,000. Not until after the American Revolution did any of these places begin to develop the population sizes we associate with a city today.

The lack of regular street patterns and stone houses in early Boston, Montreal, New York, and Quebec City gave these settlements the look of medieval towns. Even today, we can observe that original pattern of narrow, irregular streets in these historic neighborhoods. Furthermore, hard-surfaced streets were not common in the United States until well into the eighteenth and nineteenth centuries. Only Philadelphia, settled half a century later than the others, was built from the beginning on the more familiar grid system now found in many North American cities (see Chapter 6, Figure 6–3).

The underlying concept of all these cities was that they would serve as export centers for raw materials going to the European home country. Boston, for example, supplied lumber for the ships of the British Royal Navy, and for its part, Charles Town (Charleston) shipped rice and indigo back to the British Isles. New Amsterdam (New York)

BROADWAY. NEW-YORK.

North American preindustrial cities were bustling ports of commerce. Their concentrations of people and busy activity impressed visitors, but they contained only about 5 percent of the total population. Not until the nineteenth century did any reach today's minimum standard of 100,000 for large cities, as this 1830s view of New York's Broadway suggests.

and Montreal served as bases for the lucrative fur trade.

As time wore on, however, these cities, geographically distant from Europe, prospered and became more and more independent. Colonial merchants began to compete with the British (who gained control of Quebec in 1760) and established separate trade agreements with the West Indies and even with Europe.

Many new arrivals moved inland as the eighteenth century progressed, and numerous new, secondary cities, such as New Haven and Baltimore, were established. Although only a small fraction of the population lived in towns, an urban society was emerging along the eastern shore of what soon would become a new nation. By the late 1760s, the 13 colonies had at least 12 major cities and a total population (city and hinterland) of 2 million English, half a million people of other European backgrounds, and nearly 400,000 slaves, almost all of whom were in the South (Parrillo 2009b:45–49).

The City-Instigated Revolutionary War

Although the struggle for U.S. independence did not take place entirely in cities, it was in many ways a war instigated by the cities, where most of the colonial economic trade occurred. Merchants and colonists wanted freedom to pursue their life's interests as they saw fit, and economic interests were typically uppermost in their minds. The growth and development of the northern seaport towns generated numerous changes that affected labor relations, the distribution of wealth, the restructuring of social groups, and the emergence of the laboring class into the political arena (Carp 2007).

After the Revolutionary War, leadership of the new nation continued to be urban centered. New York became the first capital in 1789, and Philadelphia took over the title in 1790. Despite this urban dominance, however, most of the population was not urban at this point. The first census in 1790 identified only 5 percent residing in urban places (places with 2,500 or more persons). Only 24 such places existed, Philadelphia being the largest settlement, with a population of only 42,000.

GROWTH AND EXPANSION: 1800–1870

At the outbreak of the Revolutionary War, the western frontier of the northern colonies extended barely past the Hudson River, and the southern colonies reached outward only to the Appalachian Mountains. By the time the war was over, however, the territory of the United States extended roughly to the Mississippi River. The tremendous economic potential of this new region captured the interest of business leaders in established cities, and by the early decades of the nineteenth century, plans were under way to link the new territories with cities in the East.

The first of these links westward was established in 1818, when the National Road (now Interstate 40) pushed through the Appalachian Mountains from the city of Baltimore. This trade route, along with Baltimore's large shipbuilding industry, caused that city to grow in size and wealth. Philadelphia attempted to keep pace, opening both canal and turnpike routes west, although with more modest success. Not to be outdone, in 1825, New York opened the Erie Canal, which soon became the key to New York's increasing dominance over East Coast urban trade in the midnineteenth century. By cutting across upstate New York from the Hudson River, the canal opened a water route to the entire Great Lakes region and much of Canada. Undaunted, Baltimore began another round in this interurban rivalry by opening a railroad line to Ohio in 1828. Other cities followed suit, and soon, many railroad lines stretched westward, linking coastal cities to the hinterland.

By 1830, New York, Philadelphia, and fast-growing Baltimore had emerged as the main coastal cities, largely because of their control over the lion's share of commerce with the Ohio Valley. Table 3–1 reveals the remarkable rate of growth for these cities in comparison with Charleston, an original East Coast city still focused on tobacco and cotton production. As westward expansion proceeded, many new cities were incorporated, particularly between 1821 and 1880, the height of the westward expansion movement (see Table 3–2).

Canadian cities also benefited from new transportation links, especially in the 1850s. Toronto experienced rapid development with the coming of the Grand Trunk and Great Western railways and the signing of a trade treaty with the United States. From a population of only 9,000 in the 1830s, Toronto ballooned to 45,000 by 1861. Similarly, Montreal's railroad linkage to Toronto and initiation of shipping service with Europe brought its population to 270,000 by the end of the nineteenth century. Quebec City and

TABLE 3–1 Population Growth of Selected East Coast Cities, 1790–1870

	1790	1810	1830	1850	1870
New York	33,131	100,775	214,995	515,500	942,292
Philadelphia	44,096	87,303	161,271	340,000	674,022
Boston	18,320	38,746	61,392	136,881	250,526
Baltimore	13,503	46,555	80,620	169,054	267,354
Charleston	16,359	24,711	30,289	42,985	48,956
Total U.S. urban dwellers	202,000	525,000	1,127,000	3,543,700	9,902,000
Total percentage urban	5.1	7.3	8.8	15.3	25.7

Source: Statistics derived from U.S. Censuses in 1850, 1860, and 1910 (Washington, D.C.: U.S. Government Printing Office).

TABLE 3–2   Incorporation Dates of the Largest North American Cities by Historical Period

Pre-1776 (4)	1776–1820 (7)	1821–1860 (27)	1861–1880 (8)	1881–1910 (10)
Quebec (1608)	Nashville (1784)	Boston (1822)	Denver (1861)	Calgary (1884)
New York (1685)	Baltimore (1797)	St. Louis (1822)	Tucson (1864)	Vancouver (1886)
Philadelphia (1701)	Dayton (1805)	Detroit (1824)	Minneapolis (1867)	Virginia Beach (1887)
Charlotte (1774)	New Orleans (1805)	Memphis (1826)	Seattle (1869)	Long Beach (1888)
	San Antonio (1809)	Jacksonville (1832)	Phoenix (1871)	Oklahoma City (1890)
	Pittsburgh (1816)	Columbus (1834)	Fort Worth (1873)	Miami (1896)
	Cincinnati (1819)	Toronto (1834)	Fresno (1874)	Tulsa (1898)
		Cleveland (1836)	Indianapolis (1874)	Edmonton (1905)
		Chicago (1837)		Honolulu (1909)
		Houston (1837)		Las Vegas (1909)
		Toledo (1837)		
		Austin (1840)		
		Milwaukee (1846)		
		Atlanta (1847)		
		Albuquerque (1847)		
		Kansas City (1850)		
		Los Angeles (1850)		
		El Paso (1850)		
		Sacramento (1850)		
		San Diego (1850)		
		San Francisco (1850)		
		San Jose (1850)		
		Portland (1851)		
		Oakland (1854)		
		Ottawa (1855)		
		Dallas (1856)		
		Omaha (1857)		

Source: Based on data from Statistics Canada and the U.S. Census Bureau.

its surrounding region numbered about 1 million by 1850, mostly because of rapid natural growth. Thereafter, lack of additional fertile lands in a favorable climate for this mostly agrarian economy prompted many French Canadians to migrate to work in the new industries of the United States.

The Beginnings of Industrialization

As the nineteenth century wore on, the North American Industrial Revolution took root, giving birth to new and important inland cities. Secretary of the Treasury Alexander Hamilton played a major role in the founding of Paterson, New Jersey, in 1792, at the site of Passaic Falls—second only to Niagara Falls in width and height. Pierre L'Enfant, the French-born engineer who would later plan Washington, D.C., designed a water raceway system to harness this water power for mills. As the first planned industrial city, Paterson quickly emerged as *the* cotton town of the United States and then as a locomotive-building center. Soon, New England emerged as the leader in textiles. By the 1830s around Boston, factory towns "were rising on every hand, in Eastern Massachusetts and New Hampshire—Lawrence, Lowell, Fitchberg, Manchester, Lynn. Every village with a waterfall set up a textile mill or a paper mill, a shoe factory or an iron foundry" (Brooks 2005:4; orig. 1936). Slowly, industrialization supported by private investment began to transform the developing continent, particularly in the North, but as it did, new tensions began to mount.

Urban–Rural/North–South Tensions

The culture of the United States has always contained a streak of anti-urbanism. As long as the early North American settlements remained small and kept their relatively homogeneous character, few tensions existed between urban and rural sections. Yet some of the nation's founders worried greatly about how growing cities might transform the new nation. Thomas Jefferson, who was nurtured in the rural aristocratic tradition of Virginia, condemned cities as "ulcers on the body politic" and saw their growth as an invitation to all the corruption and evil that had befallen the Old World across the Atlantic. Commenting on an outbreak of yellow fever, Jefferson wrote to Benjamin Rush in 1800:

> When great evils happen I am in the habit of looking out for what good may arise from them as consolations to us, and Providence has in fact so established the order to things, as that most evils are the means of producing some good. The yellow fever will discourage the growth of great cities in our nation, and I view great cities as pestilential to the morals, the health and the liberties of man. (White and White 1977:28)

Despite Jefferson's wishes, the cities grew in size and prominence, and the westward movement enabled new ones to appear, bringing with them the more mechanized existence of the Industrial Age. By 1850, many rural residents were deeply alarmed about these developments, and agrarian periodicals regularly touted the superiority of country life over the deceitful ways of city life.

The debate on the pros and cons of city life soon took on a new and powerful dimension on the regional level—namely, hostility between the North and the South. Contributing to this conflict was the unparalleled growth of U.S. cities between 1820 and 1860 that was centered largely in the North. Cities such as New York, Philadelphia, and Baltimore simply outdistanced the conservative, slowly growing cities like Charleston and Savannah. The northern cities had the canal routes and the bulk of the railroad lines to the West, thereby significantly increasing their wealth

and population. Moreover, they were dominating ever-greater shares of regional and national markets, outstripping the South in overall production as industrialization spread.

The Civil War broke out in 1861. Although its causes were numerous, many historians believe that it was, in a very fundamental sense, a confrontation between urban and rural, between industrial and agricultural values. The North's victory was a symbolic turning point. The world of Jefferson was dying, thus leaving America's commitment to urban industrial expansion unchallenged. The stage was set for an urban explosion comparable to the one that had shaken Europe a century before.

THE ERA OF THE GREAT METROPOLIS: 1870–1950

The record number of small cities incorporated in North America during the 50-year period that ended in 1870 had not yet acquired many of the urban characteristics most familiar to us: towering buildings, populations in the millions, and blazing lights downtown. Two historical events would provide the impetus for this transformation: (1) the technological advance of industrialization, and (2) the migration of millions of people to urban North America.

Technological Advance

Industrialization involved much more than simply a proliferation of factories in and around the enlarging urban areas. Several inventions changed the face of the North American city. The construction of buildings with iron, and then with steel, pushed the city skyward. In 1848, a five-story factory built with an iron frame made news in New York; by 1884, a 10-story steel structure in Chicago ushered in the era of urban skyscrapers. Further ensuring the success of these taller buildings was another invention, the Otis elevator (devised in the 1850s), which became widespread in the 1880s. By the end of the nineteenth century, some buildings reached 30 stories; by 1910, a few were as high as 50. By 1913, New York had 61 buildings taller than 20 stories, and the famous city skyline was beginning to take form (Still 1994:206–207).

As cities grew upward, they also pushed outward, aided by a new technology in street-level transportation. Before the Civil War, pedestrians only had to contend with horse-drawn vehicles. By the 1870s, however, steam-powered trains were running on elevated tracks in New York. Soon after, "Els" were built in other large cities as well. People's ability to move about certainly was enhanced, but the thunderous noise, billowing smoke, and cascading sparks and cinders of these trains surely did little to preserve the peace and quiet of local neighborhoods or the quality of the environment.

In the 1880s, the electric street trolley—still in operation today in Philadelphia, Boston, New Orleans, Toronto, and Vancouver—also helped make mass transit a reality. Indeed, streetcars, and the subways that followed, were primarily responsible for making suburban life possible for millions.

Suburbs and the Gilded Age

In the mid-nineteenth century, railroads stretched outward from the central city and carried an increasing number of affluent and fashionable people to their new summer residences in outlying settlements:

> The early suburbanites usually spent only the summer months in the country, the more wealthy in their country houses and their less affluent friends in various popular boarding houses. With the improvement of rail service in the last few decades of the nineteenth century, large suburban estates began to multiply, suburban developments were built, and many families remained the year round. (Baltzell 1989:197)

Trains and trolleys allowed fast and inexpensive transportation beyond the city limits. Quick to see the possibilities, real-estate speculators built housing tracts by the dozens. For example, from 1850 to 1900, the suburbs of Roxbury, Dorchester, and West Roxbury to the south of central Boston increased in population from 60,000 to about 227,000 (Warner 1978:35). For the burgeoning middle class,

an escape from the city's dirt and din was at last possible:

> The . . . general satisfaction with suburbs came from their ability to answer some of the major needs of the day. . . . To middle class families [they] gave a safe, sanitary environment, new houses in styles somewhat in keeping with their conception of family life, and temporary neighborhoods of people with similar outlook. . . . In addition to benefiting [the middle class] the suburbs [also served that portion of the city's] population which could not afford them. The apparent openness of the new residential quarters, their ethnic variety, their extensive growth, and their wide range of prices from fairly inexpensive rental suites to expensive single-family houses—these visible characteristics of the new suburbs gave aspiring low-income families the certainty that should they earn enough money they too could possess the comforts and symbols of success. (Warner 1978:157)

The key to this increase was the streetcar, which carried people beyond the bounds of the old "walking city" of Boston, making frequent stops at stations that soon became centers of suburban housing. Suburban living and streetcar service, Warner (1978:49) concluded, "moved together"—the more there was of one, the more there was of the other. Later, cross-town service filled in the area between the original suburbs and downtown. By 1900, the old "walking city" was surrounded by a mosaic of "streetcar suburbs," which contained about half of the population of greater Boston (Warner 1978:3).

This process repeated itself across North America. As urban subway and elevated systems extended ever farther during the early twentieth century, suburbs appeared everywhere. Technology thus spawned the suburban dream, enabling the middle class to move out of the city, separating their place of work from their place of residence. Unlike the more mixed pattern of the earlier walking city, the new housing tracts created homogeneous economic and social communities that usually excluded the poor. This pattern of social class segregation and the attempt by many to escape to the suburbs remain two powerful aspects of urban history.

Nothing, however, did more to encourage people to move outward than the automobile. Before cars were common, suburbs were long corridors, stretching out along the streetcar tracks that led from the city core. Suburban settlement spread all around the city, however, as cars made every part of the region accessible to commuters. With the paving of more and more roads, the percentage of people living in suburbs moved ever upward. Even so, from 1900 to 1940, growth was moderate. "Suburban fever" did not manifest itself until the 1950s.

The Great Migration

Between 1870 and 1920, U.S. urban areas (places with over 2,500 residents) increased their populations from fewer than 10 million to more than 54 million, while Canada's urban population grew from 3.9 to 8.8 million. By 1920, both countries were predominantly urban nations, with more than 50 percent of their populations living in urban areas. The rate of growth for many of the largest cities was nothing short of astonishing. By 1920, Chicago had more than 12 times its 1870 population and was fast approaching the 3 million mark. New York, not yet a city of 1 million in 1870, was by 1920 approaching the 6 million mark. Toronto grew nearly 10-fold, from 56,000 in 1871 to 522,000 by 1921, and Montreal nearly quintupled, from 133,000 to 618,000.

The striking increases resulted primarily from the depopulation of rural areas as people moved into cities and from immigration. Prompting the movement from the countryside to the city was automation—as machinery made old forms of hand-powered labor obsolete—and the possibility of greater wealth in the city. Between 1880 and 1890, nearly 40 percent of the 25,746 U.S. townships actually lost population (Glaab and Brown 1983:176). Unable to survive in the country and lured by the cities, thousands abandoned their farms to seek their fortunes elsewhere.

The number of foreign immigrants—20 million to the United States and 5.3 million to Canada—was a bit smaller than the number who left rural areas for the cities during this period, but the changes wrought by immigrants from abroad were far greater. Representing dozens of nationalities and ethnicities, they introduced staggering cultural diversity to the large cities. Glaab and Brown give some hint of that transformation in the United States:

> The influx of immigrants to the cities, particularly during the decade of the 1880s when over five million arrived in the United States, produced some striking statistics for individual cities. In 1890, New York . . . contained more foreign born residents than any city in the world. The city had half as many Italians as Naples, as many Germans as Hamburg, twice as many Irish as Dublin, and two and a half times the number of Jews in Warsaw. In 1893, Chicago contained the third largest Bohemian community in the world; by the time of the First World War, Chicago ranked only behind Warsaw and Lodz as a city of Poles. (1983:138–39)

Clustering together in distinctive city districts, the great variety of these groups gave the

Perhaps nothing epitomizes immigrant city neighborhoods during the Great Migration more than New York City's Lower East Side. As this 1907 photograph shows, framing the streets filled with vehicles, children, pushcarts, and sidewalk vendors were the overcrowded tenements, where immigrants lived in such squalid conditions that sickness, disease, and death were constant companions.

cities a degree of diversity and excitement that was quite new—and that would affect the character of the city from that time on. To travel the breadth of Chicago, Cleveland, New York, Pittsburgh, or Toronto was—and still is—to experience a succession of differing worlds, each characterized by its own shops and products, its own sounds and smells, and its own language. Hence, in addition to upward and outward expansion and raw population growth, cultural heterogeneity became a third major characteristic of the new metropolis.

When U.S. immigration laws in 1921 and 1924 curtailed immigration, the still-developing industrial machine simply looked elsewhere for cheap labor and found African Americans in the South all too eager to find a better way of life. Between 1920 and 1929, more than 600,000 southern African Americans migrated to northern cities. By the end of the decade, Chicago's South Side and New York's Harlem had the largest concentrated black populations anywhere in the world. In Hartford, Baltimore, Washington, Philadelphia, Cincinnati, and Detroit, the black population grew enormously. Soon, racial tensions developed in many northern cities, sometimes leading to riots.

Many cities also grew through annexation. The independent suburbs of Dorchester, Roxbury, and West Roxbury, for example, became part of Boston. In Canada, between 1883 and 1900, Toronto annexed adjacent villages and towns and doubled its area, then again doubled its size by 1920 through further annexation. In 1930, Toronto's metropolitan area included the central city, four towns (Leaside, Mimico, New Toronto, and Weston), three villages (Forest Hill, Long Branch, and Swansea), and five townships (Etobicoke, East York, North York, Scarborough, and York). Montreal also annexed several cities, towns, and villages on its outskirts, thereby significantly expanding its municipal boundary as well.

Politics and Problems

With the enormous changes reshaping cities came equally enormous problems. How were the incoming millions to be provided with water, electricity, jobs, and protection against unscrupulous exploitation? Only the city government was empowered to cope with these issues; however, the pressures against fairly representing the public interest were great. Utility companies required street franchises—water and gas companies to lay pipes, electric companies to erect poles, and transit companies to lay iron rails. Local or out-of-town entrepreneurs offered to pay large sums for these lucrative franchises, and their bribes sometimes corrupted city officials.

Powerful political figures—known as "bosses"—took control of many city governments. They got the job done, but in the process, they usually lined their pockets with graft and kickbacks. By the start of the twentieth century, many city officials were as corrupt as any organized crime figure.

Another problem of the times was that large-scale immigration sparked an increasingly bitter reaction against newcomers. It was not just their numbers, however. By 1900, immigrants were more often from southern and eastern Europe, more likely to be Roman Catholic or Jewish than Protestant, and more likely to have darker eyes, hair, and skin tone than whites of northern and western European descent. Moreover, these newcomers often had manners and clothing that made them stand out as "different." These "less desirable" immigrants added significantly to anti-city sentiment, because even more than earlier arrivals, they were overwhelmingly urban settlers. By 1910, in fact, more than one-third of the inhabitants of the eight largest U.S. cities were foreign-born; another one-third were second-generation Americans. In sharp contrast, fewer than 1 in 10 nonurban Americans were foreign born (Glaab 1970:176). As a result, the towns often had a decided anti-ethnic and racist tinge.

The Quality of Life in the New Metropolis

Some profited greatly in this age of great economic expansion, making remarkable fortunes and establishing industrial empires. Yet even as the enormous mansion-retreats of the "robber-baron" industrialists rose across the urban fringe, the blight of the inner-city tenements became more and more conspicuous. With a steady stream of people entering the large cities of the North, property owners responded to the rising demand for housing by making the most profitable use of building space. New York tenements, denounced as "hideous" by Charles Dickens (2004:83; orig. 1842), became even more overcrowded by 1900, and the word *tenement* now connoted an airless, congested slum dwelling. By the turn of the century, perhaps 35 percent of New York City's population lived in such quarters, although the situation in most other industrial cities was somewhat more favorable.

Quality-of-life problems in the rapidly expanding industrial cities, unfortunately, were not limited to housing. Health hazards were greatest in high-density living areas with inadequate sewerage and generally unsanitary conditions. The frequency of typhoid epidemics was high in all cities. The *Chicago Times* summed up the problem with appropriate bluntness:

> The [Chicago] river stinks. The air stinks. Peoples' clothing, permeated by the foul atmosphere, stinks. . . . No other word expresses it so well as stink. A stench means something finite. Stink reaches the infinite and becomes sublime in the magnitude of odiousness. (quoted in Glaab and Brown 1983:172)

Urban activists did attempt to help the situation of immigrants and improve living conditions, but for decades, the battle was uphill. The cities were growing uncontrollably, a trend that ended with World War II (1941–1945) and the suburban housing boom that followed.

THE NORTH AMERICAN CITY: 1950 TO THE PRESENT

Today's cities are in the process of three major changes. First, people and businesses are still abandoning many central cities, continuing the trend toward suburbanization that began nearly 100 years ago—a process aptly called **decentralization.** Second, major population growth is occurring in areas with considerable environmental stresses, whether in U.S. cities in the South and West (the so-called **Sunbelt expansion**) or in Canadian cities, particularly around Toronto and Vancouver. Third, the work typically performed in the central city is mostly oriented toward white-collar jobs, high technology, and services, as Canadian and U.S. cities adjust to the postindustrial era of **globalization.**

Decentralization

Previously characterized by **urban implosion**— that is, ever-greater numbers of people converging on the central city itself—cities since the 1950s have been experiencing **urban explosion**—that is, people moving out from the core to the surrounding regions. Table 3–3 illustrates this decentralization with census data for major northern U.S. cities between 1910 and 2000. These cities became large metropolises by 1910, and each grew rapidly in the following few decades. By 1950, however, growth was slowing. By 1970, a decline in

TABLE 3–3   Population of Selected Northern U.S. Cities, 1910–2000 (in thousands)

	1910	1930	1950	1970	1990	2000
Baltimore	588	805	950	906	736	651
Boston	671	781	801	641	574	589
Chicago	2,185	3,376	3,621	3,367	2,784	2,896
Cleveland	561	900	915	751	506	496
Detroit	466	1,569	1,850	1,511	1,028	951
New York	4,767	6,930	7,892	7,895	7,323	8,008
Philadelphia	1,549	1,951	2,072	1,949	1,586	1,518

Source: U.S. Census Bureau.

TABLE 3–4   Population of Selected Metropolitan Areas, 2000–2006

	2006 Population (in thousands)	2000 Population (in thousands)	Percentage Change Since 2000
Canadian Metropolitan Areas			
Calgary	1,101	951	+15.8
Edmonton	1,056	938	+12.6
Hamilton	718	662	+23.4
Montreal	3,669	3,426	+7.1
Ottawa–Gatineau	1,163	1,064	+9.3
Quebec City	721	683	+5.6
Toronto	5,424	4,683	+15.8
Vancouver	2,257	1,987	+13.6
Northern Metropolitan Areas			
Baltimore–Towson	2,658	2,553	+4.1
Boston–Cambridge–Quincy	4,455	4,392	+1.4
Chicago–Naperville–Joliet	9,506	9,099	+4.5
Cleveland–Elyria–Mentor	2,114	2,148	−1.6
Detroit–Warren–Livonia	4,469	4,453	+0.4
New York–Northern NJ–Long Island	18,819	18,323	+2.7
Philadelphia–Camden–Wilmington	5,827	5,687	+2.5
Southern Metropolitan Areas			
Atlanta–Sandy Springs–Marietta	5,138	4,248	+21.0
Birmingham–Hoover	1,100	1,051	+4.6
Dallas–Fort Worth–Arlington	6,004	5,162	+16.3
Houston–Sugar Land–Baytown	5,540	4,715	+17.5
Miami–Fort Lauderdale–Miami Beach	5,464	5,008	+9.1
New Orleans–Metairie–Kenner	1,025	1,317	−22.2
Orlando–Kissimmee	1,985	1,645	+20.7
Tampa–St. Petersburg–Clearwater	2,698	2,386	+12.6
Western Metropolitan Areas			
Los Angeles–Long Beach–Santa Ana	12,950	12,366	+4.7
Phoenix–Mesa–Scottsdale	4,039	3,252	+24.2
Portland–Vancouver–Beaverton	2,138	1,928	+10.9
Salt Lake City–Ogden	1,068	969	+10.2
San Francisco–Oakland–Fremont	4,180	4,124	+1.4
Seattle–Tacoma–Bellevue	3,263	3,044	+7.2

Source: Statistics Canada and the U.S. Census Bureau.

central-city populations occurred. By the 1980s, a full-scale central-city retreat appeared to be under way, although by 2000, a few cities had reversed this trend.

Those moving are not leaving the metropolitan region, however, but rather are relocating in suburbs near the cities. Table 3–4 makes this clear by examining metropolitan area populations for selected cities across the continent, including those examined in Table 3–3. With few exceptions, suburbs are growing everywhere—and have been doing so for more than 40 years. Why?

Economic Considerations.   By the 1960s, many businesses, particularly in industry and manufacturing, were moving away from urban industrial districts. High rents and inadequate older buildings unsuitable for expansion had reduced the attraction of a city location. Furthermore, newer production procedures required large, low-level structures rather than the older, multistory buildings characteristic of an earlier era. Concerns over rising crime rates, taxes, and traffic congestion also contributed to the proliferation of new **industrial parks** outside the city. Workers often moved from the central city to be near their relocated jobs, resulting in a growth in suburban population and a decline in central-city population.

Technology. As noted earlier, technological changes in energy (steam power) and building techniques (steel-frame skyscrapers, elevators) were important in the creation of a centralized metropolis during the nineteenth century. Since then, the development of interstate highways, the telephone, computers, and telecommunications have been equally important in the decentralization of the urban area.

Technology also changed the meaning of urban space. Because we move more easily across space—in minutes by car or public transit,

or in milliseconds by telecommunications—physical proximity is no longer as necessary to tie together all the activities within the urban area. In fact, most of us routinely think in terms of time ("We live about 40 minutes from the airport.") rather than distance; we may not even know how many miles away the airport is.

The Postwar Era: 1945–1970. In the post–World War II era, North America's suburbs exploded. Millions of GIs returned home, starting new families and the baby boom. With the resultant housing shortage, these new families became caught up in the suburban dream—a place of one's own out of the congested city, with more room to raise kids in clean air and send them to good schools, without fear of crime and other urban ills. All across North America, new housing developments appeared. None, however, illustrates "suburban fever" better than Levittown on New York's Long Island.

From the 1890s until the mid-twentieth century, streetcar travel was the best means of transportation within or between cities. Acting in collusion through their partnership in a holding company, General Motors, Firestone Tire, and several oil companies bought the streetcar companies, dismantled their systems, and replaced them with buses. An actual streetcar was used in the 2008 film *The Changeling*, set in 1920s Los Angeles.

Some 30 miles east of Manhattan, Levittown rose from spinach and potato fields. Begun in 1947 by developer Abraham Levitt and his sons, the project escalated within a year from a planned 2,000 to 6,000 units, and with construction of the last house in 1951, Levittown contained 17,447 homes. Each ranch house was small (32 by 25 feet) and strikingly uniform in appearance. It sold for $7,990, with a $90 deposit and $58 monthly payment, and came in five different models, which differed only by exterior color, roofline, and the placement of windows. Built on a concrete slab with radiant heating coils, it had no garage and came with an expandable attic (Matarrese 1997). Soon, developers built similar housing developments elsewhere.

Retail businesses quickly followed the flow of population into these bedroom communities, and local shopping malls increasingly became part of suburban living. Although a suburban shopping center broke ground as early as 1907 in Baltimore and another shortly afterward in the Country Club district of Kansas City, in 1946 only eight such centers existed in the entire United States. By 1960, however, the number had soared to 3,800, and then tripled again to 13,000 "malls" by 1970. No wonder that by 1970, there were as many people working in the suburbs as there were in the central cities (Jackson 2008; Kowinski 2002).

As the white middle class moved out, the cities lost even more of the tax base that departing industry already was eroding. Left behind were minorities and the poor, who were often unable to find jobs. The city was faced with an increasing demand for services and a shrinking ability to provide them. By the mid-1960s, a true urban crisis—largely created by the phenomenon of decentralization—existed on a national level. Urban poverty was on the increase, minorities were justifiably angry over their standard of living, services were getting worse, and many cities were facing bankruptcy.

The Metropolitan Statistical Area.   With decentralization well under way, urbanization expanded as workers, unable to find adequate housing in the central city, spilled over into the surrounding towns and small cities. For example, Boston's workers began settling in Wakefield and Lynn to the north, in Wellesley and Natick to the west, and in Quincy and Braintree to the south. While technically residents of their newly adopted local communities, on another level they were still linked to Boston for jobs and under its sphere of influence.

Noticing this trend, the U.S. Census Bureau realized the need to measure more accurately the way that cities were growing. If it merely counted the residents of the central city—in this case, Boston—it would get a relatively small population count that ignored the reality of how many people living in Braintree and Wakefield were fundamentally tied to Boston. Consequently, the Census Bureau decided to count in its surveys both the central city population and the surrounding towns and cities that were interdependent with that central city. Thus was born the idea of the metropolitan area.

From 1959 until 1983, the Census Bureau used the term *standard metropolitan statistical area* (SMSA), and thereafter, it used the term **metropolitan statistical area (MSA)**. An MSA is at least one city with 50,000 or more inhabitants, the county or counties containing the city, and any surrounding counties with a high population density and a large proportion of inhabitants commuting to and from the central city. In 2000, the Census Bureau recognized 273 MSAs, containing roughly three-fourths of the total U.S. population.

The Toronto Metropolitan Area.   In 1953, Toronto created a federated form of government unique to North America in order to deal with the metropolitan phenomenon. Going beyond merely labeling a metropolitan area as such, this action created a consolidated governance system. The 13 municipalities of this metropolitan area formed a 25-member, elected Council of Metropolitan Toronto (later modified to be six municipalities with 33 members). The Council then established a common property assessment and tax rate to deal with such regional problems as water supply, sewage disposal, mass transit, school buildings, housing for the elderly, parks, and urban development. This approach to metropolitan governance exists in many European countries, but it is virtually nonexistent in the United States.

Megalopolis and the Consolidated Metropolitan Statistical Area. French geographer Jean Gottmann (1961) was one of the first urbanists to look closely at the sprawling urban regions and note the linkages between many independent urban municipalities. The first such area, which he called a **megalopolis,** was the unbroken urban region that emerged along the eastern seaboard of the United States, which he dubbed the "BosWash corridor." In the *Cityscape* on page 69, he describes this development.

The BosWash corridor was the first—but not the last—North American megalopolis. In Canada, the Quebec City–Windsor corridor (which includes Montreal, Ottawa, and Toronto) is quite comparable. Other U.S. megalopolises include Southern California ("SanSan") and the northern Midwest from Chicago ("ChiGary") to Cleveland ("CleveAk"). Once again, such growth did not go unnoticed by the U.S. Census Bureau, which coined the term **consolidated metropolitan statistical area (CMSA)** to describe these areas. By 2000, eighteen official CMSAs were part of the urban landscape.

Non-metropolitan Growth. The decentralization of the urban population has dispersed people outward from central cities not just to nearby suburbs but also to the outlying, rural hinterland as well. Small towns and rural areas lost 2.8 million people between 1900 and 1970, but during the 1970s, the trend reversed itself. Rural areas gained 8.4 million people, up some 15.4 percent. Between 1990 and 2000, the non-metropolitan population increased by 5.1 million, a 19.7 percent increase (U.S. Census Bureau 2002). Except for a small decline during the early 1970s, Canada's rural population numbers have also steadily increased, although their ratio to the urban population continues to drop, standing now at about 20 percent of the total (Statistics Canada 2008a).

No doubt improved transportation and communications are an important foundation of this change, as is the desire for a greater sense of security and a less hectic pace. Still, the newcomers are in no way traditionally rural. Most are well educated, have cosmopolitan tastes, and work in nearby cities. Local stores often spring up that supply such items as gourmet wines and sophisticated books.

The Sunbelt Expansion

A glance back at Table 3–4 (see page 65) reveals the other current trend affecting cities. Although suburban population is growing everywhere, it is growing fastest in the South and West. Figure 3–1 (see page 70) makes the point even more effectively, showing the considerable increases of population in virtually every state below the Mason– Dixon Line and west of the Rocky Mountains between 1990 and 2000.

The Northeast and Midwest regions and their cities once dominated national affairs, but an immense power shift has occurred. Table 3–5 (see page 70) illustrates the dramatic change by comparing the raw population figures and national rankings for the 10 largest U.S. cities in 2006 with those in 1950. New York, Chicago, and Philadelphia still remain in the "Top 10," but the latter two have lost significant population since 1950. If present trends continue, only New York and Los Angeles may appear on the next list. In addition, seemingly from nowhere, Houston, Dallas, San Antonio, San Diego, San Jose, and especially, Phoenix have leaped onto the list.

BosWash Assets. Despite the Sunbelt expansion, the BosWash megalopolis (also called the "Northeast Corridor") remains a major part of U.S. urban life. It is a region where more than 55 million people—almost one in five Americans—live, with a projected increase of 18 million over the next generation. Constituting 18 percent of the total U.S. population, it accounts for 20 percent of the nation's economic activity (Regional Plan Association 2006). Home to 54 of the *Fortune* Global 500 companies, it contains nearly one-half of all available global hedge fund investment capital (HedgeFund Intelligence 2007).

Why does this region still attract job-creating investments? With nearly one-fifth of the U.S.

CITYSCAPE

Megalopolis: The BosWash Corridor

The Northeastern seaboard of the United States is today the site of a remarkable development—an almost continuous stretch of urban and suburban areas from southern New Hampshire to northern Virginia and from the Atlantic shore to the Appalachian foothills. . . .

. . . As one follows the main highways or railroads between Boston and Washington, D.C., one hardly loses sight of built-up areas, tightly woven residential communities, or powerful concentrations of manufacturing plants. Flying this same route one discovers, on the other hand, that behind the ribbons of densely occupied land along the principal arteries of traffic, and in between the clusters of suburbs around the old urban centers, there still remain large areas covered with woods and brush alternating with some carefully cultivated patches of farmland. These green spaces, however, when inspected at closer range, appear stuffed with a loose but immense scattering of buildings, most of them residential but some of industrial character. That is, many of these sections that look rural actually function largely as suburbs in the orbit of some city's downtown. . . .

Thus the old distinctions between rural and urban do not apply here any more. Even a quick look at the vast area of Megalopolis reveals a revolution in land use. Most of the people living in the so-called rural areas, and still classified as "rural population" by recent censuses, have very little, if anything, to do with agriculture. In terms of their interests and work they are what used to be classified as "city folks," but their way of life and the landscapes around their residences do not fit the old meaning of urban.

In this area, then, we must abandon the idea of the city as a tightly settled and organized unit in which people, activities, and riches are crowded into a very small area clearly separated from its nonurban surroundings. Every city in this region spreads out far and wide around its original nucleus; it grows amidst an irregularly colloidal mixture of rural and suburban landscapes; it melts on broad fronts with other mixtures, of somewhat similar though different texture, belonging to the suburban neighborhoods of other cities. Such coalescence can be observed, for example, along the main lines of traffic that link New York City and Philadelphia. Here there are many communities that might be classified as belonging to more than one orbit. It is hard to say whether they are suburbs, or "satellites," of Philadelphia or New York, Newark, New Brunswick, or Trenton. The latter three cities themselves have been reduced to the role of suburbs of New York City in many respects, although Trenton belongs also to the orbit of Philadelphia. . . .

This region indeed reminds one of Aristotle's saying that cities such as Babylon had "the compass of a nation rather than a city. . . ."

Source: Jean Gottmann, *Megalopolis* (New York: Twentieth Century Fund, 1961), pp. 3, 5–7.

population on one-nineteenth of the land mass, it is the nation's most concentrated market region. Manufacturers in the BosWash corridor can reach more than half of the U.S. and Canadian industrial firms and retail sales outlets within 24 hours by truck. Also, the corridor states are, by air and by sea, close to the nearly 500 million people in the

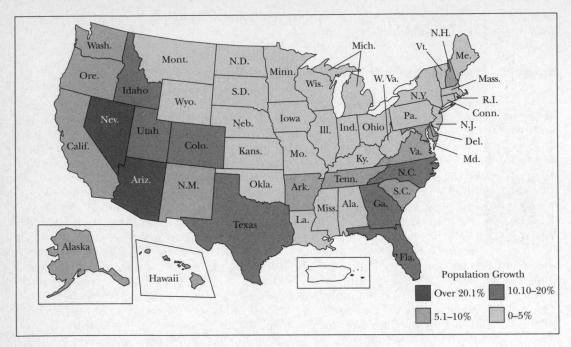

Figure 3–1   Change in State Populations as a Percentage, 2000–2006
Source: U.S. Census Bureau.

TABLE 3–5   Ten Largest U.S. Cities in 2006 Compared to 1950 (population in thousands)

	2006		1950	
	Population	Rank	Population	Rank
New York	8,214	1	7,892	1
Los Angeles	3,849	2	1,970	4
Chicago	2,833	3	3,621	2
Houston	2,144	4	596	14
Phoenix	1,513	5	107	99
Philadelphia	1,448	6	2,072	3
San Antonio	1,297	7	408	25
San Diego	1,257	8	334	31
Dallas	1,233	9	434	22
San Jose	930	10	99	—

Note: Center city data only.
Source: U.S. Census Bureau.

European Union countries. In addition, this 11-state region has the highest concentration of higher-education institutions, sending about 3 million students annually to 875 colleges and universities. Proximity to top colleges also has influenced location choices by high-technology firms. Massachusetts's famous Route 128 (now called "America's Technology Highway") is near Massachusetts Institute of Technology (MIT) and Harvard. New Jersey—the third smallest state, with about 3 percent of the nation's population—has more than 17,000 high-tech companies that employ more than 500,000 workers, including more than 184,000 scientists, engineers, and technicians (Birretteri 2001).

Sunbelt Problems.   Just as all is not negative in the Snowbelt, all is not rosy in the Sunbelt. A 2006 report by the Federal Bureau of Investigation indicated that reported violent crime in the Sunbelt region constituted 65 percent of the total (42 percent in the South and 23 percent in the West), compared with 20 percent in the Midwest and only 15 percent in the Northeast. Pollution is increasing, water is running short (particularly in the Southwest), and in many areas, population growth is just too great to absorb. Many of the fast-growth cities face high costs in developing an adequate infrastructure (roads, bridges, water and sewage systems).

THE POSTINDUSTRIAL CITY

In the 1960s, our central cities seemed to be in an irreversible process of self-destruction. Dozens of cities experienced major riots as thousands of poor minorities reacted in desperation to their poverty, lashing out at our white-dominated society. The central city was literally falling apart, and whites and the affluent were leaving for the suburbs. Industry was close behind as old factories became obsolete. Left in the decay were those who had little choice—the trapped and the poor, many of them minorities. It looked like the end of the city as we knew it, and many doubted that U.S. cities would ever rise again. In stark contrast, Canadian cities dealt with their problems more effectively, causing U.S. urbanist Jane Jacobs to refer to Toronto—by the 1960s, a cosmopolitan city with a distinct racial/ethnic mix—as "a city that works."

Deterioration and Regeneration

In the late 1960s, as central cities deteriorated—or, worse, went up in smoke—scholars, politicians, and nearly everyone else wrung their hands and wondered what could be done. One voice suggested that we need do nothing: With time, the city would save itself. That voice belonged to Edward C. Banfield (1970), whose controversial book *The Unheavenly City* (an obvious reference to Cotton Mather's wish for a "heavenly city" quoted at the beginning of this chapter) created an enormous stir. His thesis was that the city was too powerful an economic machine to remain down and out for long. Allow enough time, he argued, and new businesses and people would see that they could return to the central city and enjoy its great communicative advantages cheaply. They could buy up land; renovate deteriorated factories, houses, and apartment complexes; and thus avail themselves of the city's many benefits.

To Banfield's critics, his "do-nothing" approach toward urban destitution seemed

Unlike Sunbelt cities, Snowbelt cities such as Minneapolis–St. Paul have high-density land use. The tight clustering of buildings—and, therefore, the closer proximity of shops, offices, and restaurants, not to mention apartment residences—places more activities within walking distance and results in more crowds, congestion, and reliance on mass transit.

This night mosaic photographed from space illustrates the urban concentrations of people in North America more dramatically than could any artist or cartographer. The electric lights easily reveal where to find a megalopolis or metropolis and how much of the land is non-urban.

callous and mean-spirited. And yet, four decades later, many of his predictions have come true. Cities across the nation are in the midst of rejuvenation—and all with limited help from the federal government. The *postindustrial city* has arrived, and recent research suggests strongly that a general economic revitalization and reformulation is under way (Teaford 2006).

In many cities today, the contrast with the earlier picture of older U.S. cities in disrepair is nothing short of amazing. All over the United States—from Pittsburgh to Seattle, from New York to Phoenix—new urban construction is in progress. Office towers are multiplying almost as fast as contractors can build them. Many residential areas of the city are being totally transformed as young urban professionals—"yuppies"—move in, renovate old buildings, or settle into new apartment complexes. Although many older cities, particularly smaller ones, are still hurting, the urban economy is alive once again. In most areas of the country, a true urban renaissance is under

way as U.S. cities complete a shift to a postindustrial economy.

The reasons for this turnaround are (1) the growth of white-collar businesses tied to new computer technology and (2) a major shift in the way many industries do business. Regarding the first change, high-tech businesses were more than happy to take over, renovate, or rebuild the structures left by departing heavy industry. They needed the central-city location to maximize their efficiency. Second, many corporations are in the midst of a radical transformation, changing both their structure and their operations. In the nineteenth century, major industries believed in a "beginning-to-end" process—that is, they oversaw and controlled their product from raw material to finished, marketable item. This was true of most of the "giants," such as the Carnegie Corporation (steel) and the Ford Motor Company (which went so far as to raise sheep to produce the wool for its cars' upholstery fabric!).

Now, big industries are divesting themselves of parts of their operations that are no longer profitable as they outsource to other firms or foreign companies. Thus, General Electric no longer makes microwave ovens or the icemakers that go into its refrigerators; instead, other firms in the United States, Korea, Japan, and elsewhere supply them. Taking a more flexible approach, firms decide which components they can produce profitably themselves and which can be produced more efficiently through outsourcing (Duesterberg and Preeg 2003:45).

Such changes, which are happening all over North America, have important implications for the city. On the one hand, companies no longer require as many blue-collar workers or as many buildings geared to heavy industrial production. On the other hand, these corporations, which play so large a role in our urban scene, have created more white-collar jobs—jobs that depend on regular contact with other corporations, whether in North America or abroad.

Naturally, those employed by postindustrial, high-tech industries want to live near their work, and while some (particularly those with families) continue to commute from the suburbs, many opt to live in the central city. Illustrating this trend during the past several decades has been the process of *gentrification*, in which white-collar professionals move into and transform older, decaying neighborhoods of many cities.

The Future

The postindustrial city will likely dominate North America's future, but what form will it take? One significant worldwide trend is globalization, a subject we will explore in Chapter 7. Two other trends on this continent are occurring simultaneously, and it is uncertain which will prevail in the twenty-first century. One first trend is the appearance of *edge cities* (discussed more fully in Chapter 4). The evolution of edge cities on the fringe of older urban areas helps explain the population increase in nonmetropolitan areas. Joel Garreau (1991) suggested that North Americans have reinvented the city and that these new urban agglomerations are now the future. Numbering more

than 200 in Canada and the United States, these edge cities, with their malls and office parks, now dominate the nation's retail trade, office facilities, and cinemas.

The second trend is the revitalization of older cities, a significant process that shows no sign of stopping. More, not fewer, people are taking on the yuppie lifestyle. Because edge cities do not offer the residential ambience that young adults can find in a central city's brownstone houses, loft apartments, cozy restaurants, and shops, the upgrading of many older city neighborhoods continues. In addition, the office-building boom in many cities persists to meet the needs of postindustrial corporations (Baker 2007).

Cleveland is a good example. During the 1960s and 1970s, this Ohio city was a symbol of urban despair. Severe social problems exploded into race riots in 1966 and 1968. Pollution was thick in the air, and in 1969, the Cuyahoga River actually burned for days because of the pollutants it contained. Cleveland's heavy industry was dying, its middle class was fleeing to the suburbs, and by 1979, the city was on the verge of financial collapse.

A public–private partnership, forged by city government and business leaders during the early 1980s, attempted to breathe new life into the city. Its linchpin for revitalization was restoration of Cleveland's famous, but abandoned, landmark—the Terminal Tower commercial complex—into a rail transit station, a multilevel shopping center with upscale national stores, an 11-screen movie theater, a Ritz-Carlton hotel, and several high-rise office buildings. The Tower City Center complex created more than 3,000 permanent jobs and contributes more than $4 million in taxes to the city treasury (Greengard and Solomon 1994:65).

New tourist attractions included the six-story Rock and Roll Hall of Fame and Museum, two new stadiums, and nearby Cedar Point amusement park, with its 11 roller coasters. Yuppies turned abandoned warehouses into lofts and apartments, and city residents enjoy a new lakefront park and trendy restaurants along the Cuyahoga River, where one can sit on the patios while barges and pleasure boats navigate the river.

Nevertheless, Cleveland lost one-eighth of its population between 1990 and 2006, dropping from 506,000 to 444,000 people. Named by the U.S. Census Bureau in 2006 as the nation's poorest big city, Cleveland improved to the fourth poorest in 2007, but problems clearly remain. Even so, a resurgence appears to be under way, with $2 billion worth of infrastructure investment and a major transformation of its University Circle "eds and meds" district. In fact, so much expansion is occurring among the educational and medical institutions in this area that city officials anticipate 10,000 new jobs over the next 10 years (Chamberlain 2006). To offset the city's loss of its former industrial base, Cleveland's leaders have made renovation and land-use integration important parts of their economic strategy.

Strategy is exactly the right word. As the nation's central cities regenerate, many are engaging in a type of competition reminiscent of the interurban competition of the mid-1800s, when North American cities were growing by leaps and bounds. An increasing number of urban governments are hiring marketing professionals to spiff up the city's image so that it can attract more businesses and tourists.

The Human Cost of Economic Restructuring

The postindustrial process, unfortunately, does not benefit all of a city's residents. As gentrification progresses, the poorer residents of many city neighborhoods are simply displaced. Unable to pay the rising rents, they must find somewhere else to live. Similarly, even though a few areas within a city become havens for the affluent, this does little to change the poorest areas: New York still has its Harlem and South Bronx, Chicago its South Side, Los Angeles its Watts, and Cleveland its Hough. Even more worrisome, the postindustrial economy is exacerbating the plight of the city's poor and unskilled.

This occupational restructuring creates a "skills mismatch" as our cities' economies become more and more white collar. The cities' gradual shift away from manufacturing and goods processing eliminates many blue-collar

jobs, once the first step up for millions of unskilled migrants and immigrants. The rising skill requirements of today's urban job market, which demands educated employees to work with words and numbers in information-processing jobs, puts these new jobs out of reach for the poor. Thus, even as some urban neighborhoods improve, unemployment rates and welfare dependency among the unskilled remain high (Handel 2003; Bauder and Perle 1999). Gentrification is all well and good as far as it goes, but the changes do not benefit everyone.

In the 1980s, several urban observers viewed postindustrial cities pessimistically (Berry 1985; Downs 1985; Bradbury, Downs, and Small 1982). They saw the postindustrial city as increasingly characterized by two labor markets that fostered two dramatically unequal lifestyles—that of the well-paid, white-collar professional, and that of the low-paid service worker. Seeing these lifestyle inequities worsening in the foreseeable future, they concluded that the decline of the U.S. city was all but irreversible. In contrast, Roger Waldinger (1999) spoke of an interdependence between the city's affluent and the poor, but also that immigrants, not native-born blacks, are now filling the niches left vacant by whites moving up the economic ladder (as illustrated in the case study of the first postindustrial city, New York).

The dynamic process engaging North American cities extends from its origins—those five communities "hacked out of the wilderness" in the seventeenth century—to the present configuration—much larger and still embroiled in rapid and significant change, as decentralization, Sunbelt growth, and postindustrialization unfold. Exemplifying this process is the case study that closes this chapter, that of North America's world city, New York.

CASE STUDY
New York—The "Big Apple"

Jim said everything was in New York. Jim said that he was happy, just standing in Grand Central Station, catching scraps of people's conversations. Jim said he would not mind standing all day on Sixth Avenue where they had the joke shops and the Orange Drinks, just watching the crowds go by. Jim said he would not mind standing all day in Radio City, where the French and British shops and the travel offices were, and the evergreens at Christmas and the tulips in the spring and where the fountains sprayed ceaselessly around Mr. Manship's golden boy and where exhibition fancy skaters salved their egos in the winter. If he grew tired of skaters, Jim said he would not mind standing and staring up and up, watching the mass of buildings cut into the sky.

John P. Marquand, *So Little Time* (1943)

New York has long been the Great U.S. City. It symbolizes the United States to the world and, in many ways, reveals the rest of the world to the United States. New York not only represents the distinctive course of North American urban history, it is a timeless display of what urban life is all about. Here are just a few of the features that make it so outstanding.

First, New York is huge, an enormous concentration of population. More than 8.2 million people live within the city limits, and almost three times that many reside in the urban region that sprawls outward around the city. Second, the city is a major center for finance, insurance, real estate, media, and the arts. It has 44 of the *Fortune* 500 corporations, contains a large number of foreign corporations (1 in 10 private-sector jobs is with a foreign company), and its television and film industry is second only to Hollywood. Third, it is the third-largest U.S. port (after South Louisiana and Houston) and has dominated U.S. commerce since the early 1800s. Fourth, it is a mosaic of virtually every race and ethnic group in the world, with nearly 170 languages spoken daily and more than one-third of its residents foreign born. Many of these groups have clustered together in such well-known districts as Chinatown, Harlem, Spanish Harlem, Little Italy, and the Lower East Side. Fifth, other New York districts are world famous: Wall Street (finance), Madison Avenue (advertising), the garment district (center of the nation's clothing industry), Central Park

(arguably the greatest urban park in the world), Fifth Avenue (for fashionable shopping and living), Greenwich Village (a longtime bohemian, student, and counterculture enclave), and Broadway (center of the most vibrant theater district in the world). Sixth, New York is also a key center of the arts, music, and publishing.

At street level, New York abounds with crowds, traffic, musicians, and vendors—multiple sights and sounds that bombard the senses. Indeed, the first experience of New York City is one that many carry with them all their lives. On another level, the city is deceptive. Its very size tricks us into thinking things are other than they are—something that the *Urban Living* box on page 76 reveals about that grandest of illusion makers, Radio City Music Hall.

One cannot escape the great contradictions, contrasts, and inconsistencies of New York life. The city is home to the richest and poorest of North Americans. Some of the worst social problems stand, literally, in the shadow of the proudest cultural achievements. Inevitably, perhaps, New York is the most loved and the most hated city in the United States. Say outsiders, "A nice place to visit, but . . . I wouldn't want to live there." Some New Yorkers even boast about how awful it is—but most probably would never live anywhere else. In short, if something is to be found at all, it is to be found in New York. It is a world city par excellence. And since September 11, 2001, Americans elsewhere have expressed a special bond with New York as the symbol of an America united and defiant against terrorism.

New York, always at the center of U.S. life, has a varied history. Because its changes illustrate the themes of North American urban history generally, we shall look briefly at its development during each of the four phases discussed in this chapter.

The Colonial Era

New York was the earliest of the five major colonial settlements. By 1624, a small Dutch settlement, based primarily on the fur trade, was permanently in place on the southern tip

URBAN LIVING

All New York's a Stage

I'll tell you an old joke that will sum up Radio City Music Hall for you. It seems a man and his wife went to the Music Hall one Sunday afternoon, arriving toward the end of the film. When it ended, the house lights came up for a few minutes before the stage show and the man rose, murmuring to his wife: "I'm going to the men's room."

He located an exit on his floor—orchestra, loge, mezzanine, balcony or second balcony—but he couldn't find a men's room on it. He descended a staircase and looked on the next floor and couldn't find a men's room and descended another staircase. He walked along corridors and pushed open doors, he went along dark passages and up and down steps, getting more and more lost and more and more frantic. Just as his need became intolerably urgent, he pushed open a heavy door and found himself on a small street lined with houses, trees and shrubs. There was no one in sight and the man relieved himself in the bushes.

All this had taken time, and it took him additional time to work his way back up to his own floor and locate his own aisle and section. By the time he finally reached his seat, the stage show had ended and the movie had begun again. The man slid into his seat whispering to his wife: "How was the stage show?" To which his wife replied: "You ought to know. You were in it."

Source: Helene Hanff, *Apple of My Eye* (New York: Moyer Bell, 1989), p. 129.

---

of Manhattan Island. New Amsterdam, the center of the Dutch New Netherlands, prospered in the decades that followed: Houses were built, and farmland was cultivated. A vertical row of logs was put in place for protection along the northern edge of the settlement, which later became known as Wall Street. In 1638, a ferry service to Breukelen (later known as Brooklyn) began, and the first settlers reached Staten Island.

In 1653, Holland granted a charter to the town to organize a local government featuring a mayor and a city council. The first survey, completed in 1656, revealed that the "city" had about 1,000 people living in 120 houses on 17 irregularly shaped streets. Within a few years, some of the streets were stone covered, and a town-watch (the earliest direct ancestor of New York's police force) provided security. To the north were farms the Dutch called "boweries." This area, the point at which the irregular streets end (at about Houston Street today), was long known as "The Bowery." In 1658, the Dutch established a farming village, which they called Haarlem, much farther north at the end of a long dirt road known as "Broadway."

The first Jews arrived in the 1650s, establishing a long tradition that was to influence the city's history, and the first Quakers settled in the city during 1657. An English fleet anchored in 1664, gained control of the town, and renamed it New York in honor of Charles II's brother, James, the Duke of York. The English thereafter continued a policy of religious freedom for all groups, reaffirming the tradition of religious tolerance initiated by the Dutch.

In 1680, New York City began its climb to economic preeminence when it gained a monopoly on the sifting of flour for export. Docks multiplied, trade prospered, and support businesses of all sorts followed. The population grew steadily as well; from 4,000 in

1703, New York grew to 7,000 in 1723 and passed the 10,000 mark in 1737. The first newspaper appeared in 1725; a stagecoach link to Philadelphia started in 1730; and the New York Public Library opened in 1731.

As this growth occurred, New York, like the other colonies, began resenting ever more sharply the British impositions on trade. In 1765, the English government instituted the Stamp Act, which placed a levy on all transactions. The colonists bitterly opposed it. Swayed, Parliament repealed the act in 1766, causing a New York group dubbed the "Sons of Liberty" to build a triumphant "Liberty Pole" in the city. The British took strong offense. An altercation followed, and some of the Sons of Liberty were killed, spilling the first blood of the American Revolution.

When the Revolutionary War began, the British occupied New York for seven years. The war drove many New Yorkers temporarily out of the city, reducing its population by several thousand from a peak of 21,500. With the end of the war, however, the city leapt once more to life. George Washington was inaugurated as the first president of the United States in Federal Hall at the corner of Wall Street and Nassau Street, and for a year thereafter (1790), New York served as the U.S. capital.

Growth and Expansion

By 1800, the city's population surpassed 60,000, and spectacular growth continued. The population exceeded 96,000 by 1810 and 202,000 by 1830. Yet this was only a hint of things to come. Earlier, in 1792, a group of traders had met in the Wall Street area and planned what became the New York Stock Exchange. In 1807, the city approved its famous grid plan for street development. In 1825, the completed Erie Canal linked the Hudson River with the Great Lakes, giving New York a long-sought trade advantage over its East Coast urban competitors. With direct access to the North American heartland, the city quickly became the economic center of the United States.

Beginning in 1838, overseas steamships established a connection with Europe that truly opened the United States to immigration. In 1840, for example, more than 50,000 people arrived in New York Harbor from abroad, and most settled in the city. In 1846, the first telegraph line between New York and Philadelphia began operation. In 1848, a five-story factory (also a sign of things to come) opened its doors. Urban transportation improved with introduction of the rail-mounted horse car in 1850. This made "suburbanization" of the upper island more feasible; for the fare of a nickel, this area was within reach of most New Yorkers. In 1853, New York hosted the nation's first "expo," symbolic of the grand optimism that by now was part of the city's character. In 1858, the plan for one of the greatest of urban landmarks—Central Park—was approved (the park itself was not substantially completed until after the Civil War). In 1860, although still officially consisting of only Manhattan Island, the city boasted a population of 814,000, with another 250,000 nearby in Brooklyn, Staten Island, and Jersey City.

The Great Metropolis Emerges

After the Civil War, which temporarily slowed its growth, New York matured as a great metropolis. An unprecedented surge in the city's population occurred between 1870 and 1930, dwarfing all previous gains. Table 3–6 shows that New York City as a whole quintupled its population in the six decades after 1870.

TABLE 3–6   Population of New York City by Borough, 1870–2000 (in thousands)

	1870	1900	1930	1960	2000
New York City	1,476	3,437	6,929	7,782	8,008
Borough					
Manhattan	942	1,850	1,867	1,695	1,537
Bronx	37	201	1,265	1,425	1,333
Brooklyn	419	1,167	2,560	2,627	2,465
Queens	45	153	1,079	1,810	2,229
Staten Island	33	67	158	222	444

Note: The five boroughs were not officially incorporated as New York City until 1898.

Source: U.S. Census Bureau.

However, until January 1898, the five boroughs remained legally separate municipalities.

The period between 1870 and 1920 was an era of extensive foreign immigration to the United States, and New York was the major port of disembarkation. Chinatown began to take form in 1884; Italian immigration intensified after 1885; and Jews began to make their way through the Ellis Island immigration facility to the Lower East Side in large numbers after 1890. Many of these new urbanites went directly to work in many fields, most notably the clothing industry.

As amazing as it sounds, by 1890 four out of five people living in the New York area were either born abroad or had foreign-born parents (Glaab and Brown 1983). New York, like other U.S. metropolises, took on a characteristic "ethnic mosaic" pattern of settlement, as described by social reformer Jacob Riis in the *Cityscape* box. Although citywide residential density in 1890 was about 60 people to an acre, in immigrant areas the densities could be as much as seven times greater. The heavy concentration continued to increase to almost 750 persons per acre—about 12 times the city average—in 1898 (Glaab and Brown 1983). Today, the density of central Manhattan has fallen to about 100 persons per acre.

Sometimes, when immigrants mixed, the results were explosive. One midtown area, from about West 15th Street to West 50th Street along Eighth, Ninth, and Tenth Avenues, was home to blacks and whites of different ethnic groups. During the workweek, trouble was minimal, but on weekends in the summer, when much drinking and carousing occurred, violent fighting often broke out between groups. So intense were the confrontations that police nicknamed the area "Hell's Kitchen," and it is still called that.

Governing this incredible and growing mass of people was difficult at best. City Hall became increasingly corrupt as interest groups vied with one another for contracts, favors, and patronage. The greatest symbol of political corruption was William "Boss" Tweed. In 1870, by means of $1 million in bribes to the New York State legislature and

other groups, Tweed and his gang gained complete political control over the city. They stole an estimated $200 million in funds from the city treasury and garnered even more from kickbacks and payoffs. Finally exposed by the *New York Times* in 1871, Tweed was arrested and brought to trial. So confident that he would be acquitted, he haughtily said in response to an allegation about his misappropriation of funds, "What are ya gonna do about it?" His confidence was misplaced, however, and he went to jail in 1872. Nevertheless, extensive graft in city government continued to plague the city until well into the twentieth century.

Physical changes linked to technology contributed to the growth of the city. In 1881, the Brooklyn Bridge opened, and along with the Golden Gate Bridge in San Francisco, it remains one of the world's most beautiful. The Brooklyn Bridge was followed in 1903 by the Williamsburg Bridge and in 1904 by the first tunnel under the Hudson River, connecting the city to the New Jersey shore. In 1906, the Pennsylvania Railroad also tunneled under the Hudson River, establishing major rail transport in the heart of Manhattan at Penn Station. Subways soon followed. People now could live far from midtown and still get there cheaply and quickly.

At the lower end of Manhattan, the dazzling New York skyline began to take shape, capped by construction of the ill-fated twin towers of the World Trade Center between 1966 and 1972. Today, it is difficult to imagine New York without a forest of skyscrapers. Yet before 1890, Manhattan below Central Park was completely covered by structures of less than five stories. The first steel structure in New York appeared in 1889 and reached a "towering" 11 stories. From this point, New York grew upward as if the clouds had become great magnets. The number of buildings with 20 or more floors increased from 61 in 1913 to 188 in 1929. Indeed, half of all such buildings in the country were in New York (Douglas 2004).

Before the Great Depression stalled construction of office buildings, New York witnessed the completion of three famous

CITYSCAPE

The Crazy-Quilt Pattern of New York, 1890

A map of [New York], colored to designate nationalities, would show more stripes than the skin of a zebra, and more colors than any rainbow. . . . [G]reen for the Irish prevailing in the West Side tenement districts, and blue for the Germans on the East Side. . . . [I]ntermingled . . . would be an odd variety of tints that would give the whole the appearance of an extraordinary crazy-quilt. From down in the Sixth Ward . . . the red of the Italian would be seen forcing its way northward along the line of Mulberry Street to the quarter of the French purple on Bleecker Street and South Fifth Avenue. . . . On the West Side, the red would be seen overrunning the old Africa of Thompson Street pushing the black of the negro rapidly uptown.

. . . [T]he Russian and Polish Jew, having overrun the district between Rivington and Division Streets, east of the Bowery, to the point of suffocation, is filling the tenements of the old Seventh Ward to the river front. . . . Between the dull gray of the Jew, his favorite color, and the Italian red, would be seen squeezed in on the map a sharp streak of yellow, marking the narrow boundaries of Chinatown. . . . Dots and dashes of color here and there would show . . . the Finnish sailors . . . the Greek pedlars . . . and the Swiss. . . . And so on to the end of the long register, all toiling together in the galling fetters of the tenement.

Source: Jacob Riis, *How the Other Half Lives* (New York: Hill and Wang, 1957), pp. 18–20. Originally published in 1890.

---

architectural innovations that survive to this day. The Chrysler Building, opened in 1930, is a marvelous, 77-story example of Art Deco architecture—topped with six stories of magnificent stainless-steel arches. The following year marked the opening of the Empire State Building, which at 102 floors has symbolized New York ever since. Rockefeller Center was begun in the same year. It was designed to include "everything" in one place, as urban critic Paul Goldberger observes:

> . . . skyscrapers, plazas, movement, detail, views, stores, cafes. It is all of a piece, yet it is able to appear possessed of infinite variety at the same time. . . . It was conceived as a place in which monumental architecture would spur both business and culture to new heights, and it has come remarkably close to fulfilling that somewhat naive goal. It is surely the parent of every large scale urban complex every American downtown has built since—from Atlanta's Peachtree Center to Hartford's Constitution Center to San Francisco's Embarcadero Center—and it is no insult to say that Rockefeller Center still remains far and away the finest such development ever built (1989:168–69).

New York Today

> New York? It'll be a great place if they ever finish it.
>
> Short-story writer O. Henry

By the 1950s, New York had grown from being a metropolis to being the center of the vast BosWash megalopolis. The 2000 census placed the city at the heart of an enormous MSA covering some 4,000 square miles with more than 21 million people. Nearly 1 in 14 Americans lived in the New York MSA.

From another perspective, however, this region reflects the decentralization that has affected so many cities in contemporary North America. Bridges, highways, tunnels, cars, costs, and congestion—all led to a rapid move away from the city itself between 1970 and 1980, as New York City lost more than 860,000 people (a loss greater than the entire population of San Francisco!). Between 1980 and 1990, however, New York gained 251,000 inhabitants, and by 2000, the city had grown by another 685,000, due primarily to an influx of immigrants.

Economic Problems.   By the late 1990s, the nation had recovered all the jobs lost in the recession of the late 1980s and early 1990s, but the New York region had regained only about a third of the 770,000 jobs it lost. The numbers reflected deep structural problems in this metropolitan region, especially in the concentration of company headquarters for 46 of the nation's top 500 corporations. Many large businesses continue to shrink through mergers, downsizing, and outsourcing. The 1995 merger of Chase Manhattan and Chemical Bank, for example, eliminated about 12,000 jobs (Johnson and Lueck 1996).

Then, the destruction of the World Trade Center and its immediate surroundings dealt a severe blow to the corporate and neighborhood economies of lower Manhattan. The loss of or severe damage to 20 million square feet of office space, as well as the loss of tens of thousands of jobs, was more than that of the entire central business district of a small city. Furthermore, the damage directly affected 14,000 nearby small businesses because of the resulting reduction in pedestrians and customers (Ploeger 2002).

Beyond the Devastation.   On that infamous day of September 11, 2001, New York City suffered the worst tragedy in its history. In addition to the heartbreaking loss of so many innocent lives were the severe economic losses. These losses included billions of dollars of damaged or destroyed private capital and public infrastructure, thousands of dislocated workers, millions of dollars in lost sales as a result of business interruption, and significant disruption to the financial services industry that makes New York the capital of the global securities and banking markets.

Sudden unemployment and business losses fell not just on the many small businesses dependent on customers who worked at or visited the World Trade Center but also on those dependent on tourism—including hotels and restaurants, theaters, taxis, airlines, and airport-related industries. A study by the Center for an Urban Future found that LaGuardia and Kennedy airports suffered larger economic losses than most other major hub airports in the country. Those losses caused the elimination of 16.5 percent of all airport-related jobs—a loss of 10,000 jobs. That was by far the largest percentage loss of any industry in the city, including the securities industry, which lost 9 percent of its jobs (Kennedy 2002).

Through aid from the federal and state governments, New York City slowly rebounded. The rebuilding of Ground Zero is yet to be completed, but hopes are high. Once it is completely rebuilt, lower Manhattan will no doubt thrive again as well. In the near future, that locale will combine commercial buildings with cultural, performing arts, and transportation centers, all linked to a memorial park and pedestrian walkway. Its composition will, advocates say, "reassert New York's cosmopolitan identity" and "re-establish New York's skyline as the most thrilling in the world" (Muschamp 2002).

Major cities like New York are constantly changing. Just as immigration repeatedly remade the city throughout its history, so, too, have its economic fortunes rebounded despite the "gloom and doom" experts who sounded the city's death knell. New York and the other cities survived, and—despite past recessions—they have been working their way back to financial solvency. New York City is back for many of the same reasons that Boston, Baltimore, and other cities are coming back: The postindustrial economy is remaking New York. New positions for highly trained professional workers, particularly in the information-processing and financial sectors, are available, along with lower-paying jobs in the service sectors of food, delivery, and tourism. Parts of the city, such as midtown, thrive as white-collar service centers

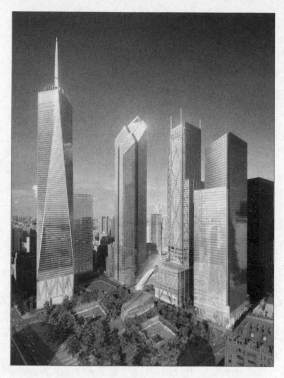

As the first of several office towers to be rebuilt on the World Trade Center site, the Freedom Tower will soar 1,776 feet into the sky and serve as an inspirational and enduring beacon in the New York City skyline. The tower's footprint, measuring 200 by 200 feet, is the same size as the footprints of the original Twin Towers, which will be left intact in the adjoining memorial park.

where business professionals can remain in close contact with one another, have lunch, and socialize after work at a wide variety of places catering to their tastes.

As in other cities, the proportion of people who work in postindustrial jobs is small—perhaps on the order of 10 percent. Many people are working in the service sector (restaurants, hotels, and retail stores) or as public employees (police, fire, transit, sanitation, and social services). Although the city's manufacturing sector has declined somewhat, its 500,000 jobs represent 15 percent of the city's labor force, and in 2005, the city initiated a comprehensive

industrial policy that involves designing new business zones and creating new incentives to encourage long-term investment in manufacturing, warehousing, and other industrial businesses throughout the five boroughs (Lyne 2005:180).

In 2008, tourism soared to a record-breaking 47 million visitors, generating about $30 billion in revenue, with its foreign visitor totals returning to the pre-2001 levels. Air passenger arrivals; hotel occupancy; attendance at Broadway shows; ticket sales at tourist attractions like the Empire State Building, Ellis Island, and the Statue of Liberty; and retail sales all improved (City of New York 2009). Its 2007 total crime index for violent and property crimes put New York among the lowest for U.S. cities with a population of 100,000 or more—and the safest city among those with 1 million or more inhabitants (Federal Bureau of Investigation 2008). More feature films and television series are now shot in the city than at any time since the 1950s, and New York hosts the second-largest concentration of motion picture activity.

Throughout the city, one can find clubs, coffee bars, chic shops, and trendy restaurants springing up, and attendance at concerts, museums, theaters, sports contests, and special events has risen as well. Rental housing is scarce and expensive, especially in Manhattan, where a month's rent for a two-bedroom apartment can be $3,500 (Messina 2008).

Upgrading the City. Construction is omnipresent. In the 1970s, completion of the twin towers of the World Trade Center in lower Manhattan boosted both the image and the economy of the city. In the 1980s, it was the construction of Battery Park City, a $1.5-billion, 92-acre commercial and residential complex that is home to the New York Mercantile Exchange, the Commodity Exchange, and American Express. There are also 2,000 apartments in eight buildings, a Ritz-Carlton and an Embassy Suites hotel, four ferry slips, and a 15-screen multiplex theater. The site also includes a museum, parks, plazas, playgrounds, public arts, and schools. In 2004, Time Warner moved into its new world headquarters, one of the largest projects ever built in New York City, the Time Warner Center at Columbus Circle. Besides its office space, the complex, with its two towers, includes one of the largest malls in the city (four floors of retail space), a screening theater, five restaurants, and a cafe with a marvelous view of Central Park.

At 125th Street in Harlem, the neighborhood's first supermarket, the New Harlem USA shopping center and cinema multiplex, and the renovation of the Apollo Theater improved the physical environment and quality of life. In lower Harlem, the completion of 3,500 new apartments in rehabilitated buildings revitalized commercial activity along 116th Street west of Malcolm X Boulevard. East New York, a once-devastated area in Brooklyn dubbed the "murder capital of New York City," was transformed into a livable area of new, multifamily homes and rental housing, with plans for 2,300 more new homes around a new mall (Hevesi 2001).

Perhaps the most dramatic symbol of New York's revival is construction in the South Bronx. Its image as a lawless, burned-out, drug-infested area whose rampant crime rate inspired the 1981 movie *Fort Apache, the Bronx* is no longer true, after what officials call the nation's largest urban rebuilding effort. With more than $1 billion in public dollars trained on the South Bronx since 1986, 19,000 apartments were refurbished and more than 4,500 new houses built for working-class home buyers. More than 50 abandoned buildings that once stood like rotten teeth along major arteries like the Cross Bronx and Major Deegan expressways were reclaimed as midrise apartment houses.

Other signs of an urban renaissance are found everywhere. They range in scale from massive residential enclaves like Queens West and Riverside South, both loosely modeled after Battery Park City, to the Starbucks-style cafes that have sprouted up all over. The transformation of 42nd Street, once a center of sex and sleaze, into a family entertainment center with Disney as the linchpin is simply amazing, and the renovation of Grand Central

Terminal with an upscale restaurant and shops is another positive sign.

Creation or restoration of parks offers another example of the improvement in the quality of life in New York. At Pier 25 in TriBeCa, for example, now stands a recreation area with miniature golf, volleyball, and a children's playground. Similar restorations at Pier 45 at Christopher Street and Pier 64 in Chelsea have made these areas available for recreation as well. Both are part of Hudson River Park, 550 acres stretching from Battery Park City to 59th Street, with esplanades, waterfront activities, biking and rollerblading paths, dog runs, athletic facilities, gardens, and sculptures. The success of the 1992 transformation of Bryant Park— once an unsafe, sequestered area overrun by drug dealers—into one of New York's busiest public spaces, where thousands go day and night for lunch, concerts, outdoor movies, or simply to mingle, surprised even city planners. Directly behind the New York Public Library and North America's first wireless zone park, it has become a hot spot for young adults, serving—in an odd manifestation of a small-town tradition—as Manhattan's town square.

On another front, 59 Business Improvement Districts (BIDs) exist in virtually every section of the city, from Harlem to Brighton Beach. More than 1,200 BIDs exist in cities across North America (including 60 in Toronto), but their greatest impact has been in cleaning up New York (particularly Times Square). The BIDs are self-taxing districts set up to clean, patrol, and upgrade their neighborhoods, providing services that were once the sole responsibility of city government. Faced with budget problems, cities have welcomed the privatization of municipal services. Once a majority of owners in a designated area agree, they work out a plan for services. After City Council approval, the city collects an annual assessment (above the property taxes) from all property owners and turns the money over to the district. The resulting services and improvements—new sidewalks, signs, street lights, planters, wastebaskets, flags and banners, street sweepers, and unarmed, uniformed security patrols—have reduced crime, cleaned up streets, and restored a sense of pride among merchants and the public (Mitchell 2001).

Changing Population. Since the end of World War II, more than 4 million whites have left the central-city area, replaced by minority migrants and immigrants. In 1950, the population of the five boroughs was 87 percent white, 9 percent black, and 3 percent Hispanic. By 2006, the city's profile had shifted to 35 percent non-Hispanic white, 24 percent non-Hispanic black, 28 percent Hispanic, and 13 percent Asian. Although these are dramatic contrasts, the change between 2000 and 2006 is far less so, with little change

in the white, black, and Hispanic ratios and an increase in the Asian presence (Beveridge 2007).

Although many minorities work in the information-processing and service sectors, unemployment and poverty are high within the city's African American and Hispanic American communities. The U.S. Census Bureau reported that about one in five of New York City residents (19 percent) lived in poverty in 2006. Yet the city also has the nation's widest income gap. In Manhattan, for example, the wealthiest 20 percent earned nearly 40 times more than the poorest 20 percent ($351,333 versus $8,855). Metropolitan New York ranked fourth among whites, 10th among blacks, 12th among Asians, and 25th among Hispanics in terms of median income (Roberts 2007).

One of the best examples of urban renaissance occurring in many North American cities is New York City's Times Square. Once the locale of sleazy porn stores and theaters and other seedy enterprises, it has undergone a facelift that is more than cosmetic. New hotels, theaters, and family-oriented businesses now dominate the area.

And so New York goes on, with its successes and failures, its ability to symbolize simultaneously all that is great and tragic about all cities. To many, New York is the quintessential city. If New York fails, in some sense cities everywhere fail, but if it succeeds, it offers hope for all.

SUMMARY

The development of North American cities has been, in its own way, as dynamic and varied as that of European cities. Neither Canada nor the United States began as an urban nation; in fact, that idea would have been anathema to many of either country's founders. Nevertheless, that is what both have become.

After beginning as places of religious and political freedom, the new colonies rapidly established themselves as major trading centers. By 1700, coastal villages were becoming bustling towns. By the late eighteenth century, these small cities had developed into major urban areas. They traded up and down the coast and with Europe and became rich by establishing links with the vast heartland of the country. Inland cities also appeared. By the mid-nineteenth century, industrialization was transforming the northern cities of the United States and, to some degree, their Canadian and newer, midwestern counterparts into manufacturing centers. The South, still operating on the "small city" pattern associated with agriculture, fell behind. With victory for the North, the Civil War effectively ended the small- versus large-city "debate" in the United States.

After 1870, North American cities, particularly in the North and the Midwest of the United States and in Lower Canada, exploded into metropolises of millions. Trade and industry were the driving forces behind this development. More and more jobs generated more and more wealth. Drawn to this opportunity, millions came from abroad, resulting in the ethnic–racial–religious mosaic that characterizes so many North American cities. With this influx came great problems, particularly in the United States. Quality of life began to deteriorate, and poverty and exploitation became rampant. New technological advances enabled many to escape to streetcar suburbs. Consequently, cities began to spread over the countryside. Losing revenue because of this exodus and seriously hampered by the Great Depression, cities began to depend on federal assistance.

After World War II, decentralization accelerated. People and businesses departed the central cities, leaving the innermost areas increasingly populated by the poor and minorities and by service-oriented or professional businesses. Huge metropolitan regions became the norm, replacing earlier central-city cores.

In the older Snowbelt cities of the United States, decentralization had particularly disastrous results. When the cities lost people and businesses, billions in tax and sales revenues and hundreds of thousands of jobs were lost as well. Many cities faced a continual threat of bankruptcy. The South and West, however, experienced an urban boom. Sunbelt cities were the direct beneficiaries of the northern cities' problems (old industrial systems, poor inner-city transportation for products, and deteriorating services). The Sunbelt cities built new plants, surrounded by efficient superhighways; provided good or brand-new service systems; and offered lower costs—particularly for energy and labor. Some Sunbelt cities were able to expand their physical boundaries—for example, in Texas, one of the states with the greatest urban expansion, suburbs were annexed almost as fast as they appeared, thus keeping the tax and business base within the city's jurisdiction.

Perhaps most important of all, North American cities are rapidly developing a postindustrial economy based on high technology, white-collar jobs, and services. They are also rebuilding the deteriorating office and housing stock left from earlier decades and improving many other amenities that define the quality of urban life. Older large cities once in the throes of economic disaster are now rebounding, although problems clearly remain, particularly affecting the poorer residents. Serving as white-collar service centers, these cities have attracted young, relatively affluent professionals whose presence has had great impact. Another trend is the formation of edge cities on the fringes of established metropolitan areas.

The evidence suggests that all three trends—decentralization, the move to the Sunbelt, and the growth of a postindustrial economy—will continue. As a result, northern cities such as New York will continue to adapt to a changing economic structure and a new population. Meanwhile, the Sunbelt picture is not as rosy as it once was. The population boom in many instances has generated infrastructure problems; crime rates are high; and racial tensions are on the rise as Hispanics move up from Mexico and Latin America and African Americans move back to the South. Furthermore, even in cities where postindustrialization is in full sway, the newfound wealth of the few who are participating in a cosmopolitan lifestyle does not extend to all city dwellers. On the contrary, the gap between the urban rich and the urban poor appears to be widening, not narrowing.

CONCLUSION

In the three centuries since urbanization took hold in the New World, North Americans have not really built Cotton Mather's hoped-for "heavenly city." Nevertheless, indicators show that cities are improving. Whether this revitalization will continue remains to be seen. If we continue to see the city as something to "use," but not as something to be collectively concerned about, then the outlook probably is not very bright. If, on the other hand, we see the city as a human creation and, thus, subject to understanding and human control, then we might be justified in being more optimistic about the outcome.

KEY TERMS

consolidated metropolitan statistical area (CMSA) (68)
decentralization (64)
globalization (64)
industrial parks (66)

megalopolis (68)
metropolitan statistical area (MSA) (67)
sunbelt expansion (64)
urban explosion (64)
urban implosion (64)

INTERNET ACTIVITIES

1. You can view different parts of the historic district of Old Québec by going to *http://www.world-heritage-tour.org/america/canada/eastern-provinces/quebec/map.html*. Once there, if you click on any small photo and then click and drag inside that enlarged image, you can get a 360° view of each part of the site.

2. You can see satellite images of many U.S. cities and of Canada if you go to *http://geology.com/satellite/cities/*. Click on "Beginner's Guide to Landsat Images" to understand the color coding so that you can enjoy the images more fully.

CHAPTER 4

TODAY'S CITIES AND SUBURBS

We can't always predict the future, but we do invent it. Today's decisions affect tomorrow's realities, just as we are living out the decisions made by preceding generations. For example, the change in public preference from urban to suburban living owes much to federal legislation in the late 1940s and 1950s that provided low-cost builder and buyer loans as well as to a massive highway-building program that made it easier to live away from city jobs and activities. That growth in middle-class suburban housing, and the subsequent exodus of many businesses to suburban campuses or shopping malls, eroded the cities' economic vitality and tax base, which, in turn, worsened the quality of urban schools and the quality of life for many city dwellers who remained. The suburban lifestyles that most North Americans favor today, as well as the problems besetting many U.S. cities, are the result of social forces unleashed two generations ago. So, too, will the decisions of recent decades affect urban and suburban lifestyles for decades to come.

Four patterns in particular—sprawl, edge cities, gated communities, and common interest developments—have grown so fast and had such a strong effect on urban areas that we can discuss both their current influence on the quality of life as well as their importance for the foreseeable future.

URBAN AND SUBURBAN SPRAWL

We must make a distinction between *growth* and *sprawl*. As Canada and the United States increase in population, additional space is necessary for the construction of residences and businesses to meet the needs of a larger populace. Moreover, the days when most people lived in cities are gone; now, most people prefer to have their own home on their own plot of land in suburbia. Therefore, the development of vacant land is a necessity, but it becomes problematic when a lack of regional planning leads to inefficient land-use management that has a negative impact on the environment and increases costs for everyone (see the *Urban Trends* box on page 88).

What Is Sprawl?

Sprawl is the term used to describe spread-out or low-density residential development beyond the edge of service and employment areas. It separates where people live from where they work, shop, and pursue leisure or an education, thereby requiring them to use cars to move between these zones. This type of development results from decades of unplanned, rapid growth and poor land-use management. Sprawl thus identifies the cumulative effects of development that is automobile-dependent, inefficient, and wasteful of natural resources.

As people move farther from core cities and into outlying regions, so do all the trappings of urban life: stores, offices, factories, hospitals, congestion, and pollution. Developments claim more and more open land as the population increases and disperses. One town looks like another; stores on the highways erect signs that shout out their wares to the fast-moving traffic going by; and every activity requires a separate trip by car.

Stretching across North America—from the West Coast to the East Coast, from Toronto to Miami, from Vancouver to Tucson—are large metropolitan areas fused into a series of megalopolises. Gobbling up the land are strip malls and large suburban tracts with cookie-cutter housing of such striking similarity that they are creating an unvarying sameness everywhere, blurring traditional regional differences. Within this vast, homogeneous panorama, one could be almost anywhere on the continent and find few visual clues as to locale (see the *Urban Trends* box on page 89).

Three striking examples of suburban sprawl development patterns consuming far more land than urban development patterns are in Pennsylvania, Arizona, and Georgia. Since 1950, Pennsylvania has lost more than 4 million acres of farmland to sprawl—an area larger than Connecticut and Rhode Island combined. The city of Phoenix now covers more than 475 square miles—nearly half the land area of the state of Rhode Island. The 13-county Atlanta region, one of the fastest-growing U.S. metropolitan areas, lost nearly

URBAN TRENDS

"As American as Apple Pie"

Critics of suburban sprawl maintain that ... sprawl—the spread-out development of separated subdivisions, office parks, malls, and strip shopping centers growing beyond existing cities and towns—has thwarted public transit development, separated rich and poor, caused unnecessary travel, consumed fragile land, and generated excessive public expenditures. On the other side of the discussion, some believe that sprawl is as American as apple pie and that citizens are getting what they want: single-family homes on large lots, safe communities with good school systems, unrestricted automobile use, and metropolitan locations far from the pace and problems of urban areas. These, and other benefits of sprawl, they argue, mean life is good. . . .

In fact, sprawl has been so well accepted by the public that the prime-rated locations for both residential and non-residential development are located increasingly farther out than closer in and are more rather than less segregated by type of land use. Gated communities, farmettes, research parks, law offices, medical groups, mega-hardware and home improvement stores, theatrical and comedy clubs, new and used car lots, and restaurants all now seek peripheral locations in pursuit of their markets. The move to the far reaches of the metropolitan area began with single-family subdivisions; shopping centers and garden apartments sprang up next, then research and industrial parks, followed by restaurants and entertainment facilities, and finally, discounters of every form.

The unique aspect of all this development is that few entities have ever failed because their decisions to move outward were in the wrong direction. Occasionally, a retailer or a residential development has gone under because an exit on the interstate or beltway was not developed as planned, but rarely has an economic entity failed in the United States because it was developed too far out.

If sprawl is so desirable, why should the citizens of the United States accept anything else? The answer is that they can no longer pay for the infrastructure necessary to develop farther and farther out in metropolitan areas. The cost to provide public infrastructure and services in new sprawling development is higher than the cost to service that same population in a more compact development form. Sprawling, "leapfrog" developments require longer public roads and water and sewer lines to provide service. . . .

Sprawl creates a never-ending upward spiral of costs. Increased usage of city roads due to the increased population makes immediate improvement necessary. The city then has to provide services to the new area. Sprawling developments also impose higher costs on police and fire departments and schools. Not as readily apparent are the costs that a new development will impose on the municipality in years to come. In all likelihood, it will not generate enough property taxes to pay for the services it requires. Farther down the road, all of the new infrastructure, originally paid for by the developer, will need maintenance and repair.

Source: From *Sprawl Costs: Economic Impacts of Unchecked Development* by Robert Burcell, Anthony Downs, Sahan Mukherji, and Barbara McCann. Copyright © 2002 by Island Press. Reproduced by permission of Island Press, Washington, D.C.

URBAN TRENDS

Something Is Wrong

Americans *sense that something is wrong* with the places where we live and work and go about our daily business. We hear this unhappiness expressed in phrases like "no sense of place" and "the loss of community." We drive up and down the gruesome, tragic suburban boulevards of commerce, and we're overwhelmed at the fantastic, awesome, stupefying ugliness of absolutely everything in sight—the fry pits, the big-box stores, the office units, the lube joints, the carpet warehouses, the parking lagoons, the jive plastic townhouse clusters, the uproar of signs, the highway itself clogged with cars—as though the whole thing had been designed by some diabolical force bent on making human beings miserable. And naturally, this experience can make us feel glum about the nature and future of our civilization.

When we drive around and look at all this cartoon architecture and other junk that we've smeared all over the landscape, we register it as ugliness. This ugliness is the surface expression of deeper problems—problems that relate to the issue of our national character. The highway strip is not just a sequence of eyesores. The pattern it represents is also economically catastrophic, an environmental calamity, socially devastating, and spiritually degrading.

. . . We reject the past and the future, and this repudiation is manifest in our graceless constructions. Our residential, commercial, and civic buildings are constructed with the fully conscious expectation that they will disintegrate in a few decades. This condition even has a name: "design life." Strip malls and elementary schools have short design lives. They are expected to fall apart in less than fifty years. Since these things are not expected to speak to any era but our own, we seem unwilling to put money or effort into their embellishment. Nor do we care about traditional solutions to the problems of weather and light, because we have technology to mitigate these problems—namely, central heating and electricity. Thus in many new office buildings the windows don't open. In especially bad buildings, like the average Wal-Mart, windows are dispensed with nearly altogether. This process of disconnection from the past and the future, and from the organic patterns of weather and light, done for the sake of expedience, ends up diminishing us spiritually, impoverishing us socially, and degrading the aggregate set of cultural patterns that we call civilization.

Source: James Howard Kunstler, "Home from Nowhere," *The Atlantic Monthly* 278 (September 1996), 46–66. Reprinted by permission of the author.

---

one-fifth of its forested lands (174,000 acres) to development between 1999 and 2005. That's an average of 80 acres a day! At the current rate of land consumption, Clayton County will run out of developable land by 2016, with the remaining 12 counties following, so that by 2040, all 2.6 million acres of land will be consumed by development (Atlanta Regional Council 2007).

Why Do We Have Sprawl?

Sprawl is like that cartoon snowball rolling down the hill, growing in size and momentum until it becomes practically unstoppable. For the past two generations, government policies on taxation, transportation, and housing—nurtured by society's embrace of *laissez faire* development—subsidized virtually unlimited

This aerial view of Las Vegas shows the spread-city phenomenon occurring in the U.S. Sunbelt area. Like other Sunbelt cities, in which climate and work opportunities attract many, the rapid growth of Las Vegas strains the existing infrastructure and water supply and gobbles up the land, and its sprawling development pattern increases dependence on the automobile.

low-density development. And the more this development occurred, the more people clamored for it.

For many, a house in the suburbs became the personification of the ideal lifestyle. Massive road-building projects and community planning designed around the car encouraged people to abandon cities for the greener pastures of suburbia. As these non-metropolitan areas grew in population, a new phenomenon—the shopping center—came into existence, with large department stores from the city serving as anchors for the variety of retail enterprises along the indoor corridors. Office and industrial parks followed, either lured by tax incentives, induced by management preferences, or prompted by the relocation of competitors. Whatever the reason, the snowball effect generated more and more growth farther and farther into outlying regions, transforming much of the natural landscape around cities in Canada and the United States.

One factor in sprawl is **political fragmentation,** the splintered governance structure of numerous local municipalities in a metropolitan region, resulting in an inability to control regional growth with a comprehensive land-use plan. This situation, a springboard for postmodernist analysis, results in each town reacting individually to a developer's proposal in terms of its own zoning regulations and gains of new tax rateable properties. Little to no thought goes into the ever-expanding settlement pattern, its furthering reliance on the automobile for ever-increasing distances, and the overall impact on the environment.

Sprawl occurs everywhere. It is most obvious and grows most spectacularly, however, in the rapid growth areas of the South and West. For instance, on the periphery of Denver, farmland is yielding to sprawl at a rate of 90,000 acres per year. Significantly, population growth only accounts for about half of sprawl; land-use decisions can decrease or increase the land-use consumption. West Palm

Beach, Florida, for example, experienced a 15 percent increase in population between 1990 and 1996 but a 25 percent decrease in population density during that same period.

Elsewhere, Cincinnati lost 25 percent of its population between 1970 and 1990 but increased its land area usage from 335 to 573 square miles. Metro Cleveland's population declined by 11 percent between 1970 and 1990, but it still consumed 33 percent more land. Similarly, Detroit declined in population by 7 percent, but its land area grew by 28 percent. Also, between 1990 and 1996, Akron, Ohio, experienced a 37 percent decrease in population but a 65 percent increase in developed land area use (Kolankiewicz and Beck 2001).

Consequences of Sprawl

The preferred lifestyle of owning a house on a large lot and enjoying the convenience of one-stop, mega-mall shopping has negative side effects. By spreading residences, medical and commercial offices, and industries throughout a region on large tracts of land, we increase residents' dependence on automobiles for transportation. Everything—and everyone—is too spread out to make public transportation economically feasible. Longer commutes take time away from families, increase gasoline consumption as well as wear and tear on cars, cause traffic congestion, and increase instances of road rage.

Nor can everyone get around by car: A lifestyle that requires a car discriminates against poor families, the elderly, the disabled, and the young. Suburban teenagers, for instance, usually lack sufficient activities in their town but are unable to travel to locations where such diversions exist. Suburban parents thus spend a large part of their time chauffeuring their children to stores, cinemas, juvenile activities, and other events, or just to the mall, where they can "hang out."

Environmentalists once stood alone in their opposition to sprawl. More recently, however, other individuals, groups, and organizations have suggested that the costs and consequences of sprawl may outweigh the benefits. This coalition includes low-income housing advocates, social service organizations, church leaders, and others concerned about the impact on cities (McMahon 1997). Those seeking to curb sprawl often base their concerns around its impact on the environment, the traffic problems it creates, its harm to cities, and the financial burden it poses on everyone.

Environmental Damage. As new construction emerges in scattered fashion across the countryside, it often disrupts wildlife habitats and fragments rural regions once abounding in farmland, fields, forests, lakes, and ponds. An example of the latter is the runoff from streets, parking lots, lawns, and farms that empties pollutants and sediment into waterways, degrading water quality and smothering habitat. In Seattle, for example, experts blame development around Puget Sound for the polluted water and habitat destruction that resulted in listing the Chinook salmon as an endangered species.

Another example is the Chesapeake Bay area, where sprawl is quickly gobbling up open space, farmlands, and forest lands. According to the Chesapeake Bay Foundation (2005), more than 90,000 acres—almost 150 square miles of the bay's surrounding land area—are lost each year to development. Today, four to five times more land is used per person compared with 40 years ago. As a result, toxins and sediments are flowing into the bay in increasing amounts and are upsetting the delicate balance of the watershed's ecosystem. Attempts to clean up Chesapeake Bay through cooperative best management practices have had only limited success: Its health remains in moderate-to-poor condition, and the overall grade in 2007 for the Bay's health status was a C–(Chesapeake EcoCheck 2008).

Sprawl has also had disastrous consequences involving the destruction of wetlands and building on flood plains. Wetlands act as natural sponges that soak up and store rain and runoff. When they are lost to residential or commercial development, water that would have been absorbed or slowed is free to flood. With few exceptions, floods are most frequent, and loss of life and property are greatest, in counties that have lost the most wetlands—especially during the past 30 years. Since the 1970s, the most extensive loss has occurred in Louisiana, Mississippi, Arkansas, Florida, South Carolina, and North Carolina (National Audubon Society 1999).

Although such natural processes as heavy rains and snowmelt can cause floods, as can the failure of dams and levees, so, too, can inadequate drainage in urbanized areas. Scientists at the U.S. Geological Survey believe that a principal cause of flooding is poor planning and unwise development that destroys the wetlands and open space that protect communities. On average, U.S. floods kill 140 people each year and cause $6 billion in damage. The remarkable flooding in 2005 caused by Hurricane Katrina cost more than $200 billion in losses in New Orleans and other Gulf Coast towns, making it the costliest natural disaster in U.S. history (U.S. Geological Survey 2008).

Sometimes, the consequence of sprawl is too little water, not too much. For example, Las Vegas is one of the fastest-growing cities in the United States. This midsized city, which increased its population by 84 percent between 1990 and 2000, gained another 75,000 residents between 2000 and 2006. Growing at the rate of 6,000 new residents every month, the city has such a serious water-supply problem that in 1999, it began paying residents $1.50 for each square foot of lawn they ripped out to conserve water. By 2007, the removal of about six square miles of grass had saved 18 billion gallons of water. Despite these efforts, Lake Mead—now at half the level it was in 2000—may run dry within the next 6 to 12 years unless water usage is further cut (Sterbentz 2008).

Three environmental groups—the National Wildlife Federation, Smart Growth America, and NatureServe—project that over the next 25 years, more than 22,000 acres of natural resources and habitat will be lost to development in 35 of the largest and most rapidly growing metropolitan areas. They also call attention to the fact that as many as 553 of the nearly 1,200 at-risk species live only in those areas (Heilprin 2005).

Traffic Problems.   Because sprawl, by definition, is low-density, automobile-dependent development on the edge of service and employment areas, it generates longer commutes and greater traffic congestion. Cars zipping along highways—or, worse, cars stuck in traffic jams—spew millions of tons of carbon dioxide and other greenhouse gases into our atmosphere each year.

The 2007 Urban Mobility Report identified worsening traffic congestion in all 437 U.S. urban areas, costing each traveler an annual average of 38 hours extra travel time and 26 gallons of fuel. For everyone, trips are taking longer, and congestion affects a greater portion of the day. The term *rush hour* is actually no longer accurate. Once, the rush hour was exactly that—typically, an hour between 7 and 8 A.M. and another between 4 and 5 P.M.—but today, the peak traffic periods last from 6 through 9 A.M. and from 3 until 7 P.M. (Schrank and Lomax 2007).

The problem is most acute in Southern California, where traffic delays have tripled during the past 20 years. The congestion will only increase as this region of 18 million absorbs a projected 6 million new residents over the next 20 years—the equivalent of twice the population of Chicago. If population growth and transportation demand continue at their current pace, the daily delay from congestion will get far worse (Southern California Association of Governments 2008:67). Elsewhere, the story is similar. For example, the typical worker in Atlanta drives 37 miles round trip to work, while those in Dallas drive 30 miles. In Los Angeles, the daily drive is 21 miles.

Americans on average commute farther to work than Canadians do. According to the U.S. Bureau of Transportation Statistics, 68 percent of workers reported a one-way commute of 15 miles or less, 22 percent traveled between 16 and 30 miles, and 11 percent traveled more than 30 miles. In contrast, Canadian workers travel only four to five miles commuting to work in Ontario, Nova Scotia, Quebec, and British Columbia (Norton 2008).

Gasoline prices, if they rise again, may well change this pattern. In mid-2008, when the price per gallon passed four dollars, tens of thousands of commuters nationwide abandoned their cars and took a bus or a train

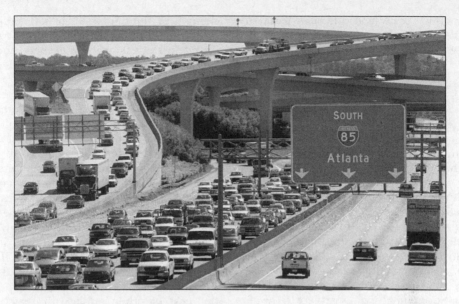

Atlanta's afternoon rush-hour traffic snarls at what commuters refer to as "spaghetti junction"—the intersection of Interstates 85 and 285. Many of these drivers are heading from their jobs to homes in suburban Gwinnett County. In two decades, Gwinnett County's population has more than tripled, to exceed 465,000. Atlanta's phenomenal growth and lack of adequate mass transit are the main reasons why the area suffers from traffic congestion, air pollution, and urban sprawl.

instead, with the biggest increases occurring in the South and West, where the driving culture is strongest. Other factors pushing people to take mass transit include expensive parking fees and technology: Wireless computers enable commuters to turn travel time into productive work time (Krauss 2008). Fuel prices, however, are the single biggest factor accounting for increased reliance on public transportation, and if these costs escalate again, mass transit ridership will also likely increase, possibly affecting future residential patterns.

Harm to Cities. Sprawl may be primarily a suburban phenomenon, but it has a powerful urban counterpart. The centrifugal shift of businesses and residences into outlying areas takes people away from the older, established central cities, downtowns, and neighborhoods, where so much of the heritage of both Canada and the United States is concentrated. This outward migration erodes the tax base, forcing cities to raise taxes on their remaining taxpayers to continue funding city services.

Sprawl destroys downtown commerce by pulling shoppers from once-thriving, locally owned stores and restaurants to large regional malls. These areas then lose their economic health, and the buildings and other historical reminders that define these once bustling places fall into disrepair. Sprawl thus robs cities of character, as abandoned factories, boarded-up homes, and decaying retail centers dominate the urban landscape.

Smaller, older cities in the northeastern United States are especially vulnerable to this process. A good example is Greensboro, North Carolina, the anchor point to Guilford County, which has been experiencing extensive development. Its population density declined by more than half after 1950, even as its boundaries more than doubled outside the old city limits:

Sprawl in Greensboro has also been associated with the movement of shopping and entertainment to the periphery and the decline of the city's once lively downtown. . . . [D]owntown Greensboro in the 1960s . . . was still a center for shopping, recreation, and many businesses. In subsequent decades, retailers, employers, and entertainment facilities followed residents to the periphery, leaving a downtown full of empty and underutilized buildings. Empty buildings pay little tax; instead they swallow large amounts of taxpayer money devoted to downtown redevelopment plans. Recent years have seen a gradual upward trend in downtown activity, but the problems of empty buildings and storefronts are far from solved. (Doss and Markham 2004:7–10)

In contrast, historic Spokane, Washington, once called "The City Beautiful," is reeling under the pressures of growth, with 50,000 newcomers expected in the next 20 years. Many city residents—believing that sprawl and automobile dependency were taking over and crushing the city's charm—banded together to form the Spokane Horizons project to develop a comprehensive plan addressing issues like parking, new roads, and infrastructure capacity while calling for a healthy downtown and surrounding neighborhoods. Adopted in 2001, the 20-year plan designates 21 mixed-use centers and corridors both within and adjacent to the city limits while maintaining the downtown as the heart of the city and the region's cultural and economic center (City of Spokane Planning Services Department 2003).

Financial Costs. Conventional wisdom says that development strengthens the municipal tax base. Although possibly true a few decades ago, this is no longer the case: The increases in tax revenues seldom make up for the increased costs of delivering new services (water and sewer lines, schools, police and fire protection, and roads) to people who live far away from the existing infrastructure.

A Maryland planning study predicted that during the first two decades of the twenty-first century, sprawl will cost state residents about $10 billion more for new roads, schools, sewers, and water than would be necessary if growth were more concentrated. Similar studies in California, Florida, and elsewhere have demonstrated a direct relationship between sprawl and the spiraling costs of government (McMahon 1997:4). Yet, in 2005, Maryland citizens found

themselves fighting a $1 billion proposal to build a new Potomac River bridge and highway, despite a study showing little need for such a bridge—except to encourage sprawl development (Solutions Not Sprawl 2005).

In contrast, a master plan for the state of New Jersey, the most densely populated of the 50 U.S. states, evaluated the costs of conventional sprawl growth patterns against a mix of "infill" development, higher-density concentrated new development, and traditional sprawl and found significant differences in cost. Infill and higher-density growth would result in a savings of $1.18 billion in roads, water, and sanitary sewer construction (or more than $12,000 per new home) and $400 million in direct annual savings to local governments. The total savings over 15 years would be $7.8 billion. This does not take into account reductions in the cost of other public infrastructure that result from infill growth: decreased spending on storm drainage, less need for school busing (and parent taxi service), fewer fire stations, and less travel time for police, ambulance, garbage collection, and other services (Clean Water Action Council 2008).

SMART GROWTH

The alternative to sprawl is **smart growth,** which is comprehensive land-use planning to revitalize and build compact, environmentally sensitive communities that are transit and pedestrian oriented and contain a mix of residential, commercial, and retail spaces. Its focus is on regional growth within already urbanized areas as well as on newly urbanizing land.

Another growing trend is an insistence on assessing the ramifications of large-scale construction projects on the environment. **Social impact analysis** is an interdisciplinary study to determine the likely consequences of a project before it is executed. This approach includes the new field of **environmental sociology,** which examines the reciprocal interactions between the physical environment, social organization, and social behavior (Sydenstricker-Neto 2008).

Population growth and continued land development are ongoing realities. For several decades now, the United States has added

5 million new housing units every five years for an additional 10 to 12 million people. Over the next 30 years, it may add another 90 million new people, most of them in metropolitan areas. That means not only additional residential space but also additional work and commercial space. Clearly, the question of how the nation grows is critical (Burchell et al. 2005:6).

Here's one example of compact growth versus sprawl. According to the Regional Plan Association—a non-profit organization dedicated to improving the quality of life in the New York metropolitan region—if the office space needed for each population increase of 5 million were built only in suburban office parks, it would cut a swath a half-mile wide and 54 miles long. In a large city with skyscrapers, however, 200 acres would fulfill the same need. The reason is that each million square feet of suburban office space requires, on average, 80 acres (25 of those acres for parking lots) as compared with only a single acre in a large city, half of which is for an office plaza. In smaller cities, the same million square feet would take up about six acres, involving the construction of 25-story buildings with landscaping and parking lots (Caldwell 1973:45–56).

Sprawl, by definition, is a regional problem, and solving the problem requires convincing people that comprehensive, rational planning and strategies to combat it are in their self-interest. "Smart growth" public policies seek ways to stop the bulldozing of forests and farms and, instead, encourage reinvestment in cities and urbanized towns through sustainability, denser development, mass transit, and pedestrian-friendly areas. An increasing number of community leaders, concerned citizens, environmental groups, and government officials are exploring approaches to growth and development that will provide alternatives to sprawl, and some of their efforts are gaining momentum (see Table 4-1).

Land Purchases

In the 1960s, the federal government began setting aside a percentage of its royalties from offshore oil drilling to acquire or expand recreational land and open space. Today, through referendums and local or state government initiatives, efforts to protect open space and

TABLE 4–1   Sprawl Versus Smart Growth

Definition	Sprawl is uncontrollable, unplanned, and unaccountable low-density development on an urban periphery beyond the edge of service and employment areas.	Smart growth is resource efficient; supports economic development and jobs; creates healthy, safe communities and neighborhoods; and protects greenspace and farmlands
Characteristics	Wide roads are designed to move automobiles rapidly, not to move people.	Pedestrian- and transit-friendly roads are designed to move people safely and allow interaction of neighbors.
	Single-use land isolates where people live from where they work, shop, enjoy recreation, and go to school.	Mixed-use land allows shops, schools, and jobs to be reached without using an automobile.
	Emphasis is on the private realm: yards, cars, and gated communities.	Emphasis is on the public realm: public facilities, parks, and pedestrian-friendly environments.
Effects	Decreases the quality of life, because it harms the environment and can cause health problems.	Preserves environmentally sensitive areas and farmlands, and reduces air pollution.
	Is costly to taxpayers because of the need for expensive infrastructure.	Provides an opportunity for community members and stakeholders to collaborate on development decisions.

Source: From *The Dark Side of the American Dream,* © 1998 Sierra Club™ Books. Reprinted by permission.

slow suburban sprawl are growing. In 1998, New Jersey voters approved a $1 billion referendum that raised the gasoline tax to pay for setting aside half the state's remaining 2 million acres of open space over the next 10 years. Earlier, voters in Monroe County, Pennsylvania, approved a $25 million bond referendum to purchase undeveloped land over a ten-year period. Voters in Austin, Texas, approved an increase in water rates to protect thousands of acres of environmentally sensitive land around the city. Maryland's Smart Growth and Neighborhood Conservation Program includes $71 million to buy agricultural, forest, or natural areas that are in danger of development. Elsewhere, such as in Florida and Michigan, communities are also purchasing land to prevent development.

Urban Growth Boundaries

Oregon and Washington require all communities to designate official boundaries in order to separate urban areas from their surrounding greenbelt of open lands, including farms, watersheds, and parks. The intent is to funnel growth into areas with existing infrastructure while protecting the wide diversity of natural resources wrapped around these population centers. Portland, Oregon—featured in this chapter's case study—has had an urban growth boundary in place since 1975. Although Portland has grown almost 50 percent in population since then, it has consumed only 2 percent more land. Builders support the growth boundaries, because there is less red tape and more flexible zoning within the designated growth areas. In addition, home prices are lower than in other major West Coast cities. As a result, Portland is one of the healthiest and most livable cities in the United States (McMahon 1997). Other cities that have been successful with this approach are Boulder, Colorado, and the California cities of San Jose, Morgan Hill, Napa, and Santa Rosa.

Revitalizing Existing Cities and Towns

The rejuvenation of once-thriving cities and towns—where mass transit, existing infrastructure, and high-density living can support

growth—will attract new residents and limit urban flight. Many communities are preserving their unique architecture through restoration and are utilizing good planning to restore a sense of community, improve livability, and enhance economic vitality. Through innovative public–private redevelopment strategies, they are creating vibrant urban environments that reconnect to their histories and cultural identities. Chattanooga, Tennessee, cleaned up its once seriously polluted river, the Tennessee, and created a riverfront park and promenade that now attract both wildlife and people. Suisun, California, in the San Francisco Bay area, converted an area containing a polluted waterway, decaying warehouses, and a high-crime neighborhood of dilapidated houses into a charming place filled with shops, affordable homes, and a canal for boating. As part of its smart growth plan to encourage revitalization by drawing people to the inner city, Maryland offered a financial incentive of at least $3,000 to people who buy a home in areas closer to their places of work.

A controversial approach to urban redevelopment is local or state government use of **eminent domain** to seize private property for public use, provided that the owner receives compensation at fair market value. This legal action, rooted in the Fifth Amendment of the U.S. Constitution, generated widespread attention in 2005 with a highly criticized, 5-4 decision by the U.S. Supreme Court in the case of *Kelo* v. *City of New London*. This small Connecticut city of about 25,000 had fallen on hard economic times, losing industry, population, and some of its tax base. In an effort to rejuvenate the city by spurring economic development, city officials offered to purchase 115 residential and commercial lots in the old Fort Trumbull neighborhood.

When 15 owners refused to sell, however, and the city acted to condemn their property, the owners sued and argued that the city had misused its power of eminent domain. After the Supreme Court ruled against them, saying that governmental taking of private property for economic development constituted a permissible "public use," critics charged the decision misinterpreted the Fifth Amendment and was a gross violation of property rights.

An excellent example of revitalizing an urban environment to reconnect to the city's history is the San Antonio River Walk, one of the world's great urban linear parks and a tourist's delight. Shops, restaurants, and hotels line the San Antonio River, as people take advantage of sightseeing boats or paddleboats, walkways, footbridges, or stairs to street level to tour historic sites.

Politicians, the general public, and numerous advocacy groups charged that a dangerous precedent had been set, allowing large corporations to benefit at the expense of individual homeowners, often minorities.

Since the *Kelo* ruling, almost all states have passed laws to limit the power of municipalities to invoke eminent domain for economic development. Meanwhile, in New London, the property owners received extra compensation, but as of February 2009, the lots are vacant, generating no tax revenues. So far, the city's redevelopment project appears to be in doubt because of the developer's problems with financing. Eminent domain continues to have vigorous advocates and opponents, and the widespread impact of the *Kelo* ruling and recent state laws are yet to be determined.

Transit-Oriented Approaches

Some proposed solutions for relieving traffic congestion focus on building more highway lanes, using "smart corridors" with synchronized traffic lights to move vehicles through congested areas, adding car pool or high-occupancy vehicle (HOV) lanes, or building more rail lines alongside the highways that connect cities and suburbs. While these proposals may alleviate traffic congestion somewhat, they do nothing to slow sprawl. Indeed, they may even intensify it. So, instead, planners seek to strengthen ridership on public transit by encouraging or requiring more compact, mixed-use development around transit stops. Some companies, worried that congested roads and long commutes hurt their ability to hire and retain workers, have taken such steps. Bell South consolidated 75 scattered work sites (with 13,000 workers) into three near the Atlanta rapid transit system. Adobe Systems moved its headquarters to downtown San Jose and now pays 300 workers $30 monthly subsidies to ride mass transit (Jones 1999).

In Vancouver, British Columbia, sprawl spread eastward and carpeted the Fraser

In 2009, Portland renovated its downtown mall area and improved its transportation system to support future population growth. With all traffic movement now controlled by a synchronized signal system, its light-rail trains and buses will share the two right lanes on Fifth and Sixth Avenues, with drivers and cyclists sharing the left lane. Refurbished sidewalks and better lighting enhance public space and create a safe pedestrian environment.

River Valley with dozens of suburbs; as a result, rush-hour traffic headed out of the city over Lion's Gate Bridge was routinely backed up for three miles. Unable to stop the sprawl, planners instead sought to reduce the traffic congestion. Determined to avoid further "Los Angelization," regional leaders rejected the idea of building more highways as the backbone of their local transportation network. Instead, they set up an extensive transit system—utilizing trains and ferries, but anchored by 1,000 buses (20 times the number in the Atlanta region). Significantly, as more suburbanites and commuters converged on the Vancouver metropolitan region, area planners opted to spread the population around by creating self-sustaining job centers in the suburbs to the east. They did so through SkyTrain, an automated light-rail train system along the Expo and Millennium lines that technically moves up to 30,000 people per hour in both directions. Its elevated electric cars zip along into the suburbs, taking passengers to and from their homes or work in far less time than would be needed on the clogged highways. Metrotown, once a suburban warehouse district on the wane, has become

SkyTrain's busiest stop, as office buildings, apartments, movie theaters, and a mall now ring the station (Wolinsky 2004).

These four approaches—land purchases, growth boundaries, revitalization, transit solutions—and other grass-roots efforts at comprehensive land-use planning to designate growth and non-growth areas are essential to revitalizing urban cores and protecting open space, outdoor lifestyles, and farmland. If public policy invests money, effort, and vision into our communities rather than into sprawl and stops subsidizing new roads, utilities, and development at the expense of our urban centers, the public will have more options to make environmentally responsible lifestyle choices.

EXURBS

A. C. Spectorsky (1957) was the first to use the term **exurb** in describing the appearance of new residential areas developing on the metropolitan fringe. He based his account of such communities from his observations (none too systematic, it should be noted) of an exclusive residential area on the fringes of the New York City metropolitan area. He noted that the lifestyle of these exurbanites was an intriguing mix of high tech, high culture, and rustic charm. Although they lived in a rural locale, they (1) commuted to jobs in the central business district, (2) combined their love for old things with attraction to new electronic gadgets, and (3) maintained a strong interest in books, theater, and art.

The small trend that Spectorsky noted in *The Exurbanites* has since morphed into a stampede. Then, the exurbanites settled heavily in counties such as Fairfield (Connecticut), Rockland and Westchester (New York), and Bucks (Pennsylvania). Today, exurban counties surround every major city, from Marin near San Francisco to Dacula near Atlanta (see *Cityscape* box on page 100). New exurbanites also now are more likely to be moving from a suburb, not from a central city, and are less likely to work in a central city (Eiesland 2000).

As Jon Teaford (2006) noted, the development of shopping malls, office towers, and sit-down restaurants within the past 20 years has expanded metropolitan areas far beyond central business districts and traditional suburbia. A diverse mixture of inner suburbs, large suburban edge cities, office parks, retail centers, "captured" small towns, and even low-density rural territory now comprise the metropolitan fringe:

> Businesses were drawn to the less crowded metropolitan periphery where—developers promised—their operations would be free from traffic congestion and would gain access to an underutilized rural population. Whether they were termed "edge cities," "techno-burbs," "outer cities," or "transformed suburbs," these relatively recent formations changed the patterns of metropolitan life as well as of small towns and rural areas now within the metropolitan orbit. (Eiesland 2000:5)

Once viewed by their residents as physically and socially distant from the city, small towns now often merge into the sprawling metropolitan region; outsiders view them as historic "subdivisions" adjacent, and economically linked, to the newly developing cities with their high-density housing, offices, shopping, and service centers (Eiesland 2000:6). As the process of exurbanization unfolds and small towns are absorbed within metropolises, there is a cost. The small-town traditions and values that first attracted the newcomers morph into more cosmopolitan ones, resulting in social tensions between old and new residents (Siskind 2006). In addition, these once-rural areas and small towns become more expensive places to live as land values, taxes, and the overall cost of living increase.

Small towns thus become new suburbs to new cities, dramatically altering the region. As Nancy Eiesland notes, "The resulting changes in demographics, organization patterns, and lifestyle in these once small towns signal a broad pattern of urban/rural spatial and social restructuring in the United States" (2000:6). We will now examine this social phenomenon of the new cities that so impact on small towns.

THE NEW CITIES

Not since the expansion of small cities into huge metropolises a century ago have we seen as profound a change in our urban world as the emergence of the **edge city**—a new, sprawling, middle-class, automobile-dependent center typically located at the fringe of an older urban area, at the intersection of major highways, where little except villages or farmland existed a few decades earlier. Today, most edge cities are rapidly emerging as less of an "edge" and more of a new center. This remains the fashionable term, however, and we will use it in this edition to discuss them more fully.

During the second half of the twentieth century, North Americans went through three waves of centrifugal movement away from the older cities. First came suburbanization, most notably after World War II, as people moved into new homes beyond city boundaries. Next came the malling of North America, particularly in the 1960s and 1970s, when we moved our stores out to where we lived. And now, says Joel Garreau (1991), we have moved our means of creating wealth, the essence of

CITYSCAPE

Atlanta's Edge Cities

He looked away from the buildings and out over the ocean of trees. Since Atlanta was not a port city and was, in fact, far inland, the trees stretched on in every direction. They were Atlanta's greatest natural resource, those trees were. People loved to live beneath them. Fewer than 400,000 people lived within the Atlanta city limits, and almost three quarters of them were black; if anything, over the past decade Atlanta's population had declined slightly. But for the past thirty years all sorts of people, most of them white, had been moving in beneath those trees, into all those delightful, leafy, rolling rural communities that surrounded the city proper. By the hundreds of thousands they had come, from all over Georgia, all over the South, all over America, all over the world, into those subdivided hills and downs and glens and glades beneath the trees, until the population of Greater Atlanta was now more than 3.5 million, and they were still pouring in. How fabulous the building booms had been!! As the G-5 banked, Charlie looked down. . . . There was Spaghetti Junction, as it was known, where Highways 85 and 285 came together in a tangle of fourteen gigantic curving concrete-and-asphalt ramps and twelve over-

passes. . . . And now he could see Perimeter Center, where Georgia 400 crossed 285. Mack Taylor and Harvey Mathis had built an office park called Perimeter Center out among all those trees, which had been considered a very risky venture at the time, because it was so far from Downtown; and now Perimeter Center was the nucleus around which an entire edge city, known by that very name, Perimeter Center, had grown. . . .

Edge city . . . Charlie closed his eyes and wished he'd never heard of the damn term. He wasn't much of a reader, but back in 1991 Lucky Putney, another developer, had given him a copy of a book called *Edge City* by somebody named Joel Garreau. He had opened it and glanced at it—and couldn't put it down, even though it was 500 pages long. He had experienced the *Aha!* phenomenon. The book put into words something he and other developers had felt, instinctively, for quite a while: namely, that from now on, the growth of American cities was going to take place not in the heart of the metropolis, not in the old Downtown or Midtown, but out on the edges, in vast commercial clusters served by highways.

Source: Excerpt from "Atlanta's Edge Cities," from *A Man in Full* by Tom Wolfe. Copyright © 1998 by Tom Wolfe. Reprinted by permission of Farrar, Straus & Giroux LLC.

urbanism—our jobs—out to where most of us have lived and shopped for two generations. This has led to the rise of edge cities, causing profound changes in the ways we live, work, and play.

The evolution of edge cities during recent decades helps explain the increases in the population of non-metropolitan areas that

were discussed in the previous chapter. Garreau suggests that North Americans have reinvented the city and that these new urban agglomerations are the future. Numbering well over 200 in the United States and Canada, these edge cities, with their malls and office parks, now dominate the nations' retail trade and office facilities.

Edge cities appeared in Canada and the United States for different reasons. Unlike the United States, the Canadian government does not provide suburb-enhancing tax deductions for home mortgages, and it has greater control over planning and development. Canada also has a greater emphasis on mass transit; a relative lack of freeways; vibrant, bustling urban centers; and a relative lack of racial problems. Nevertheless, edge cities are flourishing. Toronto, for example, has only 46 percent of the area's market. The rest is found in the nine edge cities growing up around it. These are Midtown–Yorkville and North York–North Yonge to the north; Mississauga, the Downsview Airport area, and the Etobicoke–427 area to the west; and the Don Valley Parkway–401 area, Markham–404 area, Eglington–Don Mills area, and Scarborough to the east.

Characteristics and Commonalities

The new edge cities possess many of the same characteristics of older cities: extensive office and retail space, a large-scale influx of workers each weekday morning, and a mixed use of work, shopping, and entertainment (Garreau 1991:425). What one rarely finds, however, is a clearly defined territorial boundary. Edge cities do not have the same look (the compactness of closely adjacent buildings and high pedestrian traffic), political organization (elected officials or civic codes), or even visual clues of older cities (signs, edges) to mark their perimeters. As Garreau explains:

> The reason these places are tricky to define is that they rarely have a mayor or a city council, and just about never match boundaries on a map. We're still in the process of giving each Edge City its name—a project, incidentally, that could use more flair. In New Jersey, for example, there is one with only the laconic designation "287 and 78." The reason there are no "Welcome to" signs at Edge City is that it is a judgment call where it begins and ends. (1991:6)

A common feature of edge cities is that they have sprouted far from the old downtowns, in locales where 30 or more years ago little existed save villages and farmland. They typically evolve adjacent to two or more major highways, usually with shopping malls serving as anchor points. Figures 4–1 and 4–2 show two of the more densely concentrated Edge City regions—the Los Angeles and New York areas, respectively.

Types of New Cities

Edge cities fall into one of three major categories: (1) **uptowns,** built on top of preautomobile settlements, such as Pasadena, California, or Arlington, Virginia; (2) **boomers,** the typical edge city located at the intersection of two major highways and almost always centered on a mall, such as most of those in Figure 4–1; and (3) **greenfields,** a master-planned city by one developer on thousands of farmland acres, such as Irvine, California, and Las Colinas, Texas, near the Dallas–Fort Worth airport.

> Because boomers, the most common form of edge cities, have grown so profusely throughout North America, urbanists identify three subcategories of them [see Figure 4–3 on page 104]. The strip boomer city is usually only a few hundred yards wide but extends for miles along a major highway. Most representative are the strips along Route 1 in Princeton, Route 128 near the Mass Pike outside Boston, and I-270 in Montgomery County, Maryland, in the Washington, D.C. region. All three suffer severe traffic congestion because of their extended shapes. The node boomer city is relatively dense and contained, such as The Galleria area near Houston, Tysons Corner in Virginia, and the Midtown–Yorkville and North York–North Yonge areas in Toronto. The pig-in-the-python boomer city is a cross between the previous two types. It is a strip that develops one or several nodes along it, such as the Lodge Freeway in Southfield, northwest of Detroit, or King of Prussia, Pennsylvania, northwest of Philadelphia. (Garreau 1991:115)

Evolving Middle-Class Centers

The majority of metropolitan North Americans now work, shop, and live in and around the 200-plus "new hearths of our civilization"

FIGURE 4–1 The Los Angeles Area

FIGURE 4–2 The New York Area

The Strip Boomer City

The Node Boomer City

The Pig-in-the-Python Boomer City

FIGURE 4–3 Types of Edge Cities

(Garreau 1991:3). Shopping malls function as the village squares for these new urban centers. Adjacent are the hotels, office buildings, and corporate headquarters, the tall buildings of which are not side by side as in a downtown but, instead, are located on campus-like settings of grass and trees, gazing at one another from a respectful distance. Surrounding this broad center of employment and shopping are the single-family suburban homes, whose occupants now outnumber those living next to the old downtowns.

The rise of edge cities is essentially a function of social class, not race. They are evolving in metropolitan areas with low black populations (Denver, Minneapolis, Seattle, and Toronto) as well as in metropolitan areas with high black populations (Atlanta, Chicago, New York, and Washington). In the latter areas, middle-class African Americans (presently about one-third of the total U.S. black population) are as likely to be part of edge cities as middle-class whites are. Just as the skin of the middle-class North American comes in various hues—shades of brown, black, tan, and white—so, too, do edge cities reflect this reality.

> The edge city, however, has been criticized as plastic and sterile, lacking in livability, civilization, community, neighborhood—in short, having little "urban soul." It is, however, an unfinished new city form and we do not yet know if, in its maturity, this ugly duckling will emerge as a splendid swan. Whatever their ultimate shape, we do know that our new cities have become the places in which the majority of North Americans "now live, learn, work, shop, play, pray, and die." (Garreau 1991:8)

That "unfinished new city form" is evolving further, leading planners to now speak of "turning edge cities into real cities (Barnett 2002). Some locales—such as Addison, Texas, for example—are transforming at least part of their edge cities in spaces resembling a real city, with streets that have sidewalks and frontages with stores and restaurants on ground level, apartment buildings, and landscaped urban squares.

Edge cities are appearing worldwide as well. They now mark the fringes of Bangkok, Beijing, London, Melbourne, Mexico City, Paris, Seoul, and Sydney. Increased affluence, the desire for more individual transportation, greater use of computers and telecommunications, and the existence of world financial centers are some of the important elements shaping the growth of edge cities in urban areas throughout the world.

Three New City Variations

Not all edge cities are alike, nor does their evolution occur for the same reasons everywhere. The following examples illustrate how a new city can serve as its own motivation, emerge as a solution to a problem, or simply become the problem.

Edge City as Motivator.   By 1990, Oshawa Centre, one of the oldest shopping malls in Ontario, Canada, was showing its age. Originally built for the town's blue-collar population, the place was dark and ugly. Some of the stores had outdoor-facing windows and doors plastered with newspaper and cardboard, and its sales and rental value were declining. Not anymore, however. The Toronto-based Cambridge Shopping Centres purchased it in 1991 for $145 million. It did so because Garreau had written in *Edge City* that shopping malls usually function as the village squares of the new urban centers. "So, taking that theory," said Ronald Charbon, Cambridge's director of strategic market information, "we said, 'Where are the next edge cities going to occur? Where is the next wave of growth going to occur in the greater metropolitan Toronto area? And are any of our shopping centers sufficiently located to capitalize on that growth?'" (quoted in Berman 1997:74).

Using census tracts and surveys, Cambridge Shopping Centres amassed a population profile of the area, discovering that areas surrounding Oshawa were white collar and that projections of the area's growth rate were almost three times that in the Greater Toronto Area. So, the company took the gamble, invested $40 million in a major facelift, and recruited upscale stores. That, however, was only one part of a sophisticated strategy to turn Oshawa Centre into the village square that Garreau described. Cambridge secured government approval to construct six modest-sized office towers over a 25-year period. The Oshawa Centre thus underwent a massive transformation from a jerry-built suburban mall into a mixed-use development that includes more than 200 retail stores as well as government, and community services, all inspired by Garreau's book.

Edge City as the Solution. Since incorporating in 1956, Schaumburg, Illinois, had been what Judy Pasternak (1998) called "the ultimate faceless postwar suburb." Located 26 miles northwest of Chicago, the town grew from nearly 19,000 in 1970 to about 75,000 people by 2005, with most living in townhouses and subdivisions and shopping in one or more of the 65 shopping centers that lined its streets. Along its expressway, glassy office towers provided a solid employment base. The one thing lacking in Schaumburg was that it had no center, no downtown, and no place to walk to

or for people to gather. In fact, Schaumburg hadn't had a town center since 1875.

That has now changed. The local government tore down a faded strip mall on a 30-acre site to make way for a downtown center called "Town Square." This place, however, is no small-town core like the downtowns of older suburbs that developed around train depots generations ago, even though its late nineteenth–early twentieth century architecture pays homage to the historic character of the old town center. Its design and park-like setting are intended to encourage pedestrians and shoppers, but there are no retail stores lining Main Street. In fact, there is no Main Street. Instead, a supermarket and a cluster of retail stores border a large parking lot, giving this area the look of a shopping center. Nearby are a new library, a chain restaurant, a brick clock tower, a green wrought-iron gazebo, a pond, curved benches, and a public amphitheater. Three miles away, a hotel/convention center

This view of Tysons Corner, Virginia, shows the new edge city that we now build. It has no defined borders or recognizable center, and its various buildings are not conveniently near one another. All the commercial activities but none of the charm of a city—the pedestrians, the architecture, the cultural attractions—can be found here. A car is a necessity in edge cities, and as a result, traffic congestion is unavoidable.

complex on a 45-acre parcel of land opened in 2006, with hopes of further increasing Schaumburg's commerce and tourism.

Edge City as the Problem.   The more that Tysons Corner, Virginia—located eight miles west of Washington, D.C., and one of Joel Garreau's prime examples of an edge city—continues to grow and thrive economically, the more it remains an object of derisive commentary by architects, city planners, design critics, and urban scholars. Indeed, finding a way to "fix" Tysons Corner has been the goal of several planning studies sponsored by academic institutions, professional groups, and Fairfax County, Virginia.

Home to two massive shopping malls occupying 4 million square feet, and to an impressive array of high-tech firms and major corporations filling 26 million square feet of office space, Tysons Corner today is larger, both in geographical size and in employment, than many U.S. central cities. It is, essentially, the central business district of Fairfax County, with the U.S. Census Bureau reporting its daytime population of more than 70,000 as being four times greater than its nighttime population of 18,000 residents living in 8,800 households.

Incredibly, only road transit exists, and during weekday rush hours and weekend shopping times, backups are horrendous. Clearly, mass transit would greatly alleviate the traffic congestion. Recommendations include creating an elevated rail system looping around Tysons Corner and introducing a link between Tysons Corner and the regional Metrorail network. Much more is needed, however. Tysons Corner is not pedestrian friendly; there are few sidewalks or signalized crosswalks—critical for safely traversing the extraordinarily wide, traffic-choked roads—thus making it virtually impossible to walk around Tysons Corner.

Even if traffic congestion could be reduced and pedestrian traffic encouraged, the aesthetic and visual deficiencies, the visual chaos and formlessness, would still remain. In the interest of bringing a bit of visual order to Tysons Corner, several years ago a county task force developed a plan to address streetscapes, pedestrian walkways, site planning of buildings, and open space. Still, Tysons Corner has no civic focus, or heart, and so planners have proposed a town center as a way to eliminate the soullessness often mentioned by critics as the problem with Tysons Corner. Such an undertaking is on the distant horizon, however. In the meantime, Tysons Corner continues to be emblematic of how poorly we have planned, zoned, and developed much of the landscape girdling our cities since the end of World War II (Massing 2000).

GATED COMMUNITIES

Gated communities in the United States can be traced to the late 1800s, when upper-income gated developments in New York's Tuxedo Park and private streets in St. Louis sprang up as wealthy citizens sought to "insulate themselves from the troublesome aspects of rapidly industrializing cities" (Blakely and Snyder 1999:4). These communities, however, and the fenced compounds built in the twentieth century by members of the East Coast and Hollywood aristocracies, were different from today's gated communities. They were unique places for unique people. Although a few other such exclusive communities began to appear—such as Sea Pines on Hilton Head Island, South Carolina, in 1957—they remained rare until the late 1960s and 1970s, when master-planned retirement developments first appeared. These developments were the first places where average Americans could wall themselves off from the rest of society.

Beginning in the 1980s, gated communities increased rapidly—not only in retirement villages but also in resort and country club developments, and then in middle-class suburban subdivisions, setting off a quiet but important trend that continues today. In the mid-1980s, gated communities were rare on Long Island, New York, but by the mid-1990s, they had become common, with a gatehouse included in almost every condominium of more than 50 units. Elsewhere, there are now entire incorporated cities that feature guarded entrances; one example is Canyon Lake, 60 miles east of Orange County in California.

About 10.4 million U.S. households are in developments surrounded by fences or walls. More than half of those households are in communities that also have controlled-entry systems, such as guards and electric gates (U.S. Department of Housing and Urban Development 2008:66). Whether they own or rent, Hispanics are more likely to live in such communities compared with whites or blacks, perhaps because the largest concentration of gated communities is in the West and Southwest, where there is a large Hispanic population (Sanchez et al. 2005).

Although most of these developments are in suburban areas, older, inner-city neighborhoods are also experiencing this phenomenon. Many gated communities have been built in metropolitan areas across the country, including Los Angeles, Phoenix, Dallas, Houston, Chicago, New York, and Miami. Such urban refuges exist in Canada as well. In Toronto, three older gated areas—Palmerston Avenue, Fairview Boulevard, and Wychwood Park—are city jewels that enjoy high real estate values.

What makes gated communities different from typical twentieth-century suburbs, which usually also have economic and social segregation? Gated communities are actually defended by walls, with access controlled either by electronically operated gates or 24-hour guards and grounds patrolled by private security forces. While there are a variety of approaches to living barricaded lives, the reasons why residents choose gated communities usually center on fear of crime and attempts to produce economic and physical security, free from the problems of traffic and noise. Residents enjoy their own pay-as-you-go services. They share responsibility for common areas and for enforcing the numerous rules and regulations, often through homeowners' associations, rather than relying on conventional elected local governments for many common services.

Gated communities, however, separate the people living within their walls from others even more profoundly than the most exclusive suburban jurisdiction can, and they thus accentuate patterns of segregation. Such a lifestyle reduces opportunities for positive interactions and shared experiences among people of diverse backgrounds, and it contributes to the fragmentation of the greater community (Vesselinov et al. 2007).

Types of Gated Communities

In their study regarding the development and social impact of this rapidly growing phenomenon, Edward J. Blakely and May Gail Snyder (1999) suggest that they fall into one of three categories: (1) **lifestyle communities,** (2) **prestige communities,** and (3) **security-zone communities.** Although these categories are helpful for analysis and understanding, much overlap exists; each contains some elements of the others. Still, each category caters to a different housing market and has a different approach to developing a sense of community within its walls. Moreover, each promotes a particular combination of four social values: (1) a *sense of community* (preservation and strengthening of neighborhood bonds), (2) *exclusion* (separation and protection from the outside), (3) *privatization* (the desire to privatize and internally control public services); and (4) *stability* (homogeneity and predictability).

> Where sense of community is a primary value motivating the residents of gated communities, it reflects all five aspects of community: shared territory, shared values, a shared public realm, support structure, and a shared destiny. Exclusion helps define shared territory by separating community members from outsiders. Privatization reflects a desire to protect a shared destiny through increased local control. Stability suggests shared values and support structures, and retaining stability is also a way of predicting shared destiny. (Blakely and Snyder 1999:122)

Lifestyle Communities. Lifestyle communities are an expression of conspicuous consumption and a new leisure class. They emphasize amenities and include retirement communities, such as the nationwide chain of Leisure Worlds, all of which offer senior citizens the chance to engage in a wide variety of activities close to their homes. Another type is golf and leisure communities, where the gates cordon

Gated communities, such as this one in Brentwood, California, are a rapidly growing phenomenon. Segregated from the outside world by walls, fences, electronically operated gates, and/or 24-hour guards, residents essentially live barricaded lives. Such communities typically cater to a housing market emphasizing prestige, lifestyle, or security-zone neighborhoods that promise a sense of community, exclusion, private control of public services, and the stability of homogenization.

off the leisure resources for the exclusive use of community residents. Blackhawk Country Club near San Francisco and Rancho Mirage in California's Coachella Valley cater to people with special interests, like golf or tennis. Lifestyle communities attract those who want separate, private services and amenities within a homogeneous, predictable environment.

Prestige Communities. Prestige communities are status-oriented enclaves, such as those in affluent Pacific Palisades or Marblehead in San Clemente, primarily containing the rich and famous, the affluent, the top one-fifth of Americans. These communities emphasize exclusion and image, and the gates symbolize the eminent status of their residents. Prestige communities attract those seeking a stable neighborhood of similar people where property values will be protected. For these residents, concerns about separation and privatization of services are secondary (Romig 2005).

Security-Zone Communities. Security-zone communities are "enclaves of fear" primarily concerned with protection. They are a defensive measure reflecting a fortress mentality, with walls, gates, closed streets, and various security systems. In these enclaves—often located in inner-city and lower-income neighborhoods—residents band together to shut out their neighbors, hoping that the gates will protect them from crime, traffic, and outsiders. Security-zone communities seek to strengthen and protect a sense of community, but their primary goal is to exclude the places and people their residents perceive as being threats to their safety and quality of life.

A Sense of Community

For several decades, social observers have noted a loss of community in modern life—what Robert MacIver (1962) referred to as "the great emptiness." In *Habits of the Heart*

(1985), Robert N. Bellah and his associates reported that traditional communities, where individuals have permanent emotional bonds, were yielding to "lifestyle enclaves," where relationships are often based on such superficial similarities as consumption style or leisure interests. Such enclaves diminish social life, said the authors; all residents can do is compare their own material gains with those of their neighbors to piece together some idea of "how they are doing." Robert B. Reich (1991) expressed concern that wealth was rapidly polarizing society, because the well-to-do were effectively seceding from it by walling themselves into privately policed, fortress communities. In their study of gated communities, Blakely and Snyder also lamented the loss of community:

> The fabric of civitas, communal commitment to civic and public life, has begun to rip. . . . The borders of the gated communities are emblematic of the proliferation of boundaries being set and hardened as communities fragment, looking inward. (1999:176)

As communities turn inward, motivated by security and other social needs, do the residents find what they seek? Critics, including Blakely and Snyder, charge that they do not—that gated communities reflect the social fragmentation and civic atrophy currently plaguing society. Because these barricaded neighborhoods exclude the lower classes not only from living in these residences (through prohibitive housing costs) but also from even casually passing by, they limit social contact among different members and groups of society. Such class separation is often *de facto* racial segregation, and this social distance can weaken further the civic bonds among societal members. In his comprehensive look at the impact of gated communities, Andrew Stark (2002) noted that these self-governing, private communities were redefining the grassroots level of the boundary between public and private realms.

According to various studies, the quality of community does not improve in gated developments. Even though residents move to such places in the belief that they will find their nostalgic idea of community, they do not. In fact,

these communities promote privacy within privacy: There are no front porches to induce interaction, and residents tend to stay in their own backyards and not visit one another. As a result, Blakely and Snyder found that gating often does not provide what people are seeking. Those authors discovered that although residents often expressed some satisfaction about life within these enclaves, they also expressed much disappointment, especially about the lack of a sense of shared community. In comparison with non-residents, members of gated communities do not find stronger ties with one another.

On the idea that gated communities actually serve as a deterrent to crime, the statistics are mixed. Formidable fencing and gates, by design, restrict access and therefore provide both a physical and a psychological barrier for criminals. The effectiveness of gates and fencing, however, depends on the nature of the property and the people living behind them. In the security-zone communities, crime declined right after closure of the gates, but no decline was sustained for more than a short time. Among lifestyle communities, Blakely and Snyder found that many had the same problems as other urban communities. In some cases, the gates fostered a false sense of security; police reported that crime was as likely to come from people living within the gates as from outside.

COMMON-INTEREST DEVELOPMENTS

Gated communities are often called **common-interest developments (CIDs).** Not all CIDs, however, are segregated communities (although many are), and not all gated areas are CIDs (although most are). There is a close relationship between the two phenomena, but they are not the same thing. CIDs—which require membership in a self-governing homeowners' association—include suburban planned- unit developments of single-family homes, urban condominiums, and housing cooperatives, and they have become familiar sights throughout North America. Moreover, the rapid spread of CID housing is the largest and most dramatic privatization of local government functions in

North American history. Currently, more than 300,000 of these developments exist in the United States, housing 59.5 million people in 24.1 million housing units (Community Associations Institute 2008).

Builders find CID housing profitable, because it is a mass-produced commodity and enables them to concentrate more people on less land. Buyers are willing to accept smaller lots and narrower streets, because the development contains open spaces and desirable amenities, including facilities owned in common by all residents—such as swimming pools, gyms, parks, golf courses, social centers, and often even exclusive access to shopping centers and their own schools. Public officials are willing to issue building permits for these high-density, designed communities, with their private infrastructure, because they add taxpayers at minimal public cost.

Residents must belong to homeowners' associations, pay monthly fees, and live under the rule of residential private governments. These governments perform functions for their residents that were once the province of local government—for example, police protection, trash collection, and street maintenance and lighting. In one sense, this community design is a logical, evolutionary step in the suburban ideology of territorial control (housing-market segmentation, single-use zoning, inaccessibility to mass transit, and cul-de-sacs). Some critics, however, think that the emergence of this new civic culture undermines the diversity and vitality of cities.

In *Privatopia* (1996:29-30), Evan McKenzie wrote that millions of affluent homeowners were being "encouraged to secede from urban America, with its endless flux and ferment, its spontaneity and diversity and its unpredictable rewards and hazards" and "beckoned to a privatized, artificial, utopian environment where master-planning, homogeneous populations, and private governments offer the affluent a chance to escape from urban reality." However, said McKenzie, they pay a heavy price, because they surrender a good deal of their freedom and privacy. Residents of CIDs live under the rule of their corporate board of directors, an elected group of neighbors enforcing a set of restrictions created by the developer to ensure that the master plan will never be altered. The board can dictate such things as barring holiday decorations in windows, the size and contents of your garden, even the color of paint on your front door, and it can legally impose daily fines until you comply. This private government operates outside the constitutional limits that bind local authorities, because the courts often accept the legal fiction that CID restrictions are private, voluntary arrangements among individuals. In truth, they are nonnegotiable regulations, drafted by the developer's lawyers and imposed on all residents, as the *Urban Living* box on page 112 explains.

Because CIDs contain relatively homogeneous groupings, some critics argue that such planned developments promote racial and economic segregation (Putnam 2001, Blakely and Snyder 1999). In a study of California CIDs, however, Tracy Gordon (2004) found their contributions to metropolitan segregation to be minor at this time, although their effect could be more pronounced if current trends continue.

Just as urban renewal has frequently uprooted lower-income people from their homes, so, too, have CID developments. Perhaps the most publicized of these displacements occurred on Daufuskie Island, South Carolina, near Hilton Head. Here, amid the dirt roads crisscrossing the five- by two-mile island, the black Gullah population had owned land for generations. They lived in an open community with no property line restrictions, shared in each other's good fortune, and helped one another in bad times. In the 1990s, when developers came and made more than half the island off-limits to them, placing warning signs at nearly every fork in the road, a howl of protest arose. The National Council of Churches—with 25 million members—charged that the developers of the Haig Point and Daufuskie Island Resort gated communities were committing "cultural genocide" by dislodging black residents. With the conflict publicized by national news shows and newspaper stories, the National Association for the Advancement of Colored People (NAACP) threatened to file a class-action suit against Beaufort County and the

CID Restrictions on Personal Freedom

The stories below, drawn from newspaper accounts, do not merely reflect isolated neighborhood conflicts. They are examples of the control that is exerted in walled, private, urban and suburban enclaves called common-interest developments (CIDs). Although many willingly trade some privacy and personal freedoms for the CID lifestyle, some find themselves fighting for their rights against the few residents who enforce the rules with a degree of personal power over their neighbors that the Constitution denies to public officials.

- In Monroe, New Jersey, a homeowners' association sued a married couple, because the wife, at age 45, was three years younger than the association's age-48 minimum for residency. The judge ruled in favor of the association, ordering the 60-year-old husband to sell or rent the unit—or else live there without his wife.
- In Ashland, Massachusetts, a CID board informed a Vietnam veteran that he could not fly the U.S. flag on Flag Day. He called the press, the story appeared on the front page of a local newspaper, and under public pressure, the board backed down.
- In Boca Raton, Florida, an association sued a homeowner for having a dog weighing more than 30 pounds, in violation of its rules. A court-ordered weighing revealed that the dog was just an ounce over the weight limit. The association persisted nonetheless—determined

to pay an attorney and use the courts to exclude the dog from the development for even that infraction.

- In Santa Ana, California, a condominium association issued a citation to a 51-year-old grandmother for "kissing and doing bad things" while parked one night in her circular driveway. She acknowledged kissing a friend good night, but retained an attorney to protect herself against this invasion of her privacy.
- In a development near Philadelphia, Pennsylvania, a couple bought a home and brought their sons' metal swing set with them. A year later, the association told them to take it down, despite the absence of any written rules about swing sets. When the couple challenged this order, the association passed a rule prescribing that all swing sets must be made of wood, in keeping "with what the overall community should look like." The family then submitted a petition from three-fourths of the homeowners supporting their swing set, along with data from the U.S. Environmental Protection Agency warning against the danger to children (theirs were aged two and four) from the poisonous chemicals found in pressure-treated wood used for outdoor swing sets. The association's response was to impose a daily fine of $10 until the set was removed—and to refuse offers to compromise, such as painting the swing set in earth tones.

Source: Evan McKenzie, "Trouble in Privatopia," *The Progressive* 57 (October 1993), 30–36. Reprinted by permission from The Progressive, 409 E. Main St. Madison, WI 53709, www.progressive.com.

developers for driving black families off their land. A decade later, much of the island remains undeveloped, but the families are slowly dwindling in number. And in 2005, the Daufuskie Island Resort spent $10 million to build new

luxury beach cottages and renovate existing ones (Parker 2005). Future development, however, is a virtual certainty, particularly after the resort was popularized as a romantic backdrop in a 2005 episode of *The Bachelorette* TV show.

As communities expand and evolve, they can have positive or negative consequences. Planners, sprawl opponents, and urban sociologists often cite Portland, Oregon, as a city that successfully controls its growth and development. Portland thus serves as an appropriate case study for the various themes and problems discussed in this chapter.

CASE STUDY
Portland, Oregon

Virtually all cities in western North America have undergone boom periods that gobbled up the land, strained the infrastructure, and resulted in congestion, dirty air, and tax-strained school systems. Yet Portland is a healthy, vibrant city displaying few of the problems found in other urban places. Years ago, the city determined to defy the boom mentality and set out to consciously plan its future, an effort that reflected Portland's long history of concern for urban quality of life and commitment to the common good (Jun 2004).

The Physical Setting

Portland stands in a choice location, surrounded by natural beauty and resources that greatly impressed its founders. Situated about 100 miles from the Pacific Ocean at the confluence of the Columbia and Willamette rivers, Portland is surrounded by a combination of water and lush greenery rarely found in urban settings. Snow-capped Mount Hood, Oregon's highest point (11,235 feet), is 48 miles away, and Mount Rainier, Mount St. Helens, and Mount Adams in Washington are all visible from the city. Also nearby is the spectacular Columbia Gorge and Multnomah Falls (850 feet). The city thus offers cosmopolitan living coupled with a variety of nearby outdoor activities, such as camping, canoeing, fishing, hiking, hunting, mountain climbing, and skiing.

Portland includes some of this outlying natural beauty within the city limits. Also known as "The City of Roses" for its large International Rose Test Gardens and the second-largest all-floral parade in the United States (after the Tournament of Roses Parade in Pasadena), Portland has a magnificent park system, including some 200 green spaces. The city boasts the largest forested municipal park in the nation (5,000 acres) and the world's smallest dedicated park, Mills End Park (24 inches). Three other important areas are the elm-shaded South Park blocks in the downtown area, McCall Waterfront Park, and Washington Park—home of the Rose Test Gardens, where more than 500 varieties of roses bloom, as well as of the Oregon Zoo (known for its re-created African rain forest) and the Japanese Garden. Portland is also the only U.S. city to have an extinct volcano, Mount Tabor, within the city limits.

History

Several gold rushes drew immigrants along the Oregon Trail, stimulating Portland's early growth. Deep water and abundant natural resources soon made the settlement a popular and prosperous port and commercial center, handling the farm and forest produce of the Cascade Range, Willamette Valley, and Columbia Basin.

Like many Old West centers, Portland had its seamy side, with vice and violence figuring into its nineteenth-century scene. By the start of the twentieth century, however, Portland had become a tamer place, with the city eliminating most of the seedy activities of its busy waterfront. About this time, Simon Benson, a teetotaling lumber baron, walked through one of his mills and noticed the smell of alcohol on his workers' breath. When he asked why they drank in the middle of the day, they replied that there was no fresh drinking water to be found downtown. To resolve this situation, Benson built 20 freshwater drinking fountains in the downtown area. Beer consumption reportedly fell by 25 percent after the fountains were installed. Those water fountains—now known as Benson's Bubblers—still bubble for locals and visitors alike along Portland's downtown streets. Yet Portlanders also still love their beer: The microbrewery was practically invented here, long before the concept gained popularity in other cities, and today, Portland boasts several dozen microbrews from which to choose.

Urban Decline and The Planners' Response to Sprawl

In the 1960s, Portland fell victim to the same ills afflicting other U.S. cities. Its economy nose-dived as industries closed. Shuttered mills and empty warehouses dotted the waterfront. People began moving away; unemployment rose; and those who remained found their standard of living sliding downward. One after another, downtown stores went belly up as the central business district slipped into a serious economic decline. The bus system lost so much business that it, too, went bankrupt.

The stage was set for Portland's revival, however, when Governor Tom McCall signed a new state law in 1973 requiring all of Oregon's cities to devise plans to limit urban sprawl and to protect farms, forests, and open space. Portland responded with the strictest laws in the nation. Ignoring lawsuits and pressures from commercial and development interests, Portland's leaders drew a line around their metropolitan area, banning any development beyond that point (much as London had done during its post–World War II reconstruction). The intent of this Urban Growth Boundary (UGB) was to force jobs, homes, and stores into a relatively compact area served by light rail, buses, and cars.

Automobiles, of course, are a major cause of the urban sprawl besetting most cities. Portland bucked the trend by tearing up its downtown riverfront freeway, then converting the area, along with abandoned warehouse sites, into one of the city's most-used parks, named for Governor McCall. It also limited downtown parking spaces and created an award-winning mass transit system with North America's first modern streetcar system, the

Portland's popular Tom McCall Waterfront Park attracts pedestrians at all hours of the day and is the site of numerous special events, such as the Rose Festival, Dragon Boat Races, and annual carnival. Many U.S. cities have rediscovered and revitalized their waterfronts, attracting residents and tourists alike, thereby enhancing the quality of life and ambience of the city.

MAX light rail and the TriMet bus system. These systems are fully intermodal, meaning that passengers can easily switch from one to the other. In the 330-square-block area of downtown ("Fareless Square"), rides are free.

An average of 97,000 riders have commuted daily on MAX between 2004 and 2007—more than the ridership in larger cities like Seattle, Denver, and Baltimore. No Portlander is forced to ride MAX or TriMet buses, but 70 percent of those who own cars choose a public transit option instead. The MAX has been so successful that it keeps expanding. Now a 44-mile regional light-rail system, further expansions will soon increase its miles of rails more than 50 percent (TriMet 2008). Portland is the national leader in transit ridership, its numbers increasing for 19 consecutive years. The city also encourages bike travel, placing brightly colored bikes and bike racks throughout the city for anyone to use; furthermore, its buses and MAX trains are bike accessible.

Portland also enacted a downtown development plan inspired by the ideas of Jane Jacobs, August Heckscher, William H. Whyte, and James Rouse (all of whom will be discussed in Chapter 14). All new buildings, including garages, must be people friendly at street level. Blank walls are banned in favor of stores, offices, and eating establishments. Further, Portland set aside 1 percent of public construction funds to enhance the physical attractiveness of the area through outdoor public art.

In 1996, Portland enacted an even stricter plan for its three-county metropolitan area to handle an anticipated 500,000 new residents—in essence, another Portland—within the existing urban boundaries of its now 369-square-mile metropolitan borders over 20 years, including conversion to more apartment buildings and townhouses in previously single-family neighborhoods. To keep "big box" stores from springing up in industrial areas, Portland's plan also limited retail outlets to 60,000 square feet and, in a further effort to encourage use of mass transit, restricted the number of parking spaces a new store may have. With the greater Portland area's population now projected to grow an additional 1.3 to 1.9

million over the next 50 years, it must rely on midrise building and greater density in its urban growth boundary, or it will consume all available land out to the coast (Jun 2004; Law 2008).

In becoming "the reigning model for growth management in the United States" (Stephenson 1997:259), Portland followed the visionary guide set for it by Lewis Mumford back in 1938, when he declared, "I have seen a lot of scenery in my life, but I have seen nothing so tempting as a home for man than this Oregon country.... You have the basis here for civilization on its highest scale" (cited in Stephenson 1997:259).

Portland Today

In its transition from a timber town to a high-tech hub, Portland has become a model city, one that magazines often cite as being one of the best cities in which to live. Portland is also one of the best job markets in the country. It is home to more than 1,500 technology companies, from Intel—the largest private-sector employer, with 16,000 workers—to Nike, Wells Fargo Bank, and dozens of small software firms (Portland Development Commission 2007).

Portland has a dense downtown, one that now contains about twice the work force it had 20 years ago. Yet, despite its growth, Portland has retained its nineteenth-century, small-sized block design, which yields a pedestrian-friendly city core. The central business district is virtually a walker's paradise, beckoning strollers to pass along the tree-lined streets on brick walkways and stop to enjoy fountains, benches, and small parks along the way. Pedestrians may shop at more than 1,100 retail stores, enjoy many outstanding coffee houses and restaurants, visit one of the city's microbreweries, or browse in any one of the numerous bookstores—including Powell's City of Books, the world's largest independent bookstore, which occupies an entire city block.

The city's economy is healthy, helped in large measure by the silicon forest of high-tech office campuses and factories—such as Intel, NEC, and Hewlett-Packard—that grew inside the metro area. Major department stores—Nordstrom's and Saks Fifth Avenue—enhance the central business district. Recreational activities include comedy clubs, ballet, opera, symphonies, modern dance, theater, a planetarium, hockey and baseball teams, and the Portland Trail Blazers professional basketball team.

In terms of aesthetics, amenities, economy, land use, and planning, most people applaud Portland as "a city that works," an appellation once applied only to Toronto. Another reason that Portland works is its effective, efficient, and rider-friendly transit system. As TriMet transportation planning director Ken Zatarain says, "In Portland, we try to make transit a livability choice. You can make public transportation a part of your lifestyle" (Loehndorf 2003:24). In fact, many Portland areas developed *after* mass transit. A good example is the Lloyd district, where housing, office towers, and businesses sprouted up after light rail began running through it. Zatarain calls the district a "complete community," meaning that the area is balanced with jobs and housing, and people can walk or bike (Loehndorf 2003:25).

Will Portland, with a 2007 metropolitan population of nearly 2.2 million, maintain its boundaries for urban growth to protect the surrounding countryside? So far, the results are mixed. The city did increase its urban density within the UGB, but the amount of urbanized land within the entire metropolitan area also increased by 36 percent between 1980 and 2000, from 349 to 474 square miles—the ninth highest increase among 32 metropolitan areas (Jun 2004:1337). Much of the effect of Portland's UGB was in the further suburbanization of adjoining counties, particularly in Clark County, Washington. The population projections for this region will surely test both Portland's resolve and its ability to balance big-city excitement and small-town charm. Furthermore, some bi-state cooperation between Oregon and Washington will be needed to create a consistent and compatible UGB policy to control the future direction of population growth outside the city (Jun 2004:1346).

SUMMARY

By the end of the twentieth century, four patterns of land development—sprawl, edge cities, gated communities, and CIDs—became so widespread they will most likely affect both urban and suburban lifestyles for at least the first few decades of the twenty-first century.

Sprawl refers to low-density land development beyond the edge of service and employment areas. Sprawl uses up large tracts of land (even when cities decline in population), increases the dependence of residents on automobiles, creates traffic congestion and pollution, and wastes natural resources. Solutions to sprawl include purchasing and preserving open space, setting boundaries for urban growth, revitalizing existing cities and towns, and pursuing transit-oriented approaches.

The past three decades have seen the evolution of more than 200 new cities, located at the fringes of older cities, in North America and elsewhere. Their sprawling land use and auto dependency stand in marked contrast to the compact land use of older "walking" cities. Not clearly marked by territorial boundaries but usually situated near two major highways, edge cities fall into three categories: uptown, boomer, and greenfield. Boomer cities are by far the most numerous and have three subcategories: strip, node, and pig-in-a-python. Essentially middle-class entities that cut across racial lines, edge cities have a shopping mall as their anchor point and provide more jobs, shops, and entertainment than older cities do.

Although gated communities first appeared in the United States during the late 1800s and a few other such exclusive locales during the 1950s, it was only in the late 1960s and 1970s, when retirement communities materialized, that average Americans began to wall themselves off from society. The 1980s marked a rapid increase in gated communities, both in urban and suburban locales, and today, more than 8 million people live in them. Categories of gated communities are lifestyle, prestige, and security zone. Critics charge that this residence pattern contributes to social fragmentation, does not really deter crime, and does not provide any true sense of community.

Common-interest developments may or may not include gated communities. These master-planned developments require monthly fees for shared amenities and membership in a homeowners' association, which has broad regulatory powers over residents—powers that critics charge invade both the privacy and the constitutional rights of individuals.

CONCLUSION

Although Canada has stronger central government controls over land use compared with the United States, both countries are experiencing sprawl, the development of edge cities, and an increase in exclusive communities. Some areas have more successfully contained these growth patterns than others, but they predominate nonetheless. What do these popular choices bode for the future of older cities and for the social cohesiveness of Canadian and U.S. societies?

Generations ago, zoning and planning boards throughout Canada and the United States generated building and density code variances to preserve the position of the privileged, so economic and social segregation are by no means new social phenomena. Gated communities go much further in their exclusivity, however, because they create physical barriers to entry. Moreover, they privatize not only individual space but also community space. The CIDs do even more: They privatize civic responsibilities (police protection) and communal services (street maintenance, entertainment, and recreation). This new development creates a private world that requires residents to share little with their neighbors outside the barricades—or even with the larger political system.

The recent evolution of edge cities and exclusive communities is still new, but the dominance of these urban forms in North America already suggests a need for further research. This, however, is only part of the urban picture. The next five chapters will examine how social scientists—sociologists, geographers, political economists, psychologists, and anthropologists—have come to analyze cities as living entities. Reading these chapters, you will discover that the urban story gets even more interesting.

KEY TERMS

boomers (101)
common-interest developments (CIDs) (110)
edge city (99)
eminent domain (96)
environmental sociology (94)
exurb (98)
gated communities (107)
greenfields (101)

lifestyle communities (108)
political fragmentation (90)
prestige communities (108)
security-zone communities (108)
smart growth (94)
social impact analysis (94)
sprawl (87)
uptowns (101)

INTERNET ACTIVITIES

1. Go to *http://mobility.tamu.edu/ums/congestion_ data/* to access the congestion data for any U.S. city.

2. Go to *http://www.commutesolutions.org/calc. htm* to calculate how much it really costs you to drive your car.

CHAPTER 5

URBAN SOCIOLOGY
Classic and Modern Statements

Once humans learned to harness the machine, the resulting social upheaval dramatically changed virtually everything. Nowhere were these changes more pronounced than in European cities. The emerging factory system drew in unheard-of numbers of people, and the cities exploded in population. In 1816, for example, Germany had barely 2.5 million urbanites; by 1895, that number had passed 13 million. During the nineteenth century, London grew from 861,000 to a monumental 6.5 million.

Imagine such radical change: Overwhelmed by incoming migrants, cities could not provide adequate food, safe housing, sanitary facilities, medical care, or enough jobs. As a result, poverty, disease, malnutrition, and crime were on the rise. The city streets no doubt seemed chaotic, and this was the context in which urban sociology emerged. In the *Cityscape* box on page 120, Friedrich Engels (1820–1895) vividly describes the appalling slum conditions that industrialization brought to Manchester, England.

THE EUROPEAN TRADITION: 1846–1921

Sociology was born in Europe, a child of the Industrial Revolution. Given its start by August Comte (1798–1857), it was nurtured by the sociologists who followed—including Karl Marx, Friedrich Engels, Ferdinand Tönnies, Emile Durkheim, Georg Simmel, and Max Weber—who sought to explain the great transformation wrought by urbanization and industrialization.

Karl Marx and Friedrich Engels: From Barbarism to Civilization

Karl Marx (1818–1883) spent most of his adult life in England during the heyday of the Industrial Revolution. Marx was among the first of the classical sociologists to analyze the transformation of European society.

Marx argued passionately that the economic structure of society is "the real foundation . . . [that] determines the general character of the social, political, and spiritual processes of life" (1959:49; orig. 1859). By this, he meant that the economic system serves as the base on which the social institutions of family, religion, and the political system take form. Although he conceded many causes of social change, such as technological advances, Marx contended that societal transformation primarily results from *conflict* between those who control the process of economic production (capitalists) and those who supply the necessary labor (proletariat). Thus, to argue that social problems, such as poverty and unemployment, are the fault of individuals is a form of **false consciousness** because as Marx saw it, the flaws of capitalism are the real causes of these and other problems.

Marx and his colleague Engels, however, held that the city has special importance. People, they said, live as "generic, tribal beings" in preindustrial, traditional societies. Only with the rise of the city does productive specialization begin to free individuals to act on their own. It is in cities, then, that the state emerges so that people take on a political role as citizens, deliberately planning their own environment and using new scientific skills. Thus, to Marx and Engels, the rise of the city amounted to nothing less than a transition from barbarism to civilization:

> The greatest division of material and mental labour is the separation of town and country. The antagonism between town and country begins with the transition from barbarism to civilization, from tribe to State, from locality to nation, and runs through the whole history of civilization to the present day. . . . (1976:143; orig. 1846)

Even so, Marx and Engels made it clear that not every city was liberating in this way. Under what they called "Asiatic modes of production," some cities remained chained to the bonds of the primitive community—with its limited division of labor, common property, and lack of individualism. As a result, these cities depended entirely on the agricultural surplus, and the functions of these cities—whether military, religious, or bureaucratic—lacked the dynamic drive of a commercial economy.

Even in industrial cities, however, Marx and Engels held that the social evolution of humans was not yet complete, because a capitalist elite controlled the economy. Seeing firsthand the

CITYSCAPE

Working-Class Manchester, 1844

Friedrich Engels, the son of a wealthy German manufacturer, went to Manchester, England, in 1842 to learn the textile business. During his early years there, he gathered material for his first book, *The Condition of the Working Class in England,* first published in 1844. This excerpt from that work vividly describes Manchester's appalling slum conditions:

Here one is in an almost undisguised working-men's quarter, for even the shops and beer-houses hardly take the trouble to exhibit a trifling degree of cleanliness. But all this is nothing in comparison with the courts and lanes which lie behind, to which access can be gained only through covered passages, in which no two human beings can pass at the same time. Of the irregular cramming together of dwellings in ways which defy all rational plan, of the tangle in which they are crowded literally one upon the other, it is impossible to convey an idea. And it is not the buildings surviving from the old times of Manchester which are to blame for this; the confusion has only recently reached its height when every scrap of space left by the old way of building has been filled up and patched over until not a foot of land is left to be further occupied.
 . . . Right and left a multitude of covered passages lead from the main street into numerous courts, and he who turns in thither gets into a filth and disgusting grime, the equal of which is not to be found . . . and which contain unqualifiedly the most horrible dwellings which I have yet beheld. In these courts there stands directly at the entrance, at the end of

the covered passage, a privy without a door, so dirty that the inhabitants can pass into and out of the court only by passing through foul pools of stagnant urine and excrement. . . . Below it on the river there are several tanneries which fill the whole neighborhood with the stench of animal putrefaction. Below Ducie Bridge the only entrance to most of the houses is by means of narrow, dirty stairs and over heaps of refuse and filth. . . .

The view from [Ducie] Bridge . . . is characteristic for the whole district. At the bottom flows, or rather stagnates, the Irk, a narrow, coal-black, foul-smelling stream, full of debris and refuse, which it deposits on the shallower right bank. In dry weather, a long string of the most disgusting blackish-green slime pools are left standing on this bank, from the depths of which bubbles of miasmatic gas constantly arise and give forth a stench unendurable even on the bridge forty or fifty feet above the surface of the stream. . . .

Passing along a rough bank, among stakes and washing-lines, one penetrates into this chaos of small one-storied, one-roomed huts, in most of which there is no artificial floor; kitchen, living and sleeping-room all in one. In such a hole, scarcely five feet long by six broad, I found two beds—and such bedsteads and beds!—which, with a staircase and chimney-place, exactly filled the room. In several others I found absolutely nothing, while the door stood open, and the inhabitants leaned against it. Everywhere before the doors refuse and offal; that any sort of pavement lay underneath could not be seen but only felt, here and there, with the feet. . . .

Enough! The whole side of the Irk is built in this way, a planless, knotted chaos of houses, more or less on the verge of uninhabitableness, whose unclean interiors fully correspond with

destructive aspects of early industrial capitalism, Marx and Engels believed that the historical process would further evolve, with a worldwide, anticapitalist revolution that would usher in socialism. Only in this final evolutionary phase would workers become aware of the real cause of their problems, unite, and act together to transform society into a new and just order.

their filthy external surroundings. And how could the people be clean with no proper opportunity for satisfying the most natural and ordinary wants? Privies are so rare here that they are either filled up every day, or are too remote for most of the inhabitants to use. How can people wash when they have only the dirty Irk water at hand, while pumps and water pipes can be found in decent parts of the city alone? In truth, it cannot be charged to the account of these helots of modern society if their dwellings are not more clean than the pig sties which are here and there to be seen among them. The landlords are not ashamed to let dwellings like the six or seven cellars on the quay directly below Scotland Bridge, the floors of which stand at least two feet below the low-water level of the Irk that flows not six feet away from them; or like the upper floor of the corner-house on the opposite shore directly above the bridge, where the ground-floor, utterly uninhabitable, stands deprived of all fittings for doors and windows, a case by no means rare in this region, when this open ground-floor is used as a privy by the whole neighbourhood for want of other facilities!

As for the rest, the filth, debris, and offal heaps, and the pools in the streets are common . . . and another feature most injurious to the cleanliness of the inhabitants, is the multitude of pigs walking about in all the alleys, rooting into the offal heaps, or kept imprisoned in small pens. Here, as in most of the working-men's quarters of Manchester, the pork-raisers rent the courts and build pig-pens in them. In almost every court one or even several such pens may be found, into which the inhabitants of the court throw all refuse and offal, whence the swine grow fat; and the atmosphere, confined on all four sides, is utterly corrupted by putrefying animal and vegetable substances. . . .

Such is the Old Town of Manchester, and on re-reading my description, I am forced to admit that instead of being exaggerated, it is far from black enough to convey a true impression of the filth, ruin, and uninhabitableness, the defiance of all considerations of cleanliness, ventilation, and health which characterise the construction of this single district, containing at least twenty to thirty thousand inhabitants. And such a district exists in the heart of the second city of England, the first manufacturing city in the world. If any one wishes to see in how little space a human being can move, how little air— and such air!—he can breathe, how little of civilisation he may share and yet live, it is only necessary to travel hither. . . .

Everything which here arouses horror and indignation is of recent origin, belongs to the industrial epoch. The couple of hundred houses, which belong to old Manchester, have been long since abandoned by their original inhabitants; the industrial epoch alone has crammed into them the swarms of workers whom they now shelter; the industrial epoch alone has built up every spot between these old houses to win a covering for the masses whom it has conjured hither from the agricultural districts and from Ireland; the industrial epoch alone enables the owners of these cattle sheds to rent them for high prices to human beings, to plunder the poverty of the workers, to undermine the health of thousands, in order that they alone, the owner, may grow rich. In the industrial epoch alone has it become possible that the worker scarcely freed from feudal servitude could be used as mere material, a mere chattel; that he must let himself be crowded into a dwelling too bad for every other, which he for his hard-earned wages buys the right to let go utterly to ruin. This manufacture has achieved, which, without these workers, this poverty, this slavery could not have lived.

Source: Friedrich Engels, *The Condition of the Working Class in England,* trans. by W. O. Henderson and W. H. Chaloner (New York: Macmillan, 1958).

Ferdinand Tönnies: From *Gemeinschaft* to *Gesellschaft*

In his masterwork, *Gemeinschaft and Gesellschaft* (1963; orig. 1887), the German sociologist Ferdinand Tönnies (1855–1936) described two contrasting types of human social life: *gemeinschaft,* or "community," which characterized the small country village; and *gesellschaft,* or "association," which characterized the large city. Within the village, Tönnies maintained, social life forms a "living organism," in which people have an essential unity of purpose, work together for the common good, and are united by ties of family and neighborhood. Such is not the case in the city, in which social life is a "mechanical aggregate" characterized by disunity, rampant individualism, and selfishness—even hostility. Among city dwellers, he argued, a belief in the common good is rare, and ties of family and neighborhood have little significance.

The typology of *gemeinschaft* and *gesellschaft* has had a lasting influence on urban sociology, because it was one of the first theories to understand human settlements by means of a continuum. At each "pole" of the continuum was a specific, "pure" type of settlement. Using such a formulation, one could classify any actual settlement at some point along the continuum as having a certain measure of *gemeinschaft* and a certain degree of *gesellschaft*.

In Tönnies's conceptions of *gemeinschaft* and *gesellschaft*, we can observe the influence of Karl Marx, a fact Tönnies openly acknowledged in citing "Karl Marx's masterful analysis of industrial development" (Tönnies 1963:64). In fact, Tönnies's idea of community finds its counterpart in the "primitive community" and "primitive mode of production" that Marx and Engels had written about 40 years earlier.

Gemeinschaft.   Tönnies used the concept of *gemeinschaft* to characterize the rural village and surrounding land worked communally by its inhabitants. Social life was characterized by "intimate, private, and exclusive living together," and members were bound by a common language and traditions. They recognized "common goods—common evils; common friends—common enemies" and carried within them a sense of "we-ness" and "ourness." Thornton Wilder eloquently expresses this sense of "village togetherness" in his play

Small-town America—such as here in Camden, Maine—is often idealized as today's closest approximation to a *gemeinschaft* society. In such locales, Main Street is exactly that—a place where most of the area's commercial activity, such as banking and retail sales, occurs and where people are likely to encounter known others with whom they can easily engage in personal conversations.

Our Town (see the analytical commentary about this play in the *Cityscape* box below).

Gesellschaft.   In the character of the modern city, Tönnies saw a wholly different style of life, in which the meaning of existence shifted from the group to the individual. Whereas *gemeinschaft* expresses a sense of "we-ness," *gesellschaft* is more rational, more calculating. By its very nature, *gesellschaft* conditions people

CITYSCAPE

Our Town: The Spirit of *Gemeinschaft*

Thornton Wilder's play *Our Town* is an acclaimed classic for many reasons, including its poignant portrayal of ordinary life-cycle events. To many people, however, its real charm lies in the insights it provides about life in a typical small town, where people live in what we may appropriately call a *gemeinschaft* community.

The play opens with the "Stage Manager" telling the audience about "our town," Grover's Corners, a small village in New Hampshire. He asks the audience to imagine the layout of the town and the life of its inhabitants.

To orient us, he points out what first appear to be differences—where, for example, the Polish immigrants live. They migrated to Grover's Corners to work in the mill, he tells us, as did a few "Canuck" families. Next, he tells us where the various churches are: Catholic, Congregationalist, Presbyterian, Methodist, Unitarian, and Baptist, in that order. He does not tell us that such differences may separate people's lives somewhat, but they by no means isolate them from one another. Almost intuitively, however, we know this—and it is reaffirmed through our learning that everyone here knows quite a bit about almost everyone else. They don't necessarily like everyone, or always approve of certain people's behavior—such as excessive drinking, for example—but there is nevertheless a closeness, an intimacy, among the people. This is how it also was in the medieval city—Weber's ideal form of *gemeinschaft*—where class differences, disagreements, and even conflict existed within a close-knit community dominated by traditional values and continuity.

To help us understand some of this tradition and continuity, the Stage Manager informs us that the town's earliest tombstones—dating back to 1670—are engraved with names such as Grover, Cartright, Gibbs, and Hersey. These are the same family names as exist among the townspeople in 1901, the year during which the play takes place. Emphasizing this theme of stable relationships in daily life, he tells us, "On the whole, things don't change much around here." He also offers bits of other information—the nonexistence of burglars and the daily visits by nearly everyone to the grocery store and the drug store on Main Street. These manifestations of mutual trust, daily routine, familiarity, and regular social interaction suggest a cohesiveness of community that is the essence of *gemeinschaft*.

As the play about this ordinary small town, one where "nobody remarkable ever come out of it, s'far as we know," unfolds, we learn about more than just some events in the lives of George Gibbs and Emily Webb, or in the lives of their families, friends, and neighbors, both alive or deceased. We witness the way that life once was in simpler times in North American small towns—a way of life that no doubt still exists in whatever small towns still remain. For most of us—living in a *gesellschaft* environment—it is a bygone reality, however. It is not ours.

to be concerned primarily with their own self-interest, to "look out for Number One" in contemporary terms. In *gemeinschaft,* the "natural" social institutions of kinship, neighborhood, and friendship are predominant; in *gesellschaft,* these forms of association tend to decline.

One way to distinguish easily the difference between *gemeinschaft* and *gesellschaft* is to consider, when people ask, "How are you?"—do they really want to know? Tönnies's communal relation—*gemeinschaft*—is built on broad concern for the other as a person, and such a question has significance beyond convention, beyond politeness. In the contrasting case—*gesellschaft*—each person is understood in terms of a particular role and service provided, such as teacher, computer programmer, or butcher. In the city, the question "How are you?" is usually asked only out of politeness: We don't know other people well, and what's more, we usually don't want to know them well.

Gemeinschaft **and** *Gesellschaft* **in History.** Tönnies believed that the study of European history revealed a gradual, and generally irreversible, displacement of *gemeinschaft* by *gesellschaft.* He saw the rapid rise of cities in Europe during the nineteenth century as the inevitable emergence of *gesellschaft* as the dominant form of social life. Although he did think it to be inevitable, Tönnies obviously did not think this transformation was altogether good: For him, the unity and human concern of *gemeinschaft* was gradually lost in *gesellschaft.*

Tönnies's ideas contain the beginning of a sociology of the city. He was among the first to see urban life as distinctive and worthy of study. Moreover, his use of contrasting, pure types is a pattern that numerous other urban sociologists followed.

Emile Durkheim: Mechanical and Organic Solidarity

Like Tönnies, the French sociologist Emile Durkheim (1858–1917) witnessed the urban revolution of the nineteenth century. He, too, developed a model of contrasting types:

Mechanical solidarity and organic solidarity are analogous to Tönnies's *gemeinschaft* and *gesellschaft,* respectively.

Mechanical solidarity refers to social bonds that are constructed on likeness, on common belief and custom, common ritual and symbol. Such solidarity is "mechanical," because the people who participate in it—people living in family units, tribes, or small towns—are almost identical in major respects and so are united almost automatically, without thinking. Each family, tribe, or town is relatively self-sufficient and able to meet all of life's needs without dependence on other groups.

In contrast, **organic solidarity** describes a social order based on individual differences. Characteristic of modern societies, especially cities, organic solidarity rests on a complex division of labor, in which many different people specialize in many different occupations. Like the organs of the human body, people depend more on one another to meet various needs. A lawyer depends on other people—say, restaurant owners and grocers—to supply food and, therefore, is able to specialize in legal activity. Similarly, of course, the restaurant owner and the grocer need not study law, for the same reason.

In this complex division of labor, Durkheim saw the possibility of greater freedom and choice for all of society's inhabitants. Although Durkheim acknowledged the problems that cities might create—impersonality, alienation, disagreement, and conflict—he argued for the ultimate superiority of organic over mechanical solidarity: "[The] yoke that we submit to [in modern society] is much less heavy than when society completely controls us [as it does in rural society], and it leaves much more place open for the free play of our initiative" (1964:131; orig. 1893).

Durkheim and Tönnies: A Comparison. While Durkheim agreed with Tönnies's conclusion that history was characterized by a movement from an emphasis on one type of social order to another—from mechanical solidarity (or *gemeinschaft*) to organic solidarity (or *gesellschaft*)—there are important differences in their ideas. For instance, Durkheim took exception to labeling the tribal or rural environment alone as being "natural." Rather, he asserted that "the life of large social agglomerations is just as natural as that of small groupings" (Giddens 1972:146).

This assertion reveals that Durkheim did not share Tönnies's negative view of modern society. In fact, Durkheim reversed Tönnies's terminology and labeled *gemeinschaft* "mechanical" and *gesellschaft* "organic." Although Tönnies saw little hope for truly humane life in the city (he cited parents' admonition to their city-bound children to beware of "bad *gesellschaft*"), Durkheim was more optimistic. He saw the increasing division of labor characteristic of modern urban societies as undermining traditional social integration and creating a new form of social cohesion based on mutual interdependence. Contractual agreements among individuals or groups clearly express this interdependence. Still, Durkheim cautioned, no society can exist entirely on the basis of contract: At the very least, there needs to be a moral foundation that allows agreement on how to enter into and execute all contracts fairly.

Durkheim thus provides an important counterpoint to Tönnies. Although both theorists recognized that cities were associated with the growth of social differentiation and individuality, Tönnies feared the undermining of the very fabric of social life, whereas Durkheim saw the possibility of continuing social cohesion and greater human development. The effects of the city on individuals, however, extend beyond these two visions.

Georg Simmel: The Mental Life of the Metropolis

Both Tönnies and Durkheim described the broad societal processes that produced the modern city. Although both made passing reference to the mental characteristics of city dwellers—the city dweller was more impersonal, more rational, and freer—they did not look systematically at the social psychology of city life. Another German, Georg Simmel (1858–1918), undertook that task.

Like his contemporaries, Simmel saw, in the rise of the modern world, a cause for

concern: How was the individual to maintain a spirit of freedom and creativity in the midst of the city's "overwhelming social forces"? In his famous essay "The Metropolis and Mental Life," Simmel suggested that the personality would learn to "accommodate itself" to the urban scene (Simmel 1964; orig. 1905).

The City's Characteristics.   To Simmel, the unique trait of the modern city is the intensification of nervous stimuli with which the city dweller must cope. Unlike the rural setting, where "the rhythm of life and sensory imagery flows more slowly, more habitually, more evenly" (1964:410). the city constantly bombards the individual with an enormous kaleidoscope of sights, sounds, and smells. To avoid being overwhelmed, the individual learns to discriminate such stimuli carefully—to tune in what is important and tune out what is irrelevant. In time, urban people become more sophisticated and intellectual, more rational and calculating, than their rural counterparts.

Such rationality means that urbanites are highly attuned to time. Cities, Simmel observed, are marked by the ever-present clock and wristwatch. "If," he continued, "all the clocks and watches in Berlin would suddenly go wrong in different ways, even if only by one hour, all economic life and communication of the city would be disrupted for a long time" (1964:413). In addition to the rational organization of time, Simmel saw the rationality of the city as being expressed in its advanced economic division of labor (here, he echoed Durkheim). Social life in the city is the interplay of specialists.

Perhaps the most powerful means of conveying the message of urban rationality, however, was Simmel's discussion about the importance of money. "The metropolis," he stated, "has always been the seat of a money economy" (1964:411). Why is money so important in urban life? One reason is that the advanced division of labor requires a universal means of exchange. Money performs this critical function. As Simmel (1964:414) wrote, "Money is concerned only with what is common to all: It asks for the exchange value,

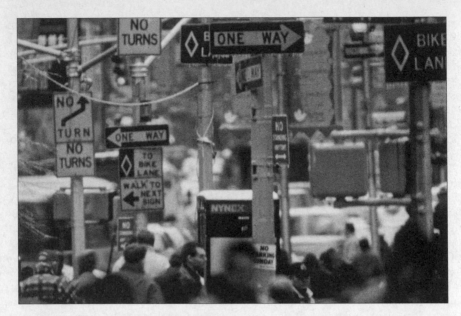

Whenever we walk along a city street, we encounter an abundance of stimuli, far more than we can absorb. This intensification of nervous stimuli—from the many signs, sounds, movements, and crowds of people—forces us, says Simmel, to discriminate carefully, to tune in what is important and tune out what is not.

it reduces all quality and individuality to the question: How much?"

The Individual's Response. How, asks Simmel, is the urbanite to behave in the midst of such powerful stimulation and unending demand for rational response? Or, on a more practical level, can you really stop to help everyone you see on the street who is in some sort of trouble? Simmel believed not. Consequently, he reasoned, the urbanite adapts to city life by developing what he called a "blasé" attitude, a social reserve or detachment. Put simply, in the city, we respond with our head rather than our heart. We learn to adopt a matter-of-fact attitude about the world around us. We simply don't care. We don't want to "get involved," as shown dramatically by the examples in the *Urban Living* box on page 127.

Even worse, Simmel speculated that the cultivated indifference necessary for living in the city may harden into a measured antagonism. "Indeed, if I do not deceive myself," he wrote, "the inner aspect of this outer reserve is not only indifference, but, more often than we are aware, it is a slight aversion, a mutual strangeness and repulsion, which will break into hatred and fight at the moment of a closer contact, however caused" (1964:415–16). Perhaps each of us can recall feeling some anger about the way someone unknown to us was behaving in a city—someone who broke into a line ahead of us, for example, or who approached us in a city park and demanded spare change.

Like Durkheim, Simmel could see freedom in the separateness fostered by city living. The urbanite, he thought, could transcend the pettiness of daily routine and reach a new height of personal and spiritual development. Simmel also detected in the city's freedom, however, a haunting specter. "It is obviously only the obverse of this freedom," he wrote, "if, under certain circumstances, one nowhere feels as lonely and lost as in the metropolitan crowd" (1964:418).

URBAN LIVING

Urban Apathy: Ignored Violent Attacks

In March 1964, the murder of Kitty Genovese near her home in the Kew Gardens section of New York's Borough of Queens exploded into a major controversy when the *New York Times* reported that dozens of Ms. Genovese's "neighbors" had observed the attacker stab her repeatedly during a period of half an hour without coming to her aid—or even calling the police until after she was dead! In an editorial the following day, the *Times* posed a frightening question: "Does residence in a great city destroy all sense of personal responsibility for one's neighbors?" The death of Kitty Genovese thus became symbolic of the argument that the city was an unhealthy setting, lacking even a rudimentary sense of human community.

A 2007 *American Psychologist* article claimed that the media exaggerated about the number of eyewitnesses, some of whom did not actually see the attack, and at least one call went to the police during the attack. Nevertheless, sad intermingling of urban violence and apathy didn't stop with Kitty Genovese, however. Hers is only the most celebrated case. On the night of November 30, 1984, the same thing happened in Brooklyn. A woman was attacked in the Gowanus Apartments, a New York City housing project. As she was beaten, she began screaming and continued her cries for 20 minutes. Many heard her—no one came to her rescue. Finally, her assailants dragged her into the lobby of a building and shot her dead. It was only then that someone deigned to call the police (*New York Times,* December 3, 1984).

In 1983, similar indifference to victims of urban crime had surfaced in St. Louis. In one case, a man was robbed at gunpoint while dozens of people watched. When the man approached the onlookers afterward and asked why they hadn't helped him, they replied that they just "didn't want to get involved." In another incident three men attacked a woman at Busch Memorial Stadium during a Cardinals baseball game. She screamed for help. No one responded. Later, she said, "I was shocked more than hurt. I just sat there and screamed and not one soul stopped. I saw all these legs going by, and I thought about reaching out and grabbing somebody" (*New York Times,* August 18, 1983). Said Sgt. Frank Baricevic of the St. Louis Police about these disturbing incidents, "Police departments are only as good as the people they protect. If [people] don't want to get involved, if they don't want to cooperate, then we're in trouble" (*New York Times,* August 18, 1983).

Such incidents still happen, and not just in the United States. In 2003, a 14-year-old girl was raped in broad daylight on a busy street in Heide, Germany, by a drunken stranger despite her calls for help to several passersby. The girl was riding home when a 19-year-old male grabbed her bicycle and dragged her to the ground. Although she immediately called out to a nearby female, who apparently understood her plea for help, the woman walked on. Soon after, a group of four people walked by and also ignored her screams, even though the attacker had pressed her to the ground in front of a pharmacy and begun to rape her. The victim told police that at the same time, at least two men watched the attack from a nearby balcony and did not move to help. Only after she was able to free herself and her father arrived did a witness alert the police, who were able to locate and detain the rapist. Because he had no previous record of sexual attacks, he was released on bail. Police said his level of intoxication could serve as a mitigating factor and save him from conviction (News24.com 2003).

If you encountered this stranger lying unconscious on your campus or in the parking lot of a suburban mall, the probability is high that you would either help him or get help. In the city, however, where sleeping vagrants, drunks, and addicts often abound, you might well ignore him and avoid getting involved, as several people here are doing.

Feeling like a cog in a giant machine, some people maintain their sense of individuality in a city by doing something "odd," by "being different" and, thereby, standing out. This sense of alienation is what Simmel would use to explain the motivation for the graffiti craze in so many cities, a process that has defaced buildings, signs, subway trains, and public monuments. For many of these vandals, their "tags" raise them out of their anonymity and shout "I'm not just another face in the project among a million others. I exist. I am here!"

In the end, then, Simmel appears to side more with Tönnies than with Durkheim in his evaluation of the city. Although Simmel depicted the city as being the setting where the great historical contest between true human liberation and alienation would occur, his analysis left little doubt that he believed the second option would likely be victorious.

Max Weber: The Historical and Comparative Study of Cities

Tönnies, Durkheim, and Simmel all analyzed a single type of city. In other words, they developed their theories by "reading" the main trends of European urban history and the main elements of life in the cities they knew.

German sociologist Max Weber (1864–1920), however, believed any theory that took account of cities in only one part of the world and at one point in time was of limited value. This concern proved to be his major methodological contribution to urban sociology.

Die Stadt.   Weber demonstrated his approach in his famous essay "*Die Stadt*," "The City" (1966; orig. 1921). Surveying cities of Europe, the Middle East, India, and China, Weber developed a definition of what he called the "full urban community":

> To constitute a full urban community, a settlement must display a relative predominance of trade–commercial relations, with the settlement as a whole displaying the following features: (1) a fortification; (2) a market; (3) a court of its own and at least partially autonomous law; (4) a related form of association; and (5) at least partial political autonomy. (1966:80–81)

This definition illustrates what Weber called an **ideal type,** a model constructed from real-world observation that highlights the crucial elements of some social phenomenon. Weber was well aware that many cities would not contain all the elements in his definition. In such cases, the city simply would not be a "full urban community" in his sense.

Let's examine the characteristics of such a community in more detail. First, Weber's urban community is based on trade or commercial relations. In rural areas, people are more or less self-sufficient—growing their own food, providing their own clothing, and so on. Trade and commerce are of limited importance there, but not so in the city. Weber clearly agreed with Tönnies, Durkheim, and Simmel that economic self-sufficiency is nearly impossible in cities, where people are economically interdependent, linked by Durkheim's organic solidarity. Indeed, the economic aspects of city life are so important that a distinct mechanism of exchange—the market—evolved to facilitate them.

Second, an urban community is relatively autonomous. Weber specified that a true city has a court and law of its own and at least partial political autonomy. It also must be militarily self-sufficient, having a fortification system and army for self-defense if and when necessary. Such autonomy is essential if urban dwellers are to identify the city as theirs, as a place demanding their allegiance in the way that a small town receives the allegiance of its inhabitants.

Third, Weber said that the urban community must have "a related form of association." By this, he meant that city living must involve social relationships and organizations through which urbanites gain a sense of meaningful participation in the life of their city.

The "Full Urban Community" in History. Like Durkheim, Weber believed that cities could be positive and liberating forces in human life. Unlike Durkheim, Weber did not see much hope for twentieth-century cities. Indeed, he thought only the fortified, self-sufficient cities of the medieval period deserved the title of "full urban community." Only in these cities had there existed the commercial relations, autonomy, and social participation that he believed were the defining characteristics of urbanism.

With the rise of the nation to preeminence as a political entity during the seventeenth, eighteenth, and nineteenth centuries, Weber claimed, cities had lost their military and, to a large extent, their legal and political autonomy—necessary elements for identifying with the city as a psychological "home." People came to identify with other units of society—the nation, country, business, or as recognized by Tönnies and Simmel, with themselves alone.

By recognizing medieval cities as examples of the full urban community, Weber hoped to show that "the good life" had existed in cities and might flourish again. Yet, by suggesting that a pinnacle of urban culture had been realized before in history, Weber implied that history might not necessarily be progressive (Sennett 1969:6–10).

The City and Culture. Weber stood apart from his colleagues, who tended to see the city itself as the cause for the distinguishing qualities of urban life. In contrast, Weber's analysis, fueled by his broad understanding of cities in other cultures and at different points in history, suggested that cities are intimately linked to larger processes—for example, to particular economic or political orientations. If a society's character is different, then the nature of its cities will be different. Thus, feudal or Chinese societies would not produce the same type of urban life that European industrial capitalism produces.

The European Tradition: An Evaluation

The ideas of Marx, Engels, Tönnies, Durkheim, Simmel, and Weber form the core of classical urban sociology and have had an enormous impact on the field ever since. It is important, however, to balance their contributions with their limitations.

Contributions.   Perhaps the most important contribution of the classical theorists was their insistence that the city is an important object of sociological study. Marx, Engels, Tönnies, and Durkheim all clearly analyzed the contrasts between rural life and urban life. Simmel and Weber went a step further, by actually developing theories of how cities worked.

In addition, all six theorists recognized that *there is something distinctive about the city and the way of life it creates.* All saw the city as increasing human choice, emphasizing rationality, being characterized by a complex division of labor, and creating a unique experience for its inhabitants. This concern with the city's unique qualities has been a major focus of the discipline ever since, as the next section will demonstrate.

Taken together, these theorists also suggested the main concerns of the discipline. Marx and Engels emphasized economics and the problems of inequality and conflict. Tönnies, Durkheim, and Weber considered the social structure of the city. Simmel suggested the importance of the urban experience.

Finally, all six Europeans made the evaluation of cities a fundamental element in their work. Each made quite clear what he thought beneficial, and what he considered detrimental, for the city's ability to produce a humane life for its population.

Limitations.   Three generations later, we can easily see how the central ideas of these theorists were an outgrowth of the times and the cities in which they lived. Cities were quickly replacing villages and countryside as the main arena of life. For all their excitement, however, one could hardly argue that these rapidly growing cities provided a good life for many of their inhabitants. Little wonder, then, that three of these theorists— Tönnies, Simmel, and Weber—saw the cities of their day as being threats to long-cherished human values. Durkheim, Marx, and Engels, however, had mixed responses to the changing cities. Durkheim acknowledged the problems of alienation and conflict in the cities, but he also saw the ultimate superiority of the new industrial age. Marx and Engels saw not the city, but the capitalist economy, as a social evil.

Of course, one can only speculate how the theories of these men might have changed had they been able to witness the growth of suburbs, major efforts at urban planning, reforms in many of the most overtly exploitative practices of turn-of-the-century cities (such as child labor), the rise of labor unions, the civil rights movement, and the recent collapse of communism in an economically bankrupt Soviet Union and a fettered Eastern Europe.

Also, the theorists show some disagreement in their interpretations. The contrast between Tönnies and Durkheim is most instructive. Tönnies saw *gemeinschaft* as humane and *gesellschaft* as brutal. Using his terms of mechanical and organic solidarity, Durkheim reversed the interpretation: The tribal or country life was cloying and undeveloped, but the life of the city was liberating and full of potential for development.

On another level, Simmel thought the social–psychological adaptations he studied were a product of the great city itself. He implied that all metropolises would produce similar mental processes. Weber, however, disagreed. He argued that only certain historical and cultural conditions produced the type of city that Simmel observed, most particularly the modern capitalist cities, and that other historical and cultural conditions would produce very different types of urban social–psychological adaptation.

Similarly, Marx and Engels maintained that the human condition in cities was the result of the economic structure. Therefore, a different economic system would produce a different city, with different patterns of social interaction.

With the evidence available at the time, it was impossible to judge such contradictory claims. Later chapters in this book, however, will show that Weber's position on this issue was closer to the truth.

URBAN SOCIOLOGY IN NORTH AMERICA: 1915–1970

About the time of World War I, urban sociology began to develop in the United States. From the outset, the discipline's character here was somewhat different from that in Europe, with U.S. researchers showing greater concern with actually going out and exploring the city. At the same time, many of the themes in the European tradition were carried into North American sociology.

The era in which this type of sociology developed is noteworthy. The early twentieth century in North America, as in Europe, was a period of industrialization and rapid urban growth. A mounting flow of immigrants— who settled mostly in cities—ensured that by 1920, the United States would become a predominantly urban society. In short, the Grover's Corners of North America (as described in the *Cityscape* box on page 123) were rapidly giving way to the expanding industrial metropolis.

No city typified this explosive growth better than Chicago. A crude outpost in 1830, Chicago was approaching a population of 2 million by 1900 and was expanding both upward and outward. The first steel-frame builing—a marvel of the age—opened its doors in Chicago in 1884, towering an incredible ten stories above the ground! By the close of World War I, Chicago boasted a population of almost 3 million. Immigrants from Europe and migrants from the countryside were everywhere. Like hundreds of exploding North American cities, Chicago factories were belching the black, smoky flag of prosperity, creating their share of severe problems along the way. It was in Chicago that the main elements of U.S. urban sociology took form.

Robert Park and Sociology at the University of Chicago

Although U.S. universities had offered courses in "social science" as early as 1865, sociology first gained intellectual respectability when the University of Chicago invited Albion W. Small (then president of Colby College) to found a sociology department in 1892 (Calhoun 2007). Within the next 30 years, the department attracted several notable scholars. One of the most outstanding was Robert Ezra Park (1864–1944).

Leaving a newspaper job in 1915 to join the department, Park established the first urban studies center in the United States. His interest in urban matters had both European and North American roots. During his early years, Park had studied with the Russian sociologist Bogdan Kistiakowski, who held much the same view of social change as Tönnies, and with Georg Simmel. Park was also deeply influenced by *The Shame of the Cities*, a book by U.S. journalist Lincoln Steffens (2004; orig. 1904) that suggested serious urban problems were everyone's responsibility. An excerpt from this critique appears in the *Urban Living* box on page 132.

Although Park was aware of both the bad and the good, there can be no question he had an almost unbounded fascination with the city. Not only did Park guide several generations of students in explorations of all aspects of Chicago, he also served as the first president of the Chicago Urban League. Dedicating his life to relentless personal exploration of the city, Park later wrote:

> I expect that I have actually covered more ground, tramping about in cities in different parts of the world, than any other living man. Out of all this I gained, among other things, a conception of the city, the community, and the region, not as geographical phenomenon [sic] merely, but as a kind of social organism. (1964, p. viii)

A Systematic Urban Sociology. Park presented the program he used to guide urban sociology at the University of Chicago in his classic article "The City: Suggestions for the Investigation of Human Behavior in the Urban Environment" (1984; orig. 1916). First, he argued that urban research had to be conducted by disciplined observation—in much the same way that anthropologists studied other cultures. Second, he conceived of the city as being a social organism, with distinct parts bound together by internal processes. Urban life was not chaos and disorder (stereotypes

URBAN LIVING

The Shame of the Cities: Who's to Blame?

When I set out on my travels, an honest New Yorker told me honestly that I would find that the Irish, the Catholic Irish, were at the bottom of it all everywhere. The first city I went to was St. Louis, a German city. The next was Minneapolis, a Scandinavian city, with a leadership of New Englanders. Then came Pittsburgh, Scotch Presbyterian, and that was what my New York friend was. "Ah, but they are all foreign populations," I heard. The next city was Philadelphia, the purest American community of all, and the most hopeless. And after that came Chicago and New York, both mongrelbred, but the one a triumph of reform, the other the best example of good government that I had seen. The "foreign element" excuse is one of the hypocritical lies that save us from the clear sight of ourselves. . . .

When I set out to describe the corrupt systems of certain typical cities, I meant to show simply how the people were deceived and betrayed. But in the very first study—St. Louis—the startling truth lay bare that corruption was not merely political; it was financial, commercial, social; the ramifications of boodle were so complex, various, and far-reaching that one mind could hardly grasp them. . . .

And it's all a moral weakness; a weakness right where we think we are strongest. Oh, we are good—on Sunday, and we are "fearfully patriotic" on the Fourth of July. But the bribe we pay to the janitor to prefer our interests to the landlord's, is the little brother of the bribe passed to the alderman to sell a city street, and the father of the air-brake stock assigned to the president of the railroad to have this life-saving invention adopted on his road. We are pathetically proud of our democratic institutions and our republican form of government, of our grand Constitution and our just laws. We are a free and sovereign people, we govern ourselves and the government is ours. But that is the point. We are responsible, not our leaders, since we follow them. We let them divert our loyalty from the United States to some "party"; we let them boss the party and turn our municipal democracies into autocracies and our republican nation into a plutocracy. We cheat our government and we let our leaders loot it, and we let them wheedle and bribe our sovereignty from us. . . . The people are not innocent.

Source: Lincoln Steffens, *The Shame of the Cities* (New York: McClure, Phillips, 1904), pp. 2–3, 7–9.

of Chicago during the Roaring Twenties notwithstanding) but, rather, tended toward an "orderly and typical grouping of its population and institutions" (1984:1). He wrote:

> Every great city has its racial colonies, like the Chinatowns of San Francisco and New York, the Little Sicily of Chicago, and the various other less pronounced types. In addition to these, most cities have their segregated vice districts . . . their rendezvous for criminals of various sorts. Every large city has its occupational suburbs, like the stockyards in Chicago, and its residential enclaves, like Brookline in Boston, the so-called "Gold Coast" in Chicago, Greenwich Village in New York, each of which has a size and character of a complete separate town, village, or city, except that its population is a select one. (1984:10)

This notion of the city's orderliness led Park to urge his students to develop detailed studies of all segments of the city's population—industrial workers, real estate officials, and

VIPs but also migrants, hobos, musicians, prostitutes, and dance hall workers. The conviction that all "parts and processes" of the city were linked was at the heart of Park's new social science, which he termed "human, as distinguished from plant and animal, ecology" (1984:2). Finally, Park also saw the city as a "moral as well as a physical organization," (1984:4) and he carried evaluative judgments of urban living deep into his sociology.

Park's Image of the City.   What was it about the city that so fascinated Park? First, like Weber, Park saw in the modern city a commercial structure that owed "its existence to the market place around which it sprang up" (1984:12). And like Marx, Weber, and Durkheim, he saw in modern city life a complex division of labor driven by industrial competition. Along with Tönnies, Park believed that this market dominance would result in the steady erosion of traditional ways of life. The past emphasis upon "family ties, local associations . . . caste, and status" would yield inevitably to a *gesellschaft*-like system "based on occupation and vocational interests" (1984:13–14).

Second, Park perceived the city as being increasingly characterized by *formal social structures* best exemplified by large-scale bureaucracies, such as police departments, courts, and welfare agencies. In time, he reasoned, these would take the place of the more "informal" means, such as neighborhood interaction, by which people historically had organized their everyday lives. Similarly, politics would develop a more formalized tone. Park contended that

> the form of government which had its origin in the town meetings and was well suited to the needs of the small community based on primary relations is not suitable to the government of the changing and heterogeneous populations of cities of three or four millions. (1984:33)

The city dweller, unable to take account of all the issues at stake in the operation of a complex city, would have to rely on either political or civic organizations run by party bosses or concerned citizens for information and action.

As an ex-newspaperman, Park could hardly have been expected to omit the media from his description of the formalization of city life. The face-to-face oral network by which information flowed in the village—*gossip* is the more precise, if less scholarly, term—would be replaced by reliance on impersonal mass media. Such was the significance of the city newspaper, and soon after that, radio and television, and eventually, the Internet.

The third dimension of Park's image of the city, showing the effects of his studies with Simmel, was his emphasis on the psychosocial dimension of urban life. Park suggested that life within the city would become *less sentimental* and *more rational.* Deep-seated sentiments and prejudices would give way to calculation based on self-interest. At the same time, however, Park was aware that the erosion of traditional sentimental ties in the city might give rise to new social bonds in the form of interest groups. In this, Park's argument has a clear Durkheimian quality: Ties based on likenesses (mechanical solidarity) give way to bonds based on the interdependence of differentiated parts (organic solidarity).

Freedom and Tolerance in the City.   As a social reformer, Park recognized that the modern city revealed problem upon problem, but like Durkheim, Park was fascinated with what he saw to be the possibilities for freedom and tolerance in the city. He wrote:

> The attraction of the metropolis is due in part to the fact that in the long run every individual finds somewhere among the varied manifestations of city life the sort of environment in which he expands and feels at ease; he finds, in short, the moral climate in which his peculiar nature obtains the stimulations that bring his innate dispositions to full and free expression. It is, I suspect, motives of this kind which have their basis, not in interest or even in sentiment, but in something more fundamental and primitive which drove many, if not most, of the young men and young women from the security of their homes in the country into the big, booming confusion and excitement of city life. (1984:41)

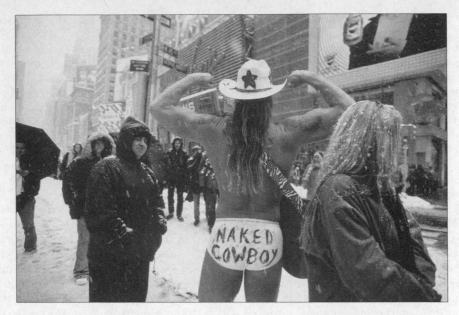

As Park suggested, urbanites typically respond to people's eccentricities with great tolerance if not amusement, sometimes even to the point of ignoring them. The "Naked Cowboy," as he bills himself, is a frequent sight in New York's Times Square area. Regardless of the weather, he appears just as you see him, posing, singing, and playing his guitar.

In short, what Tönnies saw as a steady disorganization, Park saw as the potential for greater human experience. He continued:

> In a small community it is the normal man, the man without eccentricity or genius who seems most likely to succeed. The small community often tolerates eccentricity. The city rewards it. Neither the criminal, the defective, nor the genius has the same opportunity to develop his innate disposition in a small town that he invariably finds in a great city. (1984:41)

Summing up, we see in the ideas of Robert Park a new emphasis on doing urban research and on-site investigation of the city, quite unlike the more abstract theorizing of Tönnies, Durkheim, and Simmel and the historical work of Marx, Engels, and Weber. Park's main contribution was his demand that we get out there and see how the city actually works.

Louis Wirth and Urban Theory

If the European theorists produced a great deal of theory but conducted little actual research, early Chicago sociologists did just the opposite. During the 20 years following the publication of Park's urban studies program in 1916, Chicago sociologists produced a wealth of primarily descriptive studies. Not until 1938 was this imbalance rectified, when Louis Wirth (1897–1952) published his famous essay "Urbanism as a Way of Life," in which he identified **urbanism** as that "distinctive . . . mode of life which is associated with the growth of cities" (p. 1). To Wirth, the city worked its magic by forcing people to encounter one another in a special way: In the city, large numbers of heterogeneous people come into contact within dense settings, generating a new type of behavior and awareness—an urban way of life. City dwellers become rational, self-interested, specialized, somewhat reserved, and highly tolerant.

Wirth's great contribution to urban sociology was taking the insights by previous urban sociologists and then organizing them, patiently and systematically, into the first truly sociological theory of the city. By a *theory* of the city, we mean that Wirth began his analysis by isolating several factors he argued were *universal social characteristics* of the city. He then proceeded to deduce systematically the consequences of these factors for the character of urban social life. He said, in effect, as all good theorists do: If this condition is present, then that condition will result.

Wirth began with a definition of the city as a (1) large, (2) dense, permanent settlement with (3) socially and culturally heterogeneous people. Let's examine what conditions of urban social life follow from each of these elements.

Population Size or Scale.   Wirth believed, first, that large population size by itself produces great diversity in the cultural and occupational characteristics of a city. This diversity partly results from (1) the simple fact that larger numbers of people coming together logically increase the potential differentiation among themselves and (2) the migration of diverse groups to the city (as in Chicago, where Wirth was writing). Second, the condition of cultural diversity produced by a large population has the additional effect of creating a need for formal control structures, such as a legal system. Third, a large, differentiated population supports the proliferation of specialization, and an occupational structure based on differing occupations, such as artist, politician, and cabdriver, emerges. Fourth, specialization organizes human relationships more on an "interest-specific" basis, which Wirth described as "social segmentalization":

> Characteristically, urbanites meet one another in highly segmental roles. They are, to be sure, dependent on more people for the satisfactions of their life needs than are rural people . . . but they are less dependent upon particular persons, and their dependence upon others is confined to a highly fractionalized aspect of the other's round of activity. This is essentially what is meant by saying that the city is characterized by secondary rather than primary contacts. The contacts of the city may indeed be face-to-face, but they are nevertheless impersonal, superficial, transitory, and segmental. (Wirth and Reiss 1981:71)

In other words, rather than understanding others in terms of who they are, the urbanite typically conceives of others in terms of what they do—in terms of their roles and what they can do to advance one's own ends. The qualities of rationality and sophistication are simply additional ways of suggesting that urban ties become, in essence, relationships of utility. Lastly, even with the stabilizing constraint provided by formal controls and professional codes of conduct, Wirth could not escape the conclusion that large population size carried with it the possibility of disorganization and disintegration, a fear shared by all the European theorists.

Population Density.   The consequence of population density is to *intensify* the effects of large population size on social life. Rather than manifesting the quality of sameness that one might associate with the countryside, the city separates into a mosaic of readily identifiable regions or districts. (Here, we can see the direct influence of Wirth's teacher, Park.) Both economic forces, such as differing land values, and social processes, such as attraction and avoidance based on race and ethnicity, tend to produce fairly distinct neighborhoods and districts.

For example, many U.S. cities have a predominantly Italian area, such as Boston's North End; a Chinatown, such as San Francisco's; and a high-income area, such as Chicago's North Shore. Similarly, major cities frequently have a garment district and a financial district, such as New York's Wall Street. Wirth called this process of separating the city into districts "ecological specialization." The more common term today is **natural areas,** revealing that such places evolve as unplanned clusters.

Density also operates on the social–psychological level. Exposed to "glaring contrasts . . . splendor and squalor . . . riches and poverty," Wirth (1938:14) argued, city dwellers develop mental shorthand—a mental mapping of the city, its regions, and its inhabitants. This insight (drawn from Simmel) helps us understand the urbanite's tendency toward stereotypical and categorical thinking, as well as his or her reliance on grasping the city through visible symbols and uniforms, such as clothing, cars, and fashionable street addresses.

In a city, we are almost never alone, but we may well be lonely. Most face-to-face contacts are impersonal, superficial, and segmental. Research, however, shows that although city dwellers have far more of these secondary relationships, they also have just as many meaningful primary relationships as non-urbanites.

The implication is clear—population density fosters a loss of sensitivity to the "more personal aspects" of others—and suggests why people in the city sometimes seem to be "cold and heartless."

As suggested earlier by Durkheim and Simmel, Wirth (1938:15) contended that the "juxtaposition of divergent personalities and modes of life" results in a *greater toleration of differences*. Along with this, physical closeness tends to *increase social distance* among urbanites. Forced into physical proximity, city dwellers characteristically close off or tune out those around them. (On a small scale,

this happens when people, busily chatting, enter a crowded elevator and abruptly become silent, staring up at the numbers on the elevator wall.)

Again echoing Simmel, Wirth suggested that high density might cause an increase in antisocial behavior. Wirth (1938:16) posited, "The necessary movement of great numbers of individuals in a congested habitat causes friction and irritation."

Heterogeneity. In completing his theory of urbanism, Wirth suggested several consequences of social difference or heterogeneity. First, "social interaction among such a variety of personality types in the urban milieu tends to break down the rigidity of caste lines and to complicate the class structure" (p. 16). Consequently, there tends to be heightened social mobility in the city, because the inertia of family background weakens under the force of personal achievement.

Second, physical movement typically accompanies social mobility. "Overwhelmingly the city dweller is not a homeowner and since a transitory habitat does not generate binding traditions and sentiments, only rarely is he a true neighbor" (p. 17). (Remember Kitty Genovese in the *Urban Living* box on page 127)

Finally, the concentration of diverse people leads inevitably to further depersonalization. Against a background of commercial mass production and consumption, personal relations are eroded by an emphasis on money. Thus, Wirth repeated Simmel's earlier view of the city as a "pecuniary nexus."

These three dimensions of Wirth's theory—size, density, and heterogeneity of population—interact to produce the unique way of life that he termed *urbanism*. Clearly, Wirth was pessimistic about urbanism as a way of life. He saw the city as an acid that, over time, dissolved traditional values and undermined the formation of institutions and meaningful relationships. Like Park, he touted the possibilities for greater freedom in the city, but he also worried that urbanism's positive aspects would inevitably be compromised by the disorganization he saw in turbulent Chicago. Only by massive efforts at urban planning,

Wirth imagined, could people create a humane urban environment.

As Wirth understood it, the essence of urban living was being *cosmopolitan*—literally, "belonging to all the world." Robert Merton (1968:447–53) drew a useful distinction between "localite" and "'cosmopolitan'" lifestyles. The life of the localite centers in the immediate area. Typically born in the area where they live, localites are bound up within social relations and life commitments that are encapsulated within that specific territory. Cosmopolites, on the other hand, are more rootless and think in terms of wider possibilities. They are more likely to move on (perhaps to new jobs or a better home). Whether rich or poor, cosmopolites display a certain degree of detachment, have a somewhat blasé attitude toward their immediate surroundings, and show a sophistication in matters of taste and friendship not typical of localites. Although Merton acknowledged that cosmopolites and localites could exist anywhere, there is little doubt that the cosmopolitan attitude is found more frequently among city dwellers and that the localite attitude is more typical in small towns or rural areas.

Are cosmopolitanism and localism, however, set off as clearly as Merton thought they were? For one thing, cosmopolitanism is found in many small college towns, such as Gambier, Ohio. Then, too, Chicago, Toronto, and most other large cities contain residential enclaves where localism abounds—Italian neighborhoods, Vietnamese communities, perhaps a Chinatown, or maybe an old upper-class area. If this is the case, then possibly the city doesn't produce a distinctive way of life at all. Or so argues Herbert Gans, the most outspoken critic of the Wirthian position.

Herbert Gans and the Urban Mosaic

Herbert Gans (1994) contended that the city is a mosaic of many lifestyles, only some of which resemble the cosmopolitanism described by Wirth. Furthermore, he argued that Wirth's key variables—size of population, density, and social heterogeneity—cannot account for most of these lifestyles, and that

his macrosocial analysis does not explain how most city dwellers see their own lives.

Exploring lifestyle diversity in North American cities, Gans identified four types of urban lifestyles: (1) the cosmopolites, (2) the unmarried or childless, (3) the ethnic villagers, and (4) the deprived or trapped. **Cosmopolites** are highly educated, urban sophisticates who choose to live in the city because of its wide range of activities, experiences, and social contacts. They include intellectuals, artists, musicians, writers, and students. The second urban lifestyle, the unmarried or childless, frequently overlaps with the cosmopolite category. It includes single adults or couples without children and/or people whose children are grown up and now on their own. The **ethnic villagers** show almost none of the so-called typical urban characteristics noted by Wirth. Instead, they sustain many rural life patterns in the city by claiming a local area, emphasizing traditional religious beliefs and family ties, and displaying suspicion of outsiders. Gans's remaining category—the deprived or trapped—includes the very poor, the handicapped, those in broken family situations, and those of non-white racial backgrounds who wish to move from deteriorating neighborhoods but lack the financial means to do so.

Wirth and Gans: A Comparison

We must not be too quick to accept the negative judgments from Wirth and other Chicago sociologists. Like their European colleagues, Chicago sociologists were responding to one kind of city—namely, a North American city moving into the high gear of industrialization. Neglecting historical or cross-cultural comparisons limited the significance of their work. How would their evaluation of the urban environment have changed had they, like Weber, looked at other cities in history or in a cross-cultural perspective?

Chicago sociology may be skewed for yet another reason. Park's insistence regarding on-site study, coupled with his interest in urban disorganization and problems, led him and his colleagues to concentrate on the "seamy side" of city life. A glance at the group's classic publications, brilliant though many of them are, reveals this bias: Nels Anderson, *The Hobo* (1923); Ernest Mowner, *Family Disorganization* (1927); Harvey Zorbaugh, *The Gold Coast and the Slum* (1928); Frederich Thrasher, *The Gang* (1929); Clifford Shaw and Henry McKay, *Social Factors in Juvenile Delinquency* (1931); Paul Cressey, *The Taxi Dance Hall* (1932); Norman Hayner, *Hotel Life* (1936); and Edwin H. Sutherland, *The Professional Thief* (1937). Although many other aspects of city urban life exist that might be explored, Wirth based his theory heavily on the evidence supplied by such studies.

Limitations notwithstanding, the Chicago group made great contributions. Park deserves lasting credit for his rejection of armchair theorizing in favor of studying the city firsthand, and Wirth deserves credit for the first true urban theory, which became a persuasive document that dominated the field for the next 20 years. All in all, Chicago sociologists were almost solely responsible for the early growth of urban sociology in the United States (Lofland 1985; Thomas 1983).

Gans's contribution, on the other hand, was to call our attention to the complexities of urban life. Our previous discussion of prominent urban "types" as discerned by Gans is only a partial list. Obviously, there are countless variations of all these lifestyles—and that is the point. So many urban lifestyles exist that it makes little sense to claim, as Wirth did, that the city produces a relatively uniform type of human being.

The rather hard-nosed, calculating person who Wirth hypothesized as being the typical urban dweller does appear—most frequently in the cosmopolite and unmarried or childless categories. Even among these people, however, Wirth's variables of population size, density, and heterogeneity appear to have limited effect. For instance, many cosmopolites can buy the space they need to fend off what they believe is excessive density, just as many ethnic villagers positively thrive in high-density neighborhoods. Population size or scale may increase the number of secondary or segmented relationships, said Gans. Most individuals

maintain as many primary relationships as exist elsewhere, however, because their social focus is on their neighborhood, family, co-workers, and co-religionists. With them, there is no increased social distance because of population density or increased depersonalization because of heterogeneity, as Wirth maintained. Instead, Gans noted, city residents function in smaller social worlds at home, work, and play, enjoying the same life satisfactions as others of their social class in other environments.

Thus, while cities may act on us in much the way that Wirth claimed, we need to keep several limitations in mind. First, few urban lifestyles are found exclusively in the city, and second, the determinants of these lifestyles are largely people's general social class characteristics rather than the city itself (an area we will explore more fully in Chapter 10). That is, cosmopolites live as they do because they are relatively wealthy and highly educated; likewise, the lives of the deprived and the trapped reflect poverty, a lack of skills and schooling, and often enough, racial or ethnic discrimination. We can make a similar argument for any other lifestyle on the list.

Wirth's mistake was in generalizing too much from the urban conditions of the time during which he lived. Observing the incredibly rapid growth of North American and European cities early in the twentieth century, Wirth became convinced the city was a powerful force that would come to dominate human life. A generation later, Gans and others could see that this simply wasn't happening: urban diversity continued to flourish. Today, we can conclude that *urbanization*—the clustering of population in some areas—does not necessarily generate *urbanism*—a single, distinctive way of life.

Claude Fischer and Subcultural Theory

A third approach both accepts and rejects various elements offered by Wirth and Gans. While agreeing with Wirth that something *is* different about the city and its people, Claude S. Fischer (1975, 1995), in what he calls a *subcultural theory of urbanism*, rejects Wirth's main point by

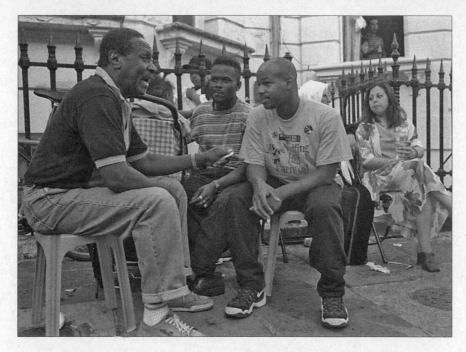

For city residents, the streets are the "rivers of life," where people-watching and social interaction are the everyday norm. This privatization of public space—setting up crates or chairs on the sidewalk, sitting on front stoops or a bench, playing games, or holding a street fair—is the urban equivalent to the suburbanites' front and back yards combined, and it is often a lot more interesting.

insisting that the urban milieu strengthens, rather than destroys, group relationships. Fischer also disagrees with Gans that the different urban lifestyles are incidental, because particular groups of people—for example, ethnic minorities, artistic avant-garde, and professionals—choose to live in the cities and, then, their lifestyles typify cities (1995:544).

Fischer's position is that unlike smaller places, a large city is more culturally heterogeneous, because it has the capacity to develop a greater number of subcultures, the larger size of which enables them to become far more intense and to resist outside influences. How? Because their large numbers in a city allow various types of people to form a **critical mass,** that level needed to generate self-sustaining momentum. Once in a city, people find out about one another, establish their own meeting places, create their own

rituals, and attract still more people (Fischer 1995:545). Examples include the entertainment community in Hollywood, the country music people in Nashville, and the gay community in Philadelphia. Such specialized places rarely exist in non-urban areas, because the critical mass of people of any one type simply isn't there (often because they have moved to a city in order to benefit from precisely the critical mass that Fischer describes).

In other words, to imply, as Gans does, that these lifestyle characteristics produce the same effects in a city of 3 million as they do in a town of 50,000 is simply wrong. The city magnifies these effects in a special way. The diversity of a city brings its residents into far more contact with people from different subcultures than can occur in a town, possibly leading to tension and conflict and, thus, reinforcing group boundaries (Fischer 1995:545).

Interestingly, says Fischer, increased contact also leads to a mutual influence through cultural diffusion—for example, hip hop music moving out of urban black culture and into mainstream urban culture. As elements of the atypical subculture infiltrate the wider urban society, the city develops an unconventionality in comparison to other settings (Fischer 1995: 545–46).

In short, Fischer's theory maintains that Wirth's size, density, and heterogeneity of cities are what generate the social dynamics to produce intense subcultures, as characterized by Gans, leading, in turn, to diffusion into the general characteristics of urban dwellers.

CLASSIC THEORIES AND MODERN RESEARCH: MYTHS AND REALITIES

Is the city a heaven or a hell? Is it a place where the best attributes of human life emerge or where people inevitably "go bad"? The seventeenth-century English poet Abraham Cowley thought he knew the answer when he wrote: "God the first garden made, and the first city, Cain." Was he right? The weight of the classic tradition—European and North American—is on Cowley's side; despite qualifiers and hopeful asides, only Durkheim was mostly optimistic. Wirth's theory symbolizes this verdict. On the one hand, he suggested that people in the city are more tolerant, but on the other hand, he asserted that city people are impersonal and detached from meaningful relationships. Wirth concluded that the city tends toward social pathology (crime, violence, and mental illness), a tendency only made worse as urban density increases.

Are these observations correct? More than seven decades have passed since the publication of Wirth's urban theory. Since then, a great many social scientists have investigated cities and urban life and gathered additional evidence.

Tolerance in the City

Early urban theory contended that the characteristic aloofness and social diversity of the city produced an atmosphere of tolerance, in contrast to the jealous parochialism of the village and small town. Most researchers who have looked closely at the relationship between urban life and tolerance have concluded that a greater tolerance of others' lifestyles and attitudes is, in fact, more prevalent in cities than in rural areas. These findings persist both across time and across different measures of tolerance, even when taking into account such related factors as education and income (Carter et al. 2005).

One factor that may lend itself to greater tolerance in the city is migration. One research study found that tolerance increased among those moving to a city, regardless of the size of the destination community (Wilson 1991). Perhaps geographical mobility—moving to a more heterogeneous locale—also enhances one's mental mobility in relating to strangers.

Impersonality in the City

The dominant characteristics of urban relationships, concluded most of the classical theorists, would be loneliness, indifference, and anonymity. At its most basic level, this argument is built on numerical logic. As the number of people interacting increases, attention becomes distributed more broadly, and so impersonality inevitably must rise. Wirth summarized this argument by saying, "Increase in the number of inhabitants of a community beyond a few hundred is bound to limit the possibility of each member of the community knowing all the others personally" (1964:70).

Yet the "urban anonymity" thesis fails to recognize that many urbanites are not the lonely lot that Wirth and others implied. For example, as early as the 1940s, William F. Whyte's *Street Corner Society* (1981; orig. 1943), a study of an Italian immigrant area in a slum district of Boston, revealed the existence of strong family, neighborhood, and friendship ties. Soon after, other studies (Bruce 1970; Greer 1962; Bell and Boat 1957) confirmed that primary ties were not incompatible with city living. Indeed, in some areas of the city—ethnic neighborhoods, for example—such ties appear to be as intense and intimate as any in rural areas. These self-segregated but close-knit communities enable residents, often with limited proficiency in English, to rely on one another and avoid whatever interethnic prejudice may exist against them (Bouma-Doff 2007).

Ethnicity is not the only bond among urban dwellers. Kinship, occupation, lifestyle, and other personal attributes also form the basis for group ties. For example, many cities contain districts of college students, elderly people, homosexuals, artists and musicians, and wealthy socialites. More broadly, people with interests in common, wherever they may live, may remain in close contact with one another through an interactional network, using the telephone, restaurants and bars, and special meeting places.

Perhaps, however, these are the exceptions. What of the lonely crowd living in all those high rises, the people who don't know any of their neighbors? Doesn't Wirth's theory accurately describe them? Recent research suggests that this notion, too, may be exaggerated. The fact that one does not necessarily know (or want to know) one's urban neighbors does not mean that the urban dweller has no personal relationships. Indeed, what seems to be significant about the urban environment is not the lack of ties of attachment but, rather, how these ties vary. That is, cities seem to encourage alternative types of relationships more than other environments do. Also, it is important to understand that the neighborhood context affects the neighboring ties (Guest et al. 2006). For example, residents in a luxury high rise who engage in similar activities—for example, dog walking, health club, or patronizing the arts—may develop closer relationships with neighbors more easily compared with those in a low-income high rise who may be less likely to engage in shared activities.

Without question, the proliferation of cell phones has had a dramatic impact on our social interactions. By providing more frequent personal conversations without the constraints of access to a landline phone, cell phones enable greater connectivity among people. Such an enhancement of social networking is an important factor in negating the potential impersonality of the city.

In the city, however, meaningful personal relationships are not dependent on spatially defined residence or place; a sense of community may evolve through social networks that integrate and separate, include and exclude, others in meaningful personal relations, communication, and exchanges (Piselli 2007). Think of urban people you know. Most have friends and relatives, but not always in the same building or neighborhood. To expect urban friendship and intimacy to be localized, as they usually are in the village or small town, is to misunderstand urban living (Freudenberg 1992).

In *The Urban Neighborhood* (1968), Suzanne Keller suggested that urban "neighboring" varies markedly—from active and intense relationships to impersonal nods. Working-class people, for example, usually live in "tighter" neighborhoods, whereas upper-middle-class people typically have networks of friends dispersed over a wide area. Similarly, people with children tend to be more "localized" in their orientation compared with single people "on the move." Here, Keller echoes Herbert Gans (1962), who, in a stinging critique, concluded that the "impersonality" Wirth saw in the city *as a whole* characterizes, at best, only the most poverty-stricken and down-and-out of the city's residents. Neighborhood context or environment—including residential stability, levels of affluence, mixed land use, and degree of upkeep in the area—are important considerations for the type of neighbor ties that prevail in urban life (Guest et al. 2006).

Other means for urban connectedness abound. The telephone and the Internet make possible extensive contact without face-to-face interaction. Consider, too, the recent proliferation in cities of voluntary associations, such as film societies, singles bars, health and natural food centers, karate clubs, meditation and yoga centers, and physical fitness centers. Participants in such organizations, living throughout the urban area, often establish primary relationships with one another. Urbanization can thus encourage all kinds of non-kin social ties that may be segmented by activity but that develop through choice and shared interests (Curtis White, and Guest 2003).

Wirth's mistake, and that of other classical theorists, was to allow the most visible aspects of city life, its *public* demeanor, to become the basis of his theory about urban living in general. Although, following Park, he did acknowledge the neighborhood element in city life, he tended to focus his attention on "street behavior." Wirth saw, of course, the hustling, competing, and apparently lonely crowd. By not examining more closely the *private* lives of the city's citizens, however, he inadvertently distorted urban life into a stereotype of impersonality.

We are led, then, to the conclusion that the early analysts took abstract constructions, such as *gemeinschaft* and *gesellschaft*, or mechanical and organic solidarity, as being synonymous with such real, concrete settings as actual villages and cities. The overall social order of the city may place greater emphasis on *gesellschaft*, and the village more toward *gemeinschaft*, but it is incorrect to assume that either *gemeinschaft* or *gesellschaft* exists in any absolute, concrete sense. An important difference exists between the statement that one commonly sees more strangers in cities and the statement that cities are impersonal. In some ways, they are; in other ways, they most certainly are not.

Density and Urban Pathology

Perhaps the most provocative idea put forth by the classical theorists—particularly Simmel, Park, and Wirth—was that human beings react to increasing population density with psychological disorder, such as mental illness, or antisocial behavior, such as crime or aggression.

One source of support for this hypothesis is our own common sense. Probably all of us have experienced some measure of frustration and aggression in crowded settings—trying to push our way through the turnstile at a football stadium, or fuming as hundreds of cars coalesce in a massive traffic jam. It is easy to assume that the place where this occurs—the city—is responsible for our feelings. But are we reacting to the condition of urban crowding, or are we merely experiencing a sense of frustration not that different from what we might feel if our car broke down along a lonely country road?

A second source of the alleged linkage between density and pathology is research that appears to have some bearing on the quality of urban life. For example, John B. Calhoun (1962:139) found that in rat populations, high density produced a reaction he termed a "behavioral sink"—an environment in which aborted pregnancies, higher infant mortality, homosexuality, and cannibalism abounded. Calhoun made no attempt to suggest that human beings would respond in a similar fashion to conditions of crowding, but Edward Hall argued that such a connection was not only plausible but also accurately described urban life. "The implosion of the world population into cities everywhere," Hall wrote, "is creating a series of destructive behavioral sinks more lethal than the hydrogen bomb" (1990:165; orig. 1966).

Hall realized that different groups of people—whites and blacks, for example—might have different cultural expectations about spatial behavior. Yet he appeared to believe that all these different reactions have a biological basis, and that the human species, like rats, has a genetically determined need for a certain amount of space. He asserted that any transgression of this built-in barrier—for example, a crowded apartment or a dense city block—would likely result in pathology.

One problem with this argument is that no one has been able to locate any genetic code for spatial behavior in humans. Until such a linkage can be demonstrated, projecting onto human beings who are living in cities what we know about animal pathology and overcrowding is highly questionable. It may well be, for example, that people's perceived needs for space are entirely *learned*, and that they react negatively to violations of their learned spatial expectations much as they would to an insult against their learned religious beliefs.

Hall also points to the high incidence of "social problems" (addiction and crime) in densely settled, low-income areas of the city. Yet addiction, crime, and crowding may appear together because of some other factor or factors, such as poverty, unemployment, and/or racial discrimination. Moreover, subsequent research has shown that when such factors are taken into account, little or no evidence remains that crowding has any of the negative effects posited by Hall (Evans, Saegert, and Harris 2001; Rousseau and Standing 1995; Lepore and Evans 1991).

Urbanites do contend with crowded conditions, such as crammed elevators and subway cars, rambunctious cabdrivers, the frustrations of traffic, and intense competition for parking spaces. People, however, have one distinct advantage over rats: superior adaptability. First, we live and work on many levels, so we are not continually milling together on the ground. Second, we have codes of urban conduct that guide us to wait in line for the bus, to keep to the right when walking, and to alternate whether we merge or stop at red lights when driving. Cities have bicycle, foot, and horse paths connecting parks and open space that make movement safer and more pleasant. Freeways permit faster travel to and from downtowns, while traffic circles, one-way streets, and coordinated traffic lights ease the traffic flow in crowded areas.

Still, what of the fact that some researchers find crowding does heighten aggression in some people? Perhaps an analogy with listening to music may explain the matter. When you listen to music that you like, turning the volume louder enhances the experience. If you don't like that music, however, an increase in volume only makes the experience more unpleasant. For people with a good support system and a high level of life satisfaction, crowding has little effect, except perhaps temporarily affecting one's mood. On the other hand, if people are already in unpleasant circumstances, have aggressive tendencies, or feel alienated or frustrated, then crowding may well generate further negative reactions. The point is that crowding, in and of itself, does not result in pathological behavior; rather, other factors people bring to the situation may have that effect (Tartaro and Levy 2007; Franklin, Franklin and Pratt 2006; Bonnes et al. 1991).

Finally, in a global context, we see that culture also mediates the experience of city living, influencing how we are affected by population density. For example, Mumbai (Bombay), India, has an extremely high rate of urban crowding but an extremely low homicide rate (National Crime Records Bureau 2007). To cite another example, Turks—whose cultural behavior favors closer interpersonal interaction—do not respond negatively to increased crowding conditions, but given Islamic codes about women in public, they do have coping strategies regarding gender and shared urban space (Mills 2007).

Urban Malaise

A last hypothesis put forth by most of the classical theorists concerned "urban malaise." They suggested that conditions of density aside, the urban environment created loneliness, depression, and anxiety more readily than other types of settlement. Research studies over the past 40 years, however, have found no significant difference in the mental health of urban versus non-urban residents. Instead, such variables as education, income, and self-perceived resources were more closely associated with mental health and depression (Eshbaugh, Lempers, and Luze 2006; Fischer 1973; Hackler 1979; Kadushin 1983; Srole 1972).

Also, as suggested earlier, the neighborhood context—whether it be people's health, social cohesion, or perceptions of problems—is a key factor (Pampalon et al. 2007). If urban residents are socioeconomically disadvantaged, they are more likely to be mistrusting,

URBAN LIVING

How City Dwellers Cope—and Cope Well

How is it possible, given the fast pace and obvious stresses of urban life, that city residents can maintain mental health comparable to that of country folks? One explanation offered by experts: The relationship between stress and mental and physical pathology is dependent not so much on the nature of the stress as on the individual's perception of it. The brain has been called a stimulus-reduction system—a means to reduce, in order to comprehend, the nearly infinite number of stimuli that reach the senses at any given moment. It is an aspect of the brain that seems to be tailor-made for life in the city.

An out-of-towner caught in midtown Manhattan at rush hour, for example, may feel under enormous pressure and strain, but New Yorkers, with their stimulus-reduction mechanism operating at full steam, hardly feel any special stress at all. By the same token, the big-city residents may ignore the loud, the profane, the drunk, and the demented—phenomena that might compromise the mental equilibrium of the uninitiated.

Related statistics support such thinking. Diala and Muntaner (2003) found that rural men reported more mood and anxiety disorders than urban men, perhaps a function of diminishing resources (steady, high-paying jobs) or increasing financial strain, particularly among whites, who comprise a majority of rural residents. No differences by place of residence existed among females. The National Center for Health Statistics (1997) conducted a national self-report survey of negative affect items related to anxiety, depression, and stress among city, suburban, and rural residents. The findings showed little difference in the prevalence of negative mood in metropolitan areas (7.7 percent) versus non-metropolitan areas (7.9 percent). A slightly higher prevalence of negative mood, however, occurred among city residents (8 percent) compared to rural residents (7 percent), but this is hardly sufficient to claim that urbanites experience more stress in their lives than those living outside the city.

especially if their neighborhoods show signs of disorder like graffiti, vandalism, abandoned buildings, noise, crime, or drug use (Ross, Mirowsky, and Pribesh 2002). In Baltimore, for example, neighborhood violent crime was found to have a direct impact on residents' depressive symptoms (Curry, Latkin, and Davey-Rothwell 2008).

Apparently, then, the city, in and of itself, does not create greater psychological distress, but problem neighborhoods do. Elsewhere, the higher population density of urban places may well have positive effects, such as making more people socially accessible to each other. When it comes to city dwellers dealing with their environment, it seems, as the *Urban Living* box on page 144 suggests, that the vast majority do quite well.

Overall, little evidence supports many of the specific claims made by the classical theorists about urban living. The city is clearly not a heaven, but neither is it the hell that some thought it to be. The city is more tolerant than other types of settlement, is not as impersonal as many thought it was, and does not produce greater rates of malaise or other pathologies. On the basis of what we now know, there is reason for more optimism than that shown by most classical theorists. The reality, in short, is both more complex—and more hopeful—than the myths.

New Directions in Urban Sociology

All this research has produced a shift in the way that many urbanists approach their subject matter, because the classic hypotheses about the city advanced by Simmel, Wirth, and others have wilted under careful scrutiny. Research has shown some to be false and others to require serious modification. Emerging from the rubble of the disproved theories was what John Walton (1981) called "the new urban sociology."

Instead of an emphasis on the role of technology or urban ecology, this newer approach of critical urban sociology directs attention toward social conflict, inequality, and change as they affect cities, and it does so within a global context. No single theory captures critical urban sociology, although neo-Marxists and conflict theorists predominate. We will explore this important approach in Chapter 7. Before we do so, however, we will first examine its predecessor, the urban ecological approach.

SUMMARY

The context in which urban sociology emerged was one of remarkable change. Indeed, the ferment associated with the Industrial Revolution was responsible for sociologists noticing the city as an object of study in the first place. What have we learned from them?

First, they suggested specific aspects of the city for urban sociologists to focus on, and second, they attempted to analyze the nature of the city in general. In the latter instance, they had both successes and failures. On the positive side, they correctly saw in the city elements of social life not prominent elsewhere. They saw the city as having more specialized occupations, more formalized interaction patterns, more rationality, and a more rapid tempo of life. On the negative side, they erred in some of their specific claims about the nature of the city. They were right about the existence of greater tolerance, but they exaggerated the city's impersonality. They also seem, on the whole, to have been wrong about urban pathology. The context in which these sociologists wrote played a significant role in their misperceptions. Seeing cities growing by millions of inhabitants with seemingly unconquerable problems, they reasoned that the city itself must be the cause of these ills.

Another limitation is the narrowness of all early theory. Marx and Engels saw cross-cultural differences in how civilization evolved in Western compared with Eastern cities, but they concentrated on the economic system as the basis for all attributes of an urban society. Tönnies and Durkheim employed the comparison of oppositional types but did not consider the city in concrete historical settings. Simmel added the social–psychological dimension, although he, too, considered only cities of one time and place. Weber argued for the importance of exploring cities in cross-cultural and historical perspective but wrote little about the modern city (perhaps a subtle way of indicating that he—like all his colleagues except Durkheim—also saw it in a negative light).

Park and Wirth both provided breakthroughs. Park demanded that on-site city research be an integral part of urban sociology, thereby providing the mechanism for getting beyond the surface impressions of the urban environment. Ironically, however, his focus on urban problems and his lack of a comparative historical frame led him to the same negative conclusions about the city as others. Wirth then tried to build a theory of the city by linking the suggestions of his colleagues. A major difficulty was that he built his theory on Park's skewed database and the somewhat misleading evaluations of the European tradition. Wirth's hypothesis was that the city's unique ecological characteristics—large numbers, density, and social heterogeneity—produce a single characteristic lifestyle. Refuting Wirth's hypothesis, Gans argued that sociocultural characteristics, such as class, age, gender, and race, are the real architects of people's lives.

Countering this claim, Fischer replied that Wirth was not all wrong. In his view, the city's ecological traits do affect people's lives, but not in quite the way that Wirth suggested. Rather than producing an effect directly, Fischer argued, large numbers, density, and heterogeneity intensify other characteristics in order to produce pronounced urban lifestyles.

Recent research has shown that many of the specific claims made by Wirth and his colleagues were incorrect. Early work saw the city as the cause of greater impersonality, poorer mental health, and various forms of stressful or pathological behavior. Modern research, however, has revealed that such broad generalizations are false; the neighborhood context is the best indicator of the attitudes and perceptions of its residents. The new urban sociology, which has emerged in the wake of the classical urbanists' failing theories, sees the city as existing in a complex historical, cultural, and economic global setting.

CONCLUSION

What we take from the classical tradition is its interest in urban studies per se and its combined model of urban analysis. A useful urban analysis must (1) examine the city in both its social–structural and psychosocial dimensions, (2) study actual cities in historical and comparative perspective, (3) be aware that no overarching theory of the city can explain urban life, and (4) evaluate cities in terms of the quality of human life. It will be the task of the remaining chapters to do justice to this tradition.

KEY TERMS

cosmopolites (137)
critical mass (139)
ethnic villagers (137)
false consciousness (119)
gemeinschaft (121)
gesellschaft (121)

ideal type (129)
mechanical solidarity (124)
natural areas (135)
organic solidarity (124)
urbanism (134)

INTERNET ACTIVITIES

1. You can find a clear, succinct list that explains classical and contemporary urban sociology theories at *http://stmarys.ca/~evanderveen/wvdv/ Urban_sociology/urban_sociology_theories.htm/*.

2. A comprehensive and readable introduction to the Chicago School of Sociology can be found at *http://userpages.umbc.edu/~lutters/pubs/ 1996_SWLNote96-1_Lutters,Ackerman.pdf*.

CHAPTER 6

SPATIAL PERSPECTIVES
Making Sense of Space

If you happen to be endowed with topographical curiosity, the hills of San Francisco fill you with an irresistible desire to walk to the top of each one of them. Whoever laid the town out took the conventional checkerboard pattern of streets and without the slightest regard for the laws of gravity planked it down blind on an irregular peninsula that was a confusion of steep slopes and sandhills. The result is exhilarating. Wherever you step out on the street there's a hilltop in one direction or the other. From the top of each hill you get a view and the sight of more hills to the right and left and ahead that offer the prospect of still broader views. The process goes on indefinitely. You can't help making your way painfully to the top of each hill just to see what you can see. . . .

This one is Nob Hill. . . . Ahead of me the hill rises higher and breaks into a bit of blue sky. Sun shines on a block of white houses at the top. Shiny as a toy fresh from a Christmas tree, a little cable car is crawling up it. Back of me under an indigo blue of mist are shadowed roofs and streets and tall buildings with wisps of fog about them, and beyond, fading off into the foggy sky, stretches the long horizontal of the Bay Bridge.

Better go back now and start about my business. The trouble is that down the hill to the right I've caught sight of accented green roofs and curved gables painted jade green and vermillion. That must be in Chinatown. Of course the thing to do is take a turn through Chinatown on the way down toward the business district. . . .

John Dos Passos, "San Francisco Looks West"

In a basic sense, cities are things—complex physical entities. Cities exist within geographic and climatic settings that naturally shape them. The hands and minds of human beings, of course, also play a part as people react to a city's physical setting. San Francisco is an excellent example—people started with an exciting geography and a pleasant climate, then added a host of their own creations (diverse neighborhoods, clattering cable cars, a lively Chinatown, and bridges that span sparkling waters) to produce a particularly enticing urban experience. While San Francisco has its unique features, all cities have a distinct "personality," which is at least partly shaped by the physical layout. This chapter explores that interrelationship between a city and its physical setting.

URBAN GEOGRAPHY

Some cities, like San Francisco, straddle hills. Others, like St. Louis, Tucson, or Oklahoma City, stretch across flat plains. No matter what the topography of the land, however, a city's design reflects its physical environment.

Take, for example, San Francisco's massive neighbor 500 miles to the south—Los Angeles. Originally a Spanish mission outpost, for decades Los Angeles remained a series of scattered communities surrounded by mountains in the relatively flat, near-desert region of California's southwest.

In the 1920s, however, coincident with the rise of the movie industry, Los Angeles began to grow rapidly. As its population surged, the city became a bowl-shaped collection of outlying suburban communities. At first, public transport—electric trains and streetcars—linked the new settlements with Los Angeles. With the mass production of the private automobile, however, public transportation ridership swiftly declined; commuters preferred the convenience and privacy of driving themselves to and from the city. This heavy reliance on automobiles fostered ever-expanding urban sprawl throughout the region and gave us Los Angeles's incredible freeways. Says Jan Morris:

These remain the city's grandest and most exciting artifacts. Snaky, sinuous, undulating, high on stilts or sunk in cuttings, they are like so many concrete tentacles, winding themselves around each block, each district, burrowing, evading, clambering, clasping every corner of the metropolis as if they are squeezing it all together to make the parts stick. They are inescapable, not just visually, but emotionally. They are always there, generally a few blocks away; they enter everyone's lives, and seem to dominate all arrangements. (2003:230)

As Los Angeles expanded, people settled the mountains themselves, with streets "forever ribbing and probing further into [the] perimeter hills, twisting like rising water ever higher, ever deeper into their canyons, and sometimes bursting through to the deserts beyond" (Morris 2003:229).

Ironically, the city's increasing population, heavy reliance on the automobile, and geography combined to produce an unexpected but monumental environmental problem: smog. Although Los Angeles is by no means the only city beset by this threat to health, its smog problem has been particularly serious, because the surrounding hills trap noxious fumes in the bowl-shaped region where most of the city's people live. Only recently has the problem lessened, thanks to California's "toughest in the nation" pollution laws. Despite its air-quality problems, the Los Angeles area continues to grow—from about 3 million in 1980 to nearly 3.9 million in 2006—and the automobile still reigns supreme.

The Location of Cities

Geography and climate, then, provide the physical conditions to which urbanites must adapt. In fact, certain physical characteristics usually determine whether an area even becomes a city at all.

Look at Figure 6–1, which shows the geographical location of the 36 most populous urban areas in North America. All but a few are located on waterways. They are either seaports (Los Angeles, New York, and Vancouver), lakeports (Chicago, Milwaukee, and Toronto), or on major rivers (Cleveland,

Memphis, and Montreal). The advantage of such sites for stimulating trade is enormous. Even cities not on important waterways (Dallas, Denver, Fort Worth, and Phoenix), however, are where they are because, at least initially, there were enough streams and lakes to support their populations.

The sole exception to the waterway thesis is Atlanta. Yet its site, too, was determined by a geographical consideration: In the 1840s, because of its centrality to the rest of the South, Atlanta was selected as the southern terminus of the Western and Atlantic Railroad. Thus, even Atlanta illustrates that environmental considerations play a key role in locating a city. With this in mind, we will consider briefly the sites of five other cities: Houston, Miami, Montreal, Salt Lake City, and Washington, D.C. What products and activities do you associate with each?

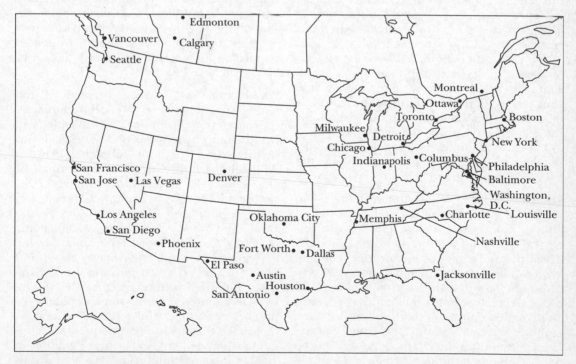

FIGURE 6–1 Geographical Location of the 36 Most Populous North American Metropolitan Areas, 2007
Source: U.S. Census Bureau, 2008, Table 20, pp. 25–6.

Houston. Located near the East Texas oil fields, this city has been booming since the 1950s. Between 1970 and 2006, its metropolitan population more than doubled, reaching 5.5 million. Because of oil—every major oil company has offices in Houston—and cheap shipping of oil via the Gulf of Mexico, the city has the nation's second-busiest port in the country (after New York) and the nation's largest port in international tonnage. Considered by many as the "energy capital of the world," Houston is home to more than 5,000 energy-related companies. It is also home to the largest medical center in the world (52,000 employees) and second only to New York City as home to the headquarters of *Fortune* 500 companies (Houston 2008).

Miami. Although Miami is a port, this city is best known for tourism and as a mecca for retirement. The winter climate is ideal, with temperatures hovering near the 80s, nearly unlimited sun, and endless beaches. "Fun in the Sun" is the city's motto. In recent years, however, Miami has become a major market for specialized goods, primarily because of its large Cuban American community. Because of the Cubans' economic success, the city has become attractive to wealthy Latin Americans. They fly to Miami, stay in or near Little Havana, speak nothing but Spanish, and buy numerous U.S. goods—clothes, computers, stereos—from Cuban merchants at prices much lower than they would pay at home. Such visitors are crucial to maintaining the city's economy (Miami 2008).

Montreal. Built on and around a mountain slope at the junction of the St. Lawrence and Ottawa River systems in the southwestern corner of Quebec, Montreal is North America's fifteenth-largest metropolitan area, containing 3.6 million people (Statistics Canada 2008a). Although Montreal has a strong, diversified industrial base, service dominates its economy. Many national and international service companies, especially in the banking, culture, finance, telecommunications, and transportation sectors, are headquartered there. Montreal also accounts for one-fourth of all corporate

research and development expenditures in Canada (twice its share by population). Long, cold winters have prompted an expansive and delightful underground network of shops, restaurants, and theaters that people enjoy year-round. Montreal also is home to four professional sports franchises, a ballet company, an opera company, and a symphony orchestra (Montreal 2008).

Salt Lake City. Situated at the foot of a mountain range near the forbidding and barren Great Salt Lake in Utah, Salt Lake City might seem an unlikely urban site. The Mormons, however, thought otherwise. Migrating westward in the mid-nineteenth century, looking for a place where they could practice their religion freely, the Mormon leaders saw the Salt Lake region as the place that God had set aside for them. In a sense, the region's remoteness was the key to its founding. As it turned out, the location is more hospitable than it appeared at first glance. Salt Lake City became a point of rest and departure for westward migration, and the salt proved to be a valuable resource. The city became the only area within hundreds of miles able to support a large metropolitan population, numbering well over 1 million in 2006 (Salt Lake City 2008).

Washington, D.C. In the capital of the United States, we have a very different case. Its founders did not look on Washington, D.C., as an economic center. The issue was politics—a wish to avoid choosing between Philadelphia and New York as the permanent U.S. capital. In addition, Washington, D.C., represented a symbolic link between two great regions: the North, and the South. Once the Potomac River basin (water again!) became the site of the nation's capital city, the emergence of the United States as a world power generated a vast government bureaucracy, hundreds of foreign embassies, countless special interest groups, and a vast array of hotels, restaurants, and national landmarks that make this urban area unique. Its metropolitan population grew from 4.1 million in 1990 to about 5.3 million in 2006 (U.S. Census Bureau 2008a:26).

Geography has played a large role in Montreal's existence. The junction of the St. Lawrence and Ottawa rivers affected its location choice, and the sloping mountain terrain dictated the layout of its expansion. Its long, cold winters influenced the building of an extensive underground mall of shops, restaurants, and theatres that are as lively as any aboveground complex found elsewhere.

Why Cities Are Where They Are

Environmental, economic, and social factors play a role in creating an urban area. On the environmental side, any setting, in order to become a city, must fulfill a number of basic conditions.

Environment. First and foremost, the location must be a *minimally hospitable environment.* It cannot be infested with disease-producing organisms, be subject to extreme heat or cold, or exist on a flood plain. On that last point, the flooding of more than 400 city blocks in Cedar Rapids, Iowa, in July 2008, and of 80 percent of New Orleans in August 2005, was the result of an unusual congruence of weather conditions (see the *Cityscape* box on page 152).

In addition, any city requires *access to adequate supplies of food, water, and building materials.* This is not to say that cities cannot overcome the limitations of some sites, but

settlers' ingenuity and technology must be up to the task. For example, gas and oil heat have made winter survival in northern cities possible for millions, just as air conditioning moderates the extreme heat of southern urban areas. Similarly, water and other resources can be imported. Las Vegas, situated in the Nevada desert, is perhaps the best example of an "impossible" city brought to life by modern technology.

Economics. Another driving force in situating cities is economics. Port cities, for example, usually thrive as centers of trade and commerce. Alfred Weber (1868–1958), the younger brother of Max Weber, formulated an **industrial location theory** that helps explain the locale of many industrial cities. He suggested that an industry would locate where the transportation costs of both raw materials and the final product would be the lowest. If the raw material, such as metal ore, weighed

CITYSCAPE

New Orleans: Paying the Price for Its Location

Its strategic location at the mouth of the Mississippi River allowed New Orleans to emerge as an important break-of-bulk city, making its port the fifth busiest in the country. Farmers in the Midwest send their crops down the river in barges, and the grains are then loaded onto 5,000 ships annually from 60 nations. As a result, the United States is the world's largest exporter of corn, soybeans, and wheat. It is not just agricultural exports, however, that make New Orleans so important. The Mississippi River links into the Ohio, Illinois, and Missouri rivers, and manufacturers from across the Midwest depend on 50,000 inland river barges to carry their products to world export through New Orleans. Leading imports include cocoa beans, coffee, rubber, and steel. In addition, more than 700,000 passengers sail through the port on cruise lines each year (Port of New Orleans 2008). Thus, the devastation to the city in 2005 as a result of Hurricane Katrina had a negative ripple effect on the economy and people far beyond the impacted area.

Moreover, the city's vulnerability to flooding—long known to government officials but never effectively countered—became painfully obvious to even the most casual observer. Although the older part of the city was built on higher ground, as New Orleans expanded, development occurred elsewhere. As a result, major portions of the city are below sea level, protected by levees and seawalls designed to guard against storm surges about 20 feet high. In 2005, however,

the damage was done by much higher surges from the Gulf's waters and by the waters of Lake Pontchartrain at the city's northern boundary. This oval-shaped lake is about 40 miles wide from east to west, and it measures about 24 miles from north to south. The heavy rains and winds of Hurricane Katrina were more than the lake's levees could withstand, and in several places, they broke, flooding about 80 percent of the city. The loss of life (1,500 dead), the struggles of the survivors, and the devastation of families, homes, businesses, and personal belongings touched people's hearts everywhere.

More than 800,000 people, mostly black, were forced to relocate, creating one of the greatest scatterings of people in U.S. history. Other cities—most notably Houston, which took in about 200,000 evacuees, giving them housing and health care and offering job fairs—stepped in to offer a place to stay. Since then, some evacuees have returned, but many others have chosen to stay where they are (Nossiter 2007). As a result, New Orleans, which had a 2005 pre-Katrina population of 452,000, had only about 240,000 by the end of 2007, and the racial mix had shifted from being two-thirds black to nearly three-fourths white (Brookings 2008).

Water was the chief reason for the settlement, growth, and destruction of New Orleans. Although it will take years and billions of dollars, the city will be rebuilt, because its strategic location demands that. The levees and walls protecting the new New Orleans, however, will be made much stronger against the forces of nature so that, hopefully, the large bodies of water to the city's north and south cannot again wreak such havoc.

more, then the processing plant would locate closer to its source; if the final product, such as bottled beer, weighed more, then the processing plant would locate closer to its market.

Weber also included cheaper labor and agglomerate—the clustering of support industries in the same area, such as a city—as being key elements in the least-cost, maximize-profits decision about where to locate. For example, the availability of cheap labor (as in Southeast Asia today) may override the greater costs of transporting raw materials or finished products over a greater distance. Critics of this theory point out its failure to recognize the many variations in market demand, transportation costs, labor availability, and the wide range of products from manufacturing plants for diverse markets, but it nonetheless offers insights regarding the role of geography (in the locational triangle of raw materials, processing, and market) in the sites of manufacturing cities during North America's industrial age (Puu 2003).

Social. After meeting basic environmental conditions and economic considerations, social factors come into play. We will look at seven such factors, using the five cities just discussed as illustrations:

1. Some cities are situated at a **natural crossroads** for a region. Montreal, for example, is the most important port on the St. Lawrence River and Seaway, lying between the Atlantic Ocean to the east and the Great Lakes to the west. Other examples are St. Louis and Chicago, with the latter nicknamed "the crossroads of the nation." Such crossroads facilitate the concentration of people, services, and especially, trade goods.

2. Other cities develop because they are located at what economists call **break-of-bulk** points. These are locations where a good—the "bulk"— is transferred from one type of transportation to another—say, from truck to ship. Houston is a break-of-bulk point for oil. In such places, goods often are warehoused for a time or processed in some way in order to make the next leg of the trip more economical. When this happens, a city develops a set of subindustries that deal with storing or processing. In Houston, oil to be shipped from the city often is stored in huge tanks before its subsequent refinement into gasoline or heating oil. A smaller city, Buffalo, rose to prominence because, as the western end of the Erie Canal, the city served as the transshipment point for grain sent eastward for the North Central states via Lake Erie and the canal. There, mills processed the grain into flour, which was then shipped by rail to the large East Coast markets (Klein 2005:316).

   Furthermore, the break-of-bulk function of cities is an enduring feature. The *Cityscape* box on page 155 describes two cases separated by

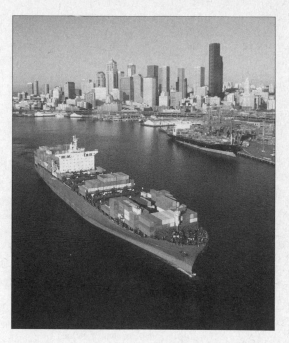

Located at Puget Sound, an inlet of the Pacific Ocean, Seattle is a major seaport and break-of-bulk city, handling more than 1,000 vessels annually. Container ships bring in such imports as wearing apparel, video games, footwear, and motor vehicle parts, while exports consist of inorganic chemicals; beef, pork, and poultry; oilseeds; and industrial equipment.

more than a century. Note the striking similarities between Charles Dickens's description of 1860 London and Vincent Parrillo's comments about contemporary Seattle.

3. Another major reason for a city's location is access to some valuable *raw material*. Montreal's early history rested heavily on its colonial fur trade. Today, this city remains an important shipping center, handling the millions of gallons of petroleum that are processed each day by Montreal-Est refineries. Similarly, Houston and its refineries are near the East Texas oilfields; San Francisco boomed in the mid-nineteenth century because it was the closest port to the Sierra Nevada gold mines; and Pittsburgh's greatness was largely a result of proximity to coal mines that afforded cheap power for its steel mills.

4. Miami suggests another reason for a city location. Here, we have an **amenity city,** located in a particular place because it provides certain surroundings—sea, surf, sand, and

The lights of a city such as Toronto at night offer strikingly beautiful visual images while simultaneously illustrating its ongoing life and activities after dark. Toronto's strategic location on the shore of Lake Ontario enhances its economic vitality, making this metropolitan area home to more than 6 million people—one-fourth of Canada's total population.

sun—that are not easily available elsewhere. In its recent guise as "Latin America's super-market," this predominantly Spanish-speaking city boasts a complete array of North American goods for sale. Much the same is true of Orlando (home of Disney World) and many other Florida cities as well. Similarly, Las Vegas offers the attraction of gambling to westerners, as Atlantic City does to people on the East Coast and Monte Carlo does to Europeans. Other amenity cities are Hot Springs, Arkansas, and Bath, England (both renowned for their hot mineral waters), as well as Innsbruck, Austria (a world-class skiing city).

5. Washington, D.C., is an example of an **administrative or political city,** a city established primarily for governmental purposes, as was Ottawa, Canada's national capital. Two international examples are Canberra, Australia, and Brasilia, Brazil, both constructed in the twentieth century.

6. Closely related historically to the administrative function has been a city's *strategic military location.* That is, many cities began in easily defensible spots (Athens and Quebec City), and

others, such as London, began because they offered military access into a whole region.

7. Finally, cities flourish for *religious or educational reasons.* Salt Lake City prospered as the home of Mormonism. In a similar way, Mecca in Saudi Arabia is the fountainhead of Islam, and Jerusalem is a focal point of no fewer than three major world religions: Christianity, Islam, and Judaism. University cities, such as Cambridge in England, Ithaca in New York (home of Cornell University), and Berkeley in California (site of one of the main campuses of the University of California), are cities that achieved prominence for educational reasons.

A combination, then, of geographic and climatic conditions and of social and economic factors explains why cities are where they are. Where many advantages come together, a city typically gains special importance. New York's prominence rests on its location as a natural port, an easily defended island, a gateway to a huge hinterland rich with raw materials, a natural break-of-bulk point, and a crossroads for people.

CITYSCAPE

Break-of-Bulk in Two Cities

In the following passage, Charles Dickens describes London's River Thames in early morning, as seen from a small boat traveling downstream.

Nineteenth-Century London

Early as it was, there were plenty of scullers going here and there that morning, and plenty of barges . . . and we went ahead among many skiffs and wherries, briskly.

Old London Bridge was soon passed, and old Billingsgate market with its oysterboats and Dutchmen, and the White Tower and Traitor's Gate, and we were in among the tiers of shipping. Here, were the Leith, Aberdeen, and Glasgow steamers, loading and unloading goods, and looking immensely high out of the water as we passed alongside; here, were colliers by the score and score, with the coal-whippers plunging off stages on deck as counterweights to measures of coal swinging up, which were then rattled over the side into barges; here, at her moorings, was tomorrow's steamer for Rotterdam . . . and here tomorrow's for Hamburg, under whose bowsprit we crossed.

In the next passage, Vincent Parrillo describes a similar morning, only this time more than a century later and in a major U.S. port.

Modern Seattle

Even to the casual observer, the Port of Seattle is a busy place, filled with freighters, tugboats, barges, commercial fishing vessels, and pleasure craft. Geographically closer to Asia than any other major U.S. port, its natural deep-water harbor attracts commercial shippers from throughout the Pacific Rim. It is one of the largest U.S. container ports, one of the leading distribution centers on the West Coast, and the top U.S. port in container tonnage exports to Asia (over 6 million metric tons annually). Today ships from Japan, Singapore, and Taiwan are anchored at the docks, each by one of 28 commercial marine terminals.

At these terminals the container cranes transfer auto parts; bamboo baskets; electronic, household, and plastic products; foods; tools; and a variety of other products to an on-dock intermodal rail facility for direct shipment to inland destinations. Elsewhere, toplifts and fork-lifts transfer shipments to the 1.5 million square feet of warehouse storage space in the Terminal 106 Complex, to other outdoor storage areas, or to the waiting trucks at the 20 loading docks.

Everywhere the eye turns, one sees the bustling activity of workers: Longshoremen, stevedores, crane and forklift operators, grain terminal operators, truckers, railway men, foremen, and supervisors—are all unloading, storing, or loading the imports or exports passing through this port.

Source: Charles Dickens, *Great Expectations* (London: Chapman and Hall, 1860), from Chapter 54; and Vincent N. Parrillo's field research in Seattle.

Finally, if the balance between a city's physical environment and people's social or economic needs and interests shifts, the city must adapt—or else it will decline. History is strewn with the ruins of cities that were unable to adapt, including the ancient Egyptian capital of Luxor and the Mayan city of El Mirador. On the other hand, cities sometimes survive great geographic and/or economic disasters. San Francisco is the best-known U.S. case, having recovered from the calamity of the 1906 earthquake to become one of the most vibrant U.S. cities.

THE SHAPE OF THE CITY

Once cities begin, what determines the form or physical shape they take? The answer depends on the city's social and economic functions.

To begin, consider that Athens is spread around the natural hilltop of the Acropolis; Edinburgh is similarly sited around a massive, extinct volcanic peak in Scotland; and Paris and Mexico City were initially situated on islands. These examples suggest that defense was one of the prime interests of these city dwellers. Durham, in northern England, provides another example. Founded about 1000 C.E., Durham is situated atop a high, steep peninsula formed by the Wear River. Even if one could get across the river, the sides of the steep ridge are extremely difficult to scale. Naturally protected on three sides, the founders of Durham only had to defend the narrow fourth side, and so here they built their heavily fortified castle.

The Radiocentric City

The importance of defense prompted preindustrial people to build cities in the form of a great container, protected by natural geographic features (Durham's steep slope) and human constructs, such as walls, moats, castles, or battlements. Urbanists characterize such cities as **radiocentric cities,** because they radiate outward from a common center.

A wonderful example of this urban form is preindustrial Baghdad, Iraq (Figure 6–2). Set within an outer wall that had four fortified gates, the inner core of the city—containing the ruling caliph's palace and the mosque—was further protected by two rings of densely packed residential quarters, where the city's poor people lived. Along the main access roads leading from the gates to the core, arcades or shops provided easy shopping access for Baghdad's inhabitants.

Not all radiocentric cities, however, have a perfectly radial shape. Ming Peking (see Figure 9–2) was heavily walled and had a moat for defense, yet it took the shape of a series of rectangles and squares attached to and within one another. These shapes reflect the Chinese cosmology of the 1400s, which led planners to arrange the city on the points of the compass—north, south, east, and west.

Other considerations also encourage cities to develop a radial shape. As any city grows,

FIGURE 6–2 The Radiocentric City: Baghdad, circa 146–762 C.E.

Source: Roberts/Hugh, *Urban Profile of the Middle East,* Palgrave, reproduced with permission of Palgrave Macmillan.

people want to be as close to the center as possible in order to make travel easier. Because a circle places the most people closest to the center, many cities grow in a ring-like fashion around a central core. As anyone who has ever gazed out an airplane window at night knows, most cities look like huge wheels, with central spokes radiating outward. These spokes—highways and rail lines—suggest another reason for the city's generally radial form. Because the shortest route to the center of a circle is a straight line, people build access roads to the city as directly as possible. That practice suggests the origin of one of history's best-known sayings: "All roads lead to Rome."

The Gridiron City

Despite the common radial pattern of most of the world's cities, the downtown areas of well-known North American cities—Atlanta, Chicago, Los Angeles, Montreal, New York, Philadelphia, Toronto, and Vancouver—are not of a radiocentric design. Indeed, while radiocentric center cities are the rule in much of the world, that form is the exception in North America.

Closer to home, we find **gridiron cities,** composed of straight streets crossing at right angles to create many regular city blocks. This form is typical of cities built after the Industrial Revolution. Only then did cities place such importance on economic activity, and a city gridiron plan facilitates the movement of people and products throughout the city. This form is also an efficient way to divide land—and to sell it as real estate. Figure 6–3 shows a notable preindustrial exception: William Penn's 1682 plan for selling lots in Philadelphia.

Grid patterns do not always result from careful planning, however. Typically, when a settlement begins, merchants favor a main-street location that allows people to shop and move from one store to another along the street. Furthermore, open-ended streets serve business well, because they allow room for growth as well as easy access to and from the shopping area. The U.S. and Canadian Midwest and West are full of such "Main Street" towns. If, in time, another major street crosses the original street, then we see the beginnings of a gridiron around "four corners" that may well expand from there.

URBAN ECOLOGY

As we discussed in Chapter 5, Robert Park and his fellow Chicago sociologists used cities as a laboratory to study social life. Their research generated the science of **human ecology,** a term coined by Park that focused on what he viewed as an orderly evolution of urban growth and development:

> There are forces at work within the limits of the urban community . . . which tend to bring about an orderly and typical grouping of its population and institutions. The science which seeks to isolate these factors and to describe the typical constellations of persons and institutions which the cooperation of these forces produce is what we call human, as distinguished from plant and animal, ecology. (1984:1–2)

Using the ecological approach that studies the relationship between living things and their environment, Park investigated how human beings live in their urban world. He believed that the evolutionary struggle for survival was evident in the everyday *competition for scarce resources,* such as food, clothing, shelter, and land.

FIGURE 6–3 The Gridiron City: William Penn's Philadelphia Plan, 1682

Boston grew from a small, walled, colonial city to an important city of commerce, annexing such adjoining municipalities as Brighton, Charlestown, Dorchester, Roxbury, and West Roxbury between 1868 and 1874. Today, it is a large metropolis, utilizing its waterways to full advantage, both commercially and recreationally.

Emerging from this competition were different clusters of activity that Park called **natural areas:** business districts, ethnic neighborhoods, skid rows, and rooming-house areas.

For Park, urban competition is not only economic; it is also about *power*. People compete for control of parks, streets, and ethnic districts—and, above all, for the prestige that comes from living in a fashionable neighborhood or having an impressive occupation.

Beyond competition, Park noted that large- scale *population movements* also influence urban development. Most of the immigrants who came to Park's Chicago and other growing North American cities a century ago had little education and few skills. They were also exceedingly poor. With few options, they poured into overcrowded housing in the center cities and took low-paying jobs in factories. As they did in cities across the continent, immigrants or their descendants later moved, leaving their old neighborhoods to the next poor group to enter the city. The Chicago sociologists called this shifting of population **invasion-succession.**

Concentric Zones

To Park, competition and population movement both shaped and reshaped cities. The more economically successful residents selected the choice city locations for their businesses and homes, leaving the less desirable locations to the less successful. In this process, claimed Park, the city as a whole took on broad, spatial patterns characteristic of an economic hierarchy. In the mid-1920s, one of Park's students, Ernest W. Burgess, suggested that a city develops somewhat the way a tree does—growing outward in a series of concentric rings or zones over time.

Although Burgess assumed that economic competition was central to urban life, he, like Park, also saw other social forces at work. Moving to a suburb, for example, is not just an economic consideration; it also confers prestige, suggesting that people have "made it." Burgess described the city in terms of four main zones, with a fifth commuter's zone

outside the city limits (see the right side of Figure 6–4). In his words:

This chart represents an ideal construction of the tendencies of any town or city to expand radially from its central business district—on the map "The Loop" (I). Encircling the downtown area there is normally an area in transition, which is being invaded by business and

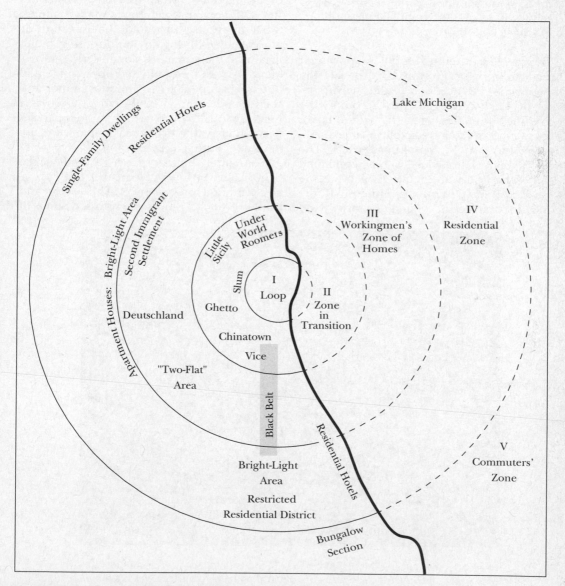

FIGURE 6–4   Chicago's Concentric Zones

Source: From "The Growth of the City," in Robert E. Park and Ernest W. Burgess, eds., *The City*. Copyright © 1967 University of Chicago Press. Reprinted with permission of the University of Chicago Press.

light manufacture (II). A third area (III) is inhabited by the workers in industries who have escaped from the area of deterioration (II) but who desire to live within easy access of their work. Beyond this zone is the "residential area" (IV) of high-class apartment buildings or of exclusive "restricted" districts of single family dwellings. Still farther, out beyond the city limits, is the commuters' zone (V)—suburban areas, or satellite cities—within a thirty- to sixty-minute ride of the central business district. (1984:50; orig. 1925).

Burgess illustrated his model by applying it directly to the Chicago of his day (the left side of Figure 6–4). Once we take the "halving effect" of Lake Michigan into account (the heavy line shows the city's edge by the lake), Burgess's theory did a creditable job in explaining the location of the city's districts. The most valuable land (Zone I) was contained within "The Loop" downtown, which was the exclusive preserve of business. In Zone II, the "zone in transition," stood factories and slums, the latter overflowing with down-and-out roomers and ethnic groups of various sorts, including Italians (Little Sicily) and Chinese (Chinatown). Zone III, the zone of working-men's homes, was predominantly inhabited by second-generation migrants, the descendants of earlier Chicago immigrants who had taken the first step in escaping the inner city by moving out of the slums. Here, too, was the "two-flat" area, in which two families occupied two-family houses instead of the usual four or more families living in multihousing buildings, as in the inner city. Zone IV was the "residential area," dominated by residential hotels, apartment areas, and most important, single-family homes. In this zone, too, was a relatively wealthy "restricted" residential district, an area that excluded people with "undesirable" ethnic or racial traits.

Soon after the emergence of the Chicago School, two other ecological growth theories achieved prominence. The sector and multiple nuclei theories addressed some of

Paterson, New Jersey—the first planned U.S. industrial city—typifies an old manufacturing city. In classic sector theory patterning, many of its factories lined the railroad tracks, and its fashionable district moved eastward along Broadway to the high ground of Manor Hill. No longer thriving, the city struggles to maintain a solid economic base.

the shortcomings of the Park and Burgess approach.

Sectors

Homer Hoyt (1939) noticed that numerous city districts did not conform to the purely concentric model suggested by Burgess. Even in Burgess's Chicago (see Figure 6–4), unusual areas like the "Deutschland Ghetto" (the home of German immigrants) and the "Black Belt" obviously cut across zones. Consequently, Hoyt studied, block-by-block, the residential patterns of 142 cities in three different time periods—1900, 1915, and 1936—adding an important historical dimension. The scope of his study was a major advance over Burgess's work, which was based almost exclusively on Chicago.

First, Hoyt found that high-prestige, fashionable districts formed sectors of varying size. Sec-

ond, despite a rough concentric shape to the cities, many sectors took on a pie-shaped form rather than resembling an entire ring (Figure 6–5). Third, lower-income districts often abutted and, sometimes, even surrounded fashionable districts. A classic example is Harlem's "Striver's Row" of the 1920s and 1930s, a wealthy, two-block oasis of pristine buildings (West 138th and 139th Streets between Seventh and Eighth Avenues) surrounded by other buildings approaching utter collapse. Fourth, Hoyt found a tendency, as time passed, for sectors to move out of the city radially, along a path begun by the sector in earlier years (Seattle provides a good example).

Fifth, in the later periods, cities revealed two or three fashionable areas in different places, with factors other than competition and population movement influencing this process. Often, the wealthy neighborhoods in many cities stood on "high ground"—Boston's

FIGURE 6–5 Shifts in the Location of Fashionable Residential Areas in Three American Cities, 1900–1936. Fashionable areas are indicated by shading.

Source: Adapted from Homer Hoyt, *The Structure and Growth of Residential Neighborhoods in American Cities* (Washington, D.C.: Federal Housing Administration, 1939), p. 115, figure 40.

Beacon Hill, for instance—indicating a preference by the wealthy to be "above" the city's poorer residents. Elsewhere, high-prestige sectors located for aesthetic reasons, such as on waterfronts, while still others located along main transportation lines that facilitated easy access to the center city.

Multiple Nuclei

Although Hoyt's study was a major advance over the Burgess model, it was limited by a focus on residential sectors. Hoyt imagined that industry, too, moved radially outward from the center city—upriver or along railroad lines, for instance—but he never investigated this hunch.

Cities experiencing their greatest growth during the automobile age, like Houston pictured above, have massive freeway approaches and interchanges as well as generally wider streets and more car-friendly services (parking and drive-in facilities) than older cities do. These cities are typically situated in warm climes, on fairly level land, and with port access being less necessary.

Chauncy Harris and Edward Ullman (1945) argued that as the contemporary city grew, it diversified, developing many distinct sectors of activity rather than retaining one center. Modern cities typically have a major central business district (CBD, sector 1 in Figure 6–6), but various historical, cultural, and economic factors specific to a given city generate other districts. For example, wholesale light manufacturing (sector 2 in Figure 6–6) might be near the CBD, with low-income residences (sector 3) in various separate districts nearby. A medium-income residential area (sector 4) might abut the CBD and give way on its outer edge to a high-income residential area (sector 5). Between these two areas might exist a secondary business district (sector 7) and, farther out, a completely separate residential suburb (sector 8). Heavy manufacturing (sector 6) might lie a relatively large distance from the CBD

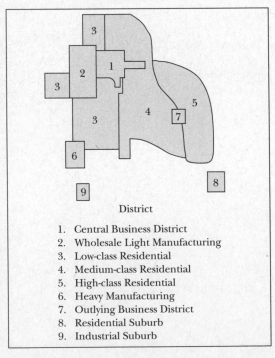

District

1. Central Business District
2. Wholesale Light Manufacturing
3. Low-class Residential
4. Medium-class Residential
5. High-class Residential
6. Heavy Manufacturing
7. Outlying Business District
8. Residential Suburb
9. Industrial Suburb

FIGURE 6–6 The Multiple Nuclei Theory

Source: From Chauncy O. Harris and Edward L. Ullman, "The Nature of Cities," *The Annals 242* (Nov. 1945), American Academy of Political and Social Science.

and evolve an industrial–residential suburb (sector 9) nearby.

Why do multiple nuclei develop? First, certain types of activities require specialized facilities. For example, heavy manufacturing requires a great deal of space. A century ago, space was plentiful downtown. In recent decades, however, space near the CBD has become hard to find and, when it can be found, expensive. Many modern factories also require more floor space on one level. As a result, much heavy manufacturing has moved from the CBD to outlying industrial areas, where land is readily available and taxes are often lower. In Chicago, for example, heavy manufacturing once located in the CBD has moved to the southeast, around Gary, Indiana.

Second, multiple CBDs can be the result of annexation. As the city absorbs a nearby municipality into its political domain, that preexisting CBD may evolve further as a secondary business district. This is particularly true of the so-called "spread cities," such as Phoenix, that have expanded greatly in the age of the private automobile. As it becomes more time-consuming to travel into the central city's CBD for shopping, entertainment, or business-related activities, other CBDs emerge within the boundaries of large, outlying areas in order to accommodate those inconvenienced by a longer commute into the city center.

Perhaps the most important contribution of Harris and Ullman's theory is that it seriously questions the notion that urban land use is predictable at all. Burgess's zonal hypothesis and, to a lesser extent, Hoyt's sector theory both implied certain inevitable patterns of land use. In contrast, Harris and Ullman's multiple nuclei theory suggests that a mix of historical, cultural, and economic situations both shapes and reshapes every city. Even the core CBD might fall into decline, as it has in some smaller cities.

Limitations

Although he based his model on Chicago, Burgess thought his concentric zone hypothesis would describe any city. Do other cities and towns conform to the concentric zone pattern? Certainly, some do. For example, an examination of changes in land use for the Moscow metropolitan area revealed concentric zones of outwardly declining land-use intensity (Ioffe and Nefedova 2001). A longitudinal study (1950–1980) of 318 U.S. metropolitan areas found that such evolving patterns occurred among industrially based, older, larger, more dispersed metropolitan communities in the Northeast (Schwirian, Hankins, and Ventresa 1990:1143).

Hoyt's sector theory offered a helpful description of urban expansion along major highways and, later, along interstate highways built through a massive federal construction program begun during the 1950s, which contributed to the development of suburbia. Still, it was a descriptive analysis only, as was the multiple nuclei model, which more effectively described a spread city or metropolitan areas with their large complexes of shopping malls as well as office and industrial parks (usually along those major highways).

Critics, however, questioned all three ecological models' suggestion of uniformity within zones and their reliance on concepts of unrestrained competition and large population movements. These vary in their intensity at different locales and time periods and, even then, may or may not play a key role in a city's growth and development. Other forces— for example, globalization, technological advances in production, communication, and transportation—can impact on how a city's spatial development occurs.

Finally, some critics dismiss the very idea of "urban ecology" as "too biological." That is, the principles of plant and animal ecology are inadequate to explain human activity. People, unlike plants, are thinking creatures who reflect and act creatively on their urban environment. The urban ecological approach pays little attention to the roles played by (1) choice, (2) culture in the city, and (3) community. In other words, this approach ignores important social considerations.

Such criticism has diminished the importance of the urban ecological approach and its various models for urban development over time—and, in fact, has even changed the essence of this field. Today, the field of **ecological sociology,** with its own organizations and journals, includes urban ecologists who use urban design, land-use planning, and policy reform to help communities plan and build neighborhoods that are environmentally sound (Urban Ecology 2008). To understand the unfolding processes of urban growth and vitality, a host of alternative theories and approaches suggest that the forces shaping land use are more complex than the early urban ecologists suspected.

SOCIAL AREA ANALYSIS AND MAPPING

One current technique to describe urban land use is comparing the socioeconomic characteristics of urbanites living in different census tracts. A **census tract** averages about 4,000 residents, and it typically contains relatively homogeneous units with respect to population characteristics, economic status, and living conditions (see the *Cityscape* box on page 165). Using these social attributes, social scientists can classify each census tract and then compare it with others to create a detailed profile of the larger urban community. For example, analysts can identify the level of segregation in a city based on the clustering of racial and ethnic groups in each census tract, or how one neighborhood differs from another in educational level, income, number of children, type of housing, or whether the mother worked. Such analysis enables social scientists to describe and distinguish the social characteristics that are found among urban neighborhoods, because numerous variations serve as the foundation of a community's social structure.

Social area analysis proved to be a helpful statistical technique, not only for identifying social class, family status, and minority patterns in cities but also for comparative studies measuring changes in these areas over time. In addition, this approach is most helpful in finding relationships between these social characteristics and any other measurable aspect of life, such as crime and mental illness rates or religious and voting behavior.

An increasingly popular way of displaying these findings is through mapping. For example, at its website, the U.S. Census Bureau offers numerous thematic maps to illustrate many of the characteristics listed above. Chapters 10 and 11 include some of these maps to illustrate text material, and at the end of this chapter, you'll find an Internet activity that deals with accessing thematic maps of cities.

GIS Mapping

A particularly valuable research tool is **GIS mapping.** Short for *Geographic Information Systems,* GIS mapping is a computer-based method to gather, transform, manipulate, and analyze information related to the surface of the earth. Called *Geomatics* in Canada, GIS mapping allows us to view, understand, question, interpret, and visualize data in many ways that reveal relationships, patterns, and trends in the form of maps, globes, and charts (GIS.com 2008).

The GIS maps serve many useful and varying purposes for all types of organizations in both the private and public sector. For example, a GIS map can be a valuable resource in land-use management and planning for future development. (Another Internet activity at the end of this chapter will give you an opportunity to look at land use where you live.)

Limitations

Like the other approaches we've discussed, social area analysis also has its limitations. One problem is that this approach is not theoretical; it merely gives a description of cities' areas. That is, social area analysis cannot predict where groups will settle, or explain why groups settled where they did, in order to aid in planning. In contrast, Park and Burgess noted the ecological forces of competition and population movements that cause concentric rings to develop. Likewise, Harris and

CITYSCAPE

Miami's Little Havana

The center of Little Havana lies along 8th Street in Southwest Miami. It is one of several areas in Miami and its environs in which substantial numbers of Cuban Americans reside. As is typical in areas that served as initial enclaves for a particular group (Chinatown in San Francisco, for example) the current population of Little Havana is older and poorer than other, later Cuban concentrations in the Miami area. . . .

Along 8th Street, for a stretch of several miles, are homes and apartments occupied primarily by Cuban families. Many of the homes have characteristically Cuban features such as decorative Spanish tiles, Catholic shrines in the backyards, and fences enclosing the front yards. There are many Cuban-owned stores, restaurants, and financial institutions catering largely, but not exclusively, to co-ethnics. . . . Some shops offer special wearing apparel such as guayaberas: lightweight, short coats traditionally worn by Cuban men. There are a number of botanicas selling religious goods, including potions for recalling saints and spirits and aerosol cans whose contents are guaranteed to improve one's love life. Many small grocery stores sell Cuban food products and almost all the pharmacies in Little Havana have signs in their windows announcing that they send medicine to Cuba. Local churches offer masses in Spanish and English.

A dozen or more daily and weekly Spanish-language newspapers are available at Little Havana's newsstands or from coin-operated boxes. Some of the newspapers are primarily oriented to news about Cuba and the Cuban population in the United States, whereas others focus on Latin America as a whole. The area is also served by WQBA, one of several Spanish-language radio stations, but the one that has historically claimed to be La Cubanisma (the most Cuban). Little Havana also contains a number of outdoor cafes and outdoor tables, where a mostly elderly male clientele gathers during the day and evening to play cards and dominos under black olive trees. A focal point in Little Havana is Domino Park, where older men play dominos throughout the day, smoke cigars, and talk about the old days in Cuba.

A number of Little Havana's restaurants offer traditional Cuban dishes such as chicken and yellow rice. Some of the restaurants are inconspicuous neighborhood eateries, others are highly ornate. The most famous among the latter is probably the Restaurant Versailles, "the mirrored palace," which was designed to closely resemble several once-popular night spots in Havana. . . .

Walking down Southwest 8th Street gives a former Cuban a feeling of being transported back in time to the Havana of yesterday. Little Havana in Miami is, in many respects, a copy of Havana in Cuba. Murals of the latter, complete with street signs, decorate the walls of restaurants, keeping alive memories of life in Cuba.

Source: From *Urban Enclaves: Identity and Place in America* by Mark Abrahamson. Copyright © 1996. Used with permission of the author.

Ullman attributed the unique form of each city to historical, cultural, or economic factors as a basis for interpreting findings. Nevertheless, even though social area analysis offers limited insights regarding the possibilities for urban land use, its utility as a systematic measurement of the complexities found in urban communities comes from how it provides us with a fuller understanding of neighborhood characteristics.

THE LOS ANGELES SCHOOL: POSTMODERNISM

Partly as a spin-off from the multiple nuclei theory, but more importantly as a rejection of the Chicago School, a new perspective—dubbed "the Los Angeles School"—emerged in the mid-1980s (see *Urban Trends* on page 168). Focusing on the five-county region of Southern California (Los Angeles, Ventura, San Bernardino, Riverside, and Orange), its

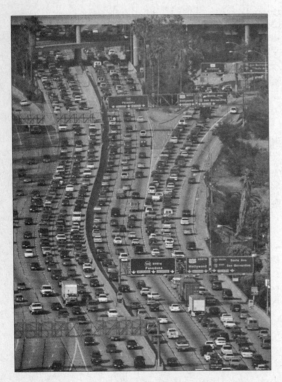

Los Angeles is a spread city held together more by an intricate freeway system than by a cohesive political system. Critics charge that neither one actually works well. Local government is too fragmented and disorganized, and the densely populated area has the nation's worst traffic congestion, leading to the average driver wasting more than 82 hours each year by sitting in traffic.

emphasis is on multicentered, dispersed patterns as the new reality of urban growth. Using Los Angeles as their model, proponents of this school argue that this city's multiple realities and decentralized structure represent the urban future. Such reasoning, with its focus on socially and spatially fragmented patterns, fits into postmodern thinking, which rejects universal truths in favor of contextual interpretations.

Building Blocks

Perhaps the origins of this new perspective lie in the vivid depiction of the Los Angeles area by Rayner Banham (2001; orig. 1973). He identified four basic "ecologies" that differed markedly from those advanced by the Chicago School: (1) *surfurbia* (the beach cities along the coast), (2) *the foothills* (the private enclaves of the privileged in such areas as Beverly Hills and Bel Air), (3) *the plains of Id* (the endless central flatlands), and (4) *autopia* (the freeways that exist as "a single comprehensible place" and "coherent state of mind"). Banham was partly harsh in his description of the "plains of Id," describing them as "gridded with endless streets, peppered endlessly with ticky-tacky houses clustered in indistinguishable neighborhoods, slashed across by endless freeways that have destroyed any community spirit that may have once existed" (p. 161).

Douglas Suisman (1990) insisted that the city's boulevards, not its freeways, are what give form to its structure and communities. As surface streets—rather than the self-contained freeways with their on-off ramps—these boulevards connect different sections of the metropolis, provide an organizational framework for local travel destinations, and serve as a "filter to adjacent residential neighborhoods" (quoted in Dear 2000:13). For Suisman, boulevards are the defining element of the city's public space in its linkage between municipalities.

Edward W. Soja (2000) helped bring a postmodern perspective to this school of thought in his argument that Los Angeles is a decentralized metropolis with a fragmented power structure that is becoming increasingly pliant and disorganized. Although the center may hold as a strategic surveillance point for social control, radiating outward is a complex, highly fragmented mishmash of "wedges" and "citadels," separated by boulevards acting as corridors. With global capitalism serving as an underlying rationale, Soja views Los Angeles as resembling "a gigantic agglomeration of theme parks" (p. 245). Moreover, he suggests that the worldwide future of urbanism will resemble Los Angeles (Miller 2000).

Main Arguments

Michael J. Dear, a leading advocate of the Los Angeles School, shares Soja's belief about the city serving as a prototype for fragmentation and social differentiation in a global economy and a postmodern culture. He also adds that as a consequence of physical sprawl, the city's "decentered politics" is one way that Los Angeles serves as a herald of the future. He describes the Los Angeles region as being "split in many separate fiefdoms, with their leaders in constant battle" (2000:14). With over 100 municipalities in Los Angeles County (total population of nearly 10 million), there are many problems of political representation. These include city–county government disputes, slow-growth/no-growth movements, and the difficulties associated with minority-group political participation. As a result, many alliances—both formal and informal, legal and illegal—form to press their claims. Either autocratic—even corrupt— power will result, or there will be "polarization along class, income, racial and ethnic lines" (2000:14–15).

Proponents of the Los Angeles School reject the old depictions of the city as outside the mainstream of U.S. urban culture with its widespread urban sprawl, insignificant architecture, and jammed freeways. Instead, Los Angeles closely resembles other emerging cities with its low-density growth, multiple ethnic enclaves, and multiple urban centers within one region. Moreover, the city contains the same dichotomy as others,

with its high concentration of wealth alongside poverty and homelessness. As a result, in contrast to the heritage of the past metropolitan form promoted by the Chicago School, those of the Los Angeles School contend their approach to urban studies is the accurate depiction of modern urban centers not just on this continent but also elsewhere in the world (Hise, Dear and Schockman 1996).

Are the postmodernists correct in saying that cities are developing in a way that is no longer rational, or even manageable, according to the old logic of urban development advocated by the urban ecologists? Is the evolution of Los Angeles that they describe truly the wave of the future? Only time will tell. Yet, with the U.S. Census Bureau projecting that the population of the Los Angeles region will increase another 6 million by 2020 (essentially by the size of three Chicagos), its ongoing growth and development as the second-largest metropolitan area in the United States is more than just an academic question.

Limitations

Once again, this approach also has its critics, who contend that advocates of the Los Angeles School overemphasize the uniqueness, importance, or widespread applicability of the Los Angeles model (Beauregard 2003). Harvey Molotch (2002) says that the Los Angeles analysts assume things are more local than they are, that there have always been cities which differed from the Chicago model of land use, and demographic distributions in western U.S. cities are but one variation of such nonconformity. Robert J. Sampson (2002) says that neither city— Los Angeles or Chicago—can be reduced to one model, because both have greater internal differentiation than either model allows and because each city actually contains spatial forms and landscape elements of the other. Essentially, all the critics argue for the need to transcend a parochial focus in favor of a theory that transcends time and place. In rebuttal, the analysts of the Los Angeles

URBAN TRENDS

The Emergence of the Los Angeles School

Just as the Chicago School emerged at a time when that city was reaching new national prominence, Los Angeles is now making its impression in the minds of urbanists worldwide. And, like the Chicago School, their theoretical inquiries focus on not only a specific city, but also on more general questions concerning urban process. . . . [O]ne theme common to all adherents of the LA School . . . is a focus on *restructuring*, which includes deindustrialization and reindustrialization, the birth of the information economy, the decline of nation-states, the emergence of new nationalisms, and the rise of the Pacific Rim. Such proliferating logics often involve multiple theoretical frameworks that overlap and co-exist in their explanations of the burgeoning global/local order. This heterodoxy is consistent with the project of postmodernism, and it is no accident that Los Angeles has come to be regarded as the prototypical postmodern metropolis.

Los Angeles undoubtedly is a special place. But adherents of the Los Angeles School do not argue that the city is unique, nor necessarily a harbinger of the future, even though both viewpoints are at some level demonstrably true. Instead, at a minimum they assert that Southern California is a suggestive archetype—a polyglot, polycentric, polycultural pastiche that is somehow engaged in the rewriting of the American social contract. The peculiar conditions that have led now to the emergence of the Los Angeles School may be coincidental: (a) that an especially powerful intersection of empirical and theoretical research projects have come together in this particular time and place; (b) that these trends are occurring in what has historically been the most understudied major city in the United States; (c) that these projects have attracted the attention of an assemblage of increasingly self-conscious scholars and practitioners; and (d) that the world is facing the prospect of a Pacific century, in which Southern California is likely to become a global capital. The validity and potential of the Los Angeles School derive principally from the intersection of these events, and the promise they hold for a re-creation of urban theory.

Source: From Michael J. Dear, *The Postmodern Urban Condition* (Malden, MA: Blackwell, 2000), p. 21.

School say that sufficient evidence exists worldwide to support their position on how to view contemporary urban growth (Scott 2001; Dear 2000).

SUMMARY

People founded cities at particular geographical sites where environmental conditions (water and climate) were favorable and where economic factors would ensure a measure of prosperity. Other human needs—political, religious, educational, and economic—played a role in locating cities as well. Spatial location of cities also results from their different types—crossroad centers, break-of-built points, and amenity, governmental, or religious entities. Industrial location theory suggests that the triangulation of minimized total costs for transportation, labor, and market, in order to maximize profits, will influence the decision about location. In addition, the type of city helps forge a city's basic shape. Radiocentric cities have a tendency to emerge where religious and political forces are of central interest to a population; gridiron cities spring up where economic concerns predominate.

Robert Park and Ernest W. Burgess (the Chicago School) saw competition and population movement as being responsible for shaping cities. Burgess's concentric zone model illustrates their ideas. Critics, however, raised questions as to whether a biologically determined competition could explain people's behavior, and they pointed out numerous exceptions to the zonal hypothesis.

Recognizing the difficulties of the Chicago theory, Homer Hoyt suggested that many cities were organized in sectors, and that the prime cause of such sectoring was socioeconomic status. This was a helpful contribution, but like the Chicago model, it ultimately failed to account for the complexity of urban life.

An additional contribution was Harris and Ullman's multiple nuclei theory. This model abandoned any idea of a deterministic pattern to urban development: It held that zones, sectors, and even the CBD were variable, with city form changing over time.

Earlier explanations of urban land use (the concentric zone, sector, and multiple nuclei theories) having been discredited as too simple, urban ecology now primarily functions as a way to use urban design, land-use planning, and policy reform to help communities plan and build neighborhoods that are environmentally sound.

Social area analysis is an approach distinguished by its lack of theory and explanation for what it reveals, but it provides a detailed description of the existing characteristics of a neighborhood and allows comparisons over time and/or with other neighborhoods. Data from the U.S. Census Bureau can offer such detailed analysis of census tracts, including thematic maps to present visually a number of various socioeconomic indicators. This form and other forms of mapping, particularly GIS mapping, can be of value in many ways, including land-use management and development planning.

The Los Angeles School is a recently evolved approach that uses a critical spatial perspective and postmodern viewpoint to understand the spread-city phenomenon. Besides more accurately explaining urbanism in Southern California than the urban ecologists could, its emphasis on political fragmentation, multiple urban centers in a region, and a multicultural/multiethnic urban entity calls our attention to the problems of governance and community within a metropolitan area increasingly affected by global capitalism. Advocates insist that Los Angeles is the prototype of the urban future, but critics insist that this claim is not justified.

CONCLUSION

Urban land use is extremely complex. This chapter has traced increasingly sophisticated efforts to capture this multifaceted reality. We can be pleased with major advances, particularly in our understanding of how cities in the modern world organize space, but we also need to understand the external forces outside the cities' control that also affect its fortunes and, therefore, its space. It is to this topic that we turn in the next chapter.

KEY TERMS

administrative or political city (154)
amenity city (153)
break-of-bulk (153)
census tract (164)
ecological sociology (164)
GIS mapping (164)
gridiron cities (157)

human ecology (157)
industrial location theory (151)
invasion-succession (158)
natural areas (158)
natural crossroads (153)
radiocentric cities (156)

INTERNET ACTIVITIES

1. Go to the U.S. Census Bureau *(http://www. census.gov)*, and click "American FactFinder." In the box "Fast Access to Information," enter a city and state, then click "Go." Change the tab to "2000." Click on any of the "map" choices. The map that appears is a social area analysis of the variable you selected.

2. Go to the Guide for Geographic Information Systems *(http://www.gis.com/whatisgis/ dowithgis.html)* for an introduction into using GIS mapping to present data. Other sublinks at this site will give you numerous real-world examples in many disciplines.

CHAPTER 7

CRITICAL URBAN SOCIOLOGY
The City and Capitalism

During the early 1970s, an alternative theoretical approach to urban sociology began to take form. In part, this development was a response to what its proponents saw as deficiencies of the Chicago School (described in Chapter 5). It was also a response to the turmoil of the times. The late 1960s and early 1970s were a period of upheaval in both the United States and Europe, prompting a more critical and political outlook on society. Not surprisingly, many scholars were led to reexamine the assumption that geography and technology were the main factors shaping urban life.

These "new" urbanists highlighted the distribution of wealth and political power in the city. They noted that the wealthiest people lived on the most desirable land and enjoyed the greatest access to the city's services. Is it any accident, they asked, that the city's best schools are situated in the city's richest neighborhoods? Or that new superhighways tear through old urban neighborhoods, with patent disregard for poor residents, to better serve the city's elite and those who have fled to the wealthy suburbs? Their answer was a resounding "No!" On the contrary, they concluded, "the structure of the city is to be explained by the pursuit of profit, which is the *raison d'être* of capitalist society, modified by the actions of the State, which has the functions of preserving and legitimizing this society" (Hall 1984:32). With the rapid globalization of the economy, many urban scholars have turned their attention to how the international economic system impacts on cities.

Also emerging in refutation to the Chicago School's emphasis on a centralized, core city that dominates a region was the postmodern perspective known as the Los Angeles School (described in Chapter 6). **Postmodernism,** you may recall, rejects the notion of any rational, overarching interpretation of reality and, instead, puts emphasis on the fragmented nature of urban growth, development, and life. Most analysts place the Los Angeles School within the larger framework of political economy models.

This alternative approach, first called "the new urban sociology" (Gottdiener and Hutchison 2006), has now existed long enough not to

be "new," so we will use the term *critical urban sociology*. In truth, however, most of its theoretical arguments are quite old, drawing heavily on the ideas of Karl Marx (1818–1883). What is new is their application to the city and, more specifically, to recent trends, such as globalization of the economy, economic restructuring in the United States, and the proliferation of megacities and edge cities.

The heart of this new approach, as already mentioned, is a central reliance on *political economy theory* and its application to urban life. That is, urban life is to be understood in terms of the social structures and processes of change that benefit some groups at the expense of others (Gottdiener and Feagin 1988). Before we examine some of the major aspects of this new perspective—which has become the dominant view in the field—we will review some earlier contributions to political and economic analysis.

URBAN ECONOMICS: THE TRADITIONAL PERSPECTIVE

People who know cities often have an image of a vibrant downtown, a place where the action is, where the buildings are taller and the lights are brighter. That is, indeed, an accurate image of North American, European, or "westernized" cities. Approaching a major city at night along a dark highway, one first sees the distant glow of the city lights, even before making out the evening skyline. Barring an electrical blackout, large areas of the center city are never dark, but why is this so? Why shouldn't the "action" be everywhere? Why should the tall buildings be concentrated in a single area?

Central Place Theory

To begin answering these questions, realize that the city is the only place where everything human comes together. Compared with the fixed life of rural areas or small towns, the city's possibilities are practically limitless. Indeed, the city is the place where the mix of people and ideas makes the creation of new things easy. The city, by its very nature, promotes "interaction and fusion" (Mumford 1989:568; orig. 1961).

Note, furthermore, that as one approaches the center of the city, the level of human activity becomes more intense. The greatest action is, literally, in the center, where people contact each other more frequently. There, in the "downtown," one finds the greatest economic advantages that cities can offer.

The Economic Advantages of Cities. Cities tend to be located where important *goods or services* are available in abundance (Winston–Salem, Raleigh, and Durham, North Carolina, are in the heart of tobacco-producing country) or where goods and services can be obtained easily (New Orleans is near the mouth of the Mississippi River). In either case, a prime location means that cities obtain, produce, and distribute their goods and services more cheaply than smaller settlements can. To ship heating oil to Albany, New York, costs a certain amount, but to transport that oil to the small town of Ticonderoga, 100 miles farther away, adds additional transportation and handling costs.

Second, cities play host to what economists call **agglomeration industries.** Take Detroit, home of the automobile industry. Because the major U.S. car manufacturers have their home bases there, this city also attracts various subindustries to serve them—companies manufacturing car paints or engine pistons, for example. The Big Three automakers share these subindustries, which benefits everyone involved, including the customer, who ultimately buys the car for less. Other examples of famous agglomeration industries are the entertainment industry in Los Angeles and Hollywood, meatpacking in Chicago, country music in Nashville, and fashion in New York. In each case, the presence of agglomeration industries keeps production costs lower than they might be in a smaller settlement.

A third economic advantage of cities, particularly those based on a free-enterprise system, is that *competition* among various producers works to keep costs down and quality up for various goods and services. Because so many businesses of the same type exist in cities, no business can charge a great deal more than its

competitors for the same product. To do so, in a competitive environment, would simply mean that customers will go elsewhere to find a better deal, with predictable consequences for the company's future. Or, if one business offers poor-quality goods for the same price at which a competitor sells a better product, which firm do you think will prosper?

What about a business in a small town with little competition? There, businesses typically offer less value to their customers, because they know it's too inconvenient and expensive for most local people to go to the city to get the lower price or the better product.

Competition also explains why so many businesses of the same type tend to cluster together in the city, what we called *natural areas* in Chapter 5. In fact, most cities have entire districts devoted solely to the computer, furniture, camera, automobile, fashion, jewelry, or entertainment businesses. The reasons for such proximity are easy to understand. Businesses of the same type, when located near one another, can (1) know what their competitors are up to simply by walking across the street, (2) provide a single locale where customers can easily engage in comparison shopping, and (3) share agglomeration services, thereby making the products cheaper for everyone.

Fourth, and finally, cities can offer higher-quality products at lower prices because they stand amidst a *greater population*. This means that urban businesses have a larger available work force than their rural counterparts do; thus, other things being equal, urban businesses can hire the more qualified people. Just as important, urban companies benefit from a larger pool of customers.

For these four reasons, the city has marked economic advantages over the hinterland. Once established, a city may operate as a "magnet" or "growth machine," becoming more and more productive as it draws raw materials and people from all around (Molotch 1976).

Within the city, economic advantages increase as one nears the city center; for this reason, people who stand to benefit from those advantages want to locate near there. This principle points out why we find, at the city's center, a **central business district (CBD)** and why, at the city's center, the action truly is greater, the buildings taller, and the lights brighter.

The Urban Hierarchy. Basic economic advantages also help explain why some cities grow much larger than others. The largest cities are just more centrally located relative to important goods or services. Chicago is a major urban center because of both its location at the southern end of Lake Michigan and its centrality to the nation's population. A century ago, Chicago thrived as the ideal location for shipping goods from the heavily settled Northeast to all other regions of the nation. Similarly, Chicago was a natural stopover for people heading westward. In comparison, Milwaukee, another major Great Lakes port, is less centrally located. Therefore, as Chicago developed into a major city, Milwaukee evolved into a second-tier urban area.

Back in the 1930s, German geographer Walter Christaller (1966; orig. 1933) incorporated this pattern into his **central place theory.** Christaller suggested that the more important a city's economic function to a region, the more its population will increase. In turn, the city's hinterland—smaller cities, towns, and rural areas—becomes dependent on the large city for many goods and services that their smaller populations cannot support. This, in turn, would make the city grow even more.

Christaller also suggested that all else being equal, cities (especially smaller ones) space themselves so that they do not cut into each other's markets. In other words, cities emerge at "distance intervals," with each serving a local hinterland. The upstate New York area provides an example: Stretched along the New York State Thruway, at least 75 miles apart, are the major urban areas of Buffalo–Niagara Falls (2006 population: 1.1 million), Rochester (1 million), Syracuse (650,000), Utica–Rome (298,000), and Albany–Schenectady–Troy (851,000).

Over a fairly large geographical region, then, we can expect cities to be distributed by size. Most numerous will be smaller, *local* cities, such as Geneva, New York; next up the scale will be fewer but larger, *regional* cities, such as Rochester, New York; then a smaller number of, large, *national* cities, such as Pittsburgh and Philadelphia; and finally, a very few, very large, *world* cities, such as New York, Paris, and Tokyo. North America's world city, New York, is centrally located within the populous Northeast and affords easy access to the entire United States and Europe. There, one can discover virtually anything from Indonesian restaurants to dozens of Broadway, off-Broadway, off-off-Broadway, and local theater groups. In smaller cities, of course, Indonesian restaurants are usually nowhere to be found, and theatergoers must be content with pre-Broadway trial runs, post-Broadway tours, or small, local theater offerings. This is why, over the last century or two, people have sometimes referred disparagingly to lower-order cities as being "one-horse towns." Or, as essayist Alexander Woollcott put it back in the 1930s, "A hick town is one where there is no place to go you shouldn't be" (Answers.com 2008).

The General Pattern of Land Use

> This vertical place is no more an accident than the Himalayas are. The city needs all these tall buildings to contain the tremendous energy there.
>
> Edward Field

Imagine you are traveling through the countryside toward any North American city. At the beginning of the trip, there are fields and, perhaps, some scattered farms or houses. As you approach the city, built-up residential areas appear, increasing in density as you near the city's center.

A Theoretical Model. Is this pattern typical of the North American cities you know? If you think it is, economist William Alonso (1971) would say that this perception is no accident, because cities definitely use their land in a patterned way. In building his land-use model, Alonso described the ideal case, assuming that (1) the city existed in a completely flat, featureless place; (2) it had a single CBD; (3) efficient transportation existed in all directions; and (4) every person in the city was motivated by economic self-interest.

Alonso was well aware, however, that in real life, many of these assumptions might not hold. For example, San Francisco exists on hills; the Minneapolis–St. Paul metropolis has two CBDs; Philadelphia's subway system runs only to certain parts of the city; and the Mormons who founded Salt Lake City were hardly motivated by purely economic interests. Similarly, Alonso knew that other factors, such as ethnic relationships, politics, and history, all play a role in urban life. Nevertheless, his model helps us see how *economic concerns* shape a city's land use. Only those who can pay the most will locate in the city's center. This is why the downtown is primarily a business district, with whatever residential property exists there taking the form of smaller apartments typically piled high on a small amount of land.

Overall, Alonso's model suggests a city with two major districts: (1) a CBD in the middle, occupied by businesses of various types (offices, industries, and warehouses), and (2) the surrounding, mostly residential areas. Circling the residential district would be yet other rings, containing businesses that require even more land and where rents are even lower. In such urban fringe areas, we might find cemeteries, golf courses, and farmland. (If one ever found a CBD golf course, however, one could bet that the cost of going nine holes would be expensive, indeed!) Still farther out, as the population dwindles away, we would begin to find little except farms.

Figure 7–1 summarizes Alonso's model of urban land use. As the figure shows, businesses pay the highest rents to be near the CBD. As the distance from the CBD grows, the number of businesses declines until, at some point, they cease altogether. This means that despite the lower rents, it is not economically feasible to operate a business there, because it requires giving up the trade advantages of being in or near the CBD.

Most residents cannot afford the high rents of the CBD, so they live some distance away. As distance increases, rents continue to drop, but at some point, no matter how low the rent, transportation problems in terms of time and money become so great that virtually

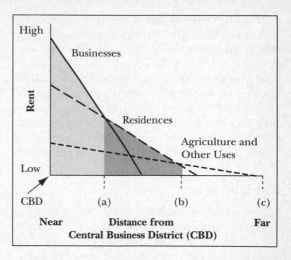

FIGURE 7–1 The Economics of Urban Land Use

no city workers choose to live there. People engaged in agriculture and other land-intensive pursuits can least afford to pay CBD rentals; thus, their businesses are a considerable distance from the CBD.

The Case of the Inner-City Poor. At this point, you may be agreeing with Alonso's general conclusions but wondering why most inner cities in North America also have many poor neighborhoods. If Alonso is correct, poor people, unable to afford high rents, should be living a long distance from the CBD.

Let's take a closer look. With little disposable income, poor people are unable to pay high rents, but they also cannot afford the high costs of travel from a remote area. Therefore, many poor people do pay higher rents than they would farther out so that they can live near the CBD. To do so, however, they live in high-density housing, perhaps sharing an apartment with another family or receiving assistance through a rent subsidy program. Also, the rents in these neighborhoods are set at what the market will bear. If it is an undesirable poor neighborhood, landlords can only charge as much rent as low-income households can afford. If this neighborhood undergoes gentrification, however, with more affluent residents moving in, the rents go much higher, forcing out those who are unable to afford them. Alonso's general conclusion then becomes applicable again.

On the other side of the coin, more affluent families can—and do—accept the higher cost of commuting from outside the CBD. These families do so mostly because they demand a great deal of space, which only a suburban neighborhood can provide within their budgets. And no doubt, many find additional "value" in having few poor people as neighbors.

Limitations

Some scholars question whether free enterprise, in the sense assumed by proponents of the economic theory just discussed, really exists at all (Todaro and Smith 2008). To them, consumers are too powerless to set the agenda for a society's economic production. The *Urban Trends* box below takes a closer look at this question.

To illustrate this criticism, consider the classic study of "Blackston," a pseudonym for a poor black area of a major eastern city. There, Betty Lou Valentine (1980) compared supermarket prices with those in surrounding, higher-income, white neighborhoods. She found that poor African Americans paid *significantly higher prices* for their groceries in Blackston than more affluent whites living elsewhere did. Why? Supermarket owners in Blackston think of African Americans as "captured customers." Because of the expense and inconvenience of going to white neighborhoods (most black families in Blackston do not own cars), and because of the overt

URBAN TRENDS

Does *Free* Enterprise Really Exist?

In economic theory, the basic questions of what and how much to produce are assumed to be determined by the aggregate preferences of all consumers as revealed by their market demand for different goods and services. Producers are assumed simply to respond to these "sovereign" consumer preferences and, motivated by the desire to maximize profits, they are assumed to compete with each other *on equal terms* in the purchase of resources and the sale of their products. . . . The ultimate rationale for the efficacy of this theory or model of economic activity is Adam Smith's famous notion of the "invisible hand" of capitalism, which postulates that if each individual consumer, producer and supplier of resources pursues his or her own self-interest, they will, "as if by an invisible hand," be promoting the overall interests of society as a whole.

Unfortunately, the facts of economic life in both the developed and the less developed nations of the world are such as to render much of [this] theory of negligible importance. . . . Consumers as a whole are rarely sovereign about anything, let alone with regard to questions of what goods and services are to be produced, in what quantities and for whom. Producers, whether private or public, have great power in determining market prices and quantities sold. The ideal of competition is typically just that—an "ideal" with little relation to reality. Finally, the so-called "invisible hand" often acts not to promote the general welfare of all, but to lift up those already well-off while pushing down that vast majority of the population which is striving to free itself from poverty, malnutrition, and illiteracy.

Source: Michael P. Todaro and Stephen C. Smith, *Economic Development,* 10th ed. (Boston: Addison-Wesley, 2008), p. 14.

prejudice those families encounter when they do, most blacks have little choice but to shop locally. Knowing this, Blackston supermarket owners can charge more than storeowners whose customers are able to climb in their cars and shop elsewhere. The point is that to the extent people cannot really choose where to shop, the free-enterprise system is an ideal rather than a reality.

Valentine's observation that people of color often encounter overt prejudice illustrates a second problem with Alonso's economic model: Important non-economic factors also influence urban land use. People in some neighborhoods may actively resist any "undesirables" who seek to move nearby. This resistance often extends beyond personal attitudes, influencing zoning laws and the practices of real estate agents that can keep people from securing housing they may be able to afford. A proposal in late 2006 for affordable, work force housing in Tarpon Springs, in the Tampa Bay region of Florida, touched off widespread resistance and dozens of impassioned letters to the local newspaper. "I am strongly opposed to any building of work force housing, better known as low-income housing," one resident wrote. "Clearly this action would create higher crimes and lower property valuations" (Quoted in Stein 2006:1). So strong was the backlash that the City Commission voted to cut the proposed density in half, resulting in no work force housing there.

A third type of criticism points out that Alonso's economic theory applies only to a limited range of cities. For example, the capitalist–industrial city (on which the economic theory is based) is only *one* of at least five major city types that have existed historically. Other types include *regal–ritual* cities (with political and religious concerns at their core), *administrative cities* (with many government activities), *colonial cities* (that manage a colonial region for another nation), and *mercantile cities* (with trade as their principal concern). Of these, only the last operates on economic principles similar to those of the modern Western city. In the other types, people are not making decisions based on the economic principles assumed by Alonso.

None of these criticisms—consumer powerlessness, non-economic factors affecting land use, and its non-universality—means that Alonso's theory is wrong. Clearly, however, it is limited in utility and is but one model of how the free market makes use of land. Let's look at the newer, more dominant economic model, as delineated in critical urban sociology.

URBAN POLITICAL ECONOMY

By the end of the 1960s, an increasing number of social scientists had found that the traditional economic model, as well as conventional theories of urban ecology, no longer accounted for many important changes in cities. In North American cities, one had to look beyond the city itself to understand the dramatic decline in industrial jobs, the movement of millions of people from the cities to the suburbs, the movement from the Snowbelt to the Sunbelt, and the intensifying financial problems of so many cities. Some other model seemed to be necessary in order to explain the new urban realities, thus setting the stage for the urban political economy approach.

Several assumptions served as the foundation for this new approach. First, any city exists within the larger political structures of county, state, and nation. Beyond that, international political processes—such as oil embargos, trade agreements, and hostilities—can affect urban life on a local level. Second, local economies do not operate independently but, rather, connect to one another and forge state, national, and international economic networks. Most important, the new breed of social scientists began to discount the notion that "natural processes" shape the physical form and social life of cities and to advance their belief that political and economic institutions—including banks, governments, and international corporations—shape urban life.

One key focus is the role of investment decisions in shaping cities. Who makes decisions that direct a city's economy, and for what purposes? In addition, the political economy approach investigates how conflicts—for example, between labor and management, between racial and ethnic populations, and between social classes—shape the physical and social character of cities.

The new political economy viewpoint drew together geographers and philosophers as well as sociologists specializing in the investigation of urban development. Drawing on the ideas of Karl Marx, such thinkers as Henri Lefebvre, David Harvey, Manuel Castells, and Allen Scott argued that urban changes must be understood in the light of historical economic and political forces. We now look at each of their contributions.

Henri Lefebvre: Redefining the Study of Cities

French philosopher Henri Lefebvre (1902–1991) sparked the application of the critical and Marxian perspective to studying the city. Drawing from the writings of Karl Marx and his associate, Friedrich Engels, Lefebvre (1991, 1970) applied the economic categories of capital, labor, profit, wages, class exploitation, and inequality to explain the unevenness of urban development. In doing so, he helped develop many ideas about cities, ideas to which Marx and Engels never devoted much attention. He thus became a seminal source of new thinking about the city, suggesting that urban development was as much a product of the capitalist economic system as was any manufactured good.

Two Circuits of Capital.   To advance his concept, Lefebvre made a distinction between two types of investment capital. He identified the commonly studied economic activity—investment to hire workers to manufacture a product to sell at a profit to be used for more investment—as the **primary circuit of capital.** Thus, in a capitalist system, the main flow of money is from investors into materials and labor costs in order to create a manufactured good, the sale of which generates profits for still more manufacturing ventures. This continual circulation of manufacturing capital generates much wealth for investors, but it is also what pumps the national economy. Hence, Lefebvre named this circular money flow the *primary* one.

To examine the unevenness of urban development, Lefebvre identified another important

profit-oriented economic activity—real estate investment—as the **second circuit of capital.** Investment in land, he maintained, almost always leads to profit and serves as an important means for acquiring wealth. One buys property expecting it to appreciate in value or develops land for residential or commercial purposes—both of which yield a profit. The circuit becomes complete when the investor takes that profit and invests it in more land-based projects.

Within a city, he suggested, profit-seeking motives determine the stability, decline, or rejuvenation of various areas. Lefebvre's focus on real estate investment pushing city growth in certain ways was a turning point that influenced subsequent theories and analyses of the dynamics of urban development.

Space as Part of Social Organization.   Lefebvre made a second important contribution with his assertion that space is more than just a social "container"; it is also closely linked to behavior. In other words, we construct our surroundings to meet particular needs and objectives, and our surroundings, in turn, affect our subsequent behavior. People thus organize their daily lives and actions—whether cultural, economic, educational, or social—within the constraints or opportunities of the environment that has been built. We need to think of planners and developers, then, as important architects of social life. Lefebvre added that comparable social systems organize space in a similar fashion, so edge cities or suburbs in Australia, Canada, and the United States, for example, closely resemble one another.

The Role of Government.   Venturing further into territory uncharted by Marx, Lefebvre also considered the actions of government, from the national level down to the local level, to be a critical factor in shaping a city's use of space. Governments are empowered to make various decisions that affect city shape and urban life—decisions that range from condemnations of structures, claims of eminent domain, provision of funding, approving new roads or alterations to roads, supervising urban renewal, and responding to zoning appeals. The federal and state governments also collect taxes from, and distribute resources to, various lower-level political units (states, counties, and municipalities). In addition, the government directly owns a great deal of urban land (fire, police, and government buildings, as well as parks and roads), and it exercises control over the rest (zoning and tax valuation). With all these forms of social control over how space is utilized, governments can strike deals to attract corporations to a certain locale or take many other actions to encourage development, or redevelopment, of an area.

Furthermore, Lefebvre distinguishes between two definitions of space: **abstract space,** and **social space.** The first is what businesspeople, investors, and government have in mind when they discuss the dimensions of size, location, and profit. The second is what individuals who live, work, and play in an area think about their environment. Often, Lefebvre claims, government and business talk about abstract space—plans, say, to build a shopping mall or construct a low-income housing project—but pay little attention to the ideas of local people. The resulting conflict, continues Lefebvre, is much the same as, but not identical to, the class conflict discussed by Marx.

These three ideas of Lefebvre—two circuits of capitalism, space as a component of social organization, and the role of government in managing space—were highly influential in charting the course that others would take. Most new theories in urban development trace their origins to this French philosopher, although many later theorists do not agree with all of Lefebvre's arguments.

Urban Areas as Themed Environments

An excellent example of Lefebvre's ideas is found in the recycling of abandoned factories and docks into redeveloped areas that emphasize a heritage and leisure experience (Ward 1998). This transformation of public space into a packaged, themed environment has been a dominant land-use pattern since the 1960s (Gottdiener 2001; Sorkin 1992). At the forefront of such efforts was developer James W. Rouse, who worked to rejuvenate dying downtowns by introducing so-called festival marketplaces: Fanueil Hall in Boston, Harborplace in Baltimore, and the South Street Seaport in Manhattan.

Although these themed public space areas are well known and prosperous, many other cities have also rediscovered their own waterfront areas. Seattle, Cincinnati, Cleveland, Louisville, and Memphis—to name just a few— have redeveloped these areas with parks, restaurants, stores, and various activities. Although each city's waterfront view may vary somewhat, one finds a generic similarity existing among all such areas in all cities. Similarly, historic districts—from San Diego's Gaslamp Quarter to Boston's Faneuil Hall marketplace—have their own unique charm, but their redevelopment to lure patrons to their shops, restaurants, and entertainment locales results in a somewhat homogeneous design.

Perhaps, however, the epitome of themed urban space is not in the rebuilding of an old urban environment but, rather, in the building of an artificial city environment as a theme park *away from* the city, such as Disney's Main Street. Built at a cost of $3 billion and opened in 1993, another such entity is City-Walk in Universal City, California. Originally intended to encourage traffic between Universal Studios' theme park and its Odeon Theatre in order to generate additional profits, it became not just a spectacular success in that regard but its own destination as well for millions of visitors.

Promoted as possessing "all the glitz and excitement of an actual urban boulevard, but with none of the problems associated with real city life . . . no carjackers, no panhandlers, no grime, no graffiti, no hookers, no muggers— yet also with no mall roof to block out the sunny skies or night time stars," CityWalk claims that, "for once, walking outside in the 'city' is completely safe" (Wayne 2008). Designed by Jon Jerde, the same architect who created the massive Mall of America in Minnesota, City-Walk features outrageous architecture that uses every visual trick imaginable to wow the passing crowds, along with numerous street performers (mimes, magicians, musicians, and entertaining street vendors). In Orlando,

Florida, Universal Studios offers a smaller City-Walk combination of shops, restaurants, cinemas, live entertainment, and nightclubs as a gateway between its two theme parks, Universal Studios and Islands of Adventure.

Whatever entertainment value these private themed environments may have, critics warn of their dangers. Michael Sorkin (1992), for example, says that they are not benign imitations but, instead, are manipulative structures designed to maximize behavior control and eliminate the authentic interaction found in traditional public space. Mark Gottdiener believes that in the aftermath of the cold, faceless public space left behind by the modernist era, the forces of capitalism have staged a "vengeful return of meaning and symbolism" to create "material space for the realization of consumer fantasies" through imitation and simulation (2001:34, 70). The problem with this is that as we buy into a visual theme, we lose our reality, turning our landscape inside out and becoming convinced that all places are the same in the built environment that excludes other forms (Zukin 1993).

David Harvey: The Baltimore Study

Geographer David Harvey (1992; orig. 1973) illustrates Lefebvre's ideas in a Marxist analysis of how the capitalist real estate system operated in Baltimore, directly shaping many of the city's problems concerning social inequality. He divided Baltimore into real estate submarkets that included the inner city, white ethnic areas, the low- to moderate-income African American area of West Baltimore, areas of high turnover, middle-income areas in northeast and southwest Baltimore, and other upper-income areas. Each of these areas revealed a distinct pattern of buying and selling, as reflected in the amount of upfront cash or investment through private loan transactions, bank financing, and government insurance. Each physical environment generated different levels of commitment by community banks, private financial institutions, and government agencies, which, in turn, influenced potential developers, speculators, homeowners, and renters.

David Harvey's study disclosed how some Baltimore neighborhoods fared better than others because of the priorities set by real estate investors and government programs. His conclusion was that these decisions, more than those by departing industrialists, are closely linked to decaying areas of a city, prompting abandonment and relocation to another area.

Harvey's detailed analysis revealed that urban development is not a monolithic growth process. Instead, it occurs unevenly. This second circuit of capital varies in its investment arrangements from place to place, influenced by different combinations of social factors, profit potential, and conflict. For example, banks showed no interest in lending to the inner-city poor, who, of necessity, financed their housing transactions by cash payment, private loans, and/or government programs. White ethnics also had trouble securing bank financing; instead, they financed their housing purchases through community-based savings and loans associations. Both inner city and white ethnic areas had difficulty obtaining Federal Housing Authority (FHA) or Veterans Administration (VA) insurance, unlike Baltimore's middle-income sections. People in more affluent sections rarely resorted to FHA guarantees, and they made far greater use of commercial and savings banks. Also, unlike residents of poor or working-class neighborhoods, they could repel, with their political and economic power, speculative incursions into their own neighborhoods.

Thus, Harvey demonstrated how discrimination by investment capitalists in the housing market affects the dynamics of buying, selling, and neighborhood transition. He also showed the role of government in shaping a city's use of space: West Baltimore improved more than other poor areas in the city did as a result of multiple government renewal programs. Essentially, Harvey's Baltimore study disclosed how the priorities of the second circuit of capital, aided by government programs, are linked directly to decay of the central city and to the suburbanization of the population. Actions by real estate investors—more so than actions by industrial capitalists, Harvey maintained—led to areas of the city becoming run-down and abandoned.

Urban change, claims Harvey, reflects the changing needs of a capitalist economy. That is, capitalists build a physical city that is appropriate to the city's needs at one point in time only to destroy that physical city later, usually in the course of some crisis. Different segments of the urban population—investors (finance capital), store owners (commerce capital), manufacturers (industrial capital), financial analysts, and even white- or blue-collar workers—have different priorities and goals. Capital interests, seeking to make a profit, and labor, seeking to protect and enhance its standard of living, often engage "in a series of running battles over a variety of issues that relate to the creation, management, and use of the built environment" (Harvey 1992:268).

Unwilling, therefore, to risk their profits by granting too much power to workers, the capitalist class seeks government intervention to secure the type of urban development that serves its narrow interests. This strategy explains widespread urban blight; finance capital has little reason to invest in poor neighborhoods, preferring instead the greater profits to be found in high-rent districts. This reluctance to aid decaying urban areas, claims Harvey, is precisely why government intervention is so important. Public urban renewal projects, however, seem to operate only to restore the area's profitability in order to attract finance and commerce capital once again, and in the process do little for the poor. Harvey's contribution, then, lies in revealing how the actions of finance capital (rather than industrial capital) affect a city's fortunes.

Manuel Castells: Updating Marx

Although influenced by Lefebvre's writings, Manuel Castells initially maintained a more orthodox Marxist approach toward the study of cities. His special contribution (1982, 1985) was extending Marxist analysis beyond the traditional conflict between labor and capital and applying it to distinct urban patterns. He also highlighted the conflict between local government and the working class arising from local administration of various social welfare programs. The federal government funds such programs as needs-based income, housing, and health care benefits for the poor, but local or city governments typically administer them. Thus, city residents seeking these resources often become entangled in conflict with city agencies.

Welfare Capitalism. Castells views welfare capitalism—that is, the government providing subsidies to workers—as an important social movement affecting urban life. To him, key issues, such as housing, education, mass transportation, health, and welfare, make sense only within the context of disputes arising over their administration by agencies of city government. Such government activity to provide resources to the working class, he says, represents an effort to "extend" capitalism and gives rise to new urban struggles and patterns of conflict unknown in Marx's time.

Changing economic conditions in the 1980s and 1990s at first lessened the impact of Castells' analysis. The once-expansive welfare states found in the advanced industrialized countries of the Western world cut back. Recessions, aging populations, tax revolts, budget deficits, and fiscal crises all curbed government spending and, in some cases, led to the dismantling of welfare programs. Thus, local governments administered fewer subsidizing programs than they once did, but then the 2009 government stimulus package brought a massive infusion of nearly one trillion dollars and an unprecedented involvement of the federal government in the economy, resulting in more welfare capitalism than ever before.

Modes of Development.   Examining industrial growth in suburbs, Castells adapted one of Marx's concepts to fit the information age. Whereas Marx had stressed the **mode of production**—the things needed to produce goods and services, such as land, tools, knowledge, wealth, or factories—Castells (1991) introduced the concept of the **mode of development.** The key element in the industrial mode of development, he explained, was discovering and applying new sources of energy. In today's informational mode of development, however, the key element is developing new forms and sources of information. One obvious consequence of this shift is that corporate decisions about location no longer rest on proximity to raw materials or a large, unskilled labor pool, as they once did.

Castells's focus was the differential effect of emerging high-tech businesses on segments of the urban region. Specifically, he found that high-tech production disproportionately

occurred in suburban rather than central-city communities. Such companies typically have facilities on the periphery of cities, thereby accelerating the pace of outward movement and sparking the rise of edge cities. Influencing the choice of suburban locations is the need for large-batch production facilities combined with automated subsidiary plants, access to a freeway system, and the typically suburban locale of research and design centers as well as military installations for testing and marketing defense-related products.

Allen Scott: Business Location and the Global Economy

Another geographer, Allen J. Scott (1988, 1980), offers additional non-Marxist insights regarding the impact of changes in the production process on urban space. His approach is not a comprehensive theory of the built environment but, rather, a study of the relationship between a city's fortunes and the globalization of the economy. Furthermore, in rejecting the urban ecology approach, Scott suggests that the economic interests of powerful transnational corporations—not a biological model of species competition over territory—determine patterns of urban growth.

Horizontal Integration.   For most of the twentieth century, until about 1970, cities evolved into metropolitan regions as corporations changed in their economic organization. Once, companies were small entities, with all their functions centralized in one location. Gradually, many industries absorbed or consolidated with competitors, sometimes taking the form of an **oligopoly**—that is, market domination by a few producers. Then, these industries maintained headquarters in a major city, with easy access to banking, marketing, and other necessary services, but they located their production plants, distribution centers, and sales divisions elsewhere, in the locales most advantageous to them. In time, many companies gained control over the manufacture of all parts that went into their final product, as when auto companies manufactured not just the engine, frame, and body of the automobile but also the batteries, headlights, radios, upholstered seats, window glass, and bumpers. Some companies even obtained ownership of raw materials needed for the manufacturing process. With their separate functions thus spatially dispersed, companies maintained a national network of command and control to reduce costs and maximize profits. This economic structure is called **horizontal integration.**

One way to maximize profits is to minimize shipping costs in the total manufacturing process. Not surprisingly, when horizontal integration was predominant, the specialized production facilities were mostly located near the main assembly plant—virtually all auto parts plants, for example, were within 150 miles of Detroit, or "Motor City," the automobile manufacturing center. The close proximity of these subsidiary agglomeration industries not only kept shipping costs low but also created an economically interdependent metropolitan region. As the companies prospered, so, too, did the cities.

Vertical Disintegration. Beginning in the 1970s, large corporations, although still maintaining some horizontal integration (especially of manufacturing, marketing, and administration activities), began to unload their production support companies—a process known as **vertical disintegration.** In other words, instead of manufacturing materials or parts needed for the production process themselves, they awarded contracts to suppliers through a process of competitive bidding. Competitiveness among subcontractors resulted in lower costs by eliminating the overhead expenses of maintaining inventory stocks, which offset concerns about shipping expenses. In addition, the advent of computer-assisted manufacturing enhanced production coordination, enabling companies to keep track of all needs and order "just-in-time" parts more easily.

Once mostly located in the office buildings of cities, many corporate businesses—lured by local tax abatements and other economic incentives—either located or relocated part or all of their operations to suburban campus areas beginning in the late twentieth century. A good example is the Pacific Shores business park in Silicon Valley, Redwood City, California, on the edge of San Francisco Bay.

A significant consequence of vertical disintegration was the creation of many new supplier companies, located where labor and energy costs were lower, either in North America or abroad. Scott sees this last development as the climax of vertical disintegration: the ability of large companies to conduct business on a global scale. In short, many businesses became transnational or multinational, investing their capital and locating their manufacturing, marketing, and administration anywhere in the world that best suited their needs. Suppliers may now be anywhere—perhaps in the non-unionized, low-energy-cost Sunbelt or, better yet, in extremely low-wage countries of the developing world.

How did this affect older industrial cities? For most, plant closings meant the loss of thousands of jobs, an out-migration of workers and their families seeking jobs elsewhere, and a depressed economy. Loss of an industrial base also adversely affected the city's commercial base, because stores no longer had the same customers as before. In contrast, the Sunbelt exploded in industrial development and population growth. As virtually every northeastern U.S. city steadily shrank in population during the second half of the twentieth century, the fastest-growing cities were those in the Sunbelt (see Chapter 3).

No longer dominated by manufacturing, older cities shifted to providing greater employment opportunities in business services. Most have not fully recovered and are still experiencing population decline. A few cities, however, such as New York, London, and Tokyo, now function as "highly concentrated command posts in the organization of the world economy." They are also important locations of finance, specialized service firms, and innovation sources, and they serve as markets for the products and innovations produced (Sassen 2001:3–4).

New economic realities thus shape the production process and, in turn, affect urban growth patterns—a subject we will now explore further through two sociological approaches, one examining local conditions and the other considering global conditions.

John Logan and Harvey Molotch: Urban Growth Machines

John Logan and Harvey Molotch (2007) employed political economy theory in an effort to identify *who* the central decision makers in North American cities are and determine *why* they do what they do. In concentrating on the battles between pro- and antigrowth factions, their study is essentially an application of Lefebvre's categories of abstract space and social space that we discussed earlier.

Urban growth coalitions—typically made up of bankers, businesspeople, corporate property owners, developers, politicians, and investors—seek to spark population growth, increase the market value of land, and stimulate the city's economy through investment and development. To accomplish these goals, they pressure the city government to create a "good business climate" (cleanliness, safety, tax incentives, low-interest loans, and relocation assistance). They also seek to enhance the image of the city, promoting its attributes, such as cultural and recreational activities, sports teams, landmarks, and nightlife. Their focus on quality of life, however, only extends to what Lefebvre termed "abstract space" issues involving the high profits that accompany urban growth.

By contrast, most local residents have a "social space" view of their community, and they may oppose growth as being against their own best interests. City residents may wish to protect the "character" of their neighborhood, preserve older buildings, limit traffic flow, and maintain parks and other open spaces.

Advocates of urban growth point out its advantages—more jobs, additional tax ratables, increased economic activity—and they are often correct in doing so. What often accompanies growth, however, is environmental degradation, higher rents, more crime, greater traffic congestion, and an infrastructure unable to handle an increased population. Tensions in the growth machine materialize as community groups seek to block a proposal or, at least, lessen its negative impact on their community and the environment.

Logan and Molotch also point out how the global economy influences many changes in the city. Today, local political action is less effective than it once was, because the deindustrialization of North American cities has caused the flight of industrial capital. The "new international division of labor" may benefit some people—major corporations and their stockholders reap huge profits from the new global economy—but the loss of jobs hurts ordinary people in cities back home. Thus, local people have less power to oppose the corporate agenda, just as corporations have more power to get their own way.

At the heart of all contemporary urban land use, then, is a focus on the most profitable use of materials and labor. The question that corporate executives ask is simply: "If we do this, will we make money?" Concerns for the welfare of the worker, the neighborhood, and the city's poor simply take a backseat—if these concerns exist at all. This "profit-bias" has international roots and consequences, as Peter Hall explains:

> In the modern world, newly industrializing countries undermine the traditional economic bases of older nations and regions. In the latter, skilled workers in declining industries lose their jobs and end up in unskilled service occupations. Entrepreneurs react to the threat of competition by closing older inner city plants and concentrating production in rural areas, where unionization is weaker and wages are lower. Multinational enterprises centralize their control functions in a few of the world's cities, where they can displace other functions to other cities and suburbs. Because profit seeking and competition are inherent and incessant, this process of change is never ending. (1984:33)

In the end, urban political economy presents an alternative to what its proponents see as the biased approach of the older urban ecology model; in the newer model, the assumption is that profit making and capitalism are the natural forces shaping cities. Those forces are global in nature and, thus, are mostly beyond the capabilities of cities to influence.

THE GLOBAL ECONOMY

Economic forces always affect cities. As discussed in Chapter 3, for example, the Industrial Revolution redefined urban life and greatly increased the size of city populations. At the midpoint of the twentieth century, the typical North American city was an industrial center. White-ethnic, blue-collar neighborhoods, built around the factories in which residents worked, peppered the urban landscape. In other parts of the city, the middle class resided. Then, in the 1950s and 1960s, the exodus of the middle class—soon followed by many businesses and industries—created a fiscal crisis from which some cities, especially smaller ones, have never recovered.

Deindustrialization

During the 1970s, U.S. manufacturers—in virtually all fields, including steel, auto, clothing, and electronics—made profit-driven decisions to dismantle and disinvest in U.S. operations. To minimize labor costs, they closed factories in the United States and outsourced to Asia and Latin America, dramatically disrupting people's lives and the welfare of many urban communities (Bluestone and Harrison 1984). For example, Youngstown, Ohio—situated between Pittsburgh, Cleveland, and Chicago—had a robust, blue-collar economy as a center of the steel industry. When its famous Jeannette Blast Furnace was shut down in 1978, cutting the heart out of the local economy, 50,000 Youngstown workers lost their jobs, and the city was rocked by economic devastation, from which it has still not fully recovered (Linkon and Russo 2003).

Other manufacturers—in appliances and electronics, for instance—quickly followed suit, and by the end of the 1970s, manufacturing in virtually every field was in decline nationwide. This transfer of much economic production to other countries dramatically changed the older cities. Gone were most of the jobs that earlier migrants and immigrants had used as a path toward economic security. Gone, too, were the ties that bound central-city

The global economy manifests itself in virtually every city. It is practically impossible, for example, to go to any urban locale worldwide as here in Tokyo and not find McDonald's, Burger King, Pizza Hut, Kodak, American cigarettes, Coke, or Pepsi. Foreign sales are an important part of all multinational corporate profits.

workers to their local employers. Also gone was a sizable portion of the cities' tax base.

Economic Restructuring

The 1980s and 1990s bore witness to **economic restructuring** and the globalization of the economy that spawned still other changes in metropolitan regions. Forced to restructure their economies away from manufacturing, North American cities evolved into service centers, specializing in advertising, corporate management, finance, and information processing. In particular, cities expanded those business services required by the finance capitalists heading up investment activity for the global economy (Sassen 2001).

Such changes are evident in the present-day character of the urban labor force. The demand for many of the entry-level factory jobs traditionally held by the urban poor with limited education and skills dropped dramatically, countered by a rising demand for computer-literate workers with verbal and quantitative skills. The reason was that even though some corporate headquarters moved outside the major cities, the latter continued to provide a necessary concentration for firms with a world-market orientation in order to have access to a corporate-services complex (Sassen 2006:96).

This is an important point. Although the evolution of a global economy prompted a new generation of cynics to sound the death knell for cities, cities still play an essential role in today's world. Ironically, those massive trends of globalization toward the spatial dispersal of economic activities at the metropolitan, national, and global levels contributed to the demand for new forms of territorial centralization of top-level management and control functions. A specialized services complex capable of handling the most advanced and complicated corporate needs is most likely to be in a city rather than a suburban office park (Sassen 2006:97). The *Urban Trends* box on page 187 further explains this reality.

URBAN TRENDS

Cities and the World Economy

If cities were irrelevant to the globalization of economic activity, the key economic and political actors could simply abandon them and not be bothered by any of this. Indeed, this is precisely what some politicians argue—that cities have become hopeless reservoirs for all kinds of social despair. The dominant economic narrative argues that place no longer matters, firms can be located anywhere, thanks to *telematics* [telecommunications and computer technologies that allow for instantaneous transmission of information over short and long distances], and major industries now are information-based and hence not place-bound. This line of argument devalues cities at a time when they are major sites for the new cultural politics. It also allows the corporate economy to extract major concessions from city governments under the notion that firms can simply leave and relocate elsewhere, which is not quite the case for a whole complex of firms . . .

In seeking to show that (1) cities are strategic to economic globalization because they are command points, global marketplaces, and production sites for the information economy; and (2) many of the devalued sectors of the urban economy actually fulfill crucial functions for the center, [we should reemphasize] the importance of cities specifically in a globalized economic system and the importance of those overlooked sectors that rest largely on the labor of women, immigrants, and, in large U.S. cities, African Americans and Latinos. In fact, the intermediary sectors of the economy (such as routine office work, headquarters that are not geared to the world markets, the variety of services demanded by the largely suburbanized middle class) and of the urban population (the middle class) can and have left cities. The two sectors that have stayed, the center and the *other*, find in the city the strategic terrain for their operations.

Source: Saskia Sassen, *Cities in a World Economy,* 3rd ed. (Thousand Oaks, CA: Pine Forge Press), 2006, p. 199.

World-Systems Analysis

With its macrosocial view, the political economy approach to understanding the conditions of cities fits nicely into a world-systems perspective. This emphasis views capitalism as evolving through a long, historical process into a single, integrated, worldwide economic and political system. This system operates as an hierarchy so that countries with various levels of economic power constitute (1) the "core," (2) the "semi-periphery," and (3) the "periphery." Within that framework, cities occupy a place in the world urban hierarchy that greatly affects their individual growth patterns (Chase-Dunn and Babones 2006; Wallerstein 2004).

The Hierarchy of Countries. The more economically developed countries—Canada, Japan, the United States, and the nations of Western Europe—constitute the core of this world system and are home to the transnational corporations that dominate the global economy. The headquarters of transnational corporations, located in large cities within affluent countries, carry out high-level decision making that guides the world's economic forces. Because so many employees are well-paid professionals, these cities benefit in the quality of housing and of the economic and social enterprises that spring up to cater to their tastes.

Large semi-peripheral countries—Argentina, Brazil, China, India, Indonesia, Mexico, and Poland—as well as smaller semi-peripheral countries—Hungary, Israel, South Africa, South Korea, and Taiwan—have close ties with the core nations. These second-tier countries serve as key nodes in the global urban system, as information technology binds their cities together in dense interaction networks. Yet, despite the integration of these cities into the cross-border economic networks, they are in the midrange of the global hierarchy, and their countries play a secondary role in global economic matters (Sassen 2002). Most of the transnational employees are lower middle class, and for the most part, their somewhat lower standard of living brings a less grand variety and quality of activities to the urban scene than are found in cities of the core countries.

Countries in the periphery are the poorer, less-developed countries in Africa, Asia, and Latin America. Jobs in these countries typically pay little and offer little opportunity to advance. These transnational workers are typically rural migrants, living in slums or shantytowns and struggling to survive. The impact of the global economy on the cities of peripheral countries is more negative than positive. A small, affluent elite exists in these cities, but most urban residents live at the lower end of the socioeconomic scale, having few of the usual social amenities of a city, which are reserved for tourists or the small, local elite. Integration into the global market encourages informal enterprises within local urban economies, but often at the cost of a serious erosion of wages and employment conditions. Essentially, the major impact of globalization on cities has been a strengthening of income inequality, an increasing vulnerability of their populations to poverty, and large-scale spatial segregation through the peripheral location of the poor (Roberts 2005; Portes, Dore-Cabral, and Landolts 1997:246).

The *maquiladoras* system locates primary manufacturing in northern Mexico, near the U.S. border, to allow multinational companies to use cheap labor and then ship finished goods north. Manufacturing in the United States has declined, but about 100 U.S.-owned and -operated companies are just south of the border, such as the BonWorth clothing factory, which produces over 10,000 garments daily to supply the company's more than 200 U.S. stores.

Thus, the three tiers of countries in the world system are unequal yet interdependent. The system operates mostly in the interest of the richest nations; it provides far less to the majority of the world's people, who live in less economically developed nations. The quality of urban life in each of the three tiers reflects this world-system hierarchy (see the *Urban Trends* box below and also Figure 7–2 on page 190).

In recent years, many governments and nonprofit organizations have taken action against one highly exploitative aspect of the global economy. Many northern hemisphere industries, such as apparel and sporting goods, rely on low-wage labor in the third-tier countries of the southern hemisphere. Those designers, researchers, executives, and other white-collar employees of these companies live and work in the large cities of the core countries and receive excellent salaries and benefits. In contrast, the workers who actually make the products live in the peripheral countries, where young children and women work long hours for little pay in hot, crowded factories. Often, they are bonded laborers, meaning they have no freedom and are kept in confined areas when not working, receive only minimal amounts of food, and even suffer verbal and physical abuse. A few years ago, some companies, like Adidas and Nike, yielded to public pressure to end their allowing such conditions in their suppliers' factories. Passage of laws in the United States, Canada, Europe, and other countries against importing products made by child labor has reduced—but not eliminated—these practices.

URBAN TRENDS

The Impact of the Global Economy on Los Angeles

In an apparent paradox, the rising pre-eminence of the local in the postmodern city has been facilitated by the appearance of a global capitalism. The emergence of post-Fordism [i.e., an increasingly flexible, disorganized regime of capitalist accumulation] has resulted in an accelerated flow of global capital, and an endless search for cheap labor supplies on an international scale. These trends have connected the local ever more effectively to the world-wide developments of post-Fordism; what happens in downtown LA tomorrow may result from yesterday's fluctuations in local labor markets in East Asia. At home, the consequences have been a rapid deindustrialization especially in the snowbelt, and (re)industrialization in the sunbelt. Los Angeles, in perhaps a typically postmodern way, is experiencing both simultaneously. Within its limits, the city has vestiges of a major automobile manufacturing industry, as well as in the glittering towers of corporate high-techdom. LA is an "informational city" with, at the same time, a proliferation of minimum-wage, part-time service industry jobs (e.g., fast food outlets) and a massive informal sector (street vendors on freeway off-ramps; can recycling efforts from the backs of trucks; etc.). In social terms, the postmodern metropolis is increasingly minoritized and polarized along class, income, race and ethnic lines. The disadvantaged classes are overwhelmingly people of color. Their family lives are increasingly disrupted by the demands of a flexible, disorganized workplace (for example, the pressure on both parents to work, or the need for families to crowd together to be able to afford housing). These trends have been aggravated by the strong dose of privatism, as well as the practical effects of privatization, that emerged during the Reagan era and show few signs of abating.

Source: From Michael J. Dear, *The Postmodern Urban Condition* (Malden, MA: Blackwell, 2000), p. 15.

FIGURE 7–2 Economic Development in Global Perspective

Source: From Macionis's *Sociology*, 12th ed. (2008), using data from the United Nations Development Programme (2006). Map projection from *Peters Atlas of the World* (2002).

Economic Development
High-income countries
Middle-income countries
Low-income countries

Nike is Vietnam's single largest private employer, with 130,000 employees. Its production of $700 million worth of footwear ranks it as the third-largest supplier behind China and Indonesia. Also among Vietnam's $6 billion in exports to the U.S. market alone are IKEA housewares and Victoria's Secret lingerie. In the global economy, Vietnam has emerged as a major player.

The Role of Cities. As mentioned earlier, cities serve as important nodes in the global network, linking together money (investment capital), people (human capital), production (industrial capital), and commodities (commercial capital). Instant communications, electronic cash transfers, rapid transportation, and the relative ease of shipping by tankers or cargo jets make cities key elements of the global economy. As such, they are locked in a reciprocal relationship: They help shape the world system, and in turn, the world system shapes them. Today, it is the importance of a city's role in the world system that largely determines its prospects for growth and prosperity (Gugler 1996:2–4).

Cities are no longer independent entities whose fortunes rise or fall according to what happens in a limited, local region. The prevailing view is that *place* no longer matters—that modern technology allows firms to locate anywhere, making cities irrelevant to the globalization of economic activity. One expert, however, disagrees. Saskia Sassen argues that cities offer an infrastructure concentration and servicing that are key dynamics in providing the capabilities for global control. Although some components of the financial district—notably in foreign currency markets—may exist in cyberspace, international cities, such as New York, London, Paris, Sydney, Tokyo, and Zurich, are examples of another aspect of the global economy: urban economic cores of banking and service activities. They are "transterritorial centers constituted via intercity electronic networks and various types of economic transactions" within "a specific complex of industries and activities" (Sassen 2006:148). Thus, these cities stand at the apex of the global urban hierarchy, because they are the financial capitals of the nations that dominate the world economy. On a smaller scale, Miami and Toronto—as significant regional sites—illustrate the locational concentration of certain industries and activities embedded in the new international

Potsdamer Platz, once a no-man's land of weeds and barbed wire between East and West, is the symbolic heart of modern Berlin. The 82-acre development is a cluster of a new mass transit system, sleek corporate high rises, shopping malls, and theaters. The district was developed mainly with global capital from corporations such as Sony, Asea Brown Boveri (an international conglomerate), and DaimlerChrysler for the sites of their European headquarters.

corporate sector. Their financial districts are of recent vintage, and their expansion is a response to the dynamics of globalization.

The place of cities in the world economy, then, is as "command points, global marketplaces, and production sites for the information economy" (Sassen 2006:199). Some intermediate sectors of the economy—the ones not geared to world markets but providing services to the mostly suburbanized middle class—may have left, but cities still provide strategic terrain for operations in a globalized economic system.

URBAN POLITICAL ECONOMY: FOUR PRINCIPLES

Although various urban political economists still emphasize different aspects of economic activity and mix the disciplinary viewpoints of economics, geography, political science, and sociology in one fashion or another, they all now agree on four principles as the foundation for studying and analyzing cities and urban life:

1. *A city's form and growth result not from "natural processes" but, rather, from decisions made by people*

and organizations that control wealth and other key resources. Rejecting the urban ecology model, urban political economists view cities as benefiting or suffering from investment decisions made by financial and business organizations. To remain competitive, companies will either expand or relocate their operations, depending on which action maximizes profits. Thus, broader economic forces and trends, not just local conditions, shape the cities, because advances in transportation and communications technologies allow the geographical mobility of capital and labor, thus freeing businesses from being rooted in a specific locale. When necessary, then, companies will move their corporate offices or production facilities, and such disinvestment in one place and investment in another impact significantly on both localities, including economic well-being, labor and population migration.

2. *Urban forms and urban social arrangements reflect conflicts over the distribution of resources.* Urban life, claim political economists, is an ongoing struggle between rich and poor, powerful and powerless, management and labor, as well as the needs of vast businesses and the desires of local communities. As the

Urban Trends box below suggests, such ongoing confrontation often brings a sense of paralysis to the people living within today's cities.

3. *Government continues to play an important role in urban life.* Local governments allocate resources and mediate conflicts among various groups that are vying for support. Decisions about zoning, tax incentives, and spending priorities, for example, still have much to do with a city's (a) business locations, (b) housing and resident population types, and (c) public space activities. And, significantly, because cities exist within a larger society, the federal government—with its enormous resources and regulatory powers—is a major influence on urban life, both directly, through its spending programs, and indirectly, through its management of the prime interest rate for loans and its rules governing investors.

4. *Urban growth patterns significantly result from economic restructuring.* The globalization of the economy changed the face of many North American cities, as manufacturing gave way to service industries. Furthermore, corporate mergers and takeovers created vast conglomerates, in the process eliminating many medium-sized firms and the jobs they provided. Downsizing, by which corporations strive to achieve a leaner, less costly organizational structure, has also reduced the number of middle-management positions. Together, these dimensions of economic restructuring dramatically reshaped cities, fostering growth or decline in metropolitan regions throughout North America and around the world.

URBAN TRENDS

Public Culture and Scarce Resources

[O]utright competition has dramatically changed the public sphere. Chronic fiscal crisis has so weakened public institutions and the members of their work force that their sense of mission has narrowed to saving their own jobs. Groups that interact in the same representative institutions, from city councils to boards of education, have radically different agendas that breed immobilism and distrust. The social practices of a public culture seem outmoded because they are "modern," along with the unquestioned hegemony of downtown and the pretended invisibility of class and ethnic cultures. The very concept of public culture seems old because it requires transcending private interests; it has been replaced by new rules of privatization, globalization, and ethnic separation. If every culture can set the rules—is individually hegemonic—it makes no sense to think of a transcendent common culture.

Yet what cities still do have in common is a "symbolic economy"—a continual production of symbols and spaces that frames and gives meaning to ethnic competition, racial change, and environmental renewal and decay. Despite the power of real estate developers, their architects, and members of public commissions, no single vision mobilizes this symbolic economy. Indeed, like the competing claims to embody "representations" of different cultures, the preeminence of culture since the 1970s has occurred despite the absence of vision, powerlessness of old elites to control the conditions of everyday urban life, and unprecedented debates over what should be built (or unbuilt) and where. A deep chasm lies between the post-1970s appreciation of visual culture and the absence of a master vision to control the chaos of urban life. This gap offers opportunities for both access and exclusion, for both elitism and democratization.

Source: Sharon Zukin, *The Cultures of Cities* (Cambridge, MA: Blackwell, 1996), p. 265.

THE URBANIZATION OF POVERTY

The world's poor once huddled mostly in rural areas, but no longer. Now, they live mostly in cities, and in 2007, one out of three city dwellers—about 1 billion people—lived in slums (UN-Habitat 2007). This urbanization of poverty creates problems that affect the quality of life for all residents—problems that cities so far have been unable to resolve.

The Developing World

In virtually every less-developed country, poverty—once found primarily in the villages of traditional agricultural societies—has moved to its cities (Figure 7–3). Significantly, however, the poverty of the world's poor is not in the same recognizable form that exists in the industrialized countries. This new form of poverty traps these unfortunate people in nations that have solved the first economic problem—the production of material goods—but not yet the second—the sufficient, if not equitable, distribution of the goods their industries produce. Food and consumer goods are not the only areas of deprivation. These cities lack sufficient housing, piped water, sewerage, public transportation, schools, police protection, doctors, hospitals, and other necessary amenities and defenses of urban life. The *Urban Living* box on page 196 illustrates one profile of urban poverty.

What is intimidating about the urbanization of poverty in less-developed countries is its scale. Between 1950 and 1990, as the first wave of industrialization came to poor, preindustrial countries, their cities expanded by 1 billion inhabitants, both through migration from villages and through natural increase. Sub-Saharan African countries—including Chad, Niger, and Sierra Leone—have some of the world's highest levels of urban poverty. Latin America has 134 million urban poor, compared with 77 million rural poor (UN-Habitat 2007).

Already exceeding the total population of cities in industrialized countries, cities in poor countries will increase by another 2 billion over the next 15 years according to the projections of demographers. These cities cannot now provide for the billion who have arrived during the past four decades, however, let alone for the 2 billion yet to come. At present, more than 1.1 billion people lack access to safe drinking water. In the megacities of Asia, more than two-thirds of the urban poor do not have access to adequate sanitation, as is the case for about three-fifths of urban Africans (UN-Habitat 2007). When the predicted 2 billion new urban poor arrive, these percentages may well increase.

Housing is no problem for most urban poor in less-developed countries, because they had previously built their own shelters in their villages. Most city land already belongs to someone else, however, so they build their makeshift dwellings in the less desirable locales—the lowlands and even wetlands around the city, or on hillsides too steep for ordinary buildings. These shantytowns go by many names: *citas miserias, bustees, bidonvilles, geccondus, favelas,* and *pueblos jovenes*. With a stubbornness and resistance to bureaucratic oppression, the residents struggle to survive, and they do so utilizing a reciprocal exchange system to help one another cope with extreme poverty. Others live an even worse existence, as homeless city dwellers. Sadly, many of them are the young, as the *Urban Living* box on page 197 reveals.

The Developed World

Unlike the less-developed countries, the more-developed countries of Asia, Europe, and North America have maintained urban societies for generations, if not centuries. Although their cities have contained large numbers of poor people for that same period of time, only recently have greater concentrations of the poor clustered in urban areas compared with elsewhere. This pattern is more pronounced in Canada than in the United States.

Canada. In a comparative demographic profile of poverty throughout Canada, the Canadian Council on Social Development reported that images of poverty as a rural

FIGURE 7-3 Prosperity and Stagnation in Global Perspective

Source: United Nations Development Programme; updated in Macionis's *Sociology*, 12th ed (2008).

URBAN LIVING

India: A Different Kind of Poverty

The statistics show that India contains about two-fifths of the world's poor, with a 2006 average annual individual income of $771. Statistics, however, do not prepare North Americans to face the reality of poverty in India. Most of the country's 1.1 billion million people live in conditions far worse than do those we label as "poor" at home. A traveler's first experience of Indian life is sobering and, sometimes, shocking. Arriving in Chennai (Madras), one of India's largest cities, with 4.3 million inhabitants, a visitor immediately recoils from the smell of human sewage that hangs over the city like a malodorous cloud. Untreated sewage also renders much of the region's water unsafe to drink. The sights and sounds of Chennai are strange and intense—as motorbikes, trucks, carts pulled by oxen, and waves of people choke the streets. Along the roads, vendors sit on burlap cloth hawking fruits, vegetables, and cooked food. Seemingly oblivious to the urban chaos all around them, people work, talk, bathe, and sleep in the streets. Tens of millions of homeless people fill the cities of India.

Chennai is also dotted by more than a thousand shanty settlements, containing more than a million people, many of whom have converged on the city from rural villages in search of something better. Shantytowns are clusters of huts constructed of branches, leaves, and discarded material. These dwellings offer little privacy and lack refrigeration, running water, and bathrooms. The visitor from the United States understandably feels uneasy entering such a community, because the poorest sections of our own inner cities seethe with frustration and, often, explode with violence.

Here again, however, India offers a sharp contrast: Its people understand poverty differently than we do. No restless young men hang out at the corner; no drug dealers work the streets; and there is surprisingly little danger. In the United States, poverty often means anger and isolation; in India, even shantytowns are built of strong families—children, parents, and perhaps, elderly grandparents—who extend a smile and a welcome.

In traditional societies like India, ways of life change slowly. To most Indians, life is shaped by *dharma,* the Hindu concept of duty and destiny that encourages them to accept their fate, whatever it may be. Mother Teresa, who won praise for her work among the poorest of India's people, went to the heart of the cultural differences: "Americans have angry poverty," she explained. "In India, there is worse poverty, but it is a happy poverty."

Perhaps we should not describe as "happy" anyone who clings to the edge of survival, but the sting of poverty in India is eased by the strength and support of families and communities, a sense that existence has a purpose, and a worldview that encourages each person to accept whatever life offers. As a result, the visitor comes away from a first encounter with Indian poverty in confusion: "How can people be so poor, and yet apparently content, vibrant, and so joyful?"

Source: Based on UN-Habitat data and John Macionis's field research in Chennai.

phenomenon are out of date. Roughly 7 of every 10 poor Canadians live in an urban area. Among Canada's largest metropolitan areas, Edmonton, Montreal, Toronto, Vancouver, Quebec City, and Winnipeg had the highest rates of poverty. Single-parent families are more likely to be poor in certain urban areas than in others. For example, in Calgary,

URBAN LIVING

Latin American "Street Children": Living on the Edge

Perhaps the greatest tragedy in Latin American cities has been the appearance of millions of "street children"—or *meninos de rua*. Like the tip of an iceberg, the presence of the street children suggests problems that run far deeper: poverty that stunts the lives of children who labor long hours each day, who work as prostitutes, or who fall victim to hunger and disease. The United Nations International Children's Emergency Children's Relief Fund (UNICEF) has estimated that there are tens of millions of street children worldwide, with half that number in Latin America, with no country excluded. Their greatest numbers are in Brazil, Colombia, Guatemala, Honduras, Mexico, and Nicaragua.

According to a study by the Casa Alianza (2006), 42 percent of the children on the streets are between 6 and 11 years old, and 49 percent are between 12 and 18 years. Many of these young people live in and around the cities' sprawling public markets, where it is easy to scavenge for food. A few work at shining shoes, cleaning windshields, or selling anything from candy to their bodies, but most beg or steal to survive. The average age of children at the garbage dump looking for items to reclaim and sell is 10 years. The average age for children involved in prostitution is 16, although 13-year-olds are also found in these activities.

The street children are orphans or come from broken or crowded homes where there is not enough to eat—and where physical and sexual abuse is commonplace. Just a couple of decades ago, the public looked on street urchins with a mixture of annoyance and affection. In Brazil, they were known as *moleques*—that is, ragamuffins, scamps, or rascals. They were streetwise kids who were cute and cunning, sometimes sexually precocious, and invariably economically enterprising. Making themselves useful in a variety of ways, honest and otherwise, they were reminiscent of Aladdin, the *Arabian Nights* character portrayed by Disney. Today, however, most people look on them as public pests who should be forcibly removed from the urban landscape (Human Rights Watch 2008).

Many cannot resist the temptation of cheap drugs to obliterate their hunger and cold. A few years ago, glue was the drug favored by street kids, but today, solvent and paint thinner are cheaper and easier to come by. A solvent-soaked rag, easily clenched in a palm, is also much more discreet than plastic bags of glue, which police have been known to seize and dump on the children's hair and clothes. All solvents have the desired effect: They stop the hunger pains, and they numb the physical and psychological effects of the brutality of the security forces. Inhaling the fumes produces hallucinations and escape, but the long-term effects are devastating: irreversible brain damage, paralysis, kidney or liver failure, and eventually, death. About 95 percent of street youth in Latin America use drugs on a daily basis, most commonly solvents or shoe glue (Arms of Love International 2008).

In other countries, the story is much the same. In the eyes of too many people, street children are not even human, so they are dispatched in much the same way that one would step on a cockroach (more than 3,200 killed in Honduras alone since 1998). It's a form of social cleansing, ridding the streets of social vermin who lie amid the rubbish or under parked cars, curled up inconspicuously on the concrete until someone comes along and kicks them. And people rarely stop to wonder why they are there in the first place (Casa Alianza 2006).

Perhaps nowhere in North America is the global economy as visible as in the daily loading and unloading of container shipments onto or off trucks and ships at its seaports, such as here in Baltimore. Many of these goods are finished products on their way to wholesalers, but others are parts destined for assembly in factories of nations other than the ones in which they were manufactured.

Richmond, Gloucester, and Burlington, the proportion of poor single-parent families is much lower than the proportion in Cape Breton, Saint John, Montreal, and Hamilton. Also, the effect of unemployment on poverty rates varies in urban areas. Vancouver and Windsor, for instance, had similar unemployment rates, but the rate of poverty was 36 percent in Vancouver but only 26 percent in Windsor (Lee 2000).

Similarly, the rate of poverty among senior citizens living in urban areas varies significantly. Less than 8 percent of elderly persons in Saskatoon, Gloucester, and Nepean live in poverty—less than the proportion in Burlington (21 percent) and in Hamilton, Quebec City, Trois-Rivieres, and Winnipeg (15–16 percent). The reasons for this may be related to the cost of living in these different urban areas and to the source of income for seniors. In some urban centers today, seniors are likely reaping the benefits of local economies that offered them good wages and benefits before they retired (Lee 2000). Furthermore, the number of homeless has increased to a level far beyond anything seen a generation ago (UN-Habitat 2007).

United States.   Central cities do not house the majority of the U.S. poor: In 2006, 38 percent of the nation's poor lived in suburban areas, 20 percent in non-metropolitan areas, and 42 percent in central cities (U.S. Census Bureau 2007a). Central cities, however, do contain the highest concentrations of poverty, and their poverty rate has been above the national average since the early 1970s. About 3.5 million people are homeless (UN-Habitat 2007). Two major reasons account for this concentration of poverty in the centers of large U.S. cities. First, many affluent residents moved to the suburbs, leaving the poor behind. Second, as more jobs moved to the suburbs, employment opportunities for city residents dwindled. Even so, the urban concentrations of poverty in central cities declined significantly during the 1990s. The primary reasons for this change are migration, suburbanization, and a nationwide drop in the poverty rate (Iceland 2005).

URBAN TRENDS

A Bold Initiative

While shelters can provide a clean and safe environment for a homeless family, the shelter system should not be simply a way station until permanent housing is secured. To address the needs of these families, shelters also must provide a variety of services and programs that enable families to build sound, independent living skills, complete their education, and obtain job training before moving to permanent housing. Not shelters, but rather Residential Education Training (RET) Centers—or American Family Inns—are required to deliver such a service intervention plan. Through RET Centers, desperately needed services such as health care, counseling, and substance abuse treatment can be economically and efficiently provided. Educational programs such as living skills workshops for adults or after-school accelerated learning programs for children are immediately accessible and responsive to the needs of parents and children. Homes for the Homeless has developed and has continued to refine the RET Center model over the past five years as a response to the changing characteristics of homeless families.

American Family Inns have proven to be a successful mechanism to start families on a secure path to independent living. *Approximately ninety-four percent of all families who have participated in the services offered by HFH's RET Centers have maintained their residences once placed in permanent housing.* When compared to New York City's return-to-shelter rate of fifty percent for formerly homeless families, RET Centers offer a successful solution by addressing the severe complexities of the poverty faced by homeless families.

The dramatic changes in the composition and characteristics of homeless families over the last several years highlight the emerging fact that homelessness is not simply a housing issue. Rather, the trends illustrate that homelessness is merely a symptom of a debilitating poverty affecting a very young and vulnerable population. Policymakers and service providers must meet the challenge of this complex issue with bold initiatives such as the RET Center model. Only then will it be possible to break the cycle of poverty and homelessness which is now plaguing the poor urban family.

Source: "A Bold Initiative" excerpted from *The Cycle of Family Homelessness: A Social Policy Reader,* Appendix B. Reprinted by permission of The Institute for Children and Poverty.

Europe. Many western European cities are beset with poverty problems, generated in large part by the influx of poor immigrants from developing countries who seek a better life. UN-Habitat (2007) reported that homelessness in Western Europe was at its highest level in 50 years, with an estimated 3 million homeless during the winter of 2003, the largest numbers being found in Germany and the United Kingdom. In recent decades, poverty escalated throughout the European Union (EU) countries, with an average of 15 percent of EU citizens at risk of poverty. In the United Kingdom, the most extreme situation exists,

with the number of poor children tripling in less than two decades (UN-Habitat 2007).

Poverty remains a concern in the cities of many advanced economies throughout the world, partially as a result of the uneven costs and benefits of economic globalization. The changing global economy eliminated many low-skill jobs in industrialized nations that once enabled the cities' poor to extricate themselves from poverty. Until innovative policies take aim at causes, not symptoms, of urban poverty and homelessness, they will not go away. See the *Urban Trends* box above for one approach to resolving this problem.

SUMMARY

The traditional economic analysis of cities highlights the advantages of particular locations and the various economic benefits those locations offer over the hinterland. Living in cities allows people to get more goods of higher quality more cheaply. These economic advantages, economists like William Alonso argue, are sufficient to explain recurrent patterns in urban land use: For example, businesses predominate at the center (the CBD), surrounded by residential areas and, farther out, agricultural areas. Even so, this theory may be descriptive only of Western (primarily North American) cities, and it ignores various non-economic forces, such as racial prejudice, that also affect urban land use.

By the 1960s, many social scientists came to the conclusion that the prevailing theories and models could not address changing patterns of urban life. French philosopher Henri Lefebvre was a major influence on the evolving political economy perspective, and he contributed ideas about the primary and secondary circuits of capital, space as a form of social organization, and the role of government. David Harvey's neo-Marxist analysis of Baltimore revealed that finance capital, not industrial capital, was now the key shaper of neighborhood quality. Manuel Castells updated Marx by suggesting welfare capitalism as a new form of class conflict probability and by discussing modes of development, in lieu of modes of production, as the key element in the information age. Allen Scott discussed horizontal integration and vertical disintegration as a basis for understanding business relocation in the global economy. John Logan and Harvey Molotch, drawing on Lefebvre's distinctions between abstract space and social space, examined the tensions arising between advocates of urban growth and residents of the current built environment who may oppose the proposed new use of that space.

Economic restructuring changed older cities from a manufacturing base to a service industries base. Recent urban economic changes must be understood in the context of an evolving world system of economic interdependence that places nations in a global hierarchy. This hierarchy consists of the "core" of highly developed countries, the "semi-periphery" of less-developed countries, and the "periphery" of the least-developed countries. Within the ever-expanding global network, cities are locked in a reciprocal relationship, serving as important nodes linking together wealth (investment capital), people (human capital), production (industrial capital), and commodities (commercial capital).

Although critical urban social scientists go in different directions, depending on their disciplinary viewpoints and areas of focus, they agree on four basic principles of political economy. First, decision makers controlling resources—not natural processes—shape the form and growth of the city, because the geographical mobility of capital and workers gives them flexibility to locate where they can maximize profits. Second, conflicts over distribution of resources also shape the form of, and social arrangements in, the city. Third, government continues to play a role in affecting urban patterns. Fourth, economic restructuring is a key influence on patterns of urban growth.

Just as the world is becoming more urbanized, so, too, is poverty. In developing countries, poverty takes a different form than in developed countries, because the equitable distribution of goods does not match the production of material goods. The rapid growth of urban poor— 1 billion over the past 40 years, and a projected 2 billion over the next 15 years—creates a serious problem for cities of the developing world in attempting to provide both necessities and amenities for this burgeoning population. Countries of the developed world, such as Canada and the United States, are experiencing greater geographical segregation based on income levels, placing a burden on their cities to cope with large concentrations of the poor, even though their numbers have declined somewhat. Poverty results in serious problems of homelessness in more-developed countries, while in less-developed countries, the wretched conditions in the many shantytowns mark their housing problem.

CONCLUSION

The economic trends that have produced major changes in the economic and employment opportunities of North American cities will continue. So, too, will the increased integration of poor countries and their cities into the world economy. Globalization is a process that no one can stop or reverse. Therefore, an understanding of global political economy remains essential in any study of cities and urban life. This perspective addresses the rapid changes that are occurring worldwide; thus, it offers a comparative approach that is lacking in ethnocentric models focusing only on individual cities located in North America.

Urban political economy, however, has two important limitations (Pahl 1989; Walton 1993). Large-scale concepts, such as Manuel Castells's modes of development, do not fully explain the differences between cities that are in the same mode of development. In other words, global political and economic forces do not fully determine the character of all cities and neighborhoods; local variations do exist. For one thing, individuals do not respond like a ball in a pinball machine, reacting to the force of a flipper by going in another direction. They reflect, interpret, and react on their own. One danger in the political economy approach is ignoring the individual factor—something researchers now realize and are striving to overcome.

Peter Hall (1984:34) further suggests that urban political economy is defined as much by what it omits as by what it stresses. On the one hand, there is much to be recommended in the political economists' critique of urban ecology. On the other hand, the political economy approach does not deal very extensively, or very deeply, with cases where capitalist cities have been successful at raising the general standard of living for the city as a whole. Nor does it offer much insight regarding the weaknesses of socialist cities in meeting the needs of many of their people.

Perhaps a fuller understanding would emerge from a synthesis of the conventional ecological and political economy approaches that would form a critical dialogue, one that draws from the strengths, yet avoids the limitations, of each. The location and shape of cities, their patterned land-use and social clustering, are important elements that enable us to grasp more fully the cities' essential qualities, but so, too, is the necessity of knowing the macroeconomic forces at play that affect their welfare. This analytical fusion could provide us with an even more sophisticated understanding of our cities.

Meanwhile, despite its limitations, political economy is now a dominant perspective in urban studies, inspiring many scientific investigations of cities throughout the world. These studies examine not only present-day patterns but also the future of cities—a subject we will turn to at the end of this book. Next, however, we will look at urban behavior as it is shaped and influenced by the physical and social environment.

KEY TERMS

abstract space   (179)
agglomeration industries   (173)
central business district (CBD)   (174)
central place theory   (174)
economic restructuring   (186)
horizontal integration   (183)
mode of development   (182)

mode of production   (182)
oligopoly   (182)
postmodernism   (172)
primary circuit of capital   (178)
second circuit of capital   (178)
social space   (179)
vertical disintegration   (183)

INTERNET ACTIVITIES

1. You will find a world map depicting the countries in the core, semi-periphery, and periphery, as defined in world-systems analysis, by going to *http://people.hofstra.edu/ geotrans/eng/ch7en/conc7en/centerperiphery.html.*

2. The illustrated evolution of the shopping center—from its nineteenth-century predecessors to suburban centers and urban festival marketplaces—is nicely presented at *http:// history.sandiego.edu/gen/soc/shoppingcenter.html.*

CHAPTER 8

SOCIAL PSYCHOLOGY
The Urban Experience

What makes cities so stimulating? Why do they pull from us reactions of either stout admiration or powerful aversion? Georg Simmel's answer was that the city is a tremendous concentration of buildings, images, and people that intensifies stimulation as no other form of human settlement does. Everywhere you turn—around a corner, breaking through a crowd, entering the subway—the city demands a response.

How do we make sense of this coming-at-you-from-all-sides, sometimes in-your-face creation that is the city? Simmel answered that we learn to categorize the city's elements, paying attention to some things while ignoring others. Louis Wirth agreed, suggesting that we mentally "map" the city. Unfortunately, neither theorist said much about how this mapping process works. But, drawing on later research, this chapter sketches the outlines of this process—the characteristic elements of the social psychology of the city.

THE PHYSICAL ENVIRONMENT

We react to the city in two ways—as a physical setting and as a social environment. First, we consider how people perceive their physical surroundings and try to make sense out of them.

Kevin Lynch: The Image of the City

To explore how people made sense of the city's physical complexity, urbanist Kevin Lynch interviewed urbanites in Boston, Jersey City, and Los Angeles. In each city, Lynch showed his respondents a map representing several square miles of the central city and asked them to describe it in their own terms. Most could offer a personal *image of the city* that Lynch defined as the individual's "generalized mental picture of the [city's] external physical world" (1982:4; orig. 1960).

To a great many people around the world, the New York City skyline is not only easily recognizable but also a symbol of the power and lure of American life. To the residents of Jersey City, living on the opposite shore of the Hudson River, the skyline is such a looming, overpowering presence that many residents mentioned it to Lynch as one of their landmarks.

Before we continue, take a moment and think of the city you know best. On a piece of paper, draw as detailed a map of it as you can, putting in everything of importance that you can recall. This exercise will make the following discussion far more meaningful.

Building an Image.   Most of Lynch's respondents developed their image of the city in a similar fashion. First, their images emerged as part of a two-way process: (1) They made distinctions among the various physical parts of the city, and (2) they organized these parts in a personally meaningful way.

For example, Figure 8–1 shows downtown Boston, where the large park known as the

Boston Common and Public Garden separates various downtown districts from one another. To the west of the park is the residential Back Bay area, with its characteristic three- and four-story apartment houses. To the north is the wealthier Beacon Hill district, where one finds the State House. To the east and south is most of Boston's central business district, full of high-rise office buildings, retail stores, restaurants, and entertainment facilities. When we say "downtown," we mean the central business district, and when we speak of the deterioration of the downtowns, we mean its loss of these interdependent commercial activities.

To a person living, say, in a small apartment just west of the Garden and the Common, the

FIGURE 8–1 Downtown Boston

Source: Kevin Lynch, *The Image of the City,* 1960. MIT Press, Cambridge, Mass.

park area may be the dominant element in an image of the city, because this person may go there frequently for walks, getting to know every bench, fountain, and footpath. This same individual, however, may know little about the rest of downtown.

On the other hand, to another Bostonian living nearby, the park may have little significance. Working in the high-rise offices on the east side of the park, this person may have little desire to use the Garden. In this case, the distinct image might be of the downtown buildings, including where the good restaurants are, and of all the shortcuts for getting from one building or street to another.

Common Elements of Images.   Lynch discovered that people built their urban images from five common elements. **Paths,** he explains, are "channels along which the observer customarily . . . moves. They may be streets, walkways, transit lines, canals, railroads" (1982:15). **Edges,** the boundaries between two areas, include shores, walls, wide streets, or breaks between buildings and open space. **Districts** represent medium-to-large sections of the city. Examples in Boston that people commonly noted were "Back Bay," "Beacon Hill," "the Common," and "the shopping district." **Nodes** stand as points of intense activity, such as a railroad terminal, a square, or a street-corner hangout. Nodes are often the places to which paths lead. Finally, Lynch's subjects built their images around **landmarks**—physical reference points including buildings, signs, stores, domes, gas stations, or hills.

Now, look back at the map you drew a few minutes ago. Were you thinking in terms of Lynch's categories?

Lynch also found that most people incorporate many of the same elements in their own images—that is, what is a path or edge to one person is a path or edge to many others. Looking back at Figure 8–1, virtually every Bostonian recognizes the Charles River as a major edge, separating one large district of the city ("downtown") from another (Cambridge). Similarly, most people also mention "Mass. Ave." to the west and the Southeast Expressway to the east as key edges. Main paths are Beacon Street, "Comm. Ave.," Boylston Street, and Tremont Street. Commonly mentioned nodes include Copley Square (site of the "BPL," the Boston Public Library), North Station (a railroad and subway terminal), and Park Street Station. Although it is below ground, Park Street Station is another classic example of an urban node: The junction of Boston's three main subway lines is constantly abuzz with activity.

Although Lynch discovered that people in every city appear to use the same elements in constructing their images, he also found that some cities stimulate their residents to conceptualize more complex images than other cities do. In Boston, virtually everyone Lynch interviewed could identify *numerous* paths, edges, nodes, districts, and landmarks. In Jersey City, by contrast, even long-term residents could identify only a few such elements, and they often confessed confusion and uncertainty about what existed in different parts of their own city. Perhaps most illustrative of their weak image of their city was the residents' frequent mention of the looming, overpowering New York City skyline to the east as a landmark. In his summary of findings about Jersey City, Lynch emphasized its nondescript character:

When asked for a general characterization of the city, one of the most common remarks was that it was not a whole, that it had no center, but was rather a collection of many hamlets. The question: "What first comes to mind with the words 'Jersey City'?," so easy to answer for Bostonians, proved to be a difficult one. Again and again, subjects repeated that "nothing special" came to mind, that the city was hard to [characterize], that it had no distinctive sections. . . . (1982:29).

Many remarks came out about the indistinguishability of the physical scene:

"It's much the same all over . . . it's more or less just common to me. I mean, when I go up and down the streets, it's more or less the same thing—Newark Avenue, Jackson Avenue, Bergen Avenue. I mean, sometimes they're more or less just the same; there's nothing to differentiate them." (1982:31)

In Los Angeles, Lynch found, residents have an even less of a sharp image for their city because of the great sprawl and uniformity of cross streets, which make it difficult to locate anything with confidence. Although the area studied was comparable in size to those of the other two cities, it included little more than a central business district. Those interviewed, most of whom worked there, could describe only a few landmarks in any specific detail, such as the "ugly" black and gold Richfield Building and the pyramid atop City Hall. The strongest element of all was Pershing Square,

> an exotically landscaped open space in the heart of the downtown, reinforced by its use as an outdoor political forum, camp meeting, and old people's hangout. Along with the Plaza–Olvera Street node (involving another open space), Pershing Square was the most sharply described element, with its immaculate central lawn, fringed first by banana trees, then by a ring of old people sitting in solid ranks on the stone walls, then by busy streets, and finally by the close files of downtown buildings. (1982:36–37)

Even so, many Angelenos were uncertain of the precise location of Pershing Square. Moreover, most residents of the city could identify only paths, and they often confused one with another. When asked to describe or symbolize Los Angeles as a whole, residents found it hard to respond, simply describing their city as "spread-out," "spacious," "formless," or "without centers." Lynch offered one person's comment as illustrating of this diffused urban image:

> "It's as if you were going somewhere for a long time, and when you got there you discovered that there was nothing there, after all." (1982:41)

The "Imagability" of Cities.   Noting how his respondents differed in their precision about urban images, Lynch suggested that cities differ markedly in terms of *imagability*.

This concept is important for two reasons. First, a clear urban image gives people a working knowledge of, and emotional security about, their city. A strong urban image makes acquisition of knowledge relatively easy, and it sets people at ease emotionally. (As the *Urban Living* box on page 207 reveals, however, the terrorist acts of September 11, 2001, make many people feel less secure in cities.) Second, a comprehensible urban environment "heightens the potential depth and intensity of the human experience" (1982:5). It invites us to experience more, to involve ourselves more in the life of the city. Lynch concluded that imagability is one of the essential aspects of a positive urban environment.

Stanley Milgram: More on Mental Maps

One of the most intriguing aspects of Lynch's work is his discovery that even people living in the same city construct different mental images of their surroundings. Most people's maps mix details with distortions as well as large gaps. To understand why **mental maps** are so distinctive, psychologist Stanley Milgram explored how New Yorkers and Parisians understood their cities. In both cases, he found that people construct mental maps *based on their personal experience, their interests, and their knowledge of the socially recognized "important areas" of the city* (Milgram 1972). In the years since, many other researchers have reaffirmed his findings (Mendoza 2006; Bembry and Norris 2005; Matei, Ball-Rokeach, and Qui 2001; Kulhavy and Stock 1996; Thill and Sui 1993).

The Individuality of Mental Maps.   Figures 8–2 and 8–3 on pages 208–209 present drawings of two people's mental maps of Manhattan. New Jersey suburbanite Beth's Manhattan, shown in Figure 8–2, emphasizes details about the streets and locations of the artistic and cultural centers that draw her to the city's midtown. She offers only sketchy information about the Upper West Side or lower Manhattan. In contrast, physical therapist Cara's Manhattan, shown in Figure 8–3, emphasizes the Upper West Side

URBAN LIVING

Living with Terrorism

In today's world, many of us are aware of the vulnerability of cities to terrorist attacks. Both Masumoto City in 1994 and Tokyo in 1995 fell victim to chemical terrorism, with use of the toxic gas sarin on defenseless civilians in subways. The 2001 attacks on the Pentagon in Washington, D.C., and the twin towers of the World Trade Center in New York City, with their horrific losses of life and mass destruction, still reverberate in the minds of hundreds of millions of people worldwide. In March 2004, terrorists in Madrid killed 191 train passengers and wounded more than 1,400 others, while in July 2005, terrorists killed 52 bus and train passengers in London, wounding an additional 700 people. In November 2008, terrorists killed 179 people in Mumbai, India.

These and other incidents remind us that urban centers attract terrorists. The large concentrations of people, tall buildings, symbolic monuments, and infrastructure of bridges and tunnels are all tempting targets for those intent on inflicting maximum damage and deaths. People once avoided cities for fear of becoming victims of violent crimes. Now, some fear not just being in major cities but even living near one in the event of a biological, chemical, or nuclear attack.

Seeing concrete barricades at many important locations and undergoing bag searches at concerts, sporting events, and airports are part of our new reality. For some, living or working in tall buildings, or viewing the cityscape from high-perched observation decks, holds little appeal. Others, refusing to allow their lives to be ruled by fear, continue their daily urban routines and lifestyles.

Whether they respond by avoidance or defiance, however, urbanites recognize that their world today is different from the one that existed before September 11, 2001. That realization is also part of the psychology of urban life.

area where she lives. Featured prominently are restaurants, parks, and high-rise apartment buildings, without the need to list streets given her familiarity with the area. Missing, save for one or two items, are midtown and lower Manhattan.

No one, Milgram found, can re-create the complexity of the whole city, as Cara's map demonstrates. Moreover, everyone's images constantly evolve as urban experiences deepen or as the city changes. A relative newcomer to a city, for example, will typically draw a map of the center city that contains prominent landmarks but almost no detail at all. Often, the few areas noted are misplaced and distorted in size. Yet, for that same person, after living there just a few more months, the city usually comes alive,

and she or he can offer far more detail as well as greater geographical accuracy. In short, with time, most people succeed in comprehending the city and using it effectively.

Multiple Urban Realities.   What all this suggests is that there are as many "New Yorks" or "Seattles," for example, as there are people living there. More broadly, each of these active mental maps contributes to the larger urban dynamic that is the full New York City or Seattle.

Mental maps, however, are not completely a matter of individual differences. Social class differences also affect what people include in their cognitive maps (Lloyd and Hooper 1991). Race plays a key part in how residents

FIGURE 8–2   Mental Maps of Manhattan: Beth's Map

understand the city as well. Researchers have found that blacks' perceptions of community undesirability differ from those of whites. Generally, blacks rate most communities as more desirable than whites do, often favoring communities in which they are the numerical minority. Whites often rate mixed-race communities as being less desirable, particularly those with higher proportions of blacks, even when blacks are the numerical minority (Krysan 2002; Sigelman and Henig 2001; Charles 2000).

FIGURE 8–3   Mental Maps of Manhattan: Cara's Map

The city is thus a dynamic, creative, ongoing mixture of perceptions and experiences, as Robert Park explained long ago:

The city ... is something more than a congeries of individual men and of social conveniences—streets, buildings, electric lights, tramways, and telephones ... something more,

also, than a mere constellation of institutions and administrative devices—courts, hospitals, schools, police, and civil functionaries of various sorts. The city is ... a state of mind (1984:1; orig. 1916).

In the *Cityscape* box on page 210, novelist Alfred Kazin describes returning to his old

CITYSCAPE

The Streets of Brownsville

All my early life lies open to my eye within five city blocks. . . . On Belmont Avenue, Brownville's great open street market, the pushcarts are still lined on each other for blocks, and the din is as deafening, marvelous, and appetizing as ever. . . . When I was a boy, they . . . reached halfway up the curb to the open stands of the stores; walking down the street was like being whirled around and around in a game of blind man's bluff. But Belmont Avenue is still the merriest street in Brownsville. As soon as I walked into it from Rockaway, caught my first whiff of the herrings and pickles in their great black barrels, heard the familiarly harsh, mocking cries and shouts from the market women—"Oh you darlings! Oh you sweet ones, oh you pretty ones! Storm us! Tear us apart! Devour us!"—I laughed right out loud, it was so good to be back among them. . . .

On my right hand the "Stadium" movie house—the sanctuary every Saturday afternoon of my childhood, the great dark place of all my dream life. On my left the little wooden synagogue where I learned my duties as a Jew and at thirteen, having reached the moral estate of a man, stood up at the high desk before the Ark (Blessed Be He, Our Lord and Our Shield!) and was confirmed in the faith of my fathers. . . .

The block: my block. It was on the Chester Street side of our house, between the grocery and the back wall of the old drugstore, that I was hammered into the shape of the streets. Everything beginning at Blake Avenue would always wear for me some delightful strangeness and mildness, simply because it was not of my block, the block, where the clang of your head sounded against the pavement when you fell in a fist fight, and the rows of store lights on each side were pitiless, watching you. . . . [I recall] smelling the sweaty sweet dampness from the pool in summer and the dust on the leaves as I passed under the ailanthus trees. . . .

We worked every inch of it, from the cellars and the backyards to the sickening space between the roofs. Any wall, any stoop, any curving metal edge on a billboard sign made a place against which to knock a ball; any bottom rung of a fire escape ladder a goal in basketball; any sewer cover a base. . . . Our life every day was fought out on the pavement and in the gutter, up against the walls of the houses and the glass fronts of the drugstore and the grocery—in and out of the fresh steaming piles of horse manure, the wheels of passing carts and automobiles, along the iron spikes of the stairway to the cellar, the jagged edge of the open garbage cans, the crumbly steps of the old farmhouses still left on one side of the street.

Source: Alfred Kazin, *A Walker in the City* (New York: MJF Books, 1997).

neighborhood in the Brownsville district of New York. Present in his image of the city are all of Lynch's visual categories, complex interpretations of sound and smell, as well as evidence of his own social background.

THE SOCIAL ENVIRONMENT: *GESELLSCHAFT*

Living in the city demands that we deal with more than just the physical environment. We must also contend with large numbers of *people,* most of whom we don't know—and probably don't want to know. How do we cope with what Ferdinand Tönnies (see Chapter 5) called the city's *gesellschaft* characteristics—its vast numbers and characteristic anonymity?

The Pedestrian: Watching Your Step

Standing on the sidewalk during rush hour along Boylston Street in Boston; State Street in Columbus, Ohio; or Kearny Street in San Francisco, anyone can observe the "faceless

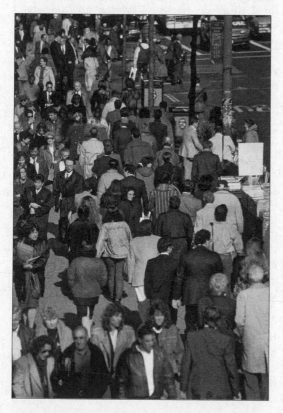

As Goffman suggested, pedestrians communally follow a sidewalk traffic code, creating two opposing streams with a dividing line somewhere in the middle of the sidewalk. Within these two streams, they share an intricate set of social rules that enable them to move easily at their own pace, without jostling or colliding with one another.

crowd" of urbanites going about their daily business. Taking such a detached perspective, the city's people seem almost like sheep—an undifferentiated, robot-like herd.

Is this really so? As most urbanites know, city life is an orderly routine, one that allows people to meet their personal needs while surrounded by an unknown mass of others. People are on the street, of course, for a reason. We move through the city to get to work, to enjoy a restaurant, to meet a friend, to catch a subway, or perhaps, just to take a walk. Simply because the observer cannot perceive such motives is no reason to think they don't exist.

Moreover, pedestrians observe an intricate set of social rules. An unwritten traffic code exists for the sidewalks, just as a written code exists for automobiles using the streets. For example, pedestrian traffic in North American cities sorts itself into two opposing streams, with the dividing line somewhere near the middle of the sidewalk. Within each stream, people "watch their step" in a variety of ways: First, they keep themselves at least slightly aware of obstacles, such as mailboxes, lampposts, or groups stopped on the sidewalk. Second, they casually note the speed of people in front of or behind them, gauging their own speed accordingly in order to avoid collisions. Third, to move faster or slower than the stream, people move to the outside of the lane. Fourth, people utilize various strategies to avoid collisions, perhaps making coughing noises or shifting packages to alert a careless walker about impending contact. Fifth, people scold one another for breaking any of these rules. After someone brushes by, one pedestrian may loudly protest: "Why don't ya look where you're going?" Such reactions show us that people know the rules for pedestrian behavior and call others to task for any transgressions. In essence, a tacit contract exists among users of public space, who come to trust each other to act like competent pedestrians (Wolfinger 1995).

Rules of pedestrian traffic vary from culture to culture, of course. This variety can puzzle—and even intimidate—a traveler, as the next *Urban Living* box on page 212 explains.

URBAN LIVING

Saigon: Learning to Cross the Street All Over Again

The first morning after we arrived in port, we left the ship early and made our way along the docks toward the center of Ho Chi Minh City—known to an earlier generation as Saigon. After looking us over—a family of U.S. visitors—the government security officers waved us through the security gates without so much as glancing at our papers. But we paused nonetheless, coming face to face with dozens of men crowded just beyond the gate, all operators of cyclos—bicycles with a small carriage attached to the front—which are the Vietnamese equivalent of taxicabs. "No, thanks," I stated firmly, breaking eye contact, and making a firm gesture with my arm. In New York, it is hard enough to find a cab; here, we spent the next twenty minutes fending off persistent drivers who cruised alongside us pleading for our business. The pressure was uncomfortable.

Let's cross the street, I suggested. We turned to the traffic and immediately realized that there were no stop signs or signal lights. In fact, there was no break at all in the steady stream of bicycles, cyclos, motorbikes, and small trucks that rattled along the rough roadway. What to do? Then the answer came, in the form of a tiny woman who walked right next to us and plunged out into the traffic without so much as batting an eye. She simply walked at a steady pace across the street; drivers saw her coming and made room for her. To us, she appeared to part the waves of vehicles as if she had some mysterious power.

We took a deep breath. From several yards back, we walked right into the traffic keeping eyes straight ahead. Amazing! It worked. Such are the rules of the road in Vietnam.

Source: Based on travel by John Macionis to Vietnam, 1994.

Escalators represent another example of cultural variety. In the United States, passengers all pile on together, making passage by anybody behind almost impossible. In most European nations, however, escalator passengers ride on the right side, leaving a lane on the left for anyone wishing to pass. Taking their first ride on a European escalator, North Americans who place themselves on the left-hand side of a ramp are often a bit puzzled to hear people behind them asking them to please move over. Conversely, Europeans riding a North American subway escalator can be quite puzzled at the "rudeness" of locals, who jam up the ramp so that no one can pass.

Finally, even in that most dense and anonymous of urban worlds, the subway, people

evolve mechanisms for ordering and personalizing their experience. The *Urban Living* box on page 213 offers a look at the subway during rush hour.

Together, these examples reveal that street behavior is not nearly as chaotic as it might appear to be at first glance. City dwellers may have to deal with larger numbers of people, often in crowded conditions, but urban life is not necessarily difficult or dehumanizing.

A World of Strangers

Besides coping with the city's sheer numbers, urbanites must also learn to deal with anonymity, living in what Lyn Lofland (1985) calls "a world of strangers." Lofland argues that we look for visual clues in order to classify strangers in much

URBAN LIVING

The Subway at Rush Hour

A crowd of people surged into the Eighth Avenue express at 59th Street. By elbowing other passengers in the back, by pushing and heaving, they forced their bodies into the coaches, making room for themselves where no room had existed before. As the train gathered speed for the long run to 125th Street, the passengers settled down into small private worlds, thus creating the illusion of space between them and their fellow passengers. The worlds were built up behind newspapers and magazines, behind closed eyes or while staring at the varicolored show cards that bordered the coaches.

Source: Ann Petry, The Street (Boston: Houghton Mifflin, 1998), p. 27.

the same way as we make sense of the city's physical environment.

Appearance and Location.   First, we identify strangers in terms of their *appearance* and their *physical location* within the city. In other words, we give strangers "the once-over," noting their clothing, hairstyle, jewelry, what they're carrying, and how they're walking. We also let location speak for people: For example, in a district of office buildings and expensive restaurants, we expect to find different types of people than we would find in a district full of all-night movie houses or pornographic bookstores.

Lofland concedes that there is nothing uniquely urban about such tactics. Even in small towns, people judge each other by appearance and by "which side of the tracks" they call home. The point is simply that in big cities, our reliance on clues like appearance and location becomes essential. After all, the odds of running into someone we know in midtown Manhattan or Chicago's downtown "loop" are small, indeed.

Worth noting is that using spatial location as a clue to people's identities is a modern practice. In preindustrial cities, public spaces, such as the town square, usually had many uses: schooling, religious services, parades, shopping, general loitering, and even executions. In short, because virtually *anybody* might be found there, location provided few clues about who strangers were. In part, then, citizens put great stock in appearance, as illustrated in the *Urban Living* box on page 214.

In modern industrial societies, however, the rules change. Dress still plays a part in identifying strangers, but costume is no longer the central clue it once was. Dress codes have relaxed, and people from all walks of life, without fear of censure, wear almost any sort of clothing. Important historical reasons explain this change.

In the preindustrial city, only the wealthy could afford clothes of silk and satin or jewelry made from gold and silver. With the Industrial Revolution, however, mass production made many types of dress much more affordable. Furthermore, a rising standard of living allowed more and more people to purchase and display such goods. The film *Hester Street* (1975) offered an example: In one scene from this view of New York in 1900, Jake, a Russian Jewish immigrant, takes his family to Central Park. Making more money than he ever did in the old country, Jake is wearing a modestly priced but very fashionable suit. As he parades around the park, he exclaims proudly: "Look at me! I'm a real American! Who could tell if I was a Jew or a Gentile?"

URBAN LIVING

Clothes Make the Man

To a degree unknown to moderns, the resident of the preindustrial city literally "donned" his identity. The Roman citizen, for example, expressed the fact of his citizenship by wearing as decreed by law, the white toga. A "gentleman" in the Colonial cities of America was known by his "periwig." . . .

Urban elites everywhere struggled to differentiate themselves from their "inferiors" not only by the design of their dress, but by the materials as well. The cap of the medieval Frenchman was made of velvet for the elites, rough cloth for the poor. In Elizabethan England, [Gideon Sjoberg reported that] "Commoners were prohibited by law from wearing clothing fashioned from gold or silver cloth, velvet, furs, and other 'luxury' materials." Hair length also indicated status. Among the Franks, only the elite had long hair. . . .

The clothing of outcaste groups . . . was often regulated by law. . . . [T]he Parsi minority in the Persian city of Yezd were forced, until the 1880s, "to twist their turbans instead of folding them, [were] denied various colors, and [were] prohibited rings, umbrellas, and other items."

Occupation, too, was signaled by dress. The lawyers of medieval France, for example, were distinguished by their round caps . . . and the executioners of the period were forced to wear a special coat of red or gold so that they would be readily recognizable in a crowd. . . . Each of the various types of itinerant peddlers of Peking . . . wore a distinctive costume as did the clergy of twelfth century Europe and the members of religious sects in numerous preindustrial cities.

Source: Lyn H. Lofland, *A World of Strangers* (Prospect Heights, IL: Waveland Press, 1985), pp. 45–46.

If dress means less to us in modern cities, then, location means more. We recognize that modern cities are composed of numerous distinct districts, such as for business, warehousing, residence, and entertainment. In business districts, we expect to encounter businesspeople, and we expect them to act in a businesslike manner.

For example, Huntington Avenue marks the boundary between two major districts of Boston (look back at Figure 8–1). On the north side of the street are the upper-middle-class Back Bay and Fenway areas, which include Symphony Hall, the Museum of Fine Arts, and numerous expensive shops and art galleries. Just across the street begins the lower-class, predominantly African American Roxbury district, with run-down housing and downscale shops.

To position oneself at the corner of Huntington Avenue and Massachusetts Avenue near Symphony Hall when the Boston Symphony Orchestra is playing is a remarkable sociological experience. On one side of the street are men sporting formal black-tie dress and women decked out in ermine and pearls. Yet just 20 feet away are people in threadbare and tattered clothes. Strangers on both sides of the street are well aware that they inhabit two different social worlds, and few people move from one side to the other.

Of course, such patterns don't mean that some people can't "work the system." We all know that it is possible for us to pass ourselves off as something we are not by manipulating the ways that we dress and act. A narcotics agent may infiltrate a drug ring, for example, and a social scientist may live anonymously in an area, hoping to learn the inside story of people's lives. Sometimes, people intentionally "perform." A sighted person may don dark eyeglasses, hold a sign saying "blind," and beg; sedate, middle-class suburbanites may come into the city to "swing" at night, retiring at evening's end to their normal routine.

Privatizing Public Space.   Lofland (1985:118–23) suggests that another way we reduce the vastness and complexity of a city is to transform areas into private or semi-private space. People can claim a street corner as a hangout; a tavern, such as television's *Cheers,* can become a club to its regular patrons; and musicians can transform a section of a park into an outdoor performance arena. Such "home territories" are rarely intentional; usually, they result from unplanned, uncoordinated actions that end up spatially segregating certain types of people. The city is full of such patterns: Yuppies appropriate plazas; skid row vagrants lay

claim to benches and steam grates; and gay people come to think of a particular neighborhood as "their own." Outsiders entering such spaces soon pick up cues of dress and behavior that indicate they are on semi-private ground.

On a larger scale, whole urban districts can become home territory—or "turf"—to a specific group. Most residential neighborhoods have a dominant character, perhaps based on class, race, ethnicity, and age. Although cities are largely impersonal, they are also (in Robert Park's phrase) "mosaics of small worlds." Within *gesellschaft,* in short, the city reveals many *gemeinschaft*-like subsocieties.

Class, Race, and the Urban Experience

People have devised strategies for making sense of the city. This hardly means that the urban experience is the same for everyone, however, because traits such as class,

In a city, many people share public space. Whether in small groups or alone, on a lunch break or resting from sight-seeing, they gather wherever there is some sun and a place to sit. Steps and low walls are popular choices, and there, they often engage in that favorite urban pastime of people-watching or enjoy some show, such as this sword-swallower in New York's Washington Square Park.

Urban ethnic neighborhoods are often places to find examples of what Lofland calls the privatizing of public space. Here, the street becomes a place to play stickball or wash a parked car, and the sidewalk becomes a site for jump rope or hopscotch games, for stores or street vendors to display their wares, or for people to sit to socialize or watch passersby.

age, gender, race, and ethnicity shape our lives in the city just as they do elsewhere.

The *Urban Living* box on pages 217–218 offers two different urban experiences. In the first passage, Jonathan Raban speaks about the difficulty he has in keeping from going "soft"—a bit crazy—"in a soft city." He writes as a "marginal man"—a freelance writer, unmarried, living alone, with few friends and no local family. In the next excerpt, Clara Rodriguez tells of growing up poor but in a stable and vibrant community, one that was largely cut off from the city as a whole. Eventually, she would witness the South Bronx collapse in urban decay—but her childhood memories convey a far different reality.

The City as *Gesellschaft:* A Reassessment

Many early urban theorists feared that people could never cope with the city's sheer physical size, its large population, and its anonymity. Yet, we *have* learned to cope. We contend with physical size by creating our personal mental image of the city. We deal with the complexities of street life by observing codes of behavior and seeking out clues to the identity of strangers. And of course, our own social characteristics place us within some part of the city. While urban life may not always be pleasant, these factors work to make it meaningful.

THE SOCIAL ENVIRONMENT: *GEMEINSCHAFT*

Then, too, the city abounds with personal relationships. Only the most extreme of urban isolates—Jonathan Raban's "marginal man," perhaps—live according to the stereotype of *gesellschaft.* For most, interpersonal bonds provide a basis for social and psychological security in the city.

URBAN LIVING

The Varieties of Urban Experience

The Marginal Man

I live here on a corner of the square in a borrowed flat, without property, at haphazard. By comparison with the right family and neighborhood life of the small town, I have few attachments or continuities. My existence is lax and unshaven. I have no proper job, just an irregular series of commissions and assignments, the chores and errands of a middle class hobo. . . . Freelance writers . . . tend to drift to the peripheral fringe of things, habitual onlookers and overhearers. My flat is pitched on the western edge of my private version of London, a place to make forays from, scavenging eastwards for material and odd jobs. I am on the rim, both geographically and socially; and this marginal position suits me very well. . . .

Cities are scary and impersonal, and the best most of us can manage is a fragile hold on our route through the streets. We cling to friends and institutions, exaggerate the importance of belonging, fear being alone too much. The freedom of the city is enormous. Here one can choose and invent one's society, and live more deliberately than anywhere else. Nothing is fixed, the possibilities of personal change and renewal are endless and open. But it is hard to learn to live as generously as real citizenship demands. I spot in others the same mouse-like caution which keeps me hugging the edge of the pavement, running from bolt hole to bolt hole, unequipped to embrace that spaciousness and privacy of city life which so often presents itself as mere emptiness and fog.

For me a city day is a succession of guarded moves, as if one was crossing a peat bog. . . . [We] need to hold on tight to avoid going completely soft in a soft city. So much of metropolitan life is just the slowing of symptoms of fright. In the city one clings to nostalgic and unreal signs of community, takes forced refuge in codes, badges and coteries; the city's life, surface and locomotion, usually seems too dangerous and demanding to live through with any confidence. The mad egotism of the man who stops you in Soho Square to tell you he is John the Baptist, or the weird rural delusions of another tramp nearby who fishes hopefully through a grating at the corner of Old Compton Street ("Caught anything?" "I had some good bites."), seem not unlikely consequences of the exercise of the freedom of the city. Its discontinuities give one vertigo; few people who aren't criminals or psychopaths will risk themselves on the rollercoaster ride of change and incongruity which the city offers. So much of city life is an elaborate process of building up defenses against the city—the self a fortified town raised against the stranger. We hedge ourselves in behind dreams and illusions, construct make-believe villages and make-believe families.

Life in the South Bronx

The South Bronx in New York City has always been home to me. As a young girl growing up there, I was surrounded by a stable family and a sense of community, even though the area was viewed as a place where only "the poorest of the poor" lived.

My earliest recollection of my neighborhood is of an energetic and alive community with a great deal of social interaction. I recall being wheeled with my sister in a huge baby carriage in front of what the *New York Times* would subsequently call those "solid, grimy five-story tenements." My parents would stop to converse with neighbors, part of a network

(*continued*)

of people who knew each other well and who helped each other.

My South Bronx had a richness of life, a dynamism and stability of relations that few other places have. However, as I matured, I came to understand that the world beyond my community's boundaries had a different view of us. That world saw us as "different" and poor and was often instinctively hostile or afraid of us. Yet, I never felt poor, deprived, or disadvantaged. I also never understood what inspired hostility toward those I held dear.

At an early age I came to puzzle over this contradiction, why the view from within was so different from the view from without; why hostility, fear, or disrespect should exist without cause. This developed in me a basic curiosity about the view of those affected and the factors that affected them.

The world within which I grew up was not all roses and pastels (a festive Puerto Rican dish). My childhood was as full of traumas, joys, and disappointments as the next person's. There were the usual struggles to survive that all people who have little money or who have strong differences of culture, color, and language experience. Life was hard, but life was manageable.

As I was growing up, I witnessed my community and others like it destroyed by forces over which we had little control: drugs, urban renewal, and housing abandonment. . . . The dynamism and stability of the communities of the South Bronx [were] destroyed by external forces.

Not all Puerto Ricans fled; some fought to maintain their neighborhoods, fought drug dealers, and organized to get support from the city and federal governments. Currently, the decline has slowed and signs of revitalization have appeared. The South Bronx has bottomed out, but the history lived there will remain a bitter chapter for all concerned.

Sources: Jonathan Raban, *Soft City*, reprint ed. (London: Harvill Press, 1998), pp. 222–27, 230; Clara E. Rodriguez, "The Puerto Rican Community in the South Bronx: View From Within and Without," in Beth B. Hess, Elizabeth W. Markson, and Peter J. Stein, *Sociology*, 5th ed. (Boston: Allyn and Bacon, 1996), p. 507.

Urban Networks

The study of interpersonal ties is called *network analysis*. As we shall see, urban networks may or may not involve organized social groups, nor need they be defined by locality.

London Couples. Examining the relationships of married couples in London, Elizabeth Bott (2003) uncovered the effects of social class on the urban experience. She found that working-class partners each maintained their own networks, whereas middle-class spouses participated in a shared network. Other studies show that strong urban networks form in stable neighborhoods, or around local schools through parenthood, or from a shared sense of group identity (Butler 2008; Robson and Butler 2001). Such findings do not discount the role of class, however. The *Urban Living* box on page 219 offers a closer look at Bott's marriage networks.

Washington, D.C., Street-Corner Men. Eliot Liebow (2003) conducted a famous participant observation study of poor African American men who frequented a street corner—"Tally's Corner"—in Washington, D.C. Most of these men, Liebow found, had believed until their late teens that they would become adult breadwinners and husbands. Driven by this ideal, many married and fathered children. Unfortunately, most of these men had few skills and little education, and they ended up with little more than menial jobs.

Many men came to hate the idea of performing degrading work. In time, many

URBAN LIVING

Two Types of Marriage Networks

Segregated Marriage Networks

At one extreme was a family in which the husband and wife carried out as many tasks as possible separately and independently of each other. There was a strict division of labor in the household, in which she had her tasks and he had his. He gave her a set amount of housekeeping money, and she had little idea of how much he earned or how he spent the money he kept for himself. In their leisure time, he went to cricket matches with his friends, whereas she visited her relatives or went to a cinema with a neighbor. With the exception of festivities with relatives, this husband and wife spent very little of their leisure time together. They did not consider that they were unusual in this respect. On the contrary, they felt their behavior was typical of their social circle.

Joint Marriage Networks

At the other extreme was a family in which husband and wife shared as many activities and spent as much time together as possible. They stressed that husband and wife should be equals: All major decisions should be made together, and even in minor household matters they should help one another as much as possible. This norm was carried out in practice. In their division of labor, many tasks were shared or interchangeable. The husband often did the cooking and sometimes the washing and ironing. The wife did the gardening and often the household repairs as well. Much of their leisure time was spent together, and they shared similar interests in politics, music, literature, and in entertaining friends. Like the first couple, this husband and wife felt their behavior was typical of their social circle, except that they felt they carried the interchangeability of household tasks a little further than most people.

Source: Elizabeth Bott, *Family and Social Network* (New York: Routledge, 2003), pp. 52–53.

---

stopped working: Some were fired; some just quit. In any case, the men soon realized they could barely provide for themselves, much less a family. This failure was evident to their wives and children and a deep source of personal pain and family tension. To make matters worse, the government offered to provide public assistance to wives and children—but only if no father were living in the home.

Men crushed by their plight could find some comfort "hanging out" together. At Tally's Corner, people commiserated and didn't ask embarrassing questions. There, a man could forget failure and get by from day to day. Before long, most men were spending more time there than at home. The *Urban Living* box on page 220 explains that networks supplied the heart and soul of life on "Tally's Corner."

Boston Neighborhoods. Many urban relationships are set in neighborhoods. Distinguished by physical or social boundaries, neighborhoods contain people who share important social characteristics, such as social class, race, and ethnicity. In a study of Boston's predominantly Italian West End neighborhood in the 1950s, Herbert Gans (1982) suggested that despite the many

URBAN LIVING

The Networks of Street-Corner Men

[The most important people in a man's network are those] with whom he is "up tight": His "walking buddies," "good" or "best" friends, girl friends, and sometimes real or putative kinsmen. These are the people with whom he is in more or less daily, face-to-face contact, and whom he turns to for emergency aid, comfort or support in time of need or crisis. He gives them and receives from them goods and services in the name of friendship, ostensibly keeping no reckoning. Routinely, he seeks them out and is sought out by them. They serve his need to be with others of his kind, and to be recognized as a discrete, distinctive personality, and he, in turn, serves them the same way. They are both his audience and his fellow actors.

It is with these men and women that he spends his waking, nonworking hours, drinking, dancing, engaging in sex, playing the fool or the wise man, passing the time at the Carry-out or on the street-corner, talking about nothing and everything, about epistemology or [Muhammad Ali], about the nature of numbers or how he would "have it made" if he could have a steady job that paid him $60 a week with no layoffs.

So important a part of daily life are these relationships that it seems like no life at all without them. Old Mr. Jenkins climbed out of his sickbed to take up a seat on the Coca-Cola case at the Carry-out for a couple of hours. "I can't stay home and play dead," he explained, "I got to get out and see my friends."

Source: Eliot Liebow, *Tally's Corner,* 2nd ed. (Lanham, MD: Rowman and Littlefield, 2003), pp. 163–64.

---

differences among residents of an urban neighborhood, many *gemeinschaft*-like relations exist.

At the time of Gans's research, the West End was a low-income, low-rent district adjacent to the elite Beacon Hill area. Traditionally home to immigrants, over the years the West End had been dominated by various categories—including Italians, Jews, Poles, and Irish, as well as a handful of artists and bohemians.

Most casual observers of the West End concluded that it was a chaotic slum. Yet living in the area revealed a different—and more accurate—picture. There, Gans found as much *gemeinschaft* as might be found in many non-urban environments, as the *Urban Living* box on page 221 suggests. This doesn't mean that everyone knew everyone else personally,

but it does mean that most West Enders forged strong ties with family, neighbors, and friends.

Other researchers reached similar conclusions after investigating other cities. For example, Gerald Suttles (1974) reported strong interpersonal ties among Italians in Chicago's Addams area, and Joseph Howell (1990) provided a similar description of life in an inner-city Washington, D.C., neighborhood. Finally, a complex study by Fischer et al. (1977) found important interpersonal networks operating throughout the Detroit metropolitan area. In sum, personal relationships, though they may be hidden to the casual observer, may be every bit as important to low-income urban neighbors as they are to people living in rural communities.

URBAN LIVING

Boston's Thriving West End

Everyday life in the West End was not much different from that in other neighborhoods, urban or suburban. The men went to work in the morning, and, for most of the day, the area was occupied largely by women and children—just as in the suburbs. . . . In the afternoon, younger women could be seen pushing baby carriages. Children of all ages played on the street, and teenagers would "hang" on the corner, or play ball in the school yard. . . . Many women went shopping every day, partly to meet neighbors and to catch up on area news in the small grocery stores, and partly to buy foods that could not be obtained in the weekly excursion to the supermarket. On Sunday mornings, the streets were filled with people who were visiting with neighbors and friends before and after church. . . .

On the whole . . . the various ethnic groups, the bohemians, transients, and others [lived together] without much difficulty, since each was responsive to totally different reference groups. . . . [For example] as Italians like to stay up late, and to socialize at high decibel levels, the bohemians' loud parties were no problem, at least to them. . . .

Many West Enders had known each other for years, if only as acquaintances who greeted each other on the street. Everyone might not know everyone else; but, as they did know something about everyone, the net effect was the same, especially within each ethnic group. Between groups, common residence and sharing of facilities—as well as the constant struggle against absentee landlords—created enough solidarity to maintain a friendly spirit. Moreover, for many families, problems were never far away. . . . Thus when emergencies occurred, neighbors helped each other readily; other problems were solved within each ethnic group.

For most West Enders, then, life in the area resembled that found in the village or small town, and even in the suburb.

Source: Reprinted with the permission of The Free Press, a division of Simon & Schuster Adult Publishing Group, from *The Urban Villagers* by Herbert J. Gans. Copyright © 1962 by The Free Press. Copyright © 1982 by Herbert J. Gans. All rights reserved.

Friendships. Many urban relationships do not involve neighbors. More affluent urbanites especially—many who move from city to city to establish their careers—are not linked to neighborhoods in any traditional sense, yet friends they have. Such people typically forge friendships involving co-workers, people with whom they have lunch or a drink and dinner, or friends they meet more casually—say, at a concert or in the park. The point is that people may not live near each other but still maintain friendships with others who share similar interests (Gibbons and Olk 2003; Whitmeyer 2002).

Industrial technology once broke up the communities of old by offering new opportunities that pulled people away from the towns of their birth. Yet technology also provides new means to stay in touch: The landline telephone served this purpose in the twentieth century, and the cell phone, e-mail, and text messaging heavily reinforce countless relationships in this century.

Scenes. One of the city's hallmarks is its many and diverse places, or **scenes,** where people gather to socialize with friends, meet new ones, and enjoy themselves. In fact, many

Many cities are filled with young adults for whom one of the most popular "scenes" is a bar or club, where they can relax and enjoy themselves with friends, fellow students, or co-workers. Some places attract a particular lifestyle crowd, such as gays, musicians, or writers; others are more open, attracting a wide range of customers.

people *invent* places where they get together. Scenes include bars, clubs, discos, or areas of a city taken over by a group, such as San Francisco's Haight–Ashbury district by hippies in the 1960s or New York's Bryant Park by yuppies in the late 1990s.

Most scenes are part-time. They usually occupy the hours away from work, such as a favorite eatery for lunch, a coffee shop, or a health club/fitness center. Second, to "make the scene" suggests that participants are, in some sense, "on stage," emphasizing only one particular aspect of themselves—their ability to dance or their knowledge of literature, for instance.

Scenes are of four main types (Irwin 1977). Most cities have *lifestyle scenes* that attract writers, musicians, gays, political radicals, and other groups. On summer evenings in Toronto, for example, young people from all over the metropolitan area descend on Yonge Street, and they often remain until the wee hours of the morning. On foot or in cars with

stereos blaring, they eat, talk, yell, buy records, and generally hang out up and down a dozen city blocks.

The *local scene* is more exclusive. A local bar, for example, may attract a particular crowd, and it may even discourage "outsiders" from coming in.

The *open scene* is more fluid in terms of clientele, yet it, too, provides the opportunity for personal relationships. Bars without a well-defined clientele fall into this category. Such public drinking places provide opportunities for those present, whether acquainted or not, to engage others in conversational interaction in a setting that promotes the near-obligation to accept these extended overtures of sociability.

Finally, the *specialized scene* involves activities, such as tennis, barbershop harmony, amateur theater, bingo, card playing, chess, skateboarding, and countless others. Like the local scene, these specialized scenes provide a sense of ingroup solidarity with others who share that particular interest. Specialized scenes, however, have a degree of openness and population fluidity that local scenes do not.

Perhaps one of the best-known specialized scenes among college students, especially those attending a city college or university, are the clubs. These typically crowded gathering places have a DJ or band, a dance floor, a bar, and room to sit or stand. For example, in Boston, some of the more popular clubs are Aria, Avalon, Liquor Store, Roxy, and Venu. Other clubs cater to different types of clientele, such as African or Hispanic Americans, or yuppies. No matter which club, though, people come to hear and dance to the music and, of course, to enjoy some good times with old or new friends.

Temporary Networks. Many urban dwellers use another type of network to make initial or short-term personal contact in the city. Examples of such networks include singles clubs, dating agencies, public ballrooms, call-in radio talk shows, and suicide hot lines.

Sometimes, such networks serve people who are extremely lonely or desperate. Just as frequently, however, they serve people who are quite happy with their lives. People who participate in late-night talk shows, for instance, need not be lonely, after all; they may just be working late, or simply be interested in speaking their mind.

Identifying with the City

The ability to know and identify with an entire city probably ended in the Middle Ages. With the dawning of the modern age, Western cities began a relentless increase in population as well as an expanding division of labor, resulting in the large, diverse cities we find today.

Still, most people have some sense of "knowing" their city, although such knowledge often rests on clichés and stereotypical images that outsiders also may share. Thus, beer has made Milwaukee famous in the same way that sunshine defines Miami and the entertainment industry has elevated Los Angeles

and Hollywood. St. Louis has its arch and Toronto its CN Tower ("world's tallest freestanding structure!"). And, while Stratford-on-Avon has its Shakespeare, Hannibal, Missouri, is proud to be the boyhood home of Mark Twain (Samuel Clemens).

In addition, sports teams foster identification with the modern city ("Minneapolis–St. Paul—Home of the Twins, Vikings, and North Stars!"), as do important local events (St. Patrick's Day in Boston, the Rose Parade in Pasadena, Inauguration Day in Washington, D.C., and Mardi Gras in New Orleans. The *Urban Living* box on page 224 examines some of these "urban rituals."

Historical events—both negative and positive—also help to define the urban experience. The San Francisco earthquake of 1906 and the devastating aftermath from Hurricane Katrina in New Orleans in 2005 are examples of costly and tragic events that remain alive in people's minds. The ride of Paul Revere through Boston, the signing of the Declaration of Independence in Philadelphia, and the battle at the Alamo in San Antonio are major events that are still well known many generations later by most of those cities' present-day inhabitants.

The City as *Gemeinschaft:* A Reassessment

A wealth of research supports the conclusion that the vast majority of urbanites are "well-connected" in their cities. On the one hand, most are engaged in a variety of networks, such as families, neighborhoods, friendships, scenes, and even temporary contacts. Similarly, most city residents have a sense of identification with their city. Although they may not always be readily apparent, characteristics of Tönnies's *gemeinschaft*—personal relationships and a sense of belonging—do flourish in the city.

THE TEXTURE OF THE CITY

Most cities convey a unique impression— a look and feel that Gerald Suttles (1984) termed a "texture" and that others call the

Great Urban Rituals

Cities, both large and small, have annual events that involve large segments of the population and serve as a means of sharing in an urban experience and, thus, identifying with the city. Here are just a few examples.

Each New Year's Day, weather permitting, about 1 million people line the streets of Philadelphia to watch the Mummers Parade. About 15,000 marchers, members of many Mummers clubs—who are capped and caped, in speckled and sequined costumes, literally strut to the music of a distinctive stringband strum. They neither walk nor march; instead, they cakewalk in a distinctive style that is difficult to imitate. It's a colorful, pleasant spectacle and a famous city tradition.

In Boston, the celebration of Patriot's Day (the third Monday in April) commemorates the events in that city that led to the American Revolution (the rides of Paul Revere and William Dawes, the battles at Lexington and Concord). Aside from reenactments of the rides and a traditional parade, the main attraction that day is the Boston Marathon. This oldest race in the United States, a marathon second only in age to the Olympics itself, attracts more than 20,000 runners and more than a half-million enthusiastic spectators along the 26.2-mile route.

Cinco de Mayo festivals celebrate Mexico's victory over French forces in Puebla, Mexico, on May 5, 1862. Though celebrated in many major U.S. cities—including Austin, Chicago, Dallas, Houston, San Antonio, and St. Paul—it is in Los Angeles where hundreds of thousands of people gather in parks and on streets, decorated in the Mexican colors (red, white, and green), to enjoy the crafts, food, music, and dancing.

On Memorial Day weekend, Detroit hosts Movement, the largest electronic music festival in the world. More than 70 well-known acts perform on multiple stages in Hart Plaza for over 1 million fans. Held in the birthplace of techno music, the event integrates musical and visual artistry, creativity, diversity, and state-of-the-art technology.

Atlanta hosts Music Midtown, one of the largest music festivals of its kind in the United States, with just about every musical genre included. The multiday, spring extravaganza in central Atlanta includes more than 100 well-known performers and attracts about 300,000 people.

Every summer since 1967, Toronto has blazed with the excitement of calypso and elaborate masquerade costumes during the annual Caribana Festival. This two-week festival is the largest Caribbean festival in North America, attracting over 1 million participants—including hundreds of thousands of American tourists.

Among the many ethnic festivals in New York City, its oldest and most popular one that cuts across ethnic boundaries is the San Gennaro Festival in Little Italy and runs for two weeks in mid-September. The street festivities, which include parades, entertainment, food stands, and a cannoli-eating contest, attract more than 1 million people annually.

Of the thousands of Oktoberfest celebrations in North America, Cincinnati's German heritage celebration is the largest, drawing over 500,000 people each year. Five downtown city blocks are transformed each September into Oktoberfest Zinzinnati, with seven stages offering live entertainment and nearly 100 booths serving German food, wine, and beer.

We cannot end this section without mentioning Mardi Gras in New Orleans, which before Hurricane Katrina included two weeks of elaborate parades, at least one a day through Fat Tuesday, the day before the Christian season of Lent began. From the parade floats, riders in outrageous costumes throw beads and other trinkets to hundreds of thousands of spectators, many of whom are also dressed in costume during this fun-filled time. As New Orleans rebounds, it once again is becoming the scene for such traditional delight.

Social researchers deflated the myth of urban alienation by documenting the pervasiveness of social networks among virtually all city dwellers, rich and poor alike. One does not need the formal trappings of social organizations to enjoy intimate ties with others. A street corner or public bench can easily serve to create a *gemeinschaft* environment.

"soul" or "personality" of the "feel" of the city. New York is the "Big Apple," a city of energy, hustle, and fear; Boston is relaxed, "cultural," and intellectual; Los Angeles is "laid back," the heart of the "new America"; and New Orleans is "The Big Easy," where life is slower, simpler, and easy-going. These are stereotypical impressions, of course, but many people share them (see the *Cityscape* box on page 226).

To what extent are such images real? Suttles argues that a city's **texture** is grounded in its history, architecture, street names, and even the nicknames for certain parts of town. Together, these elements add up to an objective reality, not just one individual's impression. A visitor to Hollywood, for example, can actually see the footprints and handprints of the stars in the cement in front of Grauman's Chinese Theater, use a map to visit the homes of the stars, and see the huge "Hollywood" sign overlooking the city. And who knows? If you're lucky, you might even end up face to face with a famed actor at a restaurant. Stars, money, and fame are all part of Hollywood's texture as "Tinsel Town."

Detroit.   The "Motor City" has been battling its negative image of urban decay and high crime for decades. With the decline of the automobile industry in the 1970s, the flight of affluent people to the suburbs, and the collapse of its center-city areas, Detroit gained a reputation as unsafe and unpleasant—a violent cultural wasteland. As both cause and effect, Detroit's population plummeted by 44 percent between 1950 and 1990, then lost another 77,000 people between 1990 and 2000 and another 80,000 people over the next six years. As a result, its population dropped

CITYSCAPE

The Personality of Cities

Author of the book that inspired the 1959 film *The Young Philadelphians* starring Paul Newman, Richard Powell gave this tongue-in-cheek, provocative commentary on his thoughts about the personalities (textures) of many U.S. cities, one that amuses some and offends others:

Of the major cities of the United States, only nine have distinct and individual personalities. These are New York, Chicago, Philadelphia, Boston, Los Angeles, San Francisco, New Orleans, Charleston, and Savannah. . . .

[Of these,] only San Francisco has a really nice one. The other eight cities often annoy people who have not had the good fortune of being born there. I hope I am not revealing anything top secret when I say that, to many outsiders, Philadelphia and Boston have highly irritating personalities. To many outsiders, these two cities are rather like a pair of sheltered maiden ladies who have become crotchety and eccentric but who happen to be awfully well-heeled.

New York, of course, has a very strong personality. Naturally, as a good Philadelphian, I dislike the place. . . .

Here is a quick review of the personality or lack of personality of other major American cities:

Chicago—Yes, it has personality. It's the neighborhood big shot of the Midwest.

Detroit—No personality. It's just the hot-rod kid of American cities.

Los Angeles—Lots of personality, but of kinds that delight a psychiatrist.

Baltimore—No more personality than one of its own Chincoteague oysters, and just about as retiring.

Cleveland, St. Louis, Cincinnati, Kansas City, Columbus, and Indianapolis—These are the great faceless cities of the Midwest, representing nothing more than the lowest common denominator of many rather interesting small towns.

Pittsburgh—It has no personality. It's merely a pro football player who struck it rich.

Washington—It's not really a city at all. It's just a big international motel whose guests only sign in for overnight.

Milwaukee—A freckle-faced kid peering wistfully through a knothole at the Milwaukee Braves.

Seattle, Rochester (New York), Portland (Oregon), Buffalo, and Minneapolis—All you can say about these is that the name is familiar but you can't place the face.

San Francisco—The most delightful personality of any American city: cultured without being snobbish, cosmopolitan without seeming foreign.

New Orleans—Like Paris, it is one of the few cities with sex appeal. It's a sort of Creole Marilyn Monroe.

Newark and Jersey City—These are nothing but a couple of dead-end kids.

Houston, Dallas, and Fort Worth—They merely pretend to have strong personalities, in the manner of cowboys whooping it up on Saturday night.

Charleston and Savannah—These are lovely old ladies, who sometimes get a bit tiresome in talking about the men who courted them when they were young.

Miami—Just a chromium-plated diner at a crossroads.

Atlanta—It has a split personality, because it can't decide whether to play the role of Scarlett O'Hara or that of Perle Mesta.

Source: From *The Philadelphian,* 50th Anniversary Edition, by Richard Powell (Medford, NJ. Plexus Publishing, Inc., www.plexuspublishing.com). Copyright © renewed 2006 by Dorothy Powell Quigley. Used by permission. All rights reserved.

from a peak of nearly 2 million in the early 1950s to less than 900,000 for the first time since 1917, falling to 871,000 in 2006 (Gray 2005; U.S. Census Bureau 2008a).

How does a city overcome such a loss in both reputation and population? City officials put more police on the streets and made concerted efforts to rebuild neighborhoods. Yet, in 2007, Detroit remained—for the eighth consecutive year in a row—the most dangerous large U.S. city as measured by the six basic crime categories of murder, rape, robbery, aggravated assault, burglary, and motor vehicle theft. Although its downtown has a relatively low crime rate, overall, Detroit ranked among 321 cities as the second most dangerous city in crime rate, behind St. Louis, Missouri (Morgan Quitno 2008).

The city has taken steps to become a more inviting cultural center. Its restored Opera House and exhibits at the Henry Ford Museum, Historical Museum, and Museum of African American History attract many visitors, as does the Institute of Arts, one of the nation's biggest art museums. A 2007 study revealed that a majority of residents in suburban Wayne, Oakland, and Macomb counties said they occasionally dine, attend cultural events, or take in professional sports events in Detroit. High earners especially come to Detroit for the restaurants. Oakland residents are the most likely to seek out culture, such as music, theater, or dance in Motown, while the appeal of the city's three professional sports teams cuts across lines of gender, geography, and all but the smallest incomes (Bailey 2007).

Another recent innovation is the People Mover—an automated, elevated train system that takes riders on a 2.9-mile loop of downtown Detroit. For just 50 cents, one can easily reach the numerous casinos, offices, restaurants, shops, nightlife, landmarks, and other attractions that are within walking distance of the People Mover's 13 stations and stops.

Perhaps the best indicator of Detroit's future potential to change its textural image, however, is the recently completed, $500 million renovation of the Renaissance Center (nicknamed "RenCen"). One of the world's largest office complexes (5.5 million square feet), its central tower (the Detroit Marriott) is the tallest all-hotel skyscraper in the western hemisphere, with the largest rooftop restaurant as well. This downtown complex of seven interconnected skyscrapers along the Detroit River houses the world headquarters of General Motors. Similarly, the $180 million renovation of the city's most famous grand hotel, the historic, 31-story, Neo-Renaissance-style Book–Cadillac Hotel, offers additional hope; it will be an upscale, mixed-use Westin Hotel, offices, and luxury condominiums. In addition, Compuware's recently built, $350 million world headquarters houses

Ethnic pride parades and street fairs, such as the International Food Festival on Ninth Avenue in New York City, are popular means by which a city not only celebrates its diversity but also provides a rich variety of activities not to be found in any other setting. Regardless of one's own background, such events are a source of interest and enjoyment.

4,100 employees and is located only a few blocks from the hotel. City officials are hopeful that these three developments will spur others so that Detroit's urban redevelopment may be fully realized.

Portland.   Our case study in Chapter 4—Portland, Oregon—already has a strong positive image, based on a revitalized downtown, new housing and businesses, and a rebuilt waterfront. Visitors take delight in strolling down tree-lined shopping streets, observing the many fountains, and traveling safely on the freely available bicycles. Portland is prospering as one of the vibrant new cities of the West. Still, it effectively controls its growth, increasing in population by only 8,000 between 2000 and 2006 (U.S. Census Bureau 2008a:33).

Streetscapes.   The "concrete canyons" formed by the tall buildings in midtown Manhattan create a different sense of place in the minds of visitors than, say, the streets of Boston's central business district, where few tall buildings abound, or the streets of San Francisco, with its many steep hills and cable cars.

In short, our senses do not deceive us when we get a different feeling from one city than we get from another. Although urban areas share many common elements, their individuality is quite real.

HUMANIZING THE CITY

People have devised ways to humanize life in today's urban environment, just as they did in the towns and villages of the past. Even when struggling with poverty, most people have found ways to maintain positive personal relationships (Henly, Danziger, and Offer 2005). Although some homeless people live on the margins in almost complete isolation, most of the urban poor generate a social network to help them cope.

Virginia Schein (1995) conducted in-depth interviews with 30 single mothers receiving public assistance. All were working or had some work experience. She found that for many, a network of family, friends, and teachers provided both emotional support

and resources, enabling these women to battle their fears and struggle onward, despite the many hardships in their daily lives. Arlene, a 34-year-old mother of three, had just earned an associate degree in business administration and moved off public assistance benefits to start a job as a customer service representative. Never, she explained, could she have done so without family support:

> I told my sister when I graduated that I owed much of it to her. My sister helped me out with the baby-sitting. She would pick them up [my kids] from day care, feed them supper, and give them baths. Then she would bring them to my house, put them to bed, and wait for me to get home, usually around 9:30 (1995:102).

For others, support came from non-family members, as another woman explained:

> It was like a three-ring circus. I have the [two] children, five classes, driving back and forth. It was quite a struggle to juggle all of that. I realized that I couldn't do this all on my own. I could ask for help and not feel disgraced. . . .
>
> I realized that there are people out there that care. They helped me. Then it got better. I knew there were people that I could call, that I had the support that I needed, that these people understood what I was going through (1995:99).

Renata, a 37-year-old high school dropout and mother of two teenagers, spoke of the positive support she received from her church:

> I just got tired of trying to fix things and nothing would get fixed. Things would change and I couldn't change them back. I started going to church and I ended up going and going. I started going a year ago and am getting to know a lot of people. I was the type that stayed home all the time. I went to work, came home, went to work, came home. I didn't associate with many people on the block. I had one neighbor on one side and a girlfriend on the other and that was it. Now I go to church every Sunday, I sing in the choir, and I talk to people all day long.
>
> One woman said, "You look so good, you have a glow, it's your aura. I don't know what it is but you look so different." A little old lady that lives up the street also said, "You should

have started going to church a long time ago—you look good." It all gives me a little more confidence each day. If I can make it this day, then I can make it the next day and the next one and the next one (1995:102–103).

Carol Stack (1997) stressed the ingenuity of poor African Americans in the inner-city area of a large midwestern city. Most of the men, she learned, were recent migrants from the South whose search for better jobs had resulted, at best, in low-paying, menial work. Most of the women struggled to raise their children with no steady source of income. Despite the odds against them, Stack discovered, these poor people had responded to their plight by constructing a diffuse family structure that allowed them to maintain a stable community and meet everyone's basic needs.

This network was a means to respond to an immediate crisis—people shared clothes, food, and rent money. Each time that help was given, however, a debt was incurred. The helping families and individuals, sure to be in need

of assistance themselves at some future point in time, expected that those they had helped would assist them in turn. As these obligations spread, the residents established an extensive network of "cooperation and mutual aid" (1997:28–31). The expanding network became one extended family, a fact suggested by the common practice of referring to the community as "all our kin." In the *Urban Living* box below, Stack describes how one particular network evolved.

Residents, Stack found, shared virtually everything, from clothes to food to child care responsibilities. Sometimes, fathers of children lived at home, and sometimes, when they could not support their families, they did not. Even then, fathers frequently contributed what they could to the upbringing of their children. When mothers had to work, they turned to their own mothers or to neighbors for help with the children. Thus, an informal day-care system evolved that ensured children always would have the attention of at least one caring adult. Through this reciprocal aid

URBAN LIVING

Helping Each Other Out

Cecil (age 35) lives in The Flats with his mother Willie Mae, his oldest sister and her two children, and his younger brother. Cecil's younger sister Lily lives with their mother's sister Bessie. Bessie has three children and Lily has two. Cecil and his mother have part-time jobs in a cafe and Lily's children are on aid. In July . . . Cecil and his mother had just put together enough money to cover their rent. Lily paid her utilities, but she did not have enough money to buy food stamps for herself and her children. Cecil and Willie Mae knew that after they paid their rent they would not have any money for food for

the family. They helped out Lily by buying her food stamps, and then the two households shared meals together until Willie Mae was paid two weeks later. A week later Lily received her second ADC [Aid to Dependent Children] check and Bessie got some spending money from her boyfriend. They gave some of this money to Cecil and Willie Mae to pay their rent, and gave Willie Mae money to cover her insurance and pay a small sum on a living room suite at the local furniture store. Willie Mae reciprocated later on by buying dresses for Bessie and Lily's daughters and by caring for all the children when Bessie got a temporary job.

Source: Carol Stack, *All Our Kin* (New York: Basic Books, 1997), p. 37.

system, people gave what was needed and expected that their kindness would be repaid later on. Or, as one woman put it,

> Sometimes I don't have a damn dime in my pocket, not a crying penny to get a box of paper diapers, milk, a loaf of bread. But you have to have help from everybody and anybody, so don't turn no one down when they come round to help. (Stack 1997:32)

In a Harlem neighborhood, Katherine S. Newman (2000) found that the same friends and family support system helps working youth as well as working parents. Living in an extended family household with her grandmother, aunts, uncles, and cousins, teenager Shaquena pools her Burger Barn earnings with her grandmother's SSI income, one aunt's unemployment insurance, an uncle's wages from working in a police station, and another uncle's car washing earnings, as all share the household expenses. Shaquena's neighborhood is one in which family and friends visit one another, eat together, and when necessary, borrow from one another, as she explains:

> My aunt . . . lives right across the street from us. She, like last night, my grandmother ran out of sugar. My grandmother called my aunt and my aunt brought her the sugar. The guy down the hall, he real cool with us, he give us stuff, and my grandmother's cool with a lot of elderly on our floor. She will ask her daughter, my aunt, for things before she asks a friend, but she's got friends [to ask]. If I need something, I go right upstairs, because my best friend lives right upstairs. Her grandmother and my grandmother are friends and they keep a kitchen full of food. (Newman 2000:197)

Such a practical arrangement also has an emotional value. The large extended family provides family stability that might otherwise be lacking, such as in the case of Shaquena, whose mother is in and out of jail on drug convictions.

In contrast, those who don't "play fair" by reciprocating are quickly sanctioned, as documented by other researchers, including Doug A. Timmer, D. Stanley Eitzen, and Kathryn D. Talley (1994), who conducted in-depth interviews of the homeless in Tampa, Denver, and Chicago. As one once-homeless woman explained:

> For six months I took [my sister] in my apartment without [the Housing Authority] knowin' about it and helped her out, fed her, bought things for her. We had holidays together. And I threw this in her face three weeks ago and told her, "This is the way it is, you know. I helped you and now you can't help me. Then you can forget about me." So we haven't called each other at all. And I won't call her. 'Til doomsday. I won't call her. Even if she comes lookin' for me, she won't find me. (1994:113)

Through this system of cooperation and mutual support, despite the conditions that hem them in, the people in study after study have invented ways to meet at least their basic needs and to soften the blow of their poverty. Such positive adaptation is a prime example of how people can make their urban experience, even under the harsh conditions of poverty, more humane.

SOCIAL MOVEMENTS AND CITY LIFE

Social movements often begin as informal, though sometimes organized, group actions to initiate or resist social change. Although these movements can begin anywhere—in eighteenth-century coffeehouses or modern universities, for example—they find the most fertile ground within cities. Here, the concentration of large numbers of people facilitate social interaction, enabling like-minded people to find one another and, in that gathering, to organize and initiate a grass-roots campaign. Indeed, whether we speak of radical social movements, such as the American and French Revolutions, the "Velvet Revolution" throughout Communist Europe in the late 1980s, or the demonstrations and massacre in Tiananmen Square in Beijing in 1989, or of reform social movements, such as the suffragette, civil rights, and gay rights actions, the stage is almost always in cities.

From the Back of the Yards meatpacking labor organizing movement of the 1930s and

1940s in Chicago, which was the prototype for all subsequent labor organizing, through creation of the Urban League, the oldest community-based organization in the United States, which originated in NYC in 1910 to crack the barriers to black employment, to the present, cities have often spawned social movements that eventually had a national impact.

Local social movements benefit from greater population density, although suburban neighborhood protests can also be effective. In many cases, their efforts, both successes and failures, are only particular to their locale, typically involving such issues as traffic safety, elimination of crack houses, drug dealers, and prostitution. We will select Seattle as an illustration for the hundreds of thousands of other kinds of local social movements, past and present. Civic engagement in this city between 1988 and 2002 involved 30,000 people guiding the development of 37 neighborhood plans. They were involved in self-help projects for the common good and built new parks and playgrounds, renovated community facilities, recorded oral histories, created public art, and cultivated community gardens (Diers 2004:19).

SUBURBAN LIFE

Much of the discussion in this chapter has concerned not just those who live in the city but also those who temporarily come to the city—whether as commuters, tourists, patrons at cultural or sports events, participants at scenes, or in some other capacity. Because the majority of people now live outside the city, however, we can also note some of the social psychology of suburban life.

The Stereotypes

When suburban migration became a mass phenomenon in the 1950s, the growing popularity of this lifestyle generated much criticism and caricature. Using the physical homogeneity of the new, Levittown-style subdivisions as their model and often reflecting their own urban bias, sociologists, journalists, and authors offered negative portraits of the supposed boredom and conformity to be found in the suburbs.

The title of David Riesman's essay, "The Suburban Sadness" (1958), easily conveys his feelings. John Keats blasted suburban developments in his best-selling book *The Crack in the Picture Window* (1956), and he named his major characters John and Mary Drone (their neighbors included the Faints and the Amicables) in order to make it indubitably clear that the people of suburbia were as prefabricated as their two-car garages. Numerous other books conveyed similar images, and William H. Whyte's influential *The Organization Man* (2002; orig. 1966)—although a carefully documented study of rootless corporate executives living in Park Forest, Illinois—conveyed another image of suburbanites moving every few years in their quest for success. Malvina Reynolds' 1963 folk song, made popular by Pete Seeger, speaks of suburban homes as "little boxes" that are "ticky tacky" and "all look just the same," as do their inhabitants.

The media helped spread this stereotypical image. TV shows like *The Adventures of Ozzie and Harriet* (1952–1966) epitomized suburban family life. More recently, the film *Edward Scissorhands* (1990) satirized suburban conformity, with its depiction of the men simultaneously leaving for work from their look-alike houses in their similar-looking cars, while the film *Pleasantville* (1998) told of two modern teenagers sucked into their TV set and then forced to live in a 1950s sitcom filled with innocence and naïveté.

In all these books, films, and TV shows, suburbanites were depicted as young, with small children who ate crunchy breakfast cereals. They socialized with each other relentlessly (coffee klatches in the morning, and barbecues in the evening), and they obsessively copied each other in tastes and styles in a demeaning attempt to "keep up with the Joneses." In these stereotypical depictions, suburbanites were portrayed as bland, shallow, and superficial.

Like all stereotypes, some elements of truth could be found in these depictions, but they hardly revealed the suburban reality.

First, they ignored the diversity of suburbs—the older ones, the industrial ones, and the working-class ones, a topic we will explore in greater depth in Chapter 10. Second, as Herbert Gans (1968) charged, many critics were more interested in exploiting a negative myth than in actually studying the suburbs (as he did for his 1967 participant-observer research in *The Levittowners*). Third, the social dynamics in a new development, with everyone of a comparable age moving in at the same time, are not the same as the years pass, people age, some move out and younger others move in, and the "frontier spirit" of the original "settlers' ebbs.

Some of those old stereotypes remain, supplemented or even surpassed by new ones. The "soccer mom" transporting her children in her gas-guzzling SUV is a common image of today's young suburban mother. The media not only promotes such a stereotype but also imprints in the public mind a soap opera quality of lust and frustration in suburban life, such as the 1999 Academy Award–winning film *American Beauty* and the Emmy Award–winning TV show *Desperate Housewives*. While such plots make for good comedy-drama, most suburban fathers do not desire their teenage daughters' girlfriends, and most suburban wives are not desperate.

The Physical Environment

Just as cities have an imagability, so, too, do suburbs. Of course, suburbs may differ from one another in their age of development, typical property values, lot size, and prestige, but they all convey some measure of open space, fresh air, trees, single-family homes, lawns, and quiet streets and neighborhoods. Front lawns are typically for display purposes only; except for mowing the grass, little activity occurs there. Instead, the backyard is the personal outdoor playground for suburbanites; here, the barbeque and patio, porch deck, swings, gym sets, tree houses, and play area set the stage for leisure activities.

By looking at the physical environment of a suburb, with just a little insight, we can ac-

tually answer the question, "What time is this place?" (Lynch 1976). Small houses—Cape Cods or bungalows—built on small lots, perhaps 50 by 75 feet, are likely to be from the 1950s. With subsequent gradations in lot size, you typically find newer and newer homes. As people's tastes changed during the late twentieth century, the size of houses increased, and the inclusion of a family room, fireplace, and greater closet space were deemed to be essential. Most recently, the mass construction of **McMansions**—any supersized, large house exceeding 4,000 square feet on too small a lot, leaving little room for yard space—has generated much criticism and local resistance. Considered by critics as "tasteless" and "ostentatious," McMansions nonetheless are an increasing part of the suburban scene, either in new developments or as replacements for older houses torn down to make way for them (Gertner 2005).

Older suburbs, with their smaller lot sizes, are more likely to have sidewalks than newer suburbs are. In fact, an inverse correlation exists between lot size and pedestrian traffic: The larger the former, the fewer the latter. Streets may be the "rivers of life" in the city, but in the suburbs, they are simply the means to get anywhere; people-watching holds little attraction. The impracticality of bus service in such low-density suburbs makes the car a necessity for adults and the bike a secondary means of transportation for teens. For parents, a great amount of time and gas is spent in chauffeuring children to school (if not on a school bus route) and after-school athletic programs or to all kinds of lessons (dance, music, karate, religious).

Few, if any, landmarks exist in the suburbs, and residents rely heavily on mental mapping to get from one locale to another. The visitor, on the other hand, requires specific directions and, even then, often gets confused in reaching that destination. There are surely multiple suburban realities, but given the diversity both within and among suburbs, their greater homogeneity when compared to cities makes the presence of these realities less intense within any given suburb.

The Social Environment

Gemeinschaft and a comprehensive social network constitute the suburban milieu, not the anonymity and widespread presence of strangers, as in the *gesellschaft* environment of the city. You might not know everyone's name, but a shared sense of community marks most everyday interactions. Moreover, especially in families with school-age children, organized activities (PTA, Little and Junior Leagues, scouting) abound, and parents are expected to be active participants. Newest residents, with or without children, often find that a local "welcome wagon" or Newcomers Club initiates contact to integrate them into the community.

Joining a church and participating in its many activities, getting involved in other local programs, and attending block or house parties and cookouts are all part of the interactive neighboring that is common in suburbia. Birthday parties and sleepovers for preteens and early teens, and sweet sixteen parties for those of that age, are just a few of the many ways in which young people are woven into the suburban social fabric.

SUMMARY

Living in cities alters our perceptions. The urban experience causes us to react to the city as a physical and social environment, and such reactions represent a social psychology of the city.

We make sense of the city by ordering it. Kevin Lynch observed that we trace the physical landscape, identifying paths, edges, districts, nodes, and landmarks. In part, such distinctions arise from the physical form of the city itself (streets, after all, are "natural" paths). In part, they also arise from our personal needs and creativity (people invent "back street" paths to get from one place to another more quickly). To this basic insight, Stanley Milgram contributed a deeper understanding of the process, with the concept of "mental mapping."

A similar ordering occurs as we respond to the city's social aspects. On the one hand, we cope with the city's *gesellschaft* characteristics (large numbers and high density) by inventing rules of behavior for riding the subway, standing in line, or walking in the street. We also size up strangers on the basis of their dress, demeanor, and location in the city. Nevertheless, despite many common strategies, we all react individually to the city. Our social characteristics—whether we are rich or poor, immigrant or native, mainstream or marginal—have much to do with the nature of our urban experience.

On another level, we have developed complex ways of establishing meaningful relationships in the city. Urban networks are a prime example. Personal networks take many forms, including kinship, neighborhood, street-corner friendships, or people frequenting some "scene." Most of us also identify with our city as a whole, merging traits of our particular city (a key industry, a winning sports team, or an important historical event) with our own personal urban experience. All these mechanisms lend a *gemeinschaft*-like character to the urban experience.

Next, there is the notion of urban texture or city personality. Recent research shows that much truth lies in people's comments that based on its history, architecture, location, and people, each city "feels" a little different.

Finally, numerous investigations reveal that people, even those facing the most desperate economic conditions, can humanize the city and turn it into a meaningful experience.

Taken together, all these elements of the urban experience provide us with a sense of order and security in this largest of human agglomerations, and they make the city meaningful, usable, and often enjoyable.

A social–psychological examination of suburban life takes us to its stereotypical images, first as a bland locale of superficial conformists promulgated by the media and biased observers to a more recent one of "soccer moms" on the one hand to the frustrated and "desperate" people on the other. A certain homogeneity does exist in the various physical elements of a suburb, even though widespread differences in lifestyle exist. A comprehensive network of interaction and organized activities involves youths and adults in numerous ways.

CONCLUSION

The city is a big place. It has more people, more buildings, more paths, more nodes, and more possibilities for interactions and relationships than any other form of settlement.

As Georg Simmel argued many years ago, cities demand a great deal of mental work from those who wish to make sense of them. In the end, such extra mental effort may be the unique element that creates the sophistication for which urban dwellers are noted. Low-density residence patterns deter pedestrian and bus traffic, and dependence on the car is high. The physical homogeneity and lack of landmarks put the visitor who lacks the detailed mental mapping of suburbanites at a disadvantage in moving about.

KEY TERMS

districts (205)
edges (205)
landmarks (205)
McMansions (232)
mental maps (206)

nodes (205)
paths (205)
scenes (221)
texture (225)

INTERNET ACTIVITIES

1. You can learn more about mental mapping and have a virtual reality, flyover experience at *http://www.mentalmaps.info/*. Once there, click on "Showcase."
2. The most recent and vivid example of urban apathy occurred in Hartford, Connecticut, in June 2008, when a 78-year-old man was the victim of a hit-and-run accident. Although several 911 calls did follow, the immediate reaction of pedestrians and other drivers caused dismay throughout the nation. Watch the horrific incident at *http://www.youtube.com/watchv=VEayX8qti1s*.

CHAPTER 9

COMPARATIVE URBANISM
The City and Culture

Something rather ironic exists in title of Louis Wirth's essay "Urbanism as a Way of Life" (1938), which we discussed in Chapter 5. You will recall Wirth argued that their size, density, and heterogeneity make cities characteristically impersonal, transient, and anonymous. His negative overgeneralizations about cities and their impact on human behavior ignored the role of **culture,** which *is* the urban way of life and often has positive effects on the lives of city dwellers.

In this chapter, we will examine the city and culture from two perspectives. First, we will look at the existence of what Daniel J. Monti calls *civic culture.* That is, in the urban way of life, the many different types of people find an appropriate form of public behavior that enables them, mostly, to get along with one another. Through ceremonies, customs, and codes, they have "worked out a way to be together in public and still carry on their private lives, peaceably and with at least a modicum of predictability" (Monti 1999:103).

Second, *the city is not an entity unto itself.* All cities reflect and intensify the world's cultures. North American culture, with its emphasis on free enterprise and the nuclear family, creates cities such as Boston, with skyscrapers downtown (to maximize trade advantages) and single-family dwellings all around the city. The culture of the Yoruba (the people who comprise the bulk of the population of Ibadan, Nigeria's second-largest city) emphasizes personalized trade relations, handicrafts, and an extended family, and it generates a city that is quite different in physical layout and social interaction. Cities are, after all, human creations that display the same variety as all human culture, and we can fully understand a city only by exploring the cultural patterns found throughout its larger society.

THE CITY AND THE COUNTRYSIDE

> . . . those that are good manners at the court are as ridiculous in the country as the behavior of the country is most mockable at the court.
>
> Shakespeare, *As You Like It,* III, 2

Interdependencies

Shakespeare noted something that everyone knows: Country ways and city ways are often quite different. Yet we must be wary of overgeneralization. For example, in Ibadan, with the city's fields so close by and farmers such a large part of the city's population, it is virtually impossible to distinguish between city ways and country ways (Lawal, Sadiku, and Dopamu 2004). Indeed, in any location, city and country are not independent of each other at all but, rather, have a symbiotic relationship.

Throughout history, the migration of people seeking a better life has transformed city and country alike. To take but one example, during the great expansion of European cities during the nineteenth century, England changed from an almost completely rural society to a nation in which more than 60 percent of the population lived in cities. Table 9–1 presents these population shifts in England and Wales during the second half of that century. In 40 years, the urban population quadrupled, as the rural population and the percentage of adult males in agriculture decreased.

The relationship between the city and its countryside involves much more than just the dynamics of migration, however. The resources that each provides create a reciprocal dependence. Because a large proportion of city dwellers (even in Ibadan) engage in specialized occupations other than agriculture, the countryside must supply the city's food. Many of the

TABLE 9–1 Urban and Rural Population in England and Wales, 1851–1891

Year	Total Urban Population	Total Rural Population	% Adult Males in Agriculture
1851	4,382,937	12,814,442	37.4
1861	6,211,464	12,880,629	34.5
1871	8,195,467	13,506,212	29.0
1881	13,824,705	12,388,102	30.1
1891	17,601,919	9,388,961	27.4

Source: Reported in Dov Friedlander, "The Spread of Urbanization in England and Wales, 1851–1951," *Population Studies* 24 (1970): 429.

Intimate, open-air markets are common in many parts of the world. Particularly in developing countries, city life—such as here in Pisac, Peru—is based on kinship and ethnic ties. Typically, the men work their farms or produce their crafts, and the women sell their products in the marketplace—and often know just about everyone with whom they do business.

specialty occupations of the city, such as weaving or steel manufacturing, depend on the country-side's raw materials. Conversely, the countryside obtains many of its goods—the clothes made by weavers, the tractors made with the steel—from the city.

Shakespeare notwithstanding, perhaps the most important link between city and coun-tryside is the reciprocal shaping of lifestyles. Migrants who swell the city's ranks bring to the city their cultural traditions. The result is a living kaleidoscope of human behavior, ranging all the way from groups who devot-edly try to continue living as they did in the "old country" (e.g., New York's Hasidic Jews) to the various ethnic Americans (e.g., Asian Americans and Hispanic Americans) who maintain only some of the old ways in their new urban setting.

At the same time, other rural influences, including traditional folk music, art, and lit-erature, continually alter the city's charac-ter. For example, at least one radio station in nearly every major U.S. city plays country music exclusively, and "country rock" is a peculiar rural–urban musical blend.

Especially common in North American and European cities (and less so in African cities like Ibadan) is the human cultural hybrid—that is, the urban person who takes a little bit from the numerous, originally rural lifestyles existing in the city and then integrates them into a new lifestyle alto-gether. Such a person was Mayor Fiorello La Guardia of New York, as described in the *Urban Living* box on page 238. Perhaps it would be fair to say that a little bit of La Guardia exists in most city dwellers today.

URBAN LIVING

Mayor Fiorello La Guardia of New York

To put it sociologically, La Guardia was a marginal man who lived in the edge of many cultures. . . . Tammany Hall may have been the first to exploit the vote-getting value of eating gefullte fish with the Jews, goulash with the Hungarians, sauerbraten with Germans, spaghetti with Italians, and so on indefinitely, but this unortho-dox Republican not only dined every bit as shrewdly but also spoke, according to the occasion, in Yiddish, Hungarian, German, Serbian-Croatian, or plain New York English. Half Jewish and half Italian, born in Greenwich Village yet raised in Arizona, married first to a Catholic and then to a Lutheran but himself a Mason and an Episcopalian, Fiorello La Guardia was a Mr. Brotherhood Week all by himself.

Source: Arthur Mann, cited in E. Digby Baltzell, *The Protestant Establishment* (New Haven, CT: Yale University Press, 1987), p. 29.

This influence works in two ways, however. Just as the city receives much from the countryside, it typically returns the favor, radiating outward an influence far beyond its borders. In fact, many sociologists think that this influence, in modern times, far outstrips the countryside's effect on urban affairs.

Urban Dominance

"I cannot see that London has any great advantage over the country," said Mrs. Bennett, "except the shops and public places. The country is a vast deal pleasanter, is it not . . . ?"

Jane Austen, *Pride and Prejudice,*
1813

Thus Mrs. Bennett, engaged in a verbal duel with some of London's high society, defended her rural environment in the early part of the nineteenth century. Her championing of the country was not well received. Everyone present—her own daughters included—subsequently told her that like it or not, London had numerous advantages over the countryside, among them a greater diversity of people, and, well, there was just so much more to do in London.

Right or wrong, Mrs. Bennett was wiser than she knew, for her allusion to what she saw as the city's one advantage—its shops and public places—suggests why the city's influence has spread so far beyond its physical boundaries. As Louis Wirth argued, the city's importance

may be regarded as a consequence of the concentration on [it] of industrial, commercial, financial, and administrative facilities and activities, transportation and communication lines, and cultural and recreational equipment such as the press, radio stations, theaters, libraries, museums, concert halls, operas, hospitals, colleges, research and publishing centers, professional organizations, and religious and welfare institutions. (Wirth and Reiss 1981:63)

Indeed, North American cities have maintained cultural dominance over society far out of proportion to the number of city dwellers since the coming of European settlers in the seventeenth century. Moreover, as we described in Chapter 3, the importance of early eastern settlements, most notably Boston, Charleston, Montreal, Newport, New York, and Philadelphia, was supplemented by that of newer cities as the population moved westward to such places as Chicago, Kansas City, St. Louis, and Toronto. In the Far West, especially following the completion of the transcontinental railroad to San Francisco in 1869, towns and cities continued to stand at the center of social life. This fact was observed by Josiah Strong, who commented in 1885, "It is the cities and towns which frame state constitutions, make laws, create public opinion, establish social usages and fix standards of morals in the West" (p. 206).

North American growth is thus intertwined with the story of the development of cities. Consistently the centers of an expanding market, the loci of advances in communication, and the sources of leadership in politics, fashion, and the arts, cities have a long linkage with cultural firsts: the first daily newspaper (Philadelphia, 1784), the first stock exchange (New York, 1792), and the first telephone system (Boston, 1877; linked to New York in 1884, to Denver in 1911, and to San Francisco in 1915).

Such a pattern of **urban dominance** over the broader society is hardly limited to North America. We find a description of the same phenomenon in Alexis de Tocqueville's historical account (1979; orig. 1856) of the French Revolution of 1789. Beginning in the 1600s as the feudal system weakened, French life became increasingly centralized in Paris. As a result, when the revolution erupted in Paris, it quickly carried the rest of French society along with it.

Tocqueville noted that in times past, Paris had been "no more than the largest town in France . . . [but by] 1789 things were very different; it [was] no exaggeration to say that Paris was France" (1979:72). The city controlled the nation's economic, intellectual, and political lifeblood. This urban dominance was also evident as one left Paris for the countryside. Inquiring as to the political climate of the outlying areas, English observer Arthur Young heard time and again: "We are only a provincial town; we must wait till Paris gives us a lead" (Tocqueville 1979:74).

By the late eighteenth century, Paris had established urban dominance over all of France in cultural, economic, and political matters. When Napoleon borrowed from ancient Roman tradition to build this massive triumphal arch at the western end of the Champs Elysées, it became a symbol of French patriotism, further strengthening the city's image as the "essence" of what is French.

That is exactly what Paris did. One of the remarkable facts of history is that the cultural ideas ("Liberty! Equality! Brotherhood!") that transformed France and much of Western civilization, in conjunction with the American Revolution a decade earlier, were largely city born.

Urban dominance is thus a central pattern of the modern and the historical world. Sometimes, however, urban influence is not so welcome, as the people of Grafton County, New Hampshire, have decided. Their views are described in the *Cityscape* box below.

In other instances, urban dominance is understated, as in the case of "Springdale," a small town in upstate New York. With its quiet streets and surrounding rural countryside, it would seem to be a world apart from the city. The appearance is deceiving. Although residents of the town displayed much pride in their traditions of independence and self-sufficiency—values they associated with small-town life—they also recognized that these sentiments were ebbing away. The average Springdaler, wrote sociologists Arthur Vidich and Joseph Bensman,

CITYSCAPE

The Invasion of the City Slickers

[What city people who move to the country] bring along is a series of unconscious assumptions. It might be better for rural America if they brought a few sticks of dynamite, or a can of arsenic.

Take a typical example. Mr. and Mrs. Nice are Bostonians. They live a couple of miles off Route 128 in a four-bedroom house. He's a partner in an ad agency; she has considerable talent as an artist. For some years they've had a second home in northern New Hampshire. The kids love it up there in Grafton County.

For some years, too, both Nices have been feeling they'd like to simplify their lives. They look with increasing envy on their New Hampshire neighbors, who never face a morning traffic jam, or an evening one, either; who don't have a long drive to the country on Friday night and a long drive back on Sunday; who aren't cramped into a suburban lot; who live in harmony with the natural rhythm of the year; who think the rat race is probably some minor event at a county fair.

One Thursday evening Don Nice says to Sue that he's been talking to the other partners, and they've agreed there's no reason he can't do some of his work at home. If he's in the office Wednesday and Thursday every week, why the rest of the time he can stay in touch by telephone. Sue, who has been trapped all year as a Brownie Scout leader and who has recently had the aerial snapped off her car in Boston, is delighted. She reflects happily that in their little mountain village you don't even need to lock your house, and there is no Brownie troop. "You're wonderful," she tells Don.

So the move occurs. In most ways Don and Sue are very happy. They raise practically all their own vegetables the first year; Sue takes up cross-country skiing. Don personally splits some of the wood they burn in their new woodstove.

But there are some problems. The first one Sue is conscious of is the school. It's just not very good. It's clear to Sue almost immediately that the town desperately needs a new school building—and also modern playground equipment, new school buses, more and better art instruction at the high school, a different princisees that the urban and metropolitan society is technically and culturally superior to his own community. He sees this in his everyday life when he confronts the fact that his community cannot provide him with everything he needs: almost everyone goes to the city for shopping and entertainment; large numbers of people are dependent on the radio and television; and everyone realizes that rural life would be drastically altered without cars and refrigerators. (2000:79; orig 1958)

It may be edge cities and not older cities that impact on many rural landscapes today, but this is merely a newer form of urban dominance. Nor are these the only links that bind the residents of Springdale to the larger urban society.

Their lives are influenced by outside specialists from organizations such as the state agricultural extension service as well as by their own college-trained professionals. Additional organizations that serve to "import" the culture of the urban society include such national organizations as the Odd Fellows and the Kiwanis Club. Perhaps more important, the economic and political life of the town is shaped more by state and federal agencies than by local entities. Taxes, education for the town's children, and the price of local farmers' milk are all increasingly subject to outside forces that are mostly city based. Vidich and Bensman concluded that despite the desires and pretensions of the townspeople, most "plans

---

pal. Don is as upset as Sue when they discover that only about 40 percent of the kids who graduate from that high school go on to any form of college. The rest do native things like becoming farmers, and mechanics, and joining the Air Force. An appalling number of the girls marry within twelve months after graduation. How are Jeanie and Don, Jr., going to get into good colleges from this school? . . . Pretty soon Sue and Don join an informal group of newcomers in town who are working to upgrade education. All they want for starters is the new building ($2.8 million) and a majority of their kind on the school board.

As for Don, though he really enjoys splitting the wood—in fact, next year he's planning to get a chainsaw and start cutting a few trees of his own—he also likes to play golf. There's no course within twenty miles. Some of the nice people he's met in the education lobby feel just as he does. They begin to discuss the possibility of a nine-hole course. The old farmer who owns the land they have in mind seems to be keeping only four or five cows on it, anyway. Besides, taxes are going up, and the old fellow is going to have to sell, sooner or later. (Which is too bad, of course. Don and Sue both admire the local farmers, and

they're sincerely sorry whenever one has to quit.)

Over the next several years, Don and Sue get more and more adjusted to rural living—and they also gradually discover more things that need changing. For example, the area needs a good French restaurant. And it needs a much better airport. At present there are only two flights a day to Boston, and because of the lack of sophisticated equipment, even they are quite often canceled. If Don wants to be sure of getting down for an important meeting, he has to drive. Sue would be glad of more organized activities for the kids. There's even talk of starting a Brownie troop.

In short, if enough upper-middle-class people move to a rural town, they are naturally going to turn it into a suburb of the nearest city. For one generation it will be a nice and truly rustic suburb, with real farms dotted around it, and real natives speaking their minds at town meeting. Then as the local people are gradually taxed out of existence (or at least out of town), one more piece of rural America has died.

Source: Text excerpt, "The Invasion of the City Slikers," reprinted from Noel Perrin, "Rural Area: Permit Required," in *Country Journal* (April 1980), pp. 34–35. Copyright © 1980. Reprinted by permission of the Estate of Noel Perrin.

and decisions that refer directly to the community are made from a distance by invisible agents and institutions" (2000:81). Thus, just as Springdalers now periodically go to the world of the city, the world of the city has subtly transformed, for better or for worse, Springdale and communities like it.

THE CITY AND CIVILIZATION

> Cities have always been the fireplaces of civilization, whence light and heat radiated out into the dark, cold world.
>
> Theodore Parker, nineteenth-
> century U.S. preacher

The reason for the city's increasing dominance in modern affairs, as we have hinted already, is that everything human—art, music, business, traditions, what we love and hate—converges there. The city does not create a way of life all its own but, rather, provides the setting where any way of life, any cultural tradition, can intensify and recreate itself in a manner not possible in other settings. For example, Socrates, Plato, and Aristotle all lived in Hellenic Athens, where they shared ideas and challenged each other. This simply would not have occurred had they all lived in rural hamlets, cut off from one another.

Nowhere is this process of intensification represented more clearly than in the suggestion that the city encapsulates a whole culture. Throughout history, writers have seen the city as capturing the essence of human civilization. Indeed, Euripides, the classical Greek playwright, maintained: "The first requisite to happiness is birth in a great city." The *Urban Trends* box on page 243 illustrates not only the connections among our most common words about cities and civilization but also the linkage between city and culture as expressed in the writings of some of history's most important urbanists.

Is the city truly synonymous with civilization? To find out, let's examine in more detail the ideas of Oswald Spengler, Lewis Mumford, and Daniel J. Monti.

Oswald Spengler: The "Soul" of the City

Oswald Spengler (1880–1936) was a German philosopher who saw in cities the drama of the rise and fall of civilization. He contended that cities developed, ultimately dominated a society, and then declined, carrying with them the culture built over generations and centuries. The cyclical element in Spengler's theory (generally considered by contemporary social scientists as being too simplistic) is less important for our purposes than his belief that "all great cultures are town-cultures" and that "world history is city history" (Spengler 1969:90; orig. 1928).

Spengler believed strongly that human civilization takes on distinctive qualities in the city. At some point in its development, the "soul" of the city emerges: "Out of the rustic group of farms and cottages . . . arises a totality. And the whole lives, breathes, grows, and acquires a face and inner form and history" (1969:65–66; orig. 1928). Spengler believed that the countryside never has a soul in this sense; it is a "landscape" at most, never a "world."

Moreover, the city senses its own power and uniqueness:

> [I]t is a place from which the countryside is henceforth regarded, felt, and experienced as "environs," as something different and subordinate. From now on there are two lives, that of the inside and that of the outside, and the peasant understands this just as clearly as the townsman. . . . The new Soul of the City speaks a new language, which soon becomes tantamount to the language of the culture itself. (1969:66, 68)

Thus, we find the essence of ancient Egypt symbolized by Thebes, ancient Greece by Athens, the Roman Empire by Rome, Islam by Baghdad, and prerevolutionary France by Paris. Indeed, Spengler believed that whole periods of European civilization were manifest only in cities. Is it not true, he asked, "that the Renaissance style flourished only in the Renaissance city, the Baroque only in the Baroque city?" (1969:68).

URBAN TRENDS

The City and Civilization

City Words

Those of us who live in the city should be grateful to our language, because the words that have to do with the city are usually flattering. We city dwellers, at least in ancient days, were supposed to be more *civil* in our manners and more *civilized* in our ways than others, for both of these words *civil* and *civilized* are the eventual children of the Latin term *civis* which meant "one who lives in a city." All city folks, you see, were regarded as automatically cultured and well housebroken. And from ancient Latin we have borrowed the word *urbs* which also meant city, and we used it to create the word *urbane* which describes the smooth manners that were presumed to be characteristic of *metropolitan* society. The Greek parts of the word *metropolitan* are *metro,* "mother," and *polis,* "city," so a *metropolis* is the "mother city" or the chief or capital city of a country, and he who lives in a *metropolis* is supposed to inherit the sophisticated ideas and manners that go with such a center. And from the Greek *polis,* "city," we inherited our word *politic.* If you are *politic,* you are expedient, shrewd, discreet, and artful in your address and your procedure, which sounds dangerously like a city slicker!

City Culture

Just as the beginning of Western Civilization is marked by permanent settlement of formerly nomadic peoples . . . so the beginning of what is distinctly modern in our civilization is best signalized by the growth of great cities. (Louis Wirth, 1938)

The city is . . . the natural habitat of civilized man. (Robert Park, 1984; orig. 1916)

[The city is] the most precious invention of civilization, second only to language itself in the transmission of culture. (Lewis Mumford, 1989; orig. 1961)

All great Cultures are town-Cultures. . . . World history is city history. Peoples, states, politics, religion, all arts, and all sciences rest upon one phenomenon . . . the town. (Oswald Spengler, 1969; orig. 1928)

Source: Wilfred Funk, *Word Origins: A Classic Exploration of Words and Language* (New York: Random House Wings Books, 1998), pp. 97–98.

Modern sociologists generally view Spengler's contribution to urban sociology as being modest, because few accept his cyclical ideas of historical change. Yet he correctly sensed the connection between city and civilization, an idea developed extensively by a U.S. urbanist whose work we will discuss next.

Lewis Mumford: The City as the Center of Civilization

Lewis Mumford (1895–1990) traced the cultural importance of cities through Western history. Based on historical and comparative evidence, he argued that the city has, indeed, been at the very center of Western civilization from its beginnings.

Mumford believed that of all creatures, only human beings seem to be aware of themselves as fundamentally distinctive. We can think, invent, and wonder about such things as life, death, sex, and god(s). In the course of human evolution, Mumford reasoned, people attached these thoughts to places. The earliest centers of this kind were probably caves and places of burial. These sites were symbolic centers to which wandering groups could return periodically to ponder the mysteries they wished to understand.

Thus began civilization. "In the earliest gathering about a grave or a painted symbol, a great stone or a sacred grove, one has the beginning of a succession of civic institutions that range from the temple to the astronomical observatory, from the theater to the university" (Mumford 1989:9; orig. 1961).

As time passed and technology improved, some people began living at these places permanently: The shrine became a camp, then a village, and finally, a town. Mumford (like Spengler) suggests that at a certain point, the cultural ideas, the people, and the place all jelled as the city emerged (see the *Urban Trends* box below).

Thenceforth, the story of civilization became the story of urban history. Yet we must be careful here. We often assume that civilization automatically means progress—that what exists today is somehow a better form of what went before. Neither Spengler nor Mumford meant to suggest this notion of cultural evolution;

URBAN TRENDS

The Crystallization of the City

This new urban mixture resulted in an enormous expansion of human capabilities in every direction. The city effected a mobilization of manpower, a command over long-distance transportation, an intensification of communication over long distances in space and time, an outburst of invention along with a large-scale development of civil engineering, and, not least, it promoted a tremendous further rise in agricultural productivity. . . . When all this happened, the archaic village culture yielded to urban "civilization," that peculiar combination of creativity and control, of expression and repression, of tension and release, whose outward manifestation has been the historic city. From its origins onward, indeed, the city may be described as a structure specially equipped to store and transmit the goods of civilization, sufficiently condensed to afford the maximum amount of facilities in a minimum space, but also capable of structural enlargement to enable it to find a place for the changing needs and the more complex forms of a growing society and its cumulative social heritage. The invention of such forms as the written record, the library, the archive, the school, and the university is one of the earliest and most characteristic achievements of the city. . . .

What happened . . . with the rise of cities, was that many functions that had heretofore been scattered and unorganized were brought together within a limited area, and the components of the community were kept in a state of dynamic tension and interaction. In this union, made almost compulsory by the strict enclosure of the city wall, the already well-established parts of the proto-city—shrine, spring, village, market stronghold—participated in the general enlargement of concentration of numbers, and underwent a structural differentiation that gave them forms recognizable in every subsequent phase of urban culture. The city proved not merely a means of expressing in concrete terms the magnification of sacred and secular power, but in a manner that went far beyond any conscious intention it also enlarged all the dimensions of life. Beginning as a representation of the cosmos, a means of bringing heaven down to earth, the city became a symbol of the possible.

rather, their idea was that the city was culture "writ large," the living embodiment of a society's or epoch's ideas. Cities did not inevitably progress. In them, as already mentioned, Spengler saw the rise and fall of civilization, and like Max Weber before him (see Chapter 5), Mumford believed that cities better than today's had existed in the past—in Hellenic Athens, for example.

Daniel J. Monti: The Civic Culture of the City

Daniel J. Monti rejects the suggestion of some social scientists that cities have become "sinkholes of civic indifference," no longer possessing the cultural or moral vision that once motivated their residents (1999:378). Instead, he argues that cities continue to inspire both a public spirit and a civic mindedness among their inhabitants. Their ability to coexist and cooperate in the everyday routines of public habits and customs is the manifestation of a **civic culture.** Its elements

borrowed from other cultures or adapted from earlier times, civic culture helps the many different peoples of a city to get along and make sense of each other's world.

Offering a detailed portrait of a civic culture is a difficult task. First, each city has its own distinctive style, temperament, and public rhythms, so generalizations are misleading. Second, civic culture is not static; it is continually changing and, thus, is hard to pinpoint. Third, some of its elements may be better or less known to certain groups in the city and, therefore, practiced unevenly or not at all in different parts of the city (Monti 1999:103–104).

Despite the unevenness of some aspects of civic culture, other parts work well throughout the city, because they are widely shared. These are found in the "ceremonies, customs, and codes for appropriate public behavior" (Monti 1999:103). Essentially, "they are expressions of how persons in that place have worked out a way to be together in public and still carry on their private lives, peaceably and

Monti suggests that civic culture in a city includes widely shared codes of appropriate public behavior, which allow strangers to be together and act with a reasonable set of expectations from each other. Such practices as alternate vehicle merging or awaiting a bus in a single line allow fair and orderly movement through unspoken, untaught norms of mutual respect.

with at least a modicum of predictability" (Monti 1999:103). For example, urbanites typically line up awaiting the arrival of a bus in a single line, not in a cluster. This unspoken, untaught norm of civic culture is quickly learned, enabling strangers to accord one another a mutual respect and an orderly entrance once the bus arrives.

In this and countless other ways, urban public behavior reflects the shared values, norms, and practices of a civic culture that makes it possible for people—different and unknown to one another—to become part of an inclusive community. Essentially minding each other's business in order to behave appropriately in urban public space, rather than focusing only on one's own actions or rituals, city people develop a common view of the world and conceive better ways to be in it together (Monti 1999:104).

> The "good city" is not necessarily a fair city or a just city, and it is most certainly not an equal city. It is instead where a people creates a viable civic culture that makes sense to them and works. The civic culture of American cities is revealed to us as an interesting and even a paradoxical mix of conservative and liberal ways of "doing community." It works well, or at least a great deal better than we have been led to believe. The good news is that the rest of us share in the civic and cultural bounty of cities anyway. The bad news is that we do not see the urban way of life made in cities as part of our cultural inheritance, and we do not appreciate the contribution it has made to our lives. (Monti 1999:379)

THE CITY AND SOCIETAL CULTURE

From Mumford and Spengler we learn that although the city and civilization are not precisely synonymous, the city definitely has a unique power to intensify and symbolize culture. From Monti, we learn the city also generates a civic culture that, to a greater or lesser degree, its residents share and practice. Another aspect of culture is that any city will dynamically and intensely reflect the characteristics of its surrounding culture. Because cultural patterns vary so widely, however,

cities may be markedly different from one another. In the following case studies, we will read about two cities, Peking during the Ming Dynasty (1368–1644 C.E.) and Hellenic Athens of the fifth century B.C.E.—capitals of vastly different civilizations and separated by more than 1,500 years.

CASE STUDY
Ming Peking

Situated on the northern seacoast, China's capital city is centered around the Forbidden City and Tiananmen Square, the world's biggest public square, with an area of 98 acres. Now a city of more than 15 million people, Beijing (formerly called Peking) has a 3,000-year history and contains fascinating remnants of its glorious past.

Established in northeastern China to protect the country from invaders out of the north, Beijing grew into a city at least several centuries before the birth of Christ. During the thirteenth century C.E., when the Yuan (Mongol) emperor ruled China, Kublai Khan transformed Beijing into a capital city. Soon after the overthrow of the Yuan by the Ming Dynasty in 1368, the Emperor Yung Lo spared no expense in turning the city into a monument to all of Chinese culture and to himself as symbolic head of that culture. It was a massive job, including the transportation of large amounts of marble a distance of 1,500 miles not only to expand the palace but also to upgrade some of the city's roads and bridges (Mote 2003:617–20).

Physical Structure

The design, deliberately created to symbolize everything vital to Chinese life, arranged the whole city on a perfect north–south axis, around which were temples and altars. Perhaps no better example exists of Lewis Mumford's idea about the city as a physical container, for Ming Beijing literally revealed the city within the city, surrounding the all-important core where the emperor lived (Figure 9–1).

The city was about 25 square miles in area and was composed of two major sections, each

FIGURE 9–1   Ming Peking

Source: Adapted from Roderick MacFarquhar, *The Forbidden City* (New York: Newsweek Books, 1972), p. 42.

roughly rectangular in shape. Beijing's southern section, known as the Outer City or Chinese City, contained most of the city's population, probably about 320,000 people at the end of the thirteenth century (Chandler 1987:356).

The northern section, however, was of quite another character. Known as the Tartar City or Inner City, this area was surrounded by a massive wall about 50 feet high and just as thick. Indeed, whereas in the West the words for *city* are linked to the words for *civilization* and *politics,* in Chinese the word for *city* literally means "wall," indicating in yet another way that the city was a container of major cultural significance (Murphy 2007:189). All city streets were arranged in a gridiron, with gates through the wall arranged symmetrically.

Centrally located within the walls of the Tartar City was another area, called the Imperial City. Protected by yet another wall, and including about 5 square miles of park-like land, complete with artificially constructed lakes and hills, this was the focus of the political and religious power and splendor of Ming civilization. In the midst of this constructed urban tranquility, and surrounded by a moat and yet another defensive wall, were the palaces and residences—facing south—of the emperor. This was called the Purple City by the Chinese and later dubbed the Forbidden City by Europeans after their realization that access was gained only through the emperor's personal decree. Just to the north was a large, artificially constructed mound of earth, Coal Hill, on which stood temples that were prominently visible above the city.

Symbolism

Ming Peking was based on elaborate Chinese cosmology, with its temples and altars serving as religious symbols of the sun, earth, and most important, heaven. Chinese astronomers had discovered long before Peking was built that the center of the heavens was the North Star, around which everything revolved. On earth— the human universe—the Chinese believed that everything revolved around the "Son of Heaven," the emperor. As the northernmost major city of China, Peking thus became the emperor's capital. The importance of the north was also evident in the city's location on a north–south axis and by the fact that the emperor could be reached only by traveling north along the Great Processional Way. Even the name of the emperor's city, the Purple City, was chosen because the North Star gave off a purple hue in the night sky (Naquin 2000).

The symbolism did not stop there, however. The colors and height of all buildings had cultural meaning. Peasants, lowly and unimportant, were allowed houses of only one story and could paint their roofs only a dull gray. In the Imperial City, various functionaries couldn't have houses of more than one story, either, but to signify their higher status, they were allowed to paint their roofs green, red, or purple, depending on their role. Only in the Forbidden City itself were buildings allowed to be more than one story. Their roofs were painted a bright golden yellow, symbolizing the life-giving (sun-like) qualities of the emperor's rule. The emperor was the pivot of the world, and ruling from the Forbidden City with the mandate of heaven, he harmonized the world, oversaw the calendar, and maintained order (Beguin and Morel 1997).

It is little wonder that the emperor, given his importance, had everything for the "good life" within a stone's throw. The construction of the Forbidden City was a marvel of urban design, as can be seen by carefully examining the buildings shown in Figure 9–2 on page 249. Note especially the buildings in the center—the emperor's sole preserve. The first group, the buildings immediately to the north of the Supreme Imperial Gate, are buildings of state: The Hall of Supreme Harmony was reserved for special state occasions, such as the New Year's ceremony and the emperor's birthday; the smaller Hall of Central Harmony was the place where the emperor prepared himself and waited for functions; the Hall of Protecting Harmony was for the reception of visitors and for day-to-day governance. The second group of central buildings—to the north of these state buildings—comprised the emperor's residences. Entering by the Gate of Heavenly Purity, one found the Palace

FIGURE 9–2 The Forbidden City

Source: Adapted from Roderick MacFarquhar, *The Forbidden City* (New York: Newsweek Books, 1972), p. 73.

of Heavenly Purity, the emperor's quarters; next was the Hall of Vigorous Fertility, which, its name notwithstanding, was where official seals were stored; finally, one found the Palace of Earthly Tranquility, where the empress lived.

Ming Peking is a striking example of the city's ability to intensify culture. Peking was a symbolic world, a whole city built on the cultural themes of harmony with nature, security (city within city), and power. Each "layer of the onion" re-emphasized the whole and led to the vital, omnipotent center—the emperor.

This particular symbolism probably means little to us, but we can imagine what it meant to the Pekingese. In a similar manner, our cities transmit and magnify our culture. What is important in our culture is "writ large" in Boston, Birmingham, and Boise. We don't have cities within cities or predominant religious symbolism, like Peking. On the site of the World Trade Center twin towers in New York City, however, contractors are presently building the "Freedom Tower," clearly a distinctive symbol and statement about U.S. culture. Flying over North American cities, we see commercial skyscrapers, fast-moving automobiles on superhighways, and private, single-family houses. What might such constructions say about the things that are culturally important to us?

CASE STUDY
Hellenic Athens

Little risk exists of exaggerating the differences between Ming Peking and Hellenic Athens, situated on the rocky northern coast of the Mediterranean. During a period of barely two generations in the fifth century B.C.E., between about 480 and the start of the Peloponnesian War in 431, a civilization took form that Mumford described as "a far richer efflorescence of human genius than history anywhere else records, except perhaps for Renaissance Florence" (1989:167). Imagine an almost simultaneous development of the arts of painting, sculpture, and architecture;

the realization of a rationally structured democracy; and the birth of a body of philosophy that remains at the center of Western thinking today. At the heart of this Golden Age was the city of Athens, leading to an almost synonymous identification of Athenian culture with Greek achievement.

The Preclassical Period

Four migrating tribes settled Athens as early as 2000 B.C.E., and eventually, the Greek peninsula came under the control of feudal overlords who called themselves, perhaps with not the greatest modesty, the *aristoi* (or aristocracy; literally, "the best people"). By the eighth century B.C.E., these overlords were in charge of several hundred independent Greek city-states, or *poli* (the source of our contemporary word *political* and of the urban suffix *-polis*). Over the next two centuries, the city-states grew rich as technology and overseas trade improved and military conquests multiplied.

Ironically, this very success is what led to the aristocrats' downfall. The improvement of trade created a wealthy middle class that began to demand participation in city rule, and the martial victories evolved a warrior class with both the skills and arms to take over the city-states. In a series of coups d'état between 660 and 550 B.C.E., they did just that in many trade and maritime city-states, earning in the process the name *tyrannos* (Burn 1970).

Tyrants or not, the preeminence of warriors during this period was to prove fortuitous. Early in the fifth century B.C.E., a series of Persian invasions threatened the Greek peninsula. Together, Athens and her rival city-state, the more militaristic Sparta, finally routed the invaders in 479 B.C.E., setting the stage for what many regard as the city's—and, perhaps, even Western history's—greatest moment.

The Golden Age

In the fifth century B.C.E., the city of Athens (about one mile square) and its surrounding villages had a population of perhaps 350,000

Athens today is strongly shaped by its culture and history. Even the physical environment reveals that social reality, as seen here. Looming above the city from its craggy hilltop site sits the Acropolis— built in the second half of the fifth century B.C.E. as the citadel of ancient Athens. Particularly prominent are the pillars of the Parthenon—the temple of Athena, patron goddess of the city.

(Waterfield 2005:149). We can best understand Athenian life in the Golden Age as the celebration of human possibilities. "Men come together in the city to live," exclaimed Aristotle in a timeless salute to the human possibilities of city life, and "they remain there in order to live the good life." What was this "good life"? In his famous funeral oration in honor of Athenian victims of the Peloponnesian War, Athenian statesman Pericles conveyed its essence: The Greek ideal, he said, began with the principle of democracy "which favors the many instead of the few."

The Athenian belief in democracy was grounded historically, for the city-states that preceded the Golden Age were independent units. Indeed, so independent were they that one cannot speak of one "nation" even at the apex of Greek culture. Each city-state pursued its own ends and believed that no one had the right to dictate otherwise.

This fierce sense of independence also characterized the Greek citizen. In 600 B.C.E.,

with dissatisfaction rife, Athens was on the verge of revolution. To avert this, Solon, an aristocrat, was chosen as arbitrator. He immediately proposed a reorganization of the Athenian constitution that allowed all "free citizens" (excluding women, slaves, and foreigners) a place in the city's governing body, the Assembly. He established the People's Council, numbering some 400 members, with the charge of preparing the Assembly's agenda. Members were chosen from the four main Athenian tribes (100 members each), thereby preventing dominance by any one group. Finally, government officials were made accountable to the Assembly for their work each year. Political participation was mandatory for all citizens; without regard to "obscurity of conditions," each was required to take part in the public life of the city.

Athenian democracy was a brilliant innovation, affording all free citizens participation in government. It also allowed the citizen the right to live as one chose within that overarching system. Classical Athens did not stand as a monument to an all-powerful god or to a ruling family but, rather, to all free citizens. In one of the great dramas of the age, Sophocles's *Antigone,* we find this statement (which could well serve as a critique of Ming Peking): "A city that is of one man is no city."

The ideals of human development and versatility were vital to Hellenic civilization. A primary cultural value was that all citizens should strive for refinement (although without extravagance) and pursue individual well-being—a fusion of the well-tutored body, mind, and spirit. Athenians developed the body through constant work, exercise, and sport, including the Olympic games, in which individuals from different city-states competed for the glory of their state. Continual dialogue provoked the mind; in their leisurely society, citizens often spent much of the day talking about the deeper matters of life. Plato's dialogues between the great philosopher Socrates and his friends are an excellent example.

Athenians even managed their spiritual life differently. For example, no system of formal or mystical religion placed the gods at great distance from the people of the city. In Peking, the priests were "specialists" who were sequestered within the walls of the Forbidden City, but in Athens, the "priest" was just another conscientious layman who made no prophecies and simply executed his religious duties as part of his civic duties. This ideal of participation meant that temples such as the Parthenon were always open to people, who typically marked their religious observances informally and, frequently, outdoors.

Indeed, as Greek civilization entered the Golden Age, the gods themselves became less abstract and more like human beings. They were the objects of jokes, criticism, and bargains, but—all the same—they were used as models for human development. The Olympian gods became the symbol of something nobler in human nature, of something within the reach of human endeavor.

A tripartite focus on body, mind, and spirit was the unique combination that formed the crux of Athens's success. By developing serious interests in all three areas, the Athenian indirectly kept any one area from becoming all-absorbing. This focus kept more practical areas of life—politics or economics, for example—in check. Too much politics breeds an overemphasis on power and control; too much economics cultivates an obsession with wealth and material goods. For a brief period, the citizens of Athens avoided these pitfalls.

Behind the Glory

Athens's moment at the pinnacle of urban history was not to last; it eventually was undermined by the culture's own egocentrism and exploitative practices. The wealth and leisurely pace of Athens during its Golden Age rested, in large measure, on the goods and services of others. During its successful expansion before the fifth century B.C.E., Athens had conquered many other city-states and regions. From them, Athens extracted tribute in materials, taxes, and people—many of whom became slaves; Waterfield (2005:149) estimates that about one-fourth of the city's population held this unhappy status, as the elite Athenian citizens benefited from the widespread use of such human servants. All women, however, were excluded from citizenship and relegated to household duties and supervision.

Elitism reared its head in yet another, more immediately destructive way. The Athenians refused citizenship to 30,000 foreigners, many of whom, as traders, had become permanent residents. This robbed the citizenry of potentially invigorating new ideas, forcing the foreign population into an exclusive concern with economic matters. Demoralized, these traders devoted their energies to money making and material consumption. In time, they became indifferent to government so long as they were free to make a profit. By the end of the fourth century B.C.E., profit making had become the center of city life, and the older idea that economic activity was simply a means to a more holistic life—so central to the health of the city—began to wane.

Into this setting came the Peloponnesian War, begun in 431 B.C.E. between Athens and Sparta. Soundly defeated, Athens surrendered in 404 B.C.E. Then, in total confusion and in public contradiction of all their democratic ideals, in 399 B.C.E the Athenians tried Socrates and condemned him to death for "undermining the state by his endless public questionings."

The handwriting was on the wall. In 338 B.C.E., the Athenians put up belated opposition to an invasion force led by Philip of Macedon. Their defeat at the Battle of Chaeronea has been called "the death of the free polis." After that, Athens became a satellite in the Macedonian Empire until the Roman overlords arrived in 148 B.C.E.

MING PEKING AND ATHENS: A COMPARISON

The culture that prevailed in classical Athens was of a radically different character from that of Ming Peking. Without doubt, the cities had certain parallels: substantial inequality; large areas of poor housing; crowded, winding streets; and important central monuments and public buildings. There were all-important differences, however. Chinese civilization rested on a fundamental cultural belief in a god-like emperor, which gave an unmistakable stamp to Peking. Monuments and buildings dwarfed the common individual as they simultaneously magnified the pomp and majesty of the emperor and his elite. Indeed, what clearer indication of a distant, exclusive power structure could there be than a citadel in the form of Peking's Forbidden City?

Athens seemed, overall, to be more humane in character. The Greek cultural ideals of citizen participation stamped that city with a human scale, encouraging openness, communication, and development among its free citizens. Such ideals can be seen in all Athens's public buildings—in the theaters (where, not by accident, the audience sat above the performers, not the other way around), in the public forums, in the temples, in the gymnasia, and in the marketplace. These buildings were not monuments to an absolute emperor; rather, Athens was much more a celebration of the "good life," an ideal that was evident despite important failings in practice.

In comparing Hellenic Athens and Ming Peking, we see just how different cities in different cultures can be, but this comparison shows us more: Athenian success at encouraging citizen participation and in developing the very best of human nature by a process of dialogue and growth shows us what the city can be. We are prompted to ask, in other words, how or why one city might be better than another. If we agree, for example, that democracy, equality, and continual mental, bodily, and spiritual development are ideals for which human beings should strive, Athens provides us with a real-life case where those ideals were encouraged. What, then, might we do to encourage the further manifestation of positive cultural values in our own modern-day cities? (See the *Cityscape* box on page 254 for a decidedly negative portrait.)

THE CULTURE OF CAPITALISM AND THE CITY

Nineteenth-century London certainly was not like either Ming Peking or Hellenic Athens. Dominated by feverish economic activity, it was the forerunner of the modern city described by U.S. urbanist Louis Wirth in Chapter 5.

Friedrich Engels, however, who first saw London in 1842—the same year he met Karl Marx and began their long collaboration—gave an interpretation radically different from that of Wirth. Whereas Louis Wirth, the Chicago urbanist, imagined he was describing the essential characteristics of all large, modern cities, Engels was aware that he was looking only at a certain cultural setting, a city intensifying the tremendous power of Western industrial capitalism. Note especially the passage in italics in the *Cityscape* box on page 254. What Wirth saw as a consequence of a large, differentiated population, Engels interpreted as cultural forces at work.

CITYSCAPE

The Industrial City: 1844

This colossal concentration, this heaping together of two and a half millions of human beings at one point . . . has raised London to the commercial capital of the world; created the giant docks and assembled the thousand vessels that continually cover the Thames. . . . all this is so vast, so impressive, that a man cannot collect himself, but is lost in the marvel of England's greatness. . . .

But the sacrifices which all this has cost become apparent later. After roaming the streets of the capital a day or two . . ., after visiting the slums of the metropolis, one realizes for the first time that these Londoners have been forced to sacrifice the best qualities of their human nature, to bring to pass all the marvels of civilization which crowd their city. . . .

The very turmoil of the streets has something repulsive, something against which human nature rebels. The hundreds of thousands of all classes and ranks crowding past each other, are they not all human beings with the same qualities and powers, and with the same interest in being happy? And have they not, in the end, to seek happiness in the same way, by the same means? And still they crowd by one another as though

they had nothing in common, nothing to do with one another. . . .

And, however much one may be aware that this isolation of the individual, this narrow self-seeking is the fundamental principle of our society everywhere, it is nowhere so shamelessly barefaced, so self-conscious as just here in the crowding of the great city. The dissolution of mankind into monads, of which each one has a separate principle and a separate purpose, the world of atoms, is here carried out to its utmost extreme. [emphasis added]

. . . here . . . people regard each other only as useful objects; each exploits the other, and the end of it all is, that the stronger treads the weaker under foot, and that the powerful few, the capitalists, seize everything for themselves, while to the weak many, the poor, scarcely a bare existence remains.

What is true of London, is true of Manchester, Birmingham and Leeds. . . . Everywhere barbarous indifference, hard egotism on one hand, and nameless misery on the other, everywhere social warfare . . . and all so shameless, so openly avowed that one shrinks before the consequences of our social state as they manifest themselves here undisguised, and can only wonder that the whole crazy fabric still hangs together.

Source: Friedrich Engels, *The Condition of the Working Class in England,* edited by David McLellan (New York: Macmillan, 2007), pp. 35–36.

Engels was mightily disturbed by what he saw. If Hellenic Athens, with its cultural ideas of developing the whole person, was the city's highest point, surely Engels believed nineteenth-century London to be its lowest point. Yet the characteristics of both cities reflect the dominant ideals and activities of the larger culture. In the same way that Greek culture produced cities in which economic activity was regarded as of decidedly secondary importance, Engels believed that Western culture, under the influence of capitalism, spawned cities where economic gain was an unrestrained obsession.

The Capitalist City

As a means of livelihood, capitalism is very old. A rich capitalist life flourished in the fifth century B.C.E. in Athens, and no doubt, such activity is centuries older. Significant commercial activity aimed at the accumulation of profit also took place on an increasing scale in medieval Europe, especially after the eleventh century C.E.

If capitalism itself was not new, the unparalleled energy with which the spirit of commerce and profit began to assert itself during the sixteenth century C.E. certainly was. Apparently, several factors prompted this change. First, the feudal order of the Middle Ages began to erode as merchants, primarily in cities, gained power. Desiring to broaden their market, these merchants established trade routes among cities all over Europe in the period between 1200 and 1500. Goods began to pour into these cities, and people in the countryside began to get wind that a better life—or at least a life with more material amenities—could be had in cities. Major urban population growth ensued and fueled increased economic vitality (Heilbroner and Milberg 2007).

Gradually, from the sixteenth century onward, the economic interests of life came to dominate Western European cities. Capitalism set the principal cultural theme, with the new order being organized around a rather different set of economic relationships than its feudal predecessor. No longer bound to lords and manors, individual workers could sell their labor to whoever would pay the highest wages. Second, under these conditions, economic activity became increasingly competitive. Because everyone was striving for profits, workers, to get the greatest economic benefits, had to outdo each other in some way. The arrival of industrialization in the mid-eighteenth century greatly enhanced capitalism's hold over Western cities.

The Industrial Revolution

Like capitalism, **industrialism**—the process of manufacturing goods in large quantities for mass consumption—had existed in Western society to a limited degree before the eighteenth century. Only after the adoption of

capitalism on a large scale, however, did the influence of industrialism begin to grow, with large-scale industrialism set in motion in England about 1750.

One important reason that English society proved to be so amenable to industrialism was the fondness, particularly evident in the upper middle classes, for engineering and guiding economic activities by the most scientific methods available. If efficient methods were not available, the innovative British invented them. Perhaps the most famous example of an invention that changed the economic order was James Watt's steam engine. This machine, perfected by 1775, had literally hundreds of applications, from textile manufacturing to flour mills to the mass production of the common pin. Its ability to save hand labor and contribute to the mass production of items was nothing short of remarkable, and in little time, entrepreneurs put this invention into widespread use. By 1781, Matthew Boulton, Watt's partner in a steam-engine manufacturing company, was claiming that "the people of London, Birmingham, and Manchester [are] all 'steam mill mad'" (Quoted in Mantoux 2006:333). From then on, the Industrial Revolution was in full force. Other inventions, such as Arkwright's spinning jenny and Maudslay's automatic screw machine, revolutionized other areas of production. "The Revolution . . . fed upon itself. The new techniques . . . simply destroyed their handicraft competition around the world and thus enormously increased their own markets" (Heilbroner and Milberg 2007: 75–77).

For the city dweller, the most important change was the invention of the factory.

The factory may be singled out as the agent which gives [the industrial–capitalist] city its structural form and social purpose. By the word "factory" I mean more than an industrial enterprise: the factory is the locus of mobilized abstract labor, of labor power as a commodity, placed in the service of commerce as well as production. Accordingly, the term applies as much to an office building and a supermarket as to a mill and a plant. Once the factory becomes an element of urban life, it takes over the city almost completely. (Bookchin 1996:51)

With the domination of the factory, the very symbolism of the city changed. The city in feudal Europe had been, above all, a Christian city, symbolically dominating the region with its Gothic cathedral. (A striking example is Venice, spread out around St. Mark's Cathedral, built in 1176.) The capitalist era, as Mumford remarked, turned the culture of feudalism on its head, transforming "six of the seven deadly sins [gluttony, pride, covetousness, envy, lust, and anger] into cardinal virtues (sloth became perhaps an even greater sin)" (1989:346). The church declined as the focal institution of society: In the place of spires appeared smokestacks, and the public plaza became a growing central business district.

> If capitalism tended to expand the market and turn every part of the city into a negotiable commodity, the change from [small-scale handicraft] to large-scale factory production transformed the industrial towns into dark hives, busily puffing, clanking, screeching, smoking for twelve and fourteen hours a day, sometimes going around the clock. The slavish routine . . . became the normal environment of the new industrial workers. None of these towns heeded the old saw, "All work and no play makes Jack a dull boy." [They] specialized in producing dull boys. (Mumford 1989:446)

In short, the dominant capitalist cultural theme, in conjunction with industrial mechanization, created a new emphasis in urban consciousness. In describing a typical schoolroom in "Coketown," a fictionalized English factory city of the nineteenth century, Charles Dickens explained the main ingredient of this consciousness, presented in the *Urban Living* box on page 257.

Urban Life as Economics

"You are never to fancy!" With this phrase, Dickens summarized what so worried Engels about the capitalist city: It reduced everything in life to objective facts and quantity. Other aspects of life—subjectivity, quality, art, music, politics, religion, and creative thought—were downplayed or consciously eradicated.

A multistory, mirrored building in Toronto's city center towers above an old stone church. The size and positioning of these buildings suggest dominant cultural themes of the past and present. Today, we see the relative importance of economics and religion in contemporary Western society, which differs from that in previous centuries, when church steeples were the highest visible points in cities.

This new consciousness not only transformed how city people acted; it transformed the physical structure of the city itself, thereby intensifying the capitalist theme even further. Land, once merely a place to live, became real estate:

> If the layout of a town has no relation to human needs and activities other than business, the pattern of the city may be simplified: The ideal layout for the business [person] is that which can be most swiftly reduced to standard monetary units for purchase and sale. The fundamental [urban] unit is no longer the neighborhood . . . but the individual building lot,

URBAN LIVING

"Nothing but the Facts, Ma'am"— Capitalist–Industrialist Consciousness

"Now, what I want is, Facts. Teach these boys and girls nothing but Facts. Facts alone are wanted in life. Plant nothing else, and root out everything else. You can only form the minds of reasoning animals upon Facts: nothing else will ever be of any service to them. This is the principle on which I bring up my own children, and this is the principle on which I bring up these children. Stick to Facts, Sir!"

The scene was a plain, bare, monotonous vault of a schoolroom, and the speaker's square forefinger emphasized his observations by underscoring every sentence with a line on the schoolmaster's sleeve. The emphasis was helped by the speaker's square wall of a forehead, which had his eyebrows for its base, while his eyes found commodious cellerage in two dark caves, overshadowed by the wall. The emphasis was helped by the speaker's mouth, which was wide, thin, and hard set. . . .

"Thomas Gradgrind, Sir. A man of realities. A man of facts and calculations. A man who proceeds upon the principle that two and two are four, and nothing over, and who is not to be talked into allowing for anything over. Thomas Gradgrind, Sir—peremptorily Thomas—Thomas Gradgrind. With a rule and a pair of scales, and the multiplication table always in his pocket, Sir, ready to weigh and measure any parcel of human nature, and tell you exactly what it comes to. It is a mere question of figures, a case of simple arithmetic. . . .

"Girl number twenty," said Mr. Gradgrind, squarely pointing with his square forefinger, "I don't know that girl. Who is that girl?"

"Sissy Jupe, Sir," explained number twenty, blushing, standing up, and curtseying.

"Sissy is not a name," said Mr. Gradgrind. "Don't call yourself Sissy. Call yourself Cecilia."

"It's father as calls me Sissy, Sir," returned the young girl in a trembling voice, and with another curtsey.

"Then he has no business to do it," said Mr. Gradgrind. "Tell him he mustn't. Cecilia Jupe. Let me see. . . .

"Give me your definition of a horse."

(Sissy Jupe thrown into the greatest alarm by this demand.)

"Girl number twenty unable to define a horse!" said Mr. Gradgrind, for the general behoof of all the little pitchers. "Girl number twenty possessed of no facts, in reference to one of the commonest of animals! Some boy's definition of a horse. Bitzer, yours. . . ."

"Quadruped. Graminivorous. Forty teeth, namely twenty-four grinders, four eye-teeth, and twelve incisive. Sheds coat in the spring; in marshy countries, sheds hoofs, too. Hoofs hard, but requiring to be shod with iron. Age known by marks in mouth." Thus (and much more) Bitzer.

"Now girl number twenty," said Mr. Gradgrind. "You know what a horse is. . . ."

["But Sir," said Cecilia Jupe, blushing] . . . "I fancy . . ."

"Ay, ay, ay! But you mustn't fancy," cried the gentleman, quite elated by coming so happily to his point. "That's it! You are never to fancy!"

Source: Excerpt from Charles Dickens, *Hard Times* (New York: Signet Classics, 1997; orig. 1854), pp. 11–16.

whose value can be gauged in terms of front feet: this favors an oblong with narrow frontage and great depth, which provides a minimum amount of light and air to the buildings, particularly the dwellings, that conform to it. Such units turned out equally advantageous for the land surveyor, the real estate speculator, the commercial builder, and the lawyer who drew up the deed of sale. In turn, the lots favored the rectangular building block, which again became the standard unit for extending the city. (Mumford 1989:421–22).

So strong was this pattern in the physical form of the city after the sixteenth century that even cities with mountainous geography, such as San Francisco, which might have benefited from a switchback or zigzag pattern in order to facilitate moving up and down the terrain, were subjected to a grid pattern.

Murray Bookchin used even stronger language to suggest the extent to which the modern Western city has been shaped by the industrial–capitalist system:

> Every esthetic urban pattern inherited from the past tends to be sacrificed to the grid system (in modern times, the factory pattern par excellence), which facilitates the most efficient transportation of goods and people. Streams are obliterated, variations in the landscape effaced without the least sensitivity to natural beauty, magnificent stands of trees removed, even treasured architectural and historical monuments demolished, and wherever possible, the terrain is leveled to resemble a factory floor. The angular and curved streets of the medieval city which at every turn delighted the eye with a new and scenic tableau, are replaced by straight monotonous vistas of the same featureless buildings and shops. Lovely squares inherited from the past are reduced to nodal points for traffic, and highways are wantonly carved into vital neighborhoods, dividing and finally subverting them. (1996:90–91).

Assets and Debits

On one level, the capitalist city has unquestionably been successful in generating a higher material standard of living for a larger proportion of its population than any other urban system in history. For example, 11.8 percent of the U.S. population in metropolitan areas was below the poverty line in 2006, compared with 15.2 percent in nonmetropolitan areas. Useful material goods and technological innovations are omnipresent, and given the "hands-off-the-individual" value that is so central to capitalism, residents of such cities experience a significant degree of political as well as other kinds of freedom. They can vote, come and go as they please, and if they have the money, live where they like.

There are debits as well, however: Millions of poor families live in cities, and many unprofitable districts have fallen into shocking decay. Within such areas, as we will see in later chapters, people suffer incredibly. Similarly, the dominant focus on material goods and technological innovations often means that many people are preoccupied with the newest MP3 or DVD player or the latest car and are less mindful of social and environmental needs that require attention.

Finally, even freedoms have their problematic side. The freedom to accumulate wealth, prestige, and power has meant, over the years, that some individuals in our cities have much more of these limited resources than others. With wealth primarily in the hands of a few (the richest 5 percent of the U.S. population control 59 percent of the wealth), these people tend to control both the economic and the political spheres of life to such a degree that others are effectively cut off from any true success or representation.

Problems such as these led to a reaction: a second type of modern city, established around and intensifying yet another set of cultural themes, those of communism.

CASE STUDY
Communist Beijing

To get a sense of the contemporary communist city, we return to Peking. The *Urban Living* box on page 259 gets us acclimated. It records the first visit to the city by Liang Heng, a

URBAN LIVING

Peking! Home of the Glorious Revolution!

Peking was cold to my sneakered feet, and the wind was like knives, but to me, it was heaven. The avenues seemed five or six times as broad as those in [my home city of] Changsha, the buildings cleaner and more splendid, if a bit austere. I immediately demanded to be taken to Tian An Men Square, and tired as they were, my friends took me, watching with amusement as I stared at everything that was legend—the Great Hall of the People, the Monument of the Heroes of the People, the Historical Museum. Like every other Red Guard coming to Peking for the first time, I took my oath in front of the huge picture of Chairman Mao, lifting my "Little Red Book" in my right hand, sticking out my chest and reciting proudly, "Chairman Mao, Liang Heng has finally come to your side. I will always be loyal to you. I will always be loyal to your Thought. I will always be loyal to your Revolutionary line." I could have stayed there all night. . . .

Source: Liang Heng and Judith Shapiro, *Son of the Revolution* (New York: Vintage, 1984), pp. 114–15.

young Red Guard supporter of Chairman Mao Zedung, during the turmoil of the Cultural Revolution of the 1960s.

Back on October 1, 1949, standing on the Meridian Gate of the old Ming Imperial City (see Figures 9–1 and 9–2), looking out over the millions assembled in Tiananmen Square, Mao had established the People's Republic of China. It was on this historic spot that Liang Heng gazed in rapture as a dedicated revolutionary on August 16, 1966. Liang was part of a youth militia, the 11-million-strong Red Guard, that Mao used for a supposed cultural revolution to purge liberals and continue the revolutionary class struggle, but it was actually a means to regain the full power that he had relinquished after his disastrous "Great Leap Forward" program. In 1957, Mao, in an attempt to speed the growth of socialism, had moved thousands of peasants into special communes to increase steel production. As a result, steel production nearly tripled, but most of it was impure and useless. Meanwhile, agricultural production plummeted, creating a famine in which more than 32 million people died from food deprivation (Thaxton 2008:5).

To appease the widespread discontent, Mao passed day-to-day control to two political allies. By 1963, however, he began criticizing his allies, and three years later, he launched the Cultural Revolution, giving the Red Guard unbridled power to act. In the violent turmoil that ensued, about half a million people died, and millions of others were persecuted, including artists, authors, educators, intellectuals, political leaders, and religious officials. During the 10 years of the Cultural Revolution, the Red Guard perpetrated one of the greatest destructions of historical artifacts in human history, devastated minority cultures, and killed hundreds of thousands of minority people, particularly Mongolian Muslims and Tibetan Buddhists. When it finally ended, even traditional Chinese culture had been weakened (Esherick, Pickowicz, and Walder. 2006).

Today, six decades after Mao made that pronouncement of a new country, Peking is a different city—its feudal and imperial past almost completely eradicated, its name reverted back to Beijing (the old name, *Peking*, was a Western transcription of *Beijing*). On the site of the old dynasties has arisen what is the most important communist city in the world, now that communism no longer dominates Russia and Eastern Europe.

Modern Beijing thus provides us with a final illustration for the consequences of different cultural themes in urban places. The great walls that protected the city and the emperor in the Ming period are gone. In their place is a city-encircling highway, while belowground, the city's modern subway system provides 88 miles of track, averages 3.4 million riders daily, and went through rapid expansion for the 2008 Summer Olympic Games. The Forbidden City is now a museum that is open to all, surrounded by great new buildings of state: the Great Hall of the People, the Historical Museum, and the Mausoleum that holds Mao's remains. The many multistoried hotels in Beijing easily dominate the old buildings of the emperor. Replaced, too, are many of the old, sonorous names of the

imperial years. For example, the Pavillion of Pleasant Sounds has given way to People's Road and Anti-Imperialist Street.

Beijing in the twenty-first century, however, is significantly different from the "austere" city that Liang Heng mentioned. Three or four decades ago, a rigid communist government controlled almost all aspects of life. Everyone dressed alike in dark, uniform-like clothes. Individuals could not own their own businesses, and residential relocation—whether from one city to another or from outlying rural areas to the city—was not allowed. Economic stagnation was the norm, and social use of public urban spaces was virtually non-existent, especially at night. In contrast, Beijing today, along with other Chinese cities, has embraced capitalistic enterprise, and city life flourishes with individual enterprises, colorful fashions and consumer goods, nightlife, and a booming economy.

Modern Beijing is an energetic city in which capitalism and consumerism flourish, as partly indicated in this view of the Wangfujing shopping street by Oriental Plaza. A lenient government policy toward individual enterprise has generated more spending money, which enables Chinese urbanites to purchase additional goods and enjoy a higher standard of living than in years past.

The Emergence of Modern Beijing

The Communists did not gain control of China easily. Ironically, the expansion of capitalist nations and their cities during the nineteenth century made it possible.

In 1644, the Ch'ing Dynasty replaced the Ming rulers who had built Imperial Peking. Like their Ming predecessors, the Ch'ing emperors were not interested in contact with the outside world, despite the fact that the world was interested in China. In the late 1700s and early 1800s—not coincidentally, the time of the industrial–capitalist revolution—various European countries made overtures to China in hopes of finding yet another trade market, for they desired China's silk, tea, and silver. When the emperor rebuked them, tensions grew. The Europeans became determined to find a way to open China to trade, and the Chinese were just as determined to keep them out.

The denouement came in the mid-nineteenth century. For many years, the British had been smuggling India-grown poppies into China. Converted into opium and mixed with tobacco for smoking, the poppies gave rise to China's infamous opium dens, which served an estimated 2 million addicts by 1835. Finally, enraged, an imperial commissioner from Beijing seized and destroyed more than 2.8 million pounds of opium in Canton in 1839. It was a fateful decision, because later that same year, the English launched the so-called Opium War as a punitive action. The English won hands down, and the resulting treaty opened five Chinese ports to unrestricted trade and established the British colony of Hong Kong. In 1860, another war and treaty forcibly opened more Chinese ports to European trade.

Severely weakened, the ruling dynasty lost the Sino-Japanese War in 1895 and, during the antiforeigner Boxer Rebellion of 1900, fled Beijing. Chinese insurgents held Peking for 55 days against an eight-nation "relief force." The insurgents' inevitable defeat placed China almost completely under foreign domination. In 1911, Dr. Sun Yat-sen overthrew the remnants of the dynasty and proclaimed a Chinese Republic. Chiang Kai-shek succeeded him in 1927, but power struggles throughout the country meant that the government remained ineffectual.

In 1934, angered by the disadvantageous trade relations that the republic still tolerated with foreign countries, China's fledgling Communist Party under Mao Zedung undertook the 6,000-mile Long March through China's countryside to escape Chiang Kai-shek's army. The Communists returned in 1948 and, after a six-week siege, occupied Peking and proclaimed the People's Republic the following year.

Urban Life as Politics

The Communists vowed to free China from centuries of domination of the many by the few and from exploitation by foreign countries. To do this, they transformed nearly all of Chinese life into an expression of the new political ideas. The job of the state was to provide equally for everyone; the job of the individual was to contribute to the state's success by participating unselfishly in the state-linked neighborhood units, school classes, factories, and party committees. Only by collectivizing everything, the Communists believed, and by constantly reminding everyone about the dangers of backsliding into individualism was true progress to be attained.

The key concept in all this was *tzu-li keng-sheng*—"self-reliance" or "regeneration through one's own efforts." In developing this concept, the party divided each city into districts (Beijing has nine), each district into neighborhoods, and each neighborhood into smaller residential areas. Each residential area developed its own "residents' committee" designed to link each individual with the city authorities, and vice versa. It became the job of these committees to oversee local services—security, fire, and sanitation—and to keep political responsibility uppermost in peoples' minds (Whyte and Parish 1987:21–22).

Study groups developed unceasing political awareness in which all neighborhood residents participated (study groups also existed in schools and factories). The tasks of these groups were (1) to communicate to all citizens the importance of participation in all areas of life; (2) to chastise political troublemakers of all kinds, such as "revisionists," "factionalists," "ultra-Leftists," "capitalists," and "imperialists"; and (3) to examine constantly, through group self-criticism, each individual's performance. The intent was to discourage individualism while encouraging both **groupthink**—conformity to opinions that supposedly reflect group consensus— and control through many eyes of each person's actions. It is difficult to imagine more contrasting views of city life than those outlined above and those held by the people of contemporary Western cities.

The Difficulties of Urban Life

Beijing's population in 1949, the year of the declaration of the People's Republic, was less than 2.5 million. (Today, its urban area contains 15 million and is bursting at the seams.) Successful in feeding and housing its people, China nevertheless remained saddled with a primitive industrial system and an inferior educational system that left it in desperate need of trained personnel. (China was an almost entirely peasant society until the 1950s.) Its standing as a world-class economic power remained elusive, and the nation was not able to provide widespread, high-quality education.

Economic Reform and Environmental Issues

With Mao's death in 1976, a great power struggle emerged in Beijing for control of the party—a struggle won by Deng Xiaoping and his followers. The new leaders de-emphasized the more extreme elements of Maoism and moved from a sluggish, Soviet-style, centrally planned economy to a more market-oriented economy, but one still within a rigid political framework of Communist Party control. To this end, the authorities switched to a system of household responsibility in place of the old collectivization in agriculture, increased the authority of local officials and plant managers in industry, permitted a wide variety of small-scale enterprise in services and light manufacturing, and opened the economy to increased foreign trade and investment.

The result has been a quadrupling of the gross domestic product (GDP) since 1978, making China the second-largest economy in the world. China's economic reforms have benefited hundreds of millions of people, but they have created a growing income disparity as well. The richest 10 percent of all Chinese families now own more than 40 percent of all private assets, and average annual income of urban residents is more than three times that of their rural counterparts. The poverty situation, however, has greatly improved. In 1990, one out of three Chinese lived in poverty, but today, it is below 1 in 10, meaning that 500 million people were lifted out of poverty in just one generation (Chowdhury 2007).

The problem is that with its rapid economic expansion, China has become a massive despoiler of the environment. One-fourth of the country is now desert, and more than three-fourths of its forests are gone. A cloud of lead, mercury, sulfur dioxide, and other elements of burned coal and car exhaust hovers over most Chinese cities. Already the world's leading emitter of carbon dioxide, China's economic development—the country has 16 of the 20 most-polluted cities in the world—is affecting its ecosystems:

> Acid rain caused by China's sulfur-dioxide emissions severely damages forests and watersheds in Korea and Japan and impairs air quality in the U.S. Every major river system flowing out of China is threatened with one sort of cataclysm or another. The surge in untreated waste and agricultural runoff pouring into the Yellow and China seas has caused frequent fish die-offs, and overfishing is endangering many ocean species. (Leslie 2008).

Many of China's cities are already paralyzed by automobile traffic, but with its car industry now the world's third largest and its 33 million cars expected to quadruple in the next 12 years, the potential impact on climate change is even worse (Leslie 2008).

A Rising Consumerism

Visitors to Beijing today find a city alive with energy. In one section of the city—just south of the old Forbidden City—is a shopping section for the capital's citizens. Beneath billboards advertising Toshiba TV sets are department stores filled with goods, with no shortage of lookers and buyers. One reason for this increasing consumerism is the additional spending money generated by the new policies encouraging individual enterprise. For example, in another part of the city is a farmers' market, where workers from a local commune sell surplus vegetables not needed for the commune or for state consumption. They are allowed to keep the profits from such transactions. Some young people, selected by the government to go abroad and teach Chinese in a North American college, earn Western salaries—astronomical by Chinese standards. When they return to Beijing, they are allowed to keep the money they have saved and, thus, are able to afford better apartments in new sections of the city and to provide their families with a variety of consumer goods.

All this change—a movement "from Marxism to Mastercard"—has its critics. Many powerful Communist Party members see the revolution of Mao being "sold out," and as an indication that the policies of Deng and his successors are not all positive, they cite extensive evidence that corruption now appears in many areas of Chinese life as people scramble for the accoutrements of a consumer society. They charge that the current policies generate self-centeredness and a kind of Western decadence. In fact, theft and prostitution, once virtually non-existent, are now as common as in Western cities. Nonetheless, the open-door policy continues, and China and its cities once again are in the throes of major social change.

Through the global economy and mass media, cultural diffusion affects any city, its culture, and its people. The result is not so much homogenization as it is accommodation of outside influences within that culture. Behind this rickshaw driver in Shanghai, China, the billboard for *Harper's Bazaar* magazine indicates the Western influence on fashion and hairstyles.

SUMMARY

The city does not exist by itself but, rather, as an intricate part of the broader society. Shaping any city's physical and social forms are the cultural values of that society and its history. For example, although some truth exists in the old idea that the ways of the country and of the city are distinct and "ne'er the twain shall meet," research reveals that cities and their countrysides are bound together in a complex interdependence that allows each to have significant influence over the other. Urban dominance, however, makes this mutual influence less than equal. Cities, once the centers for revolutions that spread nationwide, now extend their cultural influence far beyond their borders in such areas as the arts, communication, fashion, and politics.

Cities are not entirely synonymous with civilization. However, they are symbolic centers that concentrate, intensify, and re-create the cultural forces found throughout the society. Spengler envisioned a cyclical rise, dominance, and decline of cities as being reflective of their civilizations. Mumford advanced the concept that cities have always been at the center of civilization. Monti wrote about how each city creates its own civic culture that makes it unique compared to other cities in the same society.

In the cities we compared and contrasted in this chapter—Ming Peking and Hellenic Athens, nineteenth-century industrial–capitalist London and contemporary communist–capitalist Beijing—we found significant differences. These differences attest to the importance of culture in shaping the social and physical environment of the city. Only by studying cities in a comparative manner can we understand this urban variability.

CONCLUSION

If urban variety is so marked, what is left as distinctively urban? What do all the cities we've considered in this chapter have in common? To answer this question, we certainly must go beyond the factors of size, density, and heterogeneity proposed by Louis Wirth. We propose a new definition of the city, one that acknowledges the importance of the cultural dimension Wirth neglected: In comparison with other types of permanent human settlement, *a city is a relatively large, dense settlement that has a civic culture and a complex social structure that greatly reflects, intensifies, and re-creates cultural values and forms.*

A few comments are necessary to clarify this definition. The first set of characteristics—"a large, dense settlement"—is Wirth's; he seems to be quite right about them. The next characteristic—"a complex social structure"—is from V. Gordon Childe (1950). You may recall that Wirth also suggested the city is composed of "socially heterogeneous individuals." By this, he meant that people of different racial, ethnic, and religious backgrounds tend to mingle in the city. Anthropological research has shown that this more accurately describes modern Western cities (to which people of different countries migrate) than it does their non-industrial counterparts, such as Jakarta and Nairobi. Yet even if social heterogeneity is not characteristic of all cities, nearly every urbanist has noted that the city has a more complex division of labor and a more sophisticated political system (if only to handle the large numbers and density) than do other forms of human settlement. Such complexities are what we mean by "a complex social structure."

Finally, the idea that any city is a reflector, intensifier, and re-creator of cultural values and forms is a direct outgrowth of this chapter. In the final analysis, the nature of any city lies in its unique ability to interpret a particular set of cultural values in a distinctive form. By "cultural values," we mean those shared beliefs and ideas that characterize any social group of long duration. By "form," we mean the typical round of everyday activities and arrangement of urban space that characterize any city. Thus, because the cultural values of the Greeks during Athens's Golden Era (the fifth century B.C.E.) regarded money making as secondary and a holistic life as primary, we found that the daily life of the city was dominated by dialogue, politics, recreation, and ritual. While the Greeks surely went to the *agora* (the market) to trade, they just as frequently went there to talk and relax. Even their buildings reflected this cultural emphasis. The Acropolis, where the most important buildings of Greek civilization (the Parthenon, the Erechtheum, the Propylea, the Temple of Athena Nike) were located, sits on a hill overlooking the rest of the city. The *agora*, lesser in importance, lies at the bottom of the hill. All this appears to be reversed when we consider the form of contemporary capitalist cities, such as those of North America, where the round of daily activities focuses on the economic. Most people spend the bulk of their day getting, spending, and planning for more of the same. Dialogue, politics, recreation, and ritual come later—in the evenings, on the weekends, or during vacation. The city's physical layout reflects this cultural priority. Streets are arranged on a grid for easy movement and buying and selling, and the most important buildings—or at least those that dominate the skyline of any major North American city—are those of commerce.

In such comparative observations lies a crucial lesson about studying cities: Quite simply, if we don't understand the relationship between the city and culture, we can't properly understand the city. As alluded to in our discussion about the emergence of modern Beijing, however, we also need to consider the role of economic power in dictating quality of life, a subject we turn to next.

KEY TERMS

civic culture   (245)
culture   (236)
groupthink   (262)

industrialism   (255)
urban dominance   (239)

INTERNET ACTIVITIES

1. Take a virtual tour of the Forbidden City. Go to *http://www.world-heritage-tour.org/asia/ china/ming-qing/beijing/forbidden-city/map. html,* and click any photo. Then, click inside the image, and drag left or right to get a full view.

2. At *http://www.commoncensus.org/maps.php* is an intriguing, color-coded map of what viewers consider to be the cultural influence of a nearby city and to what extent that influence extends. You can add your vote to this still-unfolding national map.

CHAPTER 10

STRATIFICATION AND SOCIAL CLASS
Urban and Suburban Lifestyles

What's your stereotype of a person from the city? How about describing someone from the suburbs? Most people find it much easier to answer the second question, because conventional wisdom holds that cities are much more socially diverse than suburbs. Yet, as sociology often shows us, what people think is not necessarily true. Cities in the United States and Canada are home to people of various socioeconomic classes, races, and ethnicities, and exploring any city will reveal neighborhoods with a mix of people as well as many distinctive neighborhoods in which people have their own typical lifestyle. The same is true of suburbs. No large city or suburb is accurately described with any single stereotype.

In this chapter, we investigate the diversity found in our cities and suburbs, highlighting the social class differences within them. In Chapter 11, our attention will turn to the importance of race, ethnicity, and gender in creating urban and suburban diversity. These chapters are about social differences, but they are also about social inequality. As we examine the "structure" of the North American city, we shall see that some urbanites experience "the good life" while others contend with a host of problems. These urban problems, including inadequate housing, poor education, and high levels of crime, are the focus of Chapter 12. We begin by investigating how differences in social class create social diversity in both cities and suburbs.

SOCIAL STRATIFICATION

The United States, Canada, and all other countries are stratified societies. In every nation, people are ranked in a social hierarchy that determines their quality of life. The social hierarchy involves access to jobs, income, schooling, and other resources, which, in turn, affects people's choices about where and how to live. Keep in mind that communities are not all the same in terms of social stratification; some countries have more inequality than others. In addition, within any country, its rural communities, with somewhat more homogeneous populations, typically have fewer social levels than in cities, where people differ more in terms of occupations, incomes, and schooling.

Two classical social theorists—Karl Marx and Max Weber—offered ideas about social stratification that still influence sociological thinking today. Drawing on the work of Marx, social-conflict theorists claim that inequality in wealth and power provides some people with so many greater advantages over others that conflict between social classes is inevitable. Weber agreed with Marx that social stratification causes social conflict, but he saw Marx's two-class view of capitalists and workers as too simplistic and suggested a more complex model. To Weber, economic inequality—the issue so vital to Marx—was, indeed, important, and he referred to this as *class* position. Weber, however, viewed social class not in terms of two categories but, rather, as a continuum ranging from high to low. He also introduced the concept of *status*, or social prestige, as the second dimension of social stratification, with *power* as the third. With Weber's thinking in mind, most sociologists define **social stratification** as the *hierarchical ranking within a society of various social class groups according to wealth, power, and prestige.*

Following Weber's concepts further, sociologists use the term **socioeconomic status (SES)** to refer to *a composite ranking based on various dimensions of social inequality.* This ranking results from comparison of how many status symbol possessions one accumulates, such as the poshness of one's residence and the expensiveness of one's car, clothing, eating habits, and vacations. Of particular interest is residence, for the ability to live in a particular place—whether voluntarily or involuntarily—is an excellent illustration of social stratification. This is not an issue of city versus suburban living, however, because people in all levels of social class are living in both types of communities.

W. Lloyd Warner and his associates were the first to conduct a comprehensive study of social stratification in the United States with their examination of "Yankee City" in the 1930s. (It was actually Newburyport, Massachusetts, a small town of 17,000.) Combining objective criteria, such as income and occupation, with subjective input, using the **reputational method** in which people compared others to themselves in terms of status, Warner reported the existence of a six-tier class system (upper upper, lower upper, upper middle, lower middle, upper lower, and lower lower). Among his other findings was a significant relationship between an ethnic group's length of residence in the United States and its class status, a pattern that still holds true today for many immigrant groups.

Social Class Distinctions

Since Warner's seminal research, three generations of social scientists have studied the many manifestations of stratification and social class in all types of communities. The paradoxical coexistence of great poverty and wealth that they found in our cities is simply a condensed manifestation of what exists in society itself. Before we look at the social class segregation that we find in our cities and suburbs, therefore, it would be helpful to describe the general characteristics found among the different layers of social strata in North American society.

Although the two countries differ in their definitions of income and poverty levels, what follow are a fairly definitive portrait of U.S. society and a close approximation of Canadian society.

Upper Class. The main distinction between Warner's upper-upper and lower-upper classes was essentially that of "old money" and "new money"—that is, of either multigenerational, inherited wealth (e.g., Jay Rockefeller, with a 2008 net worth of more than $200 million) or first-generation, self-earned wealth (e.g., Bill Gates of Microsoft, with a 2008 net worth of $58 billion). The upper class constitutes about 5 percent of the total population. Whether they have "old" or "new" money, however, creates a social divide between the two levels, and they seldom have membership in the same clubs and organizations.

With their great wealth, the upper class live ostentatiously in expensive neighborhoods, enjoy high prestige, and wield considerable

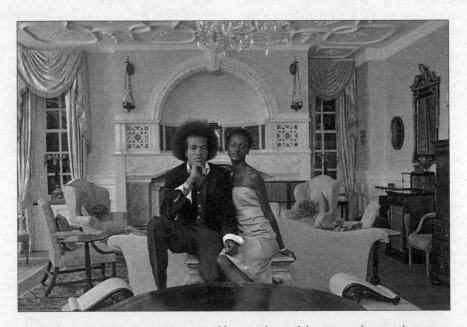

The high socioeconomic status enjoyed by members of the upper class partly rests, suggested Weber, on social prestige gained through the accumulation of prized status possessions. Among the measurable examples of such conspicuous consumption is a posh residence along with expensive cars, clothing, eating habits, vacations, and other pursuits.

political clout. They tend to be a fairly cohesive group, interacting with one another at the "right" social events, belonging to the same clubs and organizations, sending their children to the same private schools, supporting charities and the arts, and vacationing at the same elite resort areas. Upper-class women are in charge of hosting entertainments at home for guests and often do volunteer work for charitable and civic organizations, both locally and nationally; the men often are active in community service organizations (see the *Urban Living* box below).

Middle Class.   Constituting about 40 to 45 percent of society and more diverse both racially and ethnically, this population segment is the one most often depicted in films and television and most commonly targeted by advertisers. About half are upper-middle class, earning

URBAN LIVING

The "Philadelphia Gentlemen"

E. Digby Baltzell, a sociologist born into the upper class, not only gave an excellent insider's view into the world of the elite, he also provided what is probably the best study of this lifestyle in *Philadelphia Gentlemen* (1989; orig. 1958). Although his in-depth portrait was of the Philadelphia elite, his analysis is applicable to most U.S. cities that have been home to a multigenerational, "old-money" constituency.

He described these "descendants of successful individuals" as a cohesive primary group who grew up together in the same exclusive neighborhoods, attended the same private schools, vacationed in the same restrictive places, and so naturally became friends. Eventually, they intermarried, and in their adult lives, they continued their social bonding by living near one another, belonging to the same churches and clubs, and seeing each other frequently. With a strong sense of group identity and governed by social norms of what is "just not done," they maintained "a distinctive lifestyle and a kind of primary solidarity which [set] them apart from the rest of the population" (Baltzell 1989:7).

In describing the upper-class neighborhood in Philadelphia, Baltzell suggested a three-stage out-migration, which also approximates the pattern in other U.S. cities. From the colonial period through the first half of the nineteenth century, the city's elite lived in what is now the downtown business district; in Philadelphia, this was the area around Independence and Washington Squares. Following the Civil War and until World War I, the upper-upper class shifted away from the increasingly busy, noisy, congested downtown to a quieter residential neighborhood nearby; in Philadelphia, this was about 12 blocks west of the Rittenhouse Square district. In the third stage, following World War I, the elite in small and medium-size cities moved out to the suburbs; those in large cities, however, were able to maintain their upper-income enclaves. In the Philadelphia metropolitan area, the elite continued their westward out-migration to the suburbs. We should also note that throughout all three periods, the city's elite typically maintained at least two residences, one in the city and another in the country (Baltzell 1989:179; orig. 1958).

Source: Based on E. Digby Baltzell, *Philadelphia Gentlemen: The Making of a National Upper Class* (New Brunswick, NJ: Transaction Publishers, 1989).

above-average income, typically in the range of $100,000 to about $200,000 annually. That income enables them to own an expensive co-op or townhouse in the city or a good-sized suburban home, participate in local politics, send their children to universities in preparation for careers in high-prestige occupations and professions, and invest in stocks, bonds, and perhaps, property. Upper-middle-class women may or may not work: Some are in professional careers, while others prefer to be stay-at-home wives and mothers. Many will be active in local charitable, church, or civic organizations, as often are their husbands.

The other half of the middle class either work in less prestigious white-collar occupations, such as office workers, middle managers, and sales clerks, or else in highly skilled blue-collar jobs, such as electrical work and carpentry. Their family income is comparable to the national average, about $50,000 to $90,000 annually. Generally, they build up a small nest egg for their retirement, and about half their children graduate from college, often at a state-supported school. To a lesser degree than those of the upper-middle class, the women in this social stratum will also participate in local clubs and organizations, as will the men, who may be active in fraternal organizations as well. Both middle-class groups usually immerse themselves in their children's activities, such as sports programs and scouting.

Working Class. Sometimes called the lower-middle class, this population segment comprises about one-third of society and yields a family income below the national average, about $30,000 to $50,000 annually. This level of income gives them little means by which to acquire wealth, although about half of working-class families do own their own homes. They are especially vulnerable to financial crisis, however, if they experience unemployment or a serious illness. They are the classic Marxian model of workers in closely supervised jobs with little creativity and over which they have little control. Furthermore, these jobs offer fewer benefits, such as medical or dental insurance and pension plans, particularly if they are non-union jobs. About a third of the children

in these families will go to college. In many working-class families, women only work when single and become full-time homemakers once married. In many instances, however, the high cost of living has obliged these women to work as well. Both genders are likely to restrict their outside activities to church-related or neighborhood association activities. In addition, many men also enjoy participation in fraternal organizations and organized sports for themselves or their children.

Lower Class. About 20 percent of the population—poor whites as well as poor racial and ethnic minorities—fall into this category. Some are the so-called working poor, who hold low-prestige jobs with low incomes that nonetheless enable them to get by. Located in our inner cities and rural areas, about 40 percent own their own homes. Many have no medical insurance, so a serious illness or long-term unemployment could easily create the need for government assistance. About 12 to 13 percent of the population receives such welfare assistance. Researchers have found that the men and women living in these poor neighborhoods have distinctly separate social worlds (MacLeod 2004; Liebow 2003). Women are more likely to be involved in organizational activities, usually the church, and interact in more confined areas, whereas men will more often be out and about, congregating with friends to drink, talk, and enjoy sports.

Some urban neighborhoods have such extreme levels of poverty and unemployment that social scientists call them **hyperghettos** (Wacquant 1997). In Canada and the United States, the poverty rate currently hovers around 11 to 12 percent, but in hyperghettos, more than 40 percent of the residents live in poverty. The unemployment rate in both countries has been about 6 to 7 percent, compared to as high as 67 percent in hyperghettos. Other characteristics of these neighborhoods, which contain mostly rental units, are low levels of education and job skills as well as high levels of single-parent households and social isolation. Because hyperghettos are almost always racial and/or ethnic minority neighborhoods, we will explore this grim social phenomenon more fully in the next chapter.

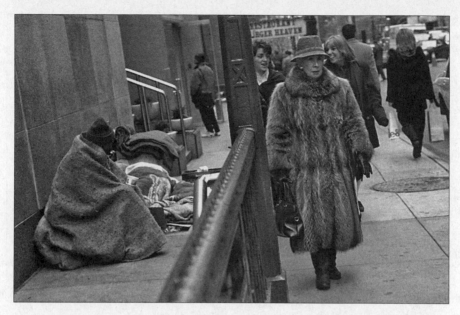

A fur-coated woman passes a blanketed homeless person on East 51st Street in New York. Not uncommonly, we can find urban scenes like this one where ostentatious displays of affluence contrast with images of poverty. Such visual dichotomy is to be expected as part of the heterogeneity of cities, in which resides a mixture of people of all social classes.

Before we examine the different social class concentrations in our cities and suburbs, we will first examine, in a larger context, three of the best measurable indicators of social stratification: (1) income, (2) wealth, and (3) poverty.

Income Distribution Nationwide

The disparity between rich and poor is not simply a matter of difference in incomes (a normal fact in any competitive society) but, rather, a difference in the proportionate share of total income that each socioeconomic group possesses and in how each group's income situation changes from year to year. This information offers helpful insight regarding macrosocial factors relating to poverty.

If family income were distributed equally across the population, each quintile, or 20 percent segment, would receive one-fifth of the total. Of all the industrialized nations, however, the United States has the most unequal distribution of wealth (Philips 2003). As Figure 10–1 on page 272 shows, the top 20 percent of all U.S. households—those earning more than $100,001 in 2007—earned 49.4 percent of all income. That is about as much as the remaining 80 percent of Americans combined! The top two-fifths earned almost three-fourths of all income, leaving the lowest 20 percent of households—those earning less than $20,300—drawing in only 3.4 percent of the total (U.S. Census Bureau 2008b). Among Canadian households, the unequal distribution is also pronounced, though not to the same level of intensity. In 2006, the top 20 percent of all Canadian households earned 47 percent of all income, while the lowest 20 percent of households earned 4 percent of the total.

Since 1968, the gap between the most affluent Americans and everyone else has been steadily widening, and by 1993, it reached its widest extent since the end of World War II in 1945. It widened still further by 2007 (U.S. Census Bureau 2008b). Similarly, the income gap has widened in Canada. Between 1996 and 2006, the income disparity between the top 20 percent and the bottom 20 percent of Canadian households widened by 27 percent (Statistics Canada 2007j).

FIGURE 10–1   Household Income, Percentage Share, 2007
Source: U.S. Census Bureau 2008b.

Incomes Within and Outside Cities

If we compare income data by residence, we find that in metropolitan areas, those living outside central cities are better off than those living within central cities. As Figure 10–2 shows, the median income of U.S. households in 2007 was $57,444 for those in suburban areas, compared to $44,205 in cities and $40,615 in non-metropolitan areas (U.S. Census Bureau 2008b). This difference of $13,239 between urban and suburban dwellers gives us an initial understanding of the greater financial resources available to many of those living beyond the city limits.

Wealth and Net Worth

Two other measures of individual or family economic well-being are wealth and net worth. *Wealth* refers to either (1) marketable assets, such as real estate and other property (boats, cars, furs, and jewelry), bank accounts, and stocks, bonds, and other securities; or (2) financial assets (all of the preceding minus owner-occupied housing). *Net worth* refers to all of one's assets minus

all liabilities (what one owes). For example, ownership of a $500,000 home that has a $400,000 mortgage results in a $100,000 net worth, which is quite a difference. Net worth thus is a more accurate indicator of economic well-being. Home ownership, in fact, is the single largest component of individual wealth. In 2004, the last year for which such data are available, homeowners (mostly in suburbia) had an average family net worth of $624,900, while renters (mostly in cities) had an average net worth of $54,100 (Federal Reserve 2006). In Canada, the median net worth of families in 2005 was $148,350 (Statistics Canada 2008a).

Because home equity is such an important element of wealth for so many people, the housing and mortgage crisis of 2007–2009 has been a major factor in creating not just a larger economic crisis but also one that negatively impacted on the wealth of many Americans. Caused, in part, by unscrupulous mortgage lenders and brokers and unregulated transactions in mortgage-backed securities, as well as buyers who didn't act responsibly, the result was 2.2 million foreclosure notices in 2007, up

FIGURE 10–2   Median Income, 2007

Source: U.S. Census Bureau 2008b.

75 percent from 2006. In 2008, more than 3 million homes experienced foreclosure, up 76 percent from 2007. Even those homeowners who could afford the higher payments from adjustable rate mortgages suffered, because the homes of tens of millions of families lost value as prices plummeted due to a glut in the market of available homes. As the economic crisis rippled outward, both investors and retirees saw their investments and annuities suffer as well. For many, their marketable and financial assets declined, thus reducing the wealth of many (Pollock 2008).

As with income, a wealth disparity exists as well. In 2004, the last year for which data are available from the Federal Reserve Bank, the top 1 percent owned 33 percent of total wealth and the next wealthiest 9 percent of families held another 36 percent. This left less than a third of the total for the remaining 90 percent of the population (Kennickell 2006:10). Although cities, some more so than others, contain extremely affluent households who are part of this vast holding of wealth, the suburbs contain the majority of these highly prosperous families (Keister 2000).

Poverty Nationwide

In 2007, the poverty threshold for a U.S. family of four was $21,386. The official poverty rate was 12.5 percent—a total of 37.3 million Americans. This was 10 percent lower than the poverty rate in 1959, the first year for which poverty data are available. In 2007, the poverty rates were as follows: non-Hispanic whites, 8.2 percent; blacks, 24.5 percent; Hispanics, 21.5 percent; and Asians, 10.2 percent. Of those living in poverty, 87.5 percent were native-born citizens, 9.5 percent naturalized citizens, and 21.3 percent foreign-born non-citizens (U.S. Census Bureau 2008b).

In Canada, 10.5 percent of its population was classified as being low income after tax in 2006. Immigrants constituted a higher proportion of those in this category compared to Canadian-born citizens. Length of residence was a factor, as immigrants who had lived in Canada less than five years had a low-income rate 2.5 times that of Canadian-born in 2003. That low-income rate falls fairly quickly with more years spent in Canada, because immigrants improve their language skills, form networks in their new country, and become more familiar with Canadian social and work norms (Picot and Hou 2003).

Poverty Within and Outside Cities

Poverty data offer an initial understanding of the greater strain put on cities' resources in order to assist those living below the poverty level. In 2007, more U.S. city residents—16.5 percent, or nearly one in six—lived in poverty compared with those living outside central cities, where the poverty rate was 9.0 percent (1 in 11). In non-metropolitan areas, 15.4 percent (one in seven) lived in poverty (Figure 10–3). In absolute numbers, this translated to about 12 million in central cities, 13.9 million outside central cities, and 7.4 million in non-metropolitan areas (U.S. Census Bureau 2008b).

We can partly explain the higher concentration of poverty in cities by the greater numbers of foreign-born residents. Throughout the history of Canada and the United States, cities have traditionally been home to many poor newcomers struggling to survive and improve their quality of life. That pattern continues today. More than two-fifths of the foreign-born (44 percent) in the United States live in a central city. (Many of the remaining foreign-born have the financial means to live in the suburbs.) Of the 38.1 million foreign-born living in the United States in 2007, 10 percent of all naturalized citizens and 21 percent of all non-U.S. citizens, much higher than the national figure of 12.5 percent, lived in poverty (U.S. Census Bureau 2008b). Although studies show that the income for most immigrants improves with the passage of time, their early presence—and particularly their large numbers—creates an ethnic underclass that competes with the long-term urban poor for socioeconomic well-being.

In Toronto, for example, while the number of families increased by 15 percent between 1981 and 2001, the number of poor families increased by almost 69 percent. There was also a dramatic increase in the number of higher-poverty neighborhoods, from 30 in 1981 to 120 in 2001 (Figure 10–4). This increase was particularly acute in the inner

FIGURE 10–3 People in Poverty, Percentage, 2007

Source: U.S. Census Bureau 2008b.

0 to 12.9

13 to 25.9

26 to 39.9

40 to 72.8

FIGURE 10–4   City of Toronto Family Poverty Rates, 1981 and 2001

Source: City of Toronto.

suburbs—in the former municipalities of Scarborough, North York, Etobicoke, York, and East York. During this 20-year period, there was a 484 percent increase in the population of poor immigrant families in these neighborhoods, from 19,700 to 115,100. Immigrant families accounted for two-thirds of the total family population living in higher poverty neighborhoods. By 2005, Toronto had a 28.8 percent low-income rate, compared to a national rate of 19.7 percent (United Way Greater Toronto 2007).

New York City offers another example. In 2007, one out of five residents (18.9 percent) were poor, compared with less than one out of eight Americans (12.5 percent) nationwide. To appreciate the enormity of the first statistic, consider this: If New York City's 1.6 million poor resided in their own municipality, they would constitute the fifth-largest city in the United States; only Houston, Chicago, Los Angeles, and the rest of New York would have a larger population. Not surprisingly, foreign-born residents are a significant component of the city's poor. New York City is home to 3.1 million foreign-born residents (37 percent of the city's total population). The largest share comes from the Caribbean (26 percent), followed by Asia (24 percent), Europe (20 percent), and Latin America (19 percent) (Levitan 2003).

A Cautionary Note

It would be a serious mistake to conclude from the foregoing information that the presence of immigrants translates into poor neighborhoods. Actually, hundreds of thousands of immigrants have the educational levels, job skills, and income to settle in middle-class suburban towns rather than in low-income city neighborhoods. It would also be equally wrong to view cities as being primarily the repositories of the poor and less affluent, while viewing suburbs as being essentially the locales of the middle and upper classes. New York City, as mentioned in the previous paragraph, has one in five residents living in poverty. That is a high proportion to be sure, but this also means that four in five New Yorkers are not poor. Instead, they are working-, middle-, or upper-class people. And remember, earlier we cited data that revealed 1 in 11 suburbanites lives in poverty. To understand more fully the socioeconomic diversity in all locales, we will first examine the layers of social stratification among urbanites and then scrutinize the diversity found in suburbs.

URBAN SOCIAL CLASS DIVERSITY

Imagine sitting in Union Square in downtown San Francisco and noting the different types of people who walk by. A well-dressed young woman carrying an attaché case hurries past, as if she is late for her next appointment. An old man, unshaven and in shabby dress, reclines on the grass enjoying the warm sun; occasionally, he removes a brown bag from his coat pocket, unscrews the top of a bottle inside, and raises it for a quick drink. Nearby, four young men in Gap shirts and jeans engage in a serious discussion about the latest violence in Iraq. A short distance away, an African American woman plays a guitar as she offers Christian messages to anyone who will listen. For a moment, she attracts the attention of a group of Chinese American children, 10 or 11 years old, who playfully skip their way through the square. A middle-class couple emerges from Macy's department store carrying a large assortment of packages. They buy ice cream from a street vendor, stroll into the square, and collapse wearily but happily on the soft grass.

Similar scenes play out daily in all the major North American cities. This brief portrait suggests the essence of urban life: tremendous human variety, which is sometimes troubling, sometimes exhilarating, but always interesting. Clearly, urban people in North America lead very diverse lives, and although their lives may touch for a moment in a place like Union Square, different interests, experiences, and life circumstances propel them in different directions. We will now go in a few of those different directions as we explore the different types of social class neighborhoods found in our larger cities.

Upper-Class Urban Neighborhoods

The upper classes typically have several homes and alternate where they live at different times of the year. In the city, they will live in the most fashionable neighborhoods, such as Nob Hill in San Francisco, or in luxury apartments or penthouses in the heart of the city, such as near Lincoln Center and Columbus Circle in Manhattan. Here, they live securely and deliberately segregated from the rest of the population, protected by doormen, security guards, and controlled entrances. Their choice of transportation is mostly likely a door-to-door limousine service, whether to some cultural event (concert, opera, or theater), social event (ball, fundraiser, or private party), or shopping (in exclusive stores, often available by appointment only).

The Upper East Side. Zip code 10065 is the most prestigious one in New York City, for it encompasses much of Manhattan's Upper East Side, the country's most affluent urban neighborhood, with some of the most expensive real estate in the United States. The Upper East Side runs from 61st Street to 68th Street between Fifth Avenue and the East River. The majestic apartment buildings lining Fifth and Park Avenues offer the ritziest addresses in town—home to advertising and public relations managers, bankers, consultants, doctors, executives, lawyers, management analysts, media stars, and socialites of old wealth alike. Although apartments closer to Fifth or Madison Avenue are generally more expensive and more elegant, the entire Upper East Side neighborhood—all the way along the narrower side streets to the East River—is filled with beautiful buildings, well-maintained parks, and abundant places to eat, drink, and shop.

Separating the two wide residential avenues is the boutique-laden Madison Avenue, the area's shopping hub, where you can find everything from Prada to Picasso. This is the most expensive retail area in the world, with blue-chip art and antiques galleries, jewelry stores, and expensive boutiques and restaurants. The valuable real estate includes such stylish landmarks as The Pierre Hotel, the penthouse of which listed on the market in 2008 for $70 million, and the renovated Lexington Avenue Barbizon Hotel, with apartments for sale at $12 million. Nearby are such familiar stores as Henri Bendel, Chanel, Gucci, Tiffany's, and Louis Vuitton, as well as many custom boutiques that devote their entire staff solely to the shopping pleasure of only one client an hour—or day (Cahalan 2008).

The appeal of this neighborhood extends beyond the elegant living spaces and retail establishments. The Upper East Side is also where you can find such world-class cultural institutions as the Metropolitan Museum of Art, the Guggenheim, and the Whitney, each located on or near New York's magnificent Central Park. Also here are the El Museo del Barrio, the Museum of the City of New York, and the Goethe Institut, a German cultural institution.

One of the biggest draws to the Upper East Side is, of course, Central Park. New York City's most famous green space borders the entire western length of the neighborhood, featuring boathouses, the Central Park Zoo and Children's Zoo, the Reservoir, and the Arsenal Building, the original site of the Museum of Natural History. And for residents with children, this area is a huge draw for its spectacular public and private schools alone. The quiet, refined pace of life spells a perfect place to live or simply a place for nonresidents to escape the "rat race" of more hectic areas in the city.

Although not everyone who lives in the Upper East Side is wealthy, a great many are. According to 2000 census data, the per-capita income in this neighborhood was $91,064, compared to the city per-capita average of $23,389. Over one-third of those households in New York City who reported incomes of more than $200,000 lived in the Upper East Side, yet the area contains only 4 percent of all households in New York City.

Other Elite Neighborhoods. Chicago's Gold Coast is the second-wealthiest urban neighborhood in the United States, after New York's Upper East Side. Located on the city's North

Side facing Lake Michigan, this premier residential area is considered to be the "old money" section of town. Luxury high-rise apartment buildings on Lake Shore Drive and rows of century-old, multimillion-dollar mansions reside in quiet contrast to the lively stores, restaurants, and nightspots of Michigan Avenue and Rush and Division Streets. Historical landmarks and preservation districts mark much of this area, including the Astor Street Historic District.

Boston's Beacon Hill is one of the oldest historic districts in the United States. Boasting one of the most outstanding and intact collections of mid- to-late-nineteenth-century homes in the country, it features exceptional examples of Federal, Greek Revival, and Victorian architecture. In 2000, the median household income in this prestigious neighborhood was nearly twice that in all of Boston (U.S. Census Bureau 2003). Louisburg Square, known as the heart of Beacon Hill in Boston, has undergone a changing of the guard from

the old elite descended from the shipping and merchant banking industries to a new elite of largely self-made millionaires from the high-tech, financial, and other industries. In essence, the old Brahmin monopoly on financial and social power that controlled Louisburg Square has given way to something more open and complex. This change reflects the process of degentrification, in which meritocracy periodically wins out over breeding in forming an elite.

Another elite neighborhood can be found in the Pacific Heights area of San Francisco. This privileged neighborhood, with its median household income well above the average for the city, contains blocks of elegant Victorian mansions and impressive views of the Bay and the Golden Gate Bridge, making the area a perennial favorite with tourists. The nouveau riche of the late 1800s first colonized this neighborhood—loosely bordered by Van Ness and Presidio Avenues and Pine and Vallejo

The elite neighborhoods in most North American cities vary according to a city's history and terrain. Some of these residential areas may contain high-rise luxury apartments, century-old mansions, or a combination of the two. Typically, they boast a special ambience at street level and often spectacular views, as here in San Francisco's Pacific Heights.

Streets—when the construction of a new cable-car line made the area accessible. That legacy of luxury has persisted, and the neighborhood remains generally quiet and residential, with the majority of its activity clustered around Fillmore Street. There, shoppers purchase expensive women's clothing and luxury items; visit exquisite gift boutiques, bath-and-body shops, and consignment stores; or else stop at a sidewalk cafe to engage in that favorite city pastime: people watching.

Middle-Class Urban Neighborhoods

Most of the middle class live in suburbia, not the city. However, even though the middle-class presence is not as proportionately high in most large cities as it was two generations ago, it is nonetheless a significant reality. Some city census blocks evolve as middle-class neighborhoods through the gentrification process, displacing the lower-income residents who can no longer afford to live there. The impetus for this change began in the 1970s as manufacturing declined in cities and their economics changed to corporate information-processing services, such as financial, legal, and marketing (Sassen 2001).

The rapid growth of the service sector generated well-paying, professional positions that brought young (late twenties to early forties), urban professionals (**yuppies**) to the city not only to work but also to live. While yuppies may be single or married, with or without children, a new term—**dinks** (dual income, no kids)—came into fashion to describe those young professional couples without children. Then, as a large number of African American college graduates entered the urban labor market, another term—**buppies**—emerged to describe this new group of black, urban professionals (Sassen 2001). The yuppies, dinks, and buppies renovated brownstones and older loft buildings, upgrading the neighborhood. Moreover, their lifestyle prompted the opening of boutiques, fitness centers, specialty stores, new restaurants, coffee shops, bookstores, and

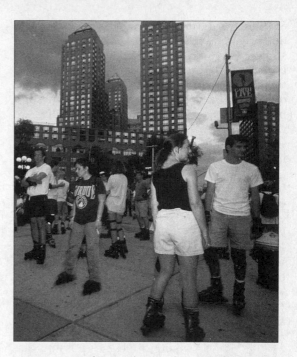

Many young urban professionals ("yuppies") find much in the city to enjoy. Eating out, shopping, concerts, theater, and clubs are all favorite pastimes. You'll also find many in the parks—biking, jogging, strolling, playing games, or as with this group in New York's Union Square Park, getting together to rollerblade around the city.

other retail establishments, thus completing the gentrification process.

Another lifestyle trend, found in both cities and suburbs, exists among adults born into upper-middle-class households who blend the trappings of their economic success (expensive choices in food, clothing, homes, appliances, and furniture) with socially responsible actions. David Brooks sees this new social class as a blend of the bourgeois (the successful capitalist middle class) and bohemians (those with unconventional appearance and behavior), which he calls **Bobos**. They work hard and emphasize their resumé accomplishments, but they also are comfortable in relaxed, informal activities. They are also into environmentalism and health, favoring recycling; cycling, jogging, and working out; frequenting coffee shops not bars; and living well, but not ostentatiously (see the *Urban Living* box below).

Not all middle-class urban neighborhoods are recently evolved entities. There are also older residential areas in cities that maintain their social-class character, sometimes despite outside forces that threaten their stability. We will look at examples of both types.

Chicago. Identified as low-income neighborhoods in 1990, Logan Square, West Town, the Near West Side, and the Near South Side experienced such significant growth in the 1990s that they are no longer low-income neighborhoods (Figure 10–5). Once struggling neighborhoods, they are now among Chicago's most desirable residential areas.

URBAN LIVING

The Bourgeois and Bohemians Merge

The members of this class . . . grapple with the trade-offs between equality and privilege ("I believe in public schooling, but the private school just seems better for my kids"), between convenience and social responsibility ("These disposable diapers are an incredible waste of resources, but they are so easy"), between rebellion and convention ("I know I did plenty of drugs in high school, but I tell my kids to Just Say No").

But the biggest tension, to put it in the grandest terms, is between worldly success and inner virtue. How do you move ahead in life without letting ambition wither your soul? How do you accumulate the resources you need to do the things you want without becoming a slave to material things? . . . These educated elites don't despair in the face of such challenges. . . . When faced with a tension between competing values, they do what any smart privileged person bursting with cultural capital would do. They find a way to have both. They reconcile opposites.

The grand achievement of the educated elites in the 1990s was to create a way of living that lets you be an affluent success and at the same time a free-spirit rebel. . . . Building gourmet companies, like Ben & Jerry's or Nantucket Nectars, they've found a way to be dippy hippies and multinational corporate fat cats. Using William S. Burroughs in ads for Nike sneakers and incorporating Rolling Stones anthems into their marketing campaigns, they've reconciled the antiestablishment style with the corporate imperative. . . . Dressing like Bill Gates in worn chinos on his way to a stockholders' meeting, they've reconciled undergraduate fashion with upper-crust occupations. . . .

When you are amidst the educated upscalers, you can never be sure if you're living in a world of hippies or stockbrokers. In reality you have entered the hybrid world in which everybody is a little of both.

Marx told us that classes inevitably conflict, but sometimes they just blur. The values of the bourgeois mainstream culture and the values of the 1960s counterculture have merged. That culture war has ended, at least within the educated class. . . . The educated elites didn't set out to create this reconciliation. It is the product of millions of individual efforts to have things both ways. But it is now the dominant tone of our age. In the resolution between the culture and the counterculture, it is impossible to tell who co-opted whom, because in reality the bohemians and the bourgeois co-opted each other. They emerge from this process as bourgeois bohemians, or Bobos.

Source: Abridged from *Bobos in Paradise: The New Upper Class and How They Got There* by David Brooks. Copyright © 2000 by David Brooks. Used by permission of Simon & Schuster, Inc.

22 - Logan Square
24 - West Town
28 - Near West Side
33 - Near South Side
32 - Loop (CBD)

Central Business District

Gentrifiers (low income in 1990,
moderate/middle income in 2000)

Predominantly black neighborhoods
(low income in 1990 and 2000)

Immigrant communities
(low income in 1990 and 2000)

New low-income communities
(moderate income in 1990, low income in 2000)

Moderate/high income neighborhoods
(not included in analysis)

FIGURE 10–5   Gentrification of Chicago, 1990 to 2000

Source: The Urban Institute.

This change occurred because each neighborhood became a destination for yuppies. Their arrival spurred further redevelopment, much of it through private developers and not the government. Mostly white, their arrival also coincided with a large exodus of blacks (the Near West Side) and Latinos (West Town). Displacement of low-income minorities did not occur on a significant scale in the Near South Side, because the new development occurred on previously unoccupied land. Logan Square went through a changeover to better-educated, higher-income Latinos (Zielenbach 2005).

The population demographics give strong evidence of a higher social class taking over these neighborhoods. The four communities saw at least a 12 percent increase in residents aged from 25 to 39, with 19 percent or greater increases in single-person households and sharp drops in the number of children. In addition, there were double-digit increases in the proportion of college graduates (Zielenbach 2005:5–6). This influx of highly educated, upwardly mobile individuals helped drive up the per-capita income and property values, in turn driving out many low-income residents and, thereby, attracting still more middle-class professionals. Although one might argue that these are actually mixed-income neighborhoods, because pockets of low-income households remain, still-developing patterns suggest that this is a temporary phase and that these neighborhoods are evolving into middle-class entities.

Milwaukee. On the northwest side, four miles from the city's downtown, is a culturally diverse, 30-block area known as Sherman Park, the history of which dates back to the 1890s. At that time, the upper class opted to remain closer to the central business district, living on the city's mansion-lined boulevards, but a steady stream of middle-class businesspeople and professionals—usually third- and fourth-generation German Americans—chose this area for building sturdy homes, noted for their ornamentation and high craftsmanship. Ever since, this neighborhood has remained a stable, middle-class residential area.

Today, the neighborhood remains one of Milwaukee's "most vibrant areas" (Curran 2003). Three of its streets have been designated as historic districts, but throughout the neighborhood, that craftsmanship and the variety of architectural styles (bungalows, Arts and Crafts, and Period Revival) have attracted people wanting to live in such fine homes on wide, quiet streets. Property values thus remain high. Most of those living here are long-term residents, however, and everyone knows everyone else.

In the 1970s, when "white flight" was occurring in Milwaukee, as in many cities, the Sherman Park Community Association (SPCA) battled racially discriminatory real estate practices, landlord neglect, and crime. What was most distinguished about the SPCA was its embrace of racial integration, encouraging blacks and whites to live together. Today, this neighborhood retains its racial diversity, although a black middle class is now the majority. Interracial couples also find a high comfort level here (Curran 2003).

Religious tolerance and integration also mark this neighborhood, which has large numbers of Catholics, Jews, and Protestants. One example is the Sherman Park Area Congregation, formed by clergy from all three faiths, which meets regularly to discuss neighborhood issues in order to reach consensus on how to tackle them.

While the neighborhood maintains residential stability, the stores along its main business thoroughfares—particularly Burleigh Street and Center Street—struggle to compete with suburban stores. Some progress has been made. The Burleigh Street Community Development Corporation, a non-profit coalition of local residents and business professionals, is dedicated to re-energizing the business district. Armed with funding from both government and private foundations, they replaced the vacant bowling alley and attached restaurant with a new business and community center. The $50 million St. Joseph Regional Medical Center is another welcome presence, and so are other new businesses attracted to this neighborhood.

What might have become a changing neighborhood has instead, thanks to the determination of its residents, remained a stable, middle-class urban neighborhood.

Working-Class Urban Neighborhoods

Often, though not always, a city's working-class neighborhoods become distinctive by the ethnic and racial minority groups who predominate. (The East End of Nashville, Tennessee, would be an example of a non-ethnic working-class neighborhood.) The many visual clues—signs, parallel social institutions (churches, clubs, stores, and newspapers), and street activities—give a distinctive sense of place, and they form an important part of the community's social life. The streets in such neighborhoods are, as William H. Whyte (2001; orig. 1980) described, "the rivers of life" of the neighborhood. Here, you will find people meeting and greeting one another, using the stoops and sidewalks as personal social space; the public space of the street becomes, in essence, their front yard. Most importantly, such neighborhoods are a *gemeinschaft* community, with shared values, intimacy, a strong sense of belonging, and a strong support network. They remain what Herbert Gans (1982) called *ethnic villages* (see the *Urban Living* box on page 284).

Newark's Ironbound. This working-class area in the East Ward of Newark, New Jersey, is one such example. It was brought to the attention of millions of moviegoers as the epicenter of the 2005 summer blockbuster *War of the Worlds*. About four miles square, it lies between the Passaic River and Newark Liberty International Airport.

The district's name derives from its being surrounded by railroad tracks. Once the industrial center of the city, with many factories, forges, and breweries, it was first home to hundreds of impoverished laborers who toiled in the nearby factories during grueling, 72-hour, six-day workweeks. In the 1920s, Portuguese immigrants began to settle in the neighborhood, joining the mixture of blacks, Germans, Irish, Italians, and Polish who were already there.

With a more liberal immigration law passed in 1965, many Portuguese immigrants, driven by political unrest, joined their compatriots as other groups moved out. By the 1970s, most of the factories and breweries in the Ironbound had closed, but more Portuguese arrivals continued to settle here. Economic conditions were worse in their homeland, and here, jobs could be found nearby. Portuguese-speaking Brazilians arrived in the late 1980s and early 1990s, drawn by the low-cost housing, close-knit community, and convenient location. Brazilians now make up half the Portuguese-speaking population in the Ironbound, where initial tensions over cultural differences between mainland Portuguese and Brazilians have largely disappeared (Lawlor 2004).

Newark, in fact, has the largest Portuguese population of any city in the United States, and the ongoing migration assures that Portuguese is often the first—and, sometimes, the only—language spoken in many Ironbound shops (Stoneback 2005). *Luso Americano*, the nation's largest Portuguese language newspaper, is published here and has a wide circulation.

The Ironbound is a mix of homes, stores, and industrial buildings, with a vibrant commercial center of shops, ethnic restaurants, cafes, and clubs on Ferry Street, each offering different elements of the European lifestyle. Residents often speak about a strong sense of community, which is easily evident in daily walks and encounters with people they know.

This closeness attracted many Portuguese immigrants to the Ironbound. Jobs were available in the many factories and there were people happy to help them find work and a place to stay. Today, there are some 20 Portuguese social clubs, most representing a single town or province of Portugal. The clubs help new immigrants, but mainly offer programs that keep the Portuguese traditions alive. (Lawlor 2004:5)

The social clubs also sponsor soccer teams, and the neighborhood parks are usually filled

URBAN LIVING

The Ethnic Villagers

To most of the West Enders, the area had been home either since birth or marriage. Some were born in the West End because this was where their parents had settled when they first came to America or where they had moved later in life. Others came as adults in the Italian "invasion" of the West End during the 1930s. Many of them had grown up in the North End and had moved at the time of marriage in order to take advantage of better and larger apartments in the West End. In any case, almost all of the West Enders came to the area as a part of a group. Even their movements within the West End—that is, from the lower end to the upper—had been made together with other Italians at about the same time. . . .

. . . West Enders were in the West End because this is where they "belonged." . . . While they do want to be left alone, they are not averse to the aural or visual closeness of their neighbors. As everyone knows everyone else's activities and problems anyway, they know that it is impossible to hide anything by physical privacy. As one West Ender put it:

> I like the noise people make. In summer people have their windows open, and everyone can hear everyone else, but nobody cares what anybody is saying; they leave their neighbors

alone. In the suburbs, people are nosier; when a car comes up the street, all the windows go up to see who is visiting whom.

While the image of the suburb is overdrawn, it is true that in the West End, where people knew so much about each other, there was no need for prying. A feeling of privacy could be maintained in the midst of high density.

In addition, hearing and seeing their neighbor's activities gave the West Enders a share in the life that went on around them, which, in turn, made them feel part of the group. . . . West Enders, living mainly in the group, have an insatiable appetite for group experience. . . .

I was told by one social worker of an experiment some years back to expose West End children to nature by taking them on a trip to Cape Cod. The experiment failed, for the young West Enders found no pleasure in the loneliness of natural surroundings and wanted to get back to the West End as quickly as possible. They were incredulous that anyone could live without people around him.

Sources: Reprinted with the permission of The Free Press, a division of Simon & Schuster Adult Publishing Group from *The Urban Villagers* by Herbert J. Gans. Copyright © 1962 by The Free Press. Copyright © 1982 by Herbert J. Gans. All rights reserved.

with adults and children playing soccer. In the bars and clubs, soccer is the spectator sport of choice, and when Brazil won the World Cup in 2002, revelers took to the streets in the middle of the night (Lawlor 2004). In fact, World Cup soccer competition remains far more important in the Ironbound than the Super Bowl is. During soccer season, the bars and restaurants are filled with fans rooting for

their teams while having lunch or dinner (Stoneback 2005).

Apartment buildings of four or more units comprise about one-fourth of the housing. Demand exceeds the supply, so most tenants are found by word of mouth. Most housing (60 percent) is two- and three-family homes; single-family homes make up the rest. Housing demand has been high since the late

As with many vibrant, urban ethnic neighborhoods, Newark's Ironbound District serves a dual purpose. Home to first-generation, working-class Americans (Portuguese-speaking, in this case), it also attracts many visitors, of the same or other backgrounds, who partake of its ethnic flavor in the stores and restaurants that line the streets.

1990s, with 900 new homes built and prices tripling, causing a problem of increased taxes for older residents. The housing boom has led to overcrowding in the Ironbound's schools and the use of classroom trailers; the city plans to build new schools in the neighborhood (Lawlor 2004).

More than 170 restaurants also attract many visitors, but it's not until 9 or 10 P.M. that they fill up with neighborhood residents who follow the Iberian pattern of late dining. On Thursday mornings, the numerous seafood shops are their busiest, as Ironbound regulars line up to buy the fresh seafood that arrives each Wednesday evening from Portugal. From morning to night, this village-within-a-city "throbs with the accents of Portugal, Spain, and Brazil" (Corcoran 2003:NJ10).

Other Ethnic Villages.   Virtually every U.S. city has one or more ethnic villages, where first-generation Americans cluster and re-create, to some extent, the world they left behind. The old European ethnic neighborhoods are fading, but new ones are taking their place with the concentrations of many African, Asian, and Hispanic immigrants. Of the thousands of examples, here are just a few: Toronto's Little India, found along Gerrard Street East between Greenwood and Coxwell Avenues, offers an active community life and array of ethnic stores. Koreatown, situated principally along Lawrence Avenue in the Albany Park neighborhood in Chicago's Northwest Side, remains a vibrant community, although other groups are making inroads. The Dominican presence is so strong in New York's Washington Heights neighborhood in upper Manhattan that it is sometimes called "Quisqueya Heights." (*Quisqueya* is the informal nickname of the Dominican Republic.) Two of Miami's better-known, cohesive ethnic neighborhoods are "Little Haiti" in the old neighborhoods of Lemon City, Edison Center, Little River, and Buena Vista East, and "Little Havana" in Miami, located west of Brickell Avenue and along Southwest Eighth Street.

Many working-class neighborhoods have mixed ethnic populations. The urban neighborhood of Ridgewood in the Queens borough of New York City, for instance, is a high-density area known for its brick and stone two-story buildings. Once a German and Italian enclave, its newer immigrants are mostly from Central and Eastern Europe (especially Poland) and from Latin America. Archer Heights on Chicago's Southwest Side has mostly brick bungalows and ranches and is home to a large Polish population and a growing Hispanic community. The Excelsior District of San Francisco is primarily a working-class neighborhood of Asian and Latino immigrant families.

Mixed-Income Urban Neighborhoods

Most cities have neighborhoods that contain people from a mixture of income levels. These neighborhoods may result from intervention, such as public housing designed to reduce the concentration of poverty, or from planned gentrification programs or be simply the non-planned result from the social dynamics of people opting to move. Whatever the cause, mixed-income neighborhoods can remain stable in their income diversity, as, indeed, many are. Otherwise, they may be in an early stage of gentrification, with low-income people moving out and higher-income people moving in, or else they are deteriorating, as the middle class moves out and more low-income people move in. The keys to the quality of life in a mixed-income neighborhood, then, are not only household income levels but also the desire and ability of residents to remain there.

Grand Rapids.   Located on the western side of Michigan, Grand Rapids is the state's second-largest city, with a population declining from 197,800 in 2000 to about 193,600 in 2007. It has a mixed economic base, with the largest employers in educational, health, and social services (22 percent); manufacturing (18 percent, down from 22 percent in 2000); and retail trade (11 percent). Median family income was $38,792 in 2007, compared to $37,224 in 2000. The percentage of city families with incomes below the poverty level was 16.8 percent, up from 11.9 percent in 2000. The city's non-Hispanic white population declined from 67.3 percent in 2000 to 66.8 percent in 2007 as population of racial minorities increased, reaching 21 percent black, 16 percent Hispanic, and 1 percent Asian (U.S. Census Bureau 2008c).

Hammered by globalization, Grand Rapids lost 40,000 manufacturing jobs between 2000 and 2004, but the city now appears to be making a comeback. Its furniture industry seems to be rebounding, Grand Valley State University recently built a downtown campus, and old buildings are being converted into office, retail, and residential space (El Nasser 2006).

June Thomas and her associates (2004) identified 11 of 131 census block groups as stable mixed-income neighborhoods, in that no significant change in the population from the lowest two income quintiles occurred over a 10-year period. Unlike other block groups, these 11 had less vacant housing, lower proportions of families in poverty, and lower family median income than found in the metropolitan statistical area. During focus group interviews in three representative neighborhoods, the researchers were able to identify five stabilizing influences of these neighborhoods. First, strong religious communities, such as Catholic parishes, kept people in the neighborhoods. Positive feelings about the schools, with the ability of children to walk to local schools, along with strong social networks both between and among neighbors were also important factors. Family connections to the neighborhood and well-organized, professionally staffed neighborhood associations completed the steadying elements.

At the same time, however, the researchers found fragility in these neighborhoods. Respondents were concerned about the increase in rental households, fearing poorly monitored properties and renters who would cause noise, visible blight, and neighborhood change. They were also anxious about the decline in the quality of the public schools and the possible relocation of parochial schools.

Many suggested that if the schools declined drastically, so would the neighborhood (Thomas, Schweitzer, and Darnton 2004).

Toronto.   The St. Lawrence neighborhood is a different example of a mixed-income area, one that was deliberately created through redevelopment of a large area previously used for warehousing and industrial activities (De Jong 2000). Now home to about 12,000 residents living in converted warehouses or new structures, it extends from Yonge Street east to Parliament and Queen Streets south to the railroad tracks.

This thriving neighborhood effectively integrates people of all ages and different socioeconomic backgrounds living side by side. Planners achieved this social mix by strategic placement of a range of housing types that included condominium apartments (39 percent), non-profit cooperatives (30 percent), private non-profit units (27 percent), and owner-occupied townhouses (4 percent). The three-story family townhouses stand on tree-lined interior roads, surrounded by seven-to ten-story apartments on busier streets. This mix nicely blends different levels of affordable housing, ranging from private ownership to rent-geared-to-income apartments (Regent Park Collaborative Team 2003).

Complementing the successful mixture of people and housing types is vibrant economic activity that includes businesses, restaurants, stores, and theaters. Nearby St. Lawrence Market—site of the city's original market and still highly popular—offers a unique shopping destination, as do other businesses on Front Street and the Esplanade. Adding to the mixed use of space and activities are a community center and a social network of civic organizations—a residents' association, a seniors' group, school-based organizations, a community center council, and various other youth and children's organizations.

The revitalized St. Lawrence neighborhood in Toronto is a mixed-income area, successfully integrating people of all ages and socioeconomic levels. What makes this area so successful is its mixture of different housing types in new structures, converted warehouses, and factories with a strategic intermingling of businesses, stores, restaurants, and theaters.

All this helps reinforce the residents' sense of commitment to stay in the area, a view that is reinforced by their sense of place. Experts further consider this to be a successful neighborhood because its excellent design ensured that the new buildings not only retained the character and scale of the older ones but also followed Toronto's nineteenth-century pattern of alignment along roads in order to encourage street-related activity. That deliberate design, augmented by excellent lighting, provides an active street life in this mixed-use neighborhood, which conveys a sense of safety to pedestrians (Regent Park Collaborative Team 2003).

All is not perfect, however. As in most mixed-income neighborhoods, an undercurrent of fear about possible negative changes exists. Some worry that neighborhood stability could be undermined if there is a high turnover rate in either the condominium units rented out for temporary lodging or some of the rent-controlled units. Residents also have expressed concern about the lack of play areas for children and of recreational spaces for seniors (Regent Park Collaborative Team 2003).

Low-Income Urban Neighborhoods

Typically, we find neighborhoods with high levels of poverty in a city's oldest districts. Many of these communities were once solidly middle-class, or even upper-class, areas that have fallen on hard times. Since these areas of high population density and substandard housing are most often located near the central business district, they came to be called **inner-city neighborhoods,** as well as **ghettos** or **slums.**

For the trapped poor who have been left behind in the inner city, the future is bleak. Lacking the necessary schooling and communication skills required for work in the service and information sectors of the economy, residents may experience unemployment rates as high as 80 percent (Bingham and Zhang 2001). High rates of substance abuse, single parents, infant mortality, violent crime, and

welfare dependency also are common. These "truly disadvantaged," in the words of William J. Wilson (1990), are poor people who rely on welfare assistance and the underground economy in order to survive.

Unlike the immigrant poor of the past, today's poor inner-city residents face social isolation. The exodus of middle- and working-class, two-parent families removes essential role models and reduces community resources. Furthermore, outsiders avoid these neighborhoods, leaving area residents to live virtually cut off from the larger society. Gary Orfield noted the magnitude of this isolation:

> To a considerable extent the residents of city ghettos are now living in separate and deteriorating societies, with separate economies, diverging family structures and basic institutions, and even growing linguistic separation within the core ghettos. (1988:103)

Current social indicators offer little cause for optimism, for such problems have structural causes that our society has yet to overcome.

Chicago.   The city of Chicago and its metropolitan region experienced significant economic growth in the 1990s, the city less so (4 percent) than its suburbs (16 percent). Still, the growth was strong enough to improve many of its low-income neighborhoods. In many of these communities, in fact, the improvement was greater than that for the city itself. For example, per-capita incomes in these low-income areas increased by 21 percent in the 1990s, compared to 16 percent in the entire city, while unemployment fell by more than 4 percent, compared to the city's decrease of 1.2 percent (Zielenbach 2005:4).

To illustrate how a neighborhood declines, we will look at Gage Park, a new low-income Chicago neighborhood that was a moderate-income neighborhood in 1990. Most common here are 80- to 115-year old bungalows, along with Georgian-style homes from the 1940s, ranches from the 1960s and 1970s, and some more recently built Cape Cods. About 30 percent of the properties are two- and three-family houses (Steele 1998).

An East European and Irish Catholic neighborhood for generations, Gage Park is now about four-fifths Hispanic. It experienced a 10 percent drop in its proportion of high school graduates by 2000, and many of the newcomers had difficulty speaking English. In fact, 36 percent of those aged 25 years or older had less than a ninth-grade education, and another 18 percent had a level higher than that but were not high school graduates. During this 10-year interval, per-capita income in the neighborhood decreased by 31 percent. Another barometer—the overall index score, which is a composite measure of per-capita income, conventional home mortgage purchase rates, and median single-family property values—declined by 52 percent in relation to the city's overall score (Zielenbach 2005:5).

Los Angeles. One of the poorest and most densely populated neighborhoods in this city is Pico-Union, which gets its name from the key intersection of Pico Boulevard and Union Avenue. Originally developed as a Los Angeles suburb in the early twentieth century, its housing and building types give testimony to that original suburban character. Its nearby location west of the downtown district made it an attractive residential locale for new immigrants, especially Scandinavian Lutherans, Russian Jews, and Greek Orthodox.

As suburbanization extended outward and residents relocated in the mid-twentieth century, Pico-Union became part of the "inner city." The shifting of economic and social resources away from the inner city and to the suburbs resulted in the decline of the physical appearance and service infrastructure of the area. Both housing and commercial buildings became run-down as a result of lack of maintenance. Landlords subdivided the large houses and then rented out those to accommodate the large number of low-income immigrant families. As a result, the neighborhood became a place characterized by overcrowding and substandard housing conditions (UCLA Department of Urban Planning 1998).

Pico-Union is now home to about 39,000 people, mostly Central Americans and Mexicans. The 2000 census revealed a population that was 88 percent Hispanic, 5 percent Asian, 4 percent black, and 3 percent non-Hispanic white (Los Angeles Almanac 2008). As is so typical in immigrant neighborhoods, many community organizations and stores are tailored to the language, culture, and service needs of the population.

The number of persons in this neighborhood who are living in poverty (44 percent) is twice that in the entire city. In 2000, per-capita income was $9,829, compared to $20,671 in Los Angeles as a whole. Median household income and median family income were also less than half those of the city overall. Educational level offers another stark contrast: In the city overall, 80 percent have a high school diploma or higher, but in Pico-Union, only 30 percent do (Los Angeles Almanac 2008). The low levels of education and the language barrier are reflected in the employment patterns and corresponding rates of economic stagnation.

Marred by graffiti and vacant stores, this neighborhood also suffers from a high crime rate. Gang activity is a serious concern, particularly by the 18th Street gang, which is involved in auto theft, drug trafficking, extortion, and murder (Valdez 2000). Both the police and community organizations attempt to make the area safer and have had some moderate success, but many problems remain.

The Homeless

Most of us encounter homeless people from time to time. Perhaps they are sleeping on benches in parks or bus stations, standing in doorways along skid-row streets, or panhandling on busy walkways. It is all too clear that they inhabit the edges of society, and we usually assume they are cut off from work and family, weeks away from their last job or even their last square meal—a familiar stereotype. The problem is much more complex, however, and no stereotype gives a complete picture of the homeless.

Recent decades have seen a new type of homeless person. Efforts to revitalize cities with new construction on the edges of the central business districts or downtowns have destroyed many of the old single-room occupancy hotels (SROs) that once provided housing to people living on the edge of poverty. Between 1970 and 1990, for example, Chicago and New York lost about 70 percent of their SROs, and Los Angeles lost more than half (Koegel, Burnam, and Baumohl 1996; Hoch and Slayton 1990). In addition, the loss of low-cost housing because of urban renewal or rent increases in an area undergoing gentrification forced many out of their neighborhoods, thereby increasing the demand on remaining low-income housing, pushing even those rents beyond what many could afford. Current estimates identify about 23 percent of all homeless as families with children, 58 percent as single men, 18 percent as single women, and 1 percent as unaccompanied youth. Sixteen percent are mentally ill, while 37 percent are substance abusers (U.S. Conference of Mayors 2008).

Particularly disturbing is the large homeless population of families with children. Each year, more than 800,000 children and youth experience homelessness, and at least one-fifth of them do not attend school (U.S. Department of Education 2007b). The average age of the homeless child is six years. One-half of homeless children attend three different schools in one year, and 75 percent perform below grade level in reading. Not surprisingly, they are four times more likely to drop out of school than other children are. Two-thirds of their parents (at least half of them women who fled domestic violence) lack a high school diploma, and 75 percent of them are unemployed. Limited schooling and little work experience are the all-too-typical attributes of the impoverished, but the added factor of homelessness denies these families any stability or community support (Institute for Children and Poverty 2008).

In terms of requests for emergency shelter in 2008, the situation improved in four cities (Cleveland, Los Angeles, Miami, and Phoenix) but worsened in 83 percent of other major cities surveyed. In most of the survey cities, emergency shelters were forced to turn away homeless persons because of a lack of resources (U.S. Conference of Mayors 2008:13–15).

Clearly, lack of affordable housing is the leading cause of homelessness. The root causes of that inability to pay for a roof over one's head—lack of education, inadequate low-income housing, poverty, and unavailable jobs—are unlikely to go away soon. For many, the images connected with this small, unfortunate segment of a city's population distort their view of the diversity of social class found in the total city population.

SUBURBAN SOCIAL CLASS DIVERSITY

Today's suburbs, particularly those closest to the city, no longer fit the white, middle-class, and family-with-kids stereotype. More and more, suburbs are home to minorities, the working class and poor, and the aged. Suburbs now vary widely in terms of average income, racial composition, average age, and length of residence.

Upper-Income Suburbs

A century ago, suburban residence symbolized the lifestyle of the well-to-do. Fabulous estates such as Lynnewood Hall—called the Versailles of America—clearly distinguished the lifestyle of early suburbanites from the lifestyle of others. The idea was to emulate the country ways of European aristocracy, as Pierre Lorillard II did better than almost anyone. In 1886, Lorillard (heir to a tobacco fortune) inherited some 600,000 acres and, at a cost of $2 million, created a millionaires' colony north of New York. Tuxedo Park was a guarded enclave where the wealthy elite "communed with nature in forty-room 'cottages' with the required ten bedrooms, gardens, stables, and housing for the small army of servants required for entertaining in style" (Conant 2002:4–5).

At Tuxedo Park Lorillard produced almost a caricature of the Victorian millionaire's mania for exclusiveness. In less than a year, he surrounded seven thousand acres with an eight-foot fence, graded some thirty miles of road, built a complete sewage and water system, a gate house which looked like "a frontispiece of an English novel," a clubhouse staffed with imported English servants, and "twenty-two casement dormered English turreted cottages." On Memorial Day, 1886, special trains brought seven hundred highly selected guests from New York to witness the Park's opening. (Baltzell 1987:122–23)

By offering his club members property within Tuxedo Park for purchase, Lorillard created, as Baltzell suggests, a sort of Levittown for aristocrats. Yet, as streetcar lines and automobiles kept increasing, new housing rippled outward from cities, and with it, a new image of the suburban lifestyle began to take hold among the masses. Its roots were the same—to live "the good life"—but the magnitude of the change ensured that the vision would be watered down.

Today's upper-class suburbs resemble the old aristocratic ones of yesteryear. They include Grosse Pointe Shores near Detroit and South Barrington near Chicago. Families have large houses on large properties, often with swimming pools, and center their social lives on churches or temples and exclusive country clubs, where golf and tennis are favorite leisure activities. This affluent lifestyle is marked by conspicuous consumption, symbols of high social status, and other attributes of class privilege.

The populations in these suburbs tend to be somewhat older, mostly white, and highly educated, with incomes significantly above the state average. Grosse Pointe Shores, for example, within its one square mile has a population of 2,800, who have a median age of 48 years, are 94 percent white, and 62 percent are at least college graduates, including 30 percent with advanced degrees. In 2005, the median household income was about $114,000, compared to a Michigan median household income of $46,000. South Barrington is larger, nearly seven square miles, with a population in 2006 of about 3,900 that was 81 percent white and 13 percent Asian. The median household income in 2005 was $182,000 (in Illinois, it was slightly more than $50,000), and 63 percent were at least college graduates, including 30 percent with advanced degrees (City-Data.com 2009).

Although the older elite suburbs long resisted the entry of racial, ethnic, and religious minorities, the newer affluent suburbs—typically located at the outer suburban edges, such as South Barrington, which is 37 miles from Chicago—accept anyone with the right-sized bank account. A good example of economic elitism prevailing over ethnic prejudice is Beverly Hills, California, where wealthy Arabs and rich Jews live harmoniously as neighbors—a far cry from their counterparts in the Middle East.

Middle-Income Suburbs

Darien, Connecticut, and Levittown, New York, closely resemble the suburban stereotype. Life here centers on the family and child-centered activities. As Robert A. Beauregard describes:

> Here people could live with others like themselves and bring up their children free from the threats and temptations of the city. . . .
>
> Central to all this was the association of middle-class values with a specific understanding of what family life meant in the suburbs. To be middle-class meant more than aspiring to a college education and a white-collar job. It also meant having a family. . . . The family was to be the center of social life. One consequence was an emphasis on family vacations and the active involvement of parents in the lives of their children through organized sports and the local parent–teacher association (2006:124–25).

In suburbs such as these, few people are poor, and almost everyone has at least finished high school. Once mostly white, these suburbs have become more racially mixed in recent years. Solon, Ohio—profiled in the *Urban Living* box on page 292—is an example of such communities, where affluent Asians, blacks, and non-Hispanic whites live harmoniously as neighbors.

Working-Class Suburbs

Some working-class suburbs developed in the early twentieth century as a home for both factories and their workers. One such town was

URBAN LIVING

Comparing Working-Class and Middle-Class Suburbs

To many people who live in the inner city or rural areas, all suburbs may seem the same. Suburbs differ in many ways, however, as portraits of two suburban Ohio towns close to the city of Cleveland show. The first, North Olmsted, is a working-class suburb. It is located 17 miles to the southwest of Cleveland, has a population of about 32,000 people, and covers about 12 square miles of land. The second, Solon, is a middle-class suburb. It is 17 miles to the southeast of Cleveland and has a far lower population density, with its 22,000 people spread over about 21 square miles.

As you might expect, the cost of housing differs in the two suburbs. In 2007, the median house value in North Olmsted was $180,000, compared to $281,300 in Solon. In Solon, there is much more new housing, with nearly half of its homes built since 1980. In North Olmstead, by contrast, just 13 percent of all homes were built since 1980. The age of homes matters, because newer homes typically are larger, with bigger rooms, and are more likely to have attached garages and amenities like central air conditioning and, perhaps, even a swimming pool.

By and large, suburbs have a smaller share of minorities than central cities. The middle-class community of Solon, however, has more racial diversity than the working-class community of North Olmstead. In Solon, 87 percent of the people are non-Hispanic whites, 6 percent

African American, 4 percent Asian American, 1 percent Hispanic, and 1 percent of two or more races. North Olmsted, by contrast, is 93 percent non-Hispanic white, with African Americans making up just 1 percent of the population, Asian Americans 2 percent, Hispanic Americans 2 percent, and the remaining 2 percent of two or more races.

One of the biggest differences between the populations of these two suburbs involves schooling. Of Solon's adult population, 50 percent have earned at least a bachelor's degree, and 22 percent have a graduate or professional degree. In North Olmstead, just 27 percent of adults have a bachelor's degree, and only 9 percent have a graduate or professional degree. Given this difference, it is no surprise that people in Solon have higher incomes: Median household earnings in Solon for 2007 were $89,358, well above the $59,500 for North Olmsted. Unemployment is typically low in suburbs, but here again, we see a difference: Solon's unemployment rate (2.5 percent) is half that in North Olmstead (4.8 percent).

As this comparison shows, suburbs display their own characteristic diversity, whether by casual observation of differences in property lot sizes and housing structures or by detailed analysis of socioeconomic data. Race and ethnicity thus appear to be less important attributes of differences in social class between the two towns than educational level and income.

Source: Data from www.city-data.com. Accessed February 27, 2009.

the South Gate suburb of Los Angeles. Some of it developer-built and some self-built on narrow lots with vegetable gardens and chickens in the back, homes became more standardized and the farm plots abandoned after World War II,

as higher wages at the unionized plants changed the town's suburban landscape. Given the residents' limited income, South Gate did not attract major retailers. With only small, mom-and-pop operations like corner grocery stores and service stations, the residents commuted to Los Angeles or other suburbs for most of their shopping, entertainment, and even employment (Nicolaides 2002).

Elsewhere in the United States during the early twentieth century, other working-class, industrial suburbs evolved. Some became more urbanized than others, but all offered blue-collar workers the opportunity to live in their own homes and work nearby. For example, Flint, Michigan, two hours from Detroit; Argo, Illinois, near Chicago; Norwood, Ohio, just outside Cincinnati; and Fairfield, Alabama, on the edge of Birmingham, are but a few of the hundreds of examples for the exodus of industry and workers that began in the early twentieth century and continued for two generations (Taylor 2001; orig. 1915).

Today, some of these older, blue-collar suburbs are suffering from a loss of jobs as industries close or move their factories abroad. With an eroding industrial and commercial tax base, these suburbs are deteriorating physically, and property taxes are on the rise. Not surprisingly, many of the more affluent residents are packing up and moving farther out. There, they hope to find a newer version of their dream home and, perhaps, a lower tax rate. Other working-class suburbs remain healthy, however, and some are even growing. One such town is the Cleveland suburb of North Olmsted, profiled in the *Urban Living* box on page 292.

Suburban Cosmopolitan Centers

In marked contrast to the working-class suburbs (and different even from Darien and Grosse Pointe Shores) are communities like Princeton, New Jersey, home of Princeton University, and Palo Alto, California, home of Stanford University. Composed mainly of academics, professionals, writers, actors, artists, and students, these communities resemble the university areas, bohemian enclaves, and cosmopolite residential neighborhoods of central cities. Their population is usually deeply interested in "high culture," and theaters, music

facilities, and elegant, unusual restaurants are found there in abundance.

Minority Suburbs

Minority suburbanization is most pronounced in metropolitan regions of 500,000 or more, where the minority population grew from 19 percent in 1990 to 27 percent in 2000. These suburbs are now 12 percent Hispanic, 9 percent black, and 5 percent Asian. In some areas, the change is even more substantial. For example, blacks are now more than 20 percent of the suburban population in such areas as Atlanta, Fort Lauderdale, Miami, New Orleans, Richmond, and Washington, D.C. Hispanics exceed 25 percent of the suburban population in Miami, Los Angeles, Riverside, and San Diego (Lewis Mumford Center 2001c).

Most suburbs are now racially diverse, and becoming more so all the time. Even so, some suburban communities remain racially segregated, as some African Americans deliberately seek out predominantly black communities. Examples of these affluent African American suburbs that attract middle-class black families who prefer socializing in a racially homogeneous environment are Rolling Oaks near Miami; Brook Glen, Panola Mill, and Wyndham Park near Atlanta; and Black Jack, Jennings, Normandy, and University City near St. Louis. Similarly, black residents in suburban Prince George's County in Maryland, who comprise 63 percent of the county's total population, find comfort from living in affluent but predominantly black communities or subdivisions. Often, though, black suburbs result from invasion–succession. That is, after some minorities enter a community, whites begin to leave, and eventually, their continuing departure results in a segregated black suburban community in many ways analogous to its center-city counterpart, the black ghetto.

Some black suburbs are "spillover" communities, such as Glenarden, Maryland, which is adjacent to Washington, D.C. These suburbs are direct outgrowths of center-city black ghettos that move, over time, beyond the center city. Significant spillover suburbs of

In the past two decades, many minority Americans, part of a growing middle class, have realized the American Dream by owning a house in suburbia. While some live in integrated neighborhoods, others prefer mostly segregated communities, finding greater comfort for themselves and their children in a homogeneous racial setting.

blacks presently exist in Cleveland, St. Louis, Chicago, Atlanta, Miami, Los Angeles, and New York, and they are becoming more and more prevalent throughout the country. The income level of spillover communities is high relative to that of other black suburbs, because, like whites who departed from the center cities, blacks moving outward tend to be middle class, wishing to leave poorer neighbors behind.

In contrast, black migration to Compton, California, in Los Angeles County, was not an example of "ghetto sprawl" but rather, at least in part, a manifestation of upwardly mobile suburbanization, fulfilling many blacks' dream of owning their own house (Sides 2006:97, 129). In fact, whether living in a predominately minority suburb or as a minority in an integrated suburb, suburbanization was not something that happened *to* them. Rather, African Americans created their own suburban dream, establishing, through property ownership, new possibilities of equity and economic opportunity (Wiese 2004).

This relationship between social mobility and residential mobility has long been an area of interest to sociologists, dating back to the Chicago School and those sociologists' observations that as the children of immigrants climbed the socioeconomic ladder, they typically moved to better housing in higher-status, suburban residential areas. Native-born blacks were no different. Compton is a minority community today, more than half-Hispanic and two-fifths black. Now an inner suburb of Los Angeles, it suffers from a higher-than-average unemployment, poverty, and crime rates.

Other minority suburbs began that way, such as Kinloch, Missouri (96 percent black in 2000), a small town just outside St. Louis, represent a second type. Often, these isolated communities originally arose as shantytowns outside the city proper, and in recent decades, white suburbs grew up around them. Colonies are poor areas (see the *Urban Living* box on page 295) with deteriorating housing and large numbers of people living

URBAN LIVING

Life in a Minority Suburb

Robbins, Illinois, is a small, minority suburb in decline. Its steadily declining population, now about 6,300 (95 percent black), is more than 3,000 less than in 1970. The town has as many people under age 18 as it does aged 65 or older (12 percent each).

Located 17 miles south of Chicago's Loop, Robbins is one of the oldest incorporated black municipalities in the United States. Largely farmland until 1910, it is characteristic of semi-rural black suburbs that developed during the Great Migration of the early twentieth century. The mostly working-class African Americans who settled here bought lots for as little as $90 each, many building their own houses and living without such amenities as electricity and indoor plumbing.

Outsiders derided the resulting makeshift landscape with its unpaved streets and called it a slum. Yet for the newly transplanted Southerners, Robbins offered numerous advantages: homeownership in a country-like environment; a safe location without risk of violence; a home near available factory jobs; and a tightly knit community. There were also work opportunities for the women, in domestic service or seasonal work in the city's canning and packing industries in Chicago. Moreover, many of the new residents could supplement their low incomes with garden produce and small livestock.

Over the next several decades, as the population increased, residents established a newspaper, the *Robbins Herald,* plus many churches and small stores. Robbins also became a popular recreation spot for black Chicagoans, who crowded its picnic grounds and nightclubs on summer weekends.

Because it was a blue-collar community with almost no commercial tax base, town officials could only undertake modest improvements, given the limited funds to upgrade services. As late as 1950, 22 percent of Robbins homes lacked indoor plumbing, and over 40 percent were considered substandard in 1960. In the 1960s, black developer Edward Starks opened the Golden Acres subdivision, which brought modern, suburban-style houses to the community. Paved streets and sewers came in the 1950s, but these costs—combined with plant layoffs in the 1970s—saddled the suburb with municipal debts. Although Robbins remained one of the few places in greater Chicago where African Americans with very limited resources could afford to buy a home of their own, declining jobs in the area put the local economy into a tailspin.

With a median household income of 27,600 in 2007, other socioeconomic statistics offer little promise of a turn-around anytime soon. Two-thirds of the residents have a high school or higher level of education, but only one in twelve has a bachelor's degree or higher. One-fourth are married, one in ten are widowed, one in ten are divorced, and nearly half the eligible population has never married. Nearly one-fourth of its population is unemployed and more than one-third live in poverty, both statistics well above the state average. One hopeful sign is that after more than 10 years of virtually no new construction, about 50 new buildings went up in 2006–2007.

Source: Adapted from Andrew Wiese, "Robbins, IL," *The Encyclopedia of Chicago* (Chicago: Chicago Historical Society, 2005) and from City-Data.com (accessed February 27, 2009).

below the poverty level (about 38 percent, in Kinloch's case). Only 53 percent of adults age 25 or older have a high school education; none has a college degree. Most work in low-skill jobs, and more than half the population lives in poverty. The outlook for them is as bleak as it is for center-city ghetto residents.

In 2000, 49 percent of all U.S. Hispanics lived in suburbs, up from 46 percent in 1990. The 10 metropolitan areas with the most Hispanic suburbanites are in just five states: California (Los Angeles–Long Branch, Riverside–San Bernardino, San Diego, Orange County, San Francisco, Oakland), Florida (Miami), Texas (Houston), Arizona (Phoenix–Mesa), and Nevada (Las Vegas). Such cities now have what are in essence Hispanic suburbs (Lewis Mumford Center 2001c).

Monterey Park near Los Angeles is an Asian suburb, its population more than 41 percent Chinese American and another 20 percent a mixture of Japanese, Vietnamese, Korean, and other Asian Americans. This is the exception, however, because Asians—a diverse racial category of many cultures—typically move to predominantly white suburbs. As the most affluent U.S. minority group, with a median household income of $66,102 in 2007, more Asians (58 percent) live in suburbia than any other racial or ethnic category.

The continuing influx of Asian and Hispanic immigrants, together with the tendency of many to settle directly in the suburbs, suggests that suburbs will become more diverse in the years to come. Clearly, the old stereotype about suburbia as a "white cocoon" no longer fits.

SUMMARY

If stereotypes about urbanites contain some truth, they also contain distortions. Research consistently points out the existence of pronounced urban variety—a range of social class lifestyles that defies easy description.

This is as true of the suburbs as it is of the center city. Proportionately, more residents in towns within the metropolitan region hold higher socioeconomic status than urban dwellers. If we look more carefully, however, we can find many examples of social class heterogeneity in both locales.

Ever since Marx and Weber offered their analyses about social stratification, sociologists have studied this aspect of community life, beginning with Warner's study of Yankee City in the 1930s and continuing ever since. The middle class is the largest grouping in the United States (about 40–45 percent), followed by the working class (about one-third), the lower class (about 20 percent), and the elite upper class (about 5 percent). Each class has distinctive characteristics in wealth, power, prestige, and lifestyles, but not necessarily in choice of urban or suburban residence.

The gap between rich and poor is so pronounced that the United States has the most unequal distribution of wealth of all industrialized countries. The top quintile of the population earns about half of all income, as much as the remaining 80 percent combined, and the top 40 percent earns three-fourths of all income. Canada's unequal income distribution is not as pronounced, but the top 20 percent still earns 41.5 percent of all income.

The median household income is significantly higher in suburbia than in the city, and the poverty rate is significantly higher in the city than in suburbia. While this broad-brush portrait of city–suburb economic contrasts is accurate, sociologists use fine-brush analysis to see the details, intricacies, and inconsistencies of that broader portrait. Rather than upholding the simplistic stereotype of affluent suburbanites and non-affluent urbanites, a much more complex picture exists, as this chapter has illustrated.

Our large cities are mosaics of enclaves containing different social classes: upper-, middle-, working-, and lower-class neighborhoods. There are also mixed-income neighborhoods, some of them stable and others changing upwardly or downwardly. Cities do, indeed, have a high proportion of people living in poverty, but most city residents maintain a higher socioeconomic status. One poverty-struck population segment, the homeless, is a mixture of families and individuals, some of them mentally ill and/or substance abusers. They are a tiny percentage of the urban population, but they do form an indelible part of many people's image of the city.

Suburbs emerged in the late nineteenth century as country estates and small enclaves for the well-to-do—people anxious to escape the immigrant lifestyles and industrial commotion of the inner city. With the invention of the automobile in the twentieth century, however, a working- and middle-class exodus accelerated, especially after World War II. The last three decades have witnessed a marked increase in suburban diversity as increased numbers of the working class and minorities moved to these outlying areas. This migration produced a lifestyle complexity that rivals that of the central city. This complexity and diversity will undoubtedly continue to increase as immigration and decentralization continue.

Suburbs fall into recognizably distinct types. There are exclusive upper-income suburbs, middle-income suburbs, working-class suburbs, minority suburbs, and—increasingly in the South, Southwest, and West—Hispanic suburbs. Social class appears to be more significant than race and ethnicity in suburban settlement patterns as more and more African Americans, Asians, and Latinos move into the newer suburbs. Some suburbs have even developed into true cosmopolitan centers, offering all the goods, services, and entertainment that once drew people to the city's center.

CONCLUSION

Ultimately, what we have learned is that the manifestations of social stratification in North America are found within *both* the city and the suburb. Any simplistic socioeconomic comparison of the two ignores the lifestyle variations existing in each and, really, does a disservice to the many positive attributes that cities possess. Of course, central cities do have their problems, as do some of the older suburbs. In addition to the diversity of social class, this chapter's topic, there is the diversity of race, ethnicity, and gender, to which we will turn in the next chapter.

KEY TERMS

bobos (279)
buppies (279)
dinks (279)
ghettos (288)
hyperghettos (270)
inner-city neighborhoods (288)

reputational method (267)
slums (288)
social stratification (267)
socioeconomic status (SES) (267)
yuppies (279)

INTERNET ACTIVITIES

1. At this *New York Times* website, *http://www. nytimes.com/packages/html/national/20050515_ CLASS_GRAPHIC/index_03.html,* you will find an interactive graphic on social class and income mobility.

2. An excellent demographic report of suburban diversity, drawing from the 2000 census, can be found at *http://www. frey-demographer.org/reports/billf.pdf.*

CHAPTER 11

RACE, ETHNICITY, AND GENDER
Urban Diversity

Everywhere and always, cities have been immigrant-luring magnets. This basic fact explains why so many cities display striking diversity—in people, in neighborhoods, and in ways of life. Indeed, part of the excitement of a city lies in precisely this heterogeneity, the range of urban choices, the countless activities and opportunities. Especially in the major immigrant-receiving nations—Britain, Canada, and the United States—racial and ethnic diversity has long been a common trait of cities. This chapter focuses on social diversity in North America and the ways in which race, ethnicity, and gender continue to play a vital part in shaping urban life.

CITIES AND IMMIGRANTS

In Canada and the United States, destinations for millions of immigrants, cities have long been mosaics of ethnic communities. At times, minorities even become the majority, as in Milwaukee back in 1850, when that city contained 6,000 Germans and 4,000 native-born citizens (Parrillo 2009a:147). At the height of the "Great Immigration" between 1880 and 1910, about 1 million immigrants came to these shores annually, and 7 out of 10 settled in cities. Not surprisingly, in most cities in the northeastern United States, foreign-born people comprised from two-thirds to three-fourths of the population.

In recent years, both Canada and the United States have been experiencing unprecedented numbers of immigrant arrivals, particularly from Africa, Asia, and Latin America, bringing ever-greater diversity to the cities. In 2006, as seen in Table 11–1, the cities with the highest percentage of foreign-born residents were Miami (57.7 percent), Toronto (45.7 percent), Los Angeles (39.9 percent), New York (37 percent), Vancouver (36.9 percent), and San Francisco—proportions significantly higher than those in 1990, but still far lower than those at the beginning of the twentieth century.

Certainly, the greater presence of immigrants affects cities' economies, but are immigrants a benefit or a problem for cities? That question—whether on a national, state, or local level—is fiercely debated. A two-year study conducted by the National Academy of Sciences (1997) for the U.S. Commission on Immigration Reform found that immigrants add about $10 billion annually in net economic output because of the increased supply of labor and resulting lower prices, and that a typical newcomer pays $80,000 more in taxes than he or she receives over the course of a

TABLE 11–1   Racial/Ethnic Population in Selected Cities, 2006 (percentage)

City	Asian	African American	Hispanic	Foreign-Born
Boston	7.9	24.5	14.9	27.2
Chicago	4.9	35.3	28.2	21.8
Dallas	2.3	24.2	43.1	26.9
Detroit	1.1	83.1	6.2	4.5
Houston	5.0	24.7	41.9	27.8
Los Angeles	10.4	9.6	48.9	39.9
Miami	0.8	22.4	69.0	57.7
New York	11.7	25.1	27.6	37.0
Philadelphia	5.3	44.3	10.5	10.9
San Francisco	31.8	6.7	14.1	36.3
Toronto	32.6	8.4	206	45.7
Vancouver	39.7	1.1	1.4	36.9
Washington, D.C.	3.4	55.4	8.2	12.7

Source: U.S. Census Bureau, *2006 American Community Survey;* Statistics Canada, *Immigration in Canada 2006: A Portrait of the Foreign-born Population.*

lifetime. At first, however, immigrant households are costly, because they tend to be younger and to have school-age children using the public schools. Even illegal immigrants make a positive contribution. The Cato Institute reported that they pay approximately 46 percent as much in taxes as American-born citizens but receive only 38 percent as much from the government (National Center for Policy Analysis 2002).

Critics argue that some urban centers receive the lion's share of immigrants, and that their concentrated presence strains the community's social fabric and places an economic burden on those areas in education, health, and welfare costs (Swain 2007). George Borjas (2001) maintains that while immigrants in general may enrich the nation, their high numbers and the growing proportion of poorly educated, low-skill workers have negative consequences, requiring a re-examination of immigration policy objectives.

Ethnic Enclaves and Ethnic Identity

Like the European immigrants of previous generations, the new immigrants create their own ethnic enclaves and distinctive social institutions. These large concentrations of ethnic peoples make cities mosaics of small worlds, abuzz with different sights, sounds, and smells reflected in ethnic celebrations, parades, restaurants, street fairs, stores, and other cultural activities. For some people, of course, cities—or at least certain neighborhoods in cities—are to be avoided precisely because of these differences; others find this variety to be one of the lures of the city.

The shifting pattern of ethnic and racial immigration underlies much of the complexity of today's cities. Table 11–2 shows that from 1861 to 1960, the vast majority of legal immigrants to the United States were white people from Europe and Canada. During this period, differences between immigrants and

Park called the city a "mosaic of small worlds," and it still is. In every major city, you can find a patchwork of communities in which the lives of individuals are embedded. Yet even as these different cultures coexist in semi-isolated worlds, they also collide with one another in the city itself, as does this multiethnic group of visitors to New York City's Little Italy.

TABLE 11–2   Legal Immigrants to the United States, 1861–2000 (percentage)

Region of Birth	1861–1900	1901–1930	1931–1960	1961–1990	1991–2000
Europe	90	79	58	18	15
Canada and Newfoundland	7	11	16	5	2
Asia	2	3	5	31	31
Latin America	0	5	17	34	38
Africa	—	—	1	2	4
Other	1	2	3	10	10

Source: U.S. Office of Immigration Statistics, 2007.

people already in this country were mostly ethnic. That is, various whites—say, the Irish, Italians, and East Europeans—differed in cultural traditions but not in race. Since 1960, however, the bulk of legal (and illegal) immigrants have been people of color from Africa, Asia, and Latin America. Racial diversity, as well as ethnic differences, compound the problems of acceptance and rejection.

Ethnic Change

A city's spatial structure reflects ethnic subcultures as immigrants arrive and, through a process known as **chain migration,** settle near friends and relatives. A vibrant ethnic community evolves—with leaders, institutions and organizations, stores, clubs, and same-language media—to help newcomers put down roots and "make it." At the same time that this pluralism manifests itself, however, the forces of assimilation also take hold as immigrants seek to be part of their adopted country. Despite the challenges of learning a new language and, for some, barriers based on skin color, virtually all immigrants gradually identify more and more with their new country, where they expect to spend the rest of their lives.

Herbert Gans (1982) noted that tight "ethnic villages" built by first-generation European immigrants did not always hold up when members of the second and third generations moved from the "old neighborhood" in the central city to the leafy (and less ethnic) suburbs. Of course, such out-migration makes room for new immigrants, an **invasion-succession** process that refreshes urban pluralism even as assimilation draws others into the mainstream.

New York City.   For most of the nation's history, New York has stood as a symbol of racial and ethnic diversity. More than a generation ago, E. Digby Baltzell noted:

> Even today [New York's] citizenry, almost half of whom are foreign born or the children of foreign born, includes more blacks than most cities in Africa, a greater concentration of Jews than at any other time or place. . . . More Puerto Ricans than any other city outside of San Juan, more persons of Italian descent than most cities in Italy, and more [Irish] than Dublin. (1987:ix; orig. 1964)

New York still holds first place as the nation's leading destination of immigrants and it is truly a multicultural city (see the *Urban Living* box on page 302). In 2007, nearly 176,000 immigrants settled in the New York City metropolitan area, compared with about 95,000 coming to Los Angeles metropolitan region (U.S. Office of Immigration Statistics 2008). Brighton Beach, Brooklyn, is known as "Little Odessa"—a place where tens of thousands of Russians live in the largest Russian immigrant community in the world. New York City also has the largest concentration of Haitians (about 200,000 living mostly in the Brooklyn neighborhoods of La Saline, Flatbush, Bedford–Stuyvesant, Bushwick, and East New York), Dominicans (more than 600,000 living mostly in Washington Heights and southwest Queens), and

URBAN LIVING

The Multicultural City and Food

Each ethnic group has its own cuisine, and part of the fun of recalling your heritage or of widening your ethnic experiences is to taste the foods associated with other groups. As any urbanite will tell you, one of the great pleasures of the city is to partake in the great variety of foods available during the numerous cultural celebrations or at the many ethnic eateries and restaurants found everywhere. And there is yet another intriguing aspect of eating these ethnic foods, brought on by the invasion-succession process of one group replacing another.

With the decline of new French, Irish, Italian, Japanese, and Jewish immigrants, and as their children move into professional fields, Asian and Hispanic newcomers are replacing the old chefs in cities throughout North America. The new arrivals learn how to prepare the other culture's foods and take over established locales, popular for their original cuisine. Some of these changes seem an easy transition because of the old countries' proximities and histories. In New York City, for example, it is not unusual to find Bangladeshis running Indian restaurants or Albanians operating Italian restaurants.

However, New York also offers more radical examples. For instance, at Second Avenue and 80th Street, there's a pizza maker who is Tibetan. Down on West 48th Street, a sushi chef at a popular Japanese restaurant is Mexican. At a French restaurant on West 55th Street, the pastry chef is Ecuadorian. A Chinese immigrant from Hong Kong, who learned his culinary art at a famous Jewish restaurant, now has his own place and serves smoked salmon and sturgeon to appreciative Jewish customers. And that wonderful nectar of the old Jewish neighborhoods, the egg cream (a wonderful, frothy drink that blends seltzer, milk, and chocolate) is served in the East Village by an Asian Indian who learned the secret recipe from the previous owner, an Italian, who learned it from the original storeowner, a Jewish immigrant.

So this is the multicultural face of the city: many different peoples serving many different kinds of food, not necessarily from their own homeland. A Central American may well have made that Middle Eastern *falafel* you get, or your Greek *moussaka* may be coming your way thanks to the efforts of a Peruvian. The city! Even its ethnic varieties have variety!

Source: Drawn from the experiences of Vincent N. Parrillo, his family, and friends.

Asian Indians (more than 170,000, living mostly in Queens).

Today, Lower Manhattan's Chinatown is five times the size it was in 1965, both in size and numbers, and is now home to more than 150,000 people. Chinatown has now all but swallowed up New York's Little Italy, with more than two-thirds of the buildings on the Little Italy stretch of Mulberry Street now being Chinese-owned. More than 90 percent of the independent greengroceries in New York City are Korean-owned, as are more than 15,000 small businesses, including import–export companies, manicure shops, gift shops, and fish markets. About 100,000 Koreans also now live in New York City.

Los Angeles.   Los Angeles grew from 3.5 million in 1990 to nearly 3.9 million in 2006, mostly because of foreign immigration (U.S. Census

Bureau 2008a:32). Today, nearly half of all residents in Los Angeles are Hispanic, and almost two-thirds of these are Mexican Americans. The city now has more people of Mexican ancestry than any other city in the Western Hemisphere except for Mexico City and Guadalajara. Salvadorans and Guatemalans are two other heavily represented populations. African Americans comprise 11 percent of the city's population, followed by Asians and Pacific Islanders (particularly Koreans, Filipinos, Japanese, Chinese, Asian Indians, and Vietnamese in descending numerical order) at 10 percent. Also, so many Iranians, perhaps 500,000, live in the city that many expatriates call it "Tehrangeles."

Before moving on to the next section, we should note that Toronto—considered to be the largest *and* most racially/ethnically diverse city—will be profiled inthe last chapter.

RACIAL AND ETHNIC MINORITIES

In past generations, particular cities were home to fewer different groups than they are today. Once, a city might be known primarily for its black, Mexican, Irish, or Italian concentrations, for example, but now, virtually any major North American city is a multicultural place, with dozens of immigrant groups from all parts of the world.

The early history of people of color in North American cities is primarily the story of people of African descent living in the United States. Their influx into Canada occurred in small numbers during the nineteenth century but increased significantly during the twentieth century as more and more blacks from the Caribbean and the United States moved north. Interestingly, in the United States, most blacks call themselves *African Americans*, but in Canada, blacks refer to themselves as *black Canadians* (Fabbi 2003). Native peoples in both Canada and the United States have seldom lived in the white people's cities, and an Asian presence did not become significant in most locales until the second half of the nineteenth century. The Muslim presence is a more recent social phenomenon.

Blacks

Canada's history with its black population is rather different from that of the United States. Although slavery existed in Canada during the eighteenth century, by the nineteenth century it had ended, and Canada became the destination for tens of thousands of fugitive slaves from the United States (Winks 1997:236–40). Afterward, other U.S. black emigrants settled in Canada, but since the late twentieth century, black immigrants from other countries have surpassed those of U.S. origin. Today, recently arrived immigrants constitute the majority of the more than 300,000 blacks living in Canada. Most live in the metropolitan areas of Toronto, Halifax, Montreal, Vancouver, Calgary, Edmonton, and Ottawa. They are somewhat less likely to have college degrees, and their incomes are generally below the rest of the population (Statistics Canada 2007a).

From the time of the first census in 1790 until the beginning of the twentieth century, about 90 percent of the U.S. black population lived in the South, mostly in rural regions. Overall, just one in four African Americans lived in an urban area. A few southern cities had sizable black populations (ranging from 25 to 50 percent of the total) in the late 1800s, a time when the black population of northeastern cities had yet to reach even 5 percent.

The Lure of the North.   The promise of schooling and better work lured black migrants to the North after 1900. By 1910, ten percent of the African American population lived in the North. Full implementation of the segregationist Jim Crow laws in the South, economic hard times, and the boll weevil's destruction of cotton crops prompted many more to head north during the next decade, raising the northern black population from 850,000 in 1910 to 1.4 million in 1920.

Hostility to labor unions in the North and **de facto segregation** (unequal treatment of people based on social customs and traditions) created a dual society there, just as **de jure segregation** (unequal treatment established by law) had done in the South. Northern blacks were an urban people, however, with some of them poor and others working class or even middle class. Black churches formed the bedrock of the segregated racial community. Economically, African Americans could immediately quadruple their income by moving north, so that promise would lead to the greatest mass migration in the country's history (Lemann 1992:41).

The Great Migration.   World War I and the restrictive legislation that followed put an end to the Great Immigration from Europe, initiating the Great Migration from the South. As cities such as Chicago, New York, and Boston grew into industrial metropolises, African Americans saw greater opportunity there than in the agricultural South. The **push–pull factors** spurring migration included the decline of southern agriculture as well as farm mechanization on the one hand and northern industries' shortage of labor and active

recruitment of black workers from southern states on the other.

During the 1920s, the net black outmigration from the South amounted to almost 1 million people. Slowing during the Great Depression of the 1930s, the massive relocation of blacks once again accelerated when industrial production rose during World War II. Migration remained high until the 1970s, when urban decentralization and minority movement to the South reversed the process.

Black Flight.   When large numbers of whites left the cities in the 1950s and 1960s, many social observers termed the movement *white flight* and offering a variety of reasons, most of them centered on fear (crime, violence, and avoidance of minorities). As Table 11–3 shows,

TABLE 11–3   African American Population in Selected U.S. Cities

Region	City	2000	2006	Percentage Change
Northeast	Boston	149,202	140,819	−5.6
	New York	2,129,762	2,062,095	−3.2
	Philadelphia	655,824	642,013	−2.1
	Baltimore	418,951	406,491	−3.0
	Washington, D.C.	343,312	322,105	−6.2
Midwest	Cleveland	243,939	216,421	−8.0
	Detroit	775,772	692,952	−10.7
	Indianapolis	199,412	210,522	+5.6
	Chicago	1,065,009	970,244	−8.9
	Milwaukee	222,933	222,999	—
	St. Louis	178,266	174,296	−2.2
	Kansas City, MO	137,879	130,879	−5.1
South	Atlanta	255,689	246,513	−3.6
	Jacksonville, FL	213,514	245,230	+14.6
	New Orleans	325,947	131,441	−59.7
	Houston	494,496	513,275	+3.8
	Dallas	307,957	288,187	−6.4
	San Antonio	78,120	85,221	+9.1
West	Denver	61,649	56,209	−8.8
	Phoenix	67,416	80,103	+18.8
	San Diego	96,216	86,503	−10.1
	Los Angeles	415,195	364,020	−12.3
	San Jose	31,349	26,803	−14.5
	San Francisco	60,515	50,012	−17.4
	Seattle	47,541	46,219	−2.8

Source: U.S. Census Bureau, *American Factfinder,* 2008.

a clear trend of blacks moving out of cities is now underway. Except for Indianapolis and Milwaukee, all northern and midwestern cities have lost black population, many of whom either chose to move south for better jobs and living conditions or else moved outward into suburbia.

Yet even in the Sunbelt, 9 of the 13 listed cities also registered a decline between 2000 and 2006. Undoubtedly, one reason for the decline is black suburbanization. New Orleans is a special case: The aftermath of Hurricane Katrina in 2005 forced the mostly black flood victims to relocate elsewhere. Similarly, part of the explanation for many Sunbelt cities gaining in black population is that they were the relocation destination of many New Orleans evacuees.

Black Majority.   In Detroit (83 percent), Baltimore (64), and Atlanta (58), blacks are the majority population, as they also are in Gary, Indiana (84); Jackson, Mississippi (76); Birmingham, Alabama (75 percent); Macon, Georgia

(66); Memphis, Tennessee (64); Savannah, Georgia (57); Newark, New Jersey (54); and Richmond, Virginia (54) (U.S. Census Bureau 2008c) . While it is conceivable that blacks may achieve a majority in a few other major cities as well, the fact that African Americans represent about 13 percent of the total U.S. population makes it statistically improbable that black majorities will appear in most other major cities.

Residential Segregation.   Most African American migrants, like earlier European immigrants, typically settled in the least desirable central-city neighborhoods. For the Europeans, this residential segregation reflected mostly lower resources and group preferences. As these immigrants gained education and income, they assimilated and moved out of these traditional ethnic enclaves. As already discussed, many blacks have also done the same, although others remain confined and isolated in racial ghettos, particularly in the Northeast and Midwest (St. Clair and Clymer 2000).

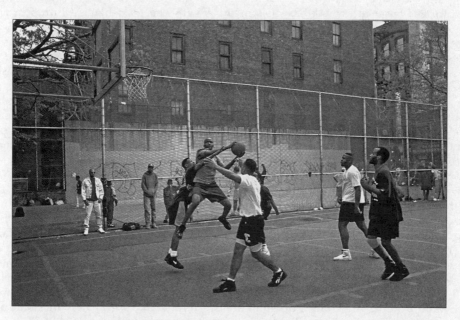

Although racial residential segregation has slowly decreased since 1970, it still remains fairly high among blacks and whites in both cities and suburbs. Most of the 10 most segregated metropolitan areas are in the North, while the 10 least segregated metropolitans areas are in the South. Even so, the 2000 Census showed high segregation levels in Atlanta, Miami, and New Orleans.

Complicating any portrait of racial segregation, however, is the relatively new presence of black immigrants from Africa and the Caribbean. Although race remains a factor, ethnicity also affects residential choice, so any examination of residential segregation requires our consideration of ethnic diversity within race and a group's length of residence in the country. We must also look at the larger picture, at the role of urban and suburban municipalities as these replace neighborhoods as the units of metropolitan segregation (Farrell 2008).

Between 1870 and 1920, segregation in the cities of the North was slight. By 1965, Karl and Alma Taeuber's classic study of racial segregation revealed a dramatic climb in the segregation index. To measure the relative separation or integration of groups across all neighborhoods, the Taeubers developed what they called an **index of dissimilarity.** Their index ranged from a low of zero (complete integration) to a high of 100 (complete segregation). Overall, in 1960, the average white–black dissimilarity index for 207 large cities was 86.2, which meant that 86.2 percent of whites would have to move to another neighborhood in order to make whites and blacks more evenly distributed across all city neighborhoods. Scores in 1960 ranged from a not-so-low 60.4 (San Jose, California) to 98.1 (Fort Lauderdale, Florida).

Since the Taeubers' findings, other researchers have used the index of dissimilarity to track trends in residential segregation. In another classic and influential study, Douglas Massey and Nancy Denton (1993) used the term **hypersegregation** for the intense geographical grouping of racial groups, as found in Fort Lauderdale and Detroit. They assigned five conceptual dimensions to hypersegregation—evenness, exposure, clustering, centralization, and concentration of the population—and if a group scored high in all five areas, it was considered to be hypersegregated. Identifying 29 metropolitan areas as fitting their criteria, they called their study *American Apartheid,* after the infamous racial structuring in old South Africa.

Although racial segregation remains, since the 1970s it has slowly but steadily decreased

in the United States. In 1980, the black–white metropolitan segregation index was 73.9, and in 2000, it dropped to 65.1. However, it still remains fairly high between blacks and whites in cities and suburbs. In 2000, the average white person in metropolitan America resided in a neighborhood that was 80 percent white and 7 percent black. In contrast, the typical black individual lived in a neighborhood that was only 33 percent white and as much as 51 percent black (Lewis Mumford Center 2001a).

Of the 50 metropolitan areas with the largest black populations, the 10 with the highest levels of segregation (in descending order) were Detroit (Figure 11–1), Milwaukee, New York City, Chicago, Newark, Cleveland, Cincinnati, Nassau–Suffolk (NY), St. Louis, and Miami. All but New York and Miami have experienced modest declines in segregation since 1990, and some are "Rust-belt" metro areas, where black–white segregation has been particularly resistant to change. At the other end, the 10 metro areas with the least black–white segregation were all Sunbelt regions in North and South Carolina, Florida, California, and Virginia. Despite signs of progress in the South, several cities in this region also display persistent segregation. For example, pre-Katrina New Orleans was above the national average, and segregation in the city of Atlanta has risen during the past 20 years and is much higher than the national city average (Lewis Mumford Center 2001a).

The Truly Disadvantaged. For the trapped African American poor left behind in the inner city, the future is bleak. Among those lacking the necessary schooling and communication skills required for work in the service and information sectors of the economy, widespread unemployment exists, and these jobless black men are concentrated, clustered, and segregated in small areas of the metropolis (Wagmiller 2007).

Unlike the immigrant poor of the past, today's poor inner-city residents face social isolation. The exodus of middle- and working-class, two-parent black families removes essential role

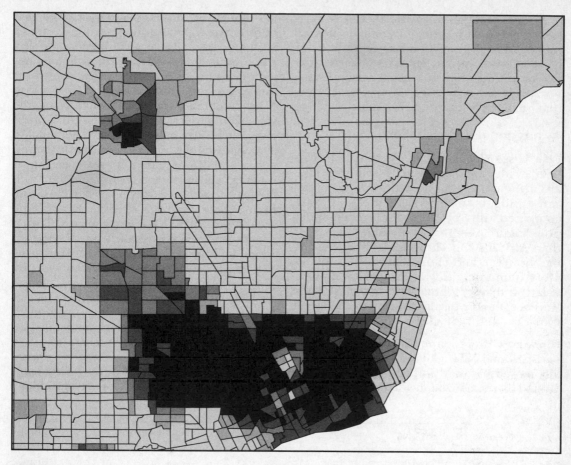

FIGURE 11–1   Percentage of Persons Who Are Black in Detroit, 2000

Source: U.S. Census Bureau.

0 to 9.9

10.0 to 34.1

34.2 to 64.1

64.2 to 86.2

86.3 to 100.0

models and reduces community resources. Furthermore, outsiders avoid these neighborhoods, leaving them plagued by massive unemployment, crime, and schools that do not promote achievement. Consequently, area residents—women and children on welfare, school dropouts, single mothers, and aggressive street criminals—live virtually cut off from the larger society. Gary Orfield noted the magnitude of this isolation:

> To a considerable extent the residents of city ghettos are now living in separate and deteriorating societies, with separate economies, diverging family structures and basic institutions, and even growing linguistic separation within the core ghettos. (1988:103)

Besides being isolated, the ghettoized poor have poor-quality schools, limited medical care, and high rates of infant mortality, substance abuse, and violent crime. Current social indicators offer little cause for optimism, because such problems have structural causes that our society has yet to overcome.

Asians and Pacific Islanders

Like Hispanics, Asians in North America reflect a wide range of distinctive cultures. They are a highly urban population, with 96 percent living in metropolitan areas in 2000, compared with 81 percent of the total population (Figure 11–2). They are also more likely than Africans and Hispanics to live in suburbia, however, and almost half, in fact, do so. Most numerous are the Chinese, Filipinos, Asian Indians, Vietnamese, Japanese, and Koreans, most typically residing in the larger Canadian and U.S. cities.

Chinese. After their initial arrival on the West Coast around 1850, Chinese immigrants gradually moved eastward in both Canada and the United States. Usually, they banded together in low-rent urban enclaves, often situated near transportation hubs (shipping docks or railroad terminals). These areas became the Chinatowns that even today still attract immigrants and, of course, tourists. San Francisco, where one in five residents are Chinese, is home to North America's largest Chinatown, and the second largest is in Vancouver, where Chinese is spoken in 30 percent of the city's households.

Canadians of Chinese origin are the largest ethnic group of non-European origin in Canada, and they are increasing fast, with 30,000 immigrants arriving annually. Numbering more than 1.2 million, they are the fifth largest of any ethnic origin in Canada other than English or French, and 72 percent reside in Toronto and Vancouver. That same percentage—72 percent—constitutes the proportion who are foreign-born, with almost 45 percent from the People's Republic of China, 30 percent from Hong Kong, and 10 percent from Taiwan (Statistics Canada 2007b).

Chinese Americans (numbering nearly 3 million and accounting for 1 percent of the total U.S. population) and Chinese Canadians (accounting for 4 percent of all Canadians)

FIGURE 11–2   U.S. Cities with the Largest Asian Populations, 2000

Source: U.S. Census Bureau.

Many large North American cities—once principally the locales of European ethnic enclaves—now often teem with thriving Asian and Hispanic neighborhoods and commercial areas reflective of changed migration patterns. Here, traffic creeps along a busy street lined with businesses displaying signs in Chinese and English in the Chinatown district of Toronto, Ontario.

currently present a bipolar occupational distribution. About 30 percent are in professional and technical positions, twice the rate among whites. However, the Chinese are also over-represented as low-skilled, low-paid service workers, with about one-fourth in this category. Median family income among Chinese Americans is above the national average, but they are likely to have more wage earners in the family. That fact, rather than a greater proportion of higher-paying positions, accounts for most of the difference.

Filipinos. More than three-fourths of all Canadians of Filipino descent arrived since 1980, and most live in either Toronto or Vancouver. Three in ten have a college degree, double the ratio for all Canadians, and while 7 in 10 are employed, a rate 10 percentage points higher than the national average, their income is $5,000 lower. About 18 percent of all Filipino children live in low-income families, the same as the national average (Statistics Canada 2007c).

In the United States, Filipinos number around 2 million, with their largest concentration in Hawaii, followed by the West and East coast metropolitan areas. More than half arrived since 1980, and the new arrivals tend to have better educational and occupational skills than most of their native-born ethnic cohorts (Parrillo 2009a:282-84).

Asian Indians. The Asian Indian presence in North America has increased dramatically during the past several decades. Census tallies reported about 466,000 Asian Indians in Canada in 2006 and 1.9 million in the United States, twice the number a decade earlier. With overpopulation being a serious problem in India (one in six of the world's people live there!), high migration rates are likely to continue. Asian Indian immigrants also arrive from East Africa and Latin America, particularly from the Caribbean and Guyana, where earlier generations had first gone as indentured plantation laborers. Almost three-fourths of the immigrants are in professional or managerial occupations;

the remainder most often operate convenience stores, gas stations, and family-managed hotels and motels. Consequently, most Asian Indians settle in large metropolitan areas, most significantly in Chicago; New York; San Jose; Washington, D.C.; and Central New Jersey (U.S. Office of Immigration Statistics 2008).

Two out of three Canadians of Asian Indian origin are foreign born, with about half arriving since 1990. Again, most live in either Toronto or Vancouver, constituting 7 percent of each city's population. About one-fourth have a college degree. Like the Chinese, they have a bipolar occupational distribution, being more likely than other Canadians to be in manufacturing jobs or in science and technological jobs. While some do well economically, other Asian Indians are more likely than other Canadians to have earnings below the official low-income cutoffs (Statistics Canada 2007d).

Vietnamese. Barely noted by the U.S. Census Bureau in 1970, more than 1.9 million Vietnamese lived in the United States, and over 160,000 in Canada in 2006. They are the largest Asian group in Texas; but by far, the largest concentration of Vietnamese—some 150,000 people—is in "Little Saigon" in Orange County, California, where the language, signs, shops, offices, and music all convey a distinctly Vietnamese character. San Jose is home to 84,000 Vietnamese Americans, and the Houston–Galveston–Brazonia area contains another 64,000 (U.S. Census Bureau 2008c).

Three-fourths of the more than 150,000 Vietnamese in Canada arrived in the past two decades. Almost all live in Ontario, Quebec, British Columbia, or Alberta, mostly in the large metropolitan areas of those provinces. Their average income is $7,000 below the national average, and more than a third live below the unofficial poverty line (Statistics Canada 2007e).

Japanese. With low annual immigration, Japanese Americans represent a steadily declining share of Asian Americans and now number about 800,000. Most are U.S.-born and have high educational and income levels, higher even than whites. Outgroup marriage now exceeds 50 percent, making Japanese

Americans the most structurally assimilated non-white group (Fu 2001; Zia 2001).

Almost all Japanese Canadians live in the provinces of British Columbia, Ontario, and Alberta, with more than half living in either Vancouver or Toronto. More than three-fourths were born in Canada, one in three has a college degree, and their average income per person is about $3,000 higher than the national average. They constitute only 0.3 percent of the total population (Statistics Canada 2007f).

Koreans. More than 1.1 million Koreans now live in the United States, making them the fourth-largest Asian American group. Their rate of self-employment is higher than that in any other racial or ethnic category, and their retail stores can be found in virtually every major city and in many small towns as well. About half buy an existing enterprise, and the rest begin their own business operations. Their higher success rate in both Canada and the United States compared to other ethnic entrepreneurs rests on their high educational achievement and a marketing strategy of scattering themselves throughout the metropolitan areas to work the mainstream market instead of an ethnic enclave (Ley 2006).

Seven of ten Canadians of Korean origin are foreign-born, and like other Asians, most live in Ontario or British Columbia, principally in Toronto or Vancouver. Although Koreans are more than twice as likely as the overall population to have a university degree, the group's average annual income is about $10,000 less per person (Statistics Canada 2007g).

The "Model Minority" Stereotype. Despite their cultural diversity, many Asians have a record of educational achievement, high income, and overall success in Canadian and U.S. metropolitan areas. Dubbed a "model minority" because of their accomplishments, they often display success in a variety of occupational roles. For example, Chinese engineers, Japanese financiers, Filipino nurses, Korean entrepreneurs, and Vietnamese restaurateurs abound, reinforcing this positive stereotype. Yet the reality is not entirely favorable. Not fitting this positive stereotype are many others, often non-citizens, who eke out an existence in low-paying jobs, often work at more than one job, and depend on multiple wage earners in the household (Kwon, Zuiker, and Bauer 2004).

Hampered by language difficulties, poor education, and weak job skills, many Southeast Asian refugees remain on welfare. Not all Asian students perform well in school. The criminal activities of Asian drug rings, extortion gangs, and youth gangs are often a brutal menace. In short, there is some truth to the "model minority" stereotype, but like other generalizations, it conceals as much as it reveals about a complex category of people.

Hispanics

By far, the fastest-growing non-white category in the United States is Hispanics—Mexicans, Puerto Ricans, Cubans, Central and South Americans, and others of Spanish origin—and they now constitute the nation's largest minority. In most U.S. cities with a population exceeding 100,000, Hispanics outnumber African Americans. These cities include Albuquerque, Dallas, Denver, Houston, Las Vegas, Los Angeles, New York, Phoenix, Salt Lake City, San Diego, San Francisco, and Tucson. In 12 other large U.S. cities, Hispanics are a majority of the population, outnumbering all other categories combined (Table 11–4).

In Canada, the Hispanic presence is not as dramatic, but it is growing significantly and now stands at more than a quarter of a million. About two-thirds are immigrants, and most prefer to live in large cities. In 2006, for

TABLE 11–4 Hispanic Majorities in Selected Cities of 100,000 or More—Percentage of Total City Population, 2000

Brownsville, TX	91.3	Miami, FL	65.8
Corpus Christi, TX	54.3	Oxnard, CA	66.2
El Monte, CA	72.4	Pomona, CA	64.5
El Paso, TX	76.6	Salinas, CA	64.1
Hialeah, FL	90.3	San Antonio, TX	58.7
Laredo, TX	94.1	Santa Ana, CA	76.1

Source: U.S. Census Bureau, 2002.

example, 33 percent lived in Toronto, 25 percent in Montreal, and 7 percent in Vancouver. The rate of those with college degrees is slightly higher than the national average (17–15 percent). The average annual income for all Canadians of Hispanic origin is lower, however, at about $7,500 per person, and more than one-fourth have incomes below the low-income cutoff, compared with 16 percent of all Canadians (Statistics Canada 2007h).

Many first-generation Hispanic Americans cluster in urban ethnic neighborhoods, repeating a centuries-old pattern of earlier immigrants. Here, they create a community support network through **parallel social institutions** (clubs, churches, organizations, and stores), where they can share the commonality of language and culture.

The U.S. Census Bureau term *Hispanic* wrongly suggests a single category of people. In truth, Hispanics differ in their race, cultural backgrounds, social class, and length of residence in North America. Some—most often Mexican Americans—live in rural areas, particularly in the U.S. Southwest. Others, such as Cuban Americans not living in Miami, often live in suburbs. In terms of residence, many Central and South Americans have been in North America for only a few years, while others, notably Puerto Ricans and the *Hispanos* of the U.S. Southwest, have lived all their lives on the U.S. mainland. Although Hispanics live in all 50 states and in all Canadian provinces, many categories of Hispanics tend to cluster in one geographical area. Florida is home to over 70,000 Nicaraguans and about three-fourths of all Cubans. Almost two-thirds of all Puerto Ricans live in the Northeast (primarily New York and New Jersey); California and Texas, by contrast, are home to three-fourths of all Mexican Americans (Lewis Mumford Center 2001a).

Cubans. Nearly 1 million Cubans have come to the United States since 1960. Although they settled in many regions, their main concentrations were in South Florida, particularly Miami, and in the New York metropolitan area. Often settling in blighted urban areas, the first wave of Cuban refugees possessed the education, motivation, and entrepreneurial skills that enabled them to restore stability to previously declining neighborhoods. While other cities experienced a depressed housing market in the 1960s, Miami experienced an economic boom as Cubans brought a new commercial vigor to the downtown area and vitality to residential neighborhoods.

Two of every three Cuban Americans live in Florida, and Miami, dubbed "Little Havana," changed from a resort town to a year-round commercial center, with linkages throughout Latin America. About 700,000 Cuban Americans now live in Miami–Dade County, and their cultural imprint on Miami's skyline, commerce, and texture is obvious (Portés and Stepick 1994).

Puerto Ricans. As U.S. citizens, Puerto Ricans enjoy open migration privileges between their island and the mainland. Before World War II, the poor living conditions on the island offered strong push factors that impelled people to migrate. After 1945, postwar prosperity and regular air flights to the mainland brought as many as 50,000 Puerto Ricans per year to the United States, primarily to New York. By 1960, some 900,000 Puerto Ricans lived within the continental United States, with about 600,000 residing in New York City. The center of the New York Puerto Rican community became East Harlem, also known as Spanish Harlem (97th Street to about 125th Street between Third and Fifth Avenues). Until the late 1970s, however, continuous shuttle migration (migrants returning to the island, and new arrivals coming to the mainland) inhibited an organized community life.

By the late 1970s, however, greater neighborhood organization was evident, as more people put down roots in the city.

More than 3.7 million people living on the mainland United States identify themselves as Puerto Rican. New York City, where most Puerto Ricans once lived, now is home to only one in four. New York State's Puerto Rican population—64 percent of the mainland total in 1970—fell to 34 percent in 2000 as a result of out-migration into other states. Primary destination states were Florida (16 percent of the total Puerto Rican population), New Jersey (12 percent), Pennsylvania (8 percent), Massachusetts (7 percent), and Connecticut (6 percent), with Illinois and California at about 5 percent each (U.S. Census Bureau 2002).

Although nearly two-fifths earned family incomes exceeding $50,000 in 2005, more Puerto Ricans live in poverty than do all other Hispanics, as shown in Table 11–5. One factor contributing to Puerto Rican poverty is a high level of female-headed families: more than one in four Puerto Rican families, compared with one in six Mexican American families. Yet 72 percent of Puerto Rican aged 25 years and older have graduated from high school, a share that is higher than the one in two for Mexican Americans (U.S. Census Bureau 2007b). Perhaps as educational attainment improves (15 percent have graduated from college), future earnings for this group will also improve.

Mexican Americans. More than 28 million Mexican Americans live in the United States, with most living in the West (53 percent) and South (35 percent). Mexican Americans make

TABLE 11–5 Income Levels of Hispanic Americans, 2007

	All Hispanics	Mexicans	Puerto Ricans	Cubans	Central Americans	South Americans
Median family income	$42,074	$40,419	$42,300	$52,113	$41,791	$52,338
Percent of families in poverty	18.5	20.0	21.2	10.2	15.6	9.7
Percent of persons in poverty	20.7	22.0	24.3	13.8	17.5	11.7
Percent of female-headed households	18.5	16.9	25.4	13.0	20.0	15.7

Source: U.S. Census Bureau, *2007 American Community Survey.*

up 34 percent of the Los Angeles population, 32 percent of Houston, 24 percent of San Diego, and 21 percent of Chicago (U.S. Census Bureau 2008c). Mexican immigration continues into both rural and urban areas, but most immigrants are settling in urban neighborhoods, although not necessarily in inner cities. About 9 in 10 Mexicans live in metropolitan areas, with half of them inside central cities. In a settlement pattern reminiscent of past German, Irish, Italian, and Jewish immigrants, many Mexicans—particularly those in California and Texas—are segregated in urban neighborhoods, where these ethnic enclaves have the potential to isolate them from the societal mainstream.

Aiding their adjustment is the Mexican American tradition of family support, which continues (although somewhat weakened) in large cities. Today's urbanites tend to follow nuclear family instead of extended-family residence patterns and to have less male dominance, higher rates of intermarriage, and more diverse occupations (Parrillo 2009a:399).

Many of the central-city residents are of low socioeconomic status and live in areas where the school dropout rate of Mexican American youths runs as high as 45 percent, with student alienation serving as a major cause. Here, drug use and gang violence are everyday realities (Mayer 2004; Wayman 2002; Lichter and Crowley 2002).

Central and South Americans.   About 200,000 immigrants from Central and South America now enter the United States each year, more than half of them from Colombia, El Salvador, Guatemala, and Peru (U.S. Office of Immigration Statistics 2008). About 700,000 Central Americans live in the Los Angeles–Long Beach metropolitan area, and more than 200,000 in the Washington, D.C., and Miami areas. New York and Houston each contain more than 150,000 Central Americans. With a population exceeding 660,000, Salvadorans constitute the majority of Central Americans in most cities, followed by Guatemalans, who number nearly 400,000. From the Caribbean, Dominicans are another significant urban presence, totaling about 1.1 million, with at least half of them living in New York City (Hernández and Rivera-Batiz 2003).

Since 1990, more than 300,000 Colombians also have settled in the United States. Although they are dispersed throughout the country, sizable Colombian communities exist in New York, Miami, and Los Angeles. Colombians are a mixture of educated professionals and low-skilled peasants seeking a better life in North America's cities.

Residential Segregation.   Hispanic residential segregation is less than that for blacks but higher than that for Asian Americans. Hispanics tend to be as segregated from blacks as they are from whites, although this pattern is declining. The degree of segregation varies by ethnic group and social class. Cubans and South Americans are far less segregated than are Dominicans, Central Americans, Puerto Ricans, and Mexicans. By far, Dominicans are the most segregated of the Latino groups. See Figure 11–3 on page 314 for a depiction of the heavy Dominican concentration in New York's Washington Heights and of other Hispanics, especially Puerto Ricans, in the Bronx.

Similar to the situation for blacks, the metro areas with the most Hispanics are also the most highly segregated. Highest among these are New York City; Newark, NJ; Los Angeles; Chicago; Philadelphia; Salinas, CA; Boston; Bergen–Passaic Counties, NJ: Ventura, CA; and Orange County, CA (Lewis Mumford Center 2001a). Such residential clustering in ethnic enclaves has historically been common among numerous immigrant populations. The traditional account of minority assimilation holds that acculturation gained through years spent in the United States—as well as through improved income, English language proficiency, and citizenship—increase geographical and residential mobility into mainstream neighborhoods. Recent research shows this also holds true for Hispanics (South, Crowder, and Chavez 2005).

Muslims

More than 500,000 Muslims, mostly post-1980 immigrants and their children, live in Canada. This population is about equally divided

0 to 12.6
12.7 to 26.7
26.8 to 45.2
45.3 to 65.3
65.3 to 100.0

FIGURE 11–3 Percentage of Persons Who Are Latino in Upper Manhattan and the Bronx, New York, 2000
Source: U.S. Census Bureau.

between Middle Eastern Muslims from Egypt to Turkey and South Asians from Pakistan, India, Bangladesh, and Indonesia, together with significant numbers from Africa and the Caribbean (Bryant 2001). More than one-third live in and around Montreal, and more than one-fifth reside in the Greater Toronto area. Like some Asian groups, they also constitute a bipolar occupation distribution, with 30 percent

holding a college degree (double the national average), yet Muslim children are twice as likely to live in low-income families (Statistics Canada 2007i).

For more than 100 years, Muslim immigrants have settled in U.S. cities, and today, about 5 million Muslims live in the United States, nearly 2 million of them black. As in Canada, most have arrived since 1980 and come from many parts of the world: 33 percent from South-Central Asia, 25 percent from Arab countries, 3 percent from Africa, and 2 percent from Europe, with native-born U.S. blacks constituting about 30 percent (Council on American-Islamic Relations 2008). Like other Americans, hundreds of thousands of Muslims are choosing the suburban life over that of the city (Karim 2006; Stewart 2005).

In the early twentieth century, work in the auto industry brought Muslims from many parts of the Middle East to Dearborn, Michigan, outside Detroit. Together with Middle Eastern Christians, these Michigan Muslims today constitute the largest Arab American settlement in the country. Significant concentrations of Muslims can also be found in such large U.S. cities as New York, Chicago, and Los Angeles, as well as in small cities like Paterson, New Jersey. Everywhere, it seems, mosques and Islamic organizations, elementary and upper-level Islamic schools, and Muslim stores and businesses have sprung up.

These are difficult times for Muslim Americans, particularly those living in cities. Almost all of them follow the non-violent teachings of their religion, but the attacks by Muslim radicals on 9/11 as well as the 2004 Madrid and 2005 London bombings, and the 2008 Mumbai attacks, have heightened prejudices and/or suspicions among non-Muslim urbanites. Muslims were killed in all those attacks as well, but this group finds itself the frequent target of **racial profiling,** both in antiterrorist law enforcement actions and in stereotyping.

Native Peoples

Throughout most of their history, few native peoples lived in cities, instead residing mostly in rural areas, on or near reservations. In recent decades, however, a steady migration to cities has brought many to urban areas. Census data indicate there were 2.5 million Native Americans in 2000, up from 800,000 in 1970, and that 70 percent live in urbanized areas. About 43 percent of U.S. natives reside in the West and another 31 percent in the South, although several hundred thousand live in various metropolitan areas across the country. Table 11–6 provides population totals for native peoples living in major Canadian and U.S. cities.

At nearly 1.2 million in 2006, aboriginals constitute 4 percent of the total Canadian population, compared to 1 percent in the United States. They can be one of three officially recognized groups: First Nations (Indians), Inuit (Eskimos), or Métis (a mixture of First Nations and French Canadians). The aboriginals are becoming increasingly urban, with 54 percent living in cities or census metropolitan areas. One-fourth lives in one of nine cities: Calgary, Edmonton, Montreal, Ottawa, Regina, Saskatoon, Toronto, Vancouver, or Winnipeg (Statistics Canada 2008b).

As always, migration to cities is prompted by the desire for a better life—most reservations are economically depressed, offering few jobs, little schooling, and insufficient services from the two federal governments. Yet for most natives, the city has not delivered much, but the situation is somewhat better in Canada. Although not living in ghettos, about three-fourths of urban Native Americans in the United States do live in poorer neighborhoods. Those who lack schooling and job skills generally experience the same poverty

TABLE 11–6   Native American Population in Selected Cities, 2006

Albuquerque	25,528	Omaha	1,703
Boston	2,013	Ottawa	20,590
Calgary	26,575	Philadelphia	3,698
Chicago	5,104	Phoenix	25,357
Cleveland	1,132	Portland	7,170
Dallas	5,232	Regina	17,105
Detroit	2,444	San Antonio	6,166
Denver	5,430	San Diego	8,155
Edmonton	52,100	San Francisco	3,067
Houston	7,820	Saskatoon	21,535
Jacksonville	2,823	Seattle	4,949
Los Angeles	21,000	Toronto	26,575
Minneapolis	4,769	Tucson	18,638
Montreal	17,865	Tulsa	18,551
New York	41,289	Vancouver	40,310
Oklahoma City	17,743	Winnipeg	68,385

Source: Statistics Canada and U.S. Census Bureau.

they left behind, but now without the tribal support system. Research suggests that Native Americans who migrate to cities are more likely to earn a higher income than those who remain behind on the reservations, but this is partly a result of their higher educational attainment (Larriviere and Kroncke 2004).

WOMEN AND URBAN LIFE

Women's lives in the city have always reflected the gender stratification of the larger society. Before the women's liberation movement, the differentiated roles that men and women played in the home, school, workplace, and community resulted in what Daphne Spain (1992) called **gendered spaces.** By this, she meant how differences in gender status resulted in the organization of space to reflect and reinforce those unequal distinctions. For example, women were once excluded from college altogether, and then secluded in women's colleges before finally being permitted to attend coed schools, at which point the gender stratification system began to change for the better (Spain 1992:4–5).

The workplace also revealed the division of labor, both in terms of occupation and in terms of place. Men and women performed different tasks that split along gender lines—for example, domestic service and teaching for women, compared to medicine and law for men—and they usually worked in segregated spaces. In fact, when women first entered the labor force, their doing factory or clerical work became controversial, because both sexes were occupying the same spaces (Spain 1992:14).

A clear distinction also existed in the use of public and private space. Men had the freedom to use public space at any time, but genteel women did not venture alone onto the streets without a male or female companion (see the *Urban Living* box on page 317). Only prostitutes or poor working women used urban public space, and then only in certain areas of the city. Public space was essentially a male domain; a woman's "place" was the private space of her home.

For the city's middle and upper classes, life in that city home—typically a two- or three-story

One dimension in the progression of gender equality is the greater use by women of urban public space. This scene at the Chelsea Piers sports complex in New York City is one such example. Not only does this facility provide an unconstrained and safe environment, it also enables women to experience such previously male-dominated activities as rock climbing.

brownstone or mansion—followed gender-specific guidelines in the use of physical space. Men rarely ventured into the kitchen, leaving that room to the women and servants. The parlor (a room designated for the reception of guests) and dining room were used by both sexes. After dinner, however, the men "retired" to the study or billiard room for cigars and brandy, while the women "withdrew" to the drawing room for tea and, perhaps, biscuits. That social segregation of private space in one's house extended to the downtown district, where exclusive men's clubs enabled the city's "wheelers and dealers" to dine, drink, socialize,

URBAN LIVING

Targets of Public Harassment

The distinctive public treatment of women in America is influenced by tradition and custom, law, and even medical and psychiatric labels. These areas share underpinnings that support and sustain the social order of public places with regard to gender and the expectations for and practices of public harassment. The prescriptions to women in public places that are supported by etiquette, crime prevention, law, and medicine contain one general theme: The competence of women is presumed to be limited when compared to that of men. Traditional rules of etiquette support this limited competence by denying women certain activities such as smoking in public, by requiring that women be accompanied in public, and by instructing women to mute their presence by wearing drab or unremarkable clothing or by keeping their voices low and their carriage dainty and graceful. Even when women are advised to take up certain strategies to "prevent crime" in public, those strategies often involve symbolic dependency and incompetence. . . .

Traditional American etiquette of public places is an expression of a shared set of norms for presentation and conduct—in short, etiquette tells us how society thinks individuals should relate to the public order.

Gender is often a central consideration in this relational behavior. . . .

Inasmuch as the requirements of etiquette demand that women demonstrate their gender in public places in ways that have connotations of, for example, frailty, incompetence, and subordination, the individual who complies implies (or is willing for the moment to seem to imply) a larger belief in the present system of gender relations as well. Part of our assumptions about behavior in public places is that, overall, this behavior serves as reliable evidence for, or clue to, private identity and behavior. Public harassment attempts to suggest there is a congruence between public and private selves. Traditional etiquette—with which women are typically acquainted, even if they choose not to meet its expectations—provides just this type of schooling. Some women choose to ignore traditional etiquette in favor of the more egalitarian model, and some men do so too, but traditional expectations in places like streets and restaurants remain an uneasy presence nonetheless. Such gender expectations, although they may not be chosen, are still part of what women (and men) know is available as acceptable behavior, one of a variety of paths of action to recognize, evaluate, choose, take, and support.

Source: Carol Brooks Gardner, *Passing By: Gender and Public Harassment.* Copyright © 1995 by the University of California Press. Reprinted with permission.

and talk business in a comfortably furnished, male domain.

In the second half of the twentieth century—as women's rights and social interactions increased during society's evolution toward greater gender equality—so, too, did the use of private and public space by women at home, work, and in the public sphere. Homes became more open, with fewer inside doors shutting off

kitchens, dining rooms, and living rooms. Family rooms, shared by all, became common instead of separate men's and women's relaxation areas. With men and women working side by side, adjustments in the work environments occurred, from the obviousness of rest rooms to what could or could not be done or displayed in order to avoid what legally came to be defined as a **hostile environment.**

Railroad commuters are a familiar part of any large city's work force. Once their ranks were mostly male, but with almost half the labor force now female, so, too, is the proportion of commuters. The greater presence of women has led to changes in the texture of urban space and in services and activities catering to their needs.

In short, the changing times and values led to greater life opportunities for women in all facets of life, which, in turn, prompted new spatial arrangements in both cities and suburbs. We now turn to these considerations.

Work

As both Canada and the United States industrialized, poor women, mostly from immigrant families, went to work at urban factories in low-skill jobs for low wages. In fact, women were the main work force in many textile mills and garment factories.

In the mid-nineteenth century, millions of Irish flocked to North American cities to seek their fortunes. The number of Irish households headed by women was high, approaching 20 percent, often because many husbands died from industrial accidents. In such cases, women commonly expanded their households to include other relatives or boarders in order to help meet living expenses. Then, too, of some 2 million Irish who came to the United States between 1871 and 1910, most

were women, unlike the common pattern by which males migrated first. Many unmarried women migrated to U.S. cities, primarily to seek domestic work as maids or jobs in textile mills (Diner 1983:73–74). For Irish women, then, the city was a place of continual hard work but economic security.

Most other immigrant women also sought work in cities. In Chicago, the needs of immigrant women and their families prompted Jane Addams to found Hull House, beginning the U.S. settlement home movement. The case study of Chicago at the end of this chapter looks more closely at her role in improving women's lives.

A very different story centers on middle- and upper-class women, usually born to prosperous U.S. merchants and industrialists. Men placed them on a pedestal, as towers of moral strength and refinement, as if to balance their own competitive world of work. Prevailing values in the nineteenth and early twentieth centuries held that the nature of women was to please and the nature of men was to achieve. By the 1920s, the expanding number of middle-class families only reinforced the notion that a woman's place was as housewife and mother, as keeper of home and hearth (Freeman 2000; Ryan 1979).

For the most part, this attitude prevailed among the middle class until World War II, when a labor shortage drew women into the work force, filling factory positions that had been vacated by men who were now in uniform. From 25 percent in 1920, the percentage of working women increased to 36 percent during the early 1940s. A postwar recession and soldiers returning to their former jobs, however, resulted in the firing of 2 million women within 15 months after the war ended. Then, as the suburban decade of the 1950s ensued, the "Ozzie and Harriet" generation (named after the popular sitcom) resumed the pattern of women's lives being confined to the house.

By 1970, however, change was under way, resulting in part from the increasing costs of a middle-class lifestyle (including the soaring costs of sending children to college) and in part from a wide range of new employment opportunities for women in the city's information and service economy. The dual-career family became the norm. By 2006, the female participation rate in the labor force reached 60 percent, way up from 46 percent in 1980. Mothers, too, joined the labor force: In 1975, 45 percent of married mothers of children under age 18 worked for pay; by 2005, that share was 68 percent (U.S. Census Bureau 2008a).

Urban Space

A key focus of recent feminist urban research is the extent to which cities use space to meet the needs of women (Garber and Turner 1994; Spain 1992; Mazey and Lee 1983). For example, how does the urban environment support the needs of today's working woman? One answer is that a host of specialized services have emerged, providing child care, household cleaning, lawn care, and shopping assistance to the working woman. Moreover, fast food and takeout restaurants, laundries, and dry cleaners carry out tasks for which she often has little time. Large merchandising stores and supermarkets, as well as malls and mini-malls, make shopping efficient by minimizing the time spent going from store to store.

Another issue concerns the allocation of public space. In a male-dominated society, planners typically allocate most open space to male-oriented activities, such as sports, giving little consideration to the needs of women. More attention needs to be given to creating safe environments in order to protect children at play, providing less-constrained places for women to walk or jog, and creating housing that promotes more contact with neighbors, especially for children. Finally, researchers suggest that spatial arrangements should not segregate the sexes, thereby reinforcing traditional ideas about gender; rather, they should allocate space to help all individuals' lives (Massey 1994).

The Public Sphere

More women than ever before now hold elected public office; tens of thousands serve as mayors or members of city councils across North America. Among major cities where women have served as mayor are Atlanta, Chicago, Oklahoma City, Ottawa, Phoenix, Portland, San Antonio, San Francisco, San Jose, and Mississauga, Ontario. As women become more active and visible in the public arena, they seek to shape and redirect policies affecting women's daily lives in the city. Many women now participate in decision making, but they have had limited success in putting on the political agenda key issues that challenge male dominance. As the number of women leaders increases, however, this situation is likely to change.

In concluding this chapter, we present a case study of what was, for a century, the "second city" of the United States—its greatest inland metropolis, Chicago. The development of Chicago illustrates all the issues raised in this chapter. As Robert Park and the University of Chicago sociologists (see Chapter 5) found out, Chicago has been a city in which class, race, ethnicity, and gender have played a central part in people's lives.

CASE STUDY
Chicago, "City of the Big Shoulders"

Hog Butcher for the World,
Tool Maker, Stacker of Wheat,
Player with Railroads and the Nation's Freight
    Handler;
Stormy, husky, brawling,
City of the Big Shoulders:
They tell me you are wicked and I believe
    them, for I have seen your painted
    women under the gas lamps luring the
    farm boys.
And they tell me you are crooked and I answer:
    Yes, it is true I have seen the gunman kill
    and go free to kill again.
And they tell me you are brutal and my reply
    is: On the faces of women and children I
    have seen the marks of wanton hunger.
And having answered so I turn once more to
    those who sneer at this my city, and I give
    them back the sneer and say to them:
Come and show me another city with lifted
    head singing so proud to be alive and
    coarse and strong and cunning.
Flinging magnetic curses amid the toil of
    piling job on job, here is a tall bold slugger
    set vivid against the little soft cities;
Fierce as a dog with tongue lapping for
    action, cunning as a savage pitted against
    the wilderness,
        Bareheaded,
        Shoveling,
        Wrecking,
        Planning,
        Building, breaking, rebuilding,
Under the smoke, dust all over his mouth,
    laughing with white teeth,
Under the terrible burden of destiny laugh-
    ing as a young man laughs,
Laughing even as an ignorant fighter laughs
    who has never lost a battle,
Bragging and laughing that under his wrist is
    the pulse, and under his ribs the heart of
    the people,
Laughing!
Laughing the stormy, husky, brawling laugh-
    ter of Youth, half-naked, sweating, proud to
    be Hog Butcher, Tool Maker, Stacker of
    Wheat, Player with Railroads and Freight
    Handler to the Nation.

                                    Carl Sandberg, "Chicago"

Carl Sandberg captures much of the flavor of turn-of-the-century Chicago in this poem he wrote in tribute to the city in 1916. Not everyone, of course, shared his enthusiasm. Visiting Chicago in the 1850s, Swedish novelist Frederika Bremer decried it as "one of the most miserable and ugly cities," a place where people come "to trade, to make money, but not to live" (cited in Glaab and Brown 1983:85–86). Rudyard Kipling, visiting the Chicago of the Gay Nineties, was more direct: "Having seen it," he wrote, "I urgently desire never to see it again. It is inhabited by savages" (cited in Rakove 1975:22).

What is it about Chicago that draws such powerful and divergent responses from observers?

Chicago's skyline offers a striking array of architectural styles that enhance its visual appeal. Within the city itself, as in all cities, a population that is also rich in diversity often grapples with problems of housing and crime that affect quality of life and satisfaction with urban living.

Perhaps it is that the most powerful themes in the United States concern wealth, prestige, power, and the drama by which they are gained or lost. Chicago, which rocketed to prominence in barely 50 years, clearly exhibits such themes. This "city of the big shoulders," at once brash and breathtaking, is a magnifier of U.S. wealth and poverty without equal.

Early Chicago

In 1673, the future site of Chicago, where the Chicago River joins Lake Michigan, caught the attention of early explorers Jacques Marquette and Louis Joliet as a possible water link between Lake Michigan and the Mississippi River.[1] The area remained under Indian and French control for almost a century, until the English took charge in 1763. Shortly thereafter, it passed into the hands of the new United States of America. Early in the next century, Native Americans vacated the area, and the U.S. Army erected Fort Dearborn amidst a sprinkling of settlers' cabins. Another generation passed before, in the shadow of a fort, the settlement of Chicago began in earnest.

By 1830, a century of spectacular growth was under way. Starting with just 50 persons, the new city (incorporated in 1833) boasted 4,000 residents by 1837. As the Erie Canal stimulated regional trade, Chicago became a boomtown. A building lot that sold for $100 in 1830 brought $15,000 by 1835. The population soared—growing by 50 percent or more between 1840 and 1900. So great was the demand for housing that the city emerged as a center for innovative architectural techniques, a tradition it has maintained. "Balloon frame" housing—assembled quickly with machined lumber rather than heavy timbers—was an early Chicago strategy to provide homes for waves of new arrivals.

The key to the economic success of the city was its position in the growing urban trade network. Chicago was linked to the East by the Great Lakes and the Erie Canal, to the South

[1]Much of the history of Chicago that follows is based on Harvey M. Mayer and Richard C. Wade, *Chicago: Growth of a Metropolis* (Chicago: University of Chicago Press, 1973).

by river and canal to the Mississippi River, and by midcentury, to the West by the railroad. On November 20, 1848, a locomotive carried the first load of wheat into the city. Although it was a trip of only 10 miles, the significance was clear: With the railroad, Chicago became the center for the entire Midwest, a break-of-bulk point for goods shipped in all directions.

By 1855, a total of 96 trains a day entered and left the city. In the 1850s, the McCormick Reaper Company made Chicago a center for farm machinery. The famed stockyards developed during the Civil War, and with the making of steel rails, Chicago also took its place as a manufacturing center. In short, "Chicago had become Chicago" (Mayer and Wade 1973:24).

In the following decades, Chicago's wealth and influence continued to grow. Railroad lines converged on the city from all directions, and water traffic expanded as trade in lumber, grain, and livestock increased dramatically. Factories proliferated, forming new industrial districts. Many industrialists became rich beyond imagination: Cyrus McCormick with his reaper and other agricultural inventions, Henry B. Clarke in hardware, and Archibald Clybourne, Gustavus Swift, and Philip Armour in beef and meat packing. By 1885, Armour employed some 10,000 workers in his meatpacking business. Prosperity seemed to be everywhere:

> The old boundaries could no longer contain the burgeoning commerce and industry. . . . Lumber yards, factories, [grain] elevators, warehouses, docks, and depots lined the river and pushed north and south along the banks of both branches; commercial facilities steadily expanded at the city's center, forcing residential construction to move out to the edge of town. . . . urban displacement. . . . had begun. (Mayer and Wade 1973:54)

Industrial giants such as McCormick, Clybourne, Clarke, Swift, and Armour became the city's first elite. As the rich did elsewhere, these men displayed their new wealth with spectacular homes away from the city's center that contrasted sharply with the working people's squalid settlements near Packingtown and other industrial areas. Further enriching the lifestyle of the privileged residents was the opening of an opera house and art gallery in 1850 and, a decade later, of Marshall Field's, the nation's first modern department store.

The Burning and Rebuilding of Chicago

According to Chicago lore, on the night of October 8, 1871, near the corner of 12th and Halsted Streets, Mrs. O'Leary left her cottage to milk her cow inside the small barn in the back. The cantankerous old cow kicked over her lamp, however, and started the fire that burned down the city of Chicago. Fanned by a stiff southwest wind, the fire swept northward along the lake, consuming 1,700 acres within 24 hours. As with London in 1666 and Atlanta in 1864, the destruction was virtually total. In a day, 100,000 Chicagoans were rendered homeless, and the heart of the city's business district lay in ashes.

Even so, the forces that had created Chicago—the quest for commercial and industrial success—were very much alive. The new Chicago became more of a "growth machine" than ever before. In 1884, the city opened the age of the urban skyscraper with the construction of a 10-story, steel building. By 1890, Chicago's population passed the 1 million mark. Pushing its borders outward, the nation's second-largest city once again dominated the Midwest.

Jane Addams and Hull House

In 1889, Jane Addams—suffragist, activist, and the first woman to win a Nobel Peace Prize—founded Hull House in an old mansion at the corner of Halsted and Polk Streets amid Chicago's West Side slums. Her house was a refuge for displaced people to "aid in the solution of social problems engendered by the modern conditions of life in a great city" and to help her neighbors "build responsible self-sufficient lives for themselves and their families" (Addams 1910).

Immigrant Aid. Hull House was situated in an ethnically diverse section, astride Italian, Bohemian, Greek, Jewish, Polish, and Russian neighborhoods. To build pride and respect for ethnic heritage, Addams implemented the Hull House Labor Museum, which portrayed the labor of immigrant parents in their native countries and connected it to the jobs held by young adults in Chicago. Unlike most of her contemporaries, Addams recognized the unique problems of African Americans and became a pioneer in the fight against racial discrimination (Addams 1930).

In *The Spirit of Youth and the City Streets* (1909), Addams voiced concern over the breakup of the sense of community that had been caused by industrialization, which tended to segregate not only social classes as well as immigrants but also even the generations within the same social class. A gifted speaker and writer, she often addressed the issue of respecting diversity in others:

> Possibly another result of our contemptuous attitude toward immigrants who differ from us is our exaggerated acceptance of standardization. Everyone wants to be like his neighbors, which is doubtless an amiable quality, but leading to one of the chief dangers of democracy—the tyranny of the herd mind. (1930:330)

Through it all, Hull House remained the center of her activism.

> Hull-House expanded to include many buildings. Eventually 70 people experienced collective living and more than 2,000 others crossed its doorway daily. It became a community center for all of Chicago; there was an art museum, a theater, a boys' club, a music school, a coffee house, meeting rooms for discussion clubs, a gymnasium, an employment bureau, a lunchroom, a library, apartments for working women and their children, a kindergarten, and much more. Scholars from the universities, leaders from Chicago society, and international leaders came to observe and learn. (Lundblad 1995:662)

Social Activism. Addams's social activism included successfully lobbying the Illinois state legislature to pass strong child labor laws as well as laws protecting women. She conceived of and helped create the juvenile court system, set up school playgrounds, demanded enforcement of housing and sanitation laws, worked for woman's suffrage, advocated for the legal protection of immigrants, and much more. Among Hull House firsts were:

- The first public swimming pool in Chicago
- The creation of four labor unions (Women Skirt Makers, Women Cloak Makers, Dorcas Federal Labor Union, and Chicago Women's Trade Union League)
- The nation's first private venture capital fund for neighborhood business development
- The first domestic violence court in Chicago, in conjunction with the Chicago Metropolitan Battered Women's Network (Domestic Violence Court Advocacy Program)
- The first infant care facility in a Chicago high school
- The first community-based foster care program of its kind in the country (Neighbor to Neighbor)

Early Feminism. Equally important, Addams believed that dramatic changes could be made in U.S. society, and to that end, she provided a forum where people of all classes, races, and genders could speak together (Deegan 1991). An especially important feature of Hull House was its role as a nurturing, fertile arena for women to engage in intellectually stimulating debates with men. With Hull House as a model, scores of settlement houses sprang up in slum neighborhoods of other cities and offered hot meals, education, and other services. Everywhere, settlement houses served as a breeding ground for feminism and activism. At least half the women residents went on to lifelong careers in some branch of social service.

Jane Addams was a close associate of George Herbert Mead, who gave lectures at Hull House. Her contributions to the founding of the science of sociology and to the first department of sociology at the University of Chicago are pivotal intellectual achievements. The noted educator John Dewey was also an associate and good friend of Jane Addams; Dewey modeled his classes at the Laboratory School, University of Chicago, after the children's activities at Hull House. Clearly, Jane Addams was a major force not only on the Chicago urban scene but at the national and international levels as well. Her achievements, contributions, and humanitarian efforts still shape our lives today.

Chicago in the Early Twentieth Century

Chicago . . . offered a world of hope and opportunity to the beginner. It was so new, so raw; everything was in the making . . . the youth, the illusions, the untrained aspirations of millions of souls. . . . Chicago [at the turn of the century] meant eagerness, hope, desire. It was a city that put vitality into almost every wavering heart. It made the beginner dream.

Theodore Dreiser, *The Genius*, 1915

Chicago plunged into the new century with clear title as the metropolis of the Midwest. The city shot upward as a towering skyline took form. Immigrants from Europe swelled the city's population: Germans, Swedes, Irish, Poles, and Italians. For many, life in Chicago's poorest neighborhoods was often brutal, unsanitary, and exceedingly crowded. An estimate at the turn of the century revealed that if all of Chicago "were as densely populated as its worst slums [900 people per acre], the whole of the Western Hemisphere could have been housed in Chicago" (Felter, as cited in Mayer and Wade 1973:256).

Over time, however, the dreams of many working-class Chicagoans became a reality. More and more sons and daughters of immigrants moved outward from the old, crowded neighborhoods into newer, middle-class housing. This outward flow spilled into newly annexed developments on the city's edge.

Success did not come to all, however. African Americans had an especially hard time. Drawn to Chicago in ever-increasing numbers during the early 1900s, blacks settled primarily on the city's South Side. There, unlike many others, they experienced little prosperity, and few migrated outward. The black ghetto simply expanded to the north and west of the city. Periodically, too, racial violence erupted. On July 27, 1919, after a confrontation on a local beach, a black youth drowned, leading to five days of rioting in the South Side ghetto. Damage was extensive, and many blacks suffered death and injury at the hands of white mobs.

By the 1920s, when the sociologists of the University of Chicago began studying their city intensively, they found Chicago to be shaped by a complex system of social stratification based on race, ethnicity, occupation, and income. Soon, organized crime asserted itself in the form of "gangsters," fed by the public's thirst for alcohol despite Prohibition. Nowhere did guns speak louder than in the smaller city of Cicero, adjacent to Chicago, where Johnny Torrio, Al Capone, and "the mob" had their headquarters. To consolidate his control of the city, Capone launched a campaign of terror on Election Day in April 1924. This represented urban political corruption at its peak of power, and the mob's victory gave gangsters control over much of the city. Still, some people fought back, and by 1931, Capone was convicted of income tax evasion and spent the rest of his life in prison.

The Great Depression of the 1930s cut deeply into Chicago's economic life. Unemployment soared, construction stalled, and even the city's second World's Fair in 1933 couldn't conceal the widespread social injury. Homeless Chicagoans sleeping in public parks or milling about street corners became commonplace. Only with World War II did the economy finally recover.

The Postwar Period

Post–World War II growth took place largely beyond Chicago's city limits. A familiar pattern changed the social character of Chicago as the more affluent population moved out, leaving behind the growing ranks of minorities and the poor. By 1960, with people demanding more services as the economic base continued to contract, some began speaking about the "death of the city." Chicago fought back under the leadership of its mayor, Richard J. Daley, whose long and controversial record lasted from his election in 1955 until his death in 1976.

The Chicago Machine

An old saying about Chicago holds that "the Jews own it, the Irish run it, and the blacks live in it" (Rakove 1975:32). This is partly incorrect—white Anglo-Saxon Protestants control the greatest wealth in the city—but the Irish have controlled the politics of the city for most of its history. Today, however, they face a growing political challenge from blacks and Hispanics, who constituted 63 percent of the city's population in 2006 (U.S. Census Bureau, 2008c).

The Chicago political machine of the Democratic Party came to power in the 1930s, later than in many other cities, and did not reach its greatest strength until Richard J. Daley became the undisputed city boss. Political life in Chicago under Daley carried the tone of the immigrant political machines of the late nineteenth century. Its leaders, from block captains to the mayor himself, tried to meet the needs of their constituents, and in return, they expected people's votes.

Daley focused on maintaining the quality of the central business district—the Loop. Centered along State Street, the Loop is the economic heart of the city, of vital concern to the city's powerful business interests. In addition, the city revitalized the lakefront to make Chicago attractive and exciting both to visitors and to Chicagoans themselves. The record of improvements was uneven, however. While all residents of the city benefited to some degree from better lighting, street cleaning, and snow removal, poorer neighborhoods continued to decay.

Chicago also boasts three of the five tallest buildings in the nation—including the Sears Tower, one of the tallest in the world—yet a commitment to improve housing for the poor was lacking until recently, a topic highlighted in the next chapter. Especially for African Americans, segregation remains all too evident, prompting a greater political voice from the black community (now 35 percent of the population). Hispanics, too, are a growing political force (28 percent of the city's people).

Since Daley's death in 1976, the Irish-dominated machine has held on in Chicago, although with considerably less power. Soon after Daley's death, Jane Byrne became the city's first woman mayor, followed by Harold Washington, Chicago's first black mayor, elected in 1983 following a divisive racial campaign. Presently, Richard Daley, son of the late mayor, is Chicago's leader.

Ordered Segmentation

Race and ethnicity are thus fundamental parts of the social organization of Chicago, as Gerald Suttles (1974) discovered through a participant–observer study of the Addams area on Chicago's West Side. Most observers considered this area, once prime turf for the Capone mob, to be little more than a disorganized slum. Suttles's most important finding was that while some housing was surely dilapidated and many people were poor, the area was far from "disorganized." Rather, Suttles found a marked social order, which he termed **ordered segmentation,** based on race and ethnicity.

How did it work? Back then, four categories—African, Italian, Mexican, and Puerto Rican Americans—made up the bulk of the area's population. Each had its own distinctive way of life, claimed its own "territory," and had its own ideas about all the others who lived nearby. Suttles found the Italians to be closely knit and trusting of one another. African Americans, in contrast, seemed to be alienated from each other, typically distrustful, and very poor. The Mexican Americans and Puerto Ricans fell somewhere in between. They were somewhat better off than the blacks economically and had more of a sense of community.

Contacts across racial and ethnic lines were rare. Most people kept their distance from others who, according to local stereotypes, were different and best avoided. The positive irony here is that such divisiveness allowed most people to establish community ties with those whom they did trust. In other words, by avoiding African Americans, Italians, and Mexican Americans, Puerto Ricans could form a sense of identity and community among themselves, thereby providing some

defense against a hostile outside world. Suttles concluded:

> For all its shortcomings . . . the moral order they have developed includes most, if not all, of their neighbors. Within limits, the residents possess a way of gaining associates, avoiding enemies, and establishing each others' intentions. In view of the difficulties encountered, the [ordered segmentation] of the Addams Area has provided a decent world within which people can live. (1974:234)

Chicago Today

Despite recent corruption scandals involving some city officials accepting bribes to award trucking contracts or illegally doling out patronage jobs, the news from Chicago these days is mostly positive. Across the city, remarkable changes are under way—physically, economically, and among its residents. Its trademark skyline now includes more rooms with a view than ever before as high-rise residences continue to sprout up throughout the downtown area and nearby neighborhoods. In 2005 alone, 4,500 new condo units were built and quickly purchased by young professionals, aging suburban empty nesters, and speculators. Other new condominium high-rises are underway, most notably the $1.5 billion Chicago Spire Condominium Tower, projected to become the nation's tallest building. Despite an increase in office vacancies—caused primarily by corporate mergers and layoffs—new commercial development continues downtown, punctuated by such new projects as the Hyatt Center, Mandarin Oriental Hotel and Condo Tower, the Legacy at Millennium Park, and the Aqua Building (Barner 2008).

New theater venues and restaurants in the Loop have brought additional vitality to the downtown. Moreover, the city's half-billion-dollar, year-round lakefront playground is the number-one Midwest tourist and leisure destination, attracting nearly 9 million visitors annually. The highlight of this leisure area is the 3,000-foot-long Navy Pier—a mix of year-round entertainment, shops, restaurants, exhibition

In the 1990s, Chicago experienced both a renaissance of its older commercial streets and a building boom along Michigan Avenue at the edge of Lake Michigan. Navy Pier—with its mix of amusements, exhibitions, restaurants, shops, theaters, and touring boats—is a year-round attraction for hundreds of thousands of residents and visitors annually.

facilities, and attractions, including a 525-seat Shakespeare Theater, a 440-seat IMAX theater, a 150-foot Ferris wheel, and a stained glass window museum (Widholm 2005; Bruno 2001).

Another significant change is in Chicago's population composition. Since 1980, the city's black and white populations have been declining as new immigrants introduce fresh dimensions of social diversity. As recently as the 1970s, most immigrants were Europeans; today, however, the European-born population of Chicago has fallen to less than 8 percent. In their place are now Hispanics, whose numbers tripled since 1970 to more than 774,000 by 2006, and Asians, who total about 135,000 (U.S. Census Bureau 2008c). As mentioned earlier, Chicago has one of the nation's highest levels of black residential segregation (Figure 11–4), but its Hispanic residents are not as intensely segregated (Figure 11–5, page 328).

In the Chicago of today, neighborhoods that once contained Germans, Poles, and Czechs bustle with African, Filipino, Korean, Mexican, Puerto Rican, and Vietnamese Americans, as well as many other ethnic groups. Within each category, of course, there is greater diversity still. Some new immigrants come to Chicago with wealth, extensive schooling, and bilingual fluency. Others, by contrast, are poor. Like immigrants throughout history, they come with little, seeking something more. As one might expect, those with the greatest social advantages tend to spread most widely throughout the city; most of Chicago's new immigrants from India, for example, are professionals and are widely

0 to 9.1
9.2 to 25.7
25.8 to 50.5
50.6 to 81.3
81.4 to 100.0

FIGURE 11–4   Percentage of Persons Who Are Black in Chicago, 2000
Source: U.S. Census Bureau.

dispersed. On the other hand, those with the fewest social advantages are re-creating the racial and ethnic enclaves that have existed in Chicago throughout its history, as evident in the clusters of signs marking Mexican, Korean, and Chinese neighborhoods.

Most of the newer racial and ethnic communities in Chicago are still too small to have a marked impact on the political scene. Yet, in the heyday of the Irish-dominated political machine, probably few could have imagined that the city would ever elect a black mayor, as it did in 1983. As new performers step to the stage in the twenty-first century, the leaders of this large and complex city will need to have big shoulders indeed.

0 to 9.8

9.9 to 25.7

25.8 to 47.8

47.9 to 71.6

71.7 to 100.0

FIGURE 11–5 Percentage of Persons Who Are Latino in Chicago, 2000

Source: U.S. Census Bureau.

SUMMARY

Cities are marked by social diversity. Throughout history, one characteristic of the city has been its ability to generate more opportunity for its people than rural living can. Seeking this opportunity, billions have streamed into cities. Certainly, this was the wheel driving the Great Immigration to North American cities that occurred between 1880 and 1920. By and large, people found much of what they were hoping for. As time passed, many immigrants, and many more of their descendants, moved from poverty into relative affluence.

This was not true for all, however. North American cities also became home to an impoverished class. Historically, the worst-off have been the city's newest arrivals: northern Europeans until 1830, southern and eastern Europeans until 1920, and "new minorities," including African, Asian, Hispanic, and Native peoples, since then.

Women with few privileges have typically worked out of necessity. Middle-class women, though, have moved in and out of the labor force over time. Today, most women work for pay, a fact that shapes the city by fostering various support services to meet the needs of dual-career families and single parents. Moreover, as women become better represented in decision-making positions, we can expect further change in how cities use space.

Finally, our case study of the Windy City, Chicago, illustrates all these themes. From its beginnings as the Midwest's regional center to its emergence as this nation's "second city," Chicago (like any other North American city we might have studied) exhibits a clear-cut stratification system based on differing amounts of wealth, prestige, and power. At the top were such industrialists as the Armours and the McCormicks. At the bottom were, first, poor European immigrants; somewhat later, African Americans; and most recently, immigrants from Latin America and Asia.

Out of the Great Depression of the 1930s arose the Democratic Party machine that reached its culmination in the 21-year administration (1955–1976) of Mayor Richard J. Daley. Like machines elsewhere, this one benefited some people and largely ignored others. Among the latter were various racial and ethnic minorities, such as those who lived in the Addams area on Chicago's West Side. It was here that Jane Addams founded Hull House and centered her highly productive career of social activism. In his later study of this district, Gerald Suttles noted the persistence of racial, ethnic, and territorial divisions, an organization pattern he termed "ordered segmentation." As European immigrants once organized themselves within urban neighborhoods in decades past, so do many of the "new immigrants" today in a city that is experiencing a building boom in new residential, commercial, and leisure space.

CONCLUSION

The larger insight from Suttles's work is that prejudice always works to distinguish some *ingroup* from some *outgroup*. Looking around them, people conclude that "they" simply don't look, think, or act the way "we" do. Kenneth Clark (1980) suggested that such prejudice and the resulting discrimination are the heart of the disadvantages faced by African Americans, a visible minority based on skin color. Much the same applies to people with a different language, who are also set apart as different and who become easy targets for discrimination. Thus, some of the success experienced by white ethnics is a result of their ability, over time, to "pass"—that is, to assimilate into the dominant urban culture. The same opportunity is not as easily afforded others with more clearly identifiable differences.

This pattern reminds us that cities do not exist in a cultural vacuum, for the values, norms, and stratification that shape the broader society also shape cities. Thus, the unequal distribution of wealth and power that characterizes North America, as well as structures of prejudice and discrimination, play out most clearly in our cities.

KEY TERMS

chain migration (301)
de facto segregation (303)
de jure segregation (303)
gendered spaces (316)

hostile environment (317)
hypersegregation (306)
index of dissimilarity (306)
invasion-succession (301)

ordered segmentation (325)

parallel social institutions (311)

push–pull factors (304)

racial profiling   (315)

INTERNET ACTIVITIES

1. Go to *http://www.censusscope.org/index. html,* and click on the "Segregation" tab. In the left box "Charts," select "Dissimilarity Indices," and then a metropolitan area or city. Then, click "View Chart," and you will see its dissimilarity indices.

2. Go to the U.S. Census Bureau (*http:// www.census. gov*), and click "American FactFinder." In the box "Fast Access to Information," enter a city and the state, then click "Go." Change the tab to "2000." Click on "map" for White, Black, Asian, or Hispanic. The map that appears gives that group's residential patterning, just like the maps in this chapter. You may want to zoom in 20 or 7 miles across (top right) to get a more detailed view.

CHAPTER 12

HOUSING, EDUCATION, CRIME
Confronting Urban Problems

I am an optimist about the possibilities and a pessimist about the probabilities.

Lewis Mumford

We did not all come over in the same ship, but we are all in the same boat.

Bernard Baruch

With four out of five North Americans living in cities, we are unquestionably an urban people. Most of us, however, recognize that urban living involves not just opportunities and excitement but also various problems. Indeed, troubles such as poor housing, poor education, and crime seem to be more intense in cities than elsewhere and often serve to convey negative images of the city.

A close look at such problems reveals that they do not exist in isolation. On the contrary, many connections exist among the problems of poverty, poor housing and education, crime, and racial and ethnic tensions. Focusing on any one alone not only hinders understanding but also frustrates any efforts at solutions. Urban problems are part of a "package," partly a product of cities and partly a product of the structure and values of society itself.

Because quality-of-life judgments often rest on the standards found in housing, education, and safety, we will examine them in an urban context. How well do our cities provide housing for everyone, including the poor? How well do they educate our children? How well do they offer safety for all citizens?

HOUSING: A PLACE TO LIVE

Chapter 10 explained that the lifestyles of the urban population are strikingly diverse, a fact that is clearly evident in people's choice of housing. Some urbanites prefer the life of a downtown apartment; others desire the liveliness of rowhouses in an ethnic neighborhood; still others are drawn to a spacious, single-family suburban home. Of course, housing and neighborhood are not simply matters of personal choice. Differences in income set the range of choices that are available. Also important are past and present economic forces that have created the city and the cultural factors that set many of our personal priorities.

Adequate Housing: Who Has It?

To define housing as either "adequate" or "substandard" is, of course, somewhat arbitrary. It is also culturally variable, because even the worst housing in the United States is of far better quality than that which exists in much of the developing world (see Chapter 13).

Still, we can all agree that housing characterized by structural defects; inadequate plumbing, heating, or sanitation; or lead paint that can be easily ingested by children poses a threat to the health and safety of those who live there. Millions of people do live in such substandard housing, and most of them live in our cities. Because most North Americans never have any direct experience with such housing, we might well be shaken if we were to confront the daily reality of the worst-housed members of our society.

Not surprisingly, the worst housing is concentrated in areas occupied by the poor and minorities who are subject to discrimination—in short, the people with the fewest social choices. Further limiting such people's options are changes in the housing market itself: a steady decline in available, low-rent housing units and a corresponding increase in higher-rent housing units. Reduced government funding for low-income housing, urban renewal, and gentrification have lowered the number of available units even as demand has risen. One unintended consequence was a worsening of homelessness in cities.

Housing Problems: A Brief History

Current housing problems have their roots in the past. Many of the older cities' tenements are nineteenth-century structures in which housing conditions were far worse than they are today despite their greater age. In an examination of conditions in New York in 1870, James D. McCabe, Jr., recorded the following impressions:

> But what shall we say of those who pass their lives in the cellars of [these] wretched buildings . . . ?
> [Most] have but one entrance and that furnishes the only means of ventilation . . . and . . . the filth of the streets comes washing down the walls into the room within. The air is always foul. The drains of the houses above pass within a few feet of the floor, and as they are generally in bad condition the filth frequently comes oozing up and poisons the air with its foul odors.

. . . The poor wretches who seek shelter here are half stupefied by it, and pass the night in this condition instead of in a healthful sleep. (1970:405, 406, 409; orig. 1872)

Despite such horrors, government leaders for generations made little effort to regulate housing. For their part, private builders, concerned mainly with profits, did little on their own. Indeed, only the collapse of the U.S. economy in the 1930s forced the government to enact a housing program—part of President Franklin Roosevelt's "New Deal."

A New Deal. Under the Roosevelt administration, the federal government became more involved in everyday life than ever before. Officials argued, first, that inadequate housing was so widespread it amounted to a serious social problem and, second, that only governmental intervention was likely to lead to a solution.

Under the New Deal, federal housing programs had four specific goals. First, government directed federal funds to encourage the construction of new housing. Second, because some 500,000 families had lost their homes because of an inability to pay their mortgage debts (not unlike the current housing crisis), agencies offered assistance to homeowners faced with foreclosure. Third, the Federal Housing Administration (FHA) guaranteed construction loans to increase the housing supply. Fourth, the Public Works Administration, begun in 1938, hired unemployed people to build low-rent public housing in 30 U.S. cities.

Taken together, these programs rapidly improved urban housing. The 1940 housing census, however, revealed that about 40 percent of urban housing in the United States still had at least some serious defect, such as a lack of running water or other inadequate plumbing.

Postwar Programs. All housing construction, public and private, slowed for the duration of World War II. Soon afterward, however, a major housing shortage loomed as military personnel returned home, started families, and launched the "baby boom." This shortage, along with the continued need to improve the overall quality of housing, led the government to devise several new strategies.

One was a broadening of federal mortgage guarantees through the FHA and the Veterans Administration (VA). The latter agency, created under the Servicemen's Readjustment Act of 1944, popularly known as the GI Bill of Rights, provided federally backed loans to military personnel and veterans. These programs greatly enhanced the home-buying ability of moderate-income families. Another major initiative, the Housing Act of 1949, initiated the suburban boom that followed. Its encouragement of new housing and home ownership outside the city relieved the urban population pressure but did little to improve the cities' housing stock.

Another component of the Housing Act of 1949 was **urban renewal,** which provided federal financing for slum clearance and the building of huge public housing projects. It rested on the principle of **eminent domain** that, in recent years, has become highly controversial in its wider application, as discussed in Chapter 7. City governments seized decaying areas, then sold the properties to private developers who would demolish old buildings and build new ones. Of course, developers sought *profitable* redevelopment, so little of the new construction was affordable to the low-income residents who had previously occupied the neighborhood. Most often, urban renewal projects created new housing for the middle class. A classic example is Boston's once-thriving Italian West End. Declaring it in need of renewal in 1953—despite the fact that the outwardly aging buildings were, on the inside, extremely well kept by residents—the city bought up the area between 1958 and 1960, evicted its residents, and let the developers have a go at renewal. The personal trauma of such displacement was often enormous. Said one evicted West Ender,

> I wish the world would end tonight. . . . I wish they'd tear the whole damn town down ... damn scab town . . . I'm going to be lost without the West End. Where the hell can I go? (Gans 1982:331)

What was built in the "new" West End were high-rise, luxury apartments beyond the reach of virtually all of the area's earlier residents. With this pattern repeating itself in many cities throughout the 1960s, critics often charged that urban renewal meant "poor or Negro removal." Many of the displaced poor had no choice but to crowd into other low-grade housing that they could afford, and the resultant overcrowding only hastened the decay of those buildings. Thus, ironically, "slum clearance" actually created more slums.

Urban renewal often made the housing crisis worse in another way: Many redevelopers did not build as many housing units as had been destroyed. A classic example is the demolition of 18 square blocks of slums (7,000 low-income apartments) in New York City to build Lincoln Center for the Performing Arts along with 4,400 new apartments, 4,000 of them luxury apartments (Caro 1975: 1013–14).

Public Housing

Public housing has never been that successful in the United States. Our cultural orientation has long viewed private home ownership as the foundation of a virtuous life and a stable social order (Bellush 2000). Therefore, people tend to judge those living in publicly supported rental housing as somehow deficient. Factor in the reality that public housing is almost exclusively the preserve of poor minorities, and we understand the stigma that is attached to housing projects. Instantly, they become ghettos, places to avoid, out-of-the-way reservations designed to contain an "unwanted" segment of society.

Originally conceived as incorporating exciting housing innovations, too many of these high-rise projects turned into unmitigated human disasters, plagued by crime, low income, overcrowding, and terrible sanitary conditions. Even poor people soon looked on them as residences of last resort. People in almost every major city can tell of such a high-rise housing project nightmare. One of the most infamous is St. Louis's Pruitt-Igoe project, described in the *Cityscape* box on page 335. Some later housing projects—notably Philadelphia's Society Hill—overcame the

mistakes of these first programs. Still, the failures far outnumber the successes.

Exactly why life in public housing is often so bad is a matter of strong disagreement. Urban critics such as Edward Banfield (1990) suggest that residents themselves are largely to blame, because many do not work, have children they cannot afford, and generally act in irresponsible ways. Architectural critics (as we'll discuss shortly) point to the design of such structures, condemning high-rise buildings as anonymous spaces vulnerable to crime and vandalism (Newman 1996). Others, such as Lee Rainwater (2006), point to the pathologies of concentrated poverty—not to the people themselves—as the fundamental cause of public housing's rather dismal record.

Different Approaches.   In the climate of criticism and social reform that characterized the late 1960s, the federal government renewed efforts to ensure a "decent home for every American," the elusive goal first put forth in 1937 and then reaffirmed in 1949. The Housing Act of 1968 attempted to place home ownership within reach of more families through loan guarantees and direct subsidies. The basic plan was laudable: Low-income families would pay only 20 percent of their income toward the home, and the government would pick up the rest. Often, however, purchasers ended up with an overpriced house in need of extensive repairs that they could not afford. The result was foreclosure, leaving the "owners" back on the street and the government saddled with 100,000 undesirable houses.

By the early 1970s, the handwriting was on the wall, and the program was cut back. By 1975, more than $4 billion had been spent, and as mentioned, the government was saddled with 100,000 bad houses. "With hindsight," Robert Green concluded, "it can safely be said that private concerns [investors, developers, banks] were given too much rope, and with it, they hung the poor" (1977:181).

An alternative approach, begun in 1974 and still active, is the Section 8 Program, which provides rent subsidies to low-income

CITYSCAPE

Pruitt-Igoe: Symbol of a Failed National Solution

It sounded so promising in 1951—a public housing project designed to improve the lives of thousands in a badly run-down area of East St. Louis. Taking advantage of the Housing Act of 1949, local officials sought to break through the "collar of slums which [was] threatening to strangle [the] downtown business section" (*Architectural Forum* 1951:129, quoted in Fogelson 2003:344).

Three years later, residents fully occupied the 2,762 apartments in 33 innovative high-rise buildings. By 1959, however, Pruitt-Igoe "had become a community scandal" (Rainwater 2006:8; orig. 1970). Crime, dirt, and accidents were rampant; the project became "a concrete shell where anarchy prevailed" (Green 1977:179). Essentially a concentration of poor, welfare-dependent African American families (57 percent were female-headed households with children), Pruitt-Igoe's population declined as more and more residents could not bear to remain. The history of Pruitt-Igoe came to a dramatic close in 1972, when the St. Louis Housing Authority dynamited the buildings into oblivion. Soon, high-rise housing projects would meet the same fate in other U.S. cities as well.

Since the dynamiting of Pruitt-Igoe in 1972, a similar fate befell other high-rise public housing as city governments attempted to correct past mistakes (not considering social as well as physical factors) with low-rise replacements. This photo shows the implosion of one of three remaining 13-story buildings of the Scudder Homes complex in Newark, New Jersey, in 1996.

tenants in private housing. This assistance program enables tenants to choose where to live instead of forcing them into a public housing project. The program offers subsidies to developers to build or rehabilitate rental housing. Developers then set aside a certain portion of the units for low-income families and—in a subsidy contract with the government—receive 30 percent of the rent from the tenant and the rest from the government. Although Section 8 and other rental assistance programs have increased the stock of low-cost rental housing, the program is severely underfunded. Waiting lists can run into the years, and many local housing authorities frequently close their waiting lists and stop accepting applications because their lists are too long.

Evaluation. Even this brief history makes clear that federally supervised urban housing programs fell well short of their lofty goals. Some specific problems are worth highlighting.

First, because of the deep involvement of private banking and construction industries in renewal programs, for many, profit overshadowed any sense of social responsibility to help the poor. Furthermore, the design of some redevelopment projects was intended for more affluent buyers, at prices out of the reach of those who originally lived there. The original intention of urban housing programs of the 1930s—to improve the housing of the poor—changed into a large-scale program to redevelop the central city in order to restore its economic health. The result was a reduction in the total amount of low-cost housing across urban North America.

A second problem is that given the tendency of investors and developers to pursue profit rather than assist the poor, local residents had little voice in the decision-making process. Herbert Gans studied the redevelopment of Boston's West End, claiming that local residents were unorganized and lacked understanding of the programs that seemed to "attack" them. Thus, for many, renewal was a bitter experience.

A similar fate befell the residents of Poletown, a mostly ethnic but racially integrated, 465-acre neighborhood in Detroit that contained more than 1,300 homes and apartments, 143 businesses, 16 churches, two schools, and a hospital. In 1981, anxious to keep a new General Motors plant and 6,000 jobs in the city, municipal leaders exercised their right of eminent domain to take over Poletown, razed it (at a cost exceeding $200 million), and sold the land to GM (for $8 million) as the location for its new plant. Residents—joined by consumer advocate Ralph Nader and Gray Panthers leader Maggie Kuhn—futilely tried to stop the forced uprooting and destruction of their homes, churches, and businesses. To this day, much bitterness remains among those displaced residents.

Third, Gans and other critics, such as Jane Jacobs, have argued that redevelopers didn't even try to understand that many areas subject to redevelopment were actually healthy, safe neighborhoods. In effect, many development programs reflected the bias of middle-class planners against the lifestyle of low-rent areas. Somehow, such areas just weren't what the planners considered to be "normal."

> Reformers [who] have long observed city people loitering on busy corners, hanging around in candy stores and bars and drinking soda pop on stoops . . . have passed a [class-biased] judgment, the gist of which is: "This is deplorable! If these people had decent homes and a more private . . . outdoor place, they wouldn't be on the street!" [Such a judgment] makes no more sense than to drop in at a testimonial banquet in a hotel and conclude that if these people . . . could cook, they would give their parties at home. (Jacobs 1993:55; orig. 1961)

At present, we find some promise for public housing, even with budget cutbacks. We will discuss the bright spots in both public and private housing shortly. First, though, we will discuss housing troubles in the private sector that also plague the cities.

Deterioration and Abandonment in the Inner City

Beginning in the 1950s, because of outward migration, the decline of manufacturing, and economic globalization, the older central cities fell on hard times. Inner-city neighborhoods lost population and deteriorated sharply, in some cases falling victim to extensive vandalism and arson. Many of the older, industrial inner cities of the Midwest and Northeast soon contained block after block of empty, dilapidated buildings, many burned, as if the area had collapsed under a full-scale bomb attack. These cities contained as many as 2 million abandoned buildings, making them look like urban "ghost towns," with 150,000 additional abandonments yearly well into the 1980s.

During the 1990s, these numbers dropped considerably, thanks to the economic revitalization in many cities and the gentrification process. Still, a recent study revealed a total of 185,000 abandoned residential units in 19 cities with a population of more than 100,000, or an average of 10,000 per city. Detroit had 45,000 abandoned buildings, Philadelphia 27,000, and St. Louis 13,000 (Mallach 2006:4).

Why would people simply walk away from otherwise usable buildings in cities where housing was in short supply? The answer is a complex, vicious circle of decline. Faced with the mounting expenses of taxes, insurance, heating fuel, and repairs because of vandalism, not to mention the loss to the suburbs of middle-income renters, and often constrained by rent control caps, some building owners reduce, or entirely eliminate, routine maintenance and repairs in an effort to retain some profit. Angered tenants often withhold rent, which, in turn, encourages owners to withhold more services in order to obtain rents. If the building eventually represents more costs or trouble than rental income warrants, some owners simply default on their mortgages or cut off the utilities. In some cases, buildings are deliberately "torched" in an effort to secure payment of insurance claims. As desperate ex-tenants scatter in search of other housing, vandals and looters seek whatever of value remains (including sinks, bathtubs, and plumbing). First the building, then the block, and eventually the whole neighborhood succumbs

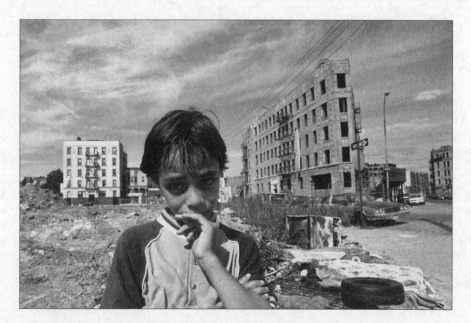

The South Bronx in the 1980s looked like a war zone, and its violent crime rate made it feel like one. Arson and abandonment led to the loss of 30,000 buildings in the 1970s, leading to a desolate environment for both children and adults. By the mid-1990s, however, urban homesteading and gentrification programs had transformed this area into a safe, pleasant place to live and raise children.

to the process. In the end, just hollow buildings remain: giant headstones marking the grave of a now-dead urban neighborhood.

Other developments in the private sector are more encouraging. During recent years, housing in major cities has vastly improved. Although much more needs to be done, notable progress is clearly evident, as we shall now explain.

The Inner City Today: A Revival?

> When a city begins to grow and spread outward from the edges, the center which was once its glory . . . goes into a period of desolation, inhabited at night by the vague ruins of men . . . . Nearly every city I know has such a dying mother of violence and despair where at night the brightness of the street lamps is sucked away and policemen walk in pairs. And then one day perhaps the city returns and rips out the sore and builds a monument to its past.
>
> John Steinbeck,
> *Travels with Charley*

Although the success of public programs has surely been limited, efforts by private groups to rebuild certain inner-city areas have achieved significant results in recent decades. Two trends deserve attention: urban homesteading and gentrification.

Urban Homesteading. In 1973, burdened with some 1,200 abandoned homes, the city of Wilmington, Delaware, revived the mid-nineteenth-century Homestead Act that gave away land and mules to pioneers if they built on vacant land in the West and lived on it for five years. The city offered buildings it acquired through default of tax payments for a token fee of a few hundred dollars to people who agreed to rehabilitate them and stay there for a minimum of three years. Wilmington's success in restoring tax ratable properties encouraged many other cities to initiate their own homesteading programs, often transferring houses to people at the top of long waiting lists for Section 8 rental housing who were willing to become "urban homesteaders"—pioneers in rebuilding an urban area.

In New York's ravaged South Bronx, where more than 30,000 buildings were abandoned in the 1970s (an average of eight a day), local citizens' groups such as the People's Development Corporation stood up against seemingly impossible odds to return deteriorating inner-city buildings to life. With little capital to invest, such groups could rely only on their own physical efforts; their collateral was not future earnings or other property but, rather, their own sweat, giving rise to the term *sweat equity*. The *Cityscape* box on page 340, which tells the story of Ramon Rueda, captures some of the 1970s spirit that inspired people to accept the challenge of building something out of almost nothing.

Ramon Rueda is just one of the thousands who reclaimed the South Bronx. Nonetheless, urban homesteading has had only limited success, because too many abandoned homes have deteriorated and been vandalized beyond rehabilitation. Others stand amid so much ruin and desolation that they are not worth salvaging. Furthermore, both the cost of repairing the building to meet occupancy code standards and the difficulty of getting rehabilitation loans eliminates most of the urban poor from participating in urban homesteading.

Demand far outstrips supply, however. A few years ago, for example, more than 2,000 people lined up in Washington, D.C., to participate in a housing lottery for 68 boarded-up buildings that were offered at a price of $250 each and a pledge to bring them up to housing code standards and live in them for five years. The mostly three- and four-bedroom houses and a few small apartment buildings had been vacant for more than a decade, with the exception of occasional visits by drug dealers, prostitutes, and the homeless. Now, they are part of the city's good housing stock (Fleishman 1999).

Another form of urban homesteading requiring the sweat equity of incoming homeowners, but overcoming some of the obstacles just mentioned, is Habitat for Humanity. Habitat is a non-profit organization that utilizes volunteer labor and some donated materials from area churches and organizations to

Habitat for Humanity is a non-profit organization that builds new, low-income family housing. It has built more than 125,000 homes around the world to date through church fundraising, volunteer labor, and donated materials, including this effort for Katrina victims. How do urban homesteading projects, such as Habitat for Humanity and gentrification, offer alternative solutions to problems of urban housing?

build new housing for low-income families. Those screened to become homeowners pay interest-free, low-mortgage loans and must work along with the volunteers to build their house. Since its founding in 1976, Habitat has built more than 30,000 houses across the United States, most in areas of massive urban blight, ultimately transforming many places into attractive, stable neighborhoods. The organization now has over 1,500 local affiliates in all 50 states, plus another 550 active affiliates in nearly 90 countries, where it has built more than 250,000 homes (Habitat for Humanity 2008).

Gentrification. Unlike urban homesteading, which is limited to the reclamation of just a few buildings or blocks at a time, gentrification is a broader process. The word **gentrification,** which was coined by the wealthy "landed gentry" during the nineteenth century to describe the renovation of run-down London homes, today refers to the movement of more affluent North Americans back into older, often decaying areas in the city. Virtually every major city in Canada and the United States is experiencing this spreading urban renaissance, following a path taken by Paris and London years earlier.

Today's gentry, like those of the past, are a rather select group of people. They are usually the cosmopolites or unmarried and childless groups discussed in Chapter 5. Or, to put it another way, they are frequently the "yuppies" we spoke of at the end of Chapter 3. More to the point, they are people with enough money to buy a brownstone in Manhattan; a Society Hill townhouse in Philadelphia; a brick cottage in the German Village of Columbus, Ohio; or a Victorian house in San Francisco's Haight–Ashbury district or in Toronto's South Parkdale. Sometimes, however, working-class neighborhoods undergo gentrification while retaining their socioeconomic group identity, as in several of Baltimore's row-house districts.

CITYSCAPE

Sweat Equity in the South Bronx

Ramon Rueda, a Puerto Rican from the South Bronx, is certainly familiar with tenements. Yet the one at 1186 Washington Avenue is very special to him. In 1976, this was just one of many abandoned buildings with no heat or water, where a few squatters camped. At age 26 and with some friends, he formed an organization known as the People's Development Corporation (PDC), and they bought this building for one dollar from the city, which had seized it for tax arrears.

Then, with no financial assistance, they worked—in the extremes of climate—at the somewhat dangerous demolition of a structure suffering from several decades of abuse and neglect. First, they cleaned and gutted the rotting six-story structure. This was a daunting task, as rubble, rats, excrement, and dead animals seemed everywhere. Worst of all was the basement with its knee-deep mud, unbelievable kinds of refuse, and fleas that embedded themselves in the workers' hair and clothing.

Slowly they restored the structure, including all the necessary plumbing, wiring, and carpentry. The work was time-consuming and difficult, but the group had an evident sense of spirit driving them on. They had a dream of creating a self-sufficient community with enough businesses, services, and jobs to keep money circulating in the neighborhood.

Sweat equity is not likely to become popular with people who have the money to buy a fashionable home, but it is one option for the poor who have the skills and strength to undertake such a monumental task. In some of the poorest neighborhoods of many cities, people like Ramon try to turn housing that is all but falling down into livable homes for themselves and other local residents. The benefits of sweat equity are very real—this one building became 28 apartments—but, just as important, a project of this kind brings neighborhood residents together with a sense of common purpose.

Urban homesteading projects are still quite rare and hardly likely to eliminate the massive housing problem in the United States. Yet people like Ramon are optimistic that they can make a real change in at least a small piece of their city. He went into the construction business and one of his next projects was a total rehabilitation of seven handsome if dilapidated turn-of-the-century brownstones on Forest Avenue north of 166th Street in the same neighborhood. Today he is project supervisor of a large low-income housing complex under construction near Yankee Stadium.

Source: Adapted from Roger M. Williams, "The New Urban Pioneers: Homesteading in the Slums," *Saturday Review,* July 23, 1977, pp. 9–14; Alan S. Oser, "Unusual Rehabilitation in the South Bronx," *New York Times* (December 9, 1983), p. A31; Amy Waldman, "Housing Radical Meets Bottom Line; In the Rebuilt South Bronx, a Pioneer of Sweat Equity Fights to Keep His Ideals," *New York Times* (January 18, 2000), p. B1.

Why, though, would middle-class people *choose* central-city neighborhoods when the trend for the last century has been to escape to the suburbs? The reasons vary, but certainly, many find that the central city still has the greatest amount of variety and stimulation. Theaters, music, and chic stores—all flourish in the greatest concentrations downtown. Second, as we noted in Chapter 7, economic restructuring increased the number of administrative and professional jobs available in central cities. The well-paid "gentry" taking these jobs need a place to live, and central-city living eases the time and costs of getting to work. Third, as more women enter the work force (70 percent of women worked for pay in 2006) and two-career couples become common (60 percent of all married couples in 2005), the time needed to maintain a single-family suburban house often makes it too burdensome (U.S. Census Bureau 2008a). Fourth, suburban housing is expensive, and while some central-city housing is extremely costly (brownstones in Manhattan often top $3 million), one can still find bargains, particularly in districts where the average income is low. Fifth, and finally, remember that much central-city housing built from about 1880 to 1910 (except tenements) has a level of craftsmanship and quality—with details like solid oak floors and stained-glass windows—rarely found in today's suburbs.

Political economy theorists see gentrification as a logical outflow of investment capital. Beginning in the 1950s, investment capital moved out of the cities and into the suburbs, where profit rates were higher. Later, with the emergence of a "rent gap" (profits above costs) in the inner city, capital returned in order to make greater profits there, as low-valued property rose in value (Zipp and Cook 1999). This return to the inner city certainly contradicts the predictions of an ever-outward migration of the affluent made by Ernest W. Burgess in the 1920s (Chapter 6).

The New Urbanism

Perhaps the best-known critique of public housing came from Jane Jacobs in *The Death and Life of Great American Cities* (1993; orig. 1961), a still-influential book on urban form and function. Critical of conventional planners, Jacobs wrote:

> One of the unsuitable ideas behind projects is the very notion that they are projects, abstracted out of the ordinary city and set apart. To think of salvaging or improving projects, as projects, is to repeat this root mistake. The aim should be to get that project, that patch upon the city, rewoven back into the fabric—and in the process of doing so, strengthen the surrounding fabric also. (1993:392)

One of the most encouraging developments in restoring the vitality of older cities has been an approach in urban design called the **New Urbanism,** which includes sociological principles in physical planning (see the *Urban Trends* box on page 342). Initially a response to the perceived lack of community in sprawling suburbs, the New Urbanism caused a rethinking of the entire city. Some of the principles of the New Urbanism are walkability, connectivity, mixed use and diversity, mixed housing types, and a traditional neighborhood structure with public space at the center. Today, in both central cities and suburbs, the goal is creating spaces that encourage people to socialize and watch out for each other.

Seaside, Florida, offers one example. Built during the mid-1980s in Florida's Panhandle, this planned community has codes mandating that houses have front porches close to the sidewalk so that residents sitting outside can converse easily with pedestrians. The town boasts corner stores that serve a function more important than simply providing provisions. They are places where friends frequently come to chat with one another over a cup of coffee.

Far more impressive is what architects and planners influenced by the New Urbanism are accomplishing in old, urban, problem-infested neighborhoods.

Columbia Point/Harbor Point.   In Boston, a government-funded housing project known as Columbia Point—built in 1953 on a small, swampy peninsula near the first suburbs of Dorchester and Roxbury—long stood as evidence for the insensitivity of urban planners. There, a full mile from the closest subway stop, architects originally laid out 28 bland, institutional-style buildings three and seven stories high. And the surrounding water and lack of roads isolated residents even more. With few stores in the area, shopping became a major effort, both more expensive and more time-consuming than for other city residents nearer the mainstream of Boston life.

Eventually, the 1,502-unit development fell victim to the same problems that plagued public housing nationwide. By the 1970s, crime was so rampant in Columbia Point that even ambulances refused to enter the project without a police escort. By 1984, only 350 families wanted to stay on when, encouraged by the U.S. Office of Housing and Urban Development, the Boston Housing Authority leased the land for 99 years at $1 a year to a partnership of the remaining tenants and a private developer. Architects for the project decided to redesign Columbia Point, modeling it after some of Boston's active, thriving neighborhoods. Also influencing their design was the New Urbanism idea that cities are enriched

by the creation of a "public realm" that highlights amenities such as waterfront views. Architects thus set down a new street pattern so that all residents would have a view of both the harbor and the Boston skyline.

Reopened in 1990, what is now called Harbor Point is a mixed-income complex that appeals to people from all ethnic backgrounds and social classes, which ensures the diversity and stability of this revitalized community (Roessner 2000). Housing is now a mixture, with two-thirds market-rate apartments and one-third low-income housing, but with no

---

URBAN TRENDS

Defining New Urbanism

The recent movement known as "New Urbanism" is attempting to reconcile competing ideas about urbanism that have been evolving in America for over a century. New Urbanism, an urban reform movement that gained prominence in the 1990s, seeks to promote qualities that urban reformers have always sought: vital, beautiful, just, environmentally benign human settlements. The significance of New Urbanism is that it is a combination of these past efforts: the culmination of a long, multifaceted attempt to define what urbanism in America should be. This revelation only comes to light in view of the history that preceded it. . . .

What has gradually evolved in the American experience are different approaches to creating good urbanism in America. Some have focused on small-scale, incremental urban improvement, like the provision of neighbourhood parks and playgrounds. Some have had larger-scale visions, drawing up grand plans and advocating for new systems of transportation and arrangements of land use. Others have looked outside the

existing city, focusing on how to build the optimal, new human habitat. And some have emphasized that urbanism should be primarily about how the human settlement relates to "nature." Multiple meanings of urbanism have, for over a century, been forming in the minds of American planners, architects, sociologists, and others who have endeavored to define in specific terms what urbanism in America is or should be. . . .

To bring these ideals together within one framework—as the New Urbanists are attempting—it is important to recognize that there are essential principles that are recurrent and embedded in the historical American consciousness. In other words, while urbanism in America involves multiple concepts, it is not "anything under the Sun."' There is a recurrent normative content, and the interrelated history of ideas about what the best possible human settlement in America should be reveals this. . . . [T]hese recurrent principles consist of, for example, diversity, equity, community, connectivity, and the importance of civic and public space.

Source: Emily Talen, *New Urbanism and American Planning: The Conflict of Cultures.* Copyright © 2005 by Routledge. Reprinted with permission.

The new urbanism design of Harbor Point, which replaced Columbia Point, was based on thriving Boston neighborhoods, such as Back Bay. Mixed building types are set close together along narrow streets canted at a 45-degree angle to the water's edge, which opens views of the harbor and Boston skyline to all residents.

physical distinctions between the two types of apartment buildings. Moreover, architects designed a variety of building types: blue and gray townhouses with wood clapboard siding as well as red and brown brick apartment houses. They kept 10 of old Columbia Point's flat-topped residential buildings, but new peaked roofs, decoration, and a reddish stain made them indistinguishable from the new buildings. To free Harbor Point completely from the stigma of public housing, they added other visual subtleties, such as rounded and pointed rooftop gables. Still other amenities were added, including a health club, swimming pool, tennis courts, and ample parking.

Along the harbor, where thieves used to dump stolen cars, is a six-acre landscaped park where a visitor hears not gunshots but screeching seagulls and water coursing over rocks. Slicing through the center of the complex is a 1,000-foot by 199-foot grassy mall with old-fashioned street lamps, benches and tennis courts patterned after Boston's Commonwealth Avenue. . . .

Narrow by design, the streets are tightly framed on each side by apartment buildings and townhouses in contrast to the open spaces and freely placed structures of tower-in-the-park urbanism. Front doors face the streets. Most apartment windows look directly at the streets. The arrangement eliminates unsupervised pockets of dead space where drug dealing and other illicit activities can occur. (Kamin 1995)

Fully leased, Harbor Point is now among Boston's safest neighborhoods. Yet some wonder whether this safety is the result of a security fence and a guard station at the main vehicular entrance to keep away outsiders. In short, Harbor Point seems to work, but is it "rewoven back into the [city's] fabric," as Jacobs urged? Critics claim that it remains physically isolated from the rest of Boston.

Today . . . Harbor Point seems too much like a world apart, a residential complex that has adopted the forms of the city without the functions, like corner bars, that fill neighborhoods with life. Harbor Point, in short, has mixed incomes but not the mixed uses that make cities hum. Its architecture, while free of cloying post-modernism, still has the contrived variety of a planned community. (Kamin 1995)

Hopefully, someday soon, greater linkage will occur. Still, many consider Harbor Point to be a success model of urban revitalization. It stands as a successful alternative to an urban nightmare and offers vivid testimony to the extraordinary transformations that the New Urbanism can achieve.

Water as an Amenity.   Just as Harbor Point's architects redesigned its grid to enable all residents to enjoy the view of surrounding water, so, too, has the New Urbanism enabled many cities to rediscover the aesthetics and possibilities for social use of public space at water's edge (Whyte 2001; orig. 1980). Baltimore's Inner Harbor and New York's South Street Seaport are thriving, rebuilt areas enjoyed by tourists and natives alike. Chicago, Cleveland, Cincinnati, Louisville, and many other cities have converted decaying piers and waterfront properties into park areas and mixed-use sites. San Antonio converted what was essentially a narrow and dirty drainage canal into the charming, 2.5-mile cobblestone River Walk—with lush green lawns, flowering shrubs and trees, and a view of paddleboats—where one delights in many interesting shops, restaurants, and night clubs. Here and at many other renovated water's-edge locales, cities have successfully merged social and commercial activities into a vibrant urban atmosphere.

Replacing High Rises.   As Harbor Point demonstrates, the New Urbanism is transforming public housing as the "superblocks" of giant high rises come down, replaced by modest townhouses and low rises that don't "look like projects."

Imagine leveling whole blocks of decaying, crime-ridden slums in one great sweep, and building in their stead modern apartments with plenty of light and fresh air and high-rise views. Think about replacing crowded streets and decrepit playgrounds with paths for pedestrians and bicycles, winding between wide lawns. (Adler and Malone 1996:70)

Many cities are addressing the failure of high-rise public housing by blowing up the buildings. Scudder Homes, seven high rises built in 1963 in Newark, New Jersey, to house 1,800 low-income families, are now gone, replaced by 150 single-family townhouses. In place of the 1,206 units in that city's seven hulking, 13-story Stella Wright homes are townhouses for low- and moderate-income residents. In Atlanta, a developer demolished more than 1,000 housing units in Techwood Homes—the first U.S. public housing project, completed in 1935—in order to build a mixed-income "village," with new stores, community facilities, schools, and apartments. Today, this once predominantly black enclave has been transformed into Centennial Place, a residential complex of 900 units that is host to a variety of races, ethnicities, and income levels.

In Chicago, the Housing Authority has been demolishing the Cabrini-Green high-rise project buildings and redeveloping its 65 acres through construction of 2,000 units of new, low-rise housing units; a new Town Center; a 145,000-square-foot shopping center; new schools; an East Chicago District police headquarters; and a library. Half the housing units are sold at market prices, with another 20 percent reserved as "affordable" units for less-affluent working families. Some of the original low-income tenants living at Cabrini-Green remain in the new housing units, thereby creating a mixed-income site similar to Harbor Point and totally unlike the all-low-income site that Cabrini-Green once was. Some old buildings still remain, though, awaiting either demolition or rehabilitation, and life in that part of the projects remains hellish (Saulny 2007; Gallun 2005). The designs of all three developments—in Newark, Atlanta, and Chicago—use grid patterns linking them to the surrounding neighborhoods rather than setting them apart, minding Jacobs's recommendation that housing projects be rewoven into the urban fabric.

These rebuilding programs seek to achieve two key goals of the New Urbanism. First, don't isolate the poor by themselves. Instead, create a mixed-income housing complex to integrate all strata of society. Second, create an environment that is physically attractive and facilitates walking and social interaction, fostering a sense of control and community among residents.

Limitations. As promising as the New Urbanism may be, three major problems prevent it from having a broader impact. First, in every case noted, there are now fewer low-income housing units than before. As with post–World War II urban renewal, displacement of the poor has also occurred in these redevelopment projects. Of course, one might argue that at least some poor people are better off living in safer and more vibrant communities, but what of the rest of those who have been displaced?

Second, weaving a housing project into the surrounding area is enormously difficult in the midst of extensive, nightmarish ghettos. If little more than empty lots or bombed-out buildings are nearby, for example, reorganizing a public housing project as an inward-facing enclave may be the only strategy, at least in the short run.

Finally, even at its best, the New Urbanism cannot, by itself, address the extensive poverty that makes public housing such a problem in the first place. For instance, in San Francisco, the Robert Pitts Plaza development project replaced a notorious, dangerous high-rise called Yerba Buena Plaza West. The new, 203-apartment, neo-Victorian complex in no way looks like a public housing development. Its architecture blends in with neighboring apartment buildings and includes projecting cornices and pastel shades of blue—a far cry from the high-rise "boxes" so common in public housing. Completed in 1991, it contained other amenities, such as an internal rectangular courtyard with lush sod, bushes, and neat lines of trees and also a colorful play set for children in a sand playground.

Three years later, though, broken glass lay everywhere. Gone were the sod and sprinkler heads; gone, too, were the bushes and plants, ripped out by vandals. Profane graffiti covered concrete seating ledges. Bars shielded ground-floor windows following a rash of burglaries suspected to have been committed by residents. Wire mesh covered many other windows, suggesting an escalating sense of fear. The problem was poverty, and all that went with it.

A Comparison. Fortunately, the situation at Robert Pitts Plaza improved once this building complex became part of a larger, 19-block redevelopment area of Yerba Buena and a successful mixture of a wide variety of housing, cultural facilities, and open space. The lesson to be learned here is that new architecture, and even new planning strategies, such as the New Urbanism, don't work if they have limited application. Robert Pitts Plaza reveals that simply replacing high-rise buildings with low-rise buildings, even if those buildings are wonderfully designed, is not enough. A more comprehensive approach is necessary. Harbor Point is a good example for at least the beginnings of connecting low-income housing to its surroundings—through a return to traditional urban forms that promote interaction *and* a mix of income groups to eliminate public housing's isolation. In short, any successful approach to improving urban life must take account of not only local planning considerations but also broader, structural concerns that include social stratification and the region's economy.

EDUCATION: THE URBAN CHALLENGE

Schools in urban settings face a variety of challenges, which are often more daunting than school districts elsewhere face. These difficulties include overcrowded schools, discipline and violence, high dropout rates, and issues of quality education and student learning outcomes. Moreover, many of these schools since the 1990s have become resegregated, heavily filled with African and Hispanic American students, reversing an earlier trend of desegregation (Orfield 2001). Cities also attract large numbers of immigrant families and children with limited English proficiency and a greater concentration of low-income families that, together with a weaker tax revenue base than most suburbs enjoy, place a heavy burden on urban schools to educate, fully and effectively, the students they serve.

Meeting the "No Child Left Behind" Challenge

The controversial No Child Left Behind Act of 2001 dramatically increased the role of the federal government in guaranteeing the quality of public education for all children. Its main provisions are increased funding for poor school districts, higher achievement standards for minority and poor students, and new measures to hold schools accountable for their students' progress. Significantly, it requires the annual administration of standardized tests in reading and math to all students in grades 3 through 8, with the results publicly reported according to income level, race, ethnicity, disability, and limited English proficiency. These results are then compared to an independent benchmark called the National Assessment of Educational Progress (NAEP).

Learning Outcomes.   Before this legislation, most urban schools had a policy of **social promotions**—that is, moving children through grades with their age peers regardless of their actual learning achievement. Whatever merit this practice had, it led to a watering-down of course content because of the gradual but steady lowering of general class ability. As a result, it produced graduates deluded into thinking they had received an education when, in reality, many of them lacked even basic skills, requiring colleges to institute non-credit, basic skills courses for freshmen. No more. Published test results will identify schools in which students are not doing well on the tests. Those schools that fall behind may be subject to various "school improvement," "corrective action," or "restructuring" measures imposed by the state.

Of particular concern are the significant differences in scores on standardized achievement tests between urban and suburban students. One of the most common arguments advanced for these different outcomes is the role of social class in providing an advantage

(for middle-class suburban students) or a disadvantage (for low-income urban students). Researchers such as anthropologist John Ogbu (2003), however, argue that even black students in affluent suburbs suffer from "academic disengagement," engendered by inappropriate sports and entertainment role models, a lack of parental involvement in their schooling, and a defeatist attitude resulting from a profound distrust of the establishment. Only an approach that reinforces positive study habits, recognizes achievement, and strengthens the students' resolve against attempts by peers to drag them down will overcome this problem (Whittle 2005).

Language Proficiency.   Immigration remains primarily an urban phenomenon, although it affects suburban and rural schools as well as communities, and students' language proficiency plays an important role in academic achievement. More than half of all immigrants now choose to live in just a dozen metropolitan areas: New York; Los Angeles; Miami; Washington, D.C.; Chicago; San Francisco; Houston; Boston; Dallas; Atlanta; Philadelphia; Riverside–San Jose, California (U.S. Office of Immigration Statistics 2008:17). Urban schools in these and other cities, therefore, must accommodate a large influx of immigrant pupils, and it is not unusual for a third or more of a school's population to lack proficiency in English (Zhou 2003). This creates the need for hiring a greater number of bilingual or English-as-a-second-language (ESL) teachers, in addition to teachers of regular subjects. The schools must also deal with other cultural adjustment issues, such as clothing, food, religious observances, role behavior, and parents whose own language and educational deficiencies may limit support for at-home study.

Environment.   Whether immigrant or native-born, many students come from home environments where poverty, family instability, or poor health may limit educational success. Other dangers or obstacles that can work against educators' goals are (1) conflicting values in the student's home or on the street about the importance of education; (2) the lack of positive, academically successful role models; and (3) the presence of gangs, street crime, drugs, and violence. In 2005, a total of 36 percent of urban students and 21 percent of suburban students aged 12 to 18 reported a street gang presence at school, a 14 percent increase from 2003 (U.S. Department of Education 2007a).

Funding. Further undermining academic achievement in many city schools is the lack of funding. Unlike affluent communities, cities lack the tax base to provide adequate per-student expenditures, even with additional state aid. As a result, students in urban schools are more likely to enter older, dilapidated buildings, where they face overcrowded classrooms with limited supplies, poor discipline, insufficient libraries and labs, and often, a shortage of qualified teachers. So far, the additional funding through the No Child Left Behind Act has not been sufficient to overcome the urban–suburban disparity in school funding.

Political Clout. Cities actually have limited control over their affairs, whether in education or in other areas, such as mass transit and poverty. Until the 1970s, cities lacked political power in the rural-dominated state and federal legislatures, despite their higher overall population. By the time the Supreme Court ruled in favor of one-person, one-vote reapportionment to balance legislative district representation, the majority of the population had shifted to the suburbs. Added to the rural–suburban bias against cities is the frequent political split between Democratic-controlled city governments and Republican-controlled state legislatures, further hindering efforts to solve urban problems.

Cities across the country are struggling to meet the federal government's demand to improve their schools. Some modest gains have occurred, but enormous challenges remain. For example, Chicago has been making a concerted effort to improve its educational system since passage of the Chicago School Reform Act in 1988. Notable improvements have occurred since then, yet even now, fewer than half of its high school students graduate (Wacquant 2007:86). Perhaps with continued improvement at the elementary level, as mandated by the No Child Left Behind Act, Chicago and other cities will also see progress at the secondary level. It will take more than wishful thinking, however, to make this a reality.

A deepening dissatisfaction with traditional public schools has engendered several innovations to give parents other options for educating their children, thus providing competition in order to force all schools to do a better job. Three of the most popular programs to improve urban education are magnet schools, school vouchers, and charter schools (see the *Urban Trends* box on page 349).

Magnet Schools

Magnet schools—schools offering special programs to attract students from many districts to achieve integration—began as an alternative to mandatory busing, but their success in raising students' scholastic achievement has gained them even more popularity. They offer special facilities and programs to promote educational excellence in a particular area, such as computer science, foreign languages, science and mathematics, or the arts. Parents can choose the school that is best suited to a particular student's talents and interests, enabling these advanced programs to attract talented students from beyond traditional neighborhood boundaries. This permits magnet schools to overcome residential segregation patterns to create a more diversified student population.

About 20 percent of U.S. students living in or around cities attend one of the nation's more than 5,000 magnet schools. Of these schools, however, about 21 percent are partial-site magnet schools (a mixture of traditional and special programs), resulting in desegregated buildings that have racially segregated classrooms. Critics charge that magnet schools are "elitist" in luring the best students and teachers, thereby relegating the majority of students to the "mediocrity" of ordinary city schools, and that they might even worsen

Magnet schools—such as this one in Schenectady, New York—enable cities to overcome residential segregation patterns by offering special programs and facilities to raise students' scholastic achievement. Despite their success, critics complain that they are expensive, that they have limited appeal, and that their elitism relegates most urban students to "mediocre" schooling.

stratification among schools by family income. Recent research, however, reveals no significance difference in school districts with or without magnet-school choice (Archbald 2004).

School Vouchers

Another option for choice in some school districts is to give parents a **school voucher** equal to the state's share of the cost to educate a child (usually about 90 percent of the average private school's tuition). Parents can then use this voucher to place their child in a public or private school of their choice. The program is limited at present, because there are not enough private-school spaces to meet demand. In such cases, a lottery usually determines who goes to choice schools. A federal voucher program operates in Washington, D.C., and among the cities utilizing their own school voucher plan are Cleveland, Indianapolis, Milwaukee, and Minneapolis. Critics (including teachers' unions) charge that this approach siphons off much-needed public education funding, thus undermining the nation's commitment to public education, and that it does little to improve central-city schools, where the need is greatest (Schemo 2006; Gorman 2003).

Because many of the private schools are church-affiliated, opponents of vouchers charge that this system violates the First Amendment provision concerning the separation of church and state. At the state level, recent court decisions have given mixed signals on this issue. The supreme courts of Arizona, Ohio, and Wisconsin ruled that voucher programs did not violate the state or federal constitution by including religious schools. In contrast, the supreme courts of Florida, Vermont, and Maine ruled against such schools on constitutional grounds. After years of conflicting lower-court opinions about parents in Cleveland using vouchers at private schools, the U.S. Supreme Court ruled in 2002 that they could do so. Experts believe

URBAN TRENDS

The New Urban Schools

On a typical morning, just north of Milwaukee, at the Marva Collins Preparatory School of Wisconsin, 180 students—kindergarten through the fifth grade—neatly dressed in their uniforms, enter an old building and climb three flights of stairs to their school on the top floor. A few miles to the east, next to a busy freeway and across from a clinic for the homeless, the 360 students at Messmer High School file in. In the hallways of this Roman Catholic institution hang portraits of Dr. Martin Luther King, Jr., Abraham Lincoln, and Jesus. Closer to the heart of the city, the 600 students in grades K–5 at the Elm Creative Arts School learn through an arts-driven curriculum. Today, while many are away performing at a concert downtown, a group of fifth graders—divided into small teams—is sprawled out on a classroom floor piecing together colorful math games while big-band music plays on the class stereo.

Welcome to public education, Milwaukee-style. These three schools, scattered throughout the city and featuring vastly different educational settings and philosophies, have one thing in common: public tax dollars.

One is a charter school adopted by the City Council; one is a private, religious school; and one is a magnet school operated by the school district. All three are part of a growing roster of alternatives available in a city that is ground zero for the school choice movement nationwide.

The definition of public schooling in the United States has changed dramatically in recent years, and nowhere is it changing faster than in Milwaukee. The city's long tradition of forward-looking views on government and politics has provided fertile soil for experiments and innovations in its public schools.

Here, in one place, are schools based on ideas that not too long ago were unheard-of in a U.S. school district: students attending religious schools with public money, a private school that has essentially been hired by the district to become a public school for a year, and a city government that has bypassed the local school board to create its own charter schools.

Yet Annette Williams, a Democratic state representative and author of the state's voucher legislation, has concerns. Williams, an African American, says she originally intended the voucher program to help mainly black-run schools and low-income students. But today, she contends, vouchers and charter schools mainly benefit white churches, white-run private schools, and white students. "Affluent folks are going to take it all on as their own," she says. "Yuppies who have choices are going to be the beneficiaries now."

Others fear in Milwaukee the emergence of a dual private and charter school system, one black, one white, and a community whose loyalty to schools is divided along racial and socioeconomic lines. Only time will tell if the alternative school programs are an improvement over traditional efforts or simply another form of racial segregation in the schools.

Source: Adapted from *Education Week* by Kerry A. White. Copyright 1999 by Editorial Projects in Education. Reproduced with permission of Editorial Projects in Education in the format Textbook via Copyright Clearance Center.

this ruling may be as significant as the 1954 *Brown* v. *Board of Education* decision on school desegregation, because it gives the green light nationwide to this program (Brokaw 2002).

Charter Schools

Charter schools are a recent alternative to traditional public schools and, in cities where a voucher plan exists, are a major beneficiary of such payments. Charters are private schools that operate with less state regulation so that teachers and administrators can try out new teaching strategies. Unlike public schools, however, they are held accountable for achieving educational results. If a school fails to meet the terms of its charter with the local school board or the state, the charter can be revoked and the school closed. In essence, then, a charter school receives greater autonomy to operate in return for greater accountability for student performance. Nationwide, charter schools enrolled 1.2 million students in 2006–2007 (Center for Education Reform 2007).

Now authorized in 40 states and the District of Columbia, spaces in charter schools are in high demand, and small class size appears to be a principal reason for this. The average enrollment of charter schools is about half that of traditional public schools. Smaller classes afford teachers the space to be more creative with curriculum and the time to provide more individualized instruction. Whether for the arts- or science-oriented or for the at-risk, these schools provide assistance to students who are otherwise underserved by the public school system (Walberg 2007).

Supporters of charter schools hope that local educators, ministers, parents, community members, school boards, and other sponsors will provide new models of schooling and exert competitive pressures on public schools that will improve the current system of public education. Others, however, fear that charter schools, at best, may be little more than escape valves that relieve pressure for genuine reform of the whole system and, at worst, may add to centrifugal forces that threaten to pull public education apart (Buckley and Schneider 2007).

In fact, some charter schools are no better than their public school counterparts. Critics say that many have weak curricula and teaching, substandard buildings, and a surprising prevalence of financial abuses. Basic classroom supplies are often lacking, labs and libraries are rare, and staff turnover is high among the low-paid, inexperienced teachers. Also, the segregation of many charter schools along ethnic, racial, and religious lines has created

church–state conflicts in conjunction with the voucher controversy (Carnoy et al. 2005).

Originally designed to provide better schooling for minority students, the single biggest group in charter schools is now non-Hispanic whites (42 percent), compared to 31 percent non-Hispanic blacks and 22 percent Hispanics (National Center on Education Statistics 2007).

CRIME: PERCEPTION AND REALITY

The problems of poor housing and poor education affect only part of the urban population. Surveys suggest, however, that almost everyone expresses concern about the extent of crime. Often, people living in outlying areas point to fears about personal safety as the primary reason they chose not to live in the city. And many city people conclude that a higher risk of crime is just part of the price one pays for the advantages of urban living. Are such perceptions correct, however? Is crime worse in the city than elsewhere? Is there more crime in bigger cities than in smaller ones? Are visitors to the city more likely than residents of the city to fall victim to crime?

Urban crime gets extensive media attention and influences public perception. Yet the public's fear about crime overlooks the important fact that the U.S. crime rate is much lower than in previous years. The property crime rate (for burglary, motor vehicle theft, and property theft) has dropped 23 percent since 1996, and the violent crime rate (for murder, rape/sexual assault, robbery, and assault) fell 26 percent, although there was a slight increase in 2005 and 2006, then a decrease in 2007 and 2008. Furthermore, all criminal victimization rates are far lower than they were in the 1970s, 1980s, and early 1990s (U.S. Bureau of Justice Statistics 2008).

Crime in Canada has dropped 30 percent since its peak year in 1991. In 2007, that country's crime rate was at its lowest level in more than 25 years. Its homicide rate, after hitting a 36-year low in 2003, increased over the next two years but has been declining ever since. Among metropolitan areas with populations exceeding 500,000, Toronto and Quebec had the lowest crime rates, while Winnipeg, Vancouver, and Edmonton had the highest (Canadian Centre for Justice Statistics 2008). A 2004 survey revealed that 94 percent of respondents said they felt safe from becoming a crime victim, up from 91 percent in 1999. Among women ages 15 to 24, 79 percent said that they felt safe walking alone in their neighborhoods at night (Statistics Canada 2008a).

Public Perception of Crime

In a 2007 Gallup poll, 71 percent of respondents thought there was more crime in the United States than in the previous year, 20 percent thought the crime problem was "extremely serious," and another 37 percent thought it was "very serious." Yet 49 percent of these same respondents did not think the problem of crime where they lived was serious (Saad 2007).

In light of the facts, why do so many think that crime is such a serious problem? Part of the answer lies in more extensive news reporting of violent crime. An ABC News poll revealed that 82 percent of Americans said their perception of crime is based on what they read or see in the news; only 17 percent said that they base their views on personal experience (ABC News 2000). One study found a positive correlation between viewing crime news and being concerned about crime (Dixon 2008). In addition, the frequent "promos" of upcoming violent crime stories, the popularity of "reality-based" crime dramas on broadcast and cable television, and tabloid sensationalism spread the image of crime well beyond the news programs themselves.

Another concern is becoming the homicide victim of a stranger, which accounts for 14 percent of all murders. Also, drug- or gang-related shootings sometimes result in stray bullets killing innocent people, even in their homes or blocks away from the source. Most vulnerable are urban black males aged 18 to 24, who are twice as likely to be victims as older black males are. Although their victimization rates are much lower now than in the late 1980s and early 1990s, they are higher than those in earlier periods (U.S. Bureau of Justice Statistics 2008).

Attitudes about crime, then, are a mix of facts and fears. To gain a more accurate sense of crime in the city, we need to look at additional statistics.

Crime and City Size.   Most violent crimes take place in cities, often growing out of street, school, or social club altercations. Indeed, the negative attitudes of non–city dwellers and their reluctance to enter cities stems in large measure from their fear of becoming an urban crime statistic, but are cities really more dangerous? Table 12–1 compares crime rates in various types of communities.

Note the steady decline of crime rates in mostly all locales. Also note that violent crime rates are higher in large metropolitan areas than in smaller cities outside metropolitan areas and, especially, in rural areas. Such data

TABLE 12-1   Crime Rates per 1,000 Residents by Type of Community, 1980, 2000, and 2007

	Property Crime			Violent Crime		
	1980	2000	2007	1980	2000	2007
U.S. Total	53	36	33	5.8	5.1	4.7
Metropolitan Areas	61	39	34	7.0	5.6	5.0
Cities Outside Metro Areas	50	41	38	3.5	4.0	3.9
Rural Areas	21	17	17	1.8	2.1	2.1

Source: Federal Bureau of Investigation, *Crime in the United States—2007.* Accessed at http://www.fbi.gov/ucr/cius2007/data/table_02.html on February 28, 2009.

would seem to support the conclusion that large cities are dangerous places. Property crime rates, however, are higher in those smaller cities than in the metropolitan regions.

Louis Wirth, whose theory of urbanism was central to Chapter 5, might claim that the size, density, and social heterogeneity of cities are to blame. If this were true, however, we would expect the largest metropolitan areas to have the highest crime rates, which is not the case. As Table 12–2 shows, the highest crime rates occur in second-tier cities (those with populations from 500,000 to 999,999) and in smaller, third-tier cities (those with populations under 500,000).

These data point to the conclusion that although cities have higher crime rates than other types of communities, city size, by itself, does not explain crime rate. How else can we explain the fact that New York, the nation's largest city, has less crime per capita than all other U.S. cities with a population of 1 million or more? On a per-capita basis, New York City has less than half the crime of such cities as Albuquerque, Miami, Memphis, New Orleans, Oklahoma City, Phoenix, and Tucson. Put differently, in 2007, New York City ranked 259 out of 385 U.S. cities with a population of 100,000 or more (having about the same crime rate as Boise, Idaho).

Before going further, however, a warning is in order. Crime statistics are notoriously imperfect. For example, many crimes are not

discovered, or reported to police, or recorded carefully. All the statistics in Tables 12–1 and 12–2 reflect official police records. Many criminologists argue that a more accurate portrait of crime comes from the U.S. Census Bureau's semi-annual, random population survey. By questioning people (rather than police), the victimization survey uncovers many unreported crimes that are missed in the crime index and crime rate calculations. While such studies confirm the decline in crime over time, they also suggest that the actual number of crimes may well be twice that of the official statistics.

Furthermore, criminologists agree that as with other problems, the amount of crime varies throughout the urban area. The greatest concentration of offenses occurs in inner-city districts with poverty-stricken, minority populations. In 2006, for example, members of the poorest U.S. households (those with incomes under $7,500) were far more likely to be assaulted or robbed than were those in higher-income households (U.S. Bureau of Justice Statistics 2008). Urbanists at the University of Chicago first identified this pattern back in the 1940s, and it still holds true for both the inner city and the suburbs.

The Race Issue. In the United States, discussions of crime almost always raise the issue of race, because many people link crime to non-white minorities. In truth, however, two-thirds of the arrests that police make for serious crimes involve white people. Even so, relative to population size, African Americans are more likely to be arrested than whites.

Keep in mind, too, that crime is largely intraracial. To illustrate, 73 percent of single-offender violent crimes committed in 2006 by blacks were against black victims, and 64 percent of such crimes committed by whites involved white victims (Federal Bureau of Investigation 2008).

Moreover, the crime problem is worst in overwhelmingly black urban ghettos, where homicide is at a crisis level. Blacks are six times more likely to be murdered than whites, and 94 percent of all black victims are killed by blacks (U.S. Bureau of Justice Statistics

TABLE 12-2   City Size and Crime Rates, 2007

Population Size	Violent Crime	Property Crime
1,000,000 or higher	8.3	36.6
500,000–999,999	9.9	54.2
250,000–499,999	9.0	48.4
100,000–249,999	6.4	43.5
50,000–99,999	4.7	36.4
25,000–49,999	3.8	33.8
10,000–24,999	3.2	31.8
Under 10,000	3.3	34.1
Suburban Areas	3.2	26.9
Rural Counties	2.2	16.8

Source: Federal Bureau of Investigation, 2008.

2008). Nationwide, the leading cause of death for black males between the ages of 15 and 34 is, by far, homicide (National Center for Health Statistics 2007:43). In 2005, blacks killed 4,497 blacks—only 258 fewer than the number of killings of whites by whites, who outnumber blacks by more than six to one (Federal Bureau of Investigation 2008).

Explaining High-Crime Areas

Why are some communities terrorized by crime? We know that the highest crime rates occur in the poorest sections of cities. Why? Social scientists offer a variety of theories to explain concentrations of urban crime. Four of the main causative explanations involve (1) cultural patterns, (2) lower intelligence, (3) persistent racial inequality and prolonged poverty, and (4) residential segregation. As we shall see, each position has both advocates and critics.

Cultural Patterns. Edward Banfield (1990) claimed that crime flourishes in urban areas that are steeped in a lower-class culture, where people share a "present-time orientation," have low aspirations, and generally are morally irresponsible. Under such conditions, he contended, people victimize anyone who seems to be an easy mark, including one another.

Moreover, parents pass on these cultural patterns to their children, which explains the persistence of crime in some neighborhoods for decades. Rather than learning values and skills that ease their way toward success, children too often learn apathy, resignation, and fatalism; indifference toward schooling; a desire for immediate gratification; and a distrust of authority. In such an environment, crime simply thrives. Add to this the fact that high-crime neighborhoods tend to have high levels of single parenting, which means that children have less supervision, especially from fathers.

Critics of such a culture-of-poverty position responded that such cultural patterns should be viewed as the *consequences*, not the *causes*, of poverty. Among people who have

few opportunities to work; are forced to live in crowded, run-down housing; and must contend with the worst schools a city has to offer, we should not be surprised that crime rates are high. Only structural changes that alleviate societal inequality are likely to bring about changes in the vicious circle of poverty and crime (Stricker 2007).

Lower Intelligence. In perhaps the most controversial effort to explain concentrations of crime and other social problems, Richard Herrnstein and Charles Murray asserted that criminality is concentrated in areas where average intelligence is low. In their book *The Bell Curve*, they suggested that crime—like poverty, welfare dependency, and illegitimacy—is strongly related to low IQ (1994:338–39). Because the more talented people have long since left the inner cities, these researchers continued, the plight of those who are left is worse than ever. And given the cause, there is little that even a compassionate public can do about it.

Critics attacked this book on many fronts, suggesting that intelligence tests are unfair to begin with and that it is far from clear what intelligence really is (Fischer et al. 1996; Willie and Taylor 1995). More specifically, numerous studies have shown that low-income people who test lower on IQ tests and scores typically find their scores improving as they achieve a higher socioeconomic status (Sowell 1977:57).

Persistent Racial Inequality and Poverty. There is far broader support for the idea that the primary problem with crime lies in social structure, including our definitions of crime itself. Manuel Castells (1982, 1979) contends that capitalism's unceasing orientation toward profit defines "crime" and "criminals" largely in terms that protect the interests of the rich. People in capitalist societies do not believe that causing people to suffer a life of poverty is criminal but, rather, that taking another's *property* is—especially if the victim is somebody "important." In a society where most wealth and power lie in the hands of the few, high rates of criminality among the more deprived are simply to be expected because of how those in power define crime and enforce the law.

Other social scientists also maintain that racial and economic inequalities breed high crime rates (Fajnzylber, Lederman, and Loayza 2002). After studying 125 large metropolitan areas, Judith and Peter Blau (1982) suggested that insofar as a city concentrates people of highly unequal incomes, those with less than others see themselves as being unjustly deprived. Therefore, even in the absence of **absolute poverty,** a city with significant **relative poverty** would still breed resentment and crime. In other words, they argue, African Americans and other poor people engage in more crime as offenders—and suffer more as victims—only because they are heavily represented among the economically deprived.

In contrast to the assertions by Banfield, Herrnstein, and Murray that poor people are *themselves* to blame for criminality, this approach sees the poor as victims of injustices within society itself. Judith and Peter Blau sum up:

> Thus, aggressive acts of violence seem to result not so much from lack of advantages as from being taken advantage of, not so much from absolute deprivation but from relative deprivation. In a society founded on the principle "that all men are created equal," economic inequalities rooted in ascribed positions [such as being born black or impoverished] violate the spirit of democracy and are likely to create alienation, despair, and conflict. (1982:126)

More recent research, however, challenges the idea that economic and racial inequality is a causal factor in crime. Some researchers have found that changing structural conditions (neighborhood demographics, competition, and racial inequality) can lead to differing rates of violence (McCall and Parker 2005). Eric Neumayer (2005) argues that the link between income inequality and crime is a misleading one, because it varies from one country to another, making cultural norms a more important factor. Some connections between racial inequality and crime may, indeed, exist, but not always.

Residential Segregation. A fourth factor noted by social scientists to explain the high rate of African American crime is that residential segregation—from the time of slavery to the present—makes the black situation unique. Recall in Chapter 11 our discussion of **hypersegregation**—the extensive segregation existing on many geographic dimensions simultaneously. Massey and Denton (1989, 1993) identified 20 hypersegregated metropolitan areas that contain nearly 40 percent of the total U.S. African American population.

In another study, researchers Ruth Peterson and Lauren Krivo (1993) examined the relationship between black segregation and black homicide in 125 metropolitan areas. They found that black–white segregation far exceeded other variables, such as income inequality and poverty, as well as several others, in explaining intercity variations in the black murder rate. In addition, they found that segregation had no bearing on homicide within families but had a clear effect on acquaintance killings and homicides involving strangers. That is, the impact of segregation on the homicide rate manifested itself in public space, not in the home. Part of the violence in inner-city neighborhoods comes out of learning the "code of the street," that toughness means survival, as illustrated in the *Urban Living* box on page 355.

As Massey puts it, "Any social process that concentrates poverty also concentrates crime and violence to create an ecological niche characterized by a high risk of physical injury, violent death, and criminal victimization" (1995:1207). Rejecting the notion that black urban crime is simply a product of individual failings, he views such crime as "an inevitable outgrowth of social conditions created by the coincidence of racial segregation and high rates of black poverty" (Anderson and Massey 2001:334). Believing that only federal policy initiatives could bring an end to the legacy of American apartheid, Massey is pessimistic. He predicts that many urban black communities will continue to deteriorate, with all of us paying a heavy economic and social price for a shameful "retreat from American democratic ideals" (1995:1231–32).

URBAN LIVING

Inner City Toughness

In the street, through their play, children pour their individual life experiences into a common knowledge pool, mixing, negating, affirming, confirming, and elaborating on what they have observed in the home and matching their skills against those of others. They also learn to fight; in particular, they learn the social meaning of fighting. In these circumstances even small children test one another, pushing and shoving others, and they seem ready to hit other children over matters not to their liking. In turn, they are readily hit by other children, and the child who is toughest prevails. Furthermore, as the violent resolution of disputes—the hitting and cursing—gains social reinforcement, the child is more completely initiated into a world that provides a strong rationale for physically campaigning for self-respect.

Moreover, younger children refine their understanding of the code by observing the disputes of the older children, which are often resolved through cursing and abusive talk, and sometimes through outright aggression or violence. They see that one child succumbs to the greater physical and mental abilities of the other. These younger children are also alert and attentive witnesses to the occasional verbal and physical fights of adults; later, they will compare notes among themselves and share their own interpretations of the event. Almost always the victor is the person who physically won the altercation, and this person often enjoys the esteem and respect of onlookers. These experiences reinforce the lessons many children have learned at home: might makes right; toughness is a virtue, humility is not. . . .

The street-oriented adults with whom children come in contact at home and on the street—including mothers, fathers, brothers, sisters, boyfriends, cousins, neighbors, and friends—help shape and reinforce this understanding by verbalizing the messages these children are getting through public experience: "Watch your back." "Protect yourself." "Don't punk out." "Respect yourself." "If someone disses you, you got to straighten them out." Many parents actually impose sanctions if a child is not sufficiently aggressive. For example, if a child loses a fight and comes home upset, the parent might respond, "Don't you come in here crying that somebody beat you up; you better get back out there and whup his ass. I didn't raise no punks! If you don't whup his ass, I'll whup yo' ass when you come home." Thus the child gains reinforcement for being tough and showing nerve.

Source: From *Code of the Street: Decency, Violence and the Moral Life of the Inner City* by Elijah Anderson. Copyright © 1999 by Elijah Anderson. Used by permission of W.W. Norton & Company, Inc.

A modest decline in racial segregation occurred during the 1980s in many U.S. metropolitan areas. Analysis of 2000 census data shows a slow change since 1980 in residential segregation of African Americans (Table 12–3, page 356). In some smaller and newer metropolitan areas, their segregation from whites has declined markedly, but in the larger places where most African Americans live, segregation has remained high. Segregation of Hispanics and Asians has not changed in the last two decades (Lewis Mumford Center 2001a).

Effects of Crime on Everyday Life

The toll of crime extends far beyond its immediate victims. For one thing, nothing pulls down property values like a high crime rate

TABLE 12-3   Most Segregated Metropolitan Areas, Black and White, 2000

Metropolitan Area	Index of Dissimilarity
1. Detroit, Michigan	85
2. Milwaukee, Wisconsin	82
3. New York, New York	82
4. Chicago, Illinois	81
5. Newark, New Jersey	80
6. Cleveland, Ohio	77
7. Nassau–Suffolk, New York	74
8. Cincinnati, Ohio	75
9. St. Louis, Missouri	74
10. Miami, Florida	74

Source: Lewis Mumford Center for Comparative Urban and Regional Research (2001a).

(Kim 2000). Owners lose equity in their investment, face high homeowners' insurance premiums, and lose neighbors or renters who otherwise would provide stability and community role models. If large numbers of people move out and cannot be replaced, owners may well abandon buildings they cannot sell, eroding the city's tax base. The vicious circle grinds on and on.

The fear of crime also reduces our use of public space. As William H. Whyte (2001:59) observed, "Streets are the rivers of life of a city. We come to partake of them, not to escape them." Certainly, in areas where people feel safe, extensive use of streets, parks, plazas, and other public places provides enjoyment for people at all hours of the day and night. Such urban areas contain the social dynamics and all the variety and excitement the city can offer. However, crime (and merely the fear of crime) restricts the use of public spaces. Another vicious circle is thus set in motion, because empty streets, plazas, and subway stations are unprotected and become ever more dangerous. In some communities, "take back the streets" campaigns have had some success, but the sad reality remains that urbanites' enjoyment of public space is more limited than it once was, especially after sunset, in too many areas.

What Is the Solution?

Can high crime rates in urban places be reduced? Is there a way to make our cities safe so that people can walk through a park in the daytime (let alone at night!) without fear? Here, again, a number of proposals are noteworthy, and New York City offers a positive model.

Physical Design.   Urban planner Oscar Newman (1996) maintained that building design plays an important part in controlling crime. High-rise apartment blocks, Newman explained, serve to encourage crime, because they isolate inhabitants from each other, creating many unwatched places where crime can easily occur. Instead, architects could design windows and entries in such a way that the paths of movement and the areas of activity provide inhabitants with continuous, natural surveillance of the street. Such designs create what Newman calls **defensible space,** allowing people to protect their own communities naturally, as they go about their daily lives, rather than relying on security guards and police for protection (see Figure 12–1 on page 357).

To support his argument, Newman compiled crime data from various low-income public housing projects, first in New York and subsequently in other cities. He found that the average crime rate is higher in taller buildings (over six stories) than in lower ones. Tall buildings with hundreds of living units are worst of all and appear to encourage isolation, stigmatization, apathy, neglect, and withdrawal, with the latter two first on the part of the residents, then by housing management, and finally, by the municipal agencies that service the project: police, education, parks and recreation, refuse collection, and social services (Newman 1996:28). Furthermore, in larger, taller buildings, crime occurs mostly in public areas—for example, elevators, halls, and lobbies—which are the places that residents cannot easily monitor. Crime in such spaces is far less frequent than in low-rise buildings, where residents can more easily supervise their surroundings.

Community Involvement.   Improving the physical design of buildings appears to be a

FIGURE 12–1   One example of defensible space is this courtyard with only one vehicular entrance route and footpaths and with many windows placed in buildings to overlook it. Such a design creates a sense of shared territorial ownership, creating an environment where the owners feel safe and the potential offender is aware of a substantial risk of scrutiny and apprehension.

Source: From http://tessellarsociety.blogspot.com/2007/05/protection-from-crime.html. Reprinted with permission of the author.

partial solution to the problem of urban crime. Regardless of architectural design, however, residents of a building must be motivated to notice and respond to potentially criminal situations. For example, neighborhoods in which a greater sense of community exists are where greater crime prevention and deterrence occurs (Lee and Earnest 2003).

Another crime-fighting strategy, advocated by Curtis Sliwa of the Guardian Angels, a volunteer crime patrol group, is street patrols by local citizens. Patrols, as well as Neighborhood Crime Watch organizations, sensitize community members to the problem as they involve everyone in watching for suspicious behavior. Studies have found that both reduce neighborhood crime (Pattavina, Byrne, and Garcia 2006; Sanders 2000).

Get Tough.   Another approach, suggested by urban critic Roger Starr (1985), is that cities adopt a "get tough, no nonsense, this has gone far enough!" approach. Specifically, he proposed that (1) cities target vulnerable areas—subways, for example—and make special efforts to control crime there; (2) cities create citizens' boards (with racially and ethnically mixed membership) to fight for more jails, more police, and to pressure legislators to reform the laws that let many criminals slip through with little or no punishment; (3) cities adopt a policy of tougher punishment, increasing the severity of the jail sentences for each subsequent offense; and (4) cities ask parents and educators to commit themselves to instilling in children and students a sense of social responsibility so that fewer young people will be drawn into crime.

A recent form of community policing in order to reduce crime in many North American cities has been the utilization of police officers on bike patrols, such as this multiethnic trio in Los Angeles. Using bicycles provides greater mobility and coverage of territory than covering a beat on foot yet allows closer observation and interaction than in a car.

New York City. Using a computerized and multifaceted tactical approach that addressed even minor infractions, such as subway turnstile jumping, New York officials succeeded in significantly dropping the city's crime rate. Following many of Starr's suggestions, they enacted stronger community and strategic policing measures as well as a "get tough" approach. **Community policing** is an approach that increases interaction and cooperation between law enforcement agencies and the people and neighborhoods they serve.

Strategic policing is an aggressive tactic of deploying increased patrols, decoys, and sting operations in locales identified through frequent computer analyses as high-crime areas. As a result, violent crime dropped almost in half, and the city became a model for other cities. Homicides, for example, dropped from 2,245 in 1990 to less than 494 in 2007, compared to 442 in Chicago, a city about one-third the size of New York. This is a truly remarkable achievement. As some critics see it, however, "get tough" approaches do little to solve the root causes of crime; rather, they deal only with the consequences.

Ultimately, achieving long-term reductions in crime probably depends on increasing economic opportunity in poor communities. Doing so may involve providing greater mobility for inner-city residents so that they are able to reach jobs on the metropolitan periphery, or providing job training and economic incentives through government to encourage businesses to locate in economically depressed areas. In addition, of course, community efforts at policing the streets, greater involvement by churches and local community groups, and efforts at upgrading neighborhoods, such as that by Habitat for Humanity, all will help. Fortunately, many city leaders recognize these needs and are taking steps to improve living and employment conditions.

SUMMARY

Poor housing, substandard education, and crime are three significant problems that plague our cities. Certainly, there are others, including environmental pollution, inadequate public transportation, and governmental corruption. This chapter highlighted housing, education, and crime, because the progress made so far in these areas offers the promise of more within our lifetimes.

All urban problems closely link to the state of a city's economy and, especially, to the extent of urban poverty. Thus, we can see that urban problems are complex, interrelated issues, such as poverty, crime, and drug abuse, with roots that extend beyond a particular city to society as a whole.

In the 1930s, as part of Franklin Roosevelt's New Deal, the federal government first enacted public housing policies. Financial assistance to homeowners and builders, together with public works programs, quickly improved urban housing. Even so, by 1940, some 40 percent of U.S. urban housing still lacked amenities such as adequate indoor plumbing. The Housing Act of 1949 launched urban renewal programs and initiated the construction of more public housing. Private developers, however, never provided anywhere near as many low-income housing units as were torn down, resulting in the displacement of the poor. Moreover, high-rise public housing stigmatized and isolated the poor and created unsafe neighborhoods. Rent subsidies were a better idea, giving families choices other than public housing.

Rising taxes and increased maintenance costs, coupled with rent levels limited by local policy and the inability of tenants to pay, eventually resulted in hundreds of thousands of landlords abandoning buildings. More recently, urban homesteading, gentrification, and the New Urbanism improved the urban scene. Each approach has limitations, however, and none can solve all the cities' housing problems.

Beset by problems of old buildings in need of repair, limited funding, a growing minority student population with limited English proficiency, a shortage of qualified teachers, and inadequate teaching resources, the nation's urban schools face serious challenges in their efforts to provide a quality education. A deepening dissatisfaction with the failure of urban schools to do their job has led to alternative approaches. Magnet schools, vouchers, and charter schools become more popular each year, but they also have their critics. Charges of elitism, violation of church–state separation, and the siphoning off of much-needed funds for urban public schools are controversies that surround these innovations.

Rates of serious crime are going down (although remaining high among juveniles). Media coverage and the fear of stranger-on-stranger violence, however, have raised public worries about crime. The greatest concentration of crime is in poor inner-city neighborhoods. Various explanations for the existence of high-crime areas highlight cultural patterns, alleged intellectual deficiencies, persistent racial inequality and poverty, and residential segregation.

Crime victimizes everyone by eroding property values, increasing insurance premiums, and generating a climate of fear. Crime also reduces the use of parks, streets, and mass transit, denying urbanites free use of their city.

Trying to build "defensible spaces" is a partial solution to the crime problem, as are "get tough" policies that target vulnerable areas for extra police protection. Yet neither approach can ultimately solve the problem of crime. Strengthening families in order to provide good adult role models for young people, generating jobs for adults, and building a sense of community through churches and other local organizations are also needed.

CONCLUSION

While there is some reason for pessimism and concern, recent decades have witnessed positive signs of improvement in urban life. For example, New York City has dramatically curtailed violent crime. Many other cities have also reduced crime, but whether this trend will persist remains to be seen. Similarly, time will tell whether the recent innovations in housing and education improve the quality of life and the life chances for all segments of the cities' population. As cities convert the failed high-rise projects to more livable, mixed-income housing complexes that no longer isolate and stigmatize the poor, they are guided by important lessons learned from the past. What is happening to cities in developing countries, however? Are they learning from Western mistakes, or is their situation even worse? In the next chapter, we will discuss Latin American, African, Middle Eastern, and Asian cities to learn the answers.

KEY TERMS

absolute poverty   (354)
charter schools   (349)
community policing   (358)
defensible space   (356)
eminent domain   (333)
gentrification   (339)
hypersegregation   (354)

magnet schools   (347)
New Urbanism   (341)
relative poverty   (354)
school voucher   (348)
social promotions   (346)
strategic policing   (358)
urban renewal   (333)

INTERNET ACTIVITIES

1. *The Condition of Education* is an annual assessment of its quality with different special features each year. At http://nces.ed.gov/programs/coe/2005/section2/indicator14.asp, you will find an analysis of student academic performance in central-city schools.

2. At http://www.fbi.gov/ucr/ucr.htm, you can access the latest statistics from the Federal Bureau of Investigation in its *Uniform Crime Reports*. Click on a year (not preliminary findings), and explore the data tables for cities, suburbs, and nonmetropolitan regions.

CHAPTER 13

CITIES IN THE DEVELOPING WORLD

When most of us think of large cities, we usually imagine towering New York City or sprawling Los Angeles. The largest city in the Western Hemisphere, however, is São Paolo, Brazil, with a population exceeding 10.2 million, and Mexico City follows, with a population of 8.5 million. The 14.9 million inhabitants of Shanghai easily surpass New York City's 8.2 million, while the 12 million people in Mumbai (Bombay) are more than three times the population of Los Angeles (3.8 million).

These major cities, and many others throughout Africa, Asia, Latin America, and the Middle East, have an urban history unlike that of Canada and the United States. That past explains, in part, their present situation. All of these regions had indigenous cities that fell under the control of colonizers but that eventually gained their political independence. Today, these areas are in the midst of rapid and far-reaching urban transformation and are growing at a startling rate, as vast numbers of people pour into their cities. Furthermore, as explained in Chapter 7, the economic well-being of these cities (as well as of those in Canada and the United States) is linked to a world-systems economic arrangement in which the more-developed countries affect the fortunes of cities in the less-developed countries.

Mexico City symbolizes in many ways the current state of poor cities around the globe. Pouring in are tens of thousands of people who must compete for extremely limited resources. Not surprisingly, those meager resources are not shared equally. Nowhere in sub-Saharan Africa is there a metropolitan area approaching the size of Cairo (at 11.1 million, it is the continent's megacity), but large cities are numerous throughout Africa. Lagos, Nigeria, boasts 9 million inhabitants, while Kinshasa, Congo (formerly Zaire), has 7.3 million inhabitants. Bangkok, Thailand, has 6.4 million.

Moreover, **primate cities** (principal cities that are extremely large compared to other cities in the country) dominate a great many

countries in the developing world. In many cases, a single city is home to more than half a country's urban population (see the *Urban Trends* box on page 363).

This chapter explores the development of cities throughout the developing world, with an eye to what they have in common, how they vary, and how they compare with Canadian and U.S. cities. This is a formidable task. Africa and Asia are vast continents of striking geographical and cultural contrasts. Africa has more than 1,000 spoken languages, and Asia has four major cultural traditions (in China, India, Japan, and Southeast Asia). Latin America, although it mostly shares a Spanish heritage, nonetheless varies significantly from one country to another in its population composition, resources, and economic development. The Middle East is a region where countries (and their cities) vary considerably in economic development, political structure, and quality of life. Still, many common elements exist in the global urbanization that we are witnessing.

From the standpoint of world-systems analysis, no developing country is a core nation in the global economy. In Latin America, Mexico, Venezuela, Argentina, Brazil, and Chile are in the semi-periphery; the rest are in the periphery. Most African countries are in the periphery, with Nigeria and South Africa in the semi-periphery. Saudi Arabia, in the Middle East, and the Asian countries that we feature in this chapter are also in the semi-periphery; all others are in the periphery. Each country's place in the global hierarchy affects the economic well-being of its cities.

Before we proceed with a look at various parts of the world, we must first remind ourselves of a point made in Chapter 1. Because countries vary widely in how they define "city" or "urban," cross-national comparisons are difficult in any urban study. For our purposes, the populations given in this book are calculated according to each country's definition and so cannot be exactly compared to the populations of cities in other countries.

URBAN TRENDS

The Evolution of Primate Cities

A *primate city* is one that grows in population and influence far beyond other cities in a nation or region. In many poor countries, the largest city may have several times the combined population of the two or three next-largest cities. Primate cities thus resemble, to use Alejandro Portés's metaphor, "gigantic heads on dwarfish bodies" (1977:68), absorbing an enormous portion of the available labor, trade, and population.

The extent of the dominance by a primate city in its own country can be shown using a **primacy ratio,** which is computed through dividing the primate city's population by the population of the second-largest city in the country. The following table shows some examples.

Note that with the exception of four cities, the primacy ratios for most of the largest cities of the developed world are relatively low. This suggests that primacy is linked to more than a good location and established trade patterns. Recent research suggests that primate cities develop more frequently in (1) small countries— Copenhagen and Vienna are clear examples; (2) countries that, for historical reasons, have only one or a few cities with anything approaching modern facilities—certainly true of poor countries around the world; and (3) countries that once were or still are under foreign control either politically or economically— colonial or postcommunist cities, for example.

Selected Developing World Cities in 2007[*]		Selected Developed World Cities in 2007[*]	
Bangkok, Thailand	17.7	Budapest, Hungary	8.3
Lima, Peru	11.3	London, England	7.5
Addis Ababa, Ethiopia	10.6	Vienna Austria	6.7
Beirut, Lebanon	8.3	Bucharest, Romania	6.1
N'Djamena, Chad	8.2	Copenhagen, Denmark	4.9
Kigali, Rwanda	7.7	Prague, Czech Republic	3.2
Santiago, Chile	6.8	Paris, France	2.6
Managua, Nicaragua	6.5	Tokyo, Japan	2.4
Havana, Cuba	5.1	Moscow, Russia	2.3
San José, Costa Rica	5.1	New York, USA	2.1
Mexico City, Mexico	5.0	Rome, Italy	2.1
Jakarta, Indonesia	3.3	Berlin, Germany	1.9

[*]All ratios computed from populations reported in "Nations of the World," 2009 *Britannica Book of the Year* (Chicago: Encyclopedia Britannica, 2009).

LATIN AMERICAN CITIES

Today's Latin American cities—Rio de Janeiro, Brazil; Buenos Aires, Argentina; Bogotá, Colombia; Santiago, Chile; Lima, Peru; Mexico City, Mexico—did not exist before the sixteenth century. They, and many others, are the products of **colonization** by Spanish and Portuguese conquerors. Before the founding of such cities, however, other complex urban centers existed. The most outstanding examples were the capitals of the Mayan and Aztec civilizations in

Central America and Mexico and of the Inca Empire on the western coast of South America.

Early Cities

Of the many pre-Columbian cities—including Teotihuacan, the Mayan capital located in central Mexico, and Cuzco, the Inca Empire's capital city in southeastern Peru—perhaps Tenochtitlán offers the most poignant example of an awe-inspiring but lost city (see the *Cityscape* box below). Originally received hospitably, Cortés and his forces encircled Tenochtitlán in April 1521, cut off its food

CITYSCAPE

The Magnificent City of Tenochtitlán

The Aztecs built Tenochtitlán into an island metropolis of incredible magnificence. Situated amid the calm, clear, turquoise waters of Lake Texcoco and linked to mainland suburbs by three great paved causeways, Tenochtitlán had a population of about 350,000 by the end of the fifteenth century.

With its pyramid temples and elegant palaces—together with its spotless streets, broad plazas, and exotic gardens—Tenochtitlán was probably, after Rome, the world's greatest city.

In 1519, the Spaniard Hernan Cortés and his men gazed with disbelief on this city. Cortés later described it as "the most beautiful city in the world," and one of his soldiers, Bernal Diaz, described the Spanish reaction this way:

We were amazed. . . . [I]t was like the enchantments they tell of in the legend of Amadis, on account of the great towers and [temples] and buildings rising from the water, and all built of masonry. And some of our soldiers even asked whether the things that we saw were not a dream. . . . I do not know how to describe it, seeing things as we did that had never been heard of or seen before, not even dreamed about (Stannard 1993:4).

Matching the city's splendor was the cleanliness of its streets, people, and water supply:

Criss-crossed with a complex network of canals, Tenochtitlán in this respect reminded the Spanish of an enormous Venice; but it also had remarkable floating gardens that reminded them of nowhere else on earth. And while European cities then, and for centuries afterward, took their drinking water from the fetid and polluted rivers nearby, Tenochtitlán's drinking water came from springs deep within the mainland and was piped into the city by a huge aqueduct system that amazed Cortés and his men—just as they were astonished by the personal cleanliness and hygiene of the colorfully dressed populace, and by their extravagant (to the Spanish) use of soaps, deodorants, and breath sweeteners (Stannard 1993:5).

Commerce was the lifeblood of the city, and especially impressive to the Spanish visitors was the enormous so-called Great Market that sprawled across the city's northern end:

This area, "with arcades all around," according to Cortés, was the central gathering place where "more than sixty thousand people come each day to buy and sell, and where every kind of merchandise produced in these lands is found . . ." (Stannard 1993:6).

So great was the variety of food, animals and birds, metals, herbs, clothing, pottery, housewares, sweets, wines, timber, tiles, firewood, and charcoal for sale, that Diaz wrote:

Some . . . among us who had been in many parts of the world, in Constantinople, all over Italy, and in Rome, said that so large a marketplace and so full of people and so well regulated and arranged, they had never beheld before. (Stannard 1993:7).

and water for three months, and then entered the city as its conquerors in August. To ensure that the remnants of the proud Aztec Empire never rose again, Cortés utterly demolished Tenochtitlán and, on its rubble, erected a city focused around a completely European culture. He called it *Ciudad Imperial de Mexico*— Mexico City. To complete his domination, the surviving Mexicans were made to serve their conquerors.

During the conquest of the Inca Empire in Peru about a decade later, Francisco Pizarro followed the same pattern. He conquered and destroyed the Inca cities and replaced them with Spanish cities. All over Latin America, new colonial cities were constructed as administrative centers for local domination and export-oriented trade. Inland settlements such as Mexico City were linked with port cities such as Vera Cruz (Figure 13–1, page 366). Where no important port existed, the Europeans built one: Lima (Peru), Valparaiso (Chile), Buenos Aires (Argentina), and Rio de Janeiro (Brazil) are examples (Figure 13–2, page 367). The "trade" of these cities, however, was a one-way operation, with precious gold, silver, tobacco, and coffee shipped to Spain and Portugal. Served in this way, these relatively poor and weak nations in Europe hoped to become rich and powerful.

European Dominance

The strategic location of most of these cities in relation to the hinterland also allowed colonists to dominate the native population. Ensconced in fortifications on the coast, the Europeans could defend themselves from internal attack and receive supplies from the sea. Such battlements also protected them from an external enemy—pirates—who lusted after the wealth these cities harbored.

Military might alone, however, did not ensure European dominance of the new cities and their hinterland. One of the most tragic aftermaths of the conquest was the literal decimation of the indigenous population. Anthropologists and historians estimate the loss of native human life in Central America during the sixteenth century at roughly 95 percent.

This means that in scarcely a single century, the native population plummeted from more than 25 million to, perhaps, 1 million. Among the many reasons for this frightening loss of life, foremost were the brutal wars with the colonists and the toll taken by European diseases, such as measles and smallpox, against which the indigenous people had no biological defense.

Imposing European culture on Latin America had other long-lasting effects. Decreeing a set of principles called the "Laws of the Indies," the Spanish constructed all their new cities along similar patterns, resulting in the breakdown of local cultural patterns. Although local geography and earlier customs brought some variations, most colonial cities were constructed around a grid plan with a central plaza—the *plaza mayor*. At one end of the plaza was an imposing Catholic church. On the other three sides were government offices, residences of the wealthy, and some businesses. Such a design established the dominant institutions of European culture—church, state, elite power, and commerce—in the heart of the city.

Around the city center, in a second district, were the residences of the city's middle class: artisans, government clerks, and small merchants. Farther out still, in a third zone, were the much more dilapidated residences of the city's poor. Finally, on the outskirts, were large parcels of land originally called *encomiendas,* which were given in trust to the local elite by the Spanish government. After independence in the nineteenth century, many of these large parcels of land became part of the equally exclusive *hacienda* system: large farms or ranches run by elites and worked by serfs.

Although physically similar to European cities, these preindustrial colonial cities were even more exclusive, favoring only a small and extremely powerful elite of European descent. Under normal circumstances, native Latin Americans could never become members of the elite. Although remnants of pre-Columbian culture remained—particularly in rural communities—the dominance of colonial cities in Latin America ensured the dominance of European culture in most areas of life (Skidmore and Smith 2004).

FIGURE 13–1 Map of Major Central American Cities

UNITED STATES

MEXICO

Mexico City ★

Gulf of
Mexico

Bahía de
Campeche

Golfo de
Tehuantepec

North
Pacific
Ocean

CUBA

Havana ★

BELIZE

GUATEMALA

Guatemala City ★

HONDURAS

Tegucigalpa ★

San Salvador ★
EL SALVADOR

NICARAGUA

Managua ★

COSTA RICA

San José ★

PANAMA

Panama
City ★

FIGURE 13–2 Map of Major South American Cities

Throughout Latin America, the Spanish influence manifests itself in both architecture and urban design. One common feature is a large church or cathedral, as well as a government palace, adjacent to or dominating a central plaza in the heart of the old city area. Illustrating this pattern is Murillo Plaza in La Paz, Bolivia.

By the early 1800s, both the willingness and the ability of the European colonists to maintain Latin American outposts were waning. The Europeans had long ago taken most of the easily extractable raw materials. Then, too, local insurgents, such as Simón Bolivar, were mounting more frequent challenges to colonial governance. Soon after a series of wars for independence (1816–1825), most Latin American nations gained their freedom.

With colonial restrictions removed, many Latin American cities began to prosper through trade with cities in England, France, and the United States. By 1900, although the population remained decidedly rural, Mexico City, São Paolo, and Santiago each grew to over a half million inhabitants, while Buenos Aires and Rio de Janeiro increased to more than a million (Eakin 2007:230). Similar patterns appeared in Montevideo, Caracas, Lima, and Havana. Indeed, by the early twentieth century, these few cities had grown so much that they dominated all the other cities in their respective countries.

Modern Cities

Not all of the growth in Latin American cities resulted from rural migrants seeking greater economic opportunity. Some was attributable to immigration between 1860 and 1930, as Latin America absorbed millions of Jews, Russians, Poles, Italians, Swiss, and Germans. Because of their generally higher level of education and greater familiarity with business, these immigrants soon came to control much of the medium-scale commerce of many Latin American cities, dominating such areas as construction, small industry, and artisan and craft activities. As a result, immigrants occupied many middle-class jobs at the expense of the impoverished indigenous population that was also streaming into the cities of Argentina, Brazil, Paraguay, and Uruguay (Eakin 2007:2 30–35).

Most Latin American cities have not followed the pattern of rapid industrialization typical of Europe, Canada, and the United States. Despite a century and a half of independence,

Latin American cities, in terms of wealth and productive capacity, lag far behind the cities of these other regions.

Why? First, most Latin American cities were, from the outset, export-oriented. Their valued products or raw materials—gold, silver, cattle, coal, oil, grains, coffee, fruits, and wool—were sent to other countries; they were not consumed by their own populations. The demand by other nations for these goods did not change after independence, and Latin American cities continued such one-way trading. The problem is that selling raw materials generates far less money than processing and marketing finished products. As a result, Latin American cities generated much less wealth than cities engaged in processing and distributing goods to consumers.

Second, with exports of raw materials as their primary source of wealth, most Latin American cities never developed much of an industrial base. Modern cities without major industries not only develop fewer jobs for their populations, they cannot compete on numerous levels (skilled labor, investment opportunities) with those cities that have them. Consequently, export-oriented cities simply fall further behind their industrialized counterparts, leading to a worsening gap between "the rich nations" and "the poor nations."

This disadvantageous situation is not simply the result of poor investment policies and lack of foresight on the part of Latin Americans. Many urbanists argue that rich nations and their corporations have contributed significantly to the problem (Greenfield 1994; Morse and Hardoy 1993; Geisse and Sabatini 1988). Still seeking raw materials and cheap labor in Latin America, these countries and corporations have thrown their aid and political support to Latin American governments that favored export over local development. Many Latin American business and government elites have become rich "playing ball" in this way, but this pattern has done little for the overall development of their countries. Thus, the old colonial pattern of external domination is preserved in another guise.

Some Latin American countries—particularly Argentina, Brazil, and Mexico—have benefited somewhat by gaining the industrial operations that closed down in postindustrial nations such as the United States. The *maquiladoras* program—creating enterprise zones in which multinational corporations control production and marketing, employ cheap labor, and often receive subsidies from the host nations—has brought some industrialization into the economies of these nations. The extensive use of female and child labor, however, helps perpetuate a culture of paternalism. Furthermore, automation, together with other modern technology and production techniques, results in these companies not generating many skilled jobs. Industrial development, therefore, is not creating enough employment opportunities to keep pace with the rural migration to the cities, so shantytowns on the cities' perimeters grow despite industrial development (Fernandez-Kelly and Shefner 2007).

AFRICAN CITIES

African urbanization is uneven, with most contemporary African cities located either on or near the continent's coastlines (Figure 13–3, page 370). The greater urbanization on Africa's northern coast is an historical legacy of trade, both with Europe and with the Islamic countries of the Middle East. To reach Europe, Africans transported their goods from the interior, crossing the forbidding Sahara Desert and then loading them onto ships that plied the Mediterranean or sailed Europe's western coast. Established during the seventeenth- and eighteenth-century European colonization to facilitate exports (including slaves), cities on Africa's western and eastern coasts soon became the most technologically and economically developed settlements on the continent.

Early Cities

Though unknown to most Westerners, complex civilizations, complete with highly developed urban centers, existed in Africa as early as 3000 B.C.E. One such civilization, Kush, with its core cities of Meroë, Musawarat, and Naga, was centered about 100 miles north of the modern

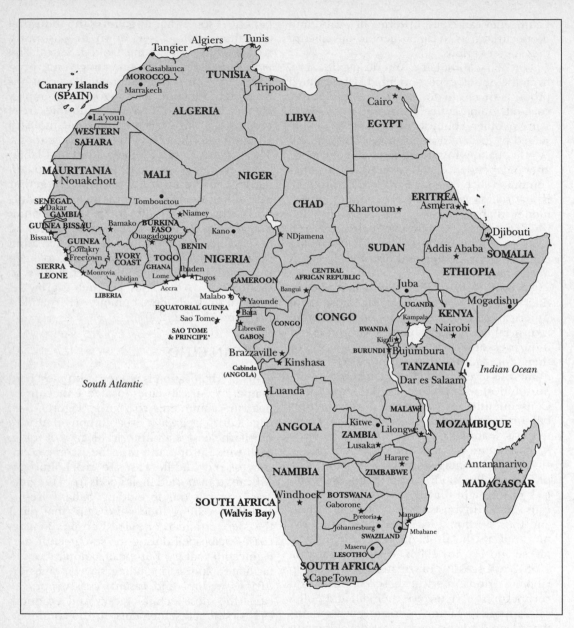

FIGURE 13–3 Map of Major African Cities

city of Khartoum. According to unearthed archaeological evidence, these Kushite cities, though originally imitators of the ancient cities of Egypt, were also highly sophisticated. By 590 B.C.E., Meroë traded extensively with Saharan and Mediterranean peoples in slaves, gold, ivory, iron, and copper (Wenke 2005). In fact, Meroë's trade in copper was so extensive that great slag heaps from the manufacturing process are still evident in the city's ruins.

Other early African cities, particularly those in the sub-Saharan region, served as capitals of indigenous African empires, as craft or manufacturing centers, or as break-of-bulk points on major trade routes. Gao, in present-day Mali, was built in the seventh century C.E. as the capital of the Songhai Empire. More impressive was Kumbi, capital of the Empire of Ghana around 1000 C.E. Backed by a large army equipped with iron weapons, Kumbi had an estimated population of 30,000, supported by a rural population numbering in the hundreds of thousands. Trade in gold and ivory—as well as in salt, kola nuts, slaves, and iron weapons—provided the empire's economic base (Wenke 2005).

Trade was crucial to these cities. In the eighth century C.E., shortly after the establishment of Islam as a major religion, cities based on trade with Arab countries and the East began to appear throughout Africa, such as Mogadishu in Somalia and Mombasa in Kenya. As exchange became more lucrative, the Muslim traders transformed the North African cities into major shipping centers to Europe. Their trade

networks linked these cities to dozens of inland, sub-Saharan cities to the south. One such city was Kano, founded in 999 C.E. Another was the legendary Timbuktu, founded in 1100 C.E. and, with its stone palaces, many-windowed homes, university, and bustling marketplace, became the intellectual capital of western Sudan.

All these early African cities were typical, preindustrial cities with a walled enclosure, narrow and winding streets, and daily life organized around religion and crafts. Residence was often determined by craft—for example, metalsmiths might cluster together—or by tribal or religious affiliation. Nothing existed that resembled the modern Western pattern of a central business district surrounded by residential rings determined by income; instead, rich and poor, commercial and residential uses, all intermingled.

European Dominance

The isolation of African cities did not continue forever, however. Although this period of empire building, trade, and urbanization

Taroudannt, Morocco, is a city of 30,000 that traces its origins to the eleventh century. Its sixteenth-century, 23-foot, fortified walls are in excellent condition and still define three-fourths of the city's borders. Walled cities once existed on all continents except Antarctica as a defensive measure, and those that remain offer vivid testimony to how cities once defined their boundaries.

(from approximately 500 B.C.E. to 1500 C.E.) was modern Africa's formative period, in which the dynamics of growth and change produced uniquely African cultures and civilizations, all became progressively submerged in the coming centuries.

Slavery has a long history; ancient Egyptians, Greeks, and Romans, for example, regularly subjugated those they conquered. Among Africans, this practice also stretches far back into the past. By the eighth through the tenth centuries B.C.E., the Islamic world inherited this tradition, initially enslaving captives from the holy wars spreading Islam across the African continent. An export trade in slaves was fairly modest, amounting to about a few thousand each year until the fifteenth century. Thereafter, the European opening of Africa stimulated the slave trade for the next 400 years, with more than 11.3 million slaves transported across the Atlantic (Lovejoy 2000: 15–18.). Traders enlisted the aid of a cadre of professional slave traders—Europeans, Muslims, and Africans—to bring the "black gold" to market at Daka in Senegal, Elmina on the coast of Ghana, Zanzibar in Tanzania, and other slave-trade towns established up and down the continent's coasts.

The first European invasion also upset many of the delicate economic, political, and interpersonal linkages of precolonial Africa. The Portuguese demolished the east coast cities and destroyed the trade alliances that had linked them to the Persian Gulf, India, and the Far East. In other parts of Africa, Europeans destroyed many of the political allegiances that had kept African tribes and empires in balance with one another. In the wake of such practices and the slave-trade abductions, much of African society was brought close to collapse.

The character of urban Africa changed radically in the nineteenth century, when Europeans arrived in force. No longer looking for a passage east, and with the slave trade waning, the rapidly industrializing colonizers now eyed Africa with much the same plundering eye that Cortés and Pizarro had cast upon Latin America more than three centuries earlier. With Africa so abundant in raw materials, they swarmed like locusts over the continent, trying to claim as much land and other wealth as they could. Between 1862 and 1915, Europeans established city after city. Where no previous cities existed, they built them; where indigenous urban centers were in place, they either "Europeanized" them or created "dual cities." In cities like Kano, Ibadan, and Kampala, the Europeans paired the African city with a new city of their own next to it. The contrast was striking: An African city constructed of mud bricks and organized around its religious life and craft associations would coexist with a European city built of stone and organized around a growing central business district.

In all cities, however, a policy of racial segregation prevailed—a form of **apartheid** (as the practice came to be known in South Africa) by which the Europeans dominated the local people. Obviously, such a system imposed tremendous economic, political, and social hardships on Africans while enriching the Europeans. Racism was at its worst in southern Africa—particularly in the then Union (now Republic) of South Africa and in Namibia—where only recently did black majorities gain power. In more northerly parts of the continent, different colonizers and different urban traditions allowed the races some contact and, thus, mitigated the racism somewhat. Thus, although racial tensions remain in West, East, and North Africa, conflict was greatest in the south, in the Republic of South Africa, Namibia, and Zimbabwe, where rigid racial segregation and stratification ended only in the late twentieth century.

Unlike Latin America, where the "Laws of the Indies" produced a continent of similar cities, the presence of many European nations in Africa resulted in a variety of different policies for urban areas. The British, for example, subscribed to a policy of indirect rule, content to let local African leaders maintain their positions as long as they bowed to the colonial government. The French, on the other hand, insisted on the eventual assimilation of

Africans into the French way of life. To promote this, they dismantled indigenous governments, taught only French in public schools, and encouraged the local population in identifying totally with French culture.

Modern Cities

During the colonial era, most African cities grew slowly. Like their Latin American counterparts, these cities were hampered by one-sided trade policies (exporting raw materials at low prices). Only a few cities—coastal ports or mining cities, for example—grew more swiftly, either because of their location or because of their special wealth.

Nationalist movements in the Cold War era led to fights for independence, and Africa became a site of confrontation for competing world ideologies. Siding with the Africans in most cases were leftist or Communist countries, prominent among them the former Soviet Union, China, and later, Cuba. Such countries often equipped local insurgents with arms to fight the colonizers. Furthermore, colonies became too costly to maintain, both economically and politically, giving Europeans second thoughts about the whole business. In the 1960s, a total of 32 former colonies in Africa gained their freedom. In 1960 alone—dubbed the "African Year"—more than 3 million square miles and 53 million of Africa's people saw an end to colonialism (Herskovits 2007). This success only further fueled independence movements, with the result that the retreating colonizers became more and more eager to let go.

In some cases, the aftermath of rapid withdrawal was debilitating political disorder, as the newfound freedom often unleashed tribal warfare and a succession of military coups. For example, after the hurried Belgian retreat from the Congo in 1960, that country endured five years of bloody civil war as factions warred for control. The civil war and horrendous slaughter in the mid-1990s between the Hutu and Tutsi tribes in the former English colony now known as Rwanda is attributable, in part, to the same legacy.

In global perspective, Africa is still the least urbanized continent, but it has the highest rate of increase in urbanization. In 1950, just 15 percent of the African population lived in cities, but by 2007, that proportion had more than doubled to 39 percent. Demographers estimate that by 2050, the number of African urbanites will reach 62 percent (United Nations Population Division 2008:5).

This increase is the result of both in-migration from the hinterland and natural population increase. Some nations—including Zambia, Zimbabwe, Gambia, Botswana, Kenya, Madagascar, Mauritania, Namibia, and Tanzania—have had success in bringing down fertility rates. Ethiopia, Nigeria, and the Congo, in contrast, have not. Nigeria is presently 1 of 10 countries with more than 100 million people, a level that Ethiopia and the Congo will reach within the next 50 years. Tragically, the AIDS epidemic is worst in sub-Saharan Africa; in 2008, this area accounted for 67 percent of the world's adult HIV infections and nearly 90 percent of the world's children inflected with HIV (24.2 million cases). In some nations, including Botswana, Lesotho, Swaziland, and Zimbabwe, more than 30 percent of the population is infected with HIV (UNAIDS and World Health Organization 2008). Despite this tragic epidemic, projections are for a sub-Saharan population growth from 809 million in 2008 to 1.16 billion in 2025 (Population Reference Bureau 2008).

Taken together, these factors help explain why Africa is a continent in severe crisis. Aside from Africa's health crisis, much of its population is starving. An example is Niger, a vast, landlocked country in central Africa that is twice the size of France and also one of the poorest countries in the world. Niger's people have a life expectancy of 57 years. In 2005, about 3.5 million people—more than a third of its total population—experienced dramatic food shortages. No statistic better captures the stunning reality of such poverty than the chilling fact that one of every six children in sub-Saharan Africa fails to reach his or her fifth birthday (UNICEF 2008).

MIDDLE EASTERN CITIES

Chapter 2 highlighted early Middle Eastern cities, including the world's first-known city, Jericho, and Catal Hüyük. Beginning in the fourth millennium B.C.E., the Persian and Egyptian empires dominated but then faded—a process hastened by the invasions of Philip of Macedon, Alexander the Great, and the Romans during the last four centuries before the birth of Christ. All left behind established cities on which more modern ones would later flourish. After 300 C.E., the declining fortunes of Rome, plus soil erosion and overgrazing, led to the eclipse of most of them.

Islamic Cities

The prophet Muhammad died in 632 C.E., unleashing a religious movement that swept over the entire Middle East, into Europe via Spain and the Balkan states, across some of sub-Saharan Africa, and eventually, as far east as Pakistan, India, Indonesia, and the southern Philippine Islands. As it spread, Islam generated an impressive array of cities. Even as European cities shrunk during the Middle Ages, Islamic cities along the coast of North Africa entered their greatest period. The Muslims, among history's greatest "middlemen," helped assure the success of these cities, as traders utilized the Middle East's geographical location to become the link between Europe and the Far East and, in the case of North Africa, between Europe and the sub-Saharan region. The inland cities, however, were probably Islam's greatest triumph. For centuries, as nomads and overland traders, the people of the Middle East had learned how to live and prosper across vast distances of inhospitable terrain. As trading centers, they established Mecca, Riyadh, Baghdad, Tehran, and Kabul, among others (Figure 13–4).

All the Islamic cities had a similar form, as described in the *Cityscape* box on page 376. By and large, the Muslim city reflected the power of the city's royal and religious elites, and many find these to be the most beautiful of all the world's cities. The following passage, excerpted from Robert Byron's writings on his travels in the Middle East during the 1930s, describes Isfahan in Iran:

> The beauty of Isfahan steals on the mind unawares. You drive about, under avenues of white tree trunks and canopies of shining twigs; past domes of turquoise and spring yellow in a sky of liquid violet-blue; along the river patched with twisting shoals, catching that blue in its muddy silver, and lined with feathery groves where the sap calls; across bridges of pale toffee brick, tier on tier of arches breaking into piled pavilions, overlooked by lilac mountains, by the Kuh-I-Sufi shaped like Punch's hump and by other ranges receding to a line of snowy surf; and before you know how, Isfahan has become indelible, has insinuated its image into that gallery of places which everyone privately treasures. (2007:166).

Yet Byron's image is misleading, for enduring internal conflict often characterized Islamic cities. Given the division of the city into multiple residential quarters—sixteenth-century Damascus contained no fewer than 70 quarters in the city itself and 30 more in the suburb of al-Salihiyyah—ingroup neighborhood solidarity often led to surging outgroup hostility, particularly when central religious values were at stake:

> So intense was neighborhood communal solidarity that at times faction fights broke out between quarters. . . . [It was] a society where economic grievances could seldom be articulated without group violence. Political communication with the ruling . . . caste was limited. Food shortages or abusive taxation provoked street demonstrations, assaults on officials, pillage of shops and the closure of markets. . . . [Youth gangs, associated with different quarters] preyed upon the quarters, running protection rackets, pillaging, and murdering. (Costello 1977:15–16)

Islamic cities reached their zenith during the Middle Ages. Thereafter, like their Persian, Egyptian, Greek, and Roman predecessors, they began to slide into decline. Again, the land near the cities became overgrazed and the topsoil depleted, leading to evaporation of precious water supplies and increasing dust and erosion. This, in turn, triggered a loss of timber, a crucial raw material any preindustrial

FIGURE 13–4   Map of Major Middle Eastern Cities

society consumes for heat, artifacts, houses, ships, and tools. City populations plummeted. For instance, in the sixteenth century, Baghdad dropped to a population of less than 100,000—one-tenth of its former size. In Syria, Egypt, Iran, and Saudi Arabia, cities were reduced to shadows of what they had been. Even in the largest cities, such as Alexandria and Aleppo (in Syria), trade slowed to a trickle.

European Dominance

Not until the nineteenth century, under European influence, did urban growth begin once more. In the Middle East, Europeans saw untapped markets for their goods, a potential source of raw materials, and in some areas, such as Suez, strategic locations for military affairs.

CITYSCAPE

The Islamic City

In the typical Islamic city, environmental and cultural elements dominant in the Middle East combined to produce a unique urban place. The surrounding wall, for example, served a dual function, first as a defense against marauders and, equally important, as a barrier to dust-laden winds coming from a variety of directions depending on the time of day or season of the year. When bush shrubs were planted along the wall, the effect on wind and dust was that of an almost-total barrier, and with strategic planting of vegetation within the settlement, wind and dust could be kept aloft and away from inhabited areas across the whole extent of the settlement.

The bustle and intensity of activity on the main thoroughfares were a notable feature of the Islamic town. The animated nature of its commercial sections and the awareness of a rich texture of human contact and activity were, and in some cases still are, the very life force of Islamic urbanism. In sharp contrast to the harsh desolation and silence of the desert, the *suqs* or bazaars provided access to a multitude of goods and services. . . .

Turning away from the main thoroughfares, a further contrast was encountered as the traveler ventured into the residential quarters on either side. Here the streets were much narrower, with walls often within touching distance on either side. The intimacy and semi-private atmosphere of these streets were borne in on the visitor as the shade provided by the dense building pattern created cool conditions in which to linger. The noise of the main streets was quickly cut to a distant murmur as the traveler moved further into the quarter. . . .

On gaining entry to a private house, yet another contrast was unveiled as the anonymous faces of the outsides of houses presented to the street were transformed by the wealth of detailed internal decoration, apparent in even quite modest homes. Houses were usually built on the courtyard principle with rooms opening onto a central space, often embellished with a fountain. This space provided the chief communal living area for the family. In keeping with the modesty of Islamic tradition, rooms of one part of the house were used only by women and the overall layout catered for the entertaining of guests without their need to encounter all members of the household.

The courtyard principle provided the ultimate achievable protection of private open space from the extremes of temperature, dust and wind outside the settlement. In an almost cell-like structure the town was set within its walls as a first line of protection from the environment. The residential quarters, often within their own walls, were then located close together in a pattern which afforded mutual protection of each building by all the others. The building density did nothing to compromise the privacy of individual houses orientated inwards as they were, so that a third and final line of protection between courtyard and residential street was afforded by the house itself. . . .

Moving finally towards the centre of the town, the traveler was confronted with the mosque. These were originally built not so much as houses of God but as a means by which to exclude unbelievers from regular prayer ceremonies. The addition of minarets, though partly only ornamental, was made to project the muezzin's call to prayer, with other mosques built once the call was out of earshot in an expanding city.

The more recent urban settlements in the Middle East often lack the high degree of unity and atmosphere found in the still-existing, specific features of the older Islamic towns. The flavor of these old urban communities, in complete contrast to the desolation all around them, was at once intimate, intricate, and intense. Thus, cities such as Baghdad, Cairo, Fez, or Tehran—situated in one of the harshest environments in the world—could provide comfortable living conditions for populations running into the hundreds of thousands.

Source: Roberts/Hugh, *Urban Profile of the Middle East*, Palgrave, reproduced with permission of Palgrave Macmillan.

The Islamic world is rich in art, architecture, culture, history, and tradition. Religion is the centerpiece of that world, and ornate mosques dominate each cityscape, much as Christian cathedrals dominate older cities in Europe. An example is the Masjed-e-Jame mosque in Isfahan, a city of 1.3 million people in central Iran.

The Europeans, however, never viewed the Middle East as the valuable prize that Latin America and Africa were, so they made limited efforts at colonization. Britain administered Egypt as a protectorate from 1882 to 1914, but otherwise was content to trade. Yet trade with outsiders was sufficient to weaken the centuries-long Islamic pattern. Despite efforts by many Muslims to bar non-believers and their way of life (including books, telephones, and automobiles), their world was changing.

As European influence spread across the region, new urban patterns emerged. For example, the French textile industry in Egypt after 1830 sparked urban growth throughout the rest of that century. From Cairo to Beirut to Tehran, suburban districts swelled beyond the quarters of the old cities, and new, wider roads were routinely clogged with motor vehicles (Cleveland 2004).

The real change, however, went deeper than the physical level. Foreign traders ventured into rural areas to make better deals for agricultural products, thereby passing up the ancient bazaars. Foreign investors opened businesses and factories in Middle Eastern cities and began undercutting the prices of the traditional guilds. This new competition altered the face of the entire region's economy. Where local sheikhs had administered land communally and restricted the open-market sale of goods, now people began to sell land, goods, and skills to the highest bidder. The ultimate cost was a weakening of traditional authority and an erosion of long-established communities. Before long, the earlier, self-sufficient, subsistence economies of Middle Eastern cities evolved into export-oriented ones that were dependent on the economies and needs of Europe and North America. Of course, this process only accelerated with the discovery of the new "black gold" of the region: oil.

Modern Cities

Economic development increased the prominence of coastal cities and undermined the significance of inland urban areas, thereby sparking a major migration to those cities. As in Latin America and Africa, this urban migration taxed the city's capacity to provide for its people. Iran's urban population, for example, increased 10-fold—from nearly 17 million in 1950 to 71.2 million in 2007, with more than two-thirds now living in cities, compared to 27 percent in 1950. The urban population in Syria also grew dramatically during the same time period, going from 1 million to more than 9.6 million, an increase from 31 to 51 percent of the total population (United Nations Population Division 2008). In addition, the free-market economy created in the Middle East, as elsewhere, a relatively large middle class of affluent entrepreneurs, who mostly live in new and exclusive suburbs outside the old cities.

Rapid urban growth also established a primate-city pattern for the entire region. Tehran, for instance, has outdistanced all other Iranian cities in size, market strength, and problems. In similar fashion, Baghdad, Kuwait City, Damascus, Beirut, Amman, and Cairo dominate their countries. As elsewhere in poor regions, some urbanists see the existence of such primate cities as curbing the growth of other cities and creating virtually insoluble problems.

In short, contemporary Middle Eastern cities are in a period of intense social change. Most are no longer the pure Islamic cities of the past millennium, yet they are not likely to become fully westernized. Like the cities of Latin America and Africa, these cities are in the process of forging a new and complex urban tradition. The emphasis here is on the word *complex*. Generalizations about cities within the context of the Arab-Islamic culture would therefore be unrealistic. The countries in which Middle Eastern cities exist include the extremely poor (Sudan, Yemen), charity cases supported by other countries (Egypt, Jordan, Lebanon), the oil rich (Kuwait, Saudi Arabia), the socialist (Syria), and those still showing a colonial imprint (Morocco, Tunisia). Middle Eastern countries and cities thus find their urban development being influenced by their economic and political context (Abu-Lughod 2007).

ASIAN CITIES

The richness and complexity of Asian culture forces us to be highly selective (Figure 13–5). Indeed, of all global regions, Asia provides the greatest challenge, because it encompasses almost 30 percent of the earth's land area and is a region of many sharp contrasts: Japan is a highly industrialized, rich nation, with one of the world's lowest birth rates. China is poorer but with a rapidly growing economy and the largest urban population of any country in the world. Southeast Asia stands out as having no real tradition of indigenous cities at all, yet despite this history, major cities now are growing at a startling rate. Despite some gains, India is still struggling to address urban problems as serious as those found anywhere in the world. We begin there.

India

Chapter 2 revealed that the Indus Valley region had thriving cities, such as Moenjo-Daro, as early as 2500 B.C.E. And in antiquity, the fabled opulence and beauty of ancient India and China held nearly mythical fascination for Westerners. These myths enticed that most famous of world travelers, Marco Polo, to set out from Venice in 1271 to find an easy route to the East.

European Domination. In the seventeenth century, the British began their colonization of India. In 1639, they established George Town (later to become Madras) at the mouth of the Cooums River on India's southeastern coast. By 1661, the British had gained control of Bombay Island from the Portuguese, and in 1690, they established the city of Calcutta. As in Latin America and Africa, such cities had a dual purpose: as centers of political control and as bases for economic exploitation.

Where cities already existed, like Delhi, the British simply constructed a second settlement next to it—in this case, New Delhi. This pattern of separation was nearly identical to the dual-city African settlements described earlier, resulting in a striking contrast between the indigenous part and the Anglicized part. One typical distinction would be a congested urban center in the old section and carefully planned, often-spacious sections nearby.

The older area (the original city) typically has a form much like that of the Islamic cities described in the last section. Crowded into a

FIGURE 13–5 Map of Major Asian Cities

379

Like many Asian and Middle Eastern cities, Delhi, a city of about 10 million people, suffers from growing pains. India's growing population increasingly worsens traffic congestion, and many roads cannot cope with the increasing volume. Streets typically are jammed with cars, bicycles, and pedestrians moving at a snail's pace, especially at the intersections.

central market or bazaar, numerous small retail shops offer a vast range of goods, including foods, cloths, hardware, and jewelry. Surrounding the marketplace is a residential area strictly divided into quarters, dividing Muslims from Hindus and separating Hindus according to their caste position. Brahmins and other high castes are usually in the best-built residential areas, either in or near the center of the old cities. The laboring castes and the menial outcastes of lowest socioeconomic status occupy the poorest houses, which tend to be located in the outskirts rather than in the center. The British part of the city, on the other hand, is very Western in form, with broad streets, often arranged in a grid pattern. At the center is a trading and manufacturing area, with a railroad leading outward.

Modern Cities. India's rate of population increase (about 1.6 percent annually) leads demographers to project that its 2008 population of 1.15 billion may grow to more than 1.7 billion in 2050, by that time easily surpassing China to become the world's most populous nation. Demographers project that India's urban areas will gain 197 million more people between 2008 and 2025, and an additional 180 million by 2050, giving it the world's second-largest urban population at 0.9 billion (United Nations Population Division 2008).

Kolkata (Calcutta). Although Kolkata is favorably located for trade in northeastern India, its land slopes away eastward and westward from the Hooghly River to marshes and swamplands, thereby confining the metropolitan area to a strip only three to five miles wide on either bank. Reclamation projects, however, have allowed some expansion. With the exception of the grid pattern in the central area where Europeans formerly lived, the narrow roads have a haphazard character. With Kazi Nazrul Islam Avenue as the only express highway, and few river crossings, Kolkata's transportation system—like its utilities and municipal facilities—is heavily overburdened. Most of the city's heavily used roads are in poor repair. The 17-mile subway system carries an estimated 25 percent of Calcutta's 7 million commuters as an alternative to the older trams and buses.

Kolkata remains the world's largest producer of jute, but the city also operates as a port, shipping coal, iron, manganese, mica, petroleum, and tea from its hinterland. Its river channel, however, enables Kolkata to handle only a small share of India's imports and exports. Although set in one of the poorest and most overpopulated regions of India, Kolkata's artistic, cultural, and intellectual life thrives. Home to three major universities and known as the "cultural capital" of India, Kolkata is unmatched among Indian cities in the volume of people who flock to its art exhibitions, book fairs, and concerts. Never very far away, however, are hundreds of shanty-towns (*bustees*), which contain fully one-third of the metropolitan area's 13.2 million residents. Worse off still are the hundreds of thousands of Kolkata's people who are entirely homeless and sleep either on the streets or wherever they can find temporary shelter. People dump all manner of human and other refuse into open sewers. Needless to say, disease is widespread.

Mumbai (Bombay).   Not only is Mumbai, a port city on India's western coast, unable to care for its people now, legions of newcomers still stream in from the countryside, where life is even worse. Such migration—the primate-city pattern—depletes the rural areas of people and creates huge, unworkable cities.

About two-thirds of Mumbai's 12 million residents are concentrated on an island, giving this city one of the highest population densities in the world. Mumbai has another distinction, as India's most culturally and religiously diverse city. More than half its residents are Hindu, with the remainder divided among Muslims, Christians, Parsis, Buddhists, Jains, and Sikhs. To make matters even more complex, Mumbai's people speak three major languages: Marathi, Gujarati, and Hindi.

The surrounding Black Cotton Soils, India's greatest cotton-growing area, has made Mumbai one of the largest cotton textile centers in the country. This industry employs almost half of Mumbai's factory workers. Most others are employed in the production of silk, artificial fibers, chemicals, and glassware or in the dyeing, bleaching, and printing industries. Most rural migrants, however, are illiterate and lack industrial skills. Unable to find factory work, they get by as best they can, typically living in deplorable conditions. Perhaps 40 percent of Mumbai's people lack an adequate diet, and virtually everyone contends with an unsanitary environment.

Outlook.   The long-run picture for India's cities may be somewhat brighter. Recent progress has occurred against hunger, and transportation, electricity, and schooling are more widely available than ever before. Some rural areas—notably the Punjab in the north—are self-sufficient, and smaller cities (those under 100,000 people) seem to be faring better than the major cities like Mumbai, Delhi, Kolkata, and Chennai.

A growing economy has improved living standards since the 1990s, particularly for an estimated 100 to 200 million middle-class consumers. Since 1994, poverty has declined by about 10 percentage points. Capitalizing on its large, growing numbers of educated people skilled in the English language, India has become a major exporter of software services and software workers. Negative factors include the desperate poverty of about one-fourth of the population and the impact of the huge and expanding population on an already overburdened environment. Whether the positive trends and hopes can finally eradicate the urban horrors in this country remains to be seen.

China

Like India, China is a land of ancient cities. Beijing (Peking), as profiled in Chapter 9, has long stood as a magnificent center of Chinese culture. Today, some of traditional China remains, but this rapidly modernizing trade nation is now a major economic power.

Foreign Domination.   From the mid-nineteenth century until the end of World War II, China was subjected to foreign control, first by Europeans and then by the Japanese. Invaders occupied the cities, particularly the so-called treaty ports that were opened to them by the Treaty of Nanking, which ended the Opium Wars in 1843. From Shanghai to Canton, Europeans remade parts of Chinese cities. Hotels, parks, tennis courts, and residential areas emerged, all catering to non-Chinese. To oversee European control of the area's economy, each city had a European-style central business district, complete with banks, corporate headquarters, and docks equipped to handle Western ships. As always, the Europeans imagined themselves as on a "civilizing" mission.

Not surprisingly, the Chinese people resented such treatment. Thus, when the People's Republic was established in 1949, Mao Zedong and his followers made a concerted effort to eradicate all aspects of European influence and privilege from China's cities. Moreover, believing that cities, by their very nature, undermined revolutionary ideals, Mao encouraged China's citizens to remain in their rural villages and transform the country from there. More extreme action was also taken. During the 1970s, the highly regimented and often brutal Maoist system forced perhaps 25 million urbanites from large cities into small towns and rural villages. Despite these efforts, however, China's urban population continued to grow. Although reliable data are hard to come by, only about 10 percent of the Chinese population was urban in 1950, while the urban share had increased to 44 percent by 2008 (*Britannica Book of the Year* 2009:548; Davis 1969, 1972).

Modern Cities.   In the 1970s, China introduced major reforms aimed at curbing population growth and stimulating economic growth in order to help Chinese cities "catch up quick." It allowed cities to introduce private enterprise in an attempt to create a flexible, market-driven economy, but one that remained under centralized, one-party political control. As a result, China's gross domestic product has grown 10-fold since 1978. China now stands as the second-largest economy in the world after the United States, although

in per capita terms, the country is still lower-middle income (Central Intelligence Agency 2008).

Special Economic Zones.   One radical innovation was the establishment of so-called Special Economic Zones, such as the city of Xiamen in southern China. With a population of about 1.6 million, Xiamen is so liberalized from the old policies that it seems to be almost capitalist. The city is a free-trade zone where China's manufacturers can wheel and deal with their Western counterparts without the restrictiveness that characterized the Mao regime. Chongqing, a city of more than 6 million people, serves as another example. The Beijing government gave the city free rein to make deals with foreign companies, and it encouraged Chongqing's citizens to use their ingenuity to find ways to make the city more productive. Another city, Guangzhou, with more than 8 million people, is alive with free enterprise. Glittering window displays of cosmetics, fashions, and video appliances on major streets like Dongfanglu look more like Nathan Road in Hong Kong than like anything previously seen in China. On the side streets, private stalls selling clothes, stir-fried food, and household commodities line block after block.

Hong Kong.   In 1997, Hong Kong once again came under Chinese sovereignty, returned by Great Britain, which had forced China to cede the 380 square miles after the First Opium War (1840–1842). Located on the southeastern coast of mainland China just 80 miles southeast of Canton, Hong Kong has 6.9 million residents, giving it a population density of more than 16,400 people per square mile, double that of Los Angeles (United Nations Population Division 2008).

Not surprisingly, overcrowding is omnipresent. Shantytowns, which have virtually disappeared from the People's Republic, house some 15 percent of the city's population despite determined efforts to provide public housing. Other, particularly older, housing is bursting at the seams. Even the port itself has become a kind of slum, housing hundreds of thousands of the city's poor

From a distance, Hong Kong, as viewed here from Victoria Peak, could easily be mistaken for a North American city, but even this highly successful city, now under Chinese communist rule after 150 years of English control, contains shantytowns. Some poor residents live in shacks on the city's outskirts, while others live in the harbor in Chinese-style boats called "junks."

on Chinese-style boats called junks. In some areas, one can literally walk across much of the harbor by simply stepping from one moored junk to another. On one level, Hong Kong has been and continues to be very successful. It has become the most important trade port on the China coast other than Shanghai, and it has generated an industrial machine that is the envy of much of the world, replacing a number of other major manufacturing points. That industrialization, however, together with high population density, has resulted in serious air pollution problems three times worse than those in New York City (Lou 2007).

Japan

Japan is a notable exception to the over-urbanization–underdevelopment pattern so common elsewhere in the non-Western world. Because it was never colonized, Japan was spared the social indignities and exploitation-oriented urban economy so characteristic of many other regions. Thus, the cities and urban life of Japan stand in marked distinction to those in most of Asia.

Early Cities. The urban roots of Japan extend back to at least the eighth century C.E., when ruling elites established a series of provincial capitals. The *samurai* (a warrior caste) protected these capitals, which were weakly linked to an emperor living in the capital city of Kyoto. Within this feudal structure, local elites kept the citizenry in subjugation over the next few centuries while they warred with each other for control of various regions. At the end of the sixteenth century, a samurai named Ieyasu emerged victorious over the warring elements, and as *shogun* (leader and protector of Japan), he established his capital at the city of Edo (now Tokyo). Ieyasu and his successors set about reorganizing the administrative system of Japan, putting greater emphasis on cities. By the eighteenth century, Edo had a population of nearly 1.5 million, making it the largest city in the world (at the time, London had a population of 900,000). Osaka and Kyoto had populations of more than half a million.

Over the centuries, the growth of Japanese cities produced, as it had in Europe and North America, a wealthy and powerful middle class. By the mid-1800s, these merchants controlled the purse strings of the country, and the power of the shogun declined considerably. Amid cries for revolution, the shogun stepped down in 1868. The new, 16-year-old emperor, Meiji, urged his country to end centuries of economic isolation and become a modern nation strong enough to resist attempts at colonization. The Japanese responded. In less than half a century, Japan became a world power economically, technologically, and militarily. As people flocked to the cities, industrialization proceeded throughout the twentieth century. Japan's lack of the natural resources needed to run its industrial machine, however, as well as its own imperialistic ambitions, led the country into foreign expansion and, finally, into the disaster of World War II.

Modern Cities. The economic success of contemporary Japanese cities is remarkable. Government–industry cooperation, a strong work ethic, mastery of high technology, and a comparatively small defense allocation (roughly 1 percent of gross domestic product) helped Japan advance with extraordinary rapidity in the past several decades to become one of the most powerful economies in the world. Another reason for Japan's success lies in its unique combination of the spirit of free enterprise and a collective orientation, in which employees hold great loyalty to their companies.

Japan's economic growth, however, has a downside. Exorbitant land costs and expensive housing either force urbanites to live in small-sized dwellings in wall-to-wall lots without any traditional Japanese gardens or else to commute long distances by subway or commuter rail lines. The typical commuter, forced to live in a satellite town because of high city housing costs, travels 1 hour and 30 minutes each way to and from work. During rush hour, commuter lines operate at 250 percent of capacity, necessitating the employment of "pushers" to force additional passengers into overcrowded cars. Heavy automobile traffic clogs the city streets, including the express roads built above the streets because of space limitations.

On the positive side, Japan has established an exemplary health care system, and its life expectancy (82 years) is among the world's highest. The Japanese have significantly reduced crime, unemployment (only 3.9 percent in 2007), and slums. They have the strictest air pollution standards in the world, and their high-quality urban lifestyle impresses visitors, who express amazement at the tidiness of urban facilities, the reliability of public transportation, and the quality of restaurants. The thriving central business districts bedazzle the first-time visitor to Japan, even a visitor from the United States or Western Europe; for example, Tokyo's Ginza district, alight at night, makes New York's Great White Way and London's Piccadilly Circus seem tawdry in comparison. In Asia, only Hong Kong and Singapore provide partial parallels.

At the same time, although Tokyo–Yokohama is a major primate city, it is only twice the size of the Osaka–Kobe–Kyoto complex and other vital urban centers—Hiroshima and Nagasaki, for example—that exist elsewhere in Japan. All have industrialized effectively, spreading wealth and opportunity throughout the country. This keeps "overload" on a single city to a minimum.

In contrast to other non-Western countries, Japan's population is shrinking. Its multiyear low birth rate and current **total fertility rate** (the average number of children a woman has during her lifetime) of 1.3 indicate that its 2008 population of 127.7 million will be only 95 million by 2050 (United Nations Population Division 2008). As a result, Japan can provide jobs for its citizens and keep the lid on the massive shortage and pollution problems that bedevil many other cities throughout the world. Because it has the world's most rapidly aging population, however, Japan faces severe economic issues in terms of health care and pension costs, which are also anticipated by all Western nations.

Southeast Asia

Unlike India and China, Southeast Asia has little tradition of large, indigenous cities. Most of its urban areas are the product of Chinese or European influence within the past few centuries. However, the principal cities of the region—Yangon, formerly Rangoon (in Myanmar, formerly Burma), Bangkok (Thailand), Ho Chi Minh City (formerly Saigon, in Vietnam), Manila (Philippines), Jakarta (Indonesia), and Singapore (Republic of Singapore)—essentially reflect the themes we have encountered throughout Asia. A few portraits will illustrate.

Singapore.   Situated at the southern end of the Malay Peninsula, Singapore is the largest port in the region and the fourth largest in the world. Despite a dearth of natural resources, it prospers as a center of East–West trade. In 2008, Singapore, which is 100 percent urban, had a population of 4.8 million, with about 75 percent Chinese, 14 percent Malayan, and 9 percent Asian Indian. Population density (nearly 18,000 people per square mile) is thus a problem (United Nations Population Division 2008). To reduce congestion and pollution, the government bans cars from the city center during working hours; only those few with an expensive entry permit may drive into the central business district during the day.

As the city's population increased throughout the twentieth century, shantytowns (*kampongs*) and squatter settlements appeared on Singapore's periphery. To alleviate the situation, the government took a novel, if heavy-handed, approach: It ripped up old neighborhoods, constructed thousands of high-rise apartment buildings, and literally forced the city's population into them. Importantly, most residents either own or are in the process of purchasing their apartments through a government-incentive program. The process has transformed an old Asian city into an ultramodern one. From a distance, today's Singapore appears Western, with a clearly recognizable downtown and apartment high rises almost as far as the eye can

see. The high rises have absorbed more than four-fifths of the city's population, and each group of well-maintained buildings boasts its own school, parking lot, community center, social facilities center, and lush landscaping.

Singapore thrives with its open-market economy, strong service and manufacturing sectors, and excellent international trading links derived from its history as a **break-of-bulk** port. The manufacturing, financial, and business services sectors dominate economic growth. Exports are booming, led by the electronics sector, particularly U.S. demand for disk drives. In applied technology, per capita output, investment, and labor discipline, Singapore is becoming Southeast Asia's financial and high-tech hub (Central Intelligence Agency 2009).

Significantly, Singapore's population growth is under control. Its growth rate of about 0.6 percent a year is much lower than that in almost all other cities of the developing world. Its success in population control is the product of an all-out attack: Singapore's government made contraceptives and abortion readily available, decreased taxes for families with fewer children, increased educational and housing benefits for small families, and raised hospital costs to families for each additional child.

All of this progress comes at a price: Singapore has a highly autocratic government. Rigid social regulations control people's lives. Violators receive harsh punishments, even for minor offenses—littering is punishable by a heavy fine, and drawing graffiti is punishable by caning. Singapore thus is a tightly controlled society, but its citizens accept the regimentation and prosper.

Jakarta.   Indonesia, lying along the equator between the Asian mainland and Australia, consists of 17,000 islands, of which only 6,000 are inhabited. As the fourth most populous country in the world, Indonesia is the largest Muslim nation. Nearly 80 percent of the country's total population (growing from 79.5 million in 1950 to 234 million in 2008) resides on the three islands of Java, Madura, and Sumatra. As a primate city, Jakarta, on the island of Java, with its 9.1 million residents has a population density of 10,500 persons per square mile, but in Java as a whole, the population density is less than one-fourth that in Jakarta (United Nations Population Division 2008).

To reduce the strain on severely crowded areas of the archipelago, Indonesia initiated a voluntary but controversial transmigration program through which poor, landless families in overpopulated areas move to underdeveloped regions and begin new lives with a house, land, and technical assistance. Since the program started in 1950, more than 12 million Indonesians have relocated, half of them without government sponsorship. Violent conflicts with the indigenous populations, resulting in hundreds of deaths, and accelerated deforestation of sensitive rainforest areas, however, have been the unintended consequences.

The Indonesian capital, Jakarta, is a primate city par excellence, with a growing number of high-rise buildings and monumental traffic jams. People migrate to Jakarta for the same reasons they trek to all cities: They want a better life, and the city's booming economy is an attractive lure. One indicator of the potential for improving the quality of life in Jakarta and its hinterland is that between 1985 and 2008, the total fertility rate dropped from 4.1 to 2.4, thereby bringing Indonesia's population more under control.

In 1965, more than 60 percent of Indonesians lived in poverty, but by 2008, that figure was about 18 percent. Indonesia also has made significant improvements in education, health care, nutrition, and housing over the past several decades. Although Indonesia remains a poor country in most respects, its rising levels of education and literacy, combined with falling fertility, may help accelerate socioeconomic development and bring greater prosperity to Jakarta and its people (Central Intelligence Agency 2009).

Bangkok. Like Jakarta, Bangkok is relatively typical of Southeast Asia's cities and serves as the capital of Thailand, a country that was never colonized. Currently with a population of 6.7 million, the city has more people than all the 118 other Thai municipal areas combined. It is also nearly 18 times as large as Samut Prakan,

the country's second-largest city, making Bangkok the premier primate city of the world.

A few figures illustrate the predominance that such primacy causes in Thai affairs. Bangkok contains more than three-fourths of the nation's telephones and half its cars, consumes over four-fifths of its electricity, holds three-fourths of all commercial bank deposits, and generates two-thirds of the country's construction. All automobile roads, railroads, and airplane routes converge on the city (so much

A new high-rise apartment building towers over old Thai houses by a lake in central Bangkok. Rapid growth fueled by foreign investment has changed the face of the once-sleepy Thai capital as the country emerges as one of Asia's most vibrant countries. This stark contrast of old and new is a common sight throughout the Asian continent.

so that to go from one place to another, you have to go through Bangkok, even if it is out of your way). Most Thai universities are in Bangkok, as are all the country's television stations. The city has about 20 daily newspapers (a few other cities have one), and it is the seat of the federal government.

With such advantages, people are drawn to the city by the millions, further strapping its meager resources. A massive "riverboat culture," much like that in Hong Kong, houses many of the city's poor. About 20 percent of the city's population—1.3 million people—live in slum communities. Population density in the inner city is more than 11,000 persons per square kilometer, which is less than the 15,270 reported in 1987. Farther out, but still within the city, are about 1,300 persons per square kilometer, and that number is increasing (UN Environment Programme 2001). Bangkok thus is a city of contrasts. Its population growth further intensifies its overcrowding, traffic jams, and pollution, yet the city's cultural, economic, and educational opportunities attract many tourists, business leaders, and students.

Southeast Asia remains one of the least urbanized areas of the world (see Chapter 1, Table 1–2), yet its urban growth rate is incredible. In the past 20 years, Jakarta, Kuala Lumpur (Malaysia), and Hanoi (Vietnam) have tripled their populations. During the same period, Surabaja (Indonesia), Yangon, Manila, and Ho Chi Minh City have doubled theirs. This pattern of over-urbanization is not likely to stop, because natural population increase and in-migration will continue for the foreseeable future. The primate cities cannot keep up with staggering growth, however, nor meet obvious needs. Unlike Singapore, they draw population from the whole geographical spans of their countries. For example, people from all over Thailand (almost 200,000 square miles) flock to Bangkok. As a result, over-urbanization is rampant, causing a scarcity of jobs and services.

COMMON LEGACIES

With the exception of some parts of the Middle East, Southeast Asia, and Japan, all of the regions covered in this chapter were colonized. Although the specifics of such colonial control varied—it lasted for a longer period in Latin America than in Africa, and it destroyed indigenous culture more thoroughly in Latin America than in Asia—its legacy has been much the same.

Economic Legacies

Colonization left behind an urban system with an underdeveloped economy. In most instances, it was a process established for the benefit of a ruling elite and the citizenry of the mother country. Most colonial cities specialized in exports, and they showed little interest in generating wealth or opportunities for the bulk of the local population or in developing industrial capabilities. Thus, these cities prospered only to a point and remained relatively small. For example, in 1780, a full two centuries after its founding, Buenos Aires was a city of only 25,000, with few roads and virtually no contact with other cities. Compare this with the postcolonial cities of the United States. Freed of their ties with England, they exploded in population and wealth as they forged links with each other and the westward frontier. When independence came for developing countries in the twentieth century, however, they found their cities to be well behind Western cities in competitive advantage and without the capability to catch up. Despite their efforts, most are still unable to provide enough jobs or wealth for their populations.

Even in areas of the developing world that were never colonized directly, economic development has been slow. In non-colonial Southeast Asia—Thailand, for example—urban industrial capacities, especially automotive and textiles, have only recently expanded, overcoming the lack of a tradition of vital indigenous cities and previous, disadvantageous export-oriented trade agreements with Western countries. In the non-colonial Middle East, the situation is much the same. Although indigenous cities have long existed, the insular policies of Islam and foreign domination of trade in the last century produced cities unable to provide for the growing needs of their populations. (This situation is changing in some countries, as oil money continues to pour into the region.)

Exceptions to this pattern are Singapore, Hong Kong, and Japan. By means of its rigid politics, Singapore controls its population growth and maintains a steadily rising standard of living. No longer a British colony, Hong Kong has accomplished the latter goal (though not for all of its people by any means) but not the goal of population control. Japan has done both, and this makes it unique among these countries. Yet Japan's history is markedly different: It has a tradition of vital indigenous cities, no colonization, a strong commitment to industrialization that began a century ago, a basically stable political system, and a social structure flexible enough to allow most of its people the chance to improve their standard of living.

A crucial factor in the rapid urbanization of less-developed countries is improved agricultural production. During the 1960s, the so-called "Green Revolution" introduced new, high-yield varieties of rice, oats, corn, and wheat into developing countries, thereby expanding their food supplies to the point of surplus. Just as agricultural advances created a food surplus to enable the creation of early cities, so, too, have modern advances been a catalyst enabling more of the world's rural population to migrate to cities.

Political Legacies

In many areas of the developing world, colonization also left political instability in its wake. The leadership vacuum created by departing colonial powers left each country's rule either to a foreign-trained, native elite or simply "up for grabs" between competing factions. Foreign-trained elites (as in much of Latin America) typically re-created the limited-opportunity social structure of colonial days—advantageous to the few, and difficult for the many. Competing factions (in much of Africa) often generated ongoing violence

and unrest in urban areas. All these conditions further retarded economic growth. What corporation wants to invest heavily in a city where a coup may cause the loss or nationalization of its entire investment? Ironically, when corporations do invest, another negative reaction often follows. Many regard this type of investment as being a contemporary form of colonialism—an alliance between multinational corporations and government elites—and see it as a continuing strategy to exploit the people.

Another political consequence concerns the irrelevance of the arbitrary national boundaries established by the European colonizers in relation to the territorial boundaries of indigenous populations. The Spanish and Portuguese carved up Latin America in terms of what they were able to conquer, without concern for any native group's natural homeland. As a result, many peoples previously separated by political, linguistic, and other cultural factors for centuries became citizens of a single, newly constructed country. Similarly, these arbitrary boundaries separated some groups who, traditionally having shared a given territory, now found their lands to be split by the European conquerors. European powers enforced a similar but much more severe carving-up process in Africa. When political independence came, many nations had yet one more barrier to their rapid entry into the modern world: a local citizenry divided against itself by an artificial historical boundary. (Many analysts see this situation as still contributing to the political instability in many African nations today.)

COMMON PROBLEMS

The diversity of history, cultural traditions, religion, and politics accounts for the differences of cities in developing countries from those in developed countries. Islamic cities of the Middle East are in many respects radically unlike cities of North America. Equally important, the cities of the developing world—Latin

America, Africa, the Middle East, and Asia—vary tremendously among themselves. No brief formula can ever grasp the diversities existing among La Paz, Kano, Kolkata, and Tokyo; however, these diverse cities do share some common concerns.

Spiraling Populations

Latin America—much more urbanized than Asia or Africa—had a population equal to that of North America as recently as 1950. By 2008, though, the total population in Latin America and the Caribbean had skyrocketed to 577 million, far more than the 338 million people in North America. The growth rate in Latin America dropped from 2.0 percent in 1994 to 1.5 percent in 2008. Still, this level of population growth (which will increase the population to 778 million by 2050) is considerably higher than the annual percentage increases of Canada (0.3) and the United States (0.6). Throughout Latin America and the Caribbean, the total fertility rate (the average number of children a woman has during her lifetime) was 2.5 in 2008, versus 1.6 in Canada and 2.1 in the United States (Population Reference Bureau 2009).

Should the AIDS epidemic now rampaging across Africa be stopped, population growth (now about 2.4 percent annually) will only increase that much faster, given that continent's 2008 total fertility rate of 4.9, by far the highest in the world (Population Reference Bureau 2009). In 1990, only six African cities had a population exceeding 1 million, but by 2020, some 30 cities will reach this level. Between Benin City and Accra, demographers anticipate a region containing 25 million inhabitants, with five cities of 1 million people or more. Accommodating these burgeoning urban populations is a challenge that will require massive investment in infrastructure and social services as well as wise, talented, and patient leaders (Brockerhoff 2000)

As for Asia—where three-fifths of the world's population live—demographers project that its 2008 population of 4.1 billion, at its present total fertility rate of 2.4, will increase by 1.2 percent annually and reach 4.8 billion by 2025. The growth rate is higher in the Middle East (2.0 percent), where the present total fertility rate of 3.3 will result in its 2008 population of 225 million increasing to 290 million by 2025 (Population Reference Bureau 2009). By 2030, the urban population will reach 73 percent in the Middle East, 54 percent in Asia, 85 percent in Latin America and the Caribbean, and 50 percent in Africa (United Nations Population Division 2008).

In the future, demographers fear, population totals in less-developed countries will soar further. In most of these nations, one-third or more of the population is under the age of 15, so they have not yet entered their childbearing years. Another factor promoting a strong population increase in the less-developed countries is that scientific advances and technological improvements (vaccinations, better sewage systems, and the like) have brought death rates down sharply. Although this is obviously good news, it also contributes to a bigger overpopulation problem as time goes on.

Quality of Life

As the cities in poor countries swell in size, they often become less able to provide sufficient employment and even basic services in water, sanitation, waste removal, gas, electricity, and police and fire protection. In Latin America alone, where only one city exceeded a million people in 1930, 50 cities reached that level by 2000. Most of these cities include large numbers of poverty-stricken people. In 2002, the National Center for Policy Analysis estimated that in the 1990s, the number of impoverished Latin Americans increased from 200 million to 211 million, or roughly 40 percent of the region's population. This poverty is increasingly visible. Almost all Latin American cities are surrounded by *cinturones de miseria,* large belts of extreme poverty that often lack even the most basic comforts, infrastructure, and social services. Similarly, in Africa, Asia, and the Middle East, cities struggle with street congestion, overcrowding, inadequate infrastructure, and pollution.

Many of the less-developed countries are extremely poor—so much so that they simply cannot generate the capital they need to solve their cities' problems. Chronic underemployment and unemployment characterize many cities—a legacy of historical dependency on one or two trade goods and the lack of a diversified industrial base. One way that many nations attempt to improve this situation is by encouraging tourism. A mixed blessing, tourism brings the world's richest citizens into contact with its poorest, a contrast only the most myopic tourists fail to see.

Finally, political corruption, crime, and urban violence are everywhere on the rise. For example, in Lagos, Nigeria, one of Africa's most economically and technologically advanced cities, violent crime is a constant risk, and many streets have become so dangerous that few people go out at night. In the Caribbean, Latin America, Africa, and Asia, one can easily become a crime victim in almost any city.

Environment

An urban population impacts on the environment more than a rural population, particularly in terms of energy consumption for electricity, transportation, cooking, and heating. Because cities radiate less heat upward than rural areas do, they create "heat islands" that can trap pollutants and affect local weather patterns, generating more rain and thunderstorms. Since they also reduce the infiltration of water and lower the water tables, runoff occurs more rapidly, increasing the likelihood of floods and water pollution downstream (Torrey 2004). In cities experiencing rapid growth without the accompanying expansion of infrastructure to handle such growth, environmental problems like an inadequate supply of safe water and sanitation, lack of rubbish disposal, air pollution from vehicle exhausts, and industrial pollution have serious health implications.

Toxic pollution is a particular threat to the health of the developing world's urbanites, affecting more than 1 billion of its citizens. The World Bank says that as much as 20 percent of all the health problems in the developing world can be attributed to environmental factors, particularly pollution (CNN 2008). In the 2008 list of the world's dirtiest cities—based on a scientific comparison of air pollution, waste management, water potability, and presence of infectious diseases, among other factors—24 of the 25 dirtiest were in developing countries. Moscow, ranked fourteenth, was the exception. The cities nearest North America were Port au Prince, Haiti, at number four and Mexico City at number five (Luck 2008).

Shantytowns

One of the major problems accompanying rapid urbanization has been the growth of city slums or squatter settlements and shantytowns on the periphery of the cities, as mentioned throughout this section (see the accompanying the *Urban Living* box on pages 391–392). They have many names: *bidonvilles* ("tin-can cities") in former French African colonies, *bustees* in India, *los villas miserias* ("cities of the miserable") throughout Latin America, and other names elsewhere. They also take many forms: mud and cardboard shacks outside Seoul, Korea; junks moored in Hong Kong harbor; and shacks in Africa and Latin America made from castoff lumber and tin. Their varying names and forms, however, are incidental to one underlying truth: They are the locales of abject poverty, malnutrition, poor sanitation, and disease. A quiet determination, strong family ties, and steadfast hope are often their positive counterparts as the inhabitants cling to the edge of survival, but these shantytowns nonetheless constitute the worst side of urban life in the developing world.

URBAN LIVING

Shantytowns Throughout the World

Africa

The hut was made of corrugated metal set on a concrete pad. It was a 10-by-10 cell. Armstrong O'Brian, Jr., shared it with three other men.

Armstrong and his friends had no water (they bought it from a nearby tap owner), no toilet (the families in his compound shared a single pit latrine), and no sewers or sanitation. They did have electricity, but it was illegal service tapped from someone else's wires and could power only one feeble bulb.

This was Southland, a small shanty community on the western side of Nairobi, Kenya. But it could have been anywhere in the city, because more than half the city of Nairobi lives like this—1.5 million people stuffed into mud or metal huts, with no services, no toilets, no rights. . . .

Outside, a mound of garbage formed the border between Southland and the adjacent legal neighborhood of Langata. It was perhaps 8 feet tall, 40 feet long, and 10 feet wide, set in a wider watery ooze. Two boys climbed the Mt. Kenya of trash. They couldn't have been more than 5 or 6 years old. They were barefoot, and with each step their toes sank into the muck, sending hundreds of flies scattering from the rancid pile. Perhaps they were playing King of the Hill. No. Once atop the pile, one of the boys lowered his shorts, squatted, and defecated. The flies buzzed hungrily around his legs.

When 20 families—one hundred people or so—share a single latrine, a boy pooping on a garbage pile is perhaps no big thing. But it stood in jarring contrast to something Armstrong had said as we were eating— that he treasured the quality of life in his neighborhood. For Armstrong, Southland wasn't constrained by its material conditions. Instead, the human spirit radiated out from the metal walls and garbage heaps to offer something no legal neighborhood could: freedom.

Asia

In the Bangladesh capital Dhaka, 3 million people—one-third of the city's population— live in slums. The working poor, who are most of the slums' inhabitants, earn their living as construction or factory workers, lorry drivers, rickshaw pullers, or work in informal sectors as domestic helpers or trash pickers.

One shantytown, named No. 2 Pura Basti or Burned Slum after it was damaged in a fire 15 years ago, is a cluster of tin and bamboo shacks that line narrow cobbled lanes flanked by open gutters. The shacks have electricity, but no running water or gas supply. The women cook food over wood-fired earthen stoves outside their shacks.

Just a few years ago, the only sources of water for the slum's 500 families were wells and an intermittent supply from an illegally connected tap to the city's water utility. For drinking water, the women and children had to wait in line for up to two hours to collect a pitcher or bucket of water from a local market or nearby houses where they often had to bribe guards and caretakers, or pay exorbitant prices. Today they use water from wells dug behind their shacks for bathing and washing, but for drinking and cooking, they get "safe" water from the slum's "water point"—two hand pumps that draw water from an underground reservoir that is filled with piped water supplied by Dhaka's water utility.

About four years ago, the Dhaka city corporation, which owns the land, paved the slum's dirt lanes and installed some community toilets. But these basic latrines, which are concrete rings set in the ground without any water or flushing facilities, drain into an

(continued)

open gutter, which in turn is linked to a nearby pond. The area reeks of garbage and human waste. Nearly 200 to 300 people, carrying pots of water, wait in long queues to use the toilets each morning, and children and the elderly, who cannot make it on time, defecate in the gutters outside their homes.

Latin America

In severely overcrowded Mexico City, one-third of its residents lack such essential services as electricity and sewage facilities. Most are squatters who live anywhere they can: in abandoned boxcars or shacks teetering on hillsides, in public parks, in roadside hovels. About a quarter-million people live illegally in 360 shantytowns built on property they don't own. Or at least, they don't own it yet, since Mexican law gives squatters property ownership rights after five years' occupancy.

Squatters often live without drainage, with frayed electric cables hooked illegally into the city's electricity grid, and drinking water from buckets or leaky rubber hoses. A fire apparently sparked by illegal electric hookups swept through about 100 shacks in "The Last Hope" squatters' camp in an industrial area of downtown Mexico City in 1998. No serious injuries were reported. Most area residents didn't even know the tarpaper shacks had been built between two factories until the squatters' burned possessions were shoveled into the street.

The problem isn't confined to the capital. A fire, also resulting from an illegal electric hookup, swept through a shantytown in Juarez in 2003, killing four women. Another similarly caused fire swept through a public market in Durango in 2004.

Sources: Adapted from numerous sources, including Robert Neuwirth, *Shadow Cities: A Billion Squatters, A New Urban World.* London: Routledge, 2004, pp. 3, 5; Mallika Wahab, "Bangladesh Slums Demand Access to Clean Water," *International Journal of Humanities and Peace* 19 (2003): 46–47; Chris Hawley, "Trying to Exorcise Mexico's 'Little Devils'," *Arizona Republic* (December 20, 2004).

Latin American shantytowns, like their African and Asian counterparts, typically exist on the outskirts of cities, such as this inappropriately named "Villa 31," with downtown Buenos Aires in the background. These squatter settlements pose the same health, economic, and psychological problems found in other slum settlements in the developing world.

SUMMARY

In decades past, social scientists debated whether economic growth was preferable to the preservation of local urban traditions. People taking the preservationist position usually argued, quite convincingly, that "creeping Westernization" by way of industrialization and foreign-oriented trade was rapidly obliterating ancient urban traditions, which were valuable not only to their peoples but also to the world as examples of the alternative forms that the urban process could take.

Although the preservation argument has lost none of its appeal today, the simple fact is that most cities in the developing world are inundated with so many people that they cannot provide adequately for their populations without major advances in economic vitality and technological efficiency. Already—as we have seen perhaps most dramatically in Kolkata—millions upon millions of the world's urban dwellers are suffering tremendous deprivation. Moreover, some of the large cities in developing nations have become so crowded and polluted that they are straining the carrying capacity of their environment.

Once again, the city is literally transforming the world, as it has twice before. In Chapter 2, we spoke of the first and second urban revolutions—the first occurring when people moved into cities in large numbers for the first time, from approximately 8000 to 2000 B.C.E., and the second occurring during the capitalist and industrial revolutions, which began around 1700 C.E. and continued through the first half of the twentieth century. This second urban revolution was responsible for a demographic transition—an unprecedented growth in population, made possible by the city's ability to provide a higher level of income, technological efficiency, and health care than those in rural areas. Now, once again, the city is fostering a demographic transition, only this time with two differences: (1) The greatest population growth is not in the developed world but, rather, in developing countries; and (2) the magnitude of the change makes the demographic transition of 1700 to 1950 look meager by comparison. This is the third urban revolution. No one ever expected the kind of growth we are seeing now.

Consider this: A generation or two ago, one correctly thought of more-developed countries as the locales of the world's largest metropolitan areas, or **urban agglomerations** as they are sometimes called. No more: Rapid growth and urban migration already have moved numerous developing world cities into this category, as the left-hand column of Table 13–1 shows. The shift to developing world dominance becomes even more pronounced

TABLE 13–1   The World's 10 Largest Urban Agglomerations, 2007 and 2025

2007		2025	
Urban Area	**Population**	**Urban Area**	**Population**
Tokyo, Japan	35,700,000	Tokyo, Japan	36,400,000
New York-Newark, USA	19,000,000	Mumbai (Bombay), India	26,400,000
Mexico City, Mexico	19,000,000	Delhi, India	22,500,000
Mumbai (Bombay), India	19,000,000	Dhaka, Bangladesh	22,000,000
São Paulo, Brazil	18,800,000	São Paulo, Brazil	21,400,000
Dhaka, Bangladesh	17,900,000	Shanghai, China	19,400,000
Delhi, India	15,900,000	Mexico City, Mexico	21,000,000
Shanghai, China	15,000,000	New York-Newark, USA	20,600,000
Kolkata (Calcutta), India	14,800,000	Kolkata (Calcutta), India	20,600,000
Buenos Aires, Argentina	12,800,000	Karachi, Pakistan	19,100,000

Source: From *World Urbanization Prospects,* 2007 Revision. Copyright © 2007 by the United Nations, Population Division. Adapted with permission.

when we consider the longer term (Table 13–1, right-hand column). The only Western city in the Top 10 is New York, and by 2025, the projections are that it will drop from third to seventh place. Next, look at the magnitude of the urban areas in the 2025 column: The smallest one is larger than nine of the Top 10 cities in the 2007 column. These will truly be **megacities,** unprecedented in human history.

CONCLUSION

Thus we come, at the end of this overview of global urbanization, to no single solution for the problems we have encountered. Scholars themselves are divided about the causes and the most efficient solutions.

One conclusion, however, seems certain. Whatever is done, most cities of the developing world are going to continue growing at enormous rates for the foreseeable future. With this growth will come, inevitably, greater problems, including congestion, pollution, and major shortages of basic necessities. As each country copes with its crises, perhaps one or a combination of two or more solutions will emerge as being clearly superior, thereby lightening the load on other overburdened cities some decades hence.

It is no small task. Millions of poor people in less-developed countries are unable to advance greatly, because given the ever-increasing population, there simply will not be enough jobs, houses, or health services to go around. The evolution of cities in the developing world thus provides a marked contrast to that of European and North American cities. Perhaps the most remarkable aspect has been the speed at which their modern development has taken place—over decades in the developing world, compared with more than a century in Canada and the United States. So-called *over-urbanization* in the developing world may well get a good deal worse before it gets better.

The evolving cities throughout the developing world each have their own complex cultural traditions and unique histories. Previously, we discussed how Herbert Gans stressed the primacy of culture over space in detailing the variety of lifestyles *within* a city (Chapter 10), and how cultural values shape a city's physical and social form (Chapter 9). In this chapter, we saw how cities throughout the developing world may share some common legacies and problems but are also different in many ways from one place to another. The expanding global economy and telecommunications networks will link these cities more closely to one another than ever before, but they will also evolve through varied patterns of development, with each nation's cities having their own distinct characteristics.

KEY TERMS

apartheid   (372)
break-of-bulk   (385)
colonization   (363)
megacities   (394)

primacy ratio   (363)
primate cities   (362)
total fertility rate   (384)
urban agglomerations   (393)

INTERNET ACTIVITIES

1. At the International Data Base of the U.S. Census Bureau, you can quickly construct population pyramids for any developed or developing nation to get a quick sense of world population trends. Go to *http:// www.census.gov/ipc/www/idb/pyramids.html.*

2. The United Nations Population Division, at *http://www.un.org/esa/population/unpop. htm,* offers the latest facts on world urbanization prospects (left menu) as well as numerous other relevant information on the subject.

CHAPTER 14

PLANNING THE URBAN ENVIRONMENT

Sometimes, cities work well (Portland, Oregon, and Toronto are frequent examples), and sometimes, they don't (Camden, New Jersey, and Detroit are often cited). Every city, however, struggles with various problems, some cities more so than others. In this chapter, we will introduce the work of individuals who responded to the shortcomings of cities with bold and provocative plans for improvement. Some tackled urban problems at the neighborhood level; others imagined radically transforming the entire city—or even society as a whole.

Not surprisingly, such plans have been controversial, because they frequently challenged cherished cultural beliefs, clashed with vested economic interests, or just seemed to be too radical. Only by giving all ideas some consideration, however, can we explore the possibilities for a better urban future.

VISIONS

In the late 1800s, what a vision Ebenezer Howard had! Deeply influenced by Edward Bellamy's novel *Looking Backward* (a utopian vision of the year 2000, in which all the problems of the city had been solved), Howard dedicated his life to realizing Bellamy's goal in England. As Howard saw it, the industrial city was a virtual nightmare: People streamed to these overcrowded cities, only to experience misery and despair.

Howard agreed that the city had advantages—opportunity, entertainment, and diversity—but he asked why cities should deny people the best of the country—a healthful environment, low population densities, and a sense of freedom. So, he set out to solve this dilemma by creating what he called the "Garden Cities of To-Morrow." In 1898, he wrote:

> The two magnets must be made one. As man and woman by their varied gifts and faculties supplement each other, so should town and country. The town is the symbol of society—of mutual help and friendly cooperation, of fatherhood, motherhood, brotherhood, sisterhood, of wide relations. . . . The country is the symbol of God's love and care. . . . All that we are and all that we have comes from it. Our bodies

are formed of it; to it they return. We are fed by it, clothed by it, and by it we are warmed and sheltered. . . . It is the source of all health, all wealth, all knowledge. . . . Town and country must be married, and out of this joyous union will spring a new hope, a new life, a new civilization. (2007:48; orig. 1898)

Celebrating the "marriage of town and country," Howard worked out the details of his **garden cities** plan, and he hoped to convince others that realizing his plan was not only desirable but also entirely possible. (The specific outline of his vision is illustrated in Figure 14–1 and described in the *Urban Trends* box on page 398.) Unfortunately, Howard's vision was one that many of his contemporaries could not understand. It struck conservatives as outlandish and liberals as too complex. Said the ultraliberal *Fabian News:*

> Mr. Howard proposes to pull [our cities] all down and substitute garden cities, each duly built according to pretty colored plans, nicely designed with a ruler and compass. . . . We have got to make the best of our existing cities, and proposals for building new ones are about as useful as would be arrangements for protection against visits from Mr. [H. G.] Wells' Martians [a reference to Wells's novel *The War of the Worlds*, which depicts a Martian invasion of earth]. (Quoted in Osborn 1965:11)

Undaunted, Howard pushed on. In 1903, in conjunction with a group of businessmen, he established his first garden city, Letchworth, about 35 miles from London. A second city, Welwyn (pronounced "well-en"), sprang up nearer London in 1919. On balance, both were quite successful, and they continue today as pleasant places to live. Still, until the 1940s, they remained Britain's only attempts at "planned" towns.

The entire history of urban planning is, in many ways, evident in the story of Howard's new towns. As the *Fabian News* noted, to alter established cities would be a massive, expensive, and disruptive undertaking. Cities are not only bricks and mortar. They are people's lives, and they rest on historical traditions, entrenched power relationships, and vested economic interests. Thus, suspicion typically greets plans for urban redesign. And given

FIGURE 14–1 The Garden Belt and Rural Belt

Source: Ebenezer Howard, *Garden Cities of To-Morrow* (Cambridge, MA: MIT Press, 1965), p. 52. Reprinted by permission of MIT Press.

the consequences of so much *bad* city planning (like urban renewal in the 1970s), suspicion is not altogether a bad thing.

CITY PLANNING IN WORLD HISTORY

Ebenezer Howard was hardly the first to undertake urban planning on a large scale. Moenjo-Daro, the Indus River Valley civilization of 2500 B.C.E. that we discussed in Chapter 2, had streets laid out in a grid pattern, broad thoroughfares, and individual houses designed for comfort and efficiency. Even more impressive were the Mexican cities of Teotihuacan, around 700 C.E., and Tenochtitlán, around 1500 C.E. Both capitals were large and richly symbolic. Expansive plazas, massive temples, and elaborate gardens were central features of

these cities. Finally, recall the case study in Chapter 9, in which we discussed the tightly controlled plan of Ming Dynasty Peking. Here, we saw planned city within planned city, all connected to convey key themes of China's culture.

Western cities also show a long history of planning. The Greeks planned Hellenic Athens, just as the Romans planned much of the pomp and majesty of Imperial Rome. Even towns of the Middle Ages showed some planning, especially in the walls built for protection and in the various "zones" set aside for specific activities. There were planned markets, squares, residential quarters, and always, the medieval church at the city's center. Still later, during the Renaissance, a veritable boom in urban planning arose, with careful efforts to achieve efficient traffic circulation

URBAN TRENDS

Sir Ebenezer Howard's Garden Cities of To-Morrow

Howard's Garden City was to cover about 1,000 acres at the center of a 6,000-acre tract. Figure 14–1 shows the idealized layout of the whole municipal area.

Six magnificent boulevards—each 120 feet wide—traverse the city from centre to circumference, dividing it into six equal parts or wards. In the centre is a circular space containing about five and a half acres, laid out as a beautiful and well-watered garden; and, surrounding this garden, each . . . in its own ample grounds, are the larger public buildings—town hall, principal concert and lecture hall, theatre, library, museum, picture-gallery, and hospital.

The rest of the large space encircled by the "Crystal Palace" is a public park, containing 145 acres, which includes ample recreation grounds within very easy access of all the people. Running all round the Central Park (except where it is intersected by the boulevards) is a wide glass arcade called the "Crystal Palace," opening on to the park. Here manufactured goods are exposed for sale, and here most of that class of shopping which requires the joy of deliberation and selection is done. The space enclosed by the Crystal Palace is, however, a good deal larger than is required for those purposes, and a considerable part of it is used as a Winter Garden—the whole forming a permanent exhibition of a most attractive character, whilst its circular form brings it near to every dweller in the town—the furthest removed inhabitant being within 600 yards.

Passing out of the Crystal Palace on our way to the outer ring of the town, we cross Fifth Avenue—lined, as are all the roads of the town, with trees—fronting which, and looking on to the Crystal Palace, we find a ring of very excellently built houses, each standing in its own ample grounds; and, as we continue our walk, we observe that the houses are for the most part built either in concentric rings, facing the various avenues (as the circular roads are termed), or fronting the boulevards and roads which all converge to the centre of the town. . . . [T]he population of this little city may be . . . about 30,000 in the city itself, and about 2,000 in the agricultural estate. . . .

On the outer ring of the town are factories, warehouses, dairies, markets, coal yards, timber yards, etc., all fronting on the circle railway, which encompasses the whole town, and which has sidings connecting it with a main line of railway which passes through the estate. This arrangement enables goods to be loaded direct into trucks from the warehouses and workshops, and so sent by railway to distant markets, or to be taken direct from the trucks into the warehouses or factories; thus not only effecting a very great saving in regard to packing and cartage, and reducing to a minimum loss from breakage, but also, by reducing the traffic on the roads of the town, lessening to a very marked extent the cost of their maintenance. The smoke fiend is kept well within bounds in Garden City; for all machinery is driven by electric energy, with the result that the cost of electricity for lighting and other purposes is greatly reduced.

Source: From Ebenezer Howard, *Garden Cities of To-Morrow,* excerpt from pages 50–56, © 1965 Massachusetts Institute of Technology, by permission of The MIT Press.

and to provide fortification against invasion. It was at this time that planners designed the radial boulevards of Paris—roadways as beautiful as they are practical.

Why Plan?

Early city planners sought, first, *to solve specific urban problems.* They planned underground sewage lines for health reasons, walls for protection, parks for leisure hours, and thoroughfares to facilitate movement.

Second, we know that the motives of city planners in Rome, Teotihuacan, Tenochtitlán, and Beijing were also *to glorify those in power.* Thus, the Emperor Augustus and his successors, declared to be gods by the Roman Senate in the first few decades of the Christian era, were "immortalized" by buildings, parks, plazas, and innumerable statues. City planners had a good reason to glorify the ruling elite: These people, after all, employed them. City planning, in short, often proceeds "from the top down." To ask "Why plan?" then, we also need to keep in mind another question: "For whom are cities planned?"

A third focus of urban planning is often the *glorification of important cultural values.* Ming Dynasty Peking was not only a monument to the all-powerful emperor but also a reminder to everyone of beliefs that were central to the Chinese way of life. Centuries later, during the Renaissance, the residency of the pope was re-established in Rome. To showcase the Catholic Church as the wealthiest and most important institution in the Western world, Pope Julius decided to replace the old St. Peter's Basilica with the greatest cathedral and piazza in Christendom. The result was the grand Piazza of St. Peter. A long processional way leads the visitor to a massive circular area before the cathedral, which leads to the cathedral itself. The faithful find a powerful religious experience in this setting; everyone is awed by the size and magnificent design of St. Peter's. Both reactions were important to the piazza's designers.

Something different is symbolized in Figure 14–2, which shows Sir Christopher Wren's plan for the rebuilding of London after the Great Fire of 1666 (see the case study in Chapter 2). Here, although the magnificent St. Paul's Cathedral (B in Figure 14–2) is a dominant focus, major roads lead not to the cathedral but to the city's stock exchange (A in Figure 14–2). The dominant feature of the plan, which ultimately was not adopted, was the financial and trade element of the city's life. London at the time was fast becoming the most powerful economic center in the world. City planning thus reflected this change.

Three concerns, then, appear again and again in the history of urban design. People plan their cities, or parts of them, in order to

A. Stock Exchange
B. St. Paul's Cathedral
C. Tower of London
D. London Bridge
E. Old Walls

THAMES RIVER

FIGURE 14–2   Sir Christopher Wren's Plan for the Rebuilding of London, 1666

Source: Arthur B. Gallion and Simon Eisner, *The Urban Pattern,* 4th ed. (New York: Van Nostrand, 1980), p. 43. Reprinted by permission of Van Nostrand Reinhold.

(1) solve specific problems, (2) serve the interests of those with wealth and power, and (3) reflect and intensify cultural ideals.

Planning in the Industrial Era: 1800–1900

Ebenezer Howard shared many concerns about the overcrowded industrial cities with the classical sociological theorists—Tönnies, Durkheim, Weber, Marx, Simmel, Park, and Wirth—whom we discussed in Chapter 5. Howard saw little hope for the industrial city, which he believed was a monument to greed and to the interests of the few rather than the many. Effective city planning, he believed, could never exist in cities of such size.

In many ways, Howard was right. Planning on a citywide scale did not exist in early cities. While quite a few industrial towns were built during the 1800s—Manchester and Birmingham in England, as well as Paterson, New Jersey, and Falls River, Massachusetts, in the United States (see Chapter 3) are good examples—by and large the underlying concern was limited to profit and efficiency.

In the early 1600s when the Dutch settled New Amsterdam at the tip of Manhattan Island, street development evolved more or less haphazardly, as in medieval European cities. Two centuries later, though, as the city expanded northward, city leaders in 1807 adopted a rigid, gridiron plan that they applied to the entire island regardless of topography. Profit and efficiency carried the day: "Straight-edged and right-angled houses," reported the city commission, when adopting the gridiron plan, "are the most cheap to build and the most convenient to live in" (Eisner, Gallion, and Eisner 1993:49).

In the new, trade-dominated city, tradition counted for little. Buildings went up only to be torn down as commercial interests dictated. Builders adopted architectural styles, such as Greek facades, "for show" and not for their deeper symbolism of a revered historic tradition (Goldberger 1989:xiv). With the major (and wonderful) exception of Central Park, the profit motive fundamentally shaped all of New York. Boston Commons, a park in midtown Boston, is another notable exception.

The "City Beautiful" Movement

In the United States, some architects, planners, and civic leaders had other ideas. The first significant innovation in U.S. city planning grew out of the 1893 Chicago World's Fair, which showcased architect Daniel Burnham's "White City" (a vision opposing grimy, sooty, industrial cities). Burnham proposed a city constructed around monumental civic centers built in a neoclassical style, with great public spaces and a network of parks all linked by spacious boulevards. Inspiring a **City Beautiful movement,** Burnham's ideas had considerable influence among urban planners across the country. Scarcely a major city exists without a city hall, courthouse, library, or train station built in imitation of ancient Roman and Greek architecture. Chicago, Cleveland, Detroit, Los Angeles, Minneapolis, St. Louis, San Francisco, and Washington, D.C., all initiated such City Beautiful projects after the fair.

The costs of this movement, however, soon led even advocates to scale back their plans. Moreover, some private interests, especially businesses, resisted compromising their narrow objectives. Before long, the City Beautiful movement simply went away. Any new communities built, whether nineteenth-century frontier towns or twentieth-century suburbs, usually lacked a large-scale plan, instead typically beginning with a non-descript Main Street center and then rippling outward in a gridiron design unless forced to adjust because of elevated terrain.

THE NEW TOWNS MOVEMENT

I will not cease from mental strife,
Nor shall my sword sleep in my hand,
Till we have built Jerusalem
In England's green and pleasant land

William Blake

This stanza by the great English poet and artist William Blake opens Sir Ebenezer Howard's book *Garden Cities of To-Morrow.* Howard's belief that his New Towns movement would solve all of urban society's ills influenced many others both in and beyond his native England.

Before we get further into this section, let's clarify what we mean by *new towns*. In this sense, we are not referring to a new settlement, such as that occurring in the development of the American and Canadian West, when railways decided where to build their station stops and a town would grow around it, or when the discovery of valuable metal ores resulted in a new boomtown. Instead, the sociological concept of a **new town** deals with the large-scale, holistic planning of a mixed-use, self-sufficient community—its physical design of streets and infrastructure; its provision of residential, commercial, educational, recreational, shopping, and service facilities; its center, squares, parks, lakes, and pathways; its blend of employment and leisure activities; and much more.

A Socialist–Feminist New Town

Howard greatly influenced Alice Constance Austin, an upper-class radical from Santa Barbara, California. Convinced that women were greatly oppressed, Austin proposed in the early 1900s a series of new towns based on communal dining and kitchenless houses. Only a "Socialist City," she maintained, could relieve women "of the thankless and unending drudgery of an inconceivably stupid and inefficient system, by which her labors are confiscated." (1935:63).

With help from co-investors, Austin founded her new town, Llano del Rio, in California, but like Howard, she soon found that such a venture could not sustain itself financially. After a brief tenure, the Llano group folded in 1917. Although they later resettled in New Llano, Louisiana, Austin's Socialist City movement never attained further success (Hayden 1978:286–87).

British New Towns

The devastation of London from repeated Nazi bombings during World War II created a desperate housing shortage and renewed interest in Ebenezer Howard's vision. In 1946, Britain passed the New Towns Act, providing for government sponsorship of new urban communities to draw population away from London and other cities. One central goal of the New Towns Act was to limit London's increasing sprawl by surrounding the city with a **green belt**—an idea

taken directly from Howard. The new towns were to be built beyond the green belt.

New communities—complete with industrial, housing, and commercial areas—were built at some distance from larger cities. In all, Great Britain built 34 new towns, with their success in large measure assured because of deep government involvement. The first new communities—called the Mark I towns—adhered closely to Howard's ideas and were modeled after Letchworth and Welwyn. Mostly single-family houses organized in neighborhoods, these communities of about 30,000 residents were completely self-sufficient centers of industry, housing, education, and transportation facilities.

A second wave of new towns—the Mark II group, built in the 1950s and 1960s—deviated rather significantly from Howard's original plan. Typified by Cumbernault, located outside Glasgow, Scotland, these towns reflected the government's concern that small cities of just 30,000 were insufficient to alleviate population problems in the larger cities. A second concern was that too many small towns would consume too much of what Britain had too little of—land. Thus, the Mark II towns (those built since the 1960s), with population projections of 80,000, began to sacrifice greenery for density and to emphasize central (rather than neighborhood) shopping and recreational facilities. The most recent new towns are larger still. One example, Milton Keynes, lies 50 miles north of London, with a population of about 185,000 living in its 120 square miles, and it is expected to grow to 300,000 by 2030.

Britain's new towns—Howard's "marriage of the city and country"—proved to be eminently successful at providing decent housing and sufficient jobs. On other levels, however, the new towns fell short. With their small number (34) and limited size, they have not had much impact on the large populations of Britain's large cities. Moreover, most of these towns are socially rather cliquish, with the same ethnic and class prejudices that one encounters in most large cities. Some critics claim that homogeneity is a product of the planning process itself, with its emphasis on neighborhoods. As sociologists often note, ingroup solidarity, which neighborhood living

Although London suburbs often contain single detached houses in close proximity to one another, these locales usually also contain a mixture of building types, such as this block of rowhouses, or else a high-density area with multiple-family dwellings. Such combinations of housing are in keeping with the new towns concept of comprehensive planning of a community.

facilitates, often creates a corresponding sense of outgroup hostility.

Another problem has been the inflexibility of many new-town plans. Rather than recognizing that cities are dynamic entities that must adjust to changing human needs, many new towns stuck rigidly to their original plans. Often, the result has been a sense of inefficiency and even oppression that, as we will see, crops up again and again in city planning efforts.

New Towns Worldwide

To some degree, early British new towns were anticity. They were small towns, their limited size suggesting a distinct dislike of large urban areas. They were also antigrowth, strictly limiting their population in the belief that more was always less. Bigness meant disorder and destruction of a delicate ecological balance between people and the environment. Several recent new towns, however, take an opposite

view. In France, the Netherlands, and Spain, new-town development has attempted to stimulate the growth of an entire urban region. Creating jobs around a cluster of industries, the new communities draw population from the countryside while also luring away people from nearby established cities. In the mid-1960s, for example, to accommodate population growth and "demagnetize" its cities, France developed five new towns near Paris, and others near Lille, Lyon, Marseille, and Rouen, in an effort to collect the population in the immediate area and lessen migration into those older cities.

Sweden. The Scandinavian countries, particularly Sweden, look on new towns as a form of "suburb control." Like many European and North American cities, Stockholm had a problem with suburban sprawl during the 1950s. In an effort to curb decentralization, the Swedish government planned a series of satellite cities linked to the central city and to each other by efficient transportation. The five cities, known as the Vallingby Complex, are distinct entities but look to the larger city for goods, many services, and jobs. Each of these small cities has about 10,000 people living in low-density housing within 300 yards of a subway-station/plaza complex.

As in Britain, the Swedes also built higher-density new towns. Instead of low-rise brick buildings that promote a sense of community and allow open space, the newer towns contain physically parallel rows of unattractive, look-alike, concrete-slab buildings with six to eight stories. These drab structures look much like sterile, low-income housing projects in the United States. Not surprisingly, these developments repel the middle class; only impoverished immigrants or low-income natives concentrate in them. Such places can also be found in France, Germany, and Italy, and there, as in Sweden, crime, drugs, and welfare dependency are common.

Australia.   Australia presents us with a different new-town concept, one designed to be the core of a new urban region and home to the national government. Located in the outback (isolated rural area), Canberra is some 180 miles from the seacoast metropolis of Sydney. Settled as early as 1912, Canberra was to be a new, inland city that would not only house the Australian government but also develop the Australian hinterland. This was no simple task. Canberra was far from Australia's normal trade routes, and it had no major resources (mineral deposits or cheap water power) to attract investors. Thus, government and planners were in complete control, which might well have pleased Ebenezer Howard.

The result is a physically beautiful city with a population now exceeding 330,000. Economically, however, the city has suffered because of its off-track location, unavoidable over-reliance on a single activity (government services), and implementation of relatively rigid plans that often put off businesspeople. For example, the government retains control of all land, so that businesses do not cluster near the center but, rather, are scattered throughout the city—a pattern that many find inefficient.

Canberra's widely dispersed single-family dwellings have also hindered the development of a sense of community. Similarly, the city's dependence on one major employer—the government—essentially created an upper- and middle-class city. Because of the high cost of living, most low-income families simply cannot afford to live there.

Brazil.   Brasilia, the inland capital of Brazil, presents a contrasting case. Conceived in the 1950s as a showcase for a modernizing Brazil, the city is about 600 miles from the coastal megalopolis of Rio de Janeiro. As with Canberra, Brasilia's location helped develop the nation's interior, with the intent of siphoning off population from the country's older cities.

An artificial lake surrounds much of the city and separates it from the suburban towns to the north. The cross-shaped plan of the central city, designed by the Brazilian architect Lúcio Costa, utilizes the North–South Axis, Brasilia's main transportation artery, and the East–West, or Monumental, Axis, lined by federal and civic buildings.

With just 12,000 people in 1957, Brasilia grew to more than 500,000 by 1970 and now exceeds 2.3 million. Expanding faster than anticipated as people streamed into the city looking for construction jobs, Brasilia abandoned or modified many parts of the original plan. As elsewhere in poor nations, migrants unable to find adequate housing constructed their own out of anything they could find. Thus, Brasilia evolved huge *favelas,* or squatter shantytowns, filled with working-class and poverty-stricken people and lacking waste removal, water, and electricity. Ironically, this "model" Brazilian city reflects all the problems that beset other Latin American cities.

All the new towns and cities that we've considered so far were government sponsored, with limited involvement of private investors. During the early history of the United States, government-planned communities were not unusual and included Williamsburg; Washington, D.C.; Indianapolis; Raleigh, North Carolina; Tallahassee, Florida; and Austin, Texas. Except for one program in the 1930s, however, U.S. new towns during the past

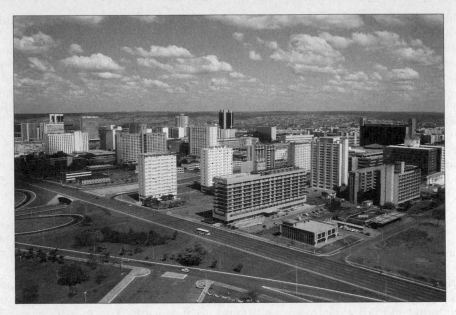

When first conceived and built in the 1950s, Brasilia was a stark example of modern architecture lacking in people-friendly usage—and, for that matter, even people, as few chose to live there. Now its population exceeds 2 million, much of its original plan has been scrapped, and squatter settlements ring this "model" city, which today exhibits many of the urban ills found elsewhere.

100 years relied upon a nearly complete dependency on the ideals, plans, and investments of private businesses.

New Towns in North America

We begin with the exceptions to the rule. Only three government-built new towns exist, all with their origins in the Great Depression of the 1930s, when millions of Americans were out of work. In 1935, President Franklin Delano Roosevelt signed the Emergency Relief Appropriation Act and the National Industrial Recovery Act. One provision in these acts, besides providing construction jobs for the unemployed, was a federally sponsored project called "Greenbelt Towns." Deeply influenced by Ebenezer Howard, this project formally stated its intent "to demonstrate in practice the soundness of planning and operating towns according to certain garden city principles, and to provide low-rent housing in healthful surroundings, both physical and social, for families in the low-income bracket" (Stein 1972:119).

The three towns constructed as part of this project were Greenbelt, Maryland (13 miles northeast of Washington, D.C.); Greendale, Wisconsin (7 miles from Milwaukee); and also Green Hills, Ohio (5 miles north of Cincinnati). Planners had high hopes that these towns would help solve big-city problems and create the jobs needed to help end the Great Depression.

These hopes soon faded. Unlike new towns in Great Britain, these settlements never attracted their own industry. Built before the age of superhighways, they simply did not provide enough economic incentive for major industry to relocate there. Then, too, soon after the towns were started, World War II intervened, diverting funding to military objectives. And by the time the war was over, the Cold War was upon us, leading many to charge that government-sponsored towns smacked of "communism." By 1949, government began selling off the new towns to private interests. The Greenbelt Towns became, and remain, more like suburbs of the large nearby cities than like the independent small cities they were envisioned to be.

After World War II, architects and private developers created more than 100 new urban environments in an attempt to follow Howard's approach. Among them were Baldwin Hills (now part of Los Angeles); Park Forest and Park Forest South near Chicago; Jonathan, Minnesota; and St. Charles, Maryland. However, most of the so-called U.S. garden cities—despite containing elements of Howard's vision, such as shared public space—lack their own industry and so are essentially middle-class suburban developments, not "new towns" as Howard proposed.

What might have been a new town fitting the Howard model—Soul City, North Carolina, championed by civil rights activist Floyd McKissick—became an unrealized dream when the federal government withdrew financial support and the economic recessions of the 1970s dissuaded major industries from locating in a rural community. Nevertheless, Soul City foreshadowed the New Urbanism movement discussed in Chapter 12 in designing "unified, mixed-use urban spaces that include multicultural neighborhoods, and that cater to families of differing economic backgrounds" (Strain 2004:70).

Among the best-known U.S. "new towns" are Radburn, New Jersey; Reston, Virginia; Columbia, Maryland; Irvine, California; and Celebration, Florida.

Radburn. Developed by architect and planner Clarence Stein, Radburn—about 20 miles west of New York City—was a direct attempt to adapt Ebenezer Howard's garden city to the United States. Radburn is laid out using what Stein called "superblocks," each surrounded by a green space. Radburn also attempted to completely separate pedestrian and automobile traffic. Stein and cofounder Henry Wright planned access roads only for service purposes, and they built houses facing the inner green areas. In 1929, Geddes Smith described Radburn as follows:

> [It is a] town built to live in—today and tomorrow. A town "for the motor age." A town turned outside-in—without any backdoors. A town where roads and parks fit together like the fingers of your right and left hands. A town in

which children need never dodge motor-trucks on their way to school (quoted in Stein 1972:44).

Like so many new towns, however, Radburn ran into financial difficulties as the years passed, and it was never completed as originally planned. About 670 families live in Radburn today, creating a population of about 3,100 within the New Jersey borough of Fair Lawn. On the other hand, Reston and Columbia, both near Washington, D.C., overcame economic crises to achieve moderate success as separate entities.

Reston. Twenty-five miles from downtown Washington, in suburban Virginia, Reston is the brainchild of developer Robert E. Simon, with the town's name made from his initials. Simon planned his "quality urban environment" around two town centers linking seven villages of approximately 10,000 residents each in a beautiful, contemporary design replete with trees, lakes, and pathways. He intended Reston to be economically self-sufficient and diverse, with mixed-income housing (high-rise luxury apartments side by side with single-family homes). Only about one-fourth of its residents live and work in Reston, however, and the rest commute. Home to about 2,000 businesses, the town's nearly 59,000 residents are 9 percent black, 9 percent Asian, 10 percent Hispanic, and 68 percent non-Hispanic white.

Reston is mostly an affluent community, with a median family income exceeding $103,000 in 2007. Its housing includes single-family homes, townhouses, condominiums, waterfront homes, homes on the golf courses, and homes that back up to woods and nature paths. The price of more than 70 homes is over $1 million. One of Reston's main focal points is Town Center, which includes high-rise offices, a Hyatt Regency hotel, boutiques, national retailers, and restaurants. Town Center has a covered outdoor ice-skating rink that doubles as a concert and events shelter during the rest of the year (City-Data.com 2009).

Columbia. For Columbia, Maryland, James Rouse, the town's developer, intended "to

The Radburn Plan:

The Radburn design provided charming, moderate-sized homes grouped on a series of cul-de-sacs, with streets designed for cars only and footways for pedestrians only. No child had to cross a street to get to school or to play. The houses backed on the street, and their fronts faced parks. Shared public space—23 acres of parks, two swimming pools, four tennis courts, other recreational facilities, and a community center—were for the use of all 3,000 residents.

create a social and physical environment which works for people and nourishes human growth and to allow private venture capital to make a profit in land development and sale" (quoted in Bailey 1990:16). To apply the best thinking available in the execution of his city, Rouse employed a host of specialists during the planning phase, including government employees, family counselors, recreationalists, sociologists, economists, educators, health specialists, psychologists, and transportation and communications experts.

Larger than Reston, Columbia, with a current population exceeding 96,000, does have low- to moderate-income housing. A racially integrated community (22 percent of its residents are African American), Columbia successfully scattered its several hundred subsidized units throughout the city. Covering more than 27 square miles, the new town is composed of communities of 800 to 900 homes, each with its own elementary school, neighborhood center and convenience store, swimming pool and recreational facilities. The plan then groups four neighborhoods into villages (of which there are nine), each with a middle school, meeting hall, supermarket, and some other shops clustered around a small plaza. In the town center are office buildings, large department stores, and a larger shopping center.

Enhancing the town's variety of programs is Howard Community College and Lincoln Technical Institute. Columbia has 5,300 acres of permanent open space, including 144 "tot lots" (children's playgrounds), 227 pedestrian bridges, the 40-acre Symphony Woods, three lakes, 19 ponds, and natural open space areas interlaced with more than 78 miles of pathways for walking, biking, and jogging. A vast network of plazas, picnic areas, public areas, tennis courts, and two par-course fitness trails also exist.

Irvine.   Also begun in the 1960s, Southern California's Irvine is the largest planned community in North America, is set on 46 square miles, and is headquarters for more than 100 major corporations. It is also home to a 15,000-acre campus of the University of California. An upper-middle-class city, with a population exceeding 201,000, its median household income in 2007 was approximately $99,000. Its racial–ethnic breakdown is 57 percent non-Hispanic white, 1 percent African American, 30 percent Asian American, and 7 percent Hispanic (City-Data.com 2009).

Celebration.   A still-developing project is the Walt Disney town of Celebration in central Florida, near Walt Disney World Resort. Planned through the collaboration of nine of the nation's leading architects, this community is the most visible example of the New Urbanism. Celebration, say Disney officials, is "sustainable and holistic," demonstrating that development can be responsive to environmental issues. It is a normal community, not an exclusive, gated enclave.

Disney began the project by building the downtown—a lively mix of retail shops, restaurants, offices and apartments, town hall, post office, grocery store, and cinema—situated along a wide promenade circling the lake in the center of town. Most notable is the Art Deco–style movie complex and a cylindrical post office. Nearly 3,000 people call Celebration their home, with an eventual total population planned to reach approximately 12,000. Oversized porches and verandas encourage old-time neighborhood socializing, and the community is surrounded by a 4,700-acre, protected green belt with miles of walking paths.

The tallest point in Celebration neighborhoods cannot exceed three stories. A model school, kindergarten through 12th grade, is run by the county school system, but with the best equipment that a $9 million cash boost from Disney can buy. A 60-acre "health campus"—a cross between a full-service gym and a hospital—enables people to keep in shape downstairs to avoid the medical wards upstairs. Unlike the average "designer suburb," where all the houses carry a similar price tag, Celebration's nearly three dozen $1-million estates coexist with other homes that have a median value of about $716,000, as well as with about 350 rental apartments, to form a social mix not often seen such communities.

Celebration is clearly an attempt to return to the pedestrian-friendly, compactly built town of the past, as compared with what the New Urbanists describe as the car-dominated, suburban sprawl of freeways, malls, and widely dispersed single-family homes. Admired by many, Celebration also receives criticism from others, who call it a retreat to a dream world of the past that only appeals to a small segment of the population.

An even larger project could have been the missed opportunity to rebuild New Orleans (see the *Urban Trends* box on pages 408-409).

Erin Mills, Ontario. The largest planned new town in Canada is located on 8,000 acres within the incorporated city of Mississauga, about 20 miles west of Toronto. Now completing the third of four building phases initiated in the 1970s, this fast-growing community of about 105,000 residents is a successful blend of residences, industry, and

URBAN TRENDS

What Will the "New" New Orleans Be Like?

The devastation of New Orleans in the aftermath of Hurricane Katrina in 2005 was so widespread that a massive rebuilding effort, lasting perhaps 10 years, is necessary. With large sections of the city uninhabited and billions of dollars pledged for rebuilding, leaders had a unique opportunity—one virtually unknown since colonial and frontier days—to envision, on a large scale, the creation of a beautiful and well-functioning city. Bruce Babbitt, former Secretary of the Interior, even called for a national commission of scientists, engineers, and planners to draw up a regional land plan and recommend a realistic course of action (Babbitt 2005).

Obviously, the first step was to secure the city against future flooding. As the flood waters receded in the weeks after the hurricane, there was no shortage of ideas on how to rebuild the city. Universal agreement occurred for constructing better seawalls and levees to hold back future high waters. Most experts also advocated rebuilding the delta and coastal barriers to enable nature to assist in the city's defenses against future storms.

For the city itself, geographers and urbanists offered a variety of ideas. A more radical proposal was to convert New Orleans into an island, surrounded by miles of open water, with an island infrastructure of relocated streets, highways, and utilities to achieve an "American Venice" (Babbitt 2005). Another bold proposal was to bring in massive amounts of earth to raise the low parts of the city above sea level, as Galveston, Texas, did after a storm surge in 1900 killed more than 6,000 residents (Petroski 2005). In contrast, another suggestion was to create higher-density neighborhoods to allow the lowest-lying parts of the city (where the floodwaters stood deepest) to return to the wetlands they once were. This would restore the marshland to absorb Lake Pontchartrain's overflow and protect the rest of the city (Colten 2005).

Standing on higher ground, the historic buildings in the French Quarter were spared. Other unique, appealing architecture in the Bywater District, where many buildings were stunningly restored after a flood in 1965, suffered only minor flood damage this time. These areas could form centerpieces for the city's renewal. In contrast, the public housing built during the 1970s in the eastern part of the city was hardest hit and needed to be replaced. Some feared their replacement with high-end housing and businesses would displace the poor, as occurred in other cities through the dynamics of gentrification. An alternative could be re-creating the city's original development pattern on the east side, just as it already exists on the west side, where grand houses line large boulevards and avenues while the interior and side streets contain more modest residences. Such a mixed-income arrangement, as found in successful new towns worldwide, could defuse commerce. This planned community contains high-rise condominiums, large low-density housing, or medium-density, single-detached, town or rowhouses; a town center; hospital; and an interconnected, tree-lined recreational trail system.

U.S. Failures.   In 1970, encouraged by the partial success of Columbia and Reston, the federal government instituted the New Communities Program, directing money toward building 13 more new towns (including Soul City). The program was a near disaster. It was reduced to a salvage operation by 1974 and completely shut down in 1983, when 12 of the 13 communities were unable to meet their financial obligations (Rodwin and Evans 1982). Except for Irvine and Celebration, the new-town movement in the United States is now all but dead. Why has such an appealing idea fared so poorly? To find out, we need to critically review the major goals of the global new-town movement.

With much housing rendered uninhabitable by the floodwaters from Hurricane Katrina in 2005, New Orleans's neighborhoods faced a massive rebuilding effort. This tragedy offered an opportunity for coordinated planning and development to build a better city and overcome its segregated areas. Instead, an uncoordinated, piecemeal effort ensued, and years later, much of the affected areas still await reconstruction.

racial tensions by keeping the races in close proximity to one another (Crutcher 2005).

It now appears that no bold plan, no holistic concept, no radical remaking of the city will occur. Instead, lack of promised federal funding and neighborhood pressure led the New Orleans City Council to adopt a settle-and-rebuild-where-you-will plan that allows each neighborhood to set its own priorities.

Under this plan, redevelopment of housing, libraries, and shopping centers and creation of parks, possibly even in the devastated lower Ninth Ward, an Afro-Cuban version of the French Quarter, will occur. This is a piecemeal plan, not a comprehensive one, but one that will attempt to preserve the architectural and cultural feel of the city (Associated Press 2007).

What Makes New Towns Succeed or Fail?

Many new towns have been built worldwide since Ebenezer Howard sounded the clarion call in 1898. Most of those that come into existence, however, do not succeed as the new towns they were intended to be. Why?

One major goal of most new towns was to distribute population more broadly. Howard and his followers thought that the congestion of big cities was destructive of human well-being and that their economic dominance sapped vitality from the rest of the region. Critics point out that new towns don't do much to meet this goal. Even in Britain, after decades of new-town development, barely 1 percent of the population lives in them. Most governments really can't raise the tax money needed to build new towns on a much larger scale. A more realistic idea may be to improve already-existing center cities and New Orleans could have been one such place.

New towns were also to be centers of employment and economic activity. Here again, however, few of them attracted much industry or other business. The problem is largely economic: At a distance from major cities, new towns present businesses with added costs for materials and transportation. Thus, especially in North America, new towns ended up with a strong suburban flavor—bedroom communities for people who, by and large, work elsewhere.

The collapse of the New Communities Program of 1970 reflected these issues. First, the costs of building new towns are enormous, taking years to return a profit to investors. Second, government only made a half-hearted commitment to such programs. New towns are the dream of a few—some city planners, a few public officials, architects, builders, and mayors. Many others think these efforts could be more effectively placed elsewhere—in inner-city development, for example, or in the elimination of slum housing. The New Communities Program is dead in the United States, and little likelihood exists that any similar program will take its place.

This is not to ignore the many contributions of the new-town idea. Columbia's developer, James Rouse, and Reston's developer, Robert E. Simon, both demonstrated broad social concern and purpose in undertaking projects of such economic magnitude and social audacity. We might also direct such tribute to Ebenezer Howard, who aspired to so much in his new-town vision. Nevertheless, no one has built "Jerusalem." Moreover, the new town is not the magic potion to cure all urban problems. There are other visions to consider.

ARCHITECTURAL VISIONS

An irony marks Ebenezer Howard's ambition—to change all of society through building cities that were very small. Some visionaries argue that solving the city's problems will demand not outlying new towns but also completely new *central cities*—more efficient, more humane, and for *everybody*. Here, we examine three large-scale "visions of the street." Each is the work of an architect; each is refreshingly different.

The Radiant City

Among the most important figures of modern architecture, Le Corbusier was also an influential urban planner. In his books *The City of Tomorrow* (1971; orig. 1927) and *The Radiant City* (1967; orig. 1933), Le Corbusier, like Howard, condemned modern cities and outlined a vision of a new urban society. His solution, though, was the opposite of Howard's. Rejecting widespread decentralization, Le Corbusier saw benefits to concentrating people in tall, architecturally magnificent buildings surrounded by huge open spaces. Such mammoth structures, Le Corbusier reasoned, allowed keeping 95 percent of available land free from any building at all (see Figure 14–3).

A second innovation was eliminating the central business district and population concentration by creating equal densities throughout the city. "Flows of people would become much more even across the whole city, instead of strong radical flows into and out of the center which characterize cities today" (Hall 2002:51).

FIGURE 14–3   Le Corbusier's Contemporary City

Source: From The Radiant City by Le Corbusier, translated by Derek Coltman. Translation copyright 1967 by Grossman Publishers, Inc., and Faber & Faber, Ltd. Used by permission of Viking Penguin, a division of Penguin Putnam, Inc. © 2003 Artists Rights Society (ARS), New York/ADAGP, Paris/FIC.

Although no such **urban utopia** was ever built, Le Corbusier's influence on city planning was great. One classic example is the Alton West estate in Roehampton, in southwest London, built after World War II. A second example of a Le Corbusier–influenced project is Manhattan's Stuyvesant Town. Red brick buildings stand between wide walkways and lawns in this park-like setting constructed in 1947.

Le Corbusier expressed his vision to its fullest extent in his 1953 design of Chandigarh, India, which calls itself "the city beautiful." Structurally, Chandigarh is a modern city, with a population exceeding 800,000. Each of the city's 49 sectors is a block about 1 square kilometer in size, with markets, shopping centers, and schools to limit people's need to travel. Citywide transportation (buses, autorickshaws, and taxicabs) links the sectors. One factor Le Corbusier was unable to control, however, was population density; as India's sixth most densely populated city, with 7,900 people per square kilometer, its density is four times what Le Corbusier wished.

Broadacre City

Frank Lloyd Wright, the most famous of all U.S. architects, viewed Le Corbusier's urban vision as a nightmare. Such high-density living

should be avoided at all costs, Wright maintained, and he championed instead "organic architecture"—the living union of architectural design with the natural environment. He reasoned that if homes could be constructed in an "organic" way, why couldn't the same be done for entire cities?

Like both Howard and Le Corbusier, Wright accepted the integral role of modern technology. Unlike them, he was antiurban and sought to increase vastly the amount of space occupied by his utopian city in order to lower greatly its density. He thought that a city, without high rises or large buildings, might easily spread over 100 square miles, or even more. With automobiles (or even personal helicopters), he contended, people could live on their own acres of farmland and still easily reach neighbors and shopping facilities. Broadacre City was a fusion of what Wright saw as the ideals of Jeffersonian democracy (fundamentally, extensive personal freedoms), the North American dream of plenty of land for personal use, and modern technology.

Broadacre City never was more than a dream, of course. The plan met with massive criticism during Wright's lifetime (1867–1959). Critics dismissed Broadacre City as too expensive, too expansive, and far too radical. Although stung by the negative reaction, Wright never gave up on his ideas. He rewrote his Broadacre treatise, *The Living City*, for the fourth time at age 90.

The Arcology

One of Wright's students was a young Italian named Paolo Soleri, who both respected and rebelled against his mentor's teaching. He accepted Wright's central notion of organic architecture, but he rejected entirely his teacher's vision of Broadacre City. Siding with Le Corbusier, Soleri advocated a dense concentration of people in an urban area. His vision, however, was even more extreme: a completely self-contained unit housing up to half a million people in a megastructure 300 stories high and occupying just the space of a few city blocks! Soleri calls such cities **arcologies,** or architectural ecologies—environmentally safe, architecturally beautiful, and totally efficient.

Babel.   Soleri's Babel IIB, designed for a population of 520,000, contained underground industrial and commercial areas; the city center at ground level; a public area and a promenade on the first level; a neighborhood and a park (both outdoors) on the second level; gardens, a community area (for recreation), and a living–working area on the third level (about 1,500 feet high!); and housing at the very top. All service facilities—elevators, heating, and exhaust systems—would be contained in the central core of the city.

Structures like these (Soleri designed dozens) are so audacious, even in the history of utopian urban planning, that few take them seriously. Critics dismiss arcologies as gigantic

beehives. Soleri counters by claiming they are "miniatures" compared with today's cities. They occupy a fraction of the land, free up the surrounding countryside for enjoyment, and allow that countryside a chance to return to nature. Imagine, he suggests, the population of Los Angeles, which now sprawls over 470 square miles, contained in 10 to 12 well-dispersed Babels, and everywhere else no freeways, no smog, just beautiful Southern California. No doubt, however, such structures would be astronomically expensive, and no one came forward to finance constructing one.

Arcosanti.   Undaunted, Soleri proceeded on his own. Rising out of the desert at Cortez Junction in Arizona, about an hour's ride north of Phoenix, is Arcosanti, Soleri's prototype to demonstrate the viability of his vision fusing architecture, ecology, and urban planning. Arcosanti, shown in model form in the

Arcosanti, Paolo Soleri's vision for the integration of architecture, ecology, and urban planning, is presently home to only 1 percent of its planned 7,000 inhabitants. This model shows Arcosanti in its planned final form. Intended to occupy less than 30 acres of the 4,060-acre preserve, it will serve as a research and study center for the social, economic, and ecological implications of its architectural framework.

If ever constructed, TRY 2004 will be the largest built structure on Earth, covering an area of 34 square miles. This utopian vision awaits the development of carbon nanotube technology, but another arcology megastructure, the Crystal Island Moscow, has preliminary planning approval from the government and would be one of the world's most ambitious building projects.

illustration on page 412, is to be completely self-sufficient. It would utilize only solar energy and food from solar greenhouses for about 5,000 people living in an urban infrastructure with workplaces, cultural centers, and service facilities, all with easy access to the surrounding natural environment.

Roughly 40 years after its inception, Arcosanti is less than 1 percent completed, although more than 6,000 people have participated in its construction. It presently consists of eight low-rise, mixed-use buildings and public spaces. Each year, its 70 residents host 50,000 visitors in the Gallery, Café, and Bakery; produce nearly 15,000 windbells in the Foundry and Ceramic Studios; and conduct educational seminars for more than 400 people (Arcosanti 2009).

TRY-2004

A bold, recent proposal for an arcology comes from Japan's leading architectural and construction firm, the Shimizu Corporation: a massive, megacity pyramid. Twelve times higher than the Great Pyramid of Giza, it would

be the largest structure on Earth. Situated over Tokyo Bay, it would stand over 1.2 miles high, with an area of 3 square miles at the base. The structure would consist of eight layers stacked on top of each other, comprising a total area of 34 square miles. Each layer would consist of smaller pyramids, each being roughly the size of the Luxor Hotel in Las Vegas, with layers 1 through 4 devoted to mixed residential and commercial usage and layers 5 through 8 devoted to leisure and social facilities (Geek About.com 2008).

With a foundation of 36 piers of special concrete, its structure would be made of superstrong, lightweight carbon nanotubes, which exist only theoretically at present. Designed to survive earthquakes, tsunamis, and strong winds, a photovoltaic film would coat the exterior façade of the hyperstructure to convert sunlight into electricity for a greener city.

Plans include 240,000 housing units to accommodate as many as 750,000 residents, with offices and commercial facilities capable of employing 800,000 people. The housing and offices would be in 80-story skyscrapers, suspended above and below and attached to the pyramid's supporting structure with nanotubes cables. Transportation within the city would consist of automated, individual pods that travel rapidly through tubes, as well as escalators and elevators.

With the nanotube technology not yet available, Japan's population dropping significantly, and the cost to build this hyperstructure with its staggering proportions, it seems unlikely any of us will witness this construction.

Then again, perhaps we should not so casually dismiss this proposal. Preliminary planning is now underway for construction of Crystal Island on Nagatino Peninsula, just 4.5 miles from the Kremlin. A self-contained city, it will soar 1,500 feet in height, with four times the floor area of the Pentagon. This megastructure will accommodate up to 30,000 residents in 900 apartments, but it will also boast 3,000 hotel rooms, a cinema, a theater, a museum, shopping malls, a sports complex, and an international school for 500 pupils (Geek About.com 2008).

Utopia's Limitations

Each of these planned urban utopias share many of the limitations found in the New Town movement. First, as Arcosanti amply demonstrates, they are financially impractical. Second, many are rigid proposals developed by visionaries who assume that everyone would see the basic logic of their vision and support it. To his credit, Paolo Soleri has been more flexible than other planners in this respect, changing his designs frequently after dialogue with others. Third, such plans seem to be sociologically naive. As Peter Hall (2002) notes, these utopians are all *architects* who believe that altering the physical world will automatically alter the social world as well, but of course, beautiful designs do not necessarily do away with social problems, such as racial prejudice or poverty.

Yet, in the final analysis, society needs utopian thinkers. They are, by their work, natural consciousness raisers. They challenge our thinking about cities, point to obvious problems, and prod us to consider visionary solutions that we "on the street" barely understand.

MORE FOCUSED URBAN PLANNING

The problem with utopian planners is that their schemes are simply too grandiose and impractical. A city is simply *too complex a phenomenon* to be controlled as though it were a programmable computer. Other planners argue that urban planning only works when it is focused on a limited segment of city life—say, a neighborhood or park. We may never be able to manage the city as a whole, but we can handle the urban scene one segment at a time.

Sidewalks and Neighborhoods

Since the 1960s, a more popular trend has been away from large-scale, comprehensive visions. Leading this reaction was Jane Jacobs, author of *The Death and Life of Great American Cities* (1993; orig. 1961). To Jacobs, the greatest value of the city is its diversity: The city's "life" lies in its countless interactions and the multiple uses of its streets, parks, sidewalks, and neighborhoods. Anything that diminishes this quality (as does comprehensive planning, by definition) leads cities to their "death." Urban living is never *planned* in any broad sense. People of the city *invent* their lives as they meet their own needs and solve their own problems.

Consider sidewalks. In any vital city, a sidewalk has uses far beyond easing the passage of pedestrians. Front steps facing the sidewalk are places for neighbors to sit and visit, just as corners are places to "hang out." Second, sidewalk street life serves as a means of public surveillance, through which people come to know each other and to identify strangers. Jacobs points out that in areas where street life abounds, crime rates are low. Third, sidewalks are environments where children explore their neighborhood, test themselves, and grasp the rules of urban social life. Finally, street life brings a sense of community to a neighborhood. South Philadelphia, New York's Lower East Side, New Orleans's French Quarter, and San Francisco's Haight–Ashbury district all maintain a positive identity based on their street life.

In general, Jacobs supports local planning initiatives but loathes grandiose designs. What city planners should do, she says, is

URBAN TRENDS

Jane Jacobs: Planning for Vitality

Consider, for a moment, the kind of goals at which city planning must begin to aim, if the object is to plan for city vitality.

Planning for vitality must stimulate and catalyze the greatest possible range and quantity of diversity among uses and among people throughout each district of a big city; this is the underlying foundation of city economic strength, social vitality and magnetism. To do this, planners must diagnose, in specific places, what is lacking to generate diversity, and then aim at helping to supply the lacks as best they can be supplied.

Planning for vitality must promote continuous networks of local street neighborhoods, whose users and informal proprietors can count to the utmost in keeping the public spaces of the city safe, in handling strangers so they are an asset rather than a menace, in keeping casual public tabs on children in places that are public.

Planning for vitality must combat the destructive presence of border vacuums [vacant land at the edges], and it must help promote people's identification with city districts that are large enough, and are varied and rich enough in inner and outer contacts to deal with the tough, inescapable, practical problems of big-city life.

Planning for vitality must aim at unslumming the slums, by creating conditions aimed at persuading a high proportion of the indigenous residents, whoever they may be, to stay put by choice over time, so there will be a steadily growing diversity among people and a continuity of community both for old residents and for newcomers who assimilate into it.

Planning for vitality must convert the self-destruction of diversity and other cataclysmic uses of money into constructive forces, by hampering the opportunities for destructiveness on the one hand, and on the other hand by stimulating more city territory into possessing a good economic environment for other people's plans.

Planning for vitality must aim at clarifying the visual order of cities, and it must do so by both promoting and illuminating functional order, rather than by obstructing or denying it.

Source: Jane Jacobs, *The Death and Life of Great American Cities* (New York: Random House, 1993), pp. 531–32.

---

facilitate diversity and vitality and let local people do the rest. The best planning, then, is sometimes the least planning. The *Urban Trends* box above outlines Jacobs's suggestions to a city planning board.

Squares and Parks

Of course, not everyone who believes in more focused city planning goes as far as Jacobs. While agreeing that holistic city planning is undesirable, some argue that good planning can be more comprehensive than Jacobs allows.

August Heckscher spent two years studying cities such as Omaha, Dallas, Cincinnati, Buffalo, Rochester, and Milwaukee. To Heckscher, the vitality of a city was fundamentally a matter of how well that city organized its space:

> Each city is a place of its own, its uniqueness determined in large measure by patterns created by the alternation of structure and void, of buildings and spaces between. The large green spaces, parks and parkways, river banks and waterfronts, give to a city a coherence that allows the urban dweller to have a feeling of the whole. . . . What is expressed in open spaces is the essential quality of urban life—its casualness and variety, its ability to crystallize community feeling. (1978:4)

In cities dominated by economic concerns, such as those in North America, Heckscher highlights the value of squares, parks, architecture, and artwork to urban life. These prompt people to remember that there are "other things" to city life. Squares provide small, natural meeting places as well as settings for more formal occasions, such as political rallies and concerts. They provide a vital physical and psychological break in the city's structure. New Orleans's Jackson Square, located in the French Quarter, is one such vital square. Others include Fountain Square in Cincinnati, Union Square in San Francisco, City Hall Square in Toronto, Rittenhouse Square in Philadelphia, and Washington Square in New York.

Parks are equally important. Sara Miller (2003) speaks for many in celebrating the first U.S. urban park, New York's Central Park, 843 acres on the upper half of Manhattan Island, which preserves a bit of country in the city. Although perhaps not as well known as Central Park, a similar public space is found in virtually every major North American city, and there, residents delight in recreation and informal activities of all kinds. Atlanta has Piedmont Park (185 acres), Chicago has Grant Park (305 acres), and San Diego has Balboa Park (1,158 acres). There is Schenley Park in Pittsburgh (456 acres), Stanley Park in Vancouver (1,000 acres), and Griffith Park in Los Angeles (4,063 acres). Philadelphia boasts the largest city park in the world, Fairmount Park (4,079 acres).

In a study of urban spaces, William H. Whyte found that many people simply thrive on the streets. Observing the Seagram Plaza in midtown Manhattan, he wrote that "On a good day, there would be a hundred and fifty people sitting, sunbathing, picnicking and schmoozing— idly gossiping, talking 'nothing talk'" (2001:14; orig., 1980). Moreover, claims Whyte,

> [People] go to the lively places where there are many people. And they go there by choice, not to escape the city but to partake of it. . . . The multiplier effect is tremendous. It is not just the number of people using these small urban places, but the larger number who pass by and enjoy them vicariously, or the even larger number who feel better about the city center for

knowledge of them. For a city such places are priceless, whatever the costs. (2001:100–101)

The Middle Ground

Later in his life, James Rouse, the creator of Columbia, Maryland, shifted his attention to midsized projects of urban regeneration. Most of these have been spectacularly successful. They are neither comprehensive, all-encompassing visions like Columbia nor small-scale, local efforts like those championed by Jane Jacobs. They are in between—the middle ground. While such planning takes account of the needs of the whole city, it targets a small portion of the city's space. The most well-known of Rouse's midsized "festival marketplace" efforts are the Faneuil Hall complex in Boston, New York's South Street Seaport, Philadelphia's Market East, Baltimore's Harborplace, Union Station in St. Louis, Pioneer Place in Portland, the Riverview Marketplace of New Orleans, and the Grand Avenue Mall in Milwaukee.

All of these projects reclaimed portions of deteriorating central cities in the 1970s and 1980s. Rouse was concerned that Americans had lived so long with grim, congested and worn-out inner cities, and with sprawling and cluttered outer cities that they subconsciously accepted such conditions as both inevitable and unavoidable. He worried that people no longer realized cities could be beautiful, humane, and truly responsive to the needs and yearnings of their people (Olsen 2004).

So, Rouse set to work. Before he began, the Faneuil Hall area of Boston had become as tawdry as one could imagine. The site of the city center in Revolutionary War days, the area abounded with old, dilapidated warehouses that abutted on the harbor. No one lived there, and only a few businesses remained. With a generous spirit, one would have called the locale "down and out."

Today, it is transformed. The old warehouses have been outwardly maintained, but the inner cores have been thoroughly modernized. Faneuil Hall has been revamped in the same manner. Inside, food shops run its football-field length. On either side of the Hall are pedestrian areas with benches, outdoor eating

The diversity in cities is also found in its variety of architectural styles. For example, this Boston cityscape spans the centuries of design and function, from the eighteenth-century structures of the revitalized Faneuil Hall and Quincy Market area to the Gothic Revival buildings of more than 100 years later to the sleek, modern skyscrapers from the mid- to late-twentieth century.

areas, and places where street musicians play. The refurbished old warehouses on either side are now the home of high-quality shops. On any summer day, the place is teeming with people—locals, tourists, and visitors from the suburbs. Looking at the project from the vantage point of one of the high-rises in the area or from the harbor, one sees how Rouse's vision works: The new buildings mimic or harmoniously blend with the old buildings of the area. Perhaps most important, the businesses in the project are profitable, and the success of the Faneuil Hall project subsequently stimulated development throughout Boston's downtown. Much the same happy story applies to his other urban projects.

Critics charge that Rouse's successes pander to the wealthier elements of urban areas and do little for the poor. Some truth lies in this accusation, but Rouse's changes helped turn around one stunning problem by replacing collapsing inner-city districts with thriving, vibrant urban places.

THE REALITIES OF URBAN PLANNING

Whatever philosophical stance one ultimately takes about urban planning, shaping the city always forces us to contend with traditions, vested interests, and environmental conditions. Such realities operate both as barriers and as opportunities.

Economics and Politics

Radical alterations in the urban landscape rarely get far off the ground. Ebenezer Howard could establish only two garden cities, and even with government support, the

British new-town effort remains limited. In the United States, Stein's Radburn, New Jersey, fell victim to financial troubles, while Columbia and Reston went through dire straits for the same reason. Partially because of expense (and partially because of its audacity), Paolo Soleri's Arcosanti has barely taken form, and Frank Lloyd Wright's Broadacre City never even began. The stark reality is that in a free market economy, urban planning rarely strays very far from the interests of business.

Local politics, too, swirls around city planning, as interest groups contend with each other to achieve their various goals. Sometimes, the complexities of even small-scale projects lead to challenges that intimidate elected officials who fear alienating voters.

The Importance of Values

In the final analysis, urban planning is always a question of values: Which ones and whose are the key issues. We have noted that city planning has always reflected cultural values.

In Catholic Rome, planning glorified the Church; in monarchic France, planning celebrated the king; in New York City, planning augmented the pursuit of the almighty dollar.

Values also permeate, explicitly or implicitly, the work of urban planners. In a review of Jane Jacobs's *Death and Life of Great American Cities*, Herbert Gans (1962) pointed out that Jacobs is a typical product of her society. She complains that too often, city planning has not been left up to the people. What could be more Western, more North American, Gans asks, than a complaint that we need more emphasis on the individual, and that we should make way for local initiative?

Of course, the values implicitly criticized by Jacobs appear in virtually all U.S. city planning. Even planners like Columbia's James Rouse, who have tried to improve people's lives in cities, do so with the expectation of being well paid for it. Said Rouse in an interview:

> The business mentality today is that the pursuit of profit is the purpose of life, and that people

Prefabricated concrete apartment buildings built throughout the old Soviet Union and Eastern European communist countries resulted in a sterile look of uniformity. This is the Nibelungen-Ring housing complex at Leipzig in eastern Germany, with other apartment buildings in traditional rows in the upper left. In most socialist cities, these gray buildings created a drab, somber look for the first-time visitor.

come second or third. I think that's deplorable. It's why development has such a bad name and why cities suffer from so much ugliness. What should be important is to produce something of benefit to mankind. If that happens, then the profit will be there (Pawlyna 1981:64).

Similarly, because most of us are deeply committed to the values of individuality and personal initiative, we are put off by all-inclusive planning that seems to demand submission to the group. Indeed, perhaps the characteristic element of North American urban planning has been the lack of comprehensive planning. From the 1600s onward, most U.S. and Canadian cities developed with very limited intervention by any governmental agency. There are notable exceptions, such as Portland, Oregon, and Toronto. Mainly, though, the national governments have no overall plans or policies for their cities, because the residents don't want them. If private investors like Jim Rouse can't make our cities better, then most people seem content to live with the consequences.

Current interest among many scholars and practitioners lies in private, market-based programs to address urban economic and social ills, in the belief that many areas of civic and commercial life do not necessarily require government involvement (Beito, Gordon, and Tabarrok 2002). Examples abound of the nongovernment sector effectively providing for roads and bridges, education, housing, social welfare, land-use planning, commercial law, and even policing and criminal prosecutions. The private, self-governing enclaves and large-scale industrial communities with complex physical infrastructure and services, such as Chicago's Manufacturing District, challenge the orthodoxy that government alone can improve community life and indicate that the private sector can play a greater role in urban planning and policy.

Some Canadian and U.S. cities, however, already illustrate the vitality wrought by good government planning. Among them are Portland, San Francisco, Seattle, and Vancouver— locales frequently cited in public opinion polls as among the "best" cities. Another city fulfilling all of these qualifications is Toronto, where planning successfully addresses the challenges of urban diversity and urban sprawl. We examine Toronto as a model of good urban planning in our final case study.

CASE STUDY
Toronto, Ontario

Toronto is a Great Lakes port and, through the St. Lawrence Seaway, an ocean port as well. With more than 5.1 million people living in the region, Toronto is the most populous metropolitan area in Canada. About one in six Canadians live there, and it continues to attract newcomers, with an average of 107,000 new immigrants each year between 2001 and 2005 (Statistics Canada 2008a). The Toronto region has that nation's major concentration of industrial jobs and serves as the commercial and financial center of Canada. The central area, downtown Toronto, is the predominant regional center, encompassing major government, financial, medical, and education services.

Toronto attracts a large number of immigrants from the developing world and has an increasing number of people requiring welfare assistance, but its school system and financial stability are stronger than those of many U.S. cities in a similar situation. Although Toronto faces suburban and edge city development as other cities do, its central city remains strong, the region's growth patterns are not wasteful of environmental resources, and the transportation systems are more efficient, with greater reliance on mass transit. What makes Toronto more successful in these areas than its sister cities elsewhere? The answer lies in a metropolitan approach to governance and policy making that enables Toronto to address spatial development and quality-of-life issues in a more comprehensive manner and with greater resources at its disposal, as we will discuss shortly.

The Physical Setting

Situated on the northern shore of Lake Ontario, Toronto is almost entirely flat, except at approximately 3 to 4 miles inland, where the land sharply rises about 40 feet at the shoreline elevation of the former glacial Lake Iroquois. Streets are in a grid design, except for the diagonal roads along the shoreline. Railroad tracks and an expressway separate the lakefront from the downtown area. The central business areas are around Bloor, Queen, and Yonge streets, while the central financial district is south of the old city hall, in the vicinity of King and Bay streets. The CN Tower (1,815 feet) dominates the city skyline—along with the Toronto-Dominion Centre, Commerce Court, and First Canadian Place—all of which are more than 50 stories high.

Situated north of the central business district is a fashionable shopping area. The Ontario Parliament Buildings and the University of Toronto rise south of Bloor Street, in a section with tall shade trees and grassy areas known for its park-like atmosphere. One of the most attractive residential areas in Toronto is Rosedale, an older neighborhood of distinguished homes set on winding, tree-lined streets close to the downtown center, which itself contains many attractive streets of modest, well-designed houses.

History

Inhabited first by the Seneca and later by the Mississauga Indians, the area was originally a trading post in the seventeenth century because of its strategic location at the crossing of ancient Indian trails going west to the Mississippi and north to Lake Simcoe and the vast wilderness beyond. The French built three small forts there in the eighteenth century; all three were subsequently destroyed after the English defeated the French in 1759. During and after the U.S. War for Independence, about 40,000 loyalists fled the United States and settled in this region.

In 1787, Lord Dorchester, the Canadian governor-in-chief, peacefully negotiated the purchase of 250,000 acres from three Indian chiefs for the future capital of Ontario. Its name was changed from Toronto to York in 1795, and U.S. forces temporarily occupied the small settlement of about 700 residents during the War of 1812. By 1834, the population grew to 9,000 and restored its original name.

The coming of the Grand Trunk and Great Western railways in the 1850s sparked rapid development. As a break-of-bulk port city, Toronto flourished, shipping agricultural products, minerals, and timber from the surrounding region. Industrialization further spurred growth, as the city and its environs soon produced more than half of Canada's manufactured goods. Through annexation of adjacent villages and towns, the city doubled in area by 1900, and then doubled again by 1920. In 1930, the metropolitan area included the central city, four towns (Leaside, Mimico, New Toronto, and Weston), three villages (Forest Hill, Long Branch, and Swansea), and five townships (Etobicoke, East York, North York, Scarborough, and York).

Creation of a Metropolitan Government

The Great Depression of the 1930s caused severe financial problems for the city that remained until the end of World War II in 1945. Already lacking the financial means to provide water and sewage systems to outlying areas, Toronto saw its municipal burden increase further with a rapid rise in population. After investigating various options, the Ottawa Municipal Board in 1953 recommended that the 13 municipalities (named in the previous paragraph) create a federated form of government unique in North America. Passage that year of the Municipality of Metropolitan Toronto Act united the metropolitan area, and the 25-member Council of Metropolitan Toronto began its task of finding ways to deal with such common concerns as revenues, education, transportation, and urban growth. This combined form of government offered greater credit than each individual municipality had, thereby enhancing financing for various public projects. A significant feature of this metropolitan system was that council members were appointed to it by virtue of their election as mayors, aldermen, or controllers of a particular municipality, which ensured good communication and a high level of coordination between the central body and the local municipalities.

The Metropolitan Council worked well. It authorized construction of new schools and renovation of older ones, and it also introduced a regional system of parks in an attempt to control future development. It greatly improved transportation by upgrading or building new roads and expressways and by constructing an excellent subway and a new airport terminal building. Toronto's transit system now consists of a grid network of streetcars, buses, three underground rapid-transit lines, and a light-rail transit system that together account for two-thirds of all trips to the central city. This transportation network is integrated with the multicentered urban structures located along the rapid transit lines and brings workers from the surrounding regions to the downtown area.

In 1967, the Corporation of Metropolitan Toronto reorganized, reducing its 13 municipalities to six and increasing the number of seats on the council from 25 to 33. The Council also considerably extended its responsibilities in education and social services and added others, such as ambulance and library services, urban renewal, and waste disposal. Also, the reorganized council resolved many of its difficult problems by creating more effective water and sewage systems.

Essentially, Toronto functioned with a two-tiered government: a local government that focused on neighborhood issues and a metropolitan government that focused on issues facing the entire region. Its regional government enabled Toronto to consolidate resources and develop a coordinated plan for the growth of both its urban and suburban schools. The Toronto region thus avoided many of the problems that plagued nearby Detroit in the areas of crime, education, and social services, because it evenly controlled use of space and distribution of resources. As a result, the council received credit for contributing substantially to shaping Toronto into "one of the most effectively planned metropolitan areas in North America" (United Nations Development Programme 1995:256).

Major achievements have included a strong industrial base, a successful mass transit system providing 70 percent of trips to an enlarged central area, concentration of office employment near subway stations, and provision of housing for an additional 1 million residents, well-located with respect to public transport. In addition [the Municipality of Metropolitan Toronto] has upgraded the road system to provide improved access to industrial and commercial employment throughout the metropolitan area and provided an effective water supply and sewerage system. (United Nations Development Programme 1995:256)

Two Phases of Urban Planning

Beginning in the 1950s and into the early 1970s, Toronto's urban planning was characterized by an all-out, prodevelopment attitude and adherence to the principles of modernist planning. This approach emphasized intense specialization of land use, massive infrastructure (particularly urban expressways), and redevelopment of older areas (Filion 1995).

City officials identified a number of districts as blighted and then obliterated them to make room for expressways, public housing projects, private high-rise apartment developments, or an expansion of downtown's commercial functions. With little regard for existing neighborhoods in these designated areas, the wrecking ball and bulldozer razed some of the city's architectural gems and destroyed communities in such places as Alexandra Park, Rusholme Road on the east side, St. Jamestown, and Regent Park. These old neighborhoods were seen as an inconvenience between two modernist sectors: the suburbs and a rapidly redeveloping central business district (Caulfield 1994:7).

Alexandra Park exemplifies the outcome of the modern planning approach that is also found in many other North American cities. Once it was an area of mixed use, consisting of old residential houses and commercial activities linked with the rest of the city. Now it is an area reflecting simplification, segmentation, withdrawal, and land use that is segregated from the day-to-day activities of the rest of the city. Most people living in Alexandra Park these days need public assistance, and the area has become an isolated, virtually impenetrable ghetto (Caulfield 1994:11–13).

Toronto officials and local developers continued to raze prominent architectural landmarks and stable working-class neighborhoods, replacing them with modern, "efficient" structures, until local activist groups began to fight city hall's urban renewal plans. The reformers pointed to the decay of U.S. inner cities and argued that Toronto could avoid their mistakes if it remained "people-oriented" and emphasized neighborhood preservation. Their arguments were persuasive; they succeeded in preserving such areas as Rusholme Road on the west side, Old City Hall, Toronto Island, Church of the Holy Trinity, Union Station, and Trefann Court. This "cultural resistance," suggests Caulfield, played an important role in the introduction of the second phase of planning: postmodern inner-city development. Postmodern urbanism is a celebration of traditional urban form and of social and cultural heterogeneity (Caulfield 1994:97).

From the late 1960s onward, the postmodernist movement—overlapping the modernist movement for a few years before emerging as the dominant force—found sufficient support in Toronto's Metropolitan Council to halt modernist redevelopment of most inner-city neighborhoods. Echoing the antimodernist perspectives of Jane Jacobs and Lewis Mumford, planners began emphasizing the benefits of a diversified, small-grained urban texture and the importance of preserving older buildings. Ironically, the preservation and upgrading of the built environment led to the loss of its social diversity, as middle- and upper-income people—seeking easy downtown access and a more stimulating environment than was available in the suburbs—displaced the working-class and ethnic populations previously there (Sewell 1993).

Toronto Today

In 1998, Toronto restructured its municipal government once more, merging its six local governments into one entity. At the same time, the city's responsibilities, revenues, and property tax base were reformed, all without disruption of city services to residents and businesses. Although the new Toronto government centralized its administration, the city still maintains community councils to deal with purely neighborhood matters, and its various local civic and social services remain in local communities.

As a result of its planning reforms and metropolitan governance, Toronto has emerged into a dynamic city with the safest urban environment in North America. It is, as Jane Jacobs remarked, "a city that works." It is Canada's top tourist destination, the financial center of Canada, and the third-largest financial center in North America. The city has the most fiber-optic telecommunications cable of any city in North America. It also contains the continent's largest continuous underground pedestrian system, connecting 1,200 stores and restaurants, 50 office towers, six major hotels, and several entertainment centers (Toronto 2009).

Toronto is also one of the world's most multicultural cities, as nearly half of all Canada's immigrants come to the Greater Toronto Area. Not surprisingly, then, half the city's population are immigrants, a much higher proportion than anywhere else in North America. The 517,000 immigrants who have settled in Toronto since 1991 are roughly equivalent to the entire population of Tucson or Halifax. With the exception of Oceania (the countries of the Pacific and South Pacific), every part of the world has sent at least 10,000 emigrants to Toronto in recent years. The 2006 Census identified more than 200 distinct ethnic origins residents. Nearly half the city's population (47 percent) were visible minorities, up from 43 percent in 2001. South Asians (12 percent) now exceed the Chinese population (11.4 percent) as the largest visible minority group, with blacks at 8.4 percent. Between 2001 and 2006, the fastest growing visible minority group were Latin Americans. The postwar suburbs of North York, Scarborough, and York have become the main immigrant settlement areas as the central city, as mentioned earlier, has proven to be an attractive locale for middle- and upper-income residents.

Toronto is also an important cultural center, with a rich fare of ballet, concerts, films, opera, and theater offerings. In fact, it is the third-largest English-language theater center after London and New York. It is home to the Toronto Symphony Orchestra, three major theaters, and many small experimental theaters, as well as the Art Gallery of Ontario, the Royal Ontario Museum, the Ontario Science Centre, and a zoo. Often called "Hollywood North," it ranks third in TV and film production. Its institutions of higher learning include the Ontario College of Art, Ryerson Polytechnical Institute, the University of Toronto, and York University. The Toronto Maple Leafs (ice hockey) and Argonauts (football) are professional sports teams that add to the city's excitement and vitality. Like any vibrant city, Toronto also offers an appealing array of restaurants, boutiques, movie theaters, festivals, exhibits, and recreational and social activities (Toronto 2009).

Toronto is not entirely free of problems. Increased traffic congestion, a shortage of affordable housing, and a need for more waste disposal sites are three of its main concerns. Following the consolidation of its six municipalities, the city set about developing and implementing a new Official Plan—a vision of how Toronto will change and grow in the new millennium—by setting priorities for social, environmental, and economic development (see the *Cityscape* box on pages 424-425). The plan's aim is to (1) protect the best of what it has, (2) invest in areas that are aging and need revitalizing, (3) ensure that new development is consistent with the existing character of the area, and (4) convert former industrial lands into uses that fit the surrounding neighborhoods and add to community vitality (Toronto 2009). Facing its future, Toronto's leaders recognize that good, people-oriented planning is essential to its continued vitality as "a city that works."

SUMMARY

Ancient, medieval, and modern cities usually evolved through the planning of their physical layout and structure, if not in their entirety

then certainly at least in part. Such planning addressed urban problems (protection, water supply, sanitation, traffic, and leisure activities), glorified the ruling elite (statues, buildings, plazas, and parks), and reflected cultural ideals (the scale of religious or commercial structures or the direction of processional routes).

In the late nineteenth century, two urban visionaries influenced many architects and planners. David Burnam's work at the 1893 World's Fair in Chicago inspired the City Beautiful movement throughout the United States. In England, Ebenezer Howard gave action to his concept of "garden cities" by building Letchworth and Welwyn in the early twentieth century. An early example in the United States of a planned new town is Radburn, New Jersey; though never completed, it served as a model for other new towns worldwide. As centers of residence, employment, and leisure activities, new towns have been more successful in countries with a strong tradition of central government planning than they have been in the United States, with its greater emphasis on individualism and home rule.

Architectural visions of a new central city—such as Le Corbusier's "radiant city," Wright's "broadacre city," Soleri's "arcology," and Shimizu's "TRY-2004"—are impractical utopias, but they do challenge our thinking about cities and prod us to consider bolder solutions to the cities' ills. The rebuilding of New Orleans provided a unique opportunity for a complete makeover of the city's design to improve the quality of life there, but it now appears unlikely that any bold initiatives will take place. Instead, the emphasis has been more in line with Jacobs' thought to let the people in neighborhoods decide for themselves.

Elsewhere, urban planners typically focus on smaller sections of the city—its neighborhoods, open spaces, water edges, and historic sections—to revitalize tourist, leisure and economy activity while making the city a more attractive locale. Economics, politics, and values are extremely significant factors in influencing what does or does not happen in urban planning. Although most cities attempt to control their destinies through good government planning, Toronto serves as a particularly impressive model with a comprehensive plan for its future.

CONCLUSION

Can we honestly say that one type of city planning has been spectacularly more effective than any other? Our review suggests a number of conclusions.

First, all the evidence suggests that changing a city's physical form does not automatically reshape social life. In new towns the world over—from Ebenezer Howard's Letchworth to James Rouse's Columbia to Lúcio Costa's Brasilia—new structures have become home to many old problems, including harmful prejudices, class antagonism, and environmental pollution. Changing the city physically, while sometimes necessary, appears not to be sufficient in itself to realize the idealistic environment envisioned by planners. The best planning blends good sociology with dramatic architecture.

CITYSCAPE

Toronto Plans Its Future

Following are introductory excerpts from an official master plan—developed, publicly discussed, and adopted in 2002 and revised in 2007—in which the city of Toronto designed its evolution over the next 30 years.

Building a successful Toronto means that we have to make sustainable choices about how we grow. We have to see connections and understand the consequences of our choices. We have to integrate environmental, social and economic perspectives in our decision making. We have to meet the needs of today without compromising the ability of future generations to meet their needs.

There is no such thing as an isolated or purely local decision. Each of us makes choices every day about where to live, work, play, shop and how to travel. They seem like small choices, but together and over time the consequences of these choices can affect everyone's quality of life. That's why planning matters. . . .

This Plan is about the basics of successful city-building. Holistic and integrated thinking is a fundamental requirement for planning a modern city like Toronto. Integrated thinking means seeing, understanding and accounting for all the connections as we go about our decision making. Sometimes it means thinking differently about solutions. Always it means searching for outcomes that demonstrate integration, balance and interdependence and that earn social, environmental and economic rewards. . . .

Toronto cannot plan in isolation or expect to stand alone in dealing with the effects of urban growth. Our view of the quality of urban life tends to be based on the local conditions in our own neighbourhoods. These conditions are in turn affected by events happening in the larger region. The quality of the air, water, services and region-wide transport systems all affect the quality of life in our neighbourhood, where we work and where we play. The way in which growth and change are managed in Toronto must mesh with that of our neighbours because we are integrally linked in many ways. . . .

Building a successful city means making choices that improve our quality of life. As our City grows and matures, we can create a more beautiful environment, healthy and vibrant communities and greater prosperity. . . .

In order to remain economically competitive in today's global economy, a city must be more than functional. It has to work well, but it also must be beautiful, vibrant, safe, and inclusive.

Second, all the planning experiments of the last century have fallen short of their goals. New towns have not solved the problems of large cities, nor have they solved many of their own troubles. Utopian designs intrigue us but offer few real solutions. Finally, small-scale efforts, such as those proposed by Jane Jacobs, August Heckscher, William H. Whyte, and James Rouse, are helpful but often leave the larger problems of the city, such as unemployment and poverty, untouched.

Third, we always must realize that urban planning occurs within a framework of certain unbending realities. Economic and political considerations limit the scope of any plan. If it costs too much, it won't be done. If sponsored by the rich, it probably won't be much help to the poor. What some people want, others are sure to resist. Urban planners, if they are to have any chance to work their craft, must become skillful politicians.

Surely, planning is vital to the future of our cities, but we must merge two often-contradictory forces—the planners' desire to shape the urban environment and a free people's need to choose. We must also overcome the tendency to think in purely local terms and, instead, recognize the need for a regional,

---

Great cities do not happen by accident—they are designed and orchestrated so that individual private and public developments work together to create cohesive blocks, neighbourhoods and districts. Good urban design is not just an aesthetic overlay, but an essential ingredient of city-building. Good urban design is good business and good social policy.

Civic pride is infectious. The City and the private sector should work together as partners in creating a great city and achieving Toronto's architectural and urban design potential. The City can play its part by organizing, designing, maintaining and improving the streets, parks and public buildings. The private sector can do its part by building the structures and landscapes that define and support these public places. This Plan demands that both the public and private sectors commit to high quality architecture, landscape architecture and urban design, consistent with energy efficient standards.

Beautiful, comfortable, safe and accessible streets, parks, open spaces and public buildings are a key shared asset. These public spaces draw people together, creating strong social bonds at the neighbourhood, city and regional level. They convey our public image to the world and unite us as a city. They set the stage for our festivals, parades and civic life as well as for daily casual contact. Public space creates communities.

This Plan recognizes how important good design is in creating a great city. Great cities are judged by the look and quality of their squares, parks, streets and public spaces and the buildings which frame and define them. People flock to the world's great cities not just to enjoy the culture, but to wander the streets, to explore their parks and plazas, to enjoy the street life, to shop and to people watch. The same characteristics and qualities that make these cities great places to visit also make them great places to live. What do these places share in common? All are very urban, high density, mixed use, mixed income, transit and pedestrian oriented vibrant places.

Great cities not only have great buildings—but the buildings work together to create great streets, plazas, parks and public places. Great cities inspire and astonish. Whether it's a bustling shopping street lined by vibrant shop windows and sidewalk cafes, an intimate, residential, tree-lined street, or a public plaza in the central business district—everywhere you look there is evidence that the place has been designed. The buildings, both public and private, work together to create the "walls" for the city's great outdoor "rooms."

Source: Toronto Urban Development Services, *Toronto Official Plan* (August 2007). Accessed online at http://www.city.toronto.on.ca/.

integrated view of metropolitan regions. Cities and suburbs do not exist independently of one another. Their fates are inextricably linked, for many of the issues and problems that affect quality of life transcend municipal boundaries. Furthermore, to ensure the vitality of cities in the twenty-first century, planners and the public need to gain an understanding of both the problems and the possibilities of urban life—and, yes, even try to learn from some of the utopian thinkers of the past.

As cities struggle to define their futures, people must ask some hard questions of themselves and of their leaders. Why should we plan in the first place? What are the issues that planners can address better than the people themselves? Whom does any plan really benefit? Guiding the discussion that such questions provoke, we also suggest, must be a fundamental commitment to the health and welfare of all people who live in the city. With such a dedication—as is evident today in the urban life of Toronto's people—it is possible that, in time, we will generate a vision of the street that perhaps all citizens can share.

KEY TERMS

arcologies   (412)
City Beautiful movement   (400)
garden cities   (396)

green belt   (401)
new town   (401)
urban utopia   (411)

INTERNET ACTIVITIES

1. The Project for Public Spaces offers a set of interesting slides on how to plan and improve public spaces (with numerous before and after examples) at *http://www. slideshare.net/metroplanning/project-for-public-spaces-streets-as-places.*

2. If you would like to see an example of architectural design that ignores the social environment (much like 1970s urban renewal did), go to *http://digitalurban. blogspot.com/2008/01/virtual-purdue-future-city-animation.html,* and play the short animated video of a futuristic Turkish city. As you watch, observe how the attractions of a city—walkability, proximity of diverse activities, people watching, public transit, and action—are noticeably missing. Hopefully, this will never be a city of the future.

3. A self-confessed geek takes you to seven futuristic cities (including Crystal Island, mentioned in this chapter) at *http:// www.geekabout.com/2008-01-21-444/arcologists-dream-7-proposed-futuristic-sky-cities.html.*

GLOSSARY

absolute poverty The lack of sufficient resources to secure the basic necessities of life.

abstract space What developers, investors, and government consider in terms of the dimensions of size, location, and profit, rather than the ideas of local people.

administrative or political city A city established primarily for governmental purposes, such as a national capital.

agglomeration industries Interdependent economic enterprises located close to one another that provide some element in the creation and distribution of a product.

amenity city A city primarily known for its specialized recreational opportunities, such as beaches, gambling, mineral springs, or skiing.

apartheid A formal policy of racial segregation that once existed in South Africa, which Massey and Denton applied to the United States because of intense residential segregation patterns.

arcologies Self-contained urban megastructures designed to be environmentally safe, architecturally beautiful, and totally efficient.

bobos Slang term for those living a lifestyle mixture of the bourgeoisie and the bohemians.

boomers Edge cities located at the intersection of two major highways and almost always centered on a mall.

bourgeoisie A term referring to the middle class, such as shopkeepers, traders, bureaucrats, government officials, and people engaged in commercial ventures.

break-of-bulk A strategic geographic location that facilitates the transfer of goods from one form of transportation to another, such as truck to ship.

buppies Slang term for black, young (late twenties to early forties) professionals.

census tract A U.S. Census Bureau population unit of about 4,000 residents who are relatively homogeneous in socioeconomic status and living conditions.

central business district (CBD) A concentration of commercial activity within a city that includes banking, entertainment, offices, restaurants, retail stores, and public transit.

central place theory Christaller's thesis that the more important a city's economic function is to a region, the more its population will increase.

chain migration The pattern of migrants settling near family or friends.

charter schools Schools that operate with less state regulation so that teachers and administrators can try out new teaching strategies.

City Beautiful movement Popular nineteenth-century idea of building cities around neoclassical civic centers, with great public spaces and parks linked by spacious boulevards.

city-states A sociopolitical organization that controls surrounding regions, including a number of other towns, villages, and rural lands.

civic culture Ability of city dwellers to coexist and cooperate in the everyday routines of public habits and customs.

colonization When a dominant group or country establishes control over another country or area, often for purposes of exploitation.

common-interest developments (CIDs) A form of gated community requiring membership in a self-governing homeowners' association thathas extensive regulatory power over residents.

community policing An approach that increases interaction and cooperation between law enforcement agencies and the people and neighborhoods they serve.

consolidated metropolitan statistical area (CMSA) The U.S. Census Bureau term for a megalopolis, or overlapping of metropolitan regions.

cosmic calendar An imaginative concept to examine the entire history of our planet compressed into a single calendar year.

cosmopolites Highly educated urban sophisticates who choose to live in the city because of its wide range of activities, experiences, and social contacts.

critical mass An amount or level of population needed to support other activities, such as churches, hospitals, or shopping centers.

culture The basic beliefs, values, and technology that characterize a city in a particular historical era.

de facto segregation Unequal treatment of people based on social customs and traditions.

de jure segregation   Unequal treatment established by law.

decentralization   The outward migration of people and business from the central city to outlying suburban regions.

defensible space   Physical design that promotes safety through ongoing natural surveillance.

dinks   Slang term for couples with dual income, no kids.

districts   Medium to large sections of the city, reinforced by physical clues to convey a sense of "being in" them.

division of labor   The way that different tasks are apportioned to different people in a given society.

ecological sociology   A subfield of sociology that focuses on urban design, land-use planning, and policy reform to create environmentally sound development.

economic restructuring   When companies or cities move away from manufacturing as their primary economic activity and evolve into more service-oriented activities.

edge city   A new, sprawling, middle-class, automobile-dependent center, typically located at the fringe of an older urban area.

edges   Boundaries, either barriers or seams, that exist between two areas.

eminent domain   The legal right of government to seize private property for public use, provided that the owner receives compensation at fair market value.

environmental sociology   The study of the reciprocal interactions between the physical environment, social organization, and social behavior.

ethnic villagers   Migrants who sustain rural life patterns in the city, cluster in a local area, emphasize traditional religious beliefs and family ties, and display suspicion of outsiders. That area is considered an "ethnic village."

exurbs   New residential areas that develop on the metropolitan fringe.

false consciousness   A misinterpretation of reality by accepting the dominant group's views and not realizing one's situation is the result of exploitation.

garden cities   Based on Howard's vision, eco-friendly pedestrian villages that attempt to blend the best of the city and the country by utilizing shared public space.

gated communities   Residential neighborhoods that restrict entry to residents and their guests.

gemeinschaft   Tönnies' depiction of one form of social life as a community, much like that of a small country village, where all share a common view of life.

gendered spaces   How differences in gender status result in the organization of space to reflect and reinforce those unequal distinctions.

gentrification   The renovation of a run-down neighborhood and the influx of people from a higher socioeconomic level.

gesellschaft   Tönnies' depiction of another form of social life as an association, much like that of a large city, where people do not necessarily share a common view of life.

ghettos   Segregated neighborhoods with high unemployment and poverty rates.

gIS mapping   A computer-based methodology to gather, transform, manipulate, and analyze information related to the surface of the Earth.

global city   Also called a world city, it is one that occupies an influential position in the global economic system, attracting global investments and exercising considerable economic power worldwide.

globalization   The development of an increasingly integrated global economy marked by connectivity and interdependence of the world's businesses and markets.

green belt   An area surrounding a city or town where no development is permitted.

gridiron cities   Cities in which the physical layout contains straight streets crossing at right angles to create regular city blocks.

groupthink   Conformity to opinions that supposedly reflect group consensus.

hierarchical power structure   The levels of power within a society.

horizontal integration   When companies gain control over the manufacture of all parts that went into their final product, sometimes even the raw materials.

hostile environment   A setting in which members of a particular group are made uncomfortable because of comments made, images displayed, or other inappropriate behavior.

human ecology   A term coined by Robert Park, reflecting his concept about the orderly evolution of urban growth and development.

hyperghettos   Segregated neighborhoods with extreme levels of poverty and unemployment.

hypersegregation   An intense grouping of a racial group within a specific geographical area.

ideal type   A model constructed from real-world observation that highlights the crucial elements of some social phenomenon.

index of dissimilarity   A measurement tool for determining the level of segregation in a neighborhood.

industrial location theory Explanation that industry would locate where the transportation costs of both raw materials and the final product would be the lowest.

industrial parks Areas zoned for a cluster of manufacturing entities on campus-like settings.

industrialism The process of manufacturing goods in large quantities for mass consumption.

inner-city neighborhoods High-density, low-income areas with substandard housing located near the central business district.

invasion-succession The ecological process in which one group or activity replaces another in a particular area.

landmarks Physical reference points, including buildings, signs, stores, domes, gas stations, or hills.

lifestyle communities Gated communities for those who want separate, private services and amenities within a homogeneous, predictable environment.

magnet schools Schools offering special programs to attract students from many districts to achieve integration.

McMansions Any supersized, large house exceeding 4,000 square feet on too small a lot, leaving little room for yard space.

mechanical solidarity Social bonds that are constructed on likeness, on common belief and custom, and on common ritual and symbol.

megacity A metropolitan area that constitutes its own megalopolis, because the population within its municipal boundary number at least 10 million people.

megalopolis When two or more metropolitan areas expand so that they intermingle with one another to form a continuous or almost continuous urban complex.

mental maps Individualized constructs of an area based on personal experience, interests, and knowledge of the socially recognized "important areas" of the city.

metropolitan area A large population center and its adjacent communies, with which it has a high degree of economic and social integration.

metropolitan statistical area (MSA) At least one city with 50,000 or more inhabitants, its county, and any surrounding urban counties from which a large proportion of inhabitants are attracted as commuters.

mode of development Castells' notion of the processing and transmission of information as the fundamental resource of productivity and power.

mode of production The things needed to produce goods and service, such as land, tools, knowledge, wealth, or factories.

natural areas Places that evolve as unplanned clusters with specialized activities.

natural crossroads A strategic geographical location that facilitates the concentration of people and services, especially trade.

new towns Large-scale, holistic planning of a mixed-use, self-sufficient community.

New Urbanism Incorporates sociological principles in physical design, such as walkability, mixed building types and activities, and social interaction.

nodes Anchor points of strategic activity, such as a major transit station or square.

oligopoly Market domination by a few producers.

ordered segmentation Suttles' term for the social organization found within a slum community.

organic solidarity A complex division of labor, in which many different people specialize in many different occupations and depend on one another to meet various needs.

parallel social institutions A minority-group, community support network of clubs, churches, organizations, stores, and media to share the commonality of language and culture.

paths Streets, walkways, transit lines, canals, and railroads along which the observer moves.

political fragmentation The splintered governance structure of numerous local municipalities in a metropolitan region.

postmodernism A reaction against the assumed certainty that rational, objective efforts can explain reality and, instead, an insistence that there are multiple interpretations based on concrete experiences, not abstract principles.

prestige communities Gated communities that are status-oriented enclaves emphasizing exclusion and image, with the gates symbolizing the eminent status of their residents.

primacy ratio The extent of the dominance of a country's primate city, computed by dividing its population by the population of the second-largest city.

primary circuit of capital Lefebvre's identification of investment to hire workers to manufacture a product to sell at a profit to be used for more investment.

primate cities Principal cities that are extremely large in comparison with other cities in the country.

productive surplus The production of a food surplus to enable some people to engage in pursuits other than farming, such as arts, crafts, and science.

push–pull factors Combination of factors that drive one from the homeland and lure that migrant to another locale.

racial profiling Targeting individuals of a specific group on the assumption they are more likely to commit illegal acts than are individuals of other groups.

radiocentric cities Cities in which the physical layout expands outward in all directions from a common center.

regal/ritual city A city with political and/or religious concerns at its core.

relative poverty The lack of resources of some people in comparison to others who have more.

reputational method Subjective input in which people compare others to themselves in terms of status.

scenes Places where people gather to socialize with friends or meet new ones, and to enjoy themselves.

school voucher Giving parents an option by applying the state's share of the cost for educating a child to the school of their choice.

second circuit of capital Lefebvre's identification of real estate investment as almost always leading to profit as an important means of acquiring wealth.

security-zone communities Gated communities with a fortress mentality of protection and the exclusion of people deemed to be a threat to the residents' safety and quality of life.

slums Low-income neighborhoods with substandard housing.

smart growth Comprehensive land-use planning to revitalize and build compact and environmentally sensitive communities.

social impact analysis The study to determine the likely consequences of a project before it is executed.

social power The ability to achieve one's goals and to shape events.

social promotions Moving children through grades with their age peers regardless of their actual learning achievement.

social space What individuals who live, work, and play in an area think about their environment.

social stratification The hierarchical ranking within a society of various social class groups according to wealth, power, and prestige.

social structure The recurrent patterns of city life that are shaped significantly by the unequal distribution of important urban resources, including wealth, power, and prestige.

sprawl Spread-out or low-density residential development beyond the edge of services and employment.

strategic policing An aggressive tactic of deploying increased patrols, decoys, and sting operations in locales identified as high-crime areas.

sunbelt expansion The growth of population, commerce, and industry in the South and West.

texture The impression that cities convey to the beholder; also called "soul" or "personality."

total fertility rate The average number of children a woman has during her lifetime.

uptowns Edge cities built on top of preautomobile settlements.

urban agglomerations A city with continuous spread around it encompassing a few other towns and outgrowths, based on the core town; a metropolitan area.

urban cluster A combination of contiguous urban areas that extend across city, county, or state boundary lines.

urban dominance A central pattern of the historical and modern world in which the city radiates its influence far beyond its borders.

urban ecology Analysis of how people and activities spread out within an urban area.

urban explosion Ever-greater numbers of people moving into the city.

urban geography A focus on the significance of a city's location and natural resources.

urban implosion Ever-greater numbers of people moving out from the city to surrounding regions.

urban political economy Critical urban sociology perspective; adherents are generally neo-Marxists, but regardless of their ideological orientation, they focus on investment decisions and economic trends that determine a city's fortunes.

urban renewal A federally funded program to demolish old buildings in decaying areas of a city and build new ones in their place.

urban utopia An idealized city in which the inhabitants are content because everything works perfectly.

urbanism The culture or way of life of city dwellers.

urbanization The changes resulting from people moving into cities and other densely populated areas.

vertical disintegration When large companies unload their production support companies.

world-systems analysis An approach suggesting that the economic well being of most cities is heavily dependent on their placement within this world hierarchy.

yuppies Slang term for young (late twenties to early forties) urban professionals.

REFERENCES

ABC NEWS. 2000. "Crime Fears Linger." Accessed at http://abcnews.go.com/sections/politics/DailyNews/poll000607.html on September 23, 2002.

ABRAHAMSON, MARK. 1996. *Urban Enclaves: Identity and Place in America.* New York: St. Martin's Press.

ABU-LUGHOD, JANET L. 2007. *Third World Urbanization.* New York: Routledge.

ADDAMS, JANE. 1909. *The Spirit of Youth and the City Streets.* New York: Macmillan.

——. 1910. *Twenty Years at Hull House.* New York: Macmillan.

——. 1930. *The Second Twenty Years at Hull House.* New York: Macmillan.

ADLER, JERRY, AND MAGGIE MALONE. 1996. "Toppling Towers." *Newsweek,* November 4, pp. 70–72.

ALONSO, WILLIAM. 1971. "A Theory of the Urban Land Market." Pp. 154–59 in *Internal Structure of the City,* edited by Larry S. Bourne. New York: Oxford University Press.

ANDERSON, ELIJAH. 2000. *Code of the Street: Decency, Violence, and the Moral Life of the Inner City.* New York: W.W. Norton & Company.

ANDERSON, ELIJAH, AND DOUGLAS S. MASSEY. 2001. *Problem of the Century: Racial Stratification in the United States.* New York: Russell Sage Foundation.

ANSWERS.COM. 2008. "Alexander Woollcott." Accessed at http://www.answers.com/topic/alexander-woollcott on December 12, 2008.

ARCHBALD, DOUGLAS A. 2004. "School Choice, Magnet Schools, and the Liberation Model: An Empirical Study." *Sociology of Education* 77 (October): 283–310.

ARCOSANTI. 2009. Accessed at http://www.arcosanti.org on March 28, 2009.

ARMS OF LOVE INTERNATIONAL. 2008. *What We Do: Street Children.* Accessed at http://www.armsoflove.org/what_street.htm on June 16, 2008.

ASSOCIATED PRESS. 2007. "New Orleans Scales Back Rebuilding Plans." Accessed at http://www.msnbc.msn.com/id/21258937/ on July 15, 2008.

ATLANTA REGIONAL COUNCIL. 2007. *Regional Snapshot: Land Development in the Atlanta Region.* Accessed at http://www.atlantaregional.com July 20, 2008.

AUSTIN, ALFREDO LOPEZ, AND LEONARDO LOPEZ LUJAN. 2001. *Mexico's Indigenous Past.* Norman: University of Oklahoma Press.

AUSTIN, ALICE CONSTANCE. 1935. *The Next Step.* Los Angeles: Institute Press.

BABBITT, BRUCE. 2005. "How to Rebuild New Orleans: Make It an Island," *New York Times,* September 9, p. A17.

BAILEY, JAMES. 1990. *New Towns in America: The Design and Development Process.* New York: Wiley Inter-Science.

BAILEY, RUBY L. 2007. "The 'D' Is a Draw: Most Suburbanites Are Repeat Visitors." *Detroit Free Press,* 22 August, p. 1.

BAKER, KERMIT. 2007. "After a Strong 2007, Nonresidential Construction Growth Projected to Moderate in 2008." *AIArchitect* (June 29), p. 14.

BALTZELL, E. DIGBY. 1980. *Puritan Boston and Quaker Philadelphia.* New York: Free Press.

——. 1987. *The Protestant Establishment.* New Haven, CT: Yale University Press; originally published 1964.

——. 1989. *Philadelphia Gentlemen: The Making of a National Upper Class.* New Brunswick, NJ: Transaction Publishers; originally published 1958.

BANFIELD, EDWARD C. 1970. *The Unheavenly City.* Boston: Little, Brown.

——. 1990. *The Unheavenly City Revisited.* Long Grove, IL: Waveland Press.

BANHAM, RAYNER. 2001. *Los Angeles: The Architecture of Four Ecologies.* Berkeley: University of California Press; originally published 1973.

BARNER, CRAIG. 2008. "Top 2008 Contractors; Battle in Iffy Market Continues in Midwest." *Midwest Construction,* 1 April, p. 33.

BARNETT, JONATHAN. 2002. "Turning Edge Cities into Real Cities." *Planning* 68 (November): 10–13.

BAUDER, H., AND E. PERLE. 1999. "Spatial and Skills Mismatch for Labor-Market Segments." *Environment and Planning* 31:959–77.

BEAUREGARD, ROBERT A. 2003. "City of Superlatives." *City & Community* 2 (September): 183–99.

——. 2006. *When America Became Suburban.* South Minneapolis: University of Minnesota Press.

BEGUIN, GILES, AND DOMINQUE MOREL. 1997. *The Forbidden City: Heart of Imperial China.* London: Thames and Hudson, Ltd.

BEITO, DAVID T., PETER GORDON, AND ALEXANDER TABARROK, eds. 2002. *The Voluntary City: Choice, Community, and Civil Society.* Ann Arbor: University of Michigan Press.

BELL, WENDELL, AND MARION BOAT. 1957. "Urban Neighborhoods and Informal Social Relations." *American Journal of Sociology* 62:391–98.

BELLAH, ROBERT N., RICHARD MADSEN, WILLIAM M. SULLIVAN, ANN SWIDLER, AND STEVEN M. TIPTON. 1985.

Habits of the Heart: Individualism and Commitment in American Life. New York: Harper & Row.

BELLUSH, JEWEL. 2000. *Urban Renewal: People, Politics, and Planning.* Garden City, NY: Doubleday.

BEMBRY, JAMES X., AND DONALD F. NORRIS. 2005. "An Exploratory Study of Neighborhood Choices among Moving to Opportunity Participants in Baltimore, Maryland." *Journal of Sociology and Social Welfare* 32 (December): 93–107.

BERMAN, DAVID. 1997. "Shopping on the Edge." *Canadian Business,* October 31, pp. 72–79.

BERRY, BRIAN J.L. 1985. "Islands of Renewal in a Sea of Decay." Pp. 69–98 in *The New Urban Reality,* edited by Paul E. Peterson. Washington, D.C.: Brookings Institution.

BEVERIDGE, ANDREW A. 2007. "The End of 'White Flight'?" *Gotham Gazette* (November). Accessed at http://www.gothamgazette.com/article/demographics/20071127/5/2358 on June 9, 2008.

BINGHAM, RICHARD, AND ZHONGCAI ZHANG. 2001. *The Economies of Central-City Neighborhoods.* Boulder, CO: Westview Press.

BIRRETTERI, ANTHONY. 2001. "All of New Jersey a High-Tech Corridor." *New Jersey Business.* Accessed at http://www.allbusiness.com/north-america/united-states-new-jersey/935175-1.html on June 7, 2008.

BLAKELY, EDWARD J., AND MARY GAIL SNYDER. 1999. *Fortress America: Gated Communities in the United States,* New Ed. Washington, D.C.: Brookings Institution Press.

BLAU, JUDITH R., AND PETER M. BLAU. 1982. "The Cost of Inequality: Metropolitan Structure and Criminal Violence." *Sociological Quarterly* 27:114–29.

BLUESTONE, BARRY, AND BENNETT HARRISON. 1984. *The Deindustrialization of America: Plant Closings, Community Abandonment, and the Dismantling of Basic Industry.* New York: Basic Books.

BONNES, MIRILIA, MARINO BONAIUTO, AND ANNA PAOLA. 1991. "Crowding and Residential Satisfaction in the Urban Environment: A Contextual Approach." *Environment and Behavior* 23 (September): 531–52.

BOOKCHIN, MURRAY. 1996. *The Limits of the City,* 2nd rev. ed. Toronto: Black Rose Books.

BORJAS, GEORGE J. 2001. *Heaven's Door: Immigration Policy and the American Economy.* Princeton, NJ: Princeton University Press.

BOTT, ELIZABETH. 2003. *Family and Social Network.* New York: Routledge.

BOUMA-DOFF, WENDA. 2007. "Involuntary Isolation: Ethnic Preferences and Residential Segregation." *Journal of Urban Affairs* 29:289–309.

BRADBURY, CATHERINE, ANTHONY DOWNS, AND KENNETH SMALL. 1982. *Urban Decline and the Future of American Cities.* Washington, D.C.: Brookings Institution.

BRASWELL, GEOFFREY E. 2004. *The Maya and Teotihuacan: Reinterpreting Early Classic Interaction.* Austin: University of Texas Press.

Britannica Book of the Year. 2008. Chicago: Encyclopedia Britannica.

BROCKERHOFF, MARTIN. 2000. "An Urbanizing World." *Population Bulletin* 55 (September).

BROKAW, TOM. 2002. NBC News, June 27.

BROOKINGS INSTITUTION AND GREATER NEW ORLEANS COMMUNITY DATA CENTER. 2008. *The New Orleans Index,* April 16. Accessed at http://www.gnocdc.org/NOLAIndex/NOLAIndex.pdf on June 18, 2008.

BROOKS, DAVID. 2001. *Bobos in Paradise: The New Upper Class and How They Got There.* New York: Simon & Schuster.

BROOKS, VAN WYCK. 2005. *The Flowering of New England, 1815–1875.* New York: AMS Press, Inc.; originally published 1936.

BRUCE, J.M. 1970. "Intergenerational Occupational Mobility and Visiting with Kin and Friend." *Social Forces* 49:117–27.

BRUNO, PAT. 2001. "Dinner and a Show: New Theaters Draw Diners Downtown." *Chicago Sun-Times,* September 7, p. 16.

BRYANT, M. DARROL. 2001. "Some Notes on Muslims in Canada and the US." Accessed at http://www.renaissance.com.pk/Seprefl2y1.html on June 29, 2008.

BUCKLEY, JACK, AND MARK SCHNEIDER. 2007. *Charter Schools: Hope or Hype?* Princeton, NJ: Princeton University Press.

BURCHELL, ROBERT, ANTHONY DOWNS, SAHAN MUKHERJI, AND BARBARA MCCANN. 2005. *Sprawl Costs: Economic Impacts of Unchecked Development.* Washington, D.C.: Island Press.

BURGESS, ERNEST W. 1984. "The Growth of the City." Pp. 47–62 in *The City,* edited by Robert E. Park and Ernest W. Burgess. Chicago: University of Chicago Press.

BURN, A.R. 1970. *Greece and Rome.* Glenview, IL: Scott, Foresman.

BUTLER, TIM. 2008. "In the City But Not of the City?" *International Journal of Social Research Methodology* 11 (April): 141–49.

BYRON, ROBERT. 2007. *The Road to Oxiana.* New York: Oxford University Press.

CAHALAN, SUSANNAH. 2008. "Code of Honor: New in-the-Money ZIP Beats Our 10021." *New York Post,* May 12, p. 3.

CALDWELL, WILLIAM A., ed. 1973. *How to Save Urban America.* New York: Signet.

CALHOUN, CRAIG, ed. 2007. *Sociology in America: A History.* Chicago: University of Chicago Press.

CALHOUN, JOHN B. 1962. "Population Density and Social Pathology." *Scientific American* 206:139–48.

CALLOW, ALEXANDER B., JR. 1982. *American Urban History: An Interpretive Reader with Commentaries* 3rd ed. New York: Oxford University Press.

CANADIAN CENTRE FOR JUSTICE STATISTICS. 2008. *Juristat* 27:5. Ottawa.

CARCOPINO, JEROME. 2003. *Daily Life in Ancient Rome: The People and City at the Height of the Empire.* New Haven, CT: Yale University Press.

CARNOY, MARTIN, REBECCA JACOBSEN, LAWRENCE MISHEL, AND RICHARD ROTHSTEIN. 2005. *The Charter School Dust-Up: Examining the Evidence on Enrollment and Achievement.* New York: Teachers College Press.

CARO, ROBERT A. 1975. *The Power Broker: Robert Moses and the Fall of New York.* New York: Vintage.

CARP, BENJAMIN. 2007. *Rebels Rising: Cities and the American Revolution.* New York: Oxford University Press.

CARTER, J. SCOTT, LALA CARR STEELMEN, LYNN M. MULKEY, AND CASEY BORCH. 2005. "When the Rubber Meets the Road: Effects of Urban and Regional Residence on

Principle and Implementation Measures of Racial Tolerance." *Social Science Research* 34 (June): 408–25.

CASA ALIANZA. 2006. *Honduras Is the Last Country Where Children and Young People Want to Live.* Accessed at http://www.casa-alianza.org/en/news.php on June 16, 2008.

CASTELLS, MANUEL. 1979. *The Urban Question.* Cambridge, MA: MIT Press.

———. 1982. *City, Class, and Power.* New York: Palgrave Macmillan.

———. 1985. *The City and the Grass Roots.* Berkeley: University of California Press.

———. 1991. *The Informational City.* Malden, MA: Blackwell.

CAULFIELD, JON. 1994. *City Form and Everyday Life: Toronto's Gentrification and Critical Social Practice.* Toronto: University of Toronto Press.

CENTER FOR EDUCATION REFORM. 2007. *Annual Survey of America's Charter Schools.* Washington, D.C.: National Center for Education Statistics.

CENTRAL INTELLIGENCE AGENCY. 2009. *World Factbook.* Accessed at https://www.cia.gov/library/publications/the-world-factbook/ on March 28, 2009.

CHADWICK, JOHN. 1999. *The Mycenaean World,* reprint ed. Cambridge, UK: Cambridge University Press.

CHAMBERLAIN, LISA. 2006. "A Resurgence in Cleveland." *New York Times,* November 8, p. C8.

CHANDLER, TERTIUS. 1987. *Four Thousand Years of Urban Growth.* Lewiston, NJ: Edwin Mellen Press.

CHARLES, CAMILLE Z. 2000. "Neighborhood Racial-Composition Preferences: Evidence from a Multiethnic Metropolis," *Social Problems* 47:379–98.

CHASE-DUNN, CHRISTOPHER, AND SALVATORE J. BABONES. 2006. *Global Social Change: Historical and Comparative Perspectives.* Baltimore: Johns Hopkins University Press.

CHESAPEAKE BAY FOUNDATION. 2005. *Vital Signs: Assessing the State of Chesapeake Agriculture in 2005.* Accessed at http://www.cbf.org/site/DocServer/StateOfAg.pdf?docID=4343 on July 20, 2008.

CHESAPEAKE ECO-CHECK. 2008. *Chesapeake Bay Health Report Card: 2007.* Accessed at http://www.eco-check.org/reportcard/chesapeake/2007/ on July 20, 2008.

CHILDE, V. GORDON. 1950. "The Urban Revolution." *Town Planning Review* 21:3–17.

CHOWDHURY, DEBASISH ROY. 2007. "Right Moves Being Made on Wealth Disparity." *China Daily,* October 16. Accessed at http://www.chinadaily.com.cn/opinion/2007-10/16/content_6728538.htm on June 21, 2008.

CHRISTALLER, WALTER. 1966. *Central Places in Southern Germany.* Englewood Cliffs, NJ: Prentice Hall; originally published 1933.

CIARDI, JOHN. 1990. *How Does a Poem Mean?* 2nd ed. New York: Random House.

CITY OF NEW YORK. 2009. "Mayor Bloomberg Announces Record Tourism Record in Weekly Radio Address." Press Release, January 13.

CITY OF SPOKANE PLANNING SERVICES DEPARTMENT. 2003. "Comprehensive Plan Background." Accessed at http://www.spokaneplanning.org/history.htm on July 21, 2008.

CITY-DATA.COM. 2009. Accessed on March 28, 2009.

CLARK, KENNETH. 1980. "The Role of Race." *New York Times Magazine,* October 5, pp. 25–33, 90–91.

CLEAN WATER ACTION COUNCIL. 2008. *Land Use & Urban Sprawl.* Accessed at http://www.cwac.net/landuse/index on July 21, 2008.

CLEVELAND, WILLIAM L. 2004. *A History of the Modern Middle East,* 3rd ed. Boulder, CO: Westview Press.

CNN. 2008. "Developing Cities and Pollution." Accessed at http://www.cnn.com/2008/WORLD/asiapcf/03/09/eco.cities/index.html on July 28, 2008.

COLTEN, CRAIG E. 2005. "How to Rebuild New Orleans: Restore the Marsh," *New York Times,* September 9, p. A17.

COMMUNITY ASSOCIATIONS INSTITUTE. 2008. "Industry Data: National Statistics. Accessed at http://www.caionline.org/about/facts.cfm on June 10, 2008.

CONANT, JENNET. 2002. *Tuxedo Park.* New York: Simon & Schuster.

CONDIE, BILL. 2008. "Global Toll Rises to 47,000 as More London Jobs Lost." *Evening Standard,* 25 April, p. 1.

CONGDON, PETER. 1995. "Socioeconomic Structure and Health in London." *Urban Studies* 32 (April): 523–49.

CORCORAN, DAVID. 2003. "Restaurants: Unbound in Ironbound, *New York Times,* July 20, p. NJ10.

COSTELLO, VINCENT F. 1977. *Urbanization in the Middle East.* New York: Cambridge University Press.

COUNCIL ON AMERICAN-ISLAMIC RELATIONS. 2008. Accessed at http://www.cair.com/Home.aspx on June 29, 2008.

CRUTCHER, MICHAEL E. 2005. "How to Rebuild New Orleans: Build Diversity," *New York Times,* September 9, p. A17.

CURRAN, DAN. 2003. "Sherman Park Still One of Milwaukee's Most Vibrant Areas." Accessed at http://www.onmilwaukee.com/visitors/articles/shermanpark.html on June 23, 2008.

CURRY, AARON, CARL LATKIN, AND MELISSA DAVEY-ROTHWELL. 2008. "Pathways to Depression: The Impact of Neighborhood Crime on Inner-City Residents in Baltimore, Maryland, USA." *Social Science & Medicine* 67 (July): 23–30.

CURTIS WHITE, KATHERINE J., AND AVERY M. GUEST. 2003. "Community Lost or Transformed? Urbanization and Social Ties." *City & Community* 2 (September): 239–59.

DANA, RICHARD HENRY. 2001. *Two Years Before the Mast.* New York: Random House Modern Library; originally published 1862.

DAVIS, KINGSLEY. 1969, 1972. *World Urbanization, 1950-1970.* Vols. 1, 2. Berkeley, CA: Institute of International Studies.

DE JONG, IAIN. 2000. "Devolution Hits Housing in Canada," *Shelterforce Online.* Accessed at http://www.nhi.org/online/issues/113/dejong.html on July 27, 2008.

DEAR, MICHAEL J. 2000. *The Postmodern Urban Condition.* Malden, MA: Blackwell.

DEEGAN, MARY JO. 1991. *Women in Sociology: A Bio-Bibliographical Sourcebook.* Westport, CT: Greenwood Press.

DIALA, CHAMBERLAIN C., AND CARLES MUNTANER. 2003. "Mood and Anxiety Disorders Among Rural, Urban, and Metropolitan Residents in the United States," *Community Mental Health Journal* 39:239–52.

DICKENS, CHARLES. 1853. *Bleak House.* London: Chapman and Hall.

———. 1860. *Great Expectations.* London: Chapman and Hall.

———. 1997. *Hard Times.* New York: Signet Classics; originally published 1854.

———. 2004. *American Notes.* Kila, MT: Kessinger Publishing; originally published 1842.

DIERS, JIM. 2004. *Neighbor Power: Building Community the Seattle Way.* Seattle: University of Washington Press.

DINER, HASIA R. 1983. *Erin's Daughters in America: Irish Immigrant Women in the Nineteenth Century.* Baltimore: Johns Hopkins University Press.

DIXON, TRAVIS L. 2008. "Crime News and Racialized Beliefs: Understanding the Relationship between Local News and Perceptions of African Americans and Crime." *Journal of Communication* 58 (March): 106–25.

DOS PASSOS, JOHN. 1969. "San Francisco Looks West." Pp. 484–89 in *City Life,* edited by Oscar Shoenfeld and Helen MacLean. New York: Grossman; essay originally published 1944.

DOSS, KELLY R., AND WILLIAM T. MARKHAM. 2004. "The Sprawl Problem in Guilford County." Accessed at http://nc.sierraclub.org/piedmont/excom/sprawl_guilford_2004.pdf on December 12, 2008.

DOUGLAS, GEORGE H. 2004. *Skyscrapers: A Social History of the Very Tall Building in America.* Jefferson, NC: McFarland & Company.

DOWNS, ANTHONY. 1985. "The Future of Industrial Cities." Pp. 281–94 in *The New Urban Reality,* edited by Paul E. Peterson. Washington, D.C.: Brookings Institution.

DUESTERBERG, THOMAS J., AND ERNEST H. PREEG. 2003. *U.S. Manufacturing: The Engine for Growth in a Global Economy.* Westport, CT: Praeger.

DURKHEIM, EMILE. 1964. *The Division of Labor in Society.* New York: Free Press; originally published 1893.

EAKIN, MARSHALL C. 2007. *The History of Latin America: Collision of Cultures.* New York: Palgrave Macmillan.

ECONOMIST. 2008. "That Sinking Feeling." (August 21), p. 49.

EIESLAND, NANCY L. 2000. *A Particular Place: Urban Restructuring and Religious Ecology in a Southern Exurb.* New Brunswick, NJ: Rutgers University Press.

EISNER, SIMON, ARTHUR GALLION, AND STANLEY EISNER. 1993. *The Urban Pattern,* 6th ed. New York: Wiley.

EL NASSER, HAYA. 2006. "Mich. Pulling Itself out of Slump." *USA Today,* April 25, p. 3A.

ENGELS, FRIEDRICH. 2007. *The Condition of the Working Class in England,* trans. by W.O. Henderson and W.H. Chaloner. New York: Macmillan; originally published 1844.

ESHBAUGH, ELAINE M., JACQUES LEMPERS, AND GAYLE L. LUZE. 2006. "Objective and Self-Perceived Resources as Predictors of Depression among Urban and Non-Urban Adolescent Mothers." *Journal of Youth and Adolescence* 35 (October): 839–47.

ESHERICK, JOSEPH W., PAUL G. PICKOWICZ, AND ANDREW G. WALDER, eds. 2006. *China's Cultural Revolution as History.* Stanford, CA: Stanford University Press.

EVANS, GARY W., SUSAN SAEGERT, AND REBECCA HARRIS. 2001. "Residential Density and Psychological Health among Children in Low-Income Families." *Environment and Behavior* 33 (March): 165–80.

FABBI, NADINE. 2003. *Early Black Canadian History.* Accessed at http://www.k12studycanada.org/files/EarlyBlackCanadianHistory.pdf on June 25, 2008.

FAJNZYLBER, PABLO, DANIEL LEDERMAN, AND NORMAN LOAYZA. 2002. "Inequality and Violent Crime," *The Journal of Law & Economics* 45 (April): 1–40.

FARRELL, CHAD R. 2008. "Bifurcation, Fragmentation, or Integration? The Racial and Geographic Structure of US Metropolitan Segregation, 1990–2000." *Urban Studies* 45 (March): 467–99.

FEDERAL BUREAU OF INVESTIGATION. 2008. *Crime in the United States—2007.* Accessed at http://www.fbi.gov/ucr/cius2007/index.html on February 28, 2009.

FEDERAL RESERVE BOARD. 2006. "Recent Changes in U.S. Family Finances." Federal Reserve Bulletin, Table 3, p. A8.

FERNANDEZ-KELLY, PATRICIA, AND JON SHEFNER, eds. 2007. *NAFTA and Beyond: Alternative Perspectives in the Study of Global Trade and Development.* Thousand Oaks, CA: Sage Publications.

FILION, PIERRE. 1995. "City Form and Everyday Life: Toronto's Gentrification and Critical Social Practice." *Journal of the American Planning Association* 61 (Spring): 281–82.

FISCHER, CLAUDE S. 1973. "Urban Malaise." *Social Problems* 52:221–35.

———. 1975. "Toward a Subcultural Theory of Urbanism." *American Journal of Sociology* 80:1319–41.

———. 1984. *The Urban Experience,* 2nd ed. Orlando: Harcourt Brace Jovanovich.

———. 1991. "Ambivalent Communities: How Americans Understand Their Localities." Pp. 79–90, in *America at Century's End,* edited by Alan Wolf. Berkeley: University of California Press.

———. 1995. "The Subcultural Theory of Urbanism: A Twentieth-Year Assessment." *American Journal of Sociology* 102 (November): 543–77.

FISCHER, CLAUDE, R.M. JACKSON, C.A. STEVE, K. GERSON, AND L.M. JONES. 1977. *Networks and Places.* New York: Free Press.

FISCHER, CLAUDE S. et al. 1996. *Inequality by Design: Cracking the Bell Curve Myth.* Princeton, NJ: Princeton University Press.

FLEISHMAN, SANDRA. 1999. "Abandoned Housing Is Now Hot Property." *Washington Post,* September 1, p. B1.

FOGELSON, ROBERT M. 2003. *Downtown.* New Haven, CT: Yale University Press.

FRANKLIN, TRAVIS W., CORTNEY A. FRANKLIN, AND TRAVIS C. PRATT. 2006. "Examining the Empirical Relationship between Prison Crowding and Inmate Misconduct: A Meta-Analysis of Conflicting Research." *Journal of Criminal Justice* 34 (July–August): 401–12.

FREEMAN, JO. 2000. *The Politics of Women's Liberation: A Case Study of an Emerging Movement and Its Relation to the Policy Process,* reprint ed. New York: David McKay.

FREUDENBERG, WILLIAM R. 1992. "Addictive Economics: Extractive Industries and Vulnerable Localities in a Changing World Economy." *Rural Sociology* 57 (3): 305–22.

Fu, Vincent K. 2001. "Racial Intermarriage Pairings," *Demography* 38:147–59.

Gallun, Alby. 2005. "Cabrini's Green," *Crain's Chicago Business* 28 (May 16): 3, 8.

Gans, Herbert. 1962. "City Planning and Urban Realities." *Commentary* 33:170–75.

———. 1967. *The Levittowners.* New York: Penguin.

———. 1968. "Urbanism and Suburbanism as Ways of Life: A Re-evaluation of Definitions." Pp. 170-95. In *Metropolis Center and Symbol of Our Time,* edited by Philip Kasinitz. New York: New York University Press, 1995.

———. 1982. *The Urban Villagers: Group and Class in the Life of Italian Americans.* New York: Free Press; originally published 1962.

———. 1994. "Urbanism and Suburbanism as Ways of Life: A Re-evaluation of Definitions." Pp. 51–69 in *People, Plans, and Policies: Essays on Poverty, Racism, and Other National Urban Problems.* New York: Columbia University Press.

Garber, Judith A., and Roby Turner, eds. 1994. *Gender in Urban Research.* Thousand Oaks, CA: Sage.

Gardner, Carol Brooks. 1995. *Passing By: Gender and Public Harassment.* Berkeley: University of California Press.

Garreau, Joel. 1991. *Edge City.* New York: Doubleday.

Geek About.Com. 2008. "Arcologists' Dream: 7 Proposed Futuristic Sky Cities." Accessed on July 16, 2008.

Geisse, G., and F. Sabatini. 1988. "Latin American Cities and Their Poor." Pp. 322–27 in *The Metropolitan Era,* edited by M. Dogan and J. Kasarda. Newbury Park, CA: Sage.

Gertner, Jon. 2005. "Chasing Ground." *New York Times Magazine,* 16 October, p. 46.

Gibbons, Deborah, and Paul M. Olk. 2003. "Individual and Structural Origins of Friendship and Social Position Among Professionals," *Journal of Personality & Social Psychology* 84:340–51.

Giddens, Anthony, ed. 1972. *Emile Durkheim: Selected Writings.* New York: Cambridge University Press.

Giovannini, Joseph. 1983. "I Love New York and L.A., Too." *New York Times Magazine,* September 11, pp. 145, 147–49.

Girardet, Herbert. 1994. "Keeping Up with Capital Growth." *Geographical Magazine* 66 (June): 12–15.

GIS.com. 2008. "What is GIS?" Accessed at http://www.gis.com/whatisgis/ on June 19, 2008.

Glaab, Charles N. 1970. *The American City: A Documentary History.* Homewood, IL: Dorsey Press.

Glaab, Charles N., and A. Theodore Brown. 1983. *A History of Urban America,* 3rd ed. New York: Macmillan.

Goldberger, Paul. 1989. *City Observed.* New York: Vintage.

Gordon, Tracy M. 2004. "Moving Up by Moving Out? Planned Developments and Residential Segregation in California." *Urban Studies* 41 (February): 441–61.

Gorman, S. 2003. "Labor Pain," *Washington Monthly* 35 (September): 20.

Gottdiener, Mark, and Joe Feagin. 1988. "The Paradigm Shift in Urban Sociology." *Urban Affairs Quarterly* 24:163–87.

Gottdiener, Mark, and Ray Hutchison. 2001. *The Theming of America,* 2nd ed. Boulder, CO: Westview Press.

———. 2006. *The New Urban Sociology,* 3rd ed. Boulder, CO: Westview Press.

Gottmann, Jean. 1961. *Megalopolis.* New York: Twentieth Century Fund.

Government Office for London. 2008. "Tourism." Accessed at http://www.gos.gov.uk/gol/Culture_leisure/Tourism/?a=42496 on June 1, 2008.

Gray, Kathleen. 2005. "Declining Numbers Give Detroit Image Problem," *Detroit Free Press,* February 8, p. 1.

Gray, Robert. 1997. *A History of London.* New York: Barnes & Noble Books.

Green, Robert L. 1977. *The Urban Challenge: Poverty and Race.* Chicago: Follett.

Greenfield, Gerald M. 1994. *Latin American Urbanization.* Westport, CT: Greenwood Publishing Group.

Greengard, Samuel, and Charlene M. Solomon. 1994. "A City Rebuilds Its Symbol—and Rejuvenates Itself." *Personnel Journal* 73 (February): 64–65.

Greer, Scott. 1962. *The Emerging City.* New York: Free Press.

Guest, Avery M., Jane K. Cover, Ross L. Matseuda, and Charis E. Kubrin. 2006. "Neighborhood Context and Neighboring Ties." *City & Community* 5 (December): 363–85.

Gugler, Josef. 1996. *The Urban Transformation of the Developing World: Regional Trajectories.* New York: Oxford University Press.

Habitat for Humanity. 2008. *Habitat for Humanity Fact Sheet.* Accessed at http://www.habitat.org/how/factsheet.html on July 27, 2008.

Hackler, Tim. 1979. "The Big City Has No Corners on Mental Illness." *New York Times Magazine,* December 19, p. A1.

Hall, Edward. 1990. *The Hidden Dimension.* Chapter 13, pp. 165–180. New York: Anchor; originally published 1966.

Hall, Peter. 1984. "Geography." Pp. 21–36 in *Cities of the Mind,* edited by Lloyd Rodwin and Robert M. Hollister. New York: Plenum.

———. 2002. *Urban and Regional Planning,* 4th ed. London: Routledge.

Hamblin, Dora Jane. 1973. *The First Cities.* New York: Little, Brown.

Handel, Michael. 2003. "Skills Mismatch in the Labor Market," *Annual Review of Sociology* 29:135–65.

Hanff, Helene. 1989. *Apple of My Eye.* Kingston, RI: Moyer Bell Ltd.

Harris, Chauncey D., and Edward L. Ullman. 1945. "The Nature of Cities." *Annals* 242:7–17.

Harvey, David. 1992. *The Condition of Postmodernity.* New York: Wiley-Blackwell.

———. 1998. *Social Justice and the City.* Malden, MA: Blackwell; originally published 1973.

Hawley, Chris. 2004. "Trying to Exorcise Mexico's 'Little Devils'," *Arizona Republic,* December 20. Accessed at http://www.azcentral.com/specials/special03/articles/1220electricity.html on August 9, 2005.

Hayden, Delores. 1978. "Two Utopian Feminists and Their Campaigns for Kitchenless Houses." *Signs: Journal of Women in Culture and Society* 4:274–90.

HEATHER, PETER. 2007. *The Fall of the Roman Empire: A New History of Rome and the Barbarians.* New York: Oxford University Press.

HECKSCHER, AUGUST. 1978. *Open Spaces: The Life of American Cities.* New York: Harper & Row.

HEDGEFUND INTELLIGENCE. 2007. "Global Hedge Fund Assets Surge 19% to $2.48 Trillion." Accessed at http://www.hedgefundintelligence.com/images/590/55595/Global%20hedge%20fund%20assets%20$2.48trillion.pdf on July 28, 2008.

HEILBRONER, ROBERT L., AND WILLIAM S. MILBERG. 2007. *The Making of Economic Society,* 12th ed. Englewood Cliffs, NJ: Prentice Hall.

HEILPRIN, JOHN. 2005. "Groups: Sprawl Threatens Plants, Animals." Associated Press, January 11.

HENG, LIANG, AND JUDITH SHAPIRO. 1984. *Son of the Revolution.* New York: Vintage.

HENLY, JULIA R., SANDRA K. DANZIGER, AND SHIRA OFFER. 2005. "The Contribution of Social Support to the Material Well-Being of Low Income Families," *Journal of Marriage and Family* 67:122–40.

HERNÁNDEZ, RAMONA, AND FRANCISCO L. RIVERA-BATIZ. 2003. *Dominicans in the United States: A Socioeconomic Profile, 2000.* New York: CUNY Dominican Studies Institute.

HERRNSTEIN, RICHARD J., AND CHARLES MURRAY. 1994. *The Bell Curve: The Reshaping of American Life by Differences in Intelligence.* New York: Free Press.

HERSKOVITS, MELVILLE J. 2007. *The Human Factor in Changing Africa.* Whitefish, MT: Kessinger Publishing.

HESS, BETH B., ELIZABETH W. MARKSON, AND PETER J. STEIN. 1996. *Sociology,* 5th ed. Boston: Allyn & Bacon.

HEVESI, DENNIS. 2001. "East New York: A Neighborhood Reborn." *New York Times,* June 10, pp. RE1, 10.

HISE, GREG, MICHAEL J. DEAR, AND ERIC H. SCHOCKMAN, eds. 1996. *Rethinking Los Angeles.* Thousand Oaks, CA: Sage Publications.

HOCH, CHARLES, AND ROBERT A. SLAYTON. 1990. *New Homeless and Old: Community and the Skid Row Hotel.* Philadelphia: Temple University Press.

HÖFLICH, JOACHIM R. 2006. "The Mobile Phone and the Dynamic between Private and Public Communication: Results of an International Exploratory Study." *Knowledge, Technology, & Policy* 19 (Summer): 58–68.

HOHENBERG, PAUL M., AND LYNN HOLLEN LEES. 1996. *The Making of Urban Europe, 1000–1950,* reprint ed. Cambridge, MA: Harvard University Press.

HOLMES, GEORGE, ed. 2002. *The Oxford History of Medieval Europe.* New York: Oxford University Press.

HOUSTON. 2008. Accessed at http://www.houstontx.gov/abouthouston/houstonfacts.html on June 17, 2008.

HOWARD, EBENEZER. 2007. *Garden Cities of To-Morrow.* New York: Routledge; originally published 1898.

HOWELL, JOSEPH T. 1990. *Hard Living on Clay Street: Portraits of Blue-Collar Families.* Long Grove, IL: Waveland Press.

HOYT, HOMER. 1939. *The Structure and Growth of Residential Neighborhoods in American Cities.* Washington, D.C.: Federal Housing Administration.

HUMAN RESOURCES AND SOCIAL DEVELOPMENT CANADA. 2008. "Financial Security-Income Distribution." Accessed at http://www4.hrsdc.gc.ca/indicator.jsp?&indicatorid=22 on June 21, 2008.

HUMAN RIGHTS WATCH. 2008. "Street Children." Accessed at http://www.hrw.org/children/street.htm on June 16, 2008.

ICELAND, JOHN. 2005. "Why Concentrated Poverty Fell in the United States in the 1990s." *Population Bulletin,* August, p. 1.

IOFFE, GRIGORY, AND TATYANA NEFEDOVA. 2001. "Land Use Changes in the Environs of Moscow." *Area* 33:273–86.

INSTITUTE FOR CHILDREN AND POVERTY. 2008. *Quick Facts.* Accessed on http://www.icpny.org/index.asp?CID=7 on June 23, 2008.

IRWIN, JOHN. 1977. *Scenes.* Beverly Hills, CA: Sage.

ISBEL, WILLIAM H., AND HELAINE SILVERMAN. 2006. *Andean Archaeology III: North and South.* New York: Springer.

JACKSON, KENNETH T. 2008. *Crabgrass Frontier: The Suburbanization of the United States,* 2nd ed. New York: Oxford University Press.

JACOBS, JANE. 1993. *The Death and Life of Great American Cities.* New York: Random House; originally published 1961.

JOHNSON, KIRK, AND THOMAS J. LUECK. 1996. "Region's Economy in Fundamental Shift." *New York Times,* February 19, p. A1.

JONES, DEL. 1999. "Employers Battle Urban Sprawl Issues." *USA Today,* June 14, p. 1B.

JUBILEE LINE EXTENSION. 1997. "Archaeological Excavation at London Bridge." Accessed at http://www.jle.lul.co.uk/arch/index.htm on August 5, 2005.

JUN, MYUNG-JIN. 2004. "The Effects of Portland's Urban Growth Boundary on Urban Development Patterns and Commuting." *Urban Studies* 41 (June): 1333–48.

KADUSHIN, CHARLES. 1983. "Mental Health and the Interpersonal Environment." *American Sociological Review* 48:188–98.

KAMIN, BLAIR. 1995. "Unifying Cities." *Chicago Tribune,* June 19, p. B1.

KARIM, JAMILLAH. 2006. "Ethnic Borders in American Muslim Communities." Pp. 121–48 in *Constructing Borders/Crossing Boundaries: Race, Ethnicity, and Immigration,* edited by Caroline Brettell. Lanham, MD: Lexington Books.

KAZIN, ALFRED. 1997. *A Walker in the City,* reprint ed. New York: MJF Books.

KEATS, JOHN. 1956. *The Crack in the Picture Window.* New York: Ballantine Books.

KEISTER, LISA A. 2000. *Wealth in America: Trends in Wealth Inequality.* New York: Cambridge University Press.

KELLER, SUZANNE. 1968. *The Urban Neighborhood.* New York: Random House.

KELLY, JOHN. 2005. *The Great Mortality: An Intimate History of the Black Death, The Most Devastating Plague of All Time.* New York: HarperCollins.

KEMP, BARRY J. 1992. *Ancient Egypt: Anatomy of a Civilization,* reprint ed. New York: Routledge.

KENNEDY, RANDY. 2002. "Study Finds Airport-Related Business in New York Hit Hard by 9/11." *New York Times,* October 25, p. B3.

KENNICKELL, ARTHUR B. 2006. "Currents and Undercurrents: Changes in the Distribution of Wealth, 1989–2004." Federal Reserve Board. Accessed February 23, 2009. http://www.federalreserve.gov/pubs/feds/2006/200613/200613pap.pdf.

KENOYER, JONATHAN M. 1998. *Ancient Cities of the Indus River Civilization.* New York: Oxford University Press.

KEYES, RALPH. 1999. *The Wit and Wisdom of Oscar Wilde.* New York: Gramercy Books, Random House.

KIM, SUNWOONG. 2000. "Race and Home Appreciation in Urban Neighborhoods." *The Review of Black Political Economy* 28:9–28.

KLEIN, MILTON M. 2005. *The Empire State: A History of New York.* Ithaca, NY: Cornell University Press.

KOEGEL, PAUL, M. AUDREY BURNAM, AND JIM BAUMOHL. 1996. "The Causes of Homelessness." Pp. 24–33 in *Homelessness in America,* edited by Jim Baumohl. Westport, CT: Oryx Press.

KOLANKIEWICZ, LEON, AND ROY BECK. 2001. *Weighing Sprawl Factors in Large U.S. Cities.* Accessed at http://www.sprawlcity. org/studyUSA/USAsprawlz.pdf on July 20, 2008.

KOWINSKI, WILLIAM SEVERINI. 2002, *The Malling of America.* Philadelphia: Xlibris.

KRAUSS, CLIFFORD. 2008. "Gas Prices Send Surge of Riders to Mass Transit." *New York Times,* 10 May, pp. A1, A15.

KRYSAN, MARIA. 2002. "Community Undesirability in Black and White: Examining Racial Residential Patterns through Community Perceptions," *Social Problems* 49:521–43.

KULHAVY, RAYMOND, W., AND WILLIAM A. STOCK. 1996. "How Cognitive Maps Are Learned and Remembered." *The Annals of the Association of American Geographers* 86 (March): 123–45.

KUNSTLER, JAMES. 1996. "Home from Nowhere." *Atlantic* (September): 43–66.

KWON, HEE-KYUNG, VIRGINIA S. ZUIKER, AND JEAN W. BAUER. 2004. "Factors Associated with the Poverty Status of Asian Immigrant Householders by Citizenship Status." *Journal of Family and Economic Issues* 25 (Spring): 101–20.

LARRIVIERE, JAMES B., AND CHARLES O. KRONCKE. 2004. "A Human Capital Approach to American Indian Earnings: The Effects of Place of Residence and Migration," *The Social Science Journal* 41:209–24.

LASEN, AMPARO. 2003. *A Comparative Study of Mobile Phone Use in Public Places in London, Madrid and Paris,* Digital World Research Centre, University of Surrey.

LAW, STEVE. 2008. "Metro Takes Long View of Growth," *Portland Tribune* (May 29), p. A1.

LAWAL, NIKE S., MATTHEW N.O. SADIKU, AND ADE DOPAMU, eds. 2004. *Understanding Yoruba Life and Culture.* Trenton, NJ: Africa World Press.

LAWLOR, JULIA. 2004. "The Ironbound: A Home Away From Home for Immigrants," *New York Times,* January 11, Section 11, p. 5.

LE CORBUSIER. 1967. *The Radiant City.* New York: Grossman–Orion; originally published 1933.

———. 1971. *The City of Tomorrow.* New York: Architectural Press; originally published 1927.

LEE, KEVIN K. 2000. *Urban Poverty in Canada: A Statistical Profile.* Canadian Council on Social Development. Accessed at http://www.ccsd.ca/pubs/2000/up/index. htm on July 29, 2005.

LEE, MATTHEW, AND TERRI L. EARNEST. 2003. "Perceived Community Cohesion and Perceived Risk of Victimization: A Cross-National Analysis." *Justice Quarterly* 20:131–57.

LEFEBVRE, HENRI. 1970. *La Revolution Urbaine.* Paris: Gallimard.

———. 1991. *The Production of Space.* Malden, MA: Blackwell.

LEMANN, NICHOLAS. 1992. *The Promised Land: The Great Migration and How It Changed America.* New York: Vintage.

LEPORE, STEPHEN J., AND GARY W. EVANS. 1991. "Social Hassles and Psychological Health in the Context of Chronic Crowding." *Journal of Health and Social Behavior* 32 (December): 357–67.

LESLIE, JACQUES. 2008. "China's Pollution Nightmare Is Now Everyone's Pollution Nightmare." *Christian Science Monitor,* March 19, p. 9.

LEVITAN, MARK. 2003. "Poverty in New York, 2002: One-Fifth of the City Lives Below the Federal Poverty Line." Accessed at http://www.cssny.org/pubs/special/ 2003_09poverty.pdf on June 27, 2005.

LEWIS MUMFORD CENTER FOR COMPARATIVE URBAN AND REGIONAL RESEARCH. 2001a. "Ethnic Diversity Grows, Neighborhood Integration Lags Behind." Accessed at http://www.s4.brown.edu/cen2000/WholePop/WPr eport/page1.html on December 13, 2008.

———. 2001b. *From Many Shores: Asians in Census 2000.* Accessed at http://www.s4.brown.edu/cen2000/ AsianPop/AsianReport/page1.html on June 28, 2008.

———. 2001c. *The New Ethnic Enclaves in America's Suburbs.* Accessed at http://mumford.albany.edu/census/ suburban/SuburbanReport/page1.html on July 27, 2008.

LEY, DAVID. 2006. "Explaining Variations in Business Performance Among Immigrant Entrepreneurs in Western Canada." *Journal of Ethnic and Migration Studies* 32 (July): 743–64.

LICHTER, DANIEL T., AND MARTHA L. CROWLEY. 2002: "Poverty in America: Beyond Welfare Reform." *Population Bulletin* 57 (June).

LIEBOW, ELIOT. 2003. *Tally's Corner,* 2nd ed. Lanham, MD: Rowman & Littlefield.

LINKON, SHERRY LEE, AND JOHN RUSSO. 2003. *Steeltown USA: Work and Memory in Youngstown.* Lawrence: University Press of Kansas.

LIVERANI, MARIO. 2006. *Uruk: The First City.* London: Equinox Publishing.

LLOYD, ROBERT, AND HARTWELL HOOPER. 1991. "Urban Cognitive Maps: Computation and Structure," *Professional Geographer* 43:15–28.

LOEHNDORF, S. 2003. "Getting on Track." *E: the Environmental Magazine* 14 (November/December): 23–25.

LOFLAND, LYN. 1985. *A World of Strangers: Order and Action in Urban Public Spaces.* Prospect Heights, IL: Waveland Press.

LOGAN, JOHN, AND HARVEY MOLOTCH. 2007. *Urban Fortunes: The Political Economy of Place,* 2nd ed. Berkeley: University of California Press.

LOS ANGELES ALMANAC. 2008. Accessed at http://www. sppsr.ucla.edu/blq/home.html on June 23, 2008.

LOU, YING. 2007. "Blue Skies May Cost Dolphins Dear," *The Standard,* April 2, p. 1.

LOVEJOY, PAUL E. 2000. *Transformations in Slavery: A History of Slavery in Africa.* New York: Cambridge University Press.

LUCK, TIFFANY M. 2008. "The World's Dirtiest Cities." *Forbes Magazine.* Accessed at http://www.forbes. com/2008/02/26/pollution-baku-oil-biz-logistics-cx_ tl_0226dirtycities.html on December 13, 2008.

LUNDBLAD, KAREN SHAFER. 1995. "Jane Addams and Social Reform: A Role Model for the 1990s." *Social Work* 40 (September): 661–69.

LYNCH, KEVIN. 1976. *What Time Is This Place?* Cambridge, MA: MIT Press.

———. 1982. *The Image of the City.* Cambridge, MA: MIT Press; originally published 1960.

LYNE, JACK. 2005. "New York Bulks Up Aid for Big Apple Manufacturers," *Site Selection* 50 (March): 180.

MACIONIS, JOHN J. 2008. *Sociology,* 12th ed. Upper Saddle River, NJ: Prentice Hall.

MACIVER, ROBERT. 1962. "The Great Emptiness." Pp. 48-55 In *The Pursuit of* Happiness. New York: Simon & Schuster.

MACLEOD, JAY. 2004. *Ain't No Makin' It,* expanded ed. Boulder, CO: Westview Press.

MACMANUS, SUSAN, AND CHARLES BULLOCK. 1995. "Electing Women to Public Office." Pp. 155-77. In *Gender in Urban Research,* edited by Judith A. Garber and Robyne S. Turner. Thousand Oaks, CA: Sage.

MAGEE, PETER. 2005. *Excavations at Tepe Yahya, Iran, 1967–1975: The Iron Age Settlement.* Cambridge, MA: Harvard University Press.

MALLACH, ALAN. 2006. *Bringing Buildings Back: From Abandoned Properties to Community Assets.* Washington, D.C.: National Housing Institute.

MANTOUX, PAUL. 2006. *The Industrial Revolution in the Eighteenth Century.* New York: Routledge.

MARQUAND, JOHN P. 1943. *So Little Time.* Boston: Little, Brown.

MARX, KARL. 1959. "A Contribution to the Critique of Political Economy." Excerpted in *Marx and Engels: Basic Writings on Politics and Philosophy,* edited by Lewis S. Feuer. Garden City, NY: Anchor Books; originally published 1859.

MARX, KARL, AND FRIEDRICH ENGELS. 1976. *The German Ideology.* New York: International Publishers; originally published 1846.

MASSEY, DOREEN. 1994. *Space, Place, and Gender.* Minneapolis: University of Minnesota Press.

MASSEY, DOUGLAS S. 1984. "Processes of Hispanic and Black Spatial Segregation." *American Journal of Sociology* 89:836–73.

———. 1995. "Getting Away With Murder: Segregation and Violent Crime in Urban America." *University of Pennsylvania Law Review* 143 (May): 1203–32.

MASSEY, DOUGLAS S., AND NANCY A. DENTON. 1989. "Hypersegregation in U.S. Metropolitan Areas: Black and Hispanic Segregation Along Five Dimensions." *Demography* 26:373–91.

———. 1993. *American Apartheid: Segregation and the Making of the Underclass.* Cambridge, MA: Harvard University Press.

MASSING, MICHAEL. 2000. "Stalled in Paradise." *American Prospect* 11 (May 22): 22–27.

MATARRESE, LYNNE. 1997. *History of Levittown, New York.* New York: Levittown Historical Society.

MATEI, SORIN, SANDRA J. BALL-ROKEACH, AND JACK L. QIU. 2001. "Fear and Misperception of Los Angeles Urban Space: A Spatial-Statistical Study of Communication-Shaped Mental Maps." *Communication Research* 28 (August): 429–63.

MAYER, HAROLD M., AND RICHARD C. WADE. 1973. *Chicago: Growth of a Metropolis.* Chicago: University of Chicago Press.

MAYER, MIRA. 2004. "The Dropout Rates of Mexican Students in Two California Cities," *Research for Educational Reform* 9:14–24.

MAZEY, MARY ELLEN, AND DAVID R. LEE. 1983. *Her Space, Her Place: A Geography of Women.* Washington, D.C.: Association of American Geographers.

MCCABE, JAMES D., JR. 1970. *Lights and Shadows of New York Life.* New York: Farrar, Straus and Giroux; originally published 1872.

MCCALL, PATRICIA L, AND KAREN F. PARKER. 2005. "A Dynamic Model of Racial Competition, Racial Inequality, and Interracial Violence," *Sociological Inquiry* 75:273–93.

MCKENZIE, EVAN. 1993. "Trouble in Privatopia." *The Progressive* 57 (October): 30–36.

———. 1996. *Privatopia: Homeowner Associations and the Rise of Residential Private Government.* New Haven: Yale University Press.

MCMAHON, EDWARD T. 1997. "Stopping Sprawl by Getting Smarter." *Planning Commissioners Journal* 26 (Spring): 4.

MENDOZA, CRISTOBAL. 2006. "Transnational Spaces Through Local Places, Mexican Immigrants in Albuquerque." *Journal of Anthropological Research* 62 (Winter): 539–61.

MERTON, ROBERT K. 1968. *Social Theory and Social Structure.* New York: Free Press.

MESSINA, JUDITH. 2008. "Unaffordable NY: Tough Choices at $150,000." *Crain's New York Business* (January 7), p. 16.

MIAMI. 2008. Accessed at http://www.miamigov.com on June 17, 2008.

MILGRAM, STANLEY. 1972. "A Psychological Map of New York City." *American Scientist* 60:194–200.

MILLER, D.W. 2000. "The New Urban Studies," *Chronicle of Higher Education,* August 18, pp. A15–16.

MILLER, SARA CEDAR. 2003. *Central Park, An American Masterpiece: A Comprehensive History of the Nation's First Urban Park.* New York: Harry N. Abrams Publishing.

MILLS, AMY. 2007. "Gender and Mahalle (Neighborhood) Space in Istanbul." *Gender, Place and Culture* 14 (June): 335–54.

MITCHELL, JERRY. 2001. "Business Improvement Districts and the 'New' Revitalization of Downtown," *Economic Development Quarterly* 15 (May): 115–23.

MOLOTCH, HARVEY. 1976. "The City as a Growth Machine." *American Journal of Sociology* 82:309–33.

———. 2002. "School's Out: A Response to Michael Dear." *City & Community* 1 (March): 39–43.

MONTI, DANIEL J. 1999. *The American City: A Social and Cultural History.* New York: Blackwell.

MONTREAL. 2008. Accessed at http://ville.montreal.qc.ca/portal on June 17, 2008.

MOORHOUSE, GEOFFREY. 1979. *Great Cities San Francisco.* Amsterdam: Time-Life.

MORGAN QUITNO. 2008. *14th Annual America's Safest/Most Dangerous Cities.* Accessed at http://www.morganquitno.com/cit07pop.htm#25 on July 18, 2008.

MORRIS, JAN. 2003. *The World: Travels 1950–2000.* New York: W.W. Norton & Company.

MORSE, RICHARD J., AND JORGE E. HARDOY, eds. 1993. *Rethinking the Latin American City.* Washington, D.C.: Woodrow Wilson Center.

MOTE, F.W. 2003. *Imperial China 900–1800.* Cambridge, MA: Harvard University Press.

MUMFORD, LEWIS. 1989. *The City in History: Its Origins, Its Transformations, and Its Prospects.* Fort Washington, PA: Harvest Books; originally published 1961.

MURPHY, RHODES. 2007. "City as a Mirror of Society." Pp. 186–204 in *The City in Cultural Context,* edited by John A. Agnew, John Mercer, and David E. Sophen. New York: Routledge.

MUSCHAMP, HERBERT. 2002. "Don't Rebuild. Imagine." *New York Times Magazine,* September 8, pp. 46–60, 63.

NAQUIN, SUSAN. 2000. *Peking: Temples and City Life, 1400–1900.* Berkeley: University of California Press.

NATIONAL ACADEMY OF SCIENCES. 1997. "Overall U.S. Economy Gains from Immigration, but It's Costly to Some States and Localities. http://www8.nationalacademies.org/onpinews/newsitem.aspx?RecordID=5779. Accessed December 12, 2008.

NATIONAL AUDUBON SOCIETY. 1999. "How Many Wetlands Have Been Destroyed? And Why?" Accessed at http://www.audubon.org/campaign/wetland/destroy.html on July 21, 2008.

NATIONAL CENTER ON EDUCATION STATISTICS. 2007. Accessed at http://nces.ed.gov/programs/coe/2007/section4/indicator32.asp on July 27, 2008.

NATIONAL CENTER FOR HEALTH STATISTICS. 2007. "Deaths: Leading Causes for 2004." *National Vital Statistics Reports* 556 (November).

NATIONAL CENTER FOR POLICY ANALYSIS. 2002. *Immigrants, Welfare, and Work.* Accessed at http://www.ncpa.org on July 27, 2008.

NATIONAL CRIME RECORDS BUREAU. 2007. *Crime in India 2006.* New Delhi, India: Ministry of Home Affairs.

NEUMAYER, ERIC. 2005. "Inequality and Violent Crime: Evidence from Data on Robbery and Violent Theft," *Journal of Peace Research* 42:101–12.

NEUWIRTH, ROBERT. 2004. *Shadow Cities: A Billion Squatters, A New Urban World.* London: Routledge.

NEW YORK TIMES. 1983. "St. Louis Reports 3 Attacks, and Nobody 'Gets Involved'," (August 18), p. D16.

NEW YORK TIMES. 1984. "Caller Reported an Attack During Assault on Woman," (December 3), p. B10.

NEWMAN, KATHERINE S. 2000. *No Shame in my Game: The Working Poor in the Inner City.* New York: Vintage.

NEWMAN, OSCAR. 1996. *Creating Defensible Space.* Washington, D.C.: U.S. Department of Housing and Urban Development.

NEWS24.COM. 2003. "Girl Raped on Busy Street," March 6. Accessed at http://www.news24.com/News24/World/News/on July 17, 2005.

NICHOLAS, DAVID. 2003. *Urban Europe, 1100–1700.* New York: Palgrave Macmillan.

NICOLAIDES, BECKY M. 2002. *My Blue Heaven: Life and Politics in the Working-Class Suburbs of Los Angeles, 1920–1965.* Chicago: University of Chicago Press.

NORTON, JADE. 2008. "Going the Distance: Commuting Patterns in BC." BC Stats. Accessed at http://www.bcstats.gov.bc.ca/pubs/es/es2008-2.pdf on July 20, 2008.

NOSSITER, ADAM. 2007. "They May Miss New Orleans," but Katrina Refugees Won't Go Back." *International Herald Tribune,* December 19, p. 4.

OGBU, JOHN. 2003. *Black Students in an Affluent Suburb: A Study of Academic Disengagement.* Mahwah, NJ: Lawrence Erlbaum.

OLSEN, JOSHUA. 2004. *Better Places, Better Lives: A Biography of James Rouse.* Washington, D.C.: Urban land Institute.

ORFIELD, GARY. 1988. "Ghettoization and Its Alternatives." Pp. 161–93. In *The New Urban Reality,* edited by Paul E. Peterson. Washington, D.C.: Brookings Institution.

———. 2001. *Schools More Separate: Consequences of a Decade of Resegregation.* Cambridge, MA: Civil Rights Project, Harvard University.

OSBORN, FREDERICK J. 1965. Pp. 9–28, "Preface" to Ebenezer Howard, *Garden Cities of To-Morrow.* Cambridge, MA: MIT Press.

PAHL, R.E. 1989. "Is the Emperor Naked? Some Questions on the Adequacy of Sociological Theory in Urban and Regional Research." *International Journal of Urban and Regional Research* 13:709.

PAMPALON, ROBERT, DENIS HAMEL, MARIA DE KONINCK, AND MARIE-JEANNE DISANT. 2007. "Perception of Place and Health: Differences between Neighbourhoods in the Québec City Region." *Social Science & Medicine* 65 (July): 95–111.

PARK, ROBERT E. 1964. *Race and Culture.* Glencoe, IL: Free Press.

———. 1984. "The City: Suggestions for the Investigation of Human Behavior in the Urban Environment." Pp. 1–46 in *The City,* reprinted, edited by Robert E. Park and Eugene W. Burgess. Chicago: University of Chicago Press; originally published 1916.

PARKER, JIM. 2005. "Daufuskie Island Vacation Spot Undergoes $10 Million Face-Lift, New Construction." *The Post and Courier,* February 26, p. 12G.

PARRILLO, VINCENT N. 2005. *Contemporary Social Problems,* 6th ed. Boston: Allyn and Bacon.

———. 2009a. *Strangers to These Shores,* 9th ed. Boston: Allyn and Bacon.

———. 2009b. *Diversity in America,* 3rd ed. Thousand Oaks, CA: Pine Forge Press.

PASTERNAK, JUDY. 1998. "'Edge City' Is Attempting to Build a Center." *Los Angeles Times,* January 1, p. 5.

PATTAVINA, APRIL, JAMES M. BYRNE, AND LUIS GARCIA. 2006. "An Examination of Citizen Involvement in Crime Prevention in High-Risk Versus Low-to-Moderate-Risk Neighborhoods." *Crime & Delinquency* 52:203–31.

PAWLYNA, ANDREA. 1981. "James Rouse, a Pioneer of the Suburban Shopping Center, Now Sets His Sights on Saving Cities." *People,* July 6, pp. 63–71.

PERRIN, NOEL. 1980. "Rural Area: Permit Required." *Country Journal,* April: 34–35.

PETERS, ARNO. 2002. *Hammond Compact Peter's World Atlas.* Union, NJ: Hammond World Atlas Corporation.

PETERSON, RUTH D., AND LAUREN J. KRIVO. 1993. "Racial Segregation and Black Urban Homicide." *Social Forces* 71:1001–26.

PETROSKI, HENRY. 2005. "How to Rebuild New Orleans: Raise the Ground," *New York Times,* September 9, p. A17.

PETRY, ANN. 1998. *The Street*. Boston: Houghton Mifflin; originally published 1946.

PHILIPS, KEVIN. 2003. *Wealth and Democracy: A Political History of the American Rich*. New York: Broadway Books.

PICOT, GARNETT, AND FENG HOU. 2003. "The Rise in Low-Income Rates Among Immigrants in Canada," *Analytical Studies Branch Research Paper No. 18*. Ottawa: Statistics Canada.

PISELLI, FORTUNATA. 2007. "Communities, Places, and Social Networks." *American Behavioral Scientist* 50 (March): 867–78.

PLOEGER, NANCY. 2002. "Six Months Later." New York: Manhattan Chamber of Commerce.

POLLOCK, ALEX J. 2008. "Your Guide to the Housing Crisis." *The American*. Accessed at http://www.american.com/ archive/2008/may-june-magazine-contents/your-guide-to-the-housing-crisis on June 21, 2008.

POPULATION REFERENCE BUREAU. 2008. "World Population Highlights." *Population Bulletin* 63 (September).

———. 2009. *2008 World Population Data Sheet*. Washington, D.C.

PORT OF NEW ORLEANS. 2008. Accessed at http://www.portno.com/pno_pages/about_overview .htm on June 18, 2008.

PORTER, ROY. 1994. "Curtains for the Capital." *New Statesman & Society* 7 (November 11): 30–31.

PORTÉS, ALEJANDRO. 1977. "Urban Latin America: The Political Condition from Above and Below." Pp. 59–70 in *Third World Urbanization*, edited by Janet Abu-Lughod and Richard Hay, Jr. Chicago: Maaroufa.

PORTÉS, ALEJANDRO, CARLOS DORE-CABRAL, AND PATRICIA LANDOLTS, eds. 1997. *The Urban Caribbean: Transition to the Global Economy*. Baltimore: Johns Hopkins University Press.

PORTÉS, ALEJANDRO, AND ALEX STEPICK. 1994, *City on the Edge: The Transformation of Miami*. Berkeley: University of California Press.

PORTLAND DEVELOPMENT COMMISSION. 2007. *Portland Metropolitan Region Fact Book*.

POUNDS, NORMAN. 2005. *The Medieval City*. Westport, CT: Greenwood Press.

POWELL, RICHARD. 2006, *The Philadelphians*, 50th anv. ed. Medford, NJ: Plexus Publishing.

PRICEWATERHOUSECOOPERS. "UK Economic Outlook, March 2007", page 5, "Table 1.2—Top 30 Urban Agglomeration GDP rankings in 2005. Accessed at http://www.ukmediacentre.pwc.com/imagelibrary/ detail.asp?MediaDetailsID=863 on December 13, 2008.

PUTNAM, ROBERT D. 2001. *Bowling Alone: The Collapse and Revival of the American Community*. New York: Simon & Schuster.

PUU, TÖNU. 2003. *Mathematical Location and Land Use Theory: An Introduction*, 2nd ed. New York: Springer.

RABAN, JONATHAN. 1998. *Soft City*, reprint ed. London: Harvill Press.

RAINWATER, LEE. 2006. *Behind Ghetto Walls: Black Families in a Federal Slum*. New Brunswick, NJ: Aldine Transaction; originally published 1970.

RAKOVE, MILTON L. 1975. *Don't Make No Waves, Don't Back No Losers*. Bloomington: Indiana University Press.

REGENT PARK COLLABORATIVE TEAM. 2003. *Lessons from Saint Lawrence for the Regent Park Redevelopment Process*. Toronto: Toronto Community Housing Corporation.

REGIONAL PLAN ASSOCIATION. 2006. "America 2050: A Prospectus." Accessed at http://www.america2050.org/ pdf/America2050prospectus.pdf on June 7, 2008.

REICH, ROBERT B. 1991. *The Work of Nations: Preparing Ourselves for 21st Century Capitalism*. New York: Alfred A. Knopf.

RICE, MICHAEL. 2003. *Egypt's Making: The Origins of Ancient Egypt 5000–2000 BC*, 2nd ed. New York; Routledge.

RIESMAN, DAVID. 1958. "The Suburban Sadness." Pp. 375–408 in *The Suburban Community*, edited by William Dobriner. New York: G.P. Putnam's Sons.

RIIS, JACOB. 1957. *How the Other Half Lives*. New York: Hill and Wang; originally published 1890.

ROBERTS, BRYAN R. 2005. "Globalization and Latin American Cities," *International Journal of Urban and Regional Research* 29:110–23.

ROBERTS, SAM. 2007. "New York's Gap Between Rich and Poor Is Nation's Widest, Census Says." *New York Times*, August 29, p. M3.

ROBSON, GARRY, AND TIM BUTLER. 2001. "Coming to Terms with London: Middle-Class Communities in a Global City." *International Journal of Urban & Regional Research* 25 (March): 70–86.

RODRIGUEZ, CLARA E. 1996. "The Puerto Rican Community in the South Bronx: View from Within and Without." P. 507. In *Sociology*, 5th ed., edited by Beth B. Hess, Elizabeth W. Markson, and Peter J. Stein. Boston: Allyn and Bacon.

RODWIN, LLOYD, AND HUGH EVANS. 1982. "The New Communities Program and Why It Failed." Pp. 115–36 in *Cities and City Planning*, edited by Lloyd Rodwin. New York: Plenum.

ROESNNER, JANE. 2000. *A Decent Place to Live: From Columbia Point to Harbor Point*. Boston: Northeastern University Press.

ROMIG, KEVIN. 2005. "The Upper Sonoran Lifestyle: Gated Communities in Scottsdale, Arizona." *City & Community* 4 (March): 67–86.

ROSS, CATHERINE E., JOHN MIROWSKY, AND SHANA PRIBESH. 2002. "Disadvantage, Disorder, and Urban Mistrust." *City & Community* 1 (March): 59–82.

ROUSSEAU, FRANCOIS, AND LIONEL STANDING. 1995. "Zero Effect of Crowding on Arousal and Performance: On 'Proving' the Null Hypothesis." *Perceptual and Motor Skills* 81 (August): 72–74.

RYAN, MARY. 1979. *Womanhood in America: From Colonial Times to the Present*, 2nd ed. New York: Franklin Watts.

SAAD, LYDIA. 2007. "Perceptions of Crime Problem Remain Curiously Negative," Gallup. Accessed at http://www. gallup.com/poll/102262/Perceptions-Crime-Problem -Remain-Curiously-Negative.aspx on February 28, 2009.

SAGAN, CARL. 1977. *The Dragons of Eden*. New York: Ballantine.

ST. CLAIRE, CLYDE, AND ROBERT CLYMER. 2000. "Racial Residential Segregation by Socioeconomic Status." *Social Science Quarterly* 81:701–15.

SALT LAKE CITY. 2008. Accessed at http://www.ci.slc.ut.us on June 17, 2008.

SAMPSON, ROBERT J. 2002. "Studying Modern Chicago." *City & Community* 1:45–48.

SANCHEZ, THOMAS W., ROBERT E. LANG, AND DAWN M. DHAVALE. 2005. "Security Versus Status?" *Journal of Planning Education and Research* 24:281–91.

SANDBURG, CARL. 1944. *Chicago Poems.* New York: Harcourt Brace Jovanovich.

SANDERS, JERRY. 2000. "Racial and Ethnic Minorities in San Diego, United States." *Policing and Society* 10:131–41.

SASSEN, SASKIA. 2001. *The Global City: New York, Tokyo, and London,* 2nd ed. Princeton: Princeton University Press; originally 1991.

——. 2002. *Global Networks: Linked Cities.* London: Brunner-Routledge.

——. 2006. *Cities in a World Economy,* 3rd ed. Thousand Oaks, CA: Pine Forge Press.

SAULNY, SUSAN. 2007. "At Housing Project, Both Fear and Renewal." *New York Times,* March 17, p. A20.

SCHEIN, VIRGINIA E. 1995. *Working from the Margins: Voices of Mothers in Poverty.* Ithaca, NY: Cornell University Press.

SCHEMO, DIANA JEAN. 2006. "Federal Program on Vouchers Draws Strong Minority Support." *New York Times,* April 6, pp. A1, A20.

SCHOMP, VIRGINIA. 2005. *Ancient Mesopotamia: The Sumerians, Babylonians, and Assyrians.* New York: Franklin Watts.

SCHRANK, DAVID, AND TIM LOMAX. 2007. *The 2007 Urban Mobility Report.* Accessed at http://tti.tamu.edu/documents/mobility_report_2007.pdf on July 19, 2008.

SCHWIRIAN, KENT P., F. MARTIN HANKINS, AND CAROL A. VENTRESCA. 1990. "The Residential Decentralization of Social Status Groups in American Metropolitan Communities, 1950–1980." *Social Forces* 68:1143–63.

SCOTT, ALLEN J. 1980. *The Urban Land Nexus and the State.* London: Pion.

——. 1988. *Metropolis.* Berkeley: University of California Press.

——. 2001. *From Chicago to L.A.: Making Sense of Urban Theory.* Thousand Oaks, CA: Sage Publications.

SENNETT, RICHARD. 1969. *Classic Essays on the Culture of Cities.* Englewood Cliffs, NJ: Prentice Hall.

SEWELL, JOHN. 1993. *The Shape of the City: Toronto Struggles with Modern Planning.* Toronto: University of Toronto Press.

SIDES, JOSH. 2006. *L.A. City Limits: African American Los Angeles from the Great Depression to the Present.* Berkeley: University of California Press.

SIGELMAN, LEE, AND JEFFREY R. HENIG. 2001. "Crossing the Great Divide: Race and Preferences for Living in the City Versus the Suburb," *Urban Affairs Review* 37:3–18.

SIMMEL, GEORG. 1964. "The Metropolis and Mental Life." Pp. 409–24 in *The Sociology of Georg Simmel,* edited by K. Wolff. New York: Free Press; originally published 1905.

SISKIND, PETER. 2006. "Suburban Growth and Its Discontents." Pp. 161–182, in *The New Suburban History,* edited by Kevin M. Kruse and Thomas J. Sugrue. Chicago: University of Chicago Press.

SJOBERG, GIDEON. 1965. *The Preindustrial City.* New York: Free Press.

SKIDMORE, THOMAS E., AND PETER H. SMITH. 2004. *Modern Latin America,* 6th ed. New York: Oxford University Press.

SOJA, EDWARD W. 2000. *Postmetropolis: Critical Studies of Cities and Regions.* New York: Wiley–Blackwell.

SOLUTIONS NOT SPRAWL. 2005. "Here We Go Again." Accessed at http://www.solutionsnotsprawl.org/issue.htm on June 21, 2005.

SORKIN, MICHAEL, ed. 1992. *Variations on a Theme Park: The New American City and the End of Public Space.* New York: The Noonday Press, Farrar, Strauss and Giroux.

SOUTH, SCOTT J., KYLE CROWDER, AND ERICK CHAVEZ. 2005. "Geographic Mobility and Spatial Assimilation among U.S. Latino Immigrants." *International Migration Review* 39 (Fall): 577–607.

SOUTHERN CALIFORNIA ASSOCIATION OF GOVERNMENTS. 2008. *Final 2008 Regional Transportation Plan: Making the Connections.* Accessed at http://www.scag.ca.gov/rtp2008/final.htm on July 21, 2008.

SOWELL, THOMAS. 1977. "New Light on Black I.Q." *New York Times Magazine,* March 27, p. 57.

SPAIN, DAPHNE. 1992. *Gendered Spaces.* Chapel Hill: University of North Carolina Press.

SPECTORSKY, A.C. 1957. *The Exurbanites.* New York: Berkley.

SPENGLER, OSWALD. 1969. *The Decline of the West.* New York: Knopf. Excerpted in *Classic Essays on the Culture of Cities,* edited by Richard Sennett. Englewood Cliffs, NJ: Prentice Hall; originally published 1928.

SROLE, LEO. 1972. "Urbanization and Mental Health: Some Reformulations." *American Scientist* 60: 576–83.

STACK, CAROL. 1997. *All Our Kin: Strategies for Survival in a Black Community.* New York: Basic Books.

STANNARD, DAVID E. 1993. *American Holocaust: The Conquest of the New World.* New York: Oxford University Press.

STARK, ANDREW. 2002. *Conflict of Interest in American Public Life.* Cambridge, MA: Harvard University Press.

STARK, MIRIAM T. 2006. *Archaeology of Asia.* Malden, MA: Blackwell.

STARR, ROGER. 1985. "Crime." *New York Times Magazine,* January 17, pp. 19–25, 58–60.

STATISTICS CANADA. 2007a. "The African Community in Canada." *Profiles of Ethnic Communities in Canada.* Ottawa: Minister of Industry.

——. 2007b. "The Chinese Community in Canada." *Profiles of Ethnic Communities in Canada.* Ottawa: Minister of Industry.

——. 2007c. "The Filipino Community in Canada." *Profiles of Ethnic Communities in Canada.* Ottawa: Minister of Industry.

——. 2007d. "The East Indian Community in Canada." *Profiles of Ethnic Communities in Canada.* Ottawa: Minister of Industry.

——. 2007e. "The Vietnamese Community in Canada." *Profiles of Ethnic Communities in Canada.* Ottawa: Minister of Industry.

——. 2007f. "The Japanese Community in Canada." *Profiles of Ethnic Communities in Canada.* Ottawa: Minister of Industry.

——. 2007g. "The Korean Community in Canada." *Profiles of Ethnic Communities in Canada.* Ottawa: Minister of Industry.

——. 2007h. "The Latin American Community in Canada." *Profiles of Ethnic Communities in Canada.* Ottawa: Minister of Industry.

———. 2007i. "The Arab Community in Canada." *Profiles of Ethnic Communities in Canada.* Ottawa: Minister of Industry.

———. 2007j. *Income in Canada-2006*, Table 8–3. http://www.statcan.gc.ca/pub/75-202-x/2006000/5215234-eng.pdf (December 12, 2008).

———. 2008a. Accessed at http://www.statcan.ca on December 12, 2008.

———. 2008b. *Aboriginal Peoples in Canada in 2006: Inuit, Métis, and First Nations, 2006 Census.* Ottawa: Minister of Industry.

STAVRIANOS, LEFTEN. 1998. *Global History: From Prehistory to the 21st Century,* 7th ed. Englewood Cliffs, NJ: Prentice Hall.

STEELE, JEFFREY. 1998. "Profile: Gage Park," *Chicago Tribune,* July 24, p. 16.

STEFFENS, LINCOLN. 2004. *The Shame of the Cities.* Mineda, NY: Dover Publications; originally published 1904.

STEIN, CLARENCE. 1972. *Toward New Towns for America.* Cambridge, MA: MIT Press.

STEIN, ROBIN. 2006. "Furor over 'Work Force Housing.'" *North Pinellas Times,* December 5, p. 1.

STEINBECK, JOHN. 1962. *Travels with Charley: In Search of America.* New York: Franklin Watts.

STEPHENSON, R. BRUCE. 1997. "A Vision of Green: Lewis Mumford's Legacy in Portland, Oregon." *Journal of the American Planning Association* 65 (Summer): 259–69.

STERBENTZ, JANEL. 2008. "Las Vegas Ripping Up Lawns to Save Water, But Is It Enough?" *Climate Science & Research,* February 20, p. 1.

STILL, BAYRD. 1994. *Mirror for Gotham: New York as Seen by Contemporaries from Dutch Days to the Present.* New York: Fordham University Press.

STEWART, NIKITA. 2005. "Muslims Find Room to Grow in D.C.'s Outer Suburbs." *The Washington Post,* August 1, p. A1.

STONEBACK, DIANE. 2005. "Ironbound Ambiance: Historic District in Newark, N.J., Is Packed with the Tasty, the Spicy and All Good Things Portuguese," *Allentown Morning Call,* June 26, p. F1.

STRAIN, CHRISTOPHER. 2004. "Soul City, North Carolina: Black Power, Utopia, and the African American Dream," *Journal of African American History* 89:57–74.

STRICKER, FRANK. 2007. *Why America Lost the War on Poverty—And How to Win It.* Chapel Hill: University of North Carolina Press.

STRONG, JOSIAH. 1885. *Our Country: Its Possible Future and Its Present Crisis.* New York: Baker and Taylor.

SUISMAN, DOUGLAS R. 1990. *Los Angeles Boulevard: 8 X-Rays of the Body Politic.* Princeton, NJ: Princeton Architectural Press.

SUTTLES, GERALD. 1974. *The Social Order of the Slum.* Chicago: University of Chicago Press.

———. 1984. "The Cumulative Texture of Local Urban Culture." *American Journal of Sociology* 90:283–304.

SWAIN, CAROL M., ed. 2007. *Debating Immigration.* New York: Cambridge University Press.

SYDENSTRICKER–NETO, JOHN. 2008. *Environmental Sociology.* Accessed at http://www.socialresearchmethods.net/Gallery/Neto/Envsoc1.html on July 25, 2008.

TAEUBER, KARL, AND ALMA TAEUBER. 2009. *Residential Segregation and Neighborhood Change.* Piscataway, NJ: Aldine Transaction; originally published 1965.

TALEN, EMILY. 2006. *New Urbanism and American Planning: The Conflict of Cultures.* New York: Routledge.

TARTARO, CHRISTINE, AND MARISSA P. LEVY. 2007. "Density, Inmate Assaults, and Direct Supervision Jails." *Criminal Justice Policy Review* 18 (December): 395–417.

TAYLOR, GRAHAM ROMEYN. 2001. *Satellite Cities: A Study of Industrial Suburbs.* Chestnut Hill, MA: Adamant Media Corporation; originally published 1915.

TEAFORD, JON C. 2006. *The Metropolitan Revolution: The Rise of Post-Urban America.* New York: Columbia University Press.

THAXTON, RALPH A., JR. 2008. *Catastrophe and Contention in Rural China* New York: Cambridge University Press.

THILL, JEAN-CLAUDE, AND DANIEL Z. SUI. 1993. "Mental Maps and Fuzziness in Space Preferences." *The Professional Geographer* 45 (August): 264–76.

THOMAS, JIM. 1983. "Toward a Critical Ethnography." *Urban Life* 11:477–90.

THOMAS, JUNE, JOHN SCHWEITZER, AND JULIA DARNTON. 2004. *Mixed-Income Neighborhoods in Grand Rapids: A Summary of Findings.* East Lansing: Michigan State University.

THORP, ROBERT L. 2005. *China in the Early Bronze Age: Shang Civilization.* Philadelphia: University of Pennsylvania Press.

TIMMER, DOUG A., D. STANLEY EITZEN, AND KATHRYN D. TALLEY. 1994. *Paths to Homelessness: Extreme Poverty and the Housing Crisis.* Boulder, CO: Westview Press.

TOCQUEVILLE, ALEXIS DE. 1979. *Old Regime and the French Revolution.* Gloucester, MA: Peter Smith Publisher; originally published 1856.

TODARO, MICHAEL P., AND STEPHEN C. SMITH. 2008. *Economic Development,* 10th ed. Boston: Addison–Wesley.

TÖNNIES, FERDINAND. 1963. *Community and Society.* New York: Harper & Row; originally published 1887.

TORONTO. 2009. Accessed at http://www.city.toronto.on.ca/ on March 8, 2009.

TORREY, BARBARA BOYLE. 2004. "Urbanization: An Environmental Force to be Reckoned With." Washington, D.C.: Population Reference Bureau.

TRIMET. 2008. *Facts About TriMet.* Accessed at http://trimet.org/pdfs/publications/factsheet.pdf on July 26, 2008.

UCLA DEPARTMENT OF URBAN PLANNING. 1998. *The Byzantine-Latino Quarter.* Accessed at http://www.sppsr.ucla.edu/blq/home.html on July 11, 2005.

UNAIDS AND WORLD HEALTH ORGANIZATION. 2008. *2008 Report on the Global AIDS Epidemic.* Geneva: UNAIDS.

UN-HABITAT. 2007. *State of the World's Cities 2006/7.* Accessed at http://www.unhabitat.org on July 27, 2008.

UNICEF. 2008. *The State of Africa's Children 2008.* Accessed at http://www.unicef.org/publications/files/SOAC_2008_EN.pdf on July 9, 2008.

UNITED NATIONS DEVELOPMENT PROGRAMME. 1995. *Human Development Report 1995.* New York: Oxford University Press.

UNITED NATIONS ENVIRONMENT PROGRAMME. 2001. *Profile of Bangkok City.* Accessed at http://www.rrcap.unedp.org/reports/soe/bangkok_profile.pdf on July 11, 2008.

UNITED NATIONS POPULATION DIVISION. 2008 http://www.un.org/esa/population/publications/wup2007/2007WUP_Highlights_web.pdf on December 12, 2008.

———. 2008. *World Urbanization Prospects*: 2007 Revision. Accessed at http://www.un.org/esa/population/publications/wup2007/2007WUP_Highlights_web.pdf on July 28, 2008.

UNITED WAY GREATER TORONTO. 2007. *Losing Ground: The Persistent Growth of Family Poverty in Canada's Largest City*. Accessed at http://www.unitedwaytoronto.com/whoWeHelp/reports/pdf/LosingGround-full-Report.pdf on February 23, 2009.

URBAN ECOLOGY. 2008. Accessed at http://www.urbanecology.org/mission.htm on July 25, 2008.

U.S. BUREAU OF JUSTICE STATISTICS. 2008. Accessed at http://www.ojp.usdoj.gov/bjs/ on July 2, 2008.

U.S. CENSUS BUREAU. 2001. *Population Change and Distribution: 1990 to 2000*. Washington, D.C.: U.S. Government Printing Office.

———. 2002. *Profile of Selected Social Characteristics: 2000*, Summary File 3.

———. 2003. "Back Bay-Beacon Hill," *2000 Census of Population and Housing*, Summary File 3 Data.

———. 2004. *The Foreign-Born Population in the United States: 2003*. Washington, D.C.: U.S. Government Printing Office.

———. 2007a. *American Housing Survey for the United States: 2006*. Washington, D.C.: U.S. Government Printing Office.

———. 2007b. "The Hispanic Population in the United States: March 2006." *Current Population Survey*. Accessed at http://www.census.gov/population/www/socdemo/hispanic/cps2006.html on June 28, 2008.

———. 2008a. *Statistical Abstract of the United States: 2008*. Washington, D.C.: U.S. Government Printing Office.

———. 2008b. *Income, Poverty, and Health Insurance Coverage in the United States, 2007*. Washington, D.C.: U.S. Government Printing Office.

———. 2008c. *American Factfinder*. Accessed at http://factfinder.census.gov on June 29, 2008.

U.S. CONFERENCE OF MAYORS. 2008. *Hunger and Homelessness Survey*. Accessed at http://www.usmayors.org on December 12, 2008.

U.S. DEPARTMENT OF EDUCATION. 2000. *The State of Charter Schools: Fourth-Year Report*. Washington, D.C.: U.S. Government Printing Office.

———. 2007a. *Indicators of School Crime and Safety: 2007*. Washington, D.C.: U.S. Government Printing Office.

———. 2007b. *Education for Homeless Children and Youths*. Accessed at http://www.ed.gov/programs/homeless/index.html on December 13, 2008.

U.S. DEPARTMENT OF HOUSING AND URBAN DEVELOPMENT. 2008. *American Housing Survey for the United States: 2007*. Washington, D.C.: U.S. Government Printing Office.

U.S. GEOLOGICAL SURVEY. 2008. "Flood Hazards—A National Threat." Accessed at http://www.usgs.gov/hazards/floods/ on July 21, 2008.

U.S. OFFICE OF IMMIGRATION STATISTICS. 2008. *2007 Statistical Yearbook*. Washington, D.C.: U.S. Government Printing Office.

VALDEZ, AL. 2000. "18th Street: California's Most Violent Export," National Alliance of Gang Investigators Associations. Accessed at http://www.streetgangs.com/topics/2002/18thexport.html on July, 27, 2008.

VALENTINE, BETTY LOU. 1980. *Hustling and Other Hard Work*. New York: Free Press.

VESSELINOV, ELENA, MATTHEW CAZESSUS, AND WILLIAM FALK. 2007. "Gated Communities and Spatial Inequality." *Journal of Urban Affairs* 29:109–27.

VIDICH, ARTHUR, AND JOSEPH BENSMAN. 2000. *Small Town in Mass Society*, rev. ed. Champaign, IL: University of Illinois Press; originally published 1958.

WACQUANT, LOÏC J.D. 1997. "Three Pernicious Premises in the Study of the American Ghetto," *International Journal of Urban & Regional Research* 21:341–53.

———. 2007. *Urban Outcasts: A Comparative Sociology of Advanced Marginality*. New York: Polity.

WAGMILLER, ROBERT L. 2007. "Race and the Spatial Segregation of Jobless Men in Urban America." *Demography* 44 (August): 539–62.

WAHAB, MALLIKA. 2003. "Bangladesh Slums Demand Access to Clean Water," *International Journal of Humanities and Peace* 19:46–47.

WALBERG, HERBERT J. 2007. *School Choice: The Findings*. Washington, D.C.: Cato Institute.

WALDINGER, ROGER. 1999. *Still the Promised City? African-Americans and New Immigrants in New York*, reprint ed. Cambridge, MA: Harvard University Press.

WALLERSTEIN, IMMANUEL. 2004. *World-Systems Analysis: An Introduction*. Durham, NC: Duke University Press.

WALTON, JOHN. 1981. "The New Urban Sociology." *International Social Science Journal* 33:374–90.

———. 1993. "Urban Sociology: The Contributions and Limits of Political Economy." *Annual Review of Sociology* 19:301–20.

WARD, STEVEN V. 1998. *Selling Places: The Marketing and Promotion of Towns and Cities 1850–2000*. London: Spon Press, Taylor & Francis Group.

WARNER, SAM BASS, JR. 1978. *Streetcar Suburbs*, 2nd ed. Cambridge, MA: Harvard University Press/MIT Press.

WATERFIELD, ROBIN. 2005. *Athens: A History, From Ancient Ideal to Modern City*. New York: Basic Books.

WAYMAN, JEFFREY C. 2002. "Student Perceptions of Teacher Ethnic Bias: A Comparison of Mexican American and Non-Latino White Dropouts and Students." *High School Journal* 85:27–37.

WAYNE, GARY. 2008. *The Universal CityWalk*. Accessed at http://www.seeing-stars.com/Shop/CityWalk.shtml on June 15, 2008.

WEBER, MAX. 1966. *The City*. New York: Free Press; originally published 1921.

WENKE, ROBERT J. 2005. *Patterns in Prehistory: Humankind's First Three Million Years*. New York: Oxford University Press.

WHITE, MORTON, AND LUCIA WHITE. 1977. *The Intellectual Versus the City*. New York: Oxford University Press.

WHITMAN, WALT. 1959. *Leaves of Grass*. New York: Viking Press; originally published 1855.

WHITMEYER, JOSEPH M. 2002. "A Deductive Approach to Friendship Networks," *Journal of Mathematical Sociology* 26:147–65.

WHITTLE, CHRIS. 2005. *Crash Course*. New York: Penguin Riverhead.

WHYTE, MARTIN K., AND WILLIAM L. PARISH. 1987. *Urban Life in Contemporary China*, reprint ed. Chicago: University of Chicago Press.

WHYTE, WILLIAM FOOTE. 1981. *Street Corner Society*, 3rd ed. Chicago: University of Chicago Press; originally published 1943.

———. 2001. *The Social Life of Small Urban Spaces*. New York: Project for Public Spaces; originally published 1980.

———. 2002. *The Organization Man*. Philadelphia: University of Pennsylvania Press; originally published 1966.

WIDHOLM, PAULA. 2005. "Chicago Is Back on the Upswing," *National Real Estate Investor* 47 (Fall): 34–38.

WIESE, ANDREW. 2004. *Places of their Own: African American Suburbanization in the Twentieth Century*. Chicago: University of Chicago Press.

———. 2005. "Robbins, IL," *The Encyclopedia of Chicago*. Chicago: Chicago Historical Society.

WILLIAMS, ROGER M. 1977. "The New Urban Pioneers: Homesteading in the Slums." *Saturday Review*, July 23, pp. 9–14.

WILLIE, CHARLES, AND HOWARD TAYLOR. 1995. "The Bell Curve Debate." Panel discussion at Eastern Sociological Society annual meeting, Philadelphia, March.

WILSON, THOMAS C. 1991. "Urbanism, Migration, and Tolerance: A Reassessment." *American Sociological Review* 56: 117–23.

WILSON, WILLIAM J. 1990. *The Truly Disadvantaged*, reprint ed. Chicago: University of Chicago Press.

WINKS, ROBIN W. 1997. *The Blacks in Canada: A History*, 2nd ed. Montreal: McGill–Queen's University Press.

WIRTH, LOUIS. 1938. "Urbanism as a Way of Life." *American Journal of Sociology* 44:1–24.

———. 1964. *On Cities and Social Life*. Chicago: University of Chicago Press.

WIRTH, LOUIS, AND ALBERT J. REISS. 1981. *On Cities and Social Life: Selected Papers*. Chicago: University of Chicago Press.

WOLFE, TOM. 1998. *A Man in Full*. New York: Farrar, Straus and Giroux.

WOLFINGER, NICHOLAS H. 1995. "Passing Moments: Some Social Dynamics of Pedestrian Interaction." *Journal of Contemporary Ethnography* 24:323–40.

WOLINSKY, JULIAN. 2004. "What Follows the Millennium?" *Railway Age* 205 (July): 27–29.

ZHOU, MIN. 2003. "Urban Education: Challenges in Educating Culturally Diverse Children," *Teachers College Record* 105:208–25.

ZIA, HELEN. 2001. *Asian American Dreams: The Emergence of an American People*. New York: Farrar, Straus and Giroux.

ZIELENBACH, SEAN. 2005. "Understanding Community Change: A Look at Low-Income Chicago Neighborhoods in the 1990s," *Neighborhood Change in America*. Washington, D.C.: The Urban Institute. Accessed at http://www.urban.org/publications/311151.html on December 13, 2008.

ZIPP, YVONNE, AND CHRISTOPHER D. COOK. 1999. "Genuine Urban Renewal, At Last in This Golden Economy, Even Bastions of Blight Start to Sparkle." *Christian Science Monitor*, August 19, p. 1.

ZUKIN, SHARON. 1993. *Landscapes of Power: From Detroit to Disney World*. Berkeley: University of California Press.

———. 1996. *The Cultures of Cities*. Malden, MA: Blackwell.

PHOTO CREDITS

INDEX